World Heritage Sites and Indigenous Peoples' Rights

Edited by Stefan Disko and Helen Tugendhat

IWGIA – Document 129

Copenhagen – 2014

World Heritage Sites and Indigenous Peoples' Rights

Editors: Stefan Disko and Helen Tugendhat

Cover and Layout: Jorge Monrás

Cover Photos: Bangaan Rice Terraces: Jacques Beaulieu (CC BY-NC 2.0); Uluṟu: unknown photographer; Ngorongoro Conservation Area: Geneviève Rose (IWGIA)

Illustrations: As indicated. Data for the little maps at the beginning of each case study provided by IUCN and UNEP-WCMC. 2013. *The World Database on Protected Areas (WDPA)*. Cambridge, UNEP-WCMC. www.protectedplanet.net

Translation: Elaine Bolton (Spanish, French); Lindsay Johnstone (French)

Proof reading: Elaine Bolton

Repress and Print: Eks-Skolens Trykkeri, Copenhagen, Denmark

© The authors, IWGIA, Forest Peoples Programme and Gundjeihmi Aboriginal Corporation 2014 – All Rights Reserved

Distribution in United States:
Transaction Publishers
Raritan Center 300 McGaw Drive, Edison, NJ 08837, USA
www.transactionpub.com

The reproduction and distribution of information contained in this book for non-commercial use is welcome as long as the source is cited. However, the translation of this book or its parts, as well as the reproduction of the book is not allowed without the consent of the copyright holders.

The articles reflect the authors' own views and opinions and not necessarily those of the editors or publishers of this book.

HURIDOCS CIP DATA

Title: World Heritage Sites and Indigenous Peoples' Rights
Editors: Stefan Disko and Helen Tugendhat
Place of publication: Copenhagen, Denmark
Publishers: IWGIA, Forest Peoples Programme, Gundjeihmi Aboriginal Corporation
Distributors: Europe: Central Books Ltd. – www.centralbooks.com; Outside Europe: Transaction Publishers – www.transactionpub.com. The title is also available from the publishers
Date of publication: November 2014
Pages: xxii, 545
ISBN: 978-87-92786-54-8
ISSN: 0105-4503
Language: English
Bibliography: Yes
Index terms: Indigenous Peoples/Human Rights/Environmental Conservation & Protection
Index codes: LAW110000/ POL035010/NAT011000
Geographical area: World

This book has been produced with financial support from The Christensen Fund and the Gundjeihmi Aboriginal Corporation.

FOREST PEOPLES PROGRAMME
1c Fosseway Business Centre, Stratford Road
Moreton-in-Marsh, GL56 9NQ, England
Tel: +44 (0)1608 652893 – Fax: +44 (0)1608 652878
Email: info@forestpeoples.org – Web: www.forestpeoples.org

GUNDJEIHMI ABORIGINAL CORPORATION
5 Gregory Place, PO Box 245, Jabiru, Northern Territory, 0886, Australia
Tel: (+61) 8 89792200 – Fax: (+61) 8 89792299
Email: gundjeihmi@mirarr.net – Web: www.mirarr.net

INTERNATIONAL WORK GROUP FOR INDIGENOUS AFFAIRS
Classensgade 11 E, DK-2100 Copenhagen, Denmark
Tel: (+45) 35 27 05 00 – Fax: (+45) 35 27 05 07
Email: iwgia@iwgia.org – Web: www.iwgia.org

Contents

Map of Case Study Locations x

Foreword
*Victoria Tauli-Corpuz, UN Special Rapporteur
on the Rights of Indigenous Peoples* xii

Preface
Annie Ngalmirama, Chairperson, Gundjeihmi Aboriginal Corporation xv

Acknowledgements xvii

Contributors xviii

PART I – BACKGROUND ARTICLES

World Heritage Sites and Indigenous Peoples' Rights: An Introduction
  Stefan Disko, Helen Tugendhat and Lola García-Alix 3
Indigenous Peoples and Protected Areas: Towards Reconciliation?
  Marcus Colchester 39
Indigenous Peoples' Heritage and Human Rights
  Jérémie Gilbert 55
World Heritage, Indigenous Peoples, Communities and Rights: An IUCN Perspective
  Peter Bille Larsen, Gonzalo Oviedo and Tim Badman 65

PART II – CASE STUDIES

Europe
The Laponian World Heritage Area: Conflict and Collaboration in Swedish *Sápmi*
  Carina Green 85

Africa
The Sangha Trinational World Heritage Site: The Experiences of Indigenous Peoples
  Victor Amougou-Amougou and Olivia Woodburne 103

'We are not Taken as People': Ignoring the Indigenous Identities and
History of Tsodilo Hills World Heritage Site, Botswana
    Michael Taylor 119
Kahuzi-Biega National Park: World Heritage Site versus the Indigenous Twa
    Roger Muchuba Buhereko 131
Bwindi Impenetrable National Park: The Case of the Batwa
    Christopher Kidd 147
Ignoring Indigenous Peoples' Rights: The Case of Lake Bogoria's
Designation as a UNESCO World Heritage Site
    Korir Sing'Oei Abraham... 163
A World Heritage Site in the Ngorongoro Conservation Area: Whose World?
Whose Heritage?
    William Olenasha 189

Asia

Western Ghats of India: A Natural Heritage Enclosure?
    C.R. Bijoy 223
Indigenous Peoples and Modern Liabilities in the Thung Yai Naresuan
Wildlife Sanctuary, Thailand: A Conflict over Biocultural Diversity
    Reiner Buergin 245
Shiretoko Natural World Heritage Area and the Ainu People
    Ono Yugo 269

Australia and Pacific

Pukulpa pitjama Ananguku ngurakutu – Welcome to Anangu Land: World
Heritage at Uluru-Kata Tjuta National Park
    Michael Adams.. 289
No Straight Thing: Experiences of the Mirarr Traditional Owners of
Kakadu National Park with the World Heritage Convention
    Justin O'Brien.. 313
Rainforest Aboriginal Peoples and the Wet Tropics of Queensland World
Heritage Area: The Role of Indigenous Activism in Achieving Effective
Involvement in Management and Recognition of the Cultural Values
    Henrietta Marrie and Adrian Marrie 341
The Tangible and Intangible Heritage of Tongariro National Park: A Ngāti
Tūwharetoa Perspective and Reflection
    George Asher.. 377
Rapa Nui National Park, Cultural World Heritage: The Struggle of the
Rapa Nui People for their Ancestral Territory and Heritage, for
Environmental Protection, and for Cultural Integrity
    Erity Teave and Leslie Cloud... 403

North America
  Protecting Indigenous Rights in Denendeh: The Dehcho First Nations
  and Nahanni National Park Reserve
    Laura Pitkanen and Jonas Antoine 423
  The Pimachiowin Aki World Heritage Project: A Collaborate Effort of
  Anishinaabe First Nations and Two Canadian Provinces to Nominate
  a World Heritage Site
    Gord Jones 441

South America
  A Refuge for People and Biodiversity: The Case of Manu National Park,
  South-East Peru
    Daniel Rodriguez and Conrad Feather 459
  Canaima National Park and World Heritage Site: Spirit of Evil?
    Iokiñe Rodríguez 489
  'We Heard the News from the Press': The Central Suriname Nature Reserve
  and its Impacts on the Rights of Indigenous and Tribal Peoples
    Fergus MacKay 515

PART III – APPENDICES

Appendix 1
  African Commission on Human and Peoples' Rights Resolution 197
  on the Protection of Indigenous Peoples' Rights in the Context
  of the World Heritage Convention 528

Appendix 2
  World Conservation Congress Resolution 5.047 on the Implementation
  of UNDRIP in the Context of the World Heritage Convention 530

Appendix 3
  Call to Action of the International Expert Workshop on the World
  Heritage Convention and Indigenous Peoples, Copenhagen, 2012 533

Appendix 4
  Report of the UN Special Rapporteur on the Rights of
  Indigenous Peoples to the UN General Assembly, 2012 (Excerpt) 539

Appendix 5
  Letter of the UN Special Rapporteur on the Rights of
  Indigenous Peoples to the World Heritage Centre, 2013 543

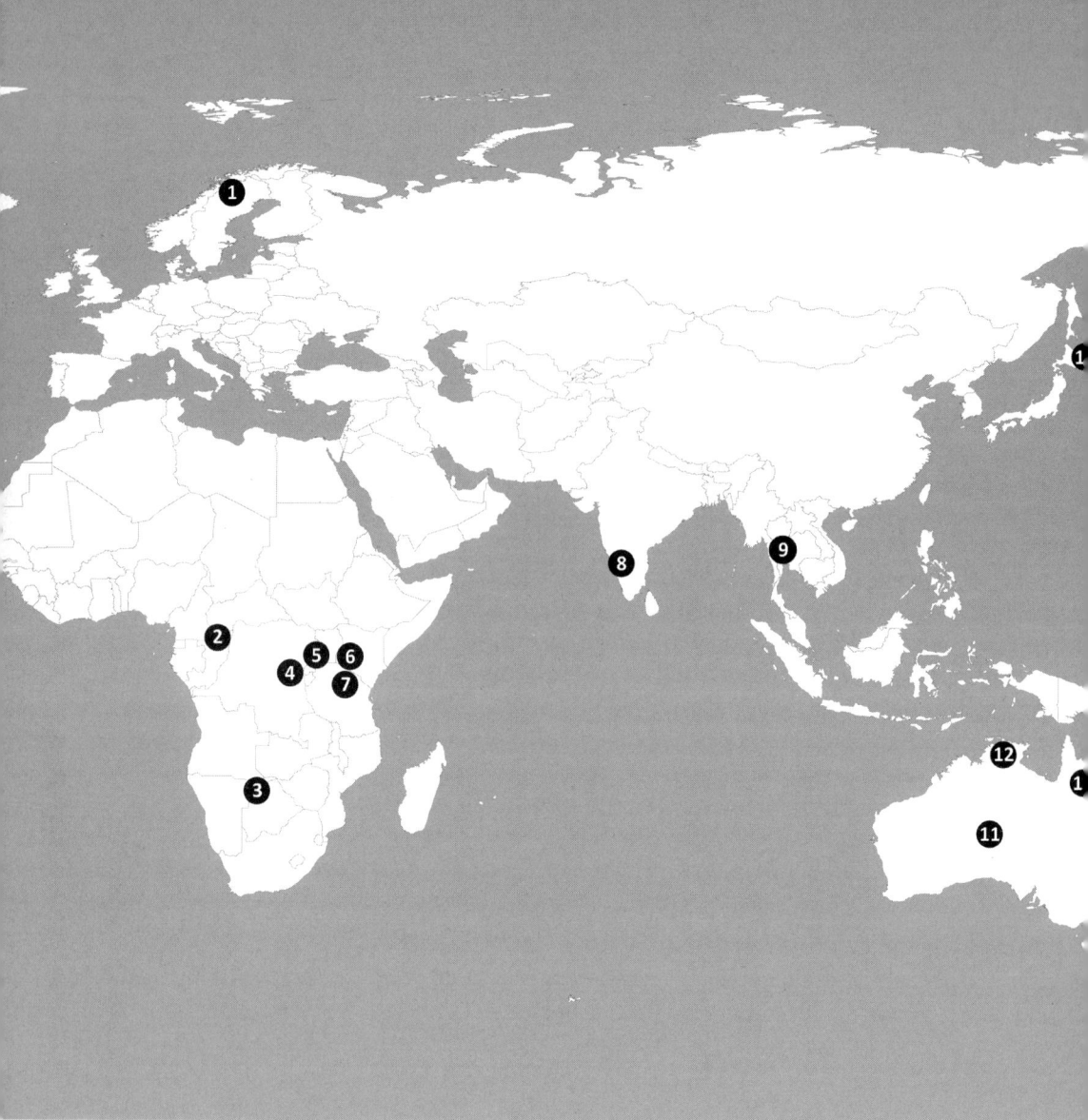

**Case study
World Heritage sites**

1. Laponian Area (Sweden)
2. Sangha Trinational (Cameroon / Central African Republic / Congo)
3. Tsodilo (Botswana)
4. Kahuzi-Biega National Park (Democratic Republic of the Congo)
5. Bwindi Impenetrable National Park (Uganda)
6. Kenya Lake System in the Great Rift Valley (Kenya)
7. Ngorongoro Conservation Area (Tanzania)
8. Western Ghats (India)
9. Thungyai-Huai Kha Khaeng Wildlife Sanctuaries (Thailand)
10. Shiretoko (Japan)

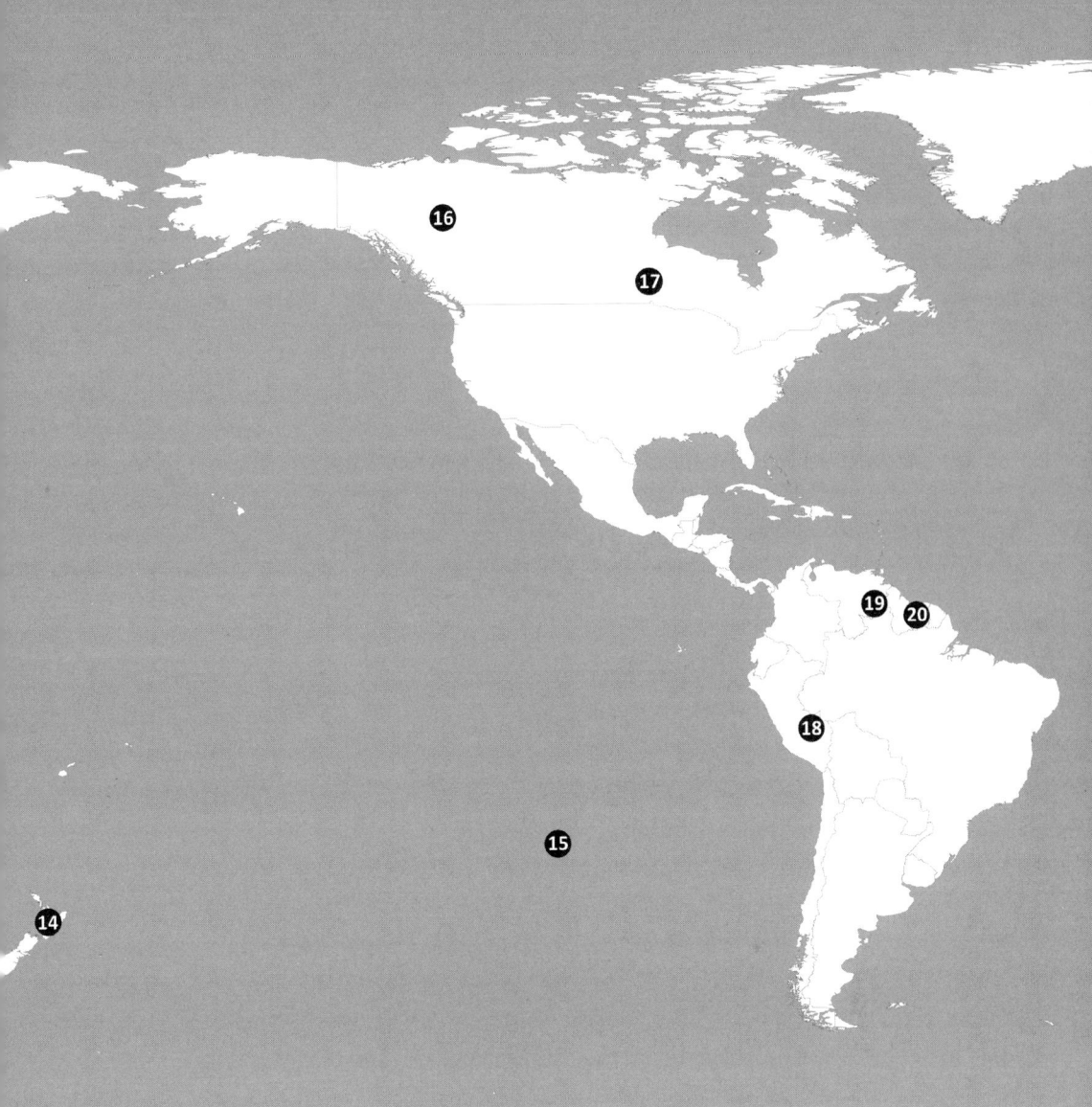

- ⑪ Uluṟu-Kata Tjuṯa National Park (Australia)
- ⑫ Kakadu National Park (Australia)
- ⑬ Wet Tropics of Queensland (Australia)
- ⑭ Tongariro National Park (New Zealand)
- ⑮ Rapa Nui National Park (Chile)
- ⑯ Nahanni National Park (Canada)
- ⑰ Pimachiowin Aki (Canada)
- ⑱ Manú National Park (Peru)
- ⑲ Canaima National Park (Venezuela)
- ⑳ Central Suriname Nature Reserve (Suriname)

Foreword

Victoria Tauli-Corpuz, UN Special Rapporteur on the Rights of Indigenous Peoples

The World Heritage Convention (formally the *Convention concerning the Protection of the World Cultural and Natural Heritage*) was adopted in 1972 to support the preservation of cultural and natural heritage for the benefit of the world and its peoples. As stated in the Preamble to the Convention, "parts of the cultural or natural heritage are of outstanding interest and therefore need to be preserved as part of the world heritage of mankind as a whole".

The Convention was adopted prior to most of the significant international steps that have been taken over the past decades to recognize and protect the rights of indigenous peoples, including the establishment of several United Nations and regional bodies dedicated to promoting and upholding the rights of indigenous peoples. The Convention therefore does not reference or reflect these important steps and is, in fact, in some ways at odds with them. Critical among these steps is the adoption of the *United Nations Declaration on the Rights of Indigenous Peoples* (UNDRIP) by the UN General Assembly in 2007.

The challenge therefore presents itself to indigenous peoples to engage with the World Heritage Convention and its organs and States Parties in order to ensure that the implementation of the Convention is amended and improved to take into consideration the new international consensus regarding the importance of recognizing, respecting and protecting the rights of indigenous peoples. This challenge is particularly urgent given the fact that World Heritage sites can be, and have often been, declared in areas that incorporate, in part or in whole, the lands, territories and resources of indigenous peoples. The result of this incorporation has not always been positive for indigenous peoples, and has usually come as part of a longer pattern of conservation policies and laws being applied at the national level.

Human rights bodies in the UN system have recognized the violations of the rights of indigenous peoples that can result from the application of conservation policies and, more specifically, from the implementation of the World Heritage Convention. All three of the UN mechanisms dedicated specifically to promoting the rights of indigenous peoples (the Permanent Forum on Indigenous Issues, the Expert Mechanism on the Rights of Indigenous Peoples and the Special Rapporteur on the Rights of Indigenous Peoples) have called for reforms in the way in which the Convention is applied, underlining the urgent need to reform the Operational Guidelines through which the Convention is implemented so that they are aligned with the UNDRIP. They have highlighted the need to adopt procedures to ensure indigenous peoples' free, prior and informed consent when sites are inscribed on the World Heritage List, the need to address the frequent lack of access by indigenous peoples to information about pending nominations and other Convention processes affecting them, and the need to take measures to ensure the protection of indigenous peoples' livelihoods and tangible and intangible cultural heritage in World Heritage areas, among many other issues.

My predecessor as Special Rapporteur, James Anaya, dedicated a whole section of his 2012 report to the UN General Assembly to the recurring issue of the impact of World Heritage sites on indigenous peoples, which contains a range of observations and recommendations on measures to prevent and remedy violations of indigenous rights in the implementation of the World Heritage Convention. Additional recommendations are contained in a communication he sent to the World Heritage Centre on 18 November 2013. I intend to follow-up these recommendations during the course of my mandate as Special Rapporteur.

It is clear that there is widespread recognition among human rights bodies of the legacy of problems in the implementation of the World Heritage Convention and the impacts that this has had on indigenous peoples. I therefore want to add my support to an important 2012 recommendation of the UN Expert Mechanism on the Rights of Indigenous Peoples, which states: "The Expert Mechanism... encourages the World Heritage Committee to establish a process to elaborate, with the full and effective participation of indigenous peoples, changes to the current procedures and operational guidelines and other appropriate measures to ensure that the implementation of the World Heritage Convention is consistent with the United Nations Declaration on the Rights of Indigenous Peoples and that indigenous peoples can effectively participate in the World Heritage Convention's decision-making processes."

The members of the Expert Mechanism highlighted both the importance of the *UN Declaration on the Rights of Indigenous Peoples* as a guide in implementing other conventions or treaties, and the importance of full and effective participation of indigenous peoples in decision-making that affects them, both themes that are explored at length in this book and which are fundamental to empowering indigenous peoples to guide their own development.

This book provides detailed case studies exploring the history and continued development and management of World Heritage sites that incorporate, in whole or in part, the lands, territories and resources of indigenous peoples. The testimonies and histories recorded in this book reveal some of the key challenges facing States and the World Heritage Convention bodies in ensuring that the implementation of the Convention does, in fact, support the aspirations of indigenous peoples to see their rights recognized and respected. The testimonies also reveal the hard work done by indigenous peoples in fighting for respect for their rights in World Heritage areas, through direct advocacy with the World Heritage Committee, engagement with international and/or regional human rights bodies, and national level efforts to achieve self-determination over their lands, territories and resources and their economic, social and cultural development as distinct peoples.

The stories contained herein reflect both the potential for the World Heritage Convention to support the self-determined development of indigenous peoples by helping them to prevent negative developments in their territories, and the difficulties inherent in the implementation of a Convention that does not explicitly recognize the rights of the peoples on which it has a direct impact. I hope that this book will form a contribution to increasing the respect between the World Heritage Convention and the rights of the indigenous peoples living in or around the natural, cultural and mixed sites protected under the Convention.

In accordance with Human Rights Council resolution 15/14 of 2010, core aspects of my mandate as Special Rapporteur are examining ways and means of overcoming existing obstacles to the full and effective protection of the rights of indigenous peoples; formulating recommendations and proposals on appropriate measures and activities to prevent and remedy violations of the rights of indigenous peoples; and developing a regular cooperative dialogue with all relevant actors, including Governments, relevant United Nations bodies, specialized agencies and programmes. As Special Rapporteur, I look forward to engaging with all the agencies and bodies involved in the implementation of the World Heritage Convention to improve its record with indigenous peoples, and to supporting indigenous peoples in the protection of their own heritage.

Preface

Annie Ngalmirama, Chairperson, Gundjeihmi Aboriginal Corporation

Since the adoption of the *UN Declaration on the Rights of Indigenous Peoples* in 2007, a great deal of attention has been paid to respecting the rights of Indigenous peoples in the implementation of the World Heritage Convention. During the Convention's 40th anniversary in 2012 (officially celebrated under the theme of "World Heritage and Sustainable Development: the Role of Local Communities"), the need to improve protection of indigenous peoples' rights in World Heritage sites was often talked about. For the Gundjeihmi Aboriginal Corporation, which represents the Mirarr Aboriginal people, this issue is very important as part of our country lies within Kakadu National Park, which has been listed as a World Heritage site for over thirty years.

Kakadu is many things to many people. It is World Heritage, it is a national park; it is where uranium mining occurs. For us Mirarr and other local Aboriginal people (Bininj), it is home. It is our ancient and long-lasting home. Our word for our land is *Gunred*. *Gunred* sustains us and we sustain it. We are obliged to care for it and for those who visit it. We do not see ourselves as separate to our land. Our land exists through us and we exist through it.

For many years, Kakadu has been a place where the Australian government and we Bininj have worked, lived and argued together. We Bininj are proud of our home and of its World Heritage recognition. For over thirty years, Mirarr have worked to protect our home against unwanted uranium mining and sometimes against the government's way of managing our land. Sometimes, we are at one with the government; at other times, we are in strong disagreement. We have also resorted to open protest and, to stop the proposed Jabiluka uranium mine, campaigned here in Kakadu and across Australia and the world. In the end we prevailed and mining at Jabiluka was stopped.

We have learned much along this journey with the Australian Government and the UNESCO World Heritage Committee. Kakadu's World Heritage status has helped us to prevail, by drawing international attention to our disagreements with the government. We have learned much about what we believe to be the denial of our fundamental international human rights because of mining and the way the Park has been managed.

We have also had positive experiences with the government. Over the years we have developed close working relationships and friendships with park rangers and other government staff. They have often helped us manage our land and they have been there during trying times. In recent years, we have also worked alongside the Djok clan and the government in partnership to secure World Heritage recognition of the Koongarra area.

Our journey with the government and the World Heritage Committee has had many twists and turns and, at the end of the day, it is an ongoing journey. We have been given great hope in recent times that our relationships with both government and industry are increasingly on a more respectful basis, that more opportunities for Bininj people are possible. Much of this is due to Kakadu's World Heritage status. It helps keep an international focus on our home and our relationships.

We stand in solidarity with other Indigenous peoples in World Heritage areas across the world and trust that their respective governments, UNESCO, and the international community will genuinely and effectively include these peoples in all their decision-making and benefit-sharing. We hope that this book will be a useful contribution to that end.

Acknowledgements

The editors of this book are grateful to the many people who supported or contributed to its successful production in one way or another. Our warmest appreciation and thanks go to Lola García-Alix who, in her capacity as IWGIA's Executive Director, guided us and supported us wherever she could throughout the production of the book and without whom this project would certainly not have been possible.

In addition to the authors who contributed book chapters and to whom we are most grateful, we would like to express our sincere acknowledgement and appreciation of those who submitted or helped with chapters which, in the end, could not be included. We are also grateful to those who reviewed chapters for us, provided comments or helped in finding authors.

We would further like to express our gratitude for the financial support received from The Christensen Fund and the Gundjeihmi Aboriginal Corporation for the production of this book.

Finally, it is important for us to thank our families for their continuous personal support, patience and encouragement.

Although it is not easy to separate out those who deserve special mention in a project that benefited from the work and efforts of so many, we would like to acknowledge the following individuals: Justin O'Brien, Mililani Trask, Victoria Tauli-Corpuz, Annie Ngalmirama, Yvonne Margarula, Mattias Åhrén, Lars-Anders Baer, Carol Sørensen, Wilson Kipkazi, Lucy Claridge, Albert Barume, Merrilyn Wasson, Bruce White, Ashish Kothari, Chris Erni, Ann-Elise Lewallen, Max Ooft, Donato Bitog, Jill Carino, Alexandra Bocharnikov, Johannes Rohr, Ndukuyakhe Ndlovu, Diana Vinding, Robert Hitchcock, Christian Strobl, Aliya Ryan, Kathrin Wessendorf, Cæcilie Mikkelsen, Annette Kjærgaard, Marianne Wiben Jensen, Alejandro Parellada, Suzanne Jasper, Dalee Sambo Dorough, Mechtild Rössler, Patricia Borraz, June Lorenzo, Ida Nicolaisen, James Tugendhat, and Caroline Maciel Lauar.

Stefan Disko and Helen Tugendhat
October 2014

Contributors

Michael Adams is Associate Professor of Geography at the University of Wollongong. He is a member of the Indigenous Peoples' Knowledges and Rights Commission of the International Geographical Union, and a member of two commissions of IUCN. His research focus has been on the relationship between Indigenous peoples and Protected Areas.

Victor Amougou-Amougou began work in rural development, helping with the capacity building of farmers' associations and cooperatives. Since 2001 he has worked primarily on Indigenous peoples' rights and livelihoods, through issues such as forestry, land and natural resource management, and has conducted detailed participatory mapping of resource use in protected areas. He is co-founder and coordinator of CEFAID (*Centre pour l'Education, la Formation et l'Appui aux Initiatives de Développement au Cameroun*), a local NGO with extensive CSO networks throughout the Congo Basin.

Jonas Antoine is a Dehcho Dene Elder from Liidlii Kue First Nation. Jonas was a member of the Nahanni Expansion Working Group, is a member of the Naha Dehe Consensus Team and represents the Dehcho First Nations in other protected areas initiatives in the Dehcho Process.

George Asher is of Maori descent and Chief Executive Officer of the Lake Taupo and Lake Rotoaira Forest Trusts in New Zealand. Both trusts comprise 55,000 hectares of ancestral lands of which 33,000 hectares are planted with commercial production forests. Parts of these lands adjoin Tongariro National Park and have been protected in their natural state. George has been actively involved in the development of his tribe, Ngāti Tūwharetoa, for the past 30 years and was also independent advisor to the 2006-07 Chairperson of the World Heritage Committee.

Tim Badman is Director of the World Heritage Programme at the International Union for Conservation of Nature (IUCN), with responsibility for managing IUCN's official advisory role to the UNESCO World Committee, and developing IUCN's wider activities related to World Heritage.

C.R. Bijoy is an independent researcher-activist who is primarily involved in indigenous peoples' struggles, for instance with the Campaign for Survival and Dignity, a national coalition of Adivasi and forest dweller organisations.

Reiner Buergin is an anthropologist with a background in forestry. He has carried out extensive field research in the Thung Yai Naresuan Wildlife Sanctuary, studying problems of local change and land use in the context of national forest policies and international environmentalism.

Leslie Cloud is a researcher in public law, legal anthropology and indigenous peoples' rights. She is currently undertaking a PhD in public law on the recognition of the rights of indigenous peoples in Chile and is working in on the SOGIP (Scales of Governance: The UN, the States and Indigenous Peoples) project, funded by the European Research Council (ERC 249236) and based at the *École des Hautes Études en Sciences Sociales* (EHESS) in Paris.

Marcus Colchester received his doctorate in social anthropology from the University of Oxford and has carried out extensive field research in applied anthropology, mainly in Amazonia, South and South-East Asia. His human rights advocacy related to development and conservation has earned him a Pew Conservation Fellowship and the Royal Anthropological Institute's Lucy Mair Medal for Applied Anthropology. He is a founder member of the World Rainforest Movement and was for many years the Director of the Forest Peoples Programme, where he now acts as Senior Policy Advisor. He has published extensively and is the author and editor of numerous books on forests, biodiversity and human rights.

Stefan Disko holds an M.A. in Ethnology, American Cultural History and International Law from the Ludwig-Maximilians-University Munich and an M.A. in World Heritage Studies from the Brandenburg University of Technology. Since 2000, his professional life has focused on working with indigenous organisations on human rights issues, mostly in the context of the United Nations. He has published various articles and reports on World Heritage and indigenous peoples' rights.

Conrad Feather is an anthropologist (PhD, University of St Andrews, UK) who has worked with indigenous peoples in south-east Peru since 2000 and is now working for the Forest Peoples Programme as a Project Officer.

Lola García-Alix holds an M.A. in Sociology from the Complutense University of Madrid. She has worked at IWGIA since 1990 and has held a variety of positions within the organisation. From 1993 until 2006 she served as Coordinator of the International Human Rights Advocacy Program. In 2004, she was appointed Vice-Director by IWGIA's Board and, in 2007, Executive Director. Since September 2014 she has resumed her position overseeing IWGIA's International Human Rights Advocacy work.

Jérémie Gilbert is a Reader in Law at the University of East London. He has published various books and articles on the rights of indigenous peoples, in particular on territorial rights, with his latest being *Nomadic Peoples and Human Rights* (Routledge, 2014). Jérémie often works with indigenous communities and NGOs on cases involving land rights. As a legal expert he has been involved in providing legal briefs, opinions and carrying out evidence gathering in several cases involving indigenous peoples' land rights, especially in Africa. He is a member of IWGIA's international board, a member of Minority Rights Group International's Advisory Board on the Legal Cases Programme and also regularly works with the Forest Peoples Programme and the Rainforest Foundation.

Carina Green holds a PhD in Cultural Anthropology from Uppsala University. Her research focuses on indigenous peoples and ethno-political mobilization. Her doctoral thesis approached the process of implementing a management plan in the Laponian World Heritage Area in Sweden. She has also carried out fieldwork in Australia and New Zealand on indigenous influence over World Heritage management and on the relationship between indigenous groups and environmental authorities in general. Carina is currently working for the Swedish Biodiversity Centre, a collaborative centre between the Swedish University of Agricultural Sciences and Uppsala University.

Gord Jones is Project Manager with the Pimachiowin Aki Corporation. Prior to joining the corporation in 2007 he worked for the Manitoba Government as Director of the Parks and Natural Areas Branch.

Chris Kidd received his M.A. and PhD in Social Anthropology from the University of Glasgow. His research and work among the Batwa of south-west Uganda focuses on the impact of development and conservation initiatives on Batwa livelihoods and futures. Chris is a Policy Advisor for the Forest Peoples Programme.

Peter Bille Larsen is a Danish anthropologist who has worked in Asia, Latin America and at the international level on conservation and social equity issues. He is a member of IUCN's Commission on Environmental, Economic and Social Policy (CEESP) and is actively involved in strengthening management approaches to World Heritage.

Fergus MacKay has worked in Suriname for over a decade, including acting for the Sa'amaka on the landmark Saramaka v Suriname case decided by the Inter-American Court on Human Rights in 2007. He works as the Legal Counsel for the Forest Peoples Programme.

Adrian Marrie serves as Bukal's company secretary. He has worked privately as a consultant with organisations such as the Foundation for Aboriginal and Islander Research Action (FAIRA), Bama Wabu Rainforest Aboriginal Corporation, the Yarrabah Community Council, and the Wungal Environment Foundation, essentially advising on cultural heritage policy and issues, community development plans and the development of reference manuals and guides. Consultancies have also included working with the Great Barrier Reef Marine Park Authority and the CSIRO.

Henrietta Marrie is a member of the Gimuy Walubara clan of the Yidinji people and Traditional Owner of the land on which the city of Cairns and southern suburbs is now located. Henrietta has wide experience of indigenous cultural and natural resource management and impact assessment, intellectual and cultural property law, heritage legislation and philanthropy. She has published over 40 papers in academic books and journals and served for six years on the Secretariat of the Convention on Biological Diversity in Montreal before becoming the Program Officer for North Australia with The Christensen Fund. She is currently an Adjunct Senior Fellow with the United Nations University – Institute of Advanced Studies (based in Yokohama, Japan) working on the Institute's Traditional Knowledge Initiative.

Roger Muchuba Buhereko is a human rights lawyer who has worked to defend the rights of Pygmy communities in Central Africa, including his home country of the Democratic Republic of Congo. He has worked as a social and environmental specialist for the World Bank, led the training programme for *Héritiers de la Justice* (Inheritors of Justice) in the DRC, and is now the National Coordinator of the Working Group on Climate and REDD, a civil society working group in the DRC.

Justin O'Brien has worked for the Mirarr people for 14 years and is currently Chief Executive Officer of the Gundjeihmi Aboriginal Corporation. He was previously Senior Policy Advisor to the Northern Land Council, a senior policy advisor with the Northern Territory Department of the Chief Minister, a media advisor to Australian Democrat Senator Lyn Allison and a journalist in rural and regional print media. Justin holds a Bachelor of Arts degree from Monash University.

William Olenasha is an advocate of the High Court of Tanzania currently practising with RAMATLaw Advocates and Legal Consultants (Arusha). A long-time activist for pastoralists' rights in Tanzania, he has worked as an Oxfam Programme Specialist for Lands and Pastoralism and as the Coordinator of the Joint Oxfam Livelihoods Initiative for Tanzania. He is currently a serving member of the Tanzania Constituent Assembly as a Presidential Appointee representing pastoralists. He is a legal advisor to the Pastoral Council in the Ngorongoro Conservation Area and has been at the forefront of championing for Maasai rights there. His publications on Ngorongoro include *Parks Without People: the Case of Ngorongoro Conservation Area*.

Gonzalo Oviedo is an anthropologist and environmentalist from Ecuador. He works as Senior Advisor on Social Policy at IUCN Headquarters in Gland, Switzerland, where he facilitates the integration of social issues into IUCN's conservation work, with particular focus on indigenous and traditional peoples, community-based natural resource management, rights and governance.

Laura Pitkanen is a political and environmental geographer. She was a representative for the Dehcho First Nations on the Nahanni Expansion Working Group and an analyst in the Dehcho Process. Laura is a PhD Candidate in Geography at the University of Toronto.

Daniel Rodriguez is a PhD student in the School of Anthropology & Conservation at the University of Kent, UK who worked as an anthropological advisor for the Isolated Peoples Programme of the Native Federation of Madre de Dios (FENAMAD) from October 2010 to December 2012.

Iokiñe Rodríguez is a Venezuelan sociologist with an M.Phil. in Environment and Development from the University of Cambridge, a PhD in Development Studies from the University of Sussex and undertook post-doctoral research at the Centre of Social Studies of Science at the Venezuela Institute of Scientific Research (IVIC). She has dedicated most of her professional life to the study of socio-environmental conflicts, with a special interest in politics of knowledge and indigenous peoples' environmental knowledge systems.

Korir Sing'Oei Abraham is a human rights lawyer specialising in minority and indigenous peoples' rights and is co-founder of the Centre for Minority Rights and Development (CEMIRIDE). He has worked particularly with the Nubian, Ogiek, Endorois, Somali, Maasai and Batwa peoples and was lead counsel for the Endorois community in Kenya, representing them in their landmark case at the African Commission on Human and Peoples' Rights (ACHPR).

Michael Taylor is Programme Manager for Global Policy and Africa at the Secretariat of the International Land Coalition in Rome, Italy. He is a citizen of Botswana and holds a PhD in Social Anthropology from the University of Edinburgh. He undertook research in Tsodilo from 1994-1996 in his role as Assistant Curator for Ethnology at the National Museum of Botswana and is one of the co-editors of the book "Tsodilo Hills: Copper Bracelet of the Kalahari" published in 2010. He has also worked in the Botswanan Ministries of Agriculture, and Environment, Wildlife and Tourism, and for UNDP.

Erity Teave is a Rapa Nui and the great-granddaughter of the great Rapa Nui leader Daniel Teave who was kidnapped, tortured and disappeared by the Chilean state in 1914. In recognition of the struggle for respect of the Rapa Nui nation's fundamental rights, continued by Erity Teave for 30 years, she was appointed Human Rights Director of the Rapa Nui Parliament and currently acts as the Rapa Nui Parliament's representative abroad. Since March 2013 she has also been the elected President of the Council of Clan Chiefs.

Helen Tugendhat is a Policy Advisor on human rights and on international financial policies and safeguards at the Forest Peoples Programme. She lived and worked with indigenous peoples in Thailand for over ten years, working both for indigenous peoples' organisations and for the United Nations Development Programme. She has authored and edited books on violence against indigenous women, human rights and dam construction, and indigenous rights in climate change mitigation policies.

Olivia Woodburne conducted her PhD research among BaAka communities in the Dzanga Sangha Reserve in the Central African Republic. Her research explored the relationship between the BaAka and the conservation project. She currently works as a communications assistant for the Forest Peoples Programme.

Ono Yugo is a professor emeritus at Hokkaido University, and professor at Hokkai Gakuen University. He is part of the non-profit organisation World Indigenous Peoples Network, Ainu (Win-Ainu) and has been closely involved in efforts to increase the role of the Ainu in the management of the Shiretoko World Heritage site.

PART I

BACKGROUND ARTICLES

World Heritage Sites and Indigenous Peoples' Rights: An Introduction

Stefan Disko, Helen Tugendhat and Lola García-Alix

In September 2007, following more than 20 years of negotiations between UN Member States and indigenous peoples' representatives, the UN General Assembly adopted the *United Nations Declaration on the Rights of Indigenous Peoples* (UNDRIP). In the Preamble to the Declaration, the General Assembly emphasized that the United Nations has an important and continuing role to play in promoting and protecting the rights of indigenous peoples. In light of this special role, Articles 41 and 42 of the Declaration provide that the organs and specialized agencies of the United Nations system and other intergovernmental organizations shall contribute to the full realization of the provisions of the Declaration through, *inter alia*, financial and technical assistance; that ways and means of ensuring the participation of indigenous peoples on issues affecting them shall be established; and that the United Nations, its bodies and agencies and Member States shall promote respect for and full application of the Declaration and follow up on its effectiveness.[1] Responsibility to promote respect for the Declaration applies throughout the United Nations system and, in particular, to United Nations institutions whose activities affect indigenous peoples, including the United Nations Educational, Scientific and Cultural Organization (UNESCO) and the World Heritage Committee.[2]

Of the roughly 1,000 areas designated as World Heritage sites under UNESCO's 1972 *Convention concerning the Protection of the World Cultural and Natural Heritage* (World Heritage Convention) as of 2014, a large number are fully or partially located within the traditional territories of indigenous peoples and are of great significance for their livelihoods and their spiritual, social and cultural well-being. While establishing an exact number of such 'indigenous sites' would require careful analysis, it is clear that there are close to 100 such sites, including well over a third of all sites designated as 'natural' World Heritage sites by the World Heritage Committee.[3]

What is also clear is that the impact of World Heritage sites on indigenous peoples has not always been positive. In his 2012 report to the UN General Assembly, the former UN Special

---

1   The commitment of the United Nations to implementing the UNDRIP was reaffirmed in September 2014 on the occasion of the high-level meeting of the General Assembly known as the World Conference on Indigenous Peoples.
2   Anaya 2012b, paras. 27, 41.
3   As of July 2014, there were a total of 1,007 World Heritage sites, including 197 'natural' sites, 779 'cultural' sites and 31 'mixed' sites (listed because of both their natural and cultural significance).

Left: Rice Terraces of the Ifugao in Batad, Philippines, inscribed on the World Heritage List in 1995 as a cultural landscape. Unlike most indigenous sites on the World Heritage List, the Ifugao Rice Terraces were included in recognition of indigenous cultural values. Photo: Adi Simionov (CC BY-SA 3.0)

Rapporteur on the rights of indigenous peoples, James Anaya, remarked that: "Indigenous peoples have expressed concerns over their lack of participation in the nomination, declaration and management of World Heritage sites, as well as concerns about the negative impact these sites have had on their substantive rights, especially their rights to lands and resources". The Special Rapporteur highlighted this as a "recurring issue" that had arisen in the context of his communications with governments regarding specific allegations of human rights violations, as well as in the context of his reports examining the situation of indigenous peoples in particular countries.[4] Concerns regarding the human rights impacts of World Heritage sites have also been raised by the two other UN mechanisms with specific mandates concerning the rights of indigenous peoples: the UN Permanent Forum on Indigenous Issues (UNPFII)[5] and the Human Rights Council's Expert Mechanism on the Rights of Indigenous Peoples (EMRIP).[6]

The purpose of this book is to analyze, through case studies of World Heritage sites in different parts of the world, the extent to which the principles of the UNDRIP are being fulfilled in the implementation of the World Heritage Convention. Case studies explore and document indigenous peoples' experiences with World Heritage sites and in particular with the processes of the World Heritage Convention at both the national/site level and the international/UNESCO level. They examine the effects of World Heritage status on indigenous peoples' lives and on the realization of their human rights (whether positive or negative) and the level of involvement of indigenous peoples in management and decision-making processes, especially their involvement in Convention processes such as the nomination of sites, the elaboration of management plans, reporting and monitoring, site evaluations and the decision-making of the World Heritage Committee. The book includes both examples of sites where indigenous peoples have been marginalized and their rights have been violated and examples where indigenous peoples' experiences with the World Heritage system have generally been positive and where indigenous peoples have benefited from the World Heritage Convention in one way or another. There are also case studies of World Heritage sites where problems that have arisen are being addressed or have been overcome, and which could therefore serve as positive examples for other sites facing challenges.

It is our hope that the book will help to identify recurring issues and concerns, as well as systemic gaps and shortcomings, in order to contribute to discussions about what changes or actions are needed to address concerns and to ensure that the World Heritage Convention can play a consistently positive role in securing human rights. We hope that the book will stimulate debate and action towards making the implementation of the World Heritage Convention consistent with the UNDRIP, will contribute ideas on the way forward and will outline possible ways for the World Heritage Committee, UNESCO, States and indigenous peoples to address the concerns identified. Our vision is for the World Heritage Convention and the UNDRIP to be mutually reinforcing.

The production of the book coincided with, and was inspired by, two unrelated but thematically connected events: the World Heritage Convention's 40th anniversary in 2012 and the World

---

4   Anaya 2012b, paras. 33-42. The section of Anaya's 2012 report discussing the World Heritage Convention is reproduced in Appendix 4 of this volume.
5   See, e.g., UNPFII 2010a, para. 131; UNPFII 2010b; UNPFII 2011, paras. 40-42; UNPFII 2013, para. 23; Cunningham 2012.
6   See, e.g., EMRIP 2011, Annex, para. 38; EMRIP 2012, p. 7 (Proposal 9: World Heritage Committee).

Conference on Indigenous Peoples in 2014. The World Heritage Convention's 40th anniversary was celebrated by UNESCO under the theme of "World Heritage and Sustainable Development: the Role of Local Communities" and was intended to provide a framework for focusing on "issues pertaining to the well-being and responsibilities of the local communities".[7] The celebration of the anniversary was meant to "present an opportunity for the international community involved in cultural and natural heritage conservation to reflect on the achievements of the *Convention* to date as well as to take stock of the challenges with which it is confronted".[8] The World Heritage Committee explicitly noted in a decision that considerations related to indigenous peoples, and in particular questions raised by the UN Permanent Forum on Indigenous Issues, "should be included in the theme of the 40th Anniversary".[9]

States Parties to the World Heritage Convention were encouraged by the Committee to "develop, support and carry out activities to promote the anniversary and to... mobilize various UNESCO related institutions, programmes and networks to join in celebrating the anniversary".[10] The Danish Agency for Culture acted on this request by partnering with IWGIA and the Government of Greenland to organize an international expert workshop on the World Heritage Convention and indigenous peoples, which took place in Copenhagen in September 2012 and involved, among others, several of the authors of articles contained in this book.[11] The workshop resulted in a Call to Action addressing the urgent need to make the implementation of UNESCO's World Heritage Convention consistent with the UNDRIP.[12]

In addition to the 40th anniversary, this book is intended as a contribution to the objectives of the World Conference on Indigenous Peoples (WCIP), a two-day high-level plenary meeting of the UN General Assembly held in New York City in September 2014, at the end of the Second International Decade of the World's Indigenous People (2005-2014). The official purpose of the World Conference was "to share perspectives and best practices on the realization of the rights of indigenous peoples, including to pursue the objectives of the United Nations Declaration on the Rights of Indigenous Peoples".[13] During the preparatory process for the WCIP, indigenous peoples organized a Global Indigenous Preparatory Conference, which took place in Alta, Norway in June 2013. One of the things highlighted by indigenous peoples in the *Alta Outcome Document* was the need for the World Heritage Committee, UNESCO and States to revise the World Heritage Convention's *Operational Guidelines* to ensure that the rights of indigenous peoples are respected in the nomination, designation, management and monitoring of World Heritage sites.[14] The outcome document of the WCIP itself, unanimously adopted by the General Assembly, reaffirms the solemn commitment of States to respect, promote and advance the rights of indigenous peoples set out in

---

7   UNESCO 2011a, para. 5.
8   UNESCO 2011a, para. 1.
9   Decision 35 COM 12D (2011), para. 10.
10 Decision 35 COM 12D (2011), para. 5.
11 For the report of the expert workshop see Disko and Tugendhat 2013.
12 See Appendix 3 at the end of this volume.
13 See General Assembly resolutions A/RES/65/198 (2011) and A/RES/66/296 (2012).
14 *Alta Outcome Document*, p. 5. Contained in UN Doc. A/67/994, Annex.

the UNDRIP, underlines the important role of the United Nations system in this regard and requests that the UN Secretary-General develop a system-wide Action Plan to ensure a coherent approach to the full realization of the provisions of the UNDRIP.[15] We hope that this book will be a useful reference for the United Nations, UNESCO and the World Heritage Committee in the elaboration and implementation of this Action Plan.

The *United Nations Declaration on the Rights of Indigenous Peoples*

Solemnly proclaimed by the UN General Assembly in 2007 with the approval of an overwhelming majority of Member States,[16] and with the support of indigenous peoples worldwide, the *United Nations Declaration on the Rights of Indigenous Peoples* reflects the existing international consensus regarding the individual and collective human rights of indigenous peoples in a way that is coherent with the provisions of other human rights instruments.[17] It represents, as affirmed by the UN Special Rapporteur James Anaya, "an authoritative common understanding, at the global level, of the minimum content of the rights of indigenous peoples, upon a foundation of various sources of international human rights law".[18] This echoes the text of the Declaration itself, according to which the rights recognized in the Declaration "constitute the *minimum standards* for the survival, dignity and well-being of the indigenous peoples of the world."[19]

Recognizing in its Preamble that "indigenous peoples have suffered from historic injustices as a result of, inter alia, their colonization and dispossession of their lands, territories and resources, thus preventing them from exercising, in particular, their right to development in accordance with their own needs and interests", the Declaration responds to "the urgent need to respect and promote the inherent rights of indigenous peoples..., especially their rights to their lands, territories and resources".[20] The Declaration therefore has, as Anaya notes, "an essentially remedial character, seeking to redress the systemic obstacles and discrimination that indigenous peoples have faced in their enjoyment of basic human rights".[21]

It is important to emphasize that the Declaration does not bestow a set of special or new rights upon indigenous peoples that are separate from the universally applicable fundamental human rights but rather provides a contextualized elaboration of general human rights principles and rights as they relate to the specific historical, cultural, social and economic circumstances of indigenous peoples.[22] In doing so, it reflects and builds upon relevant provisions of human rights instruments

---

15 *Outcome document of the high-level plenary meeting of the General Assembly known as the World Conference on Indigenous Peoples* (UN Doc. A/RES/69/2).
16 The UNDRIP was adopted by a vote of 143 in favour to 4 against, with 11 abstentions. However, all 4 opposing States (Australia, Canada, New Zealand, United States) and two of the abstaining States (Colombia, Samoa) have since reversed their positions and formally endorsed the Declaration.
17 EMRIP 2011, p. 22; Anaya 2011, para. 69.
18 Anaya 2008, para. 85.
19 Art. 43 (emphasis added).
20 Preambular paras. 6 and 7.
21 Anaya 2008, paras. 86.
22 Anaya 2008, paras. 40, 86; Anaya 2013, para. 70.

The UN General Assembly votes to adopt the Declaration on the Rights of Indigenous Peoples, United Nations, New York, 13 September 2007. Photo: Stefan Disko

of general applicability, as interpreted and applied by United Nations and regional human rights bodies, as well as the standards contained in the *Convention concerning Indigenous and Tribal Peoples in Independent Countries* (ILO Convention No. 169).

Therefore, while the UN Declaration itself is not a legally binding document, the standards found therein connect to existing State obligations under other human rights instruments that are legally binding on States. The Declaration builds upon the general human rights obligations of States under the *Charter of the United Nations*[23] and is grounded in fundamental human rights principles such as non-discrimination, self-determination and cultural integrity, which are incorporated into widely ratified human rights treaties such as the *International Covenant on Civil and Political Rights* (ICCPR), the *International Covenant on Economic, Social and Cultural Rights* (ICESCR) and the *International Convention on the Elimination of All Forms of Racial Discrimination* (ICERD).[24] Since the adoption of the UN Declaration, the human rights treaty bodies that monitor the implementation

---

23   Under the UN Charter, a binding multilateral treaty of the highest order, the United Nations and its Member States have an obligation to respect and promote human rights on a non-discriminatory basis. See Arts. 1(2), 1(3), 55 and 56 of the UN Charter.
24   Anaya 2011, para. 68; Anaya 2013, paras. 63, 65.

of these treaties have frequently interpreted and applied their provisions in ways that reflect the Declaration, and often explicitly refer to the Declaration in so doing.[25]

Additionally, the UNDRIP "includes several key provisions which correspond to existing State obligations under customary international law", as the International Law Association (ILA) found after an extensive survey of international and State practice in relation to the Declaration.[26] Norms of customary international law are binding on *all* States, irrespective of whether or not they have ratified any of the relevant treaties. They are also directly binding on international intergovernmental organizations.[27] While the Declaration as a whole cannot yet be considered as a statement of existing customary international law, the ILA notes that the provisions in the UNDRIP that do not yet correspond to customary international law nevertheless do express the aspirations of the international community to improve existing standards for the safeguarding of indigenous peoples' human rights. The fact that States recognized them in a "Declaration" adopted within the framework of the obligations established by the *Charter of the United Nations* to promote and protect human rights on a non-discriminatory basis, and passed with overwhelming support by the UN General Assembly, results in "an expectation of maximum compliance by States and the other relevant actors".[28]

Provisions of the UNDRIP which, according to the findings of the ILA, correspond not only to State obligations under the major international human rights treaties but also to existing norms of customary international law include provisions in the areas of self-determination, autonomy or self-government (including participatory rights), cultural rights and identity, land rights as well as reparation, redress and remedies.[29] While an in-depth discussion of the normative content of the UNDRIP is beyond the scope of this chapter, these five areas of rights will be briefly outlined below in order to better contextualize the issues raised in the case studies explored in this book.

Self-determination

Article 3 of the UNDRIP affirms that "Indigenous peoples have the right to self-determination. By virtue of that right they freely determine their political status and freely pursue their economic,

---

25 For a compilation of UN human rights treaty body jurisprudence pertaining to indigenous peoples, see Forest Peoples Programme 2013. Also see ILA 2010.
26 ILA 2012b (*Resolution No. 5/2012: Rights of Indigenous Peoples*), para. 2. (For the survey itself see ILA 2010 and 2012a). Likewise, the UN Special Rapporteur has noted that "some aspects of the Declaration — including core principles of non-discrimination, cultural integrity, property, self-determination and related precepts that are articulated in the Declaration — constitute, or are becoming, part of customary international law or are general principles of international law... It cannot be much disputed that at least some of the core provisions of the Declaration, with their grounding in well-established human rights principles... reflect customary international law" (Anaya 2013, para. 64).
27 See the International Law Association's report on the Accountability of International Organizations (ILA 2004), p. 22; and Reinisch 2005, p. 46 ff.
28 ILA 2012b, para. 3. Similarly, Anaya 2013, paras. 61-63.
29 ILA 2010, pp. 43, 51.

social and cultural development."[30] The wording of Article 3 mirrors a provision contained in the two international human rights Covenants (ICCPR and ICESCR) which upholds the right to self-determination for "[a]ll peoples".[31] This underscores the fact that the right to self-determination of indigenous peoples is the same right to self-determination that all peoples enjoy under international law.[32]

In essence, the right to self-determination "provides indigenous peoples with the right to control their own destiny and govern themselves... and embodies their right to live and develop as culturally distinct groups".[33] The former Chair of the UN Working Group on Indigenous Populations, Erika-Irene Daes has remarked that "[t]he true test of self-determination is not whether Indigenous Peoples have their own institutions of self-determination, legislative authorities, laws, police, or judges," but rather "whether Indigenous Peoples themselves actually feel they have choices about their way of life" and thus are able "to live well and humanly in their own ways".[34]

In the context of World Heritage, a crucial element of the right to self-determination is the right of indigenous peoples to manage, for their own benefit, their own natural resources.[35] As the UN Human Rights Committee has emphasized, referring specifically to indigenous peoples, "the right to self-determination requires, *inter alia*, that all peoples must be able to freely dispose of their natural wealth and resources and that they may not be deprived of their own means of subsistence".[36] This means, among other things, that the extinguishment of inherent aboriginal rights to lands and resources is incompatible with indigenous peoples' right to self-determination.[37]

Autonomy, self-government and the right to participate in decision-making

Directly related to indigenous peoples' exercise of their right to self-determination is their right to autonomy or self-government, affirmed in Article 4 of the UNDRIP as follows: "Indigenous peoples, in exercising their right to self-determination, have the right to autonomy or self-government in

---

30 The right to self-determination is to be exercised in conformity with relevant rules of international law and the principles of equality and non-discrimination, as the UNDRIP itself makes clear (Art. 46; preamb. para. 17). In particular, it is to be exercised in a way that is compatible with the principle of territorial integrity and political unity of States. It does not include a right for indigenous peoples to unilaterally establish their own State, i.e. a right of secession, except under such circumstances where this right exists for all peoples under general international law. See ILA 2010, pp. 9-10.
31 See identical Art. 1 of the ICCPR and the ICESCR.
32 On this aspect, see Anaya 2013, paras. 74-77; and ILA 2010, pp. 10-11. The treaty bodies that monitor the implementation of the two human rights Covenants have repeatedly invoked Art.1 of the Covenants in relation to indigenous peoples. See Forest Peoples Programme 2013.
33 ILA 2010, p. 10.
34 Daes, E.-I. 2001. The Concepts of Self-Determination and Autonomy of Indigenous Peoples in the Draft United Nations Declaration on the Rights of Indigenous Peoples. *St. Thomas Law Review* 14, p. 263 f. Quoted in ILA 2010, p. 11.
35 EMRIP 2011, Annex, para. 18.
36 CCPR 1999, para. 8. According to Art. 1, para. 2 of the two human rights Covenants, "[all] peoples may, for their own ends, freely dispose of their natural wealth and resources... In no case may a people be deprived of its own means of subsistence." Both the Human Rights Committee and the Committee on Social, Economic and Cultural Rights have repeatedly applied this provision to indigenous peoples.
37 CCPR 1999, para. 8.

matters relating to their internal and local affairs..."[38] The right of indigenous peoples to autonomy or self-government involves, on the one hand, the right to organize their social, economic, cultural and political life through their own laws, customs and practices and to establish, maintain and develop their own legal, political and cultural institutions (Articles 5, 18, 34 UNDRIP). On the other, it involves the right to effectively participate in external decision-making processes that affect them and to be consulted prior to the approval of any project or measure that may impact on their rights, lands or ways of life, with the objective of achieving agreement or consensus (Articles 18, 19, 32 UNDRIP).[39]

The participatory rights of indigenous peoples, and corresponding duties of States, are essential elements of indigenous peoples' right to self-determination and have been repeatedly affirmed by international human rights courts and treaty bodies. As will be seen in the following chapters of this book, they are crucial in the context of the World Heritage Convention.[40] The UNDRIP recognizes indigenous peoples' "right to participate in decision-making in matters which would affect their rights, through representatives chosen by themselves in accordance with their own procedures" (Article 18). At the same time, the Declaration recognizes that States have a duty to "consult and cooperate in good faith with the indigenous peoples concerned through their own representative institutions in order to obtain their free, prior and informed consent before adopting and implementing legislative or administrative measures that may affect them" (Article 19).[41]

While the modalities of indigenous participation can vary depending on the specific circumstances, it is essential for States to ensure that the participation of indigenous peoples in matters which would affect their rights is *effective*. For participation to be effective, indigenous peoples must actually be able to participate in decision-making processes through their own representative institutions and organizations and must be able to influence the outcomes of these processes. This may require special mechanisms to be created for indigenous participation, and that indigenous peoples are made aware of their existence.[42] Furthermore, for indigenous peoples to be able to make free and informed decisions about a given project, they must be "provided with full and objective information about all aspects of the project that will affect them, including the impact of the project on their lives and environment", as UN Special Rapporteur James Anaya has noted.[43] Information must be presented in a manner and form understandable to indigenous peoples, and indigenous consent must be sought sufficiently in advance of any authorization or commencement of activities, with due respect for the time requirements of indigenous decision-making processes.[44]

---

38   The ILA report on the rights of indigenous peoples notes that Art. 4 of the UNDRIP implicitly encompasses a "right to territorial self-government". Indeed, considering the extent to which the social, economic, cultural and political life of indigenous peoples is connected to their lands and territories, "control over traditional lands is the key feature of indigenous peoples' autonomy, conceived as an element of self-determination" according to the report (ILA 2010, p. 13).
39   See ILA 2010, pp. 12-16; ILA 2012a, pp. 3-7; and EMRIP 2011, Annex.
40   See EMRIP 2011, p. 24 ff.
41   Similarly, Art. 32(2) with regard to projects affecting indigenous peoples' lands, territories or resources. Also see paras. 3 and 20 of the outcome document of 2014 World Conference on Indigenous Peoples (UN Doc. A/RES/69/2), where these provisions are reaffirmed.
42   See, e.g., EMRIP 2011, pp. 24-26; Anaya 2009, paras. 36-57; ILA 2010, p. 14.
43   Anaya 2009, para. 53.

Generally, States should enable the full and effective participation of indigenous peoples in all stages of an initiative or project, from design, implementation, monitoring and evaluation to benefit-sharing.[45]

Cultural rights and identity

The protection of indigenous peoples' cultural identity and cultural rights represents a predominant theme throughout the whole text of the UNDRIP. The Declaration includes a number of provisions affirming the right of indigenous peoples to practise, develop and revitalize their cultural and spiritual traditions and customs and to maintain, control, protect and develop their tangible and intangible cultural heritage, traditional knowledge and traditional cultural expressions (Articles 11, 12, 13, 25, 31 and 34, among others). Other provisions affirm the collective right of indigenous peoples to live in freedom, peace and security as culturally distinct groups (Articles 7, 8, 9, and 33) and the right of indigenous peoples and individuals "not to be subjected to forced assimilation or destruction of their culture" (Article 8). Another key provision in terms of cultural rights and identity is Article 10 of the UNDRIP, affirming the right of indigenous peoples not to be forcibly removed from their lands or territories. Particularly relevant in the context of the World Heritage Convention, this provision "addresses the practice, quite common in the past, of removing indigenous peoples from their territories mainly for economic and development reasons, with tremendous consequences for their physical and cultural survival".[46]

The cultural rights affirmed in the UNDRIP find confirmation in a number of provisions included in international human rights treaties, such as Article 27 of the ICCPR, Article 15 of the ICESCR, or Article 5(e)(vi) of the ICERD.[47] The monitoring bodies of these treaties have on many occasions invoked these provisions in support of rights affirmed in the UNDRIP. In doing so, they have stressed that cultural rights entail the recognition of land rights for indigenous peoples, due to the fundamental importance of indigenous peoples' relationship to their lands, territories and resources for retaining their culture and cultural identity.[48]

Moreover, the ILA recognizes a customary international law norm protecting the right of indigenous peoples to recognition and preservation of their cultural identity. States are bound, according to the ILA, "to recognise, respect, protect and fulfil indigenous peoples' cultural identity (in all its elements, including cultural heritage) and to cooperate with them in good faith – through all

---

44 On the elements of free, prior and informed consent, see UNDG 2009, p. 30 and EMRIP 2011, Annex.
45 UNDESA 2008, p. 17.
46 ILA 2010, p. 18. Also see UNDRIP Art. 8, paras. 2(b)and 2(c).
47 Other instruments affirming cultural rights recognized in the UNDRIP include ILO Convention No. 169, the 2001 *UNESCO Universal Declaration on Cultural Diversity*, the 2003 UNESCO *Convention on the Safeguarding on Intangible Cultural Heritage* and the 2005 UNESCO *Convention on the Protection and Promotion of the Diversity of Cultural Expressions*.
48 See, e.g., Human Rights Committee, *General Comment No. 23: Article 27 (Rights of Minorities)*; Committee on Economic, Social and Cultural Rights, *General comment No. 21: Right of everyone to take part in cultural life*; and Committee on the Elimination of Racial Discrimination, *General Recommendation 23 on the rights of indigenous peoples*. Also see Gilbert, this volume.

possible means – in order to ensure its preservation and transmission to future generations".[49] The ILA notes that cultural rights must "be safeguarded in a way that is consistent with the perspectives, needs and expectations of the specific indigenous peoples", and that "all the prerogatives that are essential to preserve the cultural identity of indigenous peoples *according to their own perspective* must be preserved, including, e.g., the right to use ancestral lands and natural resources according to their own tradition".[50]

Land rights

As the UN Permanent Forum on Indigenous Issues has observed, lands, territories and natural resources "are of fundamental importance to indigenous peoples since they constitute the basis of their life, existence and economic livelihood, and are the sources of their spiritual, cultural and social identity". Therefore, "[l]and rights, access to land and control over it and its resources are central to indigenous peoples throughout the world, and they depend on such rights and access for their material and cultural survival."[51]

Accordingly, the UNDRIP articles on lands, territories and resources are among the most important provisions in the Declaration. The central provision in the UNDRIP dealing with land rights is Article 26, which affirms the right of indigenous peoples "to own, use, develop and control the lands, territories and resources that they possess by reason of traditional ownership or other traditional occupation or use, as well as those which they have otherwise acquired" (paragraph 2), as well as their general right to the lands, territories and resources which they have traditionally owned, occupied or used but no longer possess (paragraph 1). Article 28 provides that indigenous peoples have a right to redress for lands, territories and resources taken from them without their consent in the past.[52]

Other articles in the Declaration recognize related rights, such as the right of indigenous peoples not to be forcibly removed from their lands or territories (Article 10); their right to maintain and strengthen their spiritual relationship with their traditional lands, territories and resources (Article 25); their right to determine and develop priorities and strategies for the development or use of their lands and resources (Article 32); their right to the conservation and protection of the environment and the productive capacity of their lands and resources (Article 29); their right to be secure in the enjoyment of their own means of subsistence (Article 20); their right to the protection of their traditional medicinal plants and animals (Article 24); and their right to maintain and develop their traditional knowledge and cultural heritage associated with their lands and territories (Article 31).

The land and resource rights of indigenous peoples have been repeatedly recognized and affirmed by international human rights courts and treaty bodies, including the Human Rights

---

49 ILA 2012b, para. 6. Also see ILA 2010, pp. 16-20; 2012a, pp. 16-23.
50 ILA 2012b, para. 6; and 2010, p. 51.
51 UNPFII 2007, paras. 4 and 6.
52 Additionally, Art. 27 requires States to establish and implement processes to recognize and adjudicate the rights of indigenous peoples to their lands, territories and resources, including those that were traditionally owned, occupied or used.

Committee, the Committee on the Elimination of Racial Discrimination, the Committee on Economic, Social and Cultural Rights, the Inter-American Court of Human Rights and the African Commission on Human and Peoples' Rights. From the practice and jurisprudence of these bodies, it is clear that indigenous peoples' collective rights to their traditional lands, territories and resources are protected by international treaty law in connection with a variety of other rights, including the right to property, the right to cultural integrity, the right to self-determination and the general prohibition of racial discrimination.[53] Moreover, "[r]espect for the rights of indigenous peoples to ownership of, control over and access to their traditional lands and natural resources is a precondition for the enjoyment of other rights such as the rights to food, health, adequate housing, culture and free exercise of religion", as the former UN Special Rapporteur on the situation of human rights and fundamental freedoms of indigenous people, Rodolfo Stavenhagen, has remarked.[54]

According to the ILA, "States must comply – pursuant to customary and applicable conventional international law – with the obligation to recognise, respect, safeguard, promote and fulfil the rights of indigenous peoples to their traditional lands, territories and resources, which include the right to restitution of the ancestral lands, territories and resources of which they have been deprived in the past." The ILA underlines that "Indigenous peoples' land rights must be secured in order to preserve the spiritual relationship of the community concerned with its ancestral lands, which is an essential prerequisite to allow such a community to retain its cultural identity, practices, customs and institutions."[55] The relevant norms of customary international law also imply that indigenous peoples "must be allowed to manage their lands autonomously and according to their customary rules; this prerogative is strictly connected with the rights to self-determination and autonomy or self-government".[56]

Reparation, redress and remedies

A number of provisions in the UNDRIP affirm the rights of indigenous peoples to reparation and redress for human rights breaches they have suffered, including Articles 8(2), 11(2), 12(2), 20(2), 28, 32(3) and 40. Especially relevant in the context of World Heritage sites are Article 20(2), affirming that "Indigenous peoples deprived of their means of subsistence and development are entitled to just and fair redress", and Article 28, affirming that

> "Indigenous peoples have the right to redress, by means that can include restitution or, when this is not possible, just, fair and equitable compensation, for the lands, territories and resources which they have traditionally owned or otherwise occupied or used, and which have been confiscated, taken, occupied, used or damaged without their free, prior and informed consent."

---

53 See Feiring 2013 and Gilbert, this volume.
54 Stavenhagen 2007, para. 43.
55 ILA 2012b, para. 7.
56 ILA 2010, p. 51.

Also important in the context of the World Heritage Convention is Article 32(3) of the UNDRIP, which requires States to provide effective mechanisms for just and fair redress for any project or activities affecting the lands, territories or resources of indigenous peoples, and to take appropriate measures to mitigate adverse environmental, economic, social, cultural or spiritual impacts arising from such activities.

As shown by the ILA, States have obligations under both treaty law and customary international law to recognize and fulfil the rights of indigenous peoples to reparation and redress for wrongs they have suffered.[57] With regard to dispossession of indigenous peoples' ancestral lands, the kind of reparation that is generally preferable is the restitution of the lands, territories and resources concerned. The reason for this is "that in most cases no form of compensation is adequate to recompense effectively the deep spiritual significance that the motherland has for the very cultural identity and – in many cases – even the physical existence of indigenous communities." Consequently, "restitution is the form of redress to be granted any time that it is actually practicable."[58] In line with this, the Committee on the Elimination of Racial Discrimination has called on States parties to the ICERD:

> "to recognize and protect the rights of indigenous peoples to own, develop, control and use their communal lands, territories and resources and, where they have been deprived of their lands and territories traditionally owned or otherwise inhabited or used without their free and informed consent, to take steps to return those lands and territories. Only when this is for factual reasons not possible, the right to restitution should be substituted by the right to just, fair and prompt compensation. Such compensation should as far as possible take the form of lands and territories." [59]

Obligations and commitments of UNESCO

Promotion of respect for human rights is one of the fundamental objectives of the United Nations system as a whole. As stated in Article 1(3) of the UN Charter, one of the main purposes of the United Nations is "promoting and encouraging respect for human rights and for fundamental freedoms for all without distinction as to race, sex, language, or religion." This commitment has been reaffirmed by the UN General Assembly, other UN organs and the individual Member States in countless declarations, conventions and other instruments. It is also reflected in Article 1 of UNESCO's Constitution, which establishes the furthering of universal respect for human rights as one of the fundamental purposes of the organization. An obligation and responsibility of UNESCO to protect and promote human rights, and in particular the rights of indigenous peoples, is also

---

57 ILA 2010, p. 39 ff; ILA 2012b, para. 10.
58 ILA 2010, p. 41.
59 CERD 1997, para. 5 (*General Recommendation 23 on the rights of indigenous peoples*).

implicit in the organization's expressed commitment to principles and values such as cultural diversity, sustainable development and good governance.[60]

Moreover, the UNESCO General Conference has repeatedly emphasized that UNESCO will incorporate a human rights-based approach into all its programs and activities.[61] This means in practice that "all activities should contribute to the realization of human rights" and that "human rights principles and standards should guide the programming process in all fields and all stages, including design, implementation, monitoring and evaluation", as the *UNESCO Strategy on Human Rights* notes.[62] Programmes and activities should be conceived and designed to "contribute to the development of the capacities of 'duty-bearers' to meet their obligations and of 'rights-holders' to claim their rights".[63]

As a Declaration of the UN General Assembly, the UNDRIP represents a solemn and high-level commitment on the part of the United Nations to its provisions, within the framework of the obligations established by the UN Charter to promote and protect human rights on a non-discriminatory basis.[64] This commitment is explicit in Articles 41 and 42 of the Declaration, which require UN organs and specialized agencies to promote and act in accordance with the standards expressed in the Declaration. According to Article 41, the organs and specialized agencies of the United Nations system, as well as other intergovernmental organizations, shall establish ways and means of ensuring the participation of indigenous peoples on issues affecting them and "shall contribute to the full realization of the provisions of this Declaration through the mobilization, inter alia, of financial cooperation and technical assistance". Article 42 calls on the United Nations, its bodies and specialized agencies to "promote respect for and full application of the provisions of this Declaration and follow up the effectiveness of this Declaration", including in their action at the country level.

When the UNDRIP was adopted, UNESCO's then Director-General, Koïchiro Matsuura, officially welcomed it as "a milestone for indigenous peoples and all those who are committed to the protection and promotion of cultural diversity and intercultural dialogue", promising that the

---

60 See, e.g., UNESCO 2008, paras. 2, 3; UNESCO 2013c, para. 112. See, e.g., *UNESCO Universal Declaration on Cultural Diversity*, Art. 4: "The defence of cultural diversity is an ethical imperative, inseparable from respect for human dignity. It implies a commitment to human rights and fundamental freedoms, in particular the rights of persons belonging to minorities and those of indigenous peoples…"; *Plan of Implementation of the World Summit on Sustainable Development*, 2002, para. 5: "respect for human rights and fundamental freedoms, including the right to development, as well as respect for cultural diversity, are essential for achieving sustainable development and ensuring that sustainable development benefits all"; *The future we want* (Outcome document, United Nations Conference on Sustainable Development, 2012), para. 49: "We stress the importance of the participation of indigenous peoples in the achievement of sustainable development. We also recognize the importance of the United Nations Declaration on the Rights of Indigenous Peoples in the context of global, regional, national and subnational implementation of sustainable development strategies". On the mutually reinforcing relationship between good governance and human rights, see e.g. Human Rights Council Resolution 7/11 (2008), "The role of good governance in the promotion and protection of human rights" and the *United Nations Millennium Declaration*, Sec. V.
61 UNESCO 2003; UNESCO 2008, paras. 6, 69; UNESCO 2013c, para. 91.
62 UNESCO 2003, pp. 2 and 5.
63 Ibid., p. 5. The UNESCO Strategy on Human Rights reflects the "UN Common Understanding on the Human Rights-Based Approach to Development Cooperation". See OHCHR 2006, Annex II.
64 Anaya 2008, para. 41.

UNDRIP would "undoubtedly provide the foremost reference point [for UNESCO] in designing and implementing programmes with and for indigenous peoples".[65] On another occasion, the Director-General remarked:

> "The 2007 Declaration acknowledges the significant place that indigenous cultures occupy in the world and their vital contribution to our rich cultural diversity, which constitutes, in the words of its preamble 'the common heritage of humankind'. By approving this landmark Declaration, the UN has taken a major step forward in the protection and promotion of indigenous peoples' rights... and has sent a clear signal in this regard to the international community. It is now the responsibility of the United Nations, and in particular UNESCO..., to ensure that this message is widely disseminated, understood and – most importantly – translated into concrete policies that will enable indigenous peoples to participate fully and equally in the national and international life.
>
> Indeed, the new Declaration echoes the principles of the UNESCO Universal Declaration on Cultural Diversity (2001) and related Conventions – notably the 1972 World Heritage Convention, the 2003 Convention for the Safeguarding of the Intangible Cultural Heritage, and the 2005 Convention on the Protection and Promotion of the Diversity of Cultural Expressions. Each of these recognizes the pivotal role of indigenous peoples as custodians of cultural diversity and biodiversity." [66]

UNESCO's commitment to the UNDRIP was renewed by the General Conference in the Organization's *Medium-Term Strategy 2014-2021*, where it is declared that:

> "The needs of indigenous peoples will also be addressed by UNESCO's action. They continue to be disproportionately represented among the most marginalized and impoverished segments of society, while being recognized as the stewards of the major part of the world's biological, cultural and linguistic diversity... [T]he Organization will implement the UNDRIP across all relevant programme areas." [67]

Already in 2011, UNESCO embarked on a process of developing a house-wide Policy on Indigenous Peoples, which "will aim at positioning appropriately the Organization's programmes, procedures and activities with respect to the new institutional landscape that is emerging since the adoption of the UNDRIP, and building awareness and providing guidance to staff and committees in order to effectively implement the UNDRIP in all components of UNESCO's work." [68]

However, UNESCO has noted that implementing the UNDRIP in all components of the organization's work presents a challenge due to the fact that there are "two layers of intergovernmental governance within UNESCO on certain issues". While the main decision-making

---

65 Matsuura 2007.
66 Matsuura 2008.
67 UNESCO 2013c, para. 20.
68 UNESCO 2014a, p. 3. As of February 2014, drafting of the Policy was still in its early stages (ibid.).

bodies of UNESCO are the General Conference of Member States and the Executive Board (a smaller elected group of 58 Member States), some UNESCO Conventions and programmes have their own independent intergovernmental governance structures. Although "in many cases the same member states are sitting on these different bodies, they take decisions independently and sometimes these decisions are contradictory", according to UNESCO. "Thus, the effort of ensuring that indigenous issues are accurately reflected in all programmes, conventions and activities house-wide is complex, involving different semi-autonomous bodies." [69]

This challenge is clear in relation to the World Heritage Convention, a self-standing multilateral treaty with its own States Parties and a separate intergovernmental governance structure.[70] As further discussed below, the implementation of the Convention falls far short of the principles and requirements of the UNDRIP and there is a long history of human rights violations against indigenous peoples in relation to World Heritage sites. There can be no doubt, however, that the obligations of UNESCO to protect and promote the rights of indigenous peoples, both under its Constitution and under the UNDRIP, fully apply to the World Heritage Convention and its governing bodies. The Convention was adopted by UNESCO's General Conference pursuant to its functions under the UNESCO Constitution, and the Convention explicitly states that its central decision-making body, the World Heritage Committee, is "established within UNESCO" (Article 8.1). The Convention's Secretariat, the World Heritage Centre, is under the authority of UNESCO's Director-General, who appoints its staff pursuant to Article 14 of the Convention. It is located within UNESCO and is not autonomous of the organization.[71] Moreover, the Convention's membership is today almost identical to that of UNESCO and, with only one exception, all States Parties to the Convention are also Members of UNESCO.[72]

Implementation of the World Heritage Convention

The main purpose of the World Heritage Convention, which embodies the idea that some places are so special and important that their protection is not only the responsibility of the States in which they are located but also a duty of the international community as a whole, is the identification and collective protection of cultural and natural heritage sites of "outstanding universal value" (OUV). While no definition of this elusive term is provided in the Convention, the World Heritage Committee has adopted the following definition, contained in the *Operational Guidelines for the Implementation of the World Heritage Convention*: "Outstanding Universal Value means cultural and/or natural significance which is so exceptional as to transcend national boundaries and to be of common importance for present and future generations of all humanity." [73]

---

69 UNESCO 2014a, p. 2.
70 On the relationship between the World Heritage Committee and UNESCO see Vrdoljak 2008a, p. 224 f.
71 See Vrdoljak 2008b, p. 248 f.
72 As of 15 August 2014, there were 192 States Parties to the World Heritage Convention compared to 195 Member States of UNESCO. The only State Party that is not a UNESCO Member is the Holy See.
73 *Operational Guidelines*, para. 49. The Operational Guidelines have been regularly revised throughout the history of the Convention. Unless otherwise noted, references in this chapter refer to the July 2013 version.

The World Heritage Committee has also developed a set of ten specific criteria (six relating to cultural and four to natural values), at least one of which a given site must meet in order to be considered of OUV for the purposes of the Convention.[74] Additionally, to be deemed of OUV, a site must meet the conditions of integrity[75] and authenticity[76] (the latter only in the case of cultural sites), and must have an adequate protection and management system to ensure its safeguarding.[77] If these requirements are met, the site qualifies for inscription on UNESCO's World Heritage List, i.e. for designation as a cultural, natural or "mixed" (cultural and natural) World Heritage site (see Figure 1).[78] While the decision to include sites on the World Heritage List is the prerogative of the World Heritage Committee, sites can only be listed following a formal nomination by the State Party in whose territory they are located, and after having been included on the respective State Party's so-called 'Tentative List' (of potential World Heritage sites) for at least one year.[79] All nominated sites are visited and evaluated by the World Heritage Committee's advisory bodies IUCN and/or ICOMOS[80] before the Committee decides whether or not they will be inscribed on the World Heritage List. The Committee can also *refer* a nomination back to the State Party for additional information or *defer* a nomination for more in-depth assessment or study, or a substantial revision by the State Party.[81]

Once listed, a World Heritage site must be managed and protected with a view to maintaining its OUV as recognized by the World Heritage Committee. This is the responsibility of the State Party (or States Parties in the case of transboundary/transnational sites) in whose territory the site is located. States Parties have an obligation to regularly prepare reports about the state of conservation of the World Heritage sites in their territories and the protection measures put in place to ensure their safeguarding ("Periodic Reporting").[82] Additionally, the World Heritage Committee's advisory bodies and the World Heritage Centre report to the Committee on the state of conservation of specific World Heritage sites that are considered to be under threat ("Reactive Monitoring"). In this context, they can collect and make use of information received from sources other than the States Parties concerned, including information received from indigenous peoples

---

74 Contained in ibid., para. 77. The ten criteria have been occasionally revised by the Committee to reflect the evolution of the World Heritage concept. Now numbered (i) through (x), they were labeled cultural criteria (i)-(vi) and natural criteria (i)-(iv) until 2004.
75 See ibid., paras. 78, 87-95. Integrity is a measure of the wholeness and intactness of the natural and/or cultural heritage and its attributes.
76 See ibid., paras. 78-86. In essence, a cultural heritage site meets the condition of authenticity if it is 'genuine' (i.e. if it is truly what it claims to be) and if the information sources about its heritage values may be understood as credible or truthful. See Jokilehto 1999, p. 11 f.
77 For details, see *Operational Guidelines*, paras. 78, 96-119.
78 See ibid., paras. 45-47. A sub-category of cultural World Heritage sites are cultural landscapes, which represent the "combined works of nature and of man" mentioned in Article 1 of the World Heritage Convention. The cultural landscapes category was introduced by the World Heritage Committee in 1992. See Annex 3 of the *Operational Guidelines*.
79 *Operational Guidelines*, paras. 24(a), 63 and 65.
80 The World Heritage Committee is supported by three advisory bodies: the International Union for Conservation of Nature (IUCN), the International Council on Monuments and Sites (ICOMOS) and the International Centre for the Study of the Preservation and Restoration of Cultural Property (ICCROM). On the roles of the advisory bodies, see *Operational Guidelines*, paras. 30-37 and the chapter by Larsen, Oviedo and Badman in this volume
81 *Operational Guidelines*, Chapter III.G.
82 See *Operational Guidelines*, para. 15 and Chapter V.

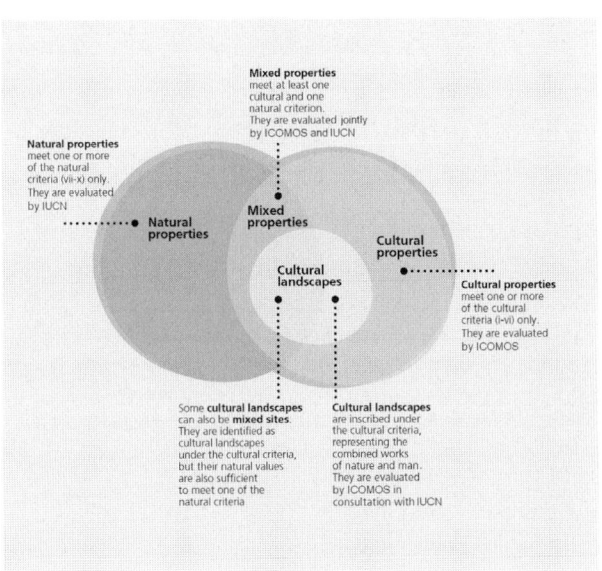

Figure 1: Types of World Heritage sites ('properties'). Adapted from UNESCO et al. 2011

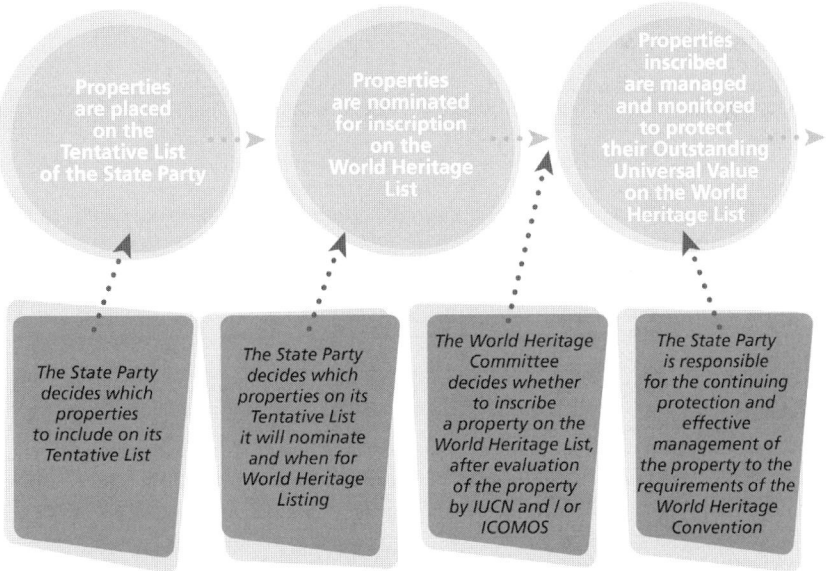

Figure 2: Summary of the different steps in the nomination process and the main responsibilities of the State Party and the UNESCO World Heritage Committee. Source: UNESCO et al. 2011

or non-governmental organizations, and may make recommendations on how to mitigate threats and outline corrective measures.[83]

Lack of implementation of the UN Declaration on the Rights of Indigenous Peoples in the context of the World Heritage Convention

The World Heritage Convention can play, and in some cases undoubtedly has played, a positive role for indigenous peoples by helping them protect their lands and territories, cultures and heritage from development pressures such as urban encroachment or extractive industry activities. A recent example is the incorporation of the uranium-rich Koongarra area into the Kakadu National Park World Heritage site, at the joint request of the State Party and the indigenous landowners, in effect barring future mineral development in the area.[84] World Heritage sites can also create business and employment opportunities for indigenous peoples, for instance in the tourism sector or directly in the management of sites. Further, in monitoring the state of conservation of inscribed World Heritage sites, the World Heritage Committee and/or its advisory bodies, IUCN and ICOMOS, may call on States Parties to improve indigenous peoples' participation in the management and decision-making processes of particular sites or to enhance benefit-sharing mechanisms.[85] These interventions have become more frequent in recent years and have in some cases contributed to positive change for indigenous peoples.[86]

However, throughout the history of the World Heritage Convention there have been frequent objections raised by indigenous peoples regarding violations of their rights in the implementation of the Convention, not only at the domestic level in the nomination and management of specific World Heritage sites but also at the international level in the practice of the World Heritage Committee, its advisory bodies IUCN and ICOMOS, and its Secretariat. Human rights concerns include, *inter alia*, frequent disrespect for indigenous peoples' participatory rights in the nomination and inscription of sites, marginalization of indigenous peoples in the on-site decision-making and management of World Heritage areas, violations of their right to share equitably in tourism benefits, a common lack of consultation with indigenous peoples by monitoring and site evaluation missions and a serious lack of transparency in some of the Convention's processes. Moreover, in some World

---

83 *Operational Guidelines*, Chapter IV.A.
84 See O'Brien, this volume.
85 See, for example, World Heritage Committee Decisions 37 COM 7B.30, para. 8b (Talamanca Range-La Amistad Reserves / La Amistad National Park, Costa Rica / Panama); 34 COM 7B.4, para. 6 (Ngorongoro Conservation Area, United Republic of Tanzania); or 35 COM 7B.34, para. 4d (Manu National Park, Peru).
86 For instance, the World Heritage Committee, IUCN and the World Heritage Centre in 2014 urged the Government of Kenya to ensure full and effective participation of the indigenous Endorois in the management and decision-making of Lake Bogoria National Reserve (see UNESCO 2014b, p. 111-113 and Committee Decision 38 COM 7B.91). This appears to have facilitated the signing of a Memorandum of Understanding in May 2014 between Kenyan government agencies and representatives of the Endorois which notes that the involvement of the Endorois in the management of the Reserve is paramount, sets out a framework for the co-management of the Reserve by Kenyan government agencies and the Endorois and recognizes that any decision-making concerning the Endorois people must have their free, prior and informed consent (for details on this case, see Sing'Oei, this volume).

The World Heritage Committee at its 35th Session in Paris in June 2011, following the decision to incorporate the Koongarra area into the Kakadu World Heritage site in Australia. In the center front row Jeffrey Lee, the senior traditional owner of the Koongarra area. Photo: Stefan Disko

Heritage areas indigenous peoples are essentially treated as threats to their own territories and tight restrictions and prohibitions are placed on traditional land-use practices such as hunting, gathering, farming or animal husbandry, in violation of indigenous peoples' cultural and subsistence rights. These restrictions and prohibitions have had severe consequences for some indigenous peoples' food security, health and well-being and can in some cases be directly linked to the World Heritage status.[87] The World Heritage List also contains several protected areas from which indigenous peoples have been forcibly removed,[88] in some instances even with the intention of "justifying inscription of an area on the World Heritage List as a place of natural importance devoid of what is perceived as the negative impact of local inhabitants", as a former staff member of the World Heritage Centre has

---

87 See, for instance, the case of the Ngorongoro Conservation Area, where a ban on subsistence cultivation imposed in 2009 resulted in a serious situation of hunger and malnutrition that affected most of the area's 70,000 residents and led to the deaths of several people (Olenasha, this volume).

88 For some examples, see the articles in this volume by Kidd (Bwindi Impenetrable National Park), Muchuba (Kahuzi-Biega National Park), Buergin (Thungyai - Huai Kha Khaeng Wildlife Sanctuaries), Sing'Oei (Lake Bogoria National Reserve) and Olenasha (Serengeti National Park).

remarked.[89] This legacy remains completely unaddressed by the World Heritage Committee although many of the affected indigenous peoples continue to suffer from the consequences to this day.

The violation of indigenous rights in World Heritage sites and in the implementation of the World Heritage Convention is facilitated by the fact that "the World Heritage Convention does not give any recognition to indigenous peoples' rights over cultural and natural heritage", as noted in the ILA's study on the rights of indigenous peoples.[90] Rather, "the Convention entrusts territorial States with all responsibilities concerning proposals for inscription of cultural and natural properties on the World Heritage List... and relating to the management of such properties after their inscription".[91] While the lack of recognition of indigenous peoples' rights in the text of the Convention can be explained by its early adoption, in 1972, when international law in this area was little developed, the subsequently devised and frequently updated *Operational Guidelines*, also, do not contain any provisions on the rights of indigenous peoples, nor other references to human rights. The ILA study therefore concludes that "the consideration devoted to indigenous peoples' rights in the context of the operation of the World Heritage Convention is far from being adequate".[92]

To its credit, in 2007 the World Heritage Committee adopted a "Strategic Objective" to "Enhance the role of communities in the implementation of the *World Heritage Convention*", in recognition of "the critical importance of involving indigenous, traditional and local communities in the implementation of the *Convention*".[93] In a 2011 Decision, the Committee also encouraged States Parties to "[i]nvolve indigenous peoples and local communities in decision making, monitoring and evaluation of the state of conservation of [World Heritage sites]" and to "[r]espect the rights of indigenous peoples when nominating, managing and reporting on World Heritage sites in indigenous peoples' territories".[94] However, the Convention's *Operational Guidelines* continue to be entirely inadequate for ensuring the meaningful participation of indigenous peoples and respect for their rights in Convention processes. Rather than upholding the right of indigenous peoples to effectively participate in decision-making affecting them, the *Operational Guidelines* merely "encourage" States Parties to ensure the participation of "a wide variety of stakeholders" in the processes of the Convention:

> "States Parties to the *Convention* are encouraged to ensure the participation of a wide variety of stakeholders, including site managers, local and regional governments, local communities, non-governmental organizations (NGOs) and other interested parties and partners in the identification, nomination and protection of World Heritage properties." [95]

---

89 Titchen 2002.
90 ILA 2012a, p. 17.
91 Ibid.
92 Ibid.
93 See World Heritage Committee Decisions 31 COM 13A and 31 COM 13B. This fifth strategic objective, also known as the "fifth C", was adopted by the World Heritage Committee during the Chairmanship of Sir Tumu Te Heuheu, Paramount Chief of Ngāti Tūwharetoa, the first indigenous person to hold this position (representing New Zealand).
94 Decision 35 COM 12E, para. 15.
95 Para. 12. Other provisions on the involvement of local communities and other stakeholders include paras. 40, 64, 123 and 211. The only provision that is couched in slightly more obligatory language relates to nominations of cultural landscapes to the World Heritage List, which "should be prepared in collaboration with and the full approval of local communities" (Annex 3, para. 12).

This approach, which subsumes indigenous peoples into a wider category of stakeholders such as local communities, NGOs and other interested parties, negates indigenous peoples' status and rights under international law, including their right to self-determination and their collective rights to their lands, territories and resources. In accordance with the principles of the UNDRIP, indigenous peoples must be treated as rights-holders and key decision-makers whose consent has to be sought in the case of activities affecting their rights, and not merely lumped together with a wide variety of 'stakeholders', who may or may not be included in decision-making processes.

The first concerted effort of indigenous peoples to enhance the consideration given to their rights in the implementation of the World Heritage Convention was in 2000 during the 24th session of the World Heritage Committee in Cairns, Australia. A forum of indigenous peoples held in conjunction with that session called for the establishment of a "World Heritage Indigenous Peoples Council of Experts (WHIPCOE)" as a consultative body to the Committee out of concern about the "lack of involvement of indigenous peoples in the development and implementation of laws, policies and plans... which apply to their ancestral lands within or comprising sites now designated as World Heritage areas".[96] The forum proposed that WHIPCOE should complement the work of the Committee's existing advisory bodies and provide "expert Indigenous advice on the holistic knowledge, traditions and cultural values of Indigenous Peoples relative to the implementation of the World Heritage Convention, including current operational guidelines".[97] Among other things, it was thought that a body such as WHIPCOE was needed "to advise on the appropriate identification, evaluation and management of 'mixed' properties and 'cultural' properties with indigenous associations and the identification, management and possible renomination of properties listed for their 'natural' World Heritage values that may also hold indigenous values".[98]

However, although the proposal was considered by the World Heritage Committee at its 24th and 25th sessions, the Committee did not approve the establishment of WHIPCOE as a consultative body or network reporting to it. The stated reasons for this decision included "a number of legal concerns and issues relating to the funding, legal status, role and relationships (with the States Parties, Advisory Bodies, World Heritage Committee and World Heritage Centre)" and the fact that "[s]ome members of the Committee questioned the definition of indigenous peoples and the relevance of such a distinction in different regions of the world."[99] The former Chairperson of the World Commission on Protected Areas, Adrian Phillips, attributed the decision to a "dismissive attitude towards indigenous peoples' issues" among some of the Committee members.[100]

In 2002, Mirarr senior traditional owner Yvonne Margarula from the Kakadu National Park World Heritage area in Australia submitted a statement on behalf of the Mirarr people to the inaugural session of the UN Permanent Forum on Indigenous Issues which recommended that the Permanent Forum undertake an independent study of indigenous peoples and World Heritage. The statement suggested that the study analyze the effectiveness of the World Heritage Convention in the protection

---

96 UNESCO 2001, p. 2.
97 Ibid., p. 3.
98 Ibid., p. 5.
99 UNESCO 2002, p. 57.
100 Quoted in IUCN 2002, p. 15.

of indigenous peoples' sacred sites and living traditions; the potential impact of the World Heritage Committee's then ongoing review of its *Operational Guidelines* on indigenous peoples living in World Heritage areas; and indigenous peoples' representation and input into the World Heritage Committee's decision-making processes.[101] Following the Permanent Forum's first session, indigenous peoples raised concerns on many occasions with the Forum about violations of their rights in World Heritage sites and in the implementation of the Convention. Having a mandate to provide expert advice and recommendations on indigenous issues to programmes and agencies of the United Nations, and to promote respect for the UNDRIP and follow up its effectiveness,[102] in 2010 the Permanent Forum for the first time sent a representative to a session of the World Heritage Committee. The purpose of this participation was to inform the Committee about the numerous concerns related to World Heritage sites that indigenous organizations had brought to the Forum's attention since its first session in 2002. In a written submission to the Committee, the Forum highlighted, among other things, that it had received complaints about a "list of indigenous sites inscribed in the World Heritage List without the adequate participation and involvement of indigenous peoples".[103]

In 2011, a broad coalition of indigenous organizations and NGOs submitted a joint statement to the World Heritage Committee, as well as the Permanent Forum, expressing "serious concern about the continuous and ongoing disrespect of the principle of free, prior and informed consent by UNESCO's World Heritage Committee when it designates sites in Indigenous peoples' territories as 'World Heritage sites'". The joint statement noted:

> "There are numerous examples of Indigenous sites on the World Heritage List that have been inscribed without the free, prior and informed consent of the Indigenous peoples concerned. In many cases Indigenous peoples were not even consulted when their territories were designated as World Heritage sites, although this designation can have far-reaching consequences for their lives and human rights, their ability to carry out their subsistence activities, and their ability to freely pursue their economic, social and cultural development in accordance with their right of self-determination."[104]

The joint statement also denounced the fact that three World Heritage nominations under consideration by the Committee at the time (Western Ghats, Sangha Trinational and Kenya Lake System in the Great Rift Valley) had been prepared without the meaningful involvement or consultation of affected indigenous peoples and that insufficient consideration had been given to indigenous peoples' cultural values and their role as stewards of the respective places. It urged

---

101 Mirarr People 2002.
102 See UN ECOSOC Resolution E/2000/22, para. 2; and UNDRIP, Art. 42.
103 UNPFII 2010b.
104 Endorois Welfare Council et al. 2011. The statement also expresses concern, in response to the 2010 designation of the Ngorongoro Conservation Area as a cultural World Heritage site (in recognition of archaeological but not indigenous cultural values), "that the concepts of 'outstanding universal value', 'integrity' and 'authenticity' are interpreted and applied in ways that are disrespectful of Indigenous peoples and their cultures, inconsiderate of their circumstances and needs, preclude cultural adaptations and changes, and serve to undermine their human rights." For more detail on the case in point, see Olenasha, this volume.

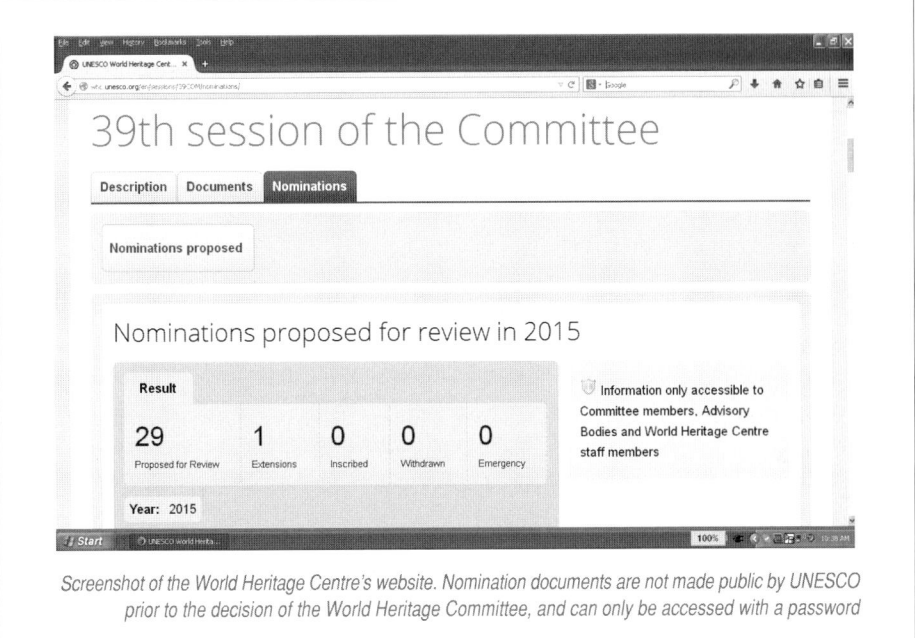

Screenshot of the World Heritage Centre's website. Nomination documents are not made public by UNESCO prior to the decision of the World Heritage Committee, and can only be accessed with a password

the Committee not to approve these nominations until the indigenous peoples concerned had been adequately consulted and involved and their free, prior and informed consent obtained.

The objections expressed in the joint statement did not, however, receive any noteworthy consideration by the World Heritage Committee. Kenya Lake System was inscribed on the World Heritage List in 2011, while Western Ghats and the Sangha Trinational were inscribed in 2012 despite the concerns not having been resolved in any of the three cases.[105] In the latter two instances, the indigenous peoples concerned had not even been able to review the final versions of the nomination documents, which had not been made publicly available by the relevant States Parties or UNESCO before the World Heritage Committee took its decision.[106]

The fact that there is no requirement under the *Operational Guidelines* for World Heritage nominations and other key documents such as state of conservation reports and monitoring mission reports to be made publicly available before the World Heritage Committee takes a decision is of serious concern to indigenous peoples.[107] It has in many cases prevented

---

105 For more detail, see the articles in this volume by Sing'Oei Abraham; Bijoy; and Amougou-Amougou and Woodburne.
106 IWGIA et al. 2012.
107 While nomination documents are never disclosed by UNESCO before a site is inscribed (see screenshot of UNESCO website), in 2013 and 2014 the World Heritage Committee encouraged States Parties to authorize UNESCO to make reports relating to the state of conservation of their World Heritage sites publicly accessible in order to contribute to improved transparency in the reactive monitoring process (see Decisions 37 COM 7C and 38 COM 7). Although most reports are now published, this is not a requirement and some reports by State Parties, as well as some of the monitoring mission reports, continue to be withheld from the public, in particular those of a contentious character.

indigenous peoples from reviewing such documents and providing their perspectives to the Committee, despite the fact that the proposals contained in these documents may have far-reaching implications for their rights and interests.[108] This remarkable lack of transparency in the processing of World Heritage nominations, as well as other processes of the World Heritage Convention, has been strongly criticized by indigenous organizations as inconsistent with the right of indigenous peoples to participate in decision-making affecting them, as well as with sustainable development principles and State obligations to ensure public participation in environmental decision-making.[109]

Response of human rights bodies

International and regional human rights bodies have, on countless occasions, expressed concerns about the impacts of the establishment and management of specific conservation areas on indigenous peoples and their ability to pursue traditional ways of life. They have underlined, among other things, that conservation areas established in the ancestral territories of indigenous peoples must allow for sustainable economic and social development that is compatible with the cultural characteristics and living conditions of the indigenous peoples concerned, that the management of such areas must ensure the effective participation of indigenous peoples in decisions affecting them, and that redress must be provided for dispossessions and land alienation suffered by indigenous peoples as a result of the establishment of such areas.[110] There are also numerous cases in which human rights bodies have expressed concern over violations of indigenous rights in conservation areas that were recognized as World Heritage sites or included on States Parties' tentative lists of potential World Heritage sites, and have urged the respective States Parties to address these concerns.[111]

---

108 Until the mid-1990s, the *Operational Guidelines* even promoted non-transparent and non-participatory nomination processes, requiring that: "In all cases, so as to maintain the objectivity of the evaluation process and to avoid possible embarrassment to those concerned, States Parties should refrain from giving undue publicity to the fact that a property has been nominated for inscription pending the final decision of the Committee on the nomination in question" (former para. 14). While this provision was deleted in 1996, similar thinking continues to be contained in Annex 6 of the *Guidelines* (Procedures of ICOMOS for the evaluation of cultural sites), where States Parties "are requested to ensure that ICOMOS evaluation missions are given a low profile so far as the media are concerned... [P]remature publicity can cause embarrassment both to ICOMOS and to the World Heritage Committee."

109 See *The future we want*, para. 43 (Outcome document of the 2012 UN Conference on Sustainable Development) and the 1998 *Aarhus Convention on Access to Information, Public Participation in Decision-Making and Access to Justice in Environmental Matters*.

110 See, e.g., CERD 2004, para. 13; CERD 2007, para. 22; CERD 2008, para. 19; CESCR. 2012, paras. 22, 29; or ACHPR 2009.

111 See, e.g., CERD 2012 (Kaeng Krachan National Park, Thailand); CCPR 2012, para. 24, CERD 2011, para. 17; and ACHPR 2011 (Kenya Lake System), Kenya); ACHPR 2000, pp. 12-16 (Bwindi Impenetrable National Park, Uganda; Kahuzi-Biega National Park, DRC; Dja Faunal Reserve, Cameroon; Ngorongoro Conservation Area, Tanzania; among other sites); Kothari 2008, para. 104 (Chitwan National Park, Nepal); Anaya 2012a, para. 13 and 2012c, para. 50 (Quebrada de Humahuaca, Argentina).

In recent years, due to the many concerns raised by indigenous peoples in relation to World Heritage sites around the world, several international human rights bodies and mandate-holders have drawn attention to systemic shortcomings in the implementation of the World Heritage Convention and called on the World Heritage Committee, UNESCO and the Advisory Bodies to take corrective action. Back in 2005, before the adoption of the UNDRIP, the UN General Assembly had already made the following recommendation to UNESCO, contained in the *Programme of Action for the Second International Decade of the World's Indigenous People*:

> "UNESCO is urged to establish mechanisms to enable indigenous peoples to participate effectively in its work relating to them, such as the... nomination of indigenous sites in the World Heritage List and other programmes relevant to indigenous peoples."[112]

Since the General Assembly's adoption of the UNDRIP in 2007, all three of the UN mechanisms with specific mandates concerning the rights of indigenous peoples (UNPFII, EMRIP and Special Rapporteur) have urged the World Heritage Committee to bring the implementation of the World Heritage Convention into line with the requirements of the UNDRIP, and to adopt changes to the existing procedures and Operational Guidelines to that end. In his 2012 report to the General Assembly, Special Rapporteur James Anaya highlighted that:

> "... there is still no specific policy or procedure which ensures that indigenous peoples can participate in the nomination and management of these sites [World Heritage sites within or near their traditional territories, or otherwise affecting them]. The Operational Guidelines for Implementation of the World Heritage Convention, which set out the procedure for the inscription of properties on the World Heritage list and the protection and conservation of sites, are silent on the issue of participation by indigenous peoples. The guidelines provide only that States parties to the Convention are encouraged to ensure the participation of a wide variety of stakeholders in the identification, nomination and protection of World Heritage properties." [113]

In 2013 the Special Rapporteur sent a letter to the World Heritage Committee drawing attention to a number of concerns raised by indigenous peoples regarding respect for their rights and worldviews in the nomination and management of World Heritage sites and the overall implementation of the Convention. He encouraged the Committee to undertake a review of its procedures and consider reforms to address these concerns, "emphasiz[ing]

---

112 UNGA 2005, para. 16.
113 Anaya 2012b, para. 35. With regard to the nomination of sites, the Special Rapporteur further criticized the fact that "States are not specifically required to provide any information on the indigenous peoples and local communities living in or around a site they nominate for World Heritage designation, or review the kind of impact a site might have on the rights of these groups" and that States are not required to "provide information about whether affected peoples have been asked about and agree with the nomination" (ibid. para. 36).

the importance of consulting with indigenous peoples throughout the entirety of such a review process".[114]

The UN Expert Mechanism on the Rights of Indigenous Peoples, a subsidiary body of the Human Rights Council, has offered the following advice to the World Heritage Committee, drawing attention to Articles 41 and 42 of the UNDRIP:

"... UNESCO must enable and ensure effective representation and participation of indigenous peoples in decision-making related to the World Heritage Convention... [R]obust procedures and mechanisms should be established to ensure that indigenous peoples are adequately consulted and involved in the management and protection of World Heritage sites, and that their free, prior and informed consent is obtained when their territories are being nominated and inscribed as World Heritage sites...

[The Expert Mechanism] Encourages the World Heritage Committee to establish a process to elaborate, with the full and effective participation of indigenous peoples, changes to the current procedures and operational guidelines and other appropriate measures to ensure that the implementation of the World Heritage Convention is consistent with the United Nations Declaration on the Rights of Indigenous Peoples and that indigenous peoples can effectively participate in the World Heritage Convention's decision-making processes."[115]

Similarly, the UN Permanent Forum on Indigenous Issues has encouraged the World Heritage Committee to revise the Convention's procedures and *Operational Guidelines* in order to ensure that the rights of indigenous peoples are respected and that their livelihoods and their tangible and intangible heritage are protected in World Heritage areas. The Permanent Forum has expressed its availability to assist in the review and revision of the *Operational Guidelines* and has also recommended that UNESCO invite indigenous representatives and experts to contribute to these efforts.[116] Additionally, the Permanent Forum has suggested that "the initial efforts to establish a World Heritage Indigenous Peoples' Council of Experts (WHIPCOE) be revisited and efforts to set up an appropriate mechanism whereby indigenous experts can provide advice to the World Heritage Committee and the World Heritage Centre be revived".[117]

Other bodies that have called on the World Heritage Committee to align the implementation of the World Heritage Convention with the UNDRIP include the African Commission on Human and Peoples' Rights (ACHPR) and the IUCN World Conservation Congress. The ACHPR, the human rights body of the African Union that oversees the implementation of the *African Charter on Human and Peoples' Rights*, adopted a specific resolution on the protection of indigenous

---

[114] See Appendix 5 of this volume and Human Rights Council 2014, p. 127, containing hyperlinks to both the letter of the Special Rapporteur and the reply received from the World Heritage Centre (Case No. OTH 10/2013). Also see UN Doc. A/HRC/27/52/Add.4.
[115] EMRIP 2012, p. 7 (Proposal 9: World Heritage Committee). Similarly, EMRIP 2011, Annex, para. 38.
[116] UNPFII 2011a, paras. 40-42; UNPFII 2011b.
[117] UNPFII 2010b; 2011b.

peoples' rights in the context of the World Heritage Convention in 2011, in which it expresses concern over the fact that "there are numerous World Heritage sites in Africa that have been inscribed without the free, prior and informed consent of the indigenous peoples in whose territories they are located and whose management frameworks are not consistent with the principles of the UN Declaration on the Rights of Indigenous Peoples".[118] In particular, the resolution condemned the World Heritage Committee's 2011 listing of Lake Bogoria National Reserve in Kenya as a World Heritage site (as part of the "Kenya Lake System in the Great Rift Valley") without involving the indigenous Endorois community in the decision-making process and without obtaining their free, prior and informed consent.[119] The ACHPR urged the World Heritage Committee:

"to review and revise current procedures and Operational Guidelines... in order to ensure that the implementation of the World Heritage Convention is consistent with the UN Declaration on the Rights of Indigenous Peoples and that indigenous peoples' rights, and human rights generally, are respected, protected and fulfilled in World Heritage areas;" [and]

"... to consider establishing an appropriate mechanism through which indigenous peoples can provide advice to the World Heritage Committee and effectively participate in its decision-making processes".[120]

Additionally, the ACHPR criticized IUCN for having recommended, in its capacity as an Advisory Body to the World Heritage Committee, the inscription of Lake Bogoria on the World Heritage List despite the lack of involvement of the Endorois in the nomination process. It therefore "urge[d] IUCN to review and revise its procedures for evaluating World Heritage nominations as well as the state of conservation of World Heritage sites, with a view to ensuring that indigenous peoples are fully involved in these processes, and that their rights are respected, protected and fulfilled in these processes and in the management of World Heritage areas".[121]

This led, in 2012, to the adoption of a resolution entitled "*Implementation of the United Nations Declaration on the Rights of Indigenous Peoples in the context of the UNESCO World Heritage*

---

118 *Resolution on the protection of indigenous peoples' rights in the context of the World Heritage Convention and the designation of Lake Bogoria as a World Heritage site* (ACHPR 2011), Preamble. The full text of the resolution is reproduced in Appendix 1 of this volume.
119 The World Heritage listing of Lake Bogoria happened less than two years after the ACHPR's landmark ruling in the Endorois case (ACHPR 2009), in which it condemned the forcible eviction of the Endorois during the creation of the Lake Bogoria reserve in the 1970s. The ACHPR ordered Kenya to "Recognise rights of ownership to the Endorois and Restitute Endorois ancestral land" and to "Pay adequate compensation to the community for all the loss suffered". The ACHPR also underlined that, in the case of any development projects that would have a major impact within the Endorois territory, "the State has a duty not only to consult with the community, but also to obtain their free, prior, and informed consent, according to their customs and traditions" (para. 291). For details on the case, see Sing'Oei, this volume.
120 ACHPR 2011, paras. 2, 3.
121 Ibid., para. 4.

Convention" by the IUCN World Conservation Congress, IUCN's highest decision-making body.[122] The resolution notes that the World Conservation Congress shares the concerns of the ACHPR and requests that IUCN's Director-General and Council (the principal governing body of IUCN) develop clear policy and practical guidelines to ensure that the principles of the UNDRIP are respected in IUCN's work as an Advisory Body and that indigenous peoples are fully informed and consulted when sites are evaluated or missions undertaken on their territories.[123] In addition, the resolution urges the World Heritage Committee to revise the *Operational Guidelines* to ensure that indigenous peoples' rights and all human rights are upheld and implemented in the management and protection of existing World Heritage sites and that no World Heritage sites are established in indigenous peoples' territories without their free, prior and informed consent. It further urges the Committee to "work with State Parties to establish mechanisms to assess and redress the effects of historic and current injustices against indigenous peoples in existing World Heritage sites" and to "establish a mechanism through which indigenous peoples can provide direct advice to the Committee in its decision-making processes in a manner consistent with the right of free, prior and informed consent and the right to participate in decision making as affirmed in the [UNDRIP]".[124]

Conclusion

The repeated violations of indigenous peoples' rights in World Heritage sites and in the processes of the World Heritage Convention are, in many ways, the result of the inadequacy of the Convention's procedures and operational guidelines. They have drawn the attention of international human rights bodies and mechanisms and stand in sharp contrast to UNESCO's mission, the principles upon which the Organization was founded and the overarching values which it promotes. The violations are damaging the reputation and credibility of UNESCO as an institution committed to furthering respect for human rights, cultural diversity, sustainable development and intercultural understanding and threaten to overshadow the positive role that the World Heritage Convention can undoubtedly play for indigenous peoples by helping them protect their lands, cultures and heritage. They are also incompatible with UNESCO's vision that World Heritage sites should "serve as an example, and become conservation models for all sites, including those of more local interest".[125]

While it is clear that awareness of the problems and the need for corrective action is growing within UNESCO, there are several factors that pose significant obstacles to aligning the implementation of the Convention with the principles and requirements of the UNDRIP. Chief

---

122 IUCN 2012. For the full resolution, see Appendix 2 of this volume.
123 IUCN 2012, para. 1.a. IUCN has begun to act on this request by making a number of improvements to its practice in evaluating World Heritage nominations. It has also concluded a review of its World Heritage evaluation processes in relation to questions related to communities and rights. See IUCN 2013, pp. ii-iii and the chapter by Larsen, Oviedo and Badman in this volume.
124 IUCN 2012, para. 2.
125 UNESCO 2004, para. 39.

among these may be the fact that, for many if not most States Parties to the Convention, including many of those serving as Members of the World Heritage Committee, the main interest in the World Heritage Convention today lies in the prestige, tourism profits and economic development that World Heritage sites can bring to a country or region. This has resulted in a climate and culture within the Committee where economic and political interests all too often override all other concerns, including human rights principles and even conservation considerations. The Director of the World Heritage Centre, Kishore Rao, recently remarked:

> "[The] question is whether safeguarding our common heritage for present and future generations is the real motivation for identifying and adding sites to the World Heritage List, or has it been eclipsed by other considerations, such as economics and national prestige… [T]he general impression is often of intense pressure to have sites designated as World Heritage because of the expected economic benefits or the prestige involved. Perhaps we are failing in our narrative to effectively communicate a coherent message about the true objectives of the Convention…" [126]

At the same time, the World Heritage Committee acts, in many ways, as if the Convention existed in a vacuum and pays little to no regard to international legal standards developed in other intergovernmental forums or the legal obligations of States under other international instruments. In particular, the Committee has been oblivious to the developments in human rights law since the Convention's adoption in 1972, as evident from the fact that the *Operational Guidelines* to this day contain no references whatsoever to human rights standards or instruments.[127] Although the Member States of UNESCO have on many occasions jointly reaffirmed their commitment to human rights through resolutions, declarations and conventions adopted by the General Conference, these commitments have not been translated into the World Heritage context. For example, the *UNESCO Strategy on Human Rights*, adopted by the General Conference in 2003, has had no perceptible impact on the implementation of the World Heritage Convention. This lack of coherence and synergy is clearly not in the interests of UNESCO, and may in fact be contrary to its Constitution, according to which the end goal of any international collaboration under the umbrella of UNESCO is the furthering of universal respect for justice, the rule of law and human rights.[128] As the international law expert Luke T. Lee once wrote, in reference to Article 1 of the UNESCO Constitution:

> "[T]he purpose of UNESCO is to further justice, the rule of law, human rights, and fundamental freedoms – a legal concept, objectively definable. International collaboration in the fields of education, science and culture is but a means to an end. To replace the

---

126 UNESCO 2013a, p. 83.
127 Noteworthy in this context is para. 44 of the *Operational Guidelines*, which contains a list of the Conventions the Committee considers relevant to the protection of cultural and natural heritage. None of the international human rights instruments are included in this list.
128 Art. 1 of the UNESCO Constitution.

end by the means, as has been done in many of its recent activities, would exceed the competence of UNESCO." [129]

There have been some efforts by UNESCO in recent years to enhance respect for indigenous peoples' rights in the implementation of the World Heritage Convention.[130] In November 2011, when UNESCO launched the process to develop the planned house-wide Policy on Indigenous Peoples, which, once adopted, shall provide "guidance to staff *and committees* in order to effectively implement the UNDRIP in all components of UNESCO's work",[131] Director-General Irina Bokova remarked that UNESCO, as the Secretariat for the World Heritage Convention, was "consciously working to improve and promote the free, prior and informed consent and the full and effective participation of indigenous peoples in the establishment and management of [World] Heritage sites".[132]

The following year, the World Heritage Convention's 40th anniversary, celebrated by UNESCO under the theme of "World Heritage and Sustainable Development: the Role of Local Communities", provided a framework for increased attention on the experiences of indigenous peoples with the Convention. UNESCO noted in a statement at the 2011 session of the Permanent Forum on Indigenous Issues that the anniversary would provide an excellent opportunity for indigenous peoples to engage with UNESCO and the World Heritage Committee and its Secretariat, "in order to address concerns that have been raised within the framework of the Permanent Forum and to work towards a constructive solution to the challenges that the [UNDRIP] brings to the international community as a whole".[133] UNESCO also dedicated an edition of its quarterly magazine *World Heritage* to the issue of "World Heritage and Indigenous Peoples" during the anniversary year, including, among other things, an interview with the then Chair of the Permanent Forum, Myrna Cunningham.[134] At the Closing Event of the 40th anniversary in November 2012 in Kyoto, Japan, the Director of the World Heritage Centre called on the World Heritage Committee to seriously consider the Permanent Forum's appeal "for the principle of free, prior and informed consent to be introduced within the *Operational Guidelines*".[135] UNESCO's Assistant Director-General for Culture, Francesco Bandarin, encouraged the Committee on the same occasion to reconsider the proposal to create a World Heritage Indigenous Peoples Council of Experts (WHIPCOE) in light of the adoption of the UNDRIP in 2007.[136]

---

129 Lee 1965, p. 740.
130 Additionally, there have been efforts by the Advisory Bodies to promote the use of human rights-based approaches in the World Heritage context. See Larsen, Oviedo and Badman, this volume; Ekern et al. 2012; and Sinding-Larsen 2012.
131 UNESCO 2014a, p. 3 (emphasis added).
132 UNESCO 2011b, at 00:06:20. Also see Bandarin 2012, p. 327: "The principle of free, prior and informed consent, as outlined in UNDRIP... will have major importance in UNESCO's policy development process with respect to indigenous peoples. In particular, as the current OGs of the World Heritage Convention do not explicitly make reference to the free, prior and informed consent of indigenous communities, continuing efforts will be made to respond to this challenge."
133 UNESCO 2011c.
134 Cunningham 2012.
135 UNESCO 2013a, p. 84.
136 Ibid., p. 43.

The 40th anniversary also provided the context for the organization of an "International Expert Workshop on the World Heritage Convention and Indigenous Peoples" by the Danish Agency for Culture, the Government of Greenland and IWGIA. Held in Copenhagen in September 2012, the workshop involved indigenous experts and human rights experts from around the world, as well as representatives of the Permanent Forum, EMRIP, UNESCO, IUCN and ICOMOS. Participants also included several of the authors of articles contained in this book. The workshop resulted in a "Call to Action" containing recommendations on how to align the implementation of the World Heritage Convention with the UNDRIP, as well as a set of proposed amendments to the Convention's *Operational Guidelines* aimed at ensuring respect for indigenous peoples' right to free, prior and informed consent in the context of World Heritage designations.[137] The workshop recommendations were presented to UNESCO and the States Parties of the World Heritage Convention during the Closing Event of the anniversary in Kyoto, Japan. Subsequently, the World Heritage Centre brought the results of the workshop to the attention of the World Heritage Committee's 37th session in June 2013 in Phnom Penh, Cambodia, suggesting that the Committee consider implications for future revisions of the *Operational Guidelines*.[138]

Unfortunately, preliminary discussions by the Committee in a working group during the Phnom Penh session revealed significant reservations and opposition among some Committee members to adding provisions related to indigenous peoples and their rights to the *Operational Guidelines*, including from governments that voted for the adoption of UNDRIP and have repeatedly expressed their commitment to advancing recognition and respect for the rights of indigenous peoples as enshrined in the UNDRIP.[139] The Committee decided, however, to "re-examine the recommendations of this meeting [the Copenhagen expert workshop] following the results of the discussions to be held by the Executive Board on the UNESCO Policy on indigenous peoples".[140]

One can therefore only hope that the adoption of the UNESCO Policy, together with the momentum generated by the World Conference on Indigenous Peoples, will provide the necessary impetus for the World Heritage Committee to finally adopt a human rights-based approach to its activities affecting indigenous peoples and take the necessary steps to ensure that the nomination, designation, management and protection of World Heritage sites consistently occurs in accordance with the principles affirmed in the UNDRIP. Considering the high visibility of the World Heritage Convention and its role as one of UNESCO's flagship programs, it is clear

---

137 For the Call to Action see Appendix 3 of this volume. The proposed amendments to the *Operational Guidelines* are available at http://www.iwgia.org/news/search-news?news_id=678 and http://whc.unesco.org/en/events/906/. For the report of the expert workshop see Disko and Tugendhat 2013.
138 UNESCO 2013d, p. 26 (Draft Decision 37 COM 5A, para. 6) and UNESCO 2013e, paras. 12, 13.
139 Personal observation by Stefan Disko. A main reason for the reservations and opposition of governments appears to be doubts about the concept and definition of 'indigenous peoples', which seem particularly prevalent in the African context. To clarify such doubts, the "Pan-African Forum for a Culture of Peace", organized jointly by UNESCO, the African Union (AU) and the Government of Angola in March 2013, made the following recommendation: "The AU, supported by the United Nations system, should ensure the wide dissemination of the reports of the [ACHPR], and the relevant clauses of the African Charter, which clarify the definition and status of indigenous peoples in the African context, so as to help dispel widespread misunderstandings and misinterpretations" (UNESCO 2013b, p. 11). For the respective reports see ACHPR 2005 and ACHPR 2006.
140 Decision 37 COM 12.II, para. 7.

that this is crucial not only for the credibility of the Convention itself but also for the credibility of UNESCO as a whole.

References

ACHPR. 2000. *Report of the African Commission's Working Group of Experts on Indigenous Populations/Communities.* Adopted by the ACHPR at its 28th ordinary session. Doc. DOC/OS(XXXIV)/345.

ACHPR. 2005. *Report of the African Commission's Working Group of Experts on Indigenous Populations/Communities.* (Adopted by the ACHPR at its 34th Ordinary Session in 2003). Copenhagen, ACHPR and IWGIA.

ACHPR. 2006. *Indigenous Peoples in Africa: the Forgotten Peoples?* [Summary of ACHPR 2005]. Copenhagen, ACHPR and IWGIA.

ACHPR. 2009. *Communication 276/2003 – Centre for Minority Rights Development (Kenya) and Minority Rights Group International on behalf of Endorois Welfare Council v Kenya.* Decision of the African Commission on Human and Peoples' Rights, adopted in November 2009, endorsed by the African Union on 2 February 2010. 27th Activity Report of the ACHPR (2009), Annex 5.

ACHPR. 2011. *Resolution on the protection of indigenous peoples' rights in the context of the World Heritage Convention and the designation of Lake Bogoria as a World Heritage site.* Res.197 (L)2011 of the African Commission on Human and Peoples' Rights adopted on 5 November 2011.

Anaya, J. 2008. *Report of the Special Rapporteur on the situation of human rights and fundamental freedoms of indigenous people, S. James Anaya* (Report to the Human Rights Council). UN Doc. A/HRC/9/9.

Anaya, J. 2009. *Report of the Special Rapporteur on the situation of human rights and fundamental freedoms of indigenous people, S. James Anaya* (Report to the Human Rights Council). UN Doc. A/HRC/12/34.

Anaya, J. 2011. *Report of the Special Rapporteur on the rights of indigenous peoples* (Report to the UN General Assembly). UN Doc. A/66/288.

Anaya, J. 2012a. *Report of the Special Rapporteur on the rights of indigenous peoples, James Anaya* (Report to the Human Rights Council). UN Doc. A/HRC/21/47.

Anaya, J. 2012b. *Report of the Special Rapporteur on the rights of indigenous peoples* (Report to the UN General Assembly). UN Doc. A/67/301.

Anaya, J. 2012c. *Report of the Special Rapporteur on the rights of indigenous peoples, James Anaya – Addendum: The situation of indigenous peoples in Argentina* (Report to the Human Rights Council). UN Doc. A/HRC/21/47/Add.2.

Anaya, J. 2013. *Report of the Special Rapporteur on the rights of indigenous peoples* (Report to the UN General Assembly). UN Doc. A/68/317.

Bandarin, F. 2012. International trade in indigenous cultural heritage: comments from UNESCO in light of its international standard-setting instruments in the field of culture. J. Graber, K. Kuprecht and Jessica Lai (eds.), *International Trade in Indigenous Cultural Heritage.* Cheltenham, Edward Elgar.

CCPR. 1994. Human Rights Committee, *General Comment No. 23: The rights of minorities (Art. 27).* UN Doc. CCPR/C/21/Rev.1/Add.5.

CCPR. 1999. *Concluding observations of the Human Rights Committee: Canada.* UN Doc. CCPR/C/79/Add.105.

CCPR. 2012. Concluding observations of the Human Rights Committee: Kenya. UN Doc. CCPR/C/KEN/CO/3.

CERD. 1997. Committee on the Elimination of Racial Discrimination, *General Recommendation No. 23, Rights of indigenous peoples.* UN Doc. A/52/18, Annex V, pp. 122-123.

CERD. 2004. *Concluding Observations of the Committee on the Elimination of Racial Discrimination: Nepal.* CERD/C/64/CO/5.

CERD. 2007. *Concluding Observations of the Committee on the Elimination of Racial Discrimination: Ethiopia.* UN Doc. CERD/C/ETH/CO/15.

CERD. 2008. *Concluding Observations of the Committee on the Elimination of Racial Discrimination: Namibia.* UN Doc. CERD/C/NAM/CO/12.

CERD. 2011. *Concluding Observations of the Committee on the Elimination of Racial Discrimination: Kenya.* UN Doc. CERD/C/KEN/CO/1-4.

CERD. 2012. Committee on the Elimination of Racial Discrimination, Early Warning and Urgent Action Procedure: Letter to Thailand regarding Kaeng Krachan National Park, 9 March 2012. http://www2.ohchr.org/english/bodies/cerd/docs/CERD_Thailand.pdf (accessed 1 June 2014).

CESCR. 2009. Committee on Economic, Social and Cultural Rights, *General comment No. 21: Right of everyone to take part in cultural life* (Art. 15, para. 1(a) of the ICESCR). UN Doc. E/C.12/GC/21.

CESCR. 2012. Concluding observations of the Committee on Economic, Social and Cultural Rights: United Republic of Tanzania. UN Doc. E/C.12/TZA/CO/1-3.

Cunningham, M. 2012. Interview with Myrna Cunningham, Chair of the United Nations Permanent Forum on Indigenous Issues (UNPFII). *World Heritage*, No. 62 ('World Heritage and Indigenous Peoples'), pp. 54-57.

Disko, S. and Tugendhat, H. 2013. *Report: International Expert Workshop on the World Heritage Convention and Indigenous Peoples, 20-21 September 2012 – Copenhagen, Denmark*. Copenhagen, IWGIA, Danish Agency for Culture and Government of Greenland.

Ekern, S. et al. 2012. Human rights and World Heritage: preserving our common dignity through rights-based approaches to site management. *International Journal of Heritage Studies*, Vol. 18, No. 3, pp. 213-225.

EMRIP. 2011. *Final report of the study on indigenous peoples and the right to participate in decision-making*. UN Doc. A/HRC/18/42.

EMRIP. 2012. *Report of the Expert Mechanism on the Rights of Indigenous Peoples on its fifth session (Geneva, 9-13 July 2012)*. UN Doc. A/HRC/21/52.

Endorois Welfare Council et al. 2011. *Joint Statement on Continuous violations of the principle of free, prior and informed consent in the context of UNESCO's World Heritage Convention*. http://www.iwgia.org/iwgia_files_news_files/0314_UNPFII_2011_Joint_Statement_on_FPIC_and_orld_Heritage.pdf (accessed 29 May 2014).

Feiring, B. 2013. *Indigenous peoples' rights to lands, territories, and resources*. Rome, International Land Coalition.

Forest Peoples Programme. 2013. *Indigenous Peoples and United Nations Human Rights Bodies - Series of Compilations of UN Treaty Body Jurisprudence and the Recommendations of the Human Rights Council*. http://www.forestpeoples.org/tags/indigenous-peoples-and-united-nations-human-rights-bodies-series-compilations-un-treaty-body-ju (accessed 14 May 2014).

Human Rights Council. 2014. *Communications report of Special Procedures*. UN Doc. A/HRC/25/74.

ILA. 2004. *Accountability of International Organisations: Final Report* (International Law Association, Berlin Conference, 2004). Adopted by ILA Res. No. 1/2004. http://www.ila-hq.org/en/committees/index.cfm/cid/9 (accessed 14 May 2014).

ILA. 2010. *Rights of Indigenous Peoples: Interim Report* (International Law Association, The Hague Conference, 2010). http://www.ila-hq.org/en/committees/index.cfm/cid/1024 (accessed 14 May 2014).

ILA. 2012a. *Rights of Indigenous Peoples: Final Report* (International Law Association, Sofia Conference, 2012). http://www.ila-hq.org/en/committees/index.cfm/cid/1024 (accessed 14 May 2014).

ILA. 2012b. *Resolution No. 5/2012: Rights of Indigenous Peoples*. Adopted by the International Law Association at its 75th Conference, Sofia, Bulgaria, 26-30 August 2012. http://www.ila-hq.org/download.cfm/docid/6784224B-04C6-490A-A0724CC6BAF63838 (accessed 14 May 2014).

IUCN. 2002. *PARKS, Vol. 12, No. 2: Local communities and protected areas*. Gland, IUCN.

IUCN. 2012. *Implementation of the United Nations Declaration on the Rights of Indigenous Peoples in the context of the UNESCO World Heritage Convention* (Resolution No. 047 of the 2012 World Conservation Congress).

IUCN. 2013. *IUCN World Heritage Evaluations 2013*. UNESCO Doc. WHC-13/37.COM/INF.8B2.

IWGIA et al. 2012. *Joint Submission on the Lack of implementation of the UN Declaration on the Rights of Indigenous Peoples in the context of UNESCO's World Heritage Convention*. http://www.forestpeoples.org/sites/fpp/files/publication/2012/05/joint-submission-unpfii.pdf (accessed 29 May 2014).

Jokilehto, J. 1999. Conservation policies in relation to cultural World Heritage Sites. *1999 Nara Seminar Report: Development and Integrity of Historic Cities*, pp. 9-16. http://unesdoc.unesco.org/images/0014/001498/149805eo.pdf (accessed 26 May 2014).

Kothari, M. 2008. *Report of the Special Rapporteur on adequate housing as a component of the right to an adequate standard of living, and on the right to non-discrimination in this context, Miloon Kothari – Addendum: Communications to and from Governments*. UN Doc. A/HRC/7/16/Add.1.

Lee, L. 1965. UNESCO: Some Comments on Purpose, Program and Administration. *Duke Law Journal*, Vol. 1965, No. 4, pp. 735-763.

Matsuura, K. 2007. *Message from Mr Koïchiro Matsuura, Director-General of UNESCO, on the occasion of the approval of the United Nations Declaration on the Rights of Indigenous Peoples by the UN General Assembly at its 62nd Session*. http://portal.unesco.org/en/ev.php-URL_ID=39604&URL_DO=DO_TOPIC&URL_SECTION=201.html (accessed 22 May 2014).

Matsuura, K. 2008. *Message from Mr Koïchiro Matsuura, Director-General of UNESCO, on the occasion of the International Day of the World's Indigenous People, 9 August 2008*. UNESCO Doc DG/ME/ID/2008/011 REV.

Mirarr People. 2002. *Submission by the Mirarr People, Kakadu, Australia to United Nations Permanent Forum for Indigenous Issues, New York, USA 13-24 May 2002.* http://www.docip.org/greenstone/collect/cendocdo/index/assoc/HASHb7cf/2987360b.dir/D_29.pdf (accessed 29 May 2014).

OHCHR. 2006. *Frequently asked questions on a human rights-based approach to development cooperation.* Geneva, Office of the UN High Commissioner for Human Rights. UN Doc. HR/PUB/06/8.

Reinisch, A. 2005. The Changing International Legal Framework for Dealing with Non-State Actors. P. Alston (ed.), *Non-State Actors and Human Rights.* Oxford, Oxford University Press, pp. 37-92.

Sinding-Larsen, A. 2012. Our Common Dignity: rights-based approaches to heritage management. *World Heritage*, No. 62, pp. 56-58.

Stavenhagen, R. 2007. *Report of the Special Rapporteur on the situation of human rights and fundamental freedoms of indigenous people, Rodolfo Stavenhagen* (Report to the Human Rights Council). UN Doc. A/HRC/6/15.

Titchen, S. 2002. *Indigenous peoples and cultural and natural World Heritage sites.* Conference presentation, New York, 15 May 2002 (transcript from audiotape). www.dialoguebetweennations.com/N2N/PFII/English/SarahTitchen.htm (accessed 26 May 2014).

UNDESA. 2008. *Resource Kit on Indigenous Peoples' Issues.* New York, UN Department of Economic and Social Affairs. http://www.un.org/esa/socdev/unpfii/documents/resource_kit_indigenous_2008.pdf (accessed 15 May 2014).

UNDG. 2009. *United Nations Development Group Guidelines on Indigenous Peoples' Issues.* New York, United Nations. UN Doc. HR/P/PT/16.

UNESCO. 2001. *Report on the Proposed World Heritage Indigenous Peoples Council of Experts (WHIPCOE).* UNESCO Doc. WHC-2001/CONF.205/WEB.3.

UNESCO. 2002. *World Heritage Committee, Twenty-fifth session, Helsinki, Finland, 11-16 December 2001: Report.* UNESCO Doc. WHC-01/CONF.208/24.

UNESCO. 2003. *UNESCO Strategy on Human Rights.* UNESCO Doc. SHS-2007/WS/15.

UNESCO. 2004. *Report by the Director-General of UNESCO on the United Nations Year for Cultural Heritage 2002 and on its Follow-up.* Paris, UNESCO.

UNESCO. 2008. *Medium-Term Strategy 2008-2013.* UNESCO Doc. 34 C/4.

UNESCO. 2011a. *Progress report on the preparation of the 40th Anniversary of the Convention.* UNESCO Doc. WHC-10/35.COM/12D.

UNESCO. 2011b. Towards a UNESCO Policy on Engaging with Indigenous Peoples: Launching event, 10 November 2011. Speech by Gretchen Kalonji on behalf of UNESCO Director-General Irina Bokova (Audio recording). http://www.unesco.org/new/en/indigenous-peoples/related-info/unesco-policy-on-indigenous-peoples/launch-event-policy-on-indigenous-people/ipp-videos/ (accessed 5 June 2014).

UNESCO. 2011c. *10th Session of the Permanent Forum on Indigenous Issues – Statement by UNESCO, Agenda Item: Free Prior and Informed Consent, 17 May 2011.* http://www.docip.org/greenstone/collect/cendocdo/index/assoc/HASHbf66/1aed222f.dir/PF11douglas071.pdf (accessed 14 June 2014).

UNESCO. 2013a. *Celebrating 40 years of the World Heritage Convention, November 2012, Kyoto, Japan: Proceedings.* Paris: UNESCO.

UNESCO. 2013b. *Final Report of the Pan-African Forum "Sources and Resources for a Culture of Peace", Luanda, Angola, 26-28 March 2013.* UNESCO Doc. 191 EX/4.INF.3.

UNESCO. 2013c. *Medium-Term Strategy 2014–2021.* UNESCO Doc. 37 C/4.

UNESCO. 2013d. *Report of the World Heritage Centre on its activities and the implementation of the World Heritage Committee's Decisions.* UNESCO Doc. WHC-13/37.COM/5A.

UNESCO. 2013e. *Revision of the Operational Guidelines* (Secretariat document prepared for the 37th session of the World Heritage Committee, Item 12 of the Provisional Agenda). UNESCO Doc. WHC-13/37.COM/12.

UNESCO. 2014a. *Report on the achievement of the goal and objectives of the Second International Decade of the World's Indigenous Peoples (2005-2014): Questionnaire Response.* February 2014. http://www.un.org/esa/socdev/unpfii/documents/2014/unesco.pdf (accessed 22 May 2014).

UNESCO. 2014b. *Item 7B of the Provisional Agenda: State of conservation of World Heritage properties inscribed on the World Heritage List* (World Heritage Committee, 38th Session). UNESCO Doc. WHC-14/38.COM/7B.Add.

UNESCO, ICCROM, ICOMOS and IUCN. 2011. *Preparing World Heritage Nominations* (Resource Manual). Paris, UNESCO.

UNGA. 2005. *Programme of Action for the Second International Decade of the World's Indigenous People.* Adopted by the UN General Assembly on 16 December 2005. UN Doc. A/60/270.

UNPFII. 2007. *Permanent Forum on Indigenous Issues: Report on the sixth session (14-25 May 2007).* UN Doc. E/2007/43-E/C.19/2007/12.

UNPFII. 2010a. *Permanent Forum on Indigenous Issues: Report on the ninth session (19-30 April 2010).* UN Doc. E/2010/43-E/C.19/2010/15.
UNPFII. 2010b. *Statement of the United Nations Permanent Forum on Indigenous Issues at the 34th Session of the UNESCO World Heritage Committee* (delivered by Victoria Tauli-Corpuz). http://xa.yimg.com/kq/groups/20674633/27593986/name/UNPFII+Statement+WHC+Final.docx (accessed 29 May 2014).
UNPFII. 2011a. *Permanent Forum on Indigenous Issues: Report on the tenth session (16-27 May 2011).* UN Doc. E/2011/43-E/C.19/2011/14.
UNPFII. 2011b. Statement of the UN Permanent Forum on Indigenous Issues at the 35th Session of the World Heritage Committee (delivered by Paul Kanyinke Sena). http://www.iwgia.org/iwgia_files_news_files/0314_UNPFII_Statement_at_HC_Paris_2011.doc (accessed 29 May 2014).
UNPFII. 2013. *Permanent Forum on Indigenous Issues: Report on the twelfth session (20-31 May 2013).* UN Doc. E/2013/43-E/C.19/2013/25.
Vrdoljak, A. F. 2008a. Article 13: World Heritage Committee and International Assistance. F. Francioni (ed.), *The 1972 World Heritage Convention: A Commentary.* Oxford, Oxford University Press, pp. 219-241.
Vrdoljak, A. F. 2008b. Article 14: The Secretariat and Support of the World Heritage Committee. F. Francioni (ed.), *The 1972 World Heritage Convention: A Commentary.* Oxford, Oxford University Press, pp. 243-268.

Indigenous Peoples and Protected Areas: Towards Reconciliation?

Marcus Colchester

"I have come here to tell you that it is the order of the Administration that you move out of Game Reserve No. 2. The reason for this order is that you are destroying the game. You may go into the Police Zone and seek work on the farms South of Windhoek, or elsewhere. You must take your women and children with you, also your stock... You will have to be out of the Game Reserve the 1st May, 1954. If you are still in the Game Reserve on that day you will be arrested and will be put in gaol. You will be regarded as trespassers... None of you will be allowed to return to Game Reserve No. 2 from Ovamboland... If you have something to say I will listen but I wish to tell you that there is no appeal against this order. The only Bushmen who will be allowed to continue to live in the Game Reserve are those in the employ of the Game Wardens. Convey what you have heard to your absent friends and relatives."

H. Eedes, Native Commissioner of Ovamboland,
to the Hai//om people of Etosha 1954[1]

Introduction: conservation and culture

As human societies have moved further and further away from a direct relationship with their environment, their tendency to treat it as a 'resource' to be controlled, exploited and managed has grown correspondingly. Classical conservation, which seeks to isolate natural areas from human influence, is one expression of this alienation. To the many peoples of the world who remain close to and live from their ancestral lands, waters and territories, these notions remain foreign. Such indigenous peoples, as they are now classed by international law, relate to their territories in a much more integrated and spiritually informed way, many of them seeing what city people call 'nature' to be part of their very lives and being. While policy dialogues today may focus on the economies, laws and institutions that now need to be reformed to accommodate indigenous peoples' rights, it is well to recall the very wide conceptual gulf that remains between indigenous peoples and most conservationists about how humans

---

1 Quoted in Widlok 2009.

Left: Roosevelt Arch at the north entrance to Yellowstone National Park, established in 1872 as the world's first national park and one of the first sites to be inscribed on the World Heritage List in 1978. Conceived as an uninhabited 'wilderness' area, the creation of the Park led to the forced removal of hundreds of indigenous people. The Yellowstone model remained the dominant approach to conservation for the next 140 years and until 1992 provided the basis for the definition of a 'national park' officially used by IUCN. Photo: Harvey Barrison (CC BY-SA 2.0)

should relate to their environment.² At the same time, it has belatedly been recognized that indigenous peoples' knowledge may be invaluable to 'resource management'.³

One of the oldest ways by which urbanised societies have sought to manage nature is through the creation of what we now call 'protected areas'. The approach has very deep roots. Indeed, the idea of setting aside areas to preserve wild species can be traced back to the royal hunting reserves of the Assyrians in 700 BCE, is later apparent in Persian traditions, and had found its way into India by the time of Ashoka in 400 BCE. These ideas were brought into Europe following the conquests of Alexander the Great. Royal hunting reserves were recorded during the reign of Emperor Charlemagne and the first 'forests', as they came to be called, were set up in Britain after the Norman Conquest. These royal hunts, game reserves set aside for the 'sport of kings', were much resented by local people as they imposed severe restrictions on their livelihoods and forbade the expansion of their farms. The first such area established in England nearly 1,000 years ago, and still known as the 'New Forest', required the forced removal of 2,000 villagers from their land.⁴

The ills of urban society have long spawned a longing for escape and, with the growth of industrialism, notions of wilderness preservation became prominent as poets, recreational hunters and nature-lovers left the cities to rejuvenate their souls. While 19th century Europe celebrated its industrial triumphs in grand exhibitions, the newly expanded United States of America celebrated its conquests of the Wild West with the setting aside of the world's first National Parks. These Parks were designed to preserve the country's most dramatic landscapes as 'wilderness' areas, which the law was to define as places where 'man himself is a visitor who does not remain'. It is important to recall, however, that both the Yosemite and the Yellowstone National Parks in the USA required the forced removal of hundreds of indigenous people, who were repeatedly attacked, killed and chased off their ancestral lands by the US Army in order to maintain the Parks free from human settlement for the enjoyment of visiting tourists.⁵

The Yellowstone model remained the dominant approach to conservation for the next 140 years. When the International Union for Conservation of Nature (IUCN) developed a global system for protected areas, the presumption was that these areas should be owned by the State and run by government agencies. National Parks were expressly defined by IUCN as areas "where one or several ecosystems are not materially altered by human exploitation and occupation..." and where "the highest competent authority of the country has taken steps to prevent or eliminate as soon as possible exploitation or occupation of the whole area...".⁶ With funds from the development agencies and the advice of international conservation organizations and legal consultants, these norms thus came to be instituted in the policies, laws and governance regimes of the majority of developing countries. Protected areas became fortresses to be protected from local inhabitants.⁷

---

2   Stevens 1997.
3   Berkes 1999.
4   Colchester 2003; Griffin 2008.
5   Kemf 1993; Keller and Turek 1998.
6   West 1991, p. xvii.
7   Brockington 2002.

Problems of exclusion

As a result of the concerted efforts of a global movement determined to achieve the goals of conservation through the establishment of protected areas, today some 12.9% of the Earth's landmass and 6.3% of its territorial waters have been designated as over 160,000 Protected Areas. It is estimated that as much as half of these protected areas have been established on indigenous peoples' lands without their agreement. The result has been serious social problems for affected peoples and long-standing abuse of their rights.

Summarising an extensive body of literature, we can note that protected areas have caused: the denial of rights to land, territories and use and access to natural resources; denial of political rights and the validity of customary institutions; the shattering of kinship systems and settlement patterns; the erosion of informal social networks, fundamental to local economies; undermining of livelihoods; loss of property; denial of compensation; impoverishment; the disruption of customary systems of environment management; the criminalization of daily life, making people into 'poachers', 'encroachers' and 'squatters' on their own land; their subjection to petty tyrannies by park guards; forced resettlement; the destruction of leadership systems, for if the community leaders accept relocation they are accused of betraying their people but if they resist they are proved powerless; the breaking of symbolic ties to environment; the weakening of cultural identity; intensified pressure on natural resources outside the protected areas; popular unrest, resistance, 'incendiarism', social conflict and ensuing repression.[8] These problems amount to systematic violations of indigenous peoples' rights as recognized in international law.

A 'new paradigm'

The exclusionary approach to conservation has always had its critics but, as the ex-Chairman of the World Commission on Protected Areas later ruefully noted:

> "At least until around the mid-1960s, the climate in which protected areas were set up around the world favoured a top-down and rather exclusive view of protected areas. Setting up large game parks without too much concern for the impact on local people fitted well with the autocratic style of colonial administration (especially in Africa); and it was equally at home in the early days of post-colonial government which followed many of the same styles of administration... Certainly the opinions and rights of indigenous peoples were of little concern to any government before about 1970; they were not organized as a political force as they are now in many countries." [9]

---

8   Chatty and Colchester 2002; Colchester 2004; Dowie 2009.
9   Phillips 2003, p. 3.

Despite this political reality, opposing voices have repeatedly spoken up in favour of alternative forms of conservation that protect indigenous rights. The IUCN's 'Kinshasa Resolution' of 1975 recognized the importance of traditional ways of life and land ownership, and called on governments to maintain and encourage customary ways of living. It urged governments to devise means by which indigenous peoples could bring their lands into conservation areas without relinquishing their ownership, use and tenure rights. It also noted that indigenous peoples should not normally be displaced from their traditional lands by protected areas, nor should protected areas be established without adequate consultation with the peoples to be directly affected.[10]

Since then, urged by a growing clamour from indigenous peoples and their supporters,[11] the IUCN has passed dozens of Resolutions, at its four-yearly World Conservation Congresses, which call for conservation efforts to respect indigenous peoples' rights, as set out in existing and emerging international laws, both inside and outside protected areas.[12] In 1994, the IUCN revised its protected area system to allow indigenous peoples, as well as others, to own and manage protected areas.[13] In 1996, the WWF adopted a progressive policy on indigenous peoples in accordance with the then draft UN Declaration on the Rights of Indigenous Peoples.[14] In 1999, the World Commission on Protected Areas adopted guidelines for the co-management of protected areas, on agreements between indigenous peoples and conservation bodies, on indigenous participation and on a recognition of indigenous peoples' rights to 'sustainable, traditional use' of their lands and territories.[15]

A significant breakthrough for indigenous peoples came at the Vth World Parks Congress, held in Durban, South Africa, in 2003, which was attended by some 150 indigenous representatives. The Durban Accord and Action Plan adopted at the Congress was promoted as a "new paradigm" for protected areas by "equitably integrating them with the interests of all affected people".[16] The Accord celebrates the conservation successes of indigenous peoples and urges the involvement of indigenous peoples in establishing and managing protected areas and their participation in decision-making on a fair and equitable basis in full respect of their human and social rights.

To implement this new vision, the Durban Action Plan requires that the rights of indigenous peoples be recognized and guaranteed in relation to natural resources and biodiversity conservation. Protected area systems must be reformed to take account of these rights, forced resettlement should be strictly eliminated and national authorities should carry out "reviews of conservation initiatives including innovative and traditional/customary governance types…". Targets were set such that:

"All existing and future protected areas shall be managed and established in full compliance with the rights of indigenous peoples, mobile peoples and local communities. Protected

---

10 Colchester 2004.
11 IAIP 1998.
12 Balasinorwala, Kothari and Goyal 2004; FPP 2012.
13 IUCN 1994.
14 WWF 1996.
15 Beltran 2000.
16 Durban Accord.

areas shall have representatives chosen by indigenous peoples and local communities in their management proportionate to their rights and interests. Participatory mechanisms for the restitution of indigenous peoples' traditional lands and territories that were incorporated in protected areas without their free and informed consent [should be] established and implemented by 2010." [17]

International environmental law

The past 30 years have also witnessed important developments in international environmental law, which has unevenly but significantly incorporated language related to indigenous peoples. For example, at the Earth Summit in 1992, indigenous peoples were recognized as a Major Group that should participate in sustainable development. Agenda 21, the action plan adopted at the Summit, devoted a whole chapter to 'Indigenous Peoples' noting that:

"Indigenous peoples and their communities and other local communities have a vital role in environmental management and development because of their knowledge and traditional practices. States should recognise and duly support their identity, culture and interests and enable their effective participation in the achievement of sustainable development."

The Earth Summit also witnessed the agreement of the *Convention on Biological Diversity* (CBD), which enjoins each State party to the Convention:

"Subject to its national legislation, [to] respect, preserve and maintain knowledge, innovations and practices of indigenous and local communities embodying traditional lifestyles relevant for the conservation and sustainable use of biological resources..." (Article 8(j))

"[To] Protect and encourage customary use of biological resources in accordance with traditional cultural practices that are compatible with conservation or sustainable use requirements." (Article 10(c))

The Conference of the Parties (COP) to the CBD meets annually to assess progress in implementing the Convention and makes Decisions, which are authoritative interpretations of how the Convention should be applied. The CBD has often been criticised for not giving proper attention to rights nor, in particular, to the importance of secure tenure. However, sustained advocacy by indigenous peoples has led to some important gains, including with respect to protected areas. At its 7th meeting, the COP explicitly welcomed the outcomes of the Durban World Parks Congress and issued Decision 7.23 of the Conference which:

---

17 Durban Action Plan.

"23. Recalls the obligations of the Parties towards indigenous and local communities in accordance with article 8(j) and related provisions and notes that the establishment, management and planning of protected areas should take place with the full and effective participation of, and *full respect for the rights* of, indigenous and local communities consistent with national law and applicable international obligations." (Emphasis added)

The same COP also adopted a 'Multi-Year Programme of Work' that included a Goal and Target on indigenous peoples as follows:

"**Goal 2.2** To enhance and secure involvement of indigenous and local communities and relevant stakeholders."

"**Target:** Full and effective participation by 2008, of indigenous and local communities, in *full respect of their rights* and recognition of their responsibilities, consistent with national law *and applicable international obligations*, and the participation of relevant stakeholders, in the management of existing, and the establishment of new, protected areas." (Emphasis added)

From principles to practice

Slower progress has been made, however, in putting such ideals into practice. An early effort to reconcile protected areas with local people, promoted since the 1970s under UNESCO's 'Man and Biosphere Programme', proposed the zoning of protected areas by surrounding strictly protected core zones from which humans were excluded with buffer zones where limited livelihoods would be managed but permitted. The experience has been mixed but not encouraging as most buffer zones have been managed as 'projects' by conservationists with little experience of social development who, as one reviewer noted, "frequently pursued objectives which were inconsistent with the aspirations of the very people they were trying to help". Tellingly, the same IUCN study concluded that better results have "not been short-term aid projects but initiatives taken by local community groups or resource managers who have made creative attempts to solve the day to day problems which they faced".[18]

Somewhat better outcomes have come from so-called 'co-management', where local people and national authorities work together to run protected areas.[19] The success of co-management, from indigenous peoples' point of view, has depended largely on the extent to which the peoples' rights are respected and they have real authority over decision-making. As one IUCN study concurred:

"Co-management is often hailed as the appropriate middle ground, within which the needs of all stakeholders can be negotiated and acceptable compromises achieved [but]... this

---

18 Sayer 1991.
19 Borrini-Feyerabend 1997; Weber, Butler and Larson 2000; Oviedo, Maffi and Larsen 2000; Eghenter 2000.

would seem to be only part of the solution. Co-management strategies can only be effective if they are accompanied by parallel efforts to address issues of tenure in the related territory. If tenure arrangements do not secure the interests of local users, there is no incentive to practice sustainable use." [20]

Successive reviews carried out by the Forest Peoples Programme and indigenous partners over the past 15 years in Latin America, Central Africa and South and Southeast Asia have found that, while there are some encouraging examples that show that it is possible to reconcile indigenous peoples' rights with protected areas, on balance conservationists are failing to implement the accords they have signed up to. Protected areas continue to be imposed in violation of indigenous peoples' rights and cause suffering, impoverishment and conflict.[21] A recent review by the CBD itself of progress in implementing its plan of action on protected areas notes that less than a third of countries report significant progress towards participation in protected areas.[22]

There are various reasons for this failure. One is that conservation continues to be funded from the top down, with strong links to the private sector and the global tourism industry, whose interests, consciously or unconsciously, are allowed to dominate decision-making and maintain the status quo.[23] The second major reason is that national polices, laws and institutions continue to be framed by the old exclusionary approach to conservation and the actors empowered by these laws now resist reforms in line with international laws and agreements.[24] Finally, there remains a lack of accessible mechanisms by which indigenous peoples can gain redress for these injustices. This in itself is a continuing abuse of the peoples' right to a remedy.[25]

In 2011, in response to yet another Resolution passed at the 2008 World Conservation Congress calling for a mechanism to reconcile protected areas with indigenous peoples' rights, indigenous peoples and the IUCN's Commission on the Environment, Economy and Social Policy, with the help of IUCN and Forest Peoples Programme, convened a high-level meeting at a Conference, entitled 'Sharing Power', held in Whakatane, New Zealand. The meeting agreed to set up the so-called 'Whakatane Mechanism' by which concerned indigenous peoples, conservationists and State agencies could work together to reconcile protected areas with indigenous rights. The mechanism contemplates field assessments made jointly by the various parties to assess a specific local situation, joint reporting of the findings, followed by national workshops involving all relevant parties to hammer out agreements on what should be done next. The Mechanism is designed to give initiative to the affected peoples and resolve problems through shared learning and dialogue.

So far two successful pilot efforts have been pioneered under the Mechanism, with the Ogiek people of Mount Elgon National Park in Kenya and the Karen and Hmong peoples of the Ob Luang National Park in Thailand. In the Ogiek case, an agreement has now been forged not to require

---

20 Forrest 1999, p. 12.
21 Gray, Parellada and Newing 1997; Colchester and Erni 2000; Nelson and Hossacks 2003; Colchester et al. 2008.
22 CBD 2012.
23 Jeanrenaud 2002; Brocking ton 2002; Chapin 2004.
24 Colchester et al. 2006.
25 MacKay 2002.

their forced removal from the Park, by itself a significant gain as they have already twice had their houses torched and been forcibly expelled since the Park was established. In Thailand, the assessment showed that moves to recognize indigenous farmers' rights in the Park under a project entitled Joint Management of Protected Areas (JoMPA) had reduced conflict and the national workshop agreed both to continue this approach in Ob Luang and extend it to other protected areas in the country. The need to reform national conservation laws to consolidate the joint management approach was also highlighted.[26] The Whakatane Mechanism now needs to be much more widely activated. It constitutes an important if modest step towards providing indigenous peoples with the means of redress that they rightfully insist upon.

Indigenous peoples, sustainable use and international environmental law

The holy grail of the environment movement is sustainability. If resource use outside of protected areas were sustainable, there would be little need for protected areas at all. However, in the meanwhile, protected areas are promoted in order to ensure that at least some areas and the biodiversity they contain are sustained. If indigenous peoples' rights are to be recognized in these areas, conservationists worry that they too will over-exploit resources. Thus, whereas human rights laws affirm indigenous peoples' rights and the CBD requires State parties to protect and encourage sustainable customary use, there remains a lack of agreement as to how such sustainability will be assessed.

Conservation biologists themselves recognize the limits of scientific knowledge on sustainability. For example, the extent to which populations of even large mammals are viable in the face of hunting is largely unknown and research continues to throw up surprises about how species and ecosystems relate.[27] Faced with this lack of knowledge, many conservationists invoke the Precautionary Principle arguing that natural areas should be off limits until sustainability can be assured, although such a simplistic approach itself has its critics.[28]

The exclusionary approach entails its own risks. Not only is it likely to perpetuate conflict with indigenous peoples but the exclusion of customary resource use may even cause a loss of biodiversity and other conservation values, for example, where shifting cultivation generates a greater variety of eco-types in a landscape than if the whole area is climax forest or where stock-grazing or controlled burning generates greater biodiversity in grasslands and semi-deserts. Indeed, recent scientific studies show that forests, including those set aside as protected areas, when under community control are more effective for conservation, provide better livelihoods and retain greater forest cover than forests and national parks under State control.[29]

There are also challenges at the level of international law that remain to be addressed. We should recall that when indigenous peoples began to have recourse to the international human

---

26 Whakatane Mechanism 2012.
27 Redford and Stearman 1993; Robinson and Bennett 2000.
28 Cooney and Dickson 2005.
29 Nepstad et al. 2006; Chhatre and Agrawal 2009; Nelson and Chomitz 2011; Persha, Agrawal and Chhatre 2011; Porter-Bolland et al. 2011.

An assessment meeting between Ogiek community members, Kenya Wildlife Service, Kenya Forest Service and other officials during the pilot Whakatane Assessment in Mount Elgon. Photo: Emmanuel Freudenthal

rights system to bolster their claims for self-determination, they had themselves to recognize that these universal principles also apply to their own societies. The *UN Declaration on the Rights of Indigenous Peoples*, which emphasises the collective rights of indigenous peoples, expressly notes that 'in the exercise of the rights enunciated in the present Declaration, human rights and fundamental freedoms of all shall be respected' (UNDRIP Article 46.2). Indigenous peoples have thus recognized in their own statements that there may be certain beliefs, customs and practices in their own societies that offend against these norms and need to be extirpated by their own efforts.[30]

There has not yet been a comparable detailed discussion about the relationship between indigenous peoples and international environmental law. Are indigenous peoples, both as self-governing polities and as human beings, not also subject to international environmental law like everyone else? Do they not also need to regulate their use of the environment to ensure that natural resources are not over-exploited?[31]

The question is more legally complex than might first be assumed. Unlike much of the international law that has evolved on indigenous rights over the past 30 years, most environmental laws were developed without indigenous participation. Moreover, most international environmental laws, including the CBD, stress the principle of sovereignty over natural resources and the United Nations has always

---

30 Tebtebba 2010.
31 Metcalf 2005.

recognised that both nations and peoples have permanent sovereignty over natural resources.[32] So, just as States insist that international environmental laws apply to them subject to their own laws and other priorities, so indigenous (and other) peoples can claim the same discretion. In line with legal norms, environmental laws cannot be imposed without taking into account other laws, including international human rights law and indigenous peoples' own systems of customary law.

Consequently, rather than impose international environmental standards on indigenous peoples without their participation or consent, it has proven more effective to work with indigenous peoples to find practical solutions. It has thus become the norm of the International Whaling Commission, for example, to negotiate hunting quotas for bowhead whales with the Inuit peoples of Alaska, thereby ensuring that whale populations and traditional practices crucial to cultural identity are both sustained. Likewise, after lengthy debate, it has been recognised by the Arctic Council that effective management of natural resources in the Arctic requires the direct involvement of the region's indigenous peoples, who attend the Council's meetings as permanent participants, albeit lacking full voting powers.[33]

Recent judgments and decisions of international human rights courts and treaty bodies help chart the way forward. States must respect indigenous peoples' rights to their lands and territories, to represent themselves through their own institutions (and not those chosen by the State) and to give or withhold their free, prior and informed consent to measures that may affect their rights.[34] Very exceptionally, where there is 'compelling public interest', there may be cause for a State to limit indigenous peoples' rights, and conceivably conservation might be one such reason. Even in such cases, however, the State cannot simply invoke the public interest but must also satisfy a number of additional requirements. Any acquisition of lands or use of those lands must be sanctioned by previously established law and in accordance with due process. The State must show that the intervention is 'necessary' and has been designed to be the least restrictive from a human rights perspective. It must likewise show that the means employed are closely tailored to the goal and that the cost to, or impact on, the affected people is 'proportional' to the benefit being sought. And, finally, the proposed intervention should not 'endanger their very survival as a people'.[35] In order to ensure 'survival as a people', four additional elements are required: effective participation in decision-making, which includes their right to Free, Prior and Informed Consent; participatory environmental and social impact assessments that conform to international standards and best practice and are undertaken in a culturally appropriate manner; mandatory benefit-sharing; and, finally, that negative impacts are effectively avoided or mitigated.[36]

In the absence of such reasons or measures, indigenous peoples do have the right to refuse protected areas on their lands and to demand the restitution of lands taken for protected areas without their consent. The African Commission on Human and Peoples' Rights affirmed the right of the Endorois pastoralists of Kenya to own their customary lands and to 'free, prior and informed

---

32 Daes 2004.
33 McIver 1997; Selin and Selin 2008.
34 Colchester 2010.
35 IACHR 2008.
36 MacKay 2009.

consent', rights which were violated when they were removed from their lands to make way for a protected area (the Lake Bogoria Game Reserve, now part of the 'Kenya Lake System' World Heritage site). The Commission recognised the right of the Endorois to restitution of their lands and compensation for losses and damages.[37]

Implications for UNESCO

Given the advances already made in global laws and policy, it seems reasonable to suggest that the most important steps now needed to reconcile protected areas with indigenous peoples lie at the national and local level. It is important, too, to celebrate the progress that has been made, without pretending that all solutions are perfect or easy.[38] National laws need to be revised to recognise indigenous peoples' rights. Conservation laws need to be changed to recognise community ownership and control of protected areas. Conservation agencies need to be overhauled so that governance systems accommodate indigenous autonomy and allow indigenous peoples' own knowledge and practices to be reaffirmed. Government staff need to be retrained so that they act as advisers and facilitators, collaborating with indigenous peoples instead of imposing exclusionary laws on them.

In putting principles and revised laws into practice at the local level, there will be real dilemmas and difficulties.[39] Even where new policies and laws have been adopted, government capacity and willingness to apply them may be lacking. Indigenous peoples' own economies, values, knowledge systems and institutions are changing. Their customary systems have been weakened or are becoming less relevant to current situations. The landscapes they inhabit are often shared with other peoples who also have rights. Environments, too, are under stress and constantly changing. Principles may be valuable but simple prescriptions can never be a substitute for locally informed action.

In its *Universal Declaration on Cultural Diversity*, UNESCO notes the importance of States adopting inclusive ways of encouraging cultural diversity through policies of cultural pluralism. Article 2 of the Declaration notes:

> "In our increasingly diverse societies, it is essential to ensure harmonious interaction among people and groups with plural, varied and dynamic cultural identities as well as their willingness to live together. Policies for the inclusion and participation of all citizens are guarantees of social cohesion, the vitality of civil society and peace. Thus defined, cultural pluralism gives policy expression to the reality of cultural diversity. Indissociable from a democratic framework, cultural pluralism is conducive to cultural exchange and to the flourishing of creative capacities that sustain public life."

---

37 Sing'Oei 2011a, 2011b.
38 Kemf 1993; MacKay 2002; Tammemagi 2012.
39 Jentoft, Minde and Nilson 2003; McShane et al. 2010; Schmidt-Soltau and Brockington 2007.

The Declaration explicitly recognises the importance of securing human rights as guarantees of cultural diversity and provides not only for the recognition of the individual human rights of persons but also for the recognition of the, implicitly collective, human rights of indigenous peoples. Article 4 of the Declaration thus notes:

> "The defence of cultural diversity is an ethical imperative, inseparable from respect for human dignity. It implies a commitment to human rights and fundamental freedoms, in particular the rights of persons belonging to minorities and those of indigenous peoples. No one may invoke cultural diversity to infringe upon human rights guaranteed by international law, nor to limit their scope."

For indigenous peoples, the key collective rights that have been recognised are their right as peoples to self-determination, as affirmed in the *UN Declaration on the Rights of Indigenous Peoples* in line with Article 1 of the *International Covenant on Civil and Political Rights*, and also their right to the collective ownership, control, management and use of their lands, territories and resources.

One of the underlying intentions of the *Convention Concerning the Protection of the World Cultural and Natural Heritage*, and of listing cultural and natural heritage areas of outstanding value as 'World Heritage Sites', is to ensure that these areas are managed and protected to the highest international standards.[40]

In 1992, the World Heritage Committee adapted its *Operational Guidelines for the Implementation of the World Heritage Convention* in order to allow for the inscription of 'cultural landscapes', sites that are recognized as 'combined works of nature and humankind'. With this change the Committee greatly enhanced the possibility of recognizing and protecting the role of indigenous peoples in managing, shaping and creating their lands and resources within World Heritage areas. These Guidelines have been periodically updated, most recently in 2013.[41]

Paragraph 12 of the latest version of the *Operational Guidelines for the Implementation of the World Heritage Convention* notes:

> "States Parties to the Convention are encouraged to ensure the participation of a wide variety of stakeholders, including site managers, local and regional governments, local communities, non-governmental organizations (NGOs) and other interested parties and partners in the identification, nomination and protection of World Heritage properties." [42]

---

40 See for example, World Heritage Committee Decision 35 COM 12E (2011): "15. Recalling that being a signatory to the World Heritage Convention entails certain responsibilities, including... management of World Heritage properties according to the highest international standards..., encourages States Parties to: e) Involve indigenous peoples and local communities in decision making, monitoring and evaluation of the state of conservation of the properties and their Outstanding Universal Value and link the direct community benefits to protection outcomes, f) Respect the rights of indigenous peoples when nominating, managing and reporting on World Heritage sites in indigenous peoples' territories;"
41 See http://whc.unesco.org/en/guidelines.
42 Doc. WHC. 13/01, July 2013. See also articles 64, 119, 123 and 211.

However, the World Heritage Convention and its Operational Guidelines make no mention of indigenous peoples or their rights to their lands and territories, so requirements for their effective participation are somewhat limited. In the past, attempts to appeal to UNESCO to ensure that governments respect indigenous peoples' rights in the nomination of areas for World Heritage listing have been rebuffed.[43]

The connection between indigenous lands and cultural integrity, as well as the need to protect both, has been recognized by UNESCO numerous times in the past. For example, the 1981 UNESCO *Declaration of San José on Ethno-Development and Ethnocide in Latin America* provides that:

"For the Indian peoples, the land is not only an object of possession and production. It forms the basis of their existence, both physical and spiritual, as an independent entity. Territorial space is the foundation and source of their relationship with the universe and the mainstay of their view of the world."

It continues that:

"The Indian peoples have a natural and inalienable right to the territories that they possess as well as the right to recover the land taken away from them. This implies the right to the natural and cultural heritage that this territory contains and the right to determine freely how it will be used and exploited." [44]

It is time such rights were explicitly recognised in the World Heritage Convention's Operational Guidelines.   ○

References

Balasinorwala, T., Kothari, A. and Goyal, M. 2004. *Participatory Conservation: paradigm shifts in international policy – a compilation of outputs from global events related to participatory conservation.* Pune, Kalpavriksh.

Beltran, J. (ed.). 2000. *Indigenous and Traditional Peoples and Protected Areas: Principles, Guidelines and Case Studies.* Gland, WCPA and IUCN.

Berkes, F. 1999. *Sacred Ecology: traditional ecological knowledge and resource management.* Philadelphia, Taylor and Francis.

Borrini-Feyerabend, G. (ed.). 1997. *Beyond Fences: Seeking Social Sustainability in Conservation* (2 Volumes). Gland, IUCN.

Brockington, D. 2002. *Fortress Conservation: the Preservation of the Mkomazi Game Reserve Tanzania.* Oxford, James Currie.

CBD. 2012. *Protected Areas: Progress in the Implementation of the Programme of Work and Achievement of the Aichi Biodiversity Target 11.* Doc. UNEP/CBD/COP/11/26, 23 July 2012.

---

43 A case in point was the efforts made by the Patamona community of Chenapau in 2001 to secure recognition of their rights prior to the World Heritage nomination of Kaieteur National Park in Guyana (Letter from Forest Peoples Programme to UNESCO and IUCN 31 January 2001).

44 UNESCO Doc. FS82/WF.32 (1982), Arts. 6 and 7.

Chapin, M. 2004. A Challenge to Conservationists. *WorldWatch Magazine*, November/December 2004, pp. 17-31.

Chatty, D. and Colchester, M. (eds.). 2002. *Conservation and Mobile Indigenous Peoples: displacement, forced settlement and sustainable development.* Oxford, Berghahn Books.

Chhatre, A. and Agrawal, A. 2009. Trade-offs and synergies between carbon storage and livelihood benefits from forest commons. *PNAS*, www.pnas.org_cgi_doi_10.1073_pnas.0905308106.

Colchester, M. 2003. *Salvaging Nature: Indigenous Peoples, Protected Areas and Biodiversity Conservation.* Montevideo, World Rainforest Movement and Forest Peoples Programme.

Colchester, M. 2004. Conservation Policy and Indigenous Peoples. *Environmental Science & Policy*, Vol. 7 (3), pp.145-153.

Colchester, M. 2010. *Free, Prior and Informed Consent: making FPIC work for forests and peoples.* New Haven, Yale (The Forests Dialogue, Research Paper, Number 11).

Colchester, M. and Erni, C. (eds.). 2000. *Indigenous Peoples and Protected Areas in South and Southeast Asia: from Principles to Practice.* Copenhagen, Forest Peoples Programme and IWGIA.

Colchester, M. et al. 2006. *Forest Peoples, Customary Use and State Forests: the case for reform.* Paper presented to the 11th Biennial Congress of the International Association for the Study of Common Property Bali, Indonesia, 19-23 June 2006. Moreton-in-Marsh, Forest Peoples Programme.

Colchester, M. et al. 2008. *Conservation and Indigenous Peoples: assessing the progress since Durban.* Moreton-in-Marsh, Forest Peoples Programme.

Cooney, R. and Dickson, B. (eds.). 2005. *Biodiversity and the Precautionary Principle: risk and uncertainty in conservation and sustainable use.* London, Earthscan.

Daes, E.-I. 2004. Indigenous Peoples' Permanent Sovereignty Over Natural Resources. Lecture at the National Native Title Conference, Adelaide, Thursday, 3 June 2004.

Dowie, M. 2009. *Conservation Refugees: the hundred year conflict between global conservation and native peoples.* Cambridge (Mass.), Massachusetts Institute of Technology.

Eghenter, C. 2000. *Mapping Peoples' Forests: the role of mapping in planning community-based management of conservation areas in Indonesia.* Washington DC, Biodiversity Support Program.

Forrest, S. 1999. *Global Tenure and Sustainable Use.* Washington DC, IUCN Sustainable Use Initiative.

FPP. 2012. *IUCN Resolutions and Recommendations on Indigenous Peoples: a comparative table.* Moreton-in-Marsh, Forest Peoples Programme (updated edition).

Gray, A., Parellada, A. and Newing, H. (eds.). 1997. *From Principles to Practice: Indigenous Peoples and Biodiversity Conservation in Latin America.* Copenhagen, Forest Peoples Programme and IWGIA.

Griffin, E. 2008. *Blood Sport: hunting in Britain since 1066.* New Haven, Yale University Press.

IACHR. 2008. *Saramaka People v. Suriname. Interpretation of the Judgment on Preliminary Objections, Merits, Reparations and Costs.* Judgment of 12th August 2008. Series C No. 185, Inter-American Court of Human Rights.

IAIP. 1998. *Indigenous Peoples, Forest and Biodiversity.* Copenhagen, International Alliance of Indigenous and Tribal Peoples of the Tropical Forests and IWGIA.

IUCN. 1994. *Guidelines for Protected Area Management Categories.* Gland, IUCN.

Jeanrenaud, S. 2002. *People-oriented Approaches in Global Conservation: is the leopard changing its spots?* London, IIED.

Jentoft, S., Minde, H. and Nilsen, R. (eds.). 2003. *Indigenous Peoples: Resource Management and Global Rights.* Delft, Eburon.

Keller, R. and Turek, M. 1998. *American Indians and National Parks.* Tucson, University of Arizona Press.

Kemf, E. 1993. *Indigenous Peoples and Protected Areas: The Law of Mother Earth.* London, Earthscan.

MacKay, F. 2002. *Addressing Past Wrongs: Indigenous Peoples and Protected Areas: the right to Restitution of Lands and Resources.* Moreton-in-Marsh, Forest Peoples Programme.

MacKay, F. 2009. *Indigenous peoples' rights and reduced emissions from reduced deforestation and forest degradation: The case of the Saramaka People v. Suriname.* Moreton-in-Marsh, Forest Peoples Programme.

McIver, J. 1997. Environmental Protection, Indigenous Rights and the Arctic Council: Rock, Paper, Scissors on the Ice? *Georgetown International Environmental Law Review*, Vol. 10, pp. 147-168.

McShane, T. O. et al. 2010. Hard Choices: making trade-offs between biodiversity conservation and human well-being. *Biological Conservation*, Vol. 144, Issue 3, pp. 966-972.

Metcalf, C. 2005. Indigenous Rights and the Environment: evolving international law. *Ottawa Law Review*, Vol. 35(1), pp. 101-140.

Nelson, A. and Chomitz, K. 2011. Effectiveness of Strict vs. Multiple Use Protected Areas in Reducing Tropical Forest Fires: A Global Analysis Using Matching Methods. *PLoS ONE* 6, No. 8: e22722.

Nelson, J. and Hossack, L. (eds.). 2003. *From Principles to Practice: Indigenous Peoples and Protected Areas in Africa.* Moreton-in-Marsh, Forest Peoples Programme.

Nepstad, D. et al. 2006. Inhibition of Amazon deforestation and fire by parks and indigenous lands. *Conservation Biology*, Vol. 20, pp. 65–73.

Oviedo, G., Maffi, L. and Larsen, P. 2000. *Indigenous and Traditional Peoples of the World and Ecoregion Conservation: an integral approach to conserving the world's biological and cultural diversity.* Gland, WWF.

Persha L., Agrawal, A., and Chhatre, A. 2011. Social and Ecological Synergy: Local Rulemaking, Forest Livelihoods, and Biodiversity Conservation. *Science*, Vol. 331, No. 6024, pp. 1606-1608.

Phillips, A. 2003. Turning Ideas on their Head: the new paradigm for protected areas. *George Wright Society Forum*, Vol. 20 (2), pp. 8–32.

Porter-Bolland, L. et al. 2011. Community managed forests and forest protected areas: an assessment of their conservation effectiveness across the tropics. *Forest Ecology and Management*, June 2011.

Redford, K. H. and Stearman, A. M. 1993. On Common Ground? Response to Alcorn. *Conservation Biology*, Vol. 7(2), pp. 427-428.

Robinson, J. and Bennett, E. (eds.). 2000. *Hunting for Sustainability in Tropical Forests.* New York, Columbia University Press.

Sayer, J. 1991. *Rainforest Buffer Zones: Guidelines for Protected Area Management.* Gland, IUCN.

Schmidt-Soltau, K. and Brockington, D. 2007. Protected Areas an Resettlement: what scope for voluntary relocation? *World Development*, Vol. 35(12), pp. 2182-2202.

Selin, H. and Selin, N. E. 2008. Indigenous Peoples in International Environmental Cooperation: Artic Management of Hazardous Substances. *Review of European Community and International Environmental Law*, Vol. 17(1), pp. 72-83.

Sing'Oei, K. 2011a. The Endorois Case and its Impacts on State and Corporate Conduct in Africa. (Unpublished manuscript).

Sing'Oei, K. 2011b. Engaging the Leviathan: National Development, Corporate Globalization and the Endorois' Quest to Recover their Herding Grounds. *International Journal on Minority and Group Rights*, Vol. 18, pp. 515-540.

Stevens, S. (ed.). 1997. *Conservation through Cultural Survival: Indigenous Peoples and Protected Areas.* Washington DC, Island Press.

Tammemagi, H. 2012. Five National Parks that Honour First Nations. *The Tyee List* #20, 4 August 2012, TheTyee.ca.

Tebtebba. 2010. The Manila Declaration of the International Conference on Conflict Resolution, Peace Building, Sustainable Development and Indigenous Peoples, organised and convened by the Tebtebba Foundation in Metro Manila, Philippines on 6-8 December 2010.

Weber, R., Butler, J. and Larson, P. 2000. *Indigenous Peoples and Conservation Organisations: Experiences in Collaboration.* Washington DC, WWF (USA).

West, P. 1991. Introduction. P. West and S. Brechin (eds.), *Resident Peoples and National Parks: Social Dilemmas in International Conservation.* Tucson, University of Arizona Press, pp. xv-xxiv.

Whakatane Mechanism. 2012. *The Whakatane Mechanism: an IUCN "One Programme" initiative to support conflict resolution on protected areas and indigenous peoples.* IUCN, CEESP, FPP and WCPA.

Widlok, T. 2009. Parks and People in Arid Africa. K. Fernandez de Larrinoa et al. (eds.), *Pueblos indigenas, paisajes culturales y protección de la naturaleza.* Pamplona, Ediciones Eunate, pp. 103-136.

WWF. 1996. *WWF Statement of principles: indigenous peoples and conservation.* Gland, WWF.

Indigenous Peoples' Heritage and Human Rights

Jérémie Gilbert

Introduction

In November 2011, the African Commission on Human and Peoples' Rights (ACHPR) took the unusual decision of adopting a specific resolution condemning the inscription of Lake Bogoria National Reserve in Kenya on the World Heritage List.[1] The Commission noted its concern that the classification of the reserve as a World Heritage site had occurred in violation of the human rights of the Endorois community, on whose ancestral land the reserve is located. Apart from the specific case of Lake Bogoria, the ACHPR also chose to highlight a general lack of integration of, and respect for, the human rights of indigenous peoples when it comes to the inscription of parts of their ancestral territories on the list of World Heritage sites. The resolution makes general comments about World Heritage in the context of indigenous peoples' human rights, notably "noting with concern that there are numerous World Heritage sites in Africa that have been inscribed without the free, prior and informed consent of the indigenous peoples in whose territories they are located and whose management frameworks are not consistent with the principles of the UN Declaration on the Rights of Indigenous Peoples." The fact that the African Commission chose to highlight the issue through the adoption of such a resolution is indicative of a common lack of respect for the rights of indigenous peoples in the implementation of the World Heritage Convention. The resolution is also an indication of the general lack of integration and understanding of the rights of indigenous peoples in the context of World Heritage.

The present chapter aims to highlight some of the main features of human rights law when it comes to the rights of indigenous peoples in the context of cultural and natural heritage sites, and in particular World Heritage sites. Cultural heritage forms an important part of the international human rights legal framework for the protection of indigenous peoples, notably through the recognition that land rights are an essential element of indigenous peoples' cultures. The connection between land rights and the cultural heritage of indigenous peoples is specifically expressed within the *UN Declaration on the Rights of Indigenous Peoples* (UNDRIP) and also more generally within the international human rights instruments relevant to the protection of indigenous peoples. To review the correlation between human

---

1   *Resolution on the Protection of Indigenous Peoples' Rights in the Context of the World Heritage Convention and the Designation of Lake Bogoria as a World Heritage Site*, adopted at the ACHPR's 50th Ordinary Session held from 24 October to 5 November 2011. For the full text of the resolution, see Appendix 1 of this volume.

Left: A view of the UN General Assembly Hall at the opening of the twelfth session of the Permanent Forum on Indigenous Issues, United Nations, New York, 20 May 2013. Photo: UN Photo/Rick Bajornas

rights law, indigenous peoples' rights, and cultural heritage, the first part of the chapter explores how human rights law has acknowledged and formally recognised the essential role that land and territories play in indigenous peoples' cosmology and cultural heritage. It then analyses how, legally, the connection between cultural heritage and indigenous peoples has been embedded into the emergence of a right to 'cultural integrity' for indigenous peoples. Thirdly, the chapter examines how the right of indigenous peoples to participate and consent before any developments take place on their lands and territories is strongly affirmed under international human rights law and how such a right is relevant in the context of World Heritage protection.

Indigenous peoples as custodians of the land

Cultural heritage has not traditionally been an issue examined in detail by international human rights institutions.[2] However, based on the importance of cultural heritage for indigenous peoples, the former UN Sub-Commission on Prevention of Discrimination and Protection of Minorities of the Commission on Human Rights gave a mandate to Erica-Irene Daes to conduct a study on the issue during the 1990s. The study notably highlighted that, for indigenous peoples, cultural heritage is often expressed via cultural practices related to the particular use of a territory.[3] The study also makes it clear that a strict separation between cultural and natural heritage is neither possible nor appropriate in the context of indigenous peoples' heritage. For indigenous peoples, 'heritage' is something holistic that includes not only products of human thought and craftsmanship but also natural features of the landscape and naturally-occurring species of plants and animals with which a people has long been connected.[4] The conduct of the study on the protection of the heritage of indigenous peoples gave a platform to many indigenous representatives to show how indigenous communities globally share a similar deep-rooted inter-relationship between their cultural heritage and their territories. Many indigenous communities throughout the world have stressed that territories and lands are not only the basis of economic livelihood but are also the source of spiritual, cultural and social identity, and form an essential part of their cultural heritage. The study therefore recommended that access and rights to land should be recognised as essential elements in ensuring that indigenous peoples can enjoy and maintain their cultural heritage.

This connection between cultural heritage and territorial rights for indigenous peoples is reflected in international legal documents. Over the years of negotiations that finally led to the adoption of the UNDRIP in 2007, indigenous peoples consistently asserted the need to reflect their specific approach to cultural rights and cultural heritage with the strong territorial component that this entails. As a result, Article 25 of the UN Declaration affirms that: "Indigenous peoples have the right to maintain and strengthen their distinctive spiritual relationship with their traditionally owned or otherwise occupied

---

2   One exception relates to protecting cultural heritage in the context of armed conflicts. See Blake 2000; and Francioni 2004.
3   "Principles and guidelines for the protection of the heritage of indigenous people". UN Commission on Human Rights 1995, Annex.
4   UN Commission on Human Rights 1993, paras. 21-24, 31.

and used lands, territories, waters and coastal seas and other resources and to uphold their responsibilities to future generations in this regard." Similarly, the *ILO Convention (No. 169) concerning Indigenous and Tribal Peoples in Independent Countries* affirms in Article 13 that, in applying the convention, "governments shall respect the special importance for the cultures and spiritual values of the peoples concerned of their relationship with the lands or territories, or both as applicable, which they occupy or otherwise use, and in particular the collective aspects of this relationship".

The connection between indigenous peoples' cultural rights and land rights has also been recognised by the Human Rights Committee (HRC) in its interpretation of Article 27 of the *International Covenant on Civil and Political Rights* (ICCPR), which concerns the cultural rights of minorities. Article 27 does not refer to land rights or to indigenous peoples but does protect the right of persons belonging to minorities, "in community with the other members of their group, to enjoy their own culture, to profess and practise their own religion, or to use their own language", thereby placing emphasis on the connection between cultural rights and the rights of minorities. Based on this affirmation, the HRC has developed specific protection for indigenous peoples' land rights by acknowledging that, for indigenous communities, their particular way of life is associated with and largely dependent on the use of their lands. In an often-quoted General Comment on Article 27 the HRC stated:

"With regard to the exercise of the cultural rights protected under article 27, the Committee observes that culture manifests itself in many forms, including a particular way of life associated with the use of land resources, especially in the case of indigenous peoples. That right may include such traditional activities as fishing or hunting and the right to live in reserves protected by law."[5]

Through this General Comment, the HRC has clearly highlighted that indigenous cultures are often strongly based on a territorial connection and that such connection is protected under the ICCPR. The connection between cultural protection and land rights for indigenous peoples has been further developed and reiterated in numerous concluding observations and individual communications of the Committee.[6] The HRC approach is that, where land is of central significance to the maintenance of a culture, the right to enjoy one's culture under Article 27 of the ICCPR requires the recognition of land rights.

A similar approach has been developed by the Committee on Economic, Social and Cultural Rights, which has also highlighted the fact that cultural rights entail the recognition of land rights for indigenous peoples. In its General Comment on Article 15 of the *International Covenant on Economic, Social and Cultural Rights* (ICESCR), which concerns the right of everyone to take part in cultural life, the Committee recognised that:

"The strong communal dimension of indigenous peoples' cultural life is indispensable to their existence, well-being and full development, and includes the right to the lands, territories and resources which they have traditionally owned, occupied or otherwise used

---

5 UN Human Rights Committee 1994, para. 7.
6 See, e.g., Scheinin 2000. The HRC has recently also highlighted this connection in relation to the forced eviction of the Endorois community from their ancestral land around Lake Bogoria. See UN Human Rights Committee 2012, para. 24.

or acquired. Indigenous peoples' cultural values and rights associated with their ancestral lands and their relationship with nature should be regarded with respect and protected, in order to prevent the degradation of their particular way of life, including their means of subsistence, the loss of their natural resources and, ultimately, their cultural identity."[7]

Likewise, the Committee on the Elimination of Racial Discrimination (CERD), which monitors implementation of the *International Convention on the Elimination of All Forms of Racial Discrimination*, has also made a direct connection between cultural rights and land rights for indigenous peoples.[8] Human rights monitoring bodies have therefore established a strong connection between cultural rights, which are an important component of the human rights treaties, and indigenous peoples' cultural attachment to their ancestral territories. There is strong recognition within international human rights law and jurisprudence that cultural rights for indigenous peoples entail rights to land and natural resources, and that there is an obligation to protect the cultural heritage of indigenous peoples through recognition of their rights to own, control and manage their ancestral territories. This approach acknowledges that indigenous peoples are the custodians of their lands and territories and that their rights to land therefore need to be protected under the banner of cultural rights.

Rights to cultural integrity and cultural heritage

Recognition of the importance of affirming and protecting the land rights of indigenous peoples as part of their human rights has become a central component of the human rights jurisprudence. Increasingly, international and regional human rights bodies have recognised the connection between land rights and cultural heritage as an essential element of indigenous peoples' human rights. This recognition of the links between the land rights and cultural rights of indigenous peoples has notably been at the core of the jurisprudence of the Inter-American Court of Human Rights (IACtHR). In the 2001 case of the Awas Tingni community against Nicaragua, the Court stated:

> "Indigenous groups, by the fact of their very existence, have the right to live freely in their own territory; the close ties of indigenous people with the land must be recognized and understood as the fundamental basis of their cultures, their spiritual life, their integrity, and their economic survival. For indigenous communities, relations to the land are not merely a matter of possession and production but a material and spiritual element which they must fully enjoy, even to preserve their cultural legacy and transmit it to future generations." [9]

It is worth noting that this ruling from the Court highlights the fact that the cultural heritage of indigenous peoples includes both the tangible and intangible relationship of the indigenous communities with their ancestral territories.

---

7   UN Committee on Economic, Social and Cultural Rights 2009, para. 36.
8   UN Committee on the Elimination of Racial Discrimination 1997.
9   Inter-American Court of Human Rights 2001, para. 149.

The Mayagna community of Awas Tingni on the Atlantic coast of Nicaragua. In 2001 the community won an historic case against the government of Nicaragua in which the Inter-American Court of Human Rights upheld their collective property rights to their ancestral lands and resources based on a pattern of use and traditional occupation.
Photo: Alianza Mesoamericana de Pueblos y Bosques

Since the Awas Tingni ruling, the IACtHR has developed further jurisprudence on land rights by integrating them as part of the right to property, the right to life and the right to health.[10] Under this approach, land rights are an essential part of the right of indigenous peoples to cultural integrity. The right to cultural integrity refers to a bundle of inter-related human rights such as rights to culture, subsistence, livelihood, and religion, which all support the protection of land rights as an important aspect of the cultural survival of indigenous peoples.[11]

References to the right to cultural integrity within the Inter-American Human Rights System found some echoes in the recent decision from the African Commission on Human and Peoples' Rights (ACHPR) in the case concerning the Endorois community in Kenya. This case concerned the forced displacement of the Endorois community from their ancestral land in the heart of the Great Rift Valley around the area of Lake Bogoria in order to create a wildlife reserve. As noted earlier, the site was recently included in the list of World Heritage sites. The forced displacement of the cattle-herding community plunged them into poverty and pushed them to the brink of cultural extinction. In front of the African Commission, the indigenous community highlighted that access to their ancestral territory "in addition to securing subsistence and livelihood, is seen as sacred, being

---

10 See Anaya and Williams 2001; Inter-American Commission on Human Rights 2009.
11 See also Inter-American Commission on Human Rights 2009, paras. 55-56.

inextricably linked to the cultural integrity of the community and its traditional way of life."[12] In its decision, the African Commission agreed that the cultural integrity of the Endorois was imperilled, acknowledging that the removal of the indigenous community from its ancestral land was a violation of their rights to freedom of religion (Article 8), culture (Article 17) and access to natural resources (Article 21) under the *African Charter on Human and Peoples' Rights*.

The right of indigenous peoples to cultural integrity is directly relevant to issues relating to cultural heritage for it directly links to the right to freedom of religion, cultural rights, and the right to access natural resources. While rights to cultural heritage are not affirmed as such in either the *American Convention on Human Rights* or the African Charter, the regional human rights bodies have acknowledged that protection of the cultural heritage of indigenous peoples is a crucial human rights issue and part of a larger bundle of rights which includes property rights, cultural rights and social rights. The approach developed by the regional human rights bodies highlights that, for indigenous peoples, the concept of cultural heritage includes both intangible and tangible anchorage to their lands and territories.

Heritage, participation and consent

Participation and consent are key rights within the human rights framework when it comes to the rights of indigenous peoples. The rights to participation, consultation and consent are strongly expressed in the UNDRIP, which includes several articles dedicated to the issue of participation.[13] Article 19 stipulates that: "States shall consult and cooperate in good faith with the indigenous peoples concerned through their own representative institutions in order to obtain their free, prior and informed consent before adopting and implementing legislative or administrative measures that may affect them." In the context of land rights, the Declaration further states:

> "Indigenous peoples have the right to determine and develop priorities and strategies for the development or use of their lands or territories and other resources. States shall consult and cooperate in good faith with the indigenous peoples concerned through their own representative institutions in order to obtain their free and informed consent prior to the approval of any project affecting their lands or territories and other resources, particularly in connection with the development, utilization or exploitation of mineral, water or other resources." [14]

It is evident that this provision also applies to decisions that would classify the lands of indigenous peoples as cultural or natural heritage sites. The importance of direct participation, consultation and consent is not limited to the UNDRIP and is part of the jurisprudence regarding the application of most other human rights treaties. For example, the Committee on Economic, Social and Cultural

---

12 African Commission on Human and Peoples' Rights 2010, para. 16.
13 See UNDRIP, Arts. 18, 19, 32, among other articles.
14 UNDRIP, Art. 32.

Rights has highlighted that "States parties should respect the principle of free, prior and informed consent of indigenous peoples in all matters covered by their specific rights."[15]

The issue of consent and participation in the specific context of World Heritage has been the focus of both the UN Permanent Forum on Indigenous Issues and the UN Expert Mechanism on the Rights of Indigenous Peoples (EMRIP), which have both highlighted the fact that indigenous peoples should be adequately consulted and involved in the management and protection of World Heritage sites. These two institutions have also emphasised that indigenous peoples' free, prior and informed consent should be obtained when their territories are being nominated and inscribed as World Heritage sites. On this very particular issue, the EMRIP has urged that:

> "Robust procedures and mechanisms should be established to ensure indigenous peoples are adequately consulted and involved in the management and protection of World Heritage sites, and that their free, prior and informed consent is obtained when their territories are being nominated and inscribed as World Heritage sites."[16]

Free, prior and informed consent implies that States have a duty to obtain indigenous peoples' consent in relation to decisions that are of fundamental importance to their rights. This includes decisions to classify their territories under the label of World Heritage sites.

The importance of recognising and upholding the land rights of indigenous peoples in the context of cultural and natural heritage is also visible in jurisprudence affirming indigenous peoples' right to free, prior and informed consent in the case of decisions that may affect their traditional territories. For instance, in 2010, in the previously mentioned Endorois case, the African Commission on Human and Peoples' Rights highlighted the fact that "any development or investment projects that would have a major impact within the Endorois territory, the State has a duty not only to consult with the community, but also to obtain their free, prior, and informed consent, according to their customs and traditions".[17] Following the classification of Lake Bogoria as a World Heritage site in 2011, the African Commission expressed deep concern that this had happened "without involving the Endorois in the decision-making process and without obtaining their free, prior and informed consent", underlining that this was a violation of their human rights under the African Charter.[18]

It is worth noting that support for respecting and implementing the right of indigenous peoples to free, prior and informed consent in the context of World Heritage sites is also emerging from other, non-human rights institutions. For example, in 2012, the International Finance Corporation (IFC) adopted a performance standard regarding indigenous peoples which states:

> "Where a project may significantly impact on critical cultural heritage that is essential to the identity and/or cultural, ceremonial, or spiritual aspects of Indigenous Peoples' lives,

---

15 UN Committee on Economic, Social and Cultural Rights 2009, para. 37.
16 UN Expert Mechanism on the Rights of Indigenous Peoples 2011, para. 38. Similarly, UN Permanent Forum on Indigenous Issues 2013, para. 58.
17 African Commission on Human and Peoples' Rights 2010, para. 291.
18 African Commission on Human and Peoples' Rights 2011.

priority will be given to the avoidance of such impacts. Where significant project impacts on critical cultural heritage are unavoidable, the client will obtain the FPIC [Free, Prior and Informed Consent] of the Affected Communities of Indigenous Peoples." [19]

The adoption of such a standard by the IFC, which plays such an important role in supporting investments globally, is very significant. Not only because the IFC may be behind several projects regarding the management of World Heritage sites but also because it shows that human rights obligations are not limited to the public sector. It is also an illustration that the human rights obligations contained in international human rights documents need to be respected and implemented by international institutions, even institutions not focusing their work on human rights issues. These obligations are not restricted to States parties but concern the international community at large. This is especially true for intergovernmental organization such as UNESCO. Article 41 of the UNDRIP specifically requires UN agencies and other intergovernmental organizations to "contribute to the full realization of the provisions of this Declaration" and to establish "ways and means of ensuring participation of indigenous peoples on issues affecting them". Likewise, Article 42 stipulates: "the United Nations, its bodies... and specialized agencies, including at the country level, and States shall promote respect for and full application of the provisions of this Declaration and follow up the effectiveness of this Declaration". From this perspective, there is no doubt that UNESCO, while being a very specialised agency, needs to integrate and respect the rights proclaimed within the UNDRIP. This includes respect for and implementation of the right of indigenous peoples to free, prior and informed consent before any decision affecting their lands is undertaken.

Conclusion

Indigenous peoples the world over have emphasised that they should be regarded as custodians of the land and that their role as actors in protecting cultural and natural heritage should be recognised and respected. Land and natural resources are part of their heritage, and human rights law strongly recognises that connection. The right of indigenous peoples to control, own and manage their ancestral territories is strongly established under human rights law. This involves recognition of the importance of land rights not only as a source of livelihood but also as an essential component of indigenous peoples' cultural integrity. This includes both the natural and cultural heritage of indigenous communities. Under international human rights law, the main principles are that indigenous peoples' rights to land need to be recognised and protected, and that no decision affecting their lands or territories must be taken without their free, prior and informed consent. Despite the fact that these principles are now strongly embedded into human rights law, there is still a lack of implementation of and respect for these principles by States parties and UNESCO when it comes to establishing and managing World Heritage sites. The World Heritage Committee

---

19 IFC Performance Standard 7, Indigenous Peoples, 1 January 2012.

needs to review its current procedures and Operational Guidelines to ensure that implementation of the World Heritage Convention is consistent with the *UN Declaration on the Rights of Indigenous Peoples*. For the time being, it is not. Not only it is morally and ethically wrong to exclude indigenous peoples from decisions that have an impact on their rights and their lives, it is also illegal under international human rights law. ○

References

African Commission on Human and Peoples' Rights. 2010. *Communication 276 / 2003 – Centre for Minority Rights Development (Kenya) and Minority Rights Group International on behalf of Endorois Welfare Council v Kenya.* Decision of 2 February 2010.

African Commission on Human and Peoples' Rights. 2011. *Resolution on the Protection of Indigenous Peoples' Rights in the Context of the World Heritage Convention and the Designation of Lake Bogoria as a World Heritage site.* ACHPR Res. 197, adopted on 5 November 2011.

Anaya, J. and Williams, R. 2001. The Protection of Indigenous Peoples' Rights over Lands and Natural Resources under the Inter-American Human Rights System. *Harvard Human Rights Journal*, Vol. 14, pp. 33-86.

Blake, J. 2000. On defining the cultural heritage. *International and Comparative Law Quarterly*, Vol. 49, No.1, pp. 61-85.

Francioni, F. 2004. Beyond state sovereignty: the protection of cultural heritage as a shared interest of humanity. *Michigan Journal of International Law*, Vol. 25, pp. 1209 ff.

Inter-American Commission on Human Rights. 2009. *Indigenous and tribal people's rights over their ancestral lands and natural resources: Norms and jurisprudence of the Inter-American human rights system.* OEA/Ser.L/V/II., Doc.56/09.

Inter-American Court of Human Rights. 2001. *The Case of the Mayagna (Sumo) Awas Tingni Community v. Nicaragua, Judgment of August 31, 2001* (Merits, Reparations and Costs). Series C No. 79.

Scheinin, M. 2000. The right to enjoy a distinct culture: indigenous and competing uses of land. T. Orlin et al. (eds.), *The jurisprudence of human rights law: a comparative interpretive approach.* Turku/Abo, Abo Akademia University.

UN Commission on Human Rights. 1993. *Study on the protection of the cultural and intellectual property of indigenous peoples, by Erica-Irene Daes, Special Rapporteur of the Sub-Commission on Prevention of Discrimination and Protection of Minorities.* UN Doc. E/CN.4/Sub.2/1993/28.

UN Commission on Human Rights. 1995. *Protection of the heritage of indigenous people. Final report of the Special Rapporteur, Mrs. Erica-Irene Daes.* UN Doc. E/CN.4/Sub.2/1995/26.

UN Committee on Economic, Social and Cultural Rights. 2009. *General comment No. 21: Right of everyone to take part in cultural life (art. 15, para. 1 (a), of the International Covenant on Economic, Social and Cultural Rights).* UN Doc. E/C.12/GC/21.

UN Committee on the Elimination of Racial Discrimination. 1997. *General Recommendation 23, Rights of indigenous peoples (Fifty-first session, 1997).* UN Doc. A/52/18, Annex V, pp. 122-123.

UN Expert Mechanism on the Rights of Indigenous Peoples. 2011. *Expert Mechanism advice No. 2 (2011): Indigenous peoples and the right to participate in decision-making.* UN Doc. A/HCR/EMRIP/2011/2, Annex.

UN Human Rights Committee. 1994. *General Comment No. 23: The rights of minorities (Art. 27).* UN Doc. CCPR/C/21/Rev.1/Add.5.

UN Human Rights Committee. 2012. Concluding observations: Kenya. UN Doc. CCPR/C/KEN/CO/3.

UN Permanent Forum on Indigenous Issues. 2013. *Follow-up to the recommendations of the Permanent Forum: Analysis of health, education and culture prepared by the secretariat of the United Nations Permanent Forum on Indigenous Issues.* Doc. E/C.19/2013/19.

World Heritage, Indigenous Peoples, Communities and Rights: An IUCN Perspective

Peter Bille Larsen, Gonzalo Oviedo and Tim Badman

Introduction

On the 40th anniversary of the World Heritage Convention, achieving a consistent and positive relationship between indigenous rights and World Heritage in respect of international standards has emerged as an important issue. There have been a series of examples where the World Heritage Convention has been positive for indigenous peoples by helping to protect areas of importance to them. However, questions of indigenous rights being infringed upon, forced relocation on the establishment of protected areas, lack of consent, little involvement in management and lack of equitable benefit-sharing are all phenomena that have been reported at World Heritage sites. It is also clear that many State Parties are taking commendable steps to nominate sites with the full consent of, and sometimes at the direct request of, the communities or peoples concerned, to engage in collaborative management, protect rights and secure local benefits. What determines whether the ultimate outcomes of a given World Heritage process are positive or negative for affected indigenous peoples and local communities is not only a matter for an individual State Party but also closely tied to the operation of the World Heritage Convention and the international support system that enables it to function.

The Advisory Bodies to the World Heritage Convention, the International Union for the Conservation of Nature (IUCN), the International Council on Monuments and Sites (ICOMOS) and the International Centre for the Study of the Preservation and Restoration of Cultural Property (ICCROM), play a central technical role in site evaluations, monitoring and standard-setting. As part of this role, each year IUCN and ICOMOS undertake independent evaluations of nominated natural, cultural and mixed sites, working in coordination with the Convention's Secretariat, UNESCO's World Heritage Centre.

In this context, in recent years there has been growing awareness that a wide range of community and rights matters may be positively or negatively affected by a given nomination process,[1] and thus evaluations in turn need to be able to capture and help State Parties and the World Heritage Committee to address such key issues. Despite the many good examples, there

---

1 Sinding-Larsen 2012.

Left: View of the Okavango Delta in Botswana, the 1,000th site to be inscribed on UNESCO's World Heritage List in June 2014. Home to various groups of San, the Delta is one of many natural World Heritage sites inhabited by indigenous peoples. Natural World Heritage sites are evaluated and monitored by IUCN, the World Heritage Committee's technical and scientific Advisory Body on natural heritage. Photo: Philip Milne (CC BY-NC-ND 2.0)

is recognition that a number of nomination processes have generated concerns and discontent due to the impacts they have had on the rights of indigenous peoples and/or local communities. Customary rights may end up being extinguished or long-standing claims and conflicts may in fact be resolved through the significant attention sites up for nomination receive from State authorities, and through the requests that can be made via the World Heritage Convention for action to be taken to support rights.

Before pursuing a specific discussion of the challenges of and perspectives on strengthening Advisory Body evaluation processes, this chapter introduces the broader World Heritage context as well as the IUCN framework on indigenous peoples, communities and rights. It then specifically presents some of the major challenges and opportunities for strengthening IUCN evaluation processes and ends with a discussion about some of the ways forward. The chapter is based on a recent study commissioned by IUCN on how IUCN could strengthen its evaluation approaches in order to better address issues related to indigenous peoples, communities and rights.[2]

World Heritage, indigenous peoples, communities and rights

Throughout the World Heritage Convention's 40-year history, community issues have gradually taken on more importance and received increasingly direct attention, not least since the adoption in 2007 of the World Heritage Committee's fifth Strategic Objective ('fifth C'): "To enhance the role of communities in the implementation of the World Heritage Convention".[3] This essentially built on what was already in the Convention in terms of Parties adopting "a general policy which aims to give the cultural and natural heritage a function in the life of the community" (Article 5a). In part, this has meant that human presence is no longer considered an anomaly in the natural World Heritage context but is, to some extent, recognized, evaluated and referred to. The Convention framework, in keeping with wider conservation policy changes, increasingly seeks to contribute to sustainable development objectives and diverse management approaches. For example, in some cases, site renominations have taken place to acknowledge the living cultural values of indigenous peoples and local communities. The 1992 recognition of cultural landscapes as a category of World Heritage site led to the addition of cultural criteria to Tongariro National Park in New Zealand and Uluru - Kata Tjuta National Park in Australia. There are now over 80 recognized World Heritage cultural landscapes worldwide.[4] The term encompasses a diversity of interactions between humankind and the natural environment, from certain forms of land-use to specific spiritual relations. Such developments increasingly seek to bridge the common separation or gap between outstanding natural and cultural values from the perspective of contemporary communities.

---

2   Larsen 2012.
3   Decisions 31 COM 13A and 13B, adopted at the Committee's 31st session in Christchurch, New Zealand.
4   See http://whc.unesco.org/en/culturallandscape/.

View of Lake Tegano, East Rennell, Solomon Islands. East Rennell is a natural World Heritage site under customary land ownership and management. Photo: Kevin Saueha, Motumahi lodge, East Rennell

This demonstrates evolving standards for linkages between the 'cultural' and the 'natural' and a move beyond 'one-size-fits-all' models of World Heritage management. East Rennell Island in the Solomon Islands is an example of a site under customary land ownership and management that was inscribed on the World Heritage List.[5] Many sites today contain a mix of different land tenure forms, although the general norm is still for a World Natural Heritage site to be an official, government-declared protected area or for it to encompass several of them.

More broadly speaking, few countries and community organizations are aware of the potential under the Convention and its Operational Guidelines for State Parties to nominate World Heritage sites harbouring distinct social, cultural and legal diversity. In practice, many sites have, for example, undertaken work to reconcile customary ownership and rights with site management. In 1985, two years prior to World Heritage listing, the traditional owners of Uluṟu,

---

[5] There was considerable debate in the World Heritage Committee, before East Rennell was listed in 1998, as to whether customary protection and management was sufficient for inscription under the terms of the Operational Guidelines. The inscription established an important standard and precedent in relation to the acceptance of customary law and management as a sufficient basis for the management and long-term protection of natural World Heritage sites (Badman et al. 2008, p. 24; UNESCO 1999, p. 26). The Operational Guidelines were subsequently amended to specifically acknowledge that traditional protection and management can be adequate to ensure a site's safeguarding (see para. 97 of the Guidelines). Nevertheless, recognition of and working with customary ownership and management practices arguably remains to be consolidated.

the Anangu, were handed back the title deeds of the national park in return for leasing it back to Parks Australia for 99 years. The Anangu and Parks Australia now jointly manage the site. However, while considerable progress is being made in many countries, this has still to be adequately reflected in international processes. It is not surprising, then, that volume 62 of UNESCO's World Heritage magazine is dedicated to indigenous peoples' concerns.[6] In practice, there is often a separation between World Heritage expertise and processes and social processes to recognize and defend rights. This partly reflects policy gaps in relation to rights in general and indigenous peoples' rights in particular.[7]

In 2003, several of the presentations at the conference 'Linking Universal and Local Values: Managing a Sustainable Future for World Heritage' were already emphasizing the centrality of rights.[8] The key issue is the uneven level of progress in relation to achieving consistent recognition of rights issues in the implementation of the Convention. UNESCO recently (late 2011) embarked on the development of an indigenous peoples' policy[9] and indigenous issues were included in the official theme of the 40th anniversary of the World Heritage Convention, 'World Heritage and Sustainable Development: The Role of Local Communities'.[10] Moreover, the UNESCO World Heritage Centre and the Advisory Bodies are in the process of developing policy guidelines for the Convention, at the request of the World Heritage Committee, which are expected to include consideration of communities and indigenous peoples.[11]

Addressing indigenous peoples, communities and rights concerns requires long-term processes rather than quick fixes – something evaluations, in turn, need to be able to capture and help State Parties to address. Whether outcomes are positive or negative in a given nomination, including for the rights of the people involved, will firstly depend on recognizing such issues, and on giving them appropriate consideration from the outset of a nomination. The earlier the issues are addressed and understood, the higher the likelihood that a nomination will contribute to the effective protection and realization of indigenous peoples' and local communities' rights.

Efforts spearheaded by ICOMOS Norway have recently sought to shed light on how a Convention without specific references to human rights may nonetheless address these concerns in cultural heritage deliberations.[12] This has led to the ICOMOS 'Our Common Dignity' agenda developed since November 2011 when the 17th General Assembly of ICOMOS recognized that an integration of human rights concerns was needed in World Heritage site designation and management, and requested that the ICOMOS Executive Committee establish the 'Our Common Dignity' initiative as part of the ICOMOS 2012-14 Action Plan.[13]

---

6   UNESCO 2012b.
7   Cunningham 2012.
8   Amsterdam, the Netherlands, 22–24 May 2003. See Merode et al. 2004.
9   It should be noted, however, that World Heritage affairs, while hosted by UNESCO, are not *per se* governed by UNESCO policy.
10 See World Heritage Committee Decision 35 COM 12D (2011); UNESCO 2011c, para. 5.
11 See UNESCO 2013 and World Heritage Committee Decision 37 COM 13.
12 Sinding-Larsen 2012.
13 Resolution 17GA 2011/30 of the ICOMOS General Assembly (*Our Common Dignity: Rights-based Approaches to Heritage Management*).

Following an ICOMOS Norway-organized workshop on World Heritage and Human Rights (Oslo, March 2011), ICOMOS, IUCN and ICCROM, in coordination with UNESCO's World Heritage Centre, established a working group seeking, among other things, to develop good practice in World Heritage site evaluations and monitoring. Although not explicitly involved in the preparation of nominations given their role in evaluating them, IUCN and ICOMOS can through the evaluation process help clarify - in a sound and well-documented manner - the extent to which nomination processes and documents have addressed rights concerns adequately. They can also make sure that site-specific recommendations reflect and support action to address indigenous peoples, communities and rights concerns as fully as possible. The working group has had several discussions to coordinate and advance this work and has developed a roadmap focusing especially on the opportunities created by the 40th Anniversary of the World Heritage Convention.

IUCN framework in relation to World Heritage and rights

What constitutes the IUCN framework in relation to World Heritage and rights? There are two major building blocks to take into consideration from an IUCN perspective. On the one hand, there is the specific mandate of IUCN in relation to the World Heritage Convention as a technical Advisory Body. On the other, there is a wider move within IUCN and its membership to analyze, promote and address community and rights concerns as a scientific, policy and practice field in the nature conservation context; integral to this effort are IUCN's policies that seek to ensure that human rights are respected, promoted and fulfilled for just and equitable conservation (see Box 1, Guiding Principles on Conservation and Human Rights).

Overall, the IUCN evaluation process is defined in relation to the specific mandate provided under the World Heritage Convention in articles 8, 13 and 14. This positions IUCN as a formally-recognized technical and scientific Advisory Body on natural heritage and the general implementation of the programme and project work of the World Heritage Committee. Article 14 speaks of the World Heritage Committee using the services of its Advisory Bodies in their respective "areas of competence and capability". For more than three decades (since 1979), IUCN has supported the World Heritage Committee by providing technical advisory services on eight general functions. These services are the subject of a combination of contracted work and a substantial voluntary contribution of IUCN and its networks. Each of these functions offers opportunities for the mainstreaming of rights, as outlined in the following matrix.

IUCN WH functions	Rights linkages
Evaluation of new nominations	Integrating indigenous peoples, communities and rights issues into the evaluation of nominations and associated processes
Monitoring the status of existing sites	Monitoring progress on addressing rights concerns (respect, protection and realization)
Participating in training and technical workshops	Facilitating training and technical workshops on community and rights concerns (targeted training for duty-bearers and rights-holders)
Management of information (with the UNEP World Conservation Monitoring Centre (UNEP-WCMC))	Facilitating the integration of indigenous peoples, communities and rights concerns as part of the information system and site data sheets
Communication and promotion activities	Communicating good practice and state-of-the-art guidance on indigenous peoples, communities and rights concerns in the WH context
Advice on international assistance requests	Facilitating inputs on assistance requests related to community and tenure concerns
General standard-setting on protected area management	Advising the WH Committee and the UNESCO WH Centre on possibilities for strengthening standards in relation to indigenous peoples, communities and rights in the context of natural sites, mixed sites and cultural landscapes
Contributing to the Global Strategy for a representative World Heritage List (e.g. identification of gaps in WH List)	Strengthening the integration of nature-culture inter-linkages, indigenous heritage priorities and broader issues linked to bio-cultural diversity in the global strategy

Table 1: IUCN World Heritage functions and opportunities for rights inter-linkages[14]

IUCN's work on World Heritage is, however, only a small part of the work of the Union, and questions of indigenous peoples, local communities and rights are a mainstream focus of IUCN's work as a whole. This wider focus and mandate within IUCN and its membership to analyze, promote and address indigenous peoples, communities and rights in relation to conservation concerns is part of the technical capabilities IUCN brings to the World Heritage Convention and its Operational Guidelines.

---

14 Built from Thorsell and Hogan 2009; UNESCO 2011a.

Delegates at the 2012 World Conservation Congress in Jeju, Republic of Korea. The Congress is IUCN's highest decision-making body and sets the general policy of the organization. Photo: Brähler ICS

This includes the very mission of the IUCN and its overall body of policy in relation to human rights and conservation and broader policies on social equity. It also includes resolutions and policies in relation to specific concerns such as indigenous peoples and their collective rights.

IUCN World Conservation Congress Resolution 4.056 from 2008 (*Rights-based approaches to conservation*) "promote[s] the analysis of rights-based approaches as a crosscutting principle within IUCN and its membership", and calls on the IUCN Council and the Director General to "undertake further work to support and guide IUCN on the implementation of policies and actions reflecting a rights-based approach to conservation". The overall objective for IUCN in promoting rights-based approaches is to ensure that the protection of rights and biodiversity conservation become mutually reinforcing.

The 2012 World Conservation Congress adopted an overall IUCN *Policy on Conservation and Human Rights for Sustainable Development*,[15] including a set of 'Guiding Principles' (Box 1). The scope of the Policy is "human rights, which are the rights that all people are entitled to regardless of nationality, sex, origin, race, religion, language, political association or other, and which are protected and recognized in international and national laws, and rights in a broader sense... such as many of the customary rights of indigenous peoples or local communities (e.g. tenure rights)".[16] IUCN's policies on rights include the integration of relevant international standards for indigenous peoples, such as those of the *UN Declaration on the Rights of Indigenous Peoples* (UNDRIP) and ILO *Convention (No. 169) concerning Indigenous and Tribal Peoples in Independent Countries*, as

---

15 Res. 5.099 *IUCN Policy on Conservation and Human Rights for Sustainable Development*, Annex.
16 Ibid.

well as the human rights standards laid out in the *Universal Declaration of Human Rights* and other international instruments.[17]

The same World Conservation Congress also adopted two resolutions on World Heritage, one of which called on the World Heritage Committee to develop new processes and standards that would ensure that the Convention appropriately recognizes the rights of indigenous peoples.[18] The second resolution specifically focused on the implementation of UNDRIP in the context of the World Heritage Convention and called on the Committee and State Parties to ensure that indigenous peoples' rights and all human rights are upheld and implemented in the management and protection of existing World Heritage sites, and to revise the Convention's Operational Guidelines to ensure that "no World Heritage sites are established in indigenous peoples' territories without their free, prior and informed consent".[19]

IUCN Guiding Principles on Conservation and Human Rights

- Respect, protect, promote and fulfil all procedural and substantive rights, including environmental and customary rights, for just and equitable conservation;
- Promote the implementation of the provisions of international conventions and policy processes which respect human rights in all approaches to conservation [...];
- Consider and realize the rights of people that can be affected in development and conservation activities such as women, indigenous peoples and other most vulnerable groups and who could, at the same time, benefit from rights-inclusive and socially sensitive development measures [...];
- Work towards ensuring the respect for, and seeking further protection and the realization of general livelihood and human well-being considerations always keeping in mind gender balance as an essential component;
- Focus on the roles and corresponding responsibilities of duty-bearers, rights-holders and all other actors involved [...];
- Promote transparency and develop tools to address and be accountable for the social effects of IUCN's work [...]
- Ensure that IUCN programmes, projects, and activities undertaken, sponsored or supported by the IUCN are assessed using international human rights standards [...];
- In line with UNDRIP standards, require free, prior and informed consent when IUCN projects, activities, and/or initiatives take place on indigenous peoples' lands and territories and/or impact [their] natural and cultural resources, sites, assets etc.

Box 1: IUCN Guiding Principles on Conservation and Human Rights [20]

---

17 In addition to World Conservation Congress Resolution 4.056, see in particular Res. 4.048 *Indigenous peoples, protected areas and implementation of the Durban Accord* and Res. 4.052 *Implementing the United Nations Declaration on the Rights of Indigenous Peoples*, all adopted in 2008.
18 Res. 5.046 *Strengthening the World Heritage Convention*.
19 Res. 5.047 *Implementation of the United Nations Declaration on the Rights of Indigenous Peoples in the context of the UNESCO World Heritage Convention*. See Appendix 2 of this volume.
20 *IUCN Policy on Conservation and Human Rights for Sustainable Development*. .

In addition, with seven other international conservation organizations, IUCN created the Conservation Initiative on Human Rights (CIHR) in 2008, which adopted the following principles:

CIHR Conservation and Human Rights Framework

CIHR members commit to:

1. **Respect human rights:** Respect internationally proclaimed human rights and make sure that we do not contribute to infringements of human rights while pursuing our mission.
2. **Promote human rights within conservation programmes:** Support and promote the protection and realization of human rights within the scope of our conservation programmes.
3. **Protect the vulnerable:** Make special efforts to avoid harm to those who are vulnerable to infringements of their rights and to support the protection and fulfilment of their rights within the scope of our conservation programmes.
4. **Encourage good governance:** Support the improvement of governance systems that can secure the rights of indigenous peoples and local communities in the context of our work on conservation and sustainable natural resource use, including elements such as legal, policy and institutional frameworks, and procedures for equitable participation and accountability.

Box 2: CIHR Conservation and Human Rights Framework [21]

The above policies, translated into IUCN's Advisory Body mandate, imply:

1. Promoting the use of rights-based approaches in a World Heritage context both by IUCN itself and its membership (i.e. State Parties nominating World Heritage sites and undertaking tentative listing);

2. Undertaking further work to support and guide IUCN on rights-based approaches in a World Heritage context;

3. Collaborating with the World Heritage Committee, the Secretariat and other Advisory Bodies to apply these policies and principles;

4. Strengthening the evaluation process to enhance State and rights-holder capacity to identify links between human rights and World Heritage conservation, and to do the same for other World Heritage processes, such as monitoring.

---

21 Available in English, French and Spanish through https://community.iucn.org/cihr/

It should be underlined that IUCN's Advisory Body mandate also involves supporting and complementing work by the other actors within the Convention, notably the central role of the State Parties themselves, and the work of the other Advisory Bodies and the World Heritage Centre. IUCN's responsibility to undertake evaluations of a given World Heritage site nomination is not primarily focused on identifying rights issues and engaging with affected groups, but rather on providing technical support to the process, whether through wider guidance (see further discussion below) or specific evaluations. States may, for example, in specific World Heritage contexts, put efforts in place to respect, protect and fulfil rights, which IUCN can then address and assess in its evaluations.

Challenges and opportunities in evaluation processes

It is well-established that the relationship between rights and conservation is complex, and this is equally true in relation to World Heritage. While there are many good examples, it must be recognized that a number of nomination processes, and subsequent inscriptions, have generated problems and discontent due to the impact of inscription on the rights of those affected. At the same time, it must be noted that some State Parties are spearheading far more proactive engagement with and use of rights as an integral dimension of the nomination process. Heritage conservation has the potential to allow for improved protection of rights, including rights to land and resources, just as it has the potential to clash with or infringe upon them. The following synthesis of issues lists *some* of the major concerns identified in discussions with a broad range of actors and the literature reviewed. The list is far from comprehensive but seeks to illustrate the breadth and diversity of issues at stake.

Overall guidance on World Heritage and communities and rights is growing but still insufficient

There has been a marked increase in World Heritage Committee references to and recommendations on indigenous peoples, communities and rights issues, including requesting State Parties to address and resolve outstanding matters or commending them for having done so. In response, State Parties are increasingly presenting detailed information in this respect, just as wording is increasingly apparent in guidance material. Yet, there are also inconsistencies, in part stemming from the lack of a comprehensive approach to indigenous peoples, communities and rights concerns. Human rights standards and technical frameworks have been rapidly developed at international and national levels, making it challenging to put them into practice in short timeframes.

New standards and practices generate new needs, also in the World Heritage context. While references to participation and local values have become more common, the approach to incorporating these issues needs to be far more systematic. This needs to be revisited in the Operational Guidelines as well as other guidance documents. The current (2011) UNESCO manual for 'Preparing World Heritage Nominations',[22] for example, includes no specific wording on either rights or community tenure issues, although these issues are addressed in the subsequent manual on 'Managing Natural World Heritage'.[23] Core nomination guidance therefore does not yet fully reflect the importance attached to community concerns and rights by the World Heritage Committee and the Advisory Bodies in a comprehensive manner. While some countries have advanced such work, stimulated by domestic policies or international standards, there is a need for upstream guidance to facilitate State Party engagement on the issues. Although some aspects have been strengthened, the fact that others are lacking reflects the deficiency of specific consideration of these issues in the Operational Guidelines.

Working with different stakeholders requires different approaches

'Stakeholders' is a term commonly used to encompass all social and institutional groups that have some kind of interest in a given conservation area or action, such as a World Heritage nomination or site. In the current processes, the diversity of 'stakes' of such groups is rarely recognized and addressed, and little or no distinction is made between the nature of these different stakes, for example, of indigenous peoples, local communities, government officials, researchers, commercial interests and NGOs, all of whom are identified as stakeholders.[24] This undifferentiated approach affects the situation of indigenous peoples and local communities, whose livelihoods and cultures may be historically connected to a site. In cases where these groups have customary rights to an area due to their long-standing occupation and use of it, they can be called 'rights-holders' to distinguish them from other stakeholders. The use of the term 'rights-holders' for the indigenous peoples and communities concerned does not negate the existence of other rights vested in other groups – for example, the people of the country a site belongs to also have the right to have their national heritage protected and well managed. At a given World Heritage site, however, if there are indigenous peoples or local communities with customary rights to the lands, territories and resources, the specificities of engaging with these rights-holders need to be reflected in the approaches.

Nomination processes that have been inclusive of specific rights-holders illustrate the range of rights and processes this may imply. Whereas the identification of indigenous peoples and traditional communities in nomination processes is growing, in some cases it remains contested by government officials or experts, which could prevent the systematic identification of indigenous peoples and community rights concerns in IUCN's evaluation processes. While the topic receives fairly comprehensive treatment in evaluations in some countries with relatively strong legal recognition of indigenous rights and long-standing indigenous engagement with heritage processes, evaluations are much weaker in countries lacking such law and practice. Paradoxically, the latter

---

22 UNESCO 2011b.
23 UNESCO 2012a.
24 See e.g. UNESCO 2011b.

are often the countries where reviewing how rights have been addressed in the nomination is most needed. In addition to indigenous and community rights-holders, most sites will involve a complex of other types of rights-holders potentially affected by World Heritage nomination. These may include children, migrants, settlers or women, for example. Again, nominations differ markedly in terms of the extent to which such different right-holders are adequately identified in the evaluation process.

Rights concerns not identified in evaluation processes

Cases of indigenous peoples' and local communities' rights not being identified during the evaluation process undertaken by IUCN have appeared throughout the years. One particular case, that of the Lake Bogoria National Reserve (part of the Kenya Lake System in the Great Rift Valley, inscribed as a World Heritage site in 2011), has highlighted some of the disconnections in the system that need to be addressed. The Lake Bogoria area was declared a Game Reserve in 1978, at which moment, following national legislation, the resident Endorois community was forcibly removed from the area, according to a legal complaint filed by the community in 2003 with the African Commission on Human and Peoples' Rights (ACHPR).[25] The ACHPR ruled in favour of the plaintiffs, finding that as a result of their forced eviction from their ancestral lands the Endorois had suffered violations of several of their human rights under the *African Charter on Human and Peoples' Rights*. The grievances of the community were not mentioned in the nomination, and although the Endorois representatives raised these complaints in letters to UNESCO, these were not conveyed to IUCN during the evaluation process. The complaints were also not mentioned during the stakeholder consultations and public hearings that took place during the field evaluation (although other concerns were raised and addressed). Complaints from the Endorois Welfare Council and organizations who supported them even reached international venues such as the UN Permanent Forum on Indigenous Issues, yet they were not detected during the IUCN evaluation process. A petition specifically prepared to articulate rights concerns in relation to nominations to the 35th Session of the World Heritage Committee raised concerns about ineffective consultation and lack of consent but did not mention the judgement of the ACHPR, despite its evident relevance to rights concerns.[26] Furthermore, the State Party presented documented evidence of an extensive 10-year consultation process.

Accessing appropriate and sufficient information on rights issues and making consultations around the nomination process and documentation as inclusive as possible is challenging, as this example illustrates. It has been suggested that evaluation arrangements could, in the most extreme cases, be easily 'stage managed' by State Parties interested in avoiding problematic areas, including possible human rights violations; this might manifest itself in community meetings and

---

25 *Communication 276 / 2003 – Centre for Minority Rights Development (Kenya) and Minority Rights Group International on behalf of Endorois Welfare Council v Kenya.*
26 Endorois Welfare Council et al. 2011.

consultations organized and selected by State officials etc. Furthermore, it is also a concern that key rights-holders may be unaware of the nomination process, suggesting the need for more proactive outreach to indigenous peoples' and local communities' representatives if genuine participation is sought. This is particularly clear at natural sites often involving large distances, poor infrastructure and weak communication means.

Despite the difficulties and complexity, there is a clear need for evaluation processes to include greater and more systematic consultation of indigenous peoples, and to include specific assessment of the degree to which consultation has been undertaken by State Parties. Structured relationships with key organizations with expertise in this area that can assist Advisory Body evaluations also need to be formed and/or strengthened. The United Nations Permanent Forum on Indigenous Issues, as the recognized UN body considering indigenous peoples' issues in general, may provide particularly appropriate opportunities for collaborative work with the Advisory Bodies, and could also offer advice to UNESCO. UN Special Rapporteurs with theme- or country-specific mandates may also be important interlocutors.

Recognizing complexity and working systematically

The complexity of dealing with indigenous peoples, communities and rights issues in the World Heritage context is an important reason for strengthening the Advisory Bodies' engagement with these issues in their evaluations. Firstly, some sites harbour particularly complex make-ups of different rights- and stakeholders, whose interests and claims may be overlapping and, in some cases, conflicting. Understanding such complexity requires prolonged engagement. Secondly, community engagement is rarely a simple 'either or' scenario but involves a whole range of issues and challenges, including in relation to opportunities for participation, and questions regarding who speaks for or represents a particular community or people. In some cases, there is a perception that field missions, due to their short durations, easily (and perhaps inevitably) risk missing the complexity of a given topic, especially if evaluators lack knowledge of the region and issues. For State Parties investing time and resources in addressing these issues, it is important that the Advisory Bodies' evaluations pay due credit to both the complexity of the issue and the wide range of efforts being made. A more systematic approach to the range of issues around indigenous peoples, local communities and rights is critical in order both to recognize what is being done and, equally, to allow evaluations to clarify complexity and identify workable follow-up solutions where problems are identified.

Rights may be misunderstood as problematic for World Heritage recognition and site management

In a number of countries, World Heritage processes have led to concerns regarding possible expropriation of lands from communities or indigenous peoples and relocation of settlements.

Any such actions may reflect a misconception that World Heritage nomination requires community presence and rights to be extinguished for site recognition. This may, in part, also result from the fact that State-governed IUCN Category 2 protected areas ('National Parks') are often presented as a preferred management model for World Heritage sites, without fully exploring alternatives, and such a category in the national legislation of many countries excludes resident communities.

Depending on the site and the level of civil society involvement, such neglect of rights would, in some cases, only be raised and addressed in the nomination and evaluation process. In recent years, IUCN has been actively promoting new policies and practices in the protected area community not only in terms of addressing social impacts but also in terms of avoiding blueprint approaches based on Western notions of nature that neglect long-standing human ecological relationships and other management possibilities. This confirms the importance of further upstream guidance in this respect, while reinforcing the need for the Advisory Bodies to identify and evaluate how rights are being addressed in the nomination process and its preceding steps. Fundamentally important in this regard but insufficiently known is the fact that the World Heritage Convention has long regarded traditional management systems as fully appropriate for providing the protection and management expected of listed World Heritage sites.[27] A growing number of World Heritage sites have been listed on this basis, including at the specific request of indigenous peoples.

Legacy issues: 'Rights were already infringed upon before the nomination process, so recognition does not change anything'

An important point is that World Heritage nomination or inscription of a natural area does not anticipate a direct change in tenure and protection arrangements existing therein. Inscription of a site merely recognizes its Outstanding Universal Values and its form of land-use, including the protection and management of standards and practices that have been put in place for its conservation. Typically, for example, a national park would have been declared well before the nomination, following national legislation and policies. The relocation of people or other actions negative for indigenous peoples and/or local communities in the area may thus have happened years before the initiation of a World Heritage nomination process, that is, at the time when the national park was established.

As an example, the Wildlife Sanctuaries of Thung Yai Naresuan and Huai Kha Khaeng in Thailand became a World Heritage site in 1991; Thung Yai Naresuan had been declared a Wildlife Sanctuary 17 years earlier, in 1974. Ethnic Pwo Karen communities had been living in Thung Yai Naresuan for possibly 200 years before the establishment of the Sanctuary yet, since the creation of the Sanctuary, they had been subject to a number of measures aimed at their relocation and

---

27 See para. 97 of the Operational Guidelines.

restriction of their subsistence practices.[28] The challenges that the Pwo Karen communities have faced are not therefore primarily the result of the inscription of the area as a World Heritage site in 1991 but of the creation of the Wildlife Sanctuary in 1974.

The question that follows from this and similar examples is whether such antecedents should be used as an argument against the World Heritage nomination and inscription of the sites, or whether the nomination process itself could be an opportunity to redress wrongdoings that happened decades before and, if so, what it would require to change the tenure and rights set-up, including through reforming national laws.

The debate is important. It is the view of the authors that more emphasis is needed on the transformative potential of World Heritage nominations in situations with legacies of rights issues. Recognition of pre-existing rights problems in an evaluation process as such may not in principle change a given situation but it can influence change through practical recommendations from the evaluations, for example the inclusion or exclusion of certain areas, the adoption of specific management practices or recommendations related to buffer zones.

An important policy principle in this context for IUCN is that relocation or other actions negatively affecting communities should never be directly caused, accelerated or intensified as a result of World Heritage nomination processes. Furthermore, measures proposed regarding communities linked to a site should be based on agreements with them and should result in demonstrable improvements in the lives and capacities of the communities for engaging in World Heritage management.

Unless community land and tenure is adequately addressed in the preparation process, indigenous peoples and local communities may suffer from increased land and housing prices and other problems that the World Heritage inscription can sometimes trigger. Conversely, World Heritage recognition may be a leverage point to revoke or repair prior infringements, restore relationships with land and resources, and pursue socially beneficial management and economic relations. What is clear is that unless infringements and concerns regarding rights that took place prior to World Heritage processes are addressed in explicit terms during the evaluation of nominations, the real potential to resolve and repair the rights deficit will be lost, and there could be the risk that rights concerns are further deepened.

Lack of clear performance criteria for indigenous peoples, communities and rights issues

It is clear that overall protected area standards are being consolidated in relation to concerns about indigenous peoples, communities and rights through processes such as the CBD Programme of Work on Protected Areas;[29] however, similar standards are less clear in relation to World Heritage

---

28 Buergin 2003; Delang and Wong 2006.
29 Adopted at the seventh meeting of the Conference of Parties to the *Convention on Biological Diversity* (Kuala Lumpur, 2004) and reaffirmed with additional elements in 2010 (Nagoya, Japan). Available at https://www.cbd.int/protected/pow.

nominations. The uneven treatment of issues related to indigenous peoples and local community concerns across different evaluations raises the need for a more structured framework or checklist allowing for evaluators to assess performance on key community and rights topics.

Such a checklist would involve developing specific questions and, when applicable, performance criteria, along with key concerns about indigenous peoples, local communities and rights. The sources of such performance criteria would include existing and future World Heritage Committee decisions, Operational Guidelines and policies, as well as applicable international standards such as the UNDRIP. For IUCN, it is specifically important to better reflect its own standards (and those international standards that IUCN regards as the most significant) in relation to indigenous peoples, local communities and rights as part of the evaluation process. The underlying issue is the need for a consolidated set of policy principles and performance indicators on indigenous peoples, local communities and rights to guide World Heritage Committee decisions on specific site nominations. Until these are agreed, one option for the Advisory Bodies such as IUCN is to make more use of their own standards on indigenous peoples, local communities and rights and share relevant good practice with State Parties when undertaking evaluations. In grey-zone areas where standards are still being developed, IUCN could make use of its own standards as a reference agreed upon by its membership. This may form part of technical inputs to help strengthen the World Heritage Convention's own policy framework. It is also clear that this effort would benefit substantially from upstream work to ensure that guidance to State Parties is provided, and also for nomination formats to be strengthened in terms of more explicit policy standards and dedicated space to address community and rights issues.

In response, IUCN has initiated a learning-by-doing process to introduce consideration of rights explicitly into its World Heritage evaluation processes. This included, in 2012-13, the addition of a dedicated space in field evaluation reports for community and rights concerns, a new protocol to ensure field evaluators are prompted to consider rights issues before evaluation missions, enhanced consultation procedures with both external networks and IUCN's own expert groups on rights, the introduction of the heading of 'Community' with relevant content in IUCN reports to the World Heritage Committee, and explicit attention to these issues in the agenda of the IUCN World Heritage Panel. Complementing these efforts is a growing dialogue and partnership with ICOMOS on these issues, on the relationships between the 'natural heritage' and 'cultural heritage' mandates of both organizations, and on the need to better coordinate evaluation activities.

Unresolved rights issues and World Heritage as a turning point for change

Deep-running structural conflicts in any given place are unlikely to be resolved unless problems are addressed in a comprehensive manner. This is true in the case of national protected areas laws and policies, as well as institutional setups and practices. World Heritage nomination typically involves significant public and governmental attention to a given area and its on-going conflicts, problems and unresolved issues. From this perspective, nominations can offer important opportunities for catalyzing attention and resources to resolve a given conflict, particularly if evaluations identify the concerns at stake. The most obvious cases are sites which specifically make reference to indigenous peoples' and local communities' rights in the nomination itself.

World Heritage processes can have problem-solving effects on seemingly intractable issues. In one area, concerns raised anonymously with the field evaluator about a waste landfill being planned between two conservation areas making up the nominated site created an opportunity for dialogue between the technical mission and the State Party, as a result of which a solution was found to the problem – while debates had run on for years unproductively. Similar problem-solving effects could likely appear in relation to indigenous peoples, local communities and rights issues; for this, more explicit questions and formalized and structured attention to community and rights issues by the evaluators would significantly heighten opportunities for undertaking dialogue with State Parties and resolving many of the matters currently either neglected or only addressed when conflict erupts.

Ways forward

Concerns regarding rights clearly need a new and more active approach in the World Heritage Convention, recognizing the balance of issues at stake, including resolving problems, realizing opportunities and celebrating successes. There is a need to ensure that the minimum standards applied to World Heritage nominations correspond to international norms, as well as to develop approaches that will enable the Convention to set standards of best practice in line with its flagship role. The site-specific focus of the World Heritage Convention also ensures that results in the real world can be seen and evaluated so that a connection from policy to practice can be achieved in a tangible way.

As a first step in a new phase of active and systematic consideration of rights in the World Heritage evaluation process, IUCN has embarked on a learning-by-doing exercise in the 2012/2013 evaluation cycle, as mentioned above. It is expected that this experience will be integrated into IUCN processes, with a consolidated report to the 2016 World Conservation Congress, as well as to the World Heritage Committee. Consultations with other Advisory Bodies have moreover cemented community and rights concerns as a collective challenge also in need of collective solutions. This includes collaborating with ICOMOS both in terms of its specific mandate in relation to cultural sites and in terms of joint responsibilities in relation to mixed sites and collaboration taking place in relation to cultural landscapes.

Yet it is also clear that reforming World Heritage processes so that they adequately build on a rights-based approach will take much more than strengthened evaluation practices. Across the whole World Heritage system and cycles, from guidance to nomination processes to monitoring of sites, there are good opportunities and entry points for addressing rights issues and securing positive results. A much deeper and more inclusive debate is required to resolve the disconnections blocking positive change, to communicate and learn from both positive and negative experiences, and to agree on the changes that could be made to the expectations set for State Parties and their listed World Heritage sites via the Operational Guidelines and procedures of the World Heritage

Convention. Such debate is needed to make World Heritage sites not only effective conservation areas but also places for just, equitable and sustainable development for communities and peoples.

References

Badman, T., Bomhard, B., Fincke, A., Langley, J., Rosabal, P., and D. Sheppard. 2008. *Outstanding Universal Value: Standards for Natural World Heritage*. Gland, IUCN.

Buergin, R. 2003. Shifting frames for local people and forests in a global heritage: the Thung Yai Naresuan Wildlife Sanctuary in the context of Thailand's globalization and modernization. *Geoforum*, Vol. 34, pp. 375–393.

Cunningham, M. 2012. Interview with Myrna Cunningham, Chair of the United Nations Permanent Forum on Indigenous Issues (UNPFII). *World Heritage*, Vol. 62, February 2012, pp. 52-55.

Delang, C. O. and Wong, T. 2006. The Livelihood-based Forest Classification System of the Pwo Karen in Western Thailand. *Mountain Research and Development*, Vol. 26, No. 2, May 2006, pp. 138–145.

Endorois Welfare Council et al. 2011. *Joint Statement on Continuous violations of the principle of free, prior and informed consent in the context of UNESCO's World Heritage Convention*. 17 May 2011.

Larsen, P. B. 2012. *IUCN, World Heritage and Evaluation Processes Related to Communities and Rights: An independent review*. Gland, IUCN World Heritage Programme.

Merode, E. de, Smeets, R. and Westrik, C. (eds,). 2004. Linking Universal and Local Values: Managing a Sustainable Future for World Heritage. *World Heritage Papers*, Vol. 13. Paris, UNESCO.

Sinding-Larsen, A. 2012. Our common dignity: rights-based approaches to heritage management. *World Heritage*, Vol. 62, February 2012, pp. 56-58.

Thorsell, J. and Hogan, R. 2009. *IUCN Evaluation of World Heritage Nominations: Some Suggestions to Evaluators for IUCN Evaluation Missions and IUCN Technical Evaluation Reports*. Gland, IUCN.

UNESCO. 1999. *World Heritage Committee, Twenty-second session, Kyoto, Japan, 30 November – 5 December 1998: Report*. Doc. WHC-98/CONF.203/18.

UNESCO. 2011a. *Operational Guidelines for the Implementation of the World Heritage Convention*. Doc. WHC. 11/01, November 2011. Paris, World Heritage Centre.

UNESCO. 2011b. *Preparing World Heritage Nominations (Second edition, 2011)*. World Heritage Resource Manual. Paris, UNESCO/ICCROM/ICOMOS/IUCN.

UNESCO. 2011c. *Progress report on the preparation of the 40th Anniversary of the Convention*. Doc. WHC-10/35.COM/12D.

UNESCO. 2012a. *Managing Natural World Heritage*. World Heritage Resource Manual. Paris, UNESCO/ICCROM/ICOMOS/IUCN.

UNESCO. 2012b. *World Heritage*, Vol. 62 (Special issue on "World Heritage and Indigenous Peoples"). Paris, World Heritage Centre.

UNESCO. 2013. *Draft Policy Guidelines* [for the implementation of the World Heritage Convention]. Doc. WHC-13/37.COM/13.

PART II

CASE STUDIES

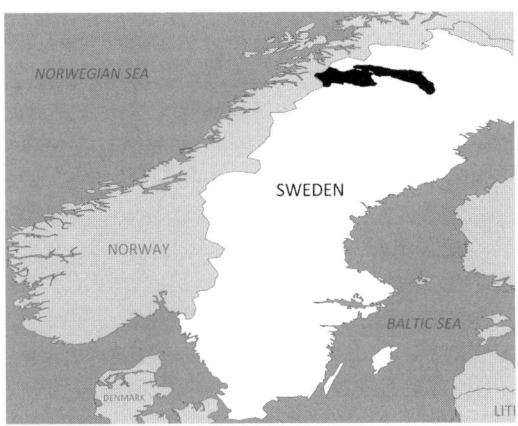

The Laponian World Heritage Area: Conflict and Collaboration in Swedish *Sápmi*

Carina Green[1]

Introduction

The Laponian World Heritage Area is situated just above the Arctic Circle in the north of Sweden, and stretches across the mountain range towards the Norwegian border. Established in 1996, it consists of some of the oldest and most well-known national parks and nature reserves in Sweden, such as *Stuor Muorkke, Sarek* and *Sjávnja* (see Map 1).[2]

This article will discuss some of the events that occurred locally when the area gained its World Heritage status.[3] In 1996, a finished and detailed management plan was not a prerequisite when

---

[1] The author would like to thank Lars-Anders Baer and Mattias Åhrén for valuable comments on a previous draft of this article.
[2] Named here in Sami, these areas are called *Stora Sjöfallet, Sarek* and *Sjaunja* in Swedish.
[3] The empirical material for this article rests on the results of research in the Laponian Area specifically and on the World Heritage phenomenon in more general terms. The research was carried out over different periods between 1999 and 2009, and was sponsored predominantly by consecutive grants from the Swedish Research Council and the Swedish National Heritage Board. For a more detailed account, see my Doctoral Thesis (Green 2009).

*Left: Gathering of a reindeer herd by members of the Sirges sameby in November 2012 near Lake Kutjaure on the border of the Laponian Area (Padjelanta National Park). At the beginning of winter, the reindeer herds are gathered from their grazing areas in the Laponian Area and moved down to their winter pastures in the lowland forests to the east of Laponia .
Photo: Carl-Johan Utsi*

nominating sites. As the area had been under national environmental protection for such a long time (the earliest declaration of protected status was 1909), existing national regulations for the area were considered sufficient for the nomination, and were supposed to be developed further once the site was inscribed on the World Heritage List. However, it proved difficult to achieve a management plan that all actors involved could agree upon, and there was a clear polarization between the local authorities and the indigenous Sami community involved. The Laponian case shows that local and indigenous people's involvement in environmental protection schemes is, above all, a political issue that ultimately leads to reassessed and restructured relations with the state authorities.

The Sami in Sweden – a short background

The Sami people are indigenous to northern Norway, Sweden, Finland and the Kola Peninsula of Russia. In total, the population is estimated at approximately 70 000 individuals[4] and, out of these, around 20 000 live in Sweden. The Laponian Area has traditionally been inhabited by Sami people and lies in the heart of the Sami core area, *Sápmi* (Samiland). Until today the area is of vital importance for many Sami reindeer herding families. Although famous throughout the world for being a pastoral, reindeer herding people, most Sami today are not engaged in reindeer herding. In Sweden, approximately 10-15% of the total Sami population of 20 000 are active in herding. Nevertheless, there are strong Sami cultural and symbolic values attached to reindeer and the herding lifestyle and, as such, reindeer herding remains an important ethnic marker for the Sami community as a whole.[5]

The reindeer herders are organized into *samebys*. A *sameby* is an economic association of a group of reindeer herders who collaboratively use a specific traditionally occupied geographical area for herding.[6] There are 51 *samebys* in Sweden today. Only reindeer herders are members of *samebys* and, under Swedish law, only *sameby* members can legally exercise the collective inherent resource use rights of the Sami people, including special rights to hunt and fish. In practice, this means that only a small percentage of the total Sami population today are able to enjoy those rights. This 'split' between reindeer herding Sami and non-herding Sami in terms of their ability to legally exercise their collective rights goes back to reindeer herding laws from the beginning of the 20th century, and was generated by both issues of resource conflict and of Social Darwinist influences on the government's Sami policies at the time.[7]

---

4 Sami Information Centre 2006. This number is taken from the official information site on the Sami people, under the control of the Sami Parliament in Sweden. However, a proper census of the population has never been taken. Moreover, it would be difficult to come up with an exact estimation since the definition of who is and who is not Sami is often arbitrary and, to many people of 'mixed' origin, the Sami identity will be of significance only on specific occasions or at specific periods in life.
5 In Sweden, reindeer herding is an exclusive right of the Sami population, based on customary use since time immemorial.
6 For details, see Beach 1981, pp. 360-393.
7 For more details, see Beach 1981; Lundmark 1998, 2002; Mörkenstam 1999, 2002.

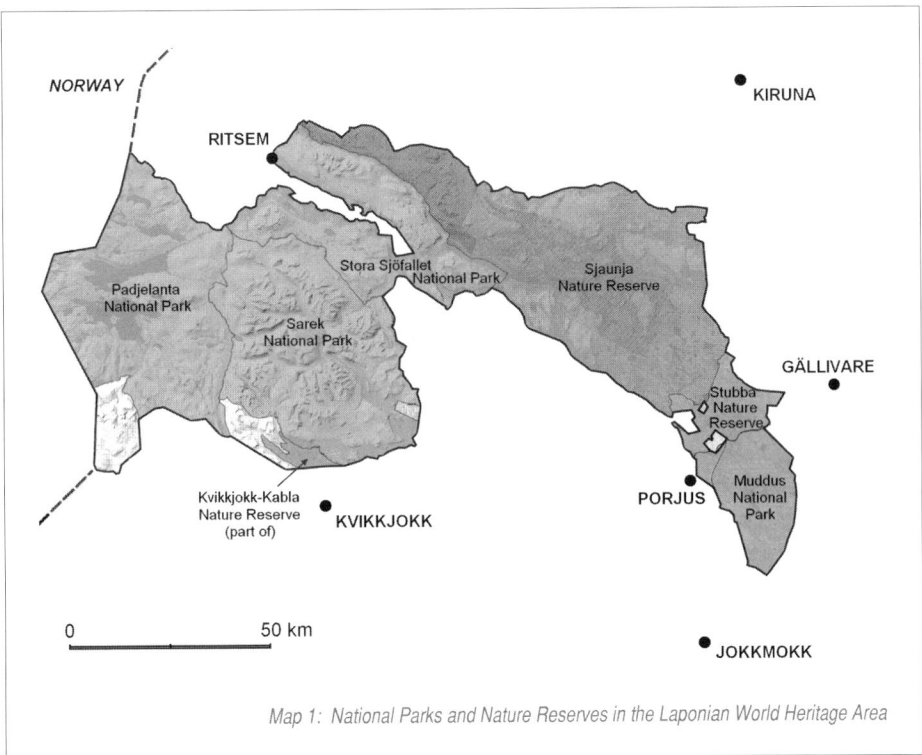

Map 1: National Parks and Nature Reserves in the Laponian World Heritage Area

Nine *samebys* have grazing land for their reindeer inside the World Heritage area.[8] No one lives there permanently but, each summer, the reindeer herders in the area move up with their families from the populated areas to the mountains to be close to the reindeer and their summer pastures.

Compared to indigenous peoples in other countries, the Sami in Sweden are well-integrated into the welfare system, and there are in general terms no major socio-economic differences between the Sami and other citizens. The colonization process was slow and rested mostly on administrative and religious assimilation into the majority society.[9] The majority population has had a long and mostly peaceful interaction with the Sami community, and non-Sami farmers settled early in large parts of *Sápmi*. However, injustices and atrocities have historically occurred and should not be downplayed. The colonial rule, mentality and attitude of the state authorities, both historically and today, is an issue that many Sami are aware of and have to deal with. Many Sami (and non-Sami) would argue that there is still a prevailing structural colonization that hinders Sami individuals as well as Sami ideas and values in playing a full role in the development of

---

8   The nine *samebys* with grazing areas inside the Laponian Area are *Baste Čearru* (Mellanbyn), *Unna Čearuš* (Sörkaitum), *Sirges* (Sirkas), *Jåhkågasska, Tuorpon, Luokta Mávas, Gällivare, Sierri* and *Udtja*.
9   Rydving 1993; Lehtola 2004.

society, both locally and nationally. Frequently, the relationship between state officials and the Sami (especially reindeer herding Sami) is somewhat strained. In most countries with an indigenous population, the relations between government agencies tasked with environmental protection and the indigenous population is a specific and often difficult one. Even though colonization to a large extent involves non-material perspectives (religion, values, language and so on), confiscation of inhabited and traditionally used territories nevertheless stands out as the most tangible proof of colonization. It is here that the basic resources, including both intrinsic and material values, rest. Since the land is still often under the claim of national authorities, these agencies and their staff are frequently seen as the concrete testimony of both historical and current colonial rule. In the process of establishing a management plan for Laponia, the Sami representatives would all agree that this colonial structure, sometimes so difficult to discern, became visible and came to affect the negotiations among the local actors.[10]

The Sami community in Sweden today is active in international indigenous affairs and there is a Sami Parliament in Sweden, established in 1993. In some regions in Sweden, children can attend Sami schools and Sami have the right to use their own language when interacting with the authorities. Culturally, academically and politically the Sami community has seen a rapid and positive development in the last decades. However, when it comes to concrete rights to lands and waters, and increased political autonomy more generally, there have been fewer signs of progress, and knowledge of Sami history, culture and current situation among the majority population remains weak.

Background to the World Heritage nomination

Laponia is a 'mixed' World Heritage site. Its 'outstanding universal value', as defined by the World Heritage Committee, is based both on natural criteria and on the Sami culture (both historical and current) in the area. The official inscription in 1996 reads as follows:

> "The Committee decided to inscribe the nominated property on the basis of natural criteria (i), (ii) and (iii) and cultural criteria (iii) and (v). The Committee considered that the site is of outstanding universal value as it contains examples of ongoing geological, biological and ecological processes, a great variety of natural phenomena of exceptional beauty and significant biological diversity including a population of brown bear and alpine flora. It was noted that the site meets all conditions of integrity. The site has been occupied continuously by the Sami people since prehistoric times, is of the last and unquestionably largest and best preserved examples of an area of transhumance, involving summer grazing by large reindeer herds, a practice that was widespread at one time and which dates back to an early stage in human economic and social development." [11]

---

10 Dahlström 2003, Green 2009.
11 World Heritage Committee 1996.

View of the Rapa Valley in the Laponian Area (Sarek National Park). Photo: distantranges (CC BY-NC 2.0)

The Committee also "underlined the importance of the interaction between people and the natural environment".[12]

The story of the World Heritage nomination of Laponia can be said to have begun as early as the 1980s when the Swedish government submitted an application to the World Heritage Committee nominating the Sjávnja nature reserve (today part of the Laponian Area) on the basis of natural criteria only. This first initiative was not accepted by the World Heritage Committee. The Committee, based on the reports from its advisory body, IUCN, thought the area lacking in exceptionality and informally advised the Swedish authorities to withdraw the application with a view to nominating an extended area in the future.[13] Voices were now also raised, both from government departments and from the Sami Parliament, suggesting that the new nomination should also include Sami culture in the area. After all, reindeer herding had a significant impact in shaping the biological characteristics of the landscape, and the Sami cultural and spiritual connections to the land were and still are strong. This was an idea that would indeed increase the possibility of a successful outcome for the nomination.

---

12 Ibid.
13 See IUCN 1990; UNESCO 1990; and Dahlström 2003, p. 242.

The Sami had not been very involved in the process for the 'old' nature-based Sjávnja nomination, apart from a few discussions and talks with authority officials on the matter. With the mixed-site nomination, however, their participation in the process became more direct. The first thing that happened was that the cultural part of the application had to be inserted into the document, containing the already completed description of the site's natural values.[14] This assignment was given to the head of the Ájtte Swedish Mountain and Sami Museum. However, it was expected that the cultural part of the application should be completed in only three months, compared to the years and years of work that had been put into the natural part of the application. The County Administration of Norrbotten had previously been criticized by other actors (Sami and non-Sami) for placing too much focus on the biology and geology of the area, without properly emphasizing the Sami cultural heritage. The short time given to the head of the museum confirmed these opinions and this was something that many of the members of the local *samebys* talked about at the time. Less time and fewer resources were spent on the cultural parts of the application and on the parts acknowledging the Sami interest in the area, and this was something that would continue to echo throughout the negotiations over how to manage the area.[15]

From collaboration to conflict

As stated earlier, the Laponian Area consists of previously established national parks and nature reserves. This means that a large part of what is today called Laponia had been the object of nature conservation legislation for a long time, the first national park having been established as early as 1909 (Sarek). Laponia consists almost entirely of Crown Land, according to the official interpretation of the law. However, this assumed ownership has never been officially registered and has been contested and debated.[16] The authority responsible for nature conservation management in Sweden is the County Administrative Board (*Länsstyrelsen*), and its regional offices. Consequently, the County Administration of Norrbotten (henceforward the County Administration), the northernmost regional office of the County Administration Board, was from the start responsible for the maintenance and management of the World Heritage area. The County Administration, together with the Swedish Environmental Protection Agency (SEPA), had been very active in forming the application for World Heritage status ever since the first attempts in the 1980s with the Sjávnja application.

As mentioned, nine *samebys* have some or most of their reindeer herding land inside the World Heritage area. Of these nine *samebys*, two (*Sierri* and *Udtja*) only use these lands occasionally

---

14 In the original draft of the nomination document, the area was referred to as "The Lapponian Wilderness Area" and portrayed as more or less untouched by humans (with the exception of the traditional influence of the Sami and their reindeer herding). The Sami Parliament objected to this depiction, pointing out that the area was a Sami cultural landscape that had been inhabited and influenced from time immemorial (Dahlström 2003, pp. 246-253; Green 2009, p. 103).
15 Dahlström 2003, pp. 242, 255; Green 2009, p. 106.
16 Cramér 1966-2009; Korpijaako-Labba 1994; Allard 2006.

and chose to remain outside the negotiations. However the seven remaining *samebys* (*Báste, Unna Čearus, Sirkas, Jåkkåkaska, Tourpon, Luokta-Mavas,* and *Gällivare skogssameby*) were from the start active in trying to influence the process. They had both concerns and expectations for the new World Heritage site. The local reindeer herders were especially worried that the World Heritage designation would lead to restrictions on their immemorial rights and that they would not be allowed to use the area for fishing and hunting, or collect wood for fire or handicraft materials to the same extent as before. Another concern was how the nomination of Laponia would affect the predator policy. Large predators are a constant threat to the reindeer and most herders find the regulations regarding the possibilities of protecting their herds from these animals too strict. A discussion regarding what was considered a rather rigid definition of 'culture' was also taking place at this point in time. Some local *sameby* members expressed a worry that there would be an increased demand on them to behave 'more traditionally' in order to fit the stereotypical image of the Sami and please tourists. Another fear from some *sameby* members was that World Heritage status would increase the number of tourists and that the *samebys* would not have enough influence over where and when tourists would reside in the area, and therefore that tourism would disturb the reindeer. Nevertheless, there were also many hopes and expectations from the *samebys* regarding the new World Heritage status. Tourism was also talked about in positive terms, and many *sameby* members saw a possibility of engaging in the tourism industry or even establishing their own tourism enterprises. Another positive opinion raised by many was that the very fact that the Sami reindeer herding culture was now part of a World Heritage site was something to be proud of. Many hoped that this, in some way, would mean additional international support for the Sami ethno-political struggle. Above all, many *sameby* members expressed how important it was that they would be able to have a say in the future of the World Heritage area and in the management of it. Broad underlying issues of accessibility to land, responsibility, influence and control were at stake for the local *samebys* at the beginning of what would be a long and often painstaking process.

Immediately after the approval of the Laponian nomination by the World Heritage Committee in December 1996, a Laponian Council was formed consisting of representatives from the two municipalities[17] of Jokkmokk and Gällivare, the County Administration, the local *samebys*, the Ájtte museum and tourist departments of the municipalities. In spite of the intention to cooperate and jointly form a management module for the World Heritage site, it soon became obvious that the different actors had very different views on how to go about the process and what to prioritize.

The main difference of opinion among the various representatives on the Laponian Council was regarding how much emphasis should be placed on Sami cultural heritage in relation to natural heritage. The representatives from the *samebys* articulated their status as a separate and clearly defined actor in relation to the other groupings, and in discussions raised the importance

---

17 In Sweden, municipalities (*kommuner*) are administrative units, as well as geographically demarcated areas that are governed by a Municipal County (*kommunfullmäktige*), elected by local voters. The two closest municipalities to the Laponian Area, Jokkmokk and Gällivare, were, together with the County Administration, the local authorities that from the beginning had a strong interest in the development of the new World Heritage site.

of reindeer herding interests and Sami control in the future management of the World Heritage site as vital for the development of the area. At this point in time, it was not self-evident that the *samebys* would be counted as an actor on their own behalf, equal in status to the municipalities and the County Administration. Voices were even raised that questioned the organization of the *samebys* as a stakeholder group in their own right. After all, it was argued, they could and should be represented by the municipalities in the negotiation of the future of Laponia just as any other citizen, for they had elected the current politicians in the latest municipal elections.[18] Even though far from everybody agreed with this standpoint, it is an indication of the difficulties that the *sameby* members faced in the very beginning, after Laponia had been inscribed on the World Heritage List, to position themselves as a separate and equal partner in the decision making regarding the area. This fact was prominent throughout the years of negotiation that followed, and very much shaped the relations among the local actors, along with the characteristics of the negotiation process.

Years of disagreement

After only a few meetings, the Laponian Council was disbanded. From this point on, it was primarily the three main local actors (the *samebys*, the municipalities and the County Administration) that continued to be involved in working out a future management plan for Laponia albeit more often separately than in collaboration with each other. The representatives from the nine *samebys* were now determined to have a real influence over the development of the World Heritage site. They realized that strong Sami involvement in the management was of importance not only locally but could have effects for the Sami community as a whole. It was seen as a potential stepping stone towards increased self-governance in a broader sense. The representatives from the *samebys* launched one clear demand: to have the majority of seats on a future management board.[19] This was, however, strongly rejected by the other actors.

It was decided that each of the three local actors should produce a proposal for a management plan in which they articulated their visions for the World Heritage site and sketched what a management organization could look like in practice. The *samebys* involved had now employed a coordinator to help them coordinate the work regarding Laponia, and they also employed an editor, skilled in international conservation management issues and indigenous issues, to help them write the proposal. The County Administration financially supported the *samebys* in producing their proposal. The representatives came to work as a reference group in this task, and many meetings and discussions finally led to the finished product in the year 2000. They called their proposal *Mijá Ednam* (Our Land)[20] and they also later established an economic association with that same name in order to better safeguard their

---

18   This argument was never seen in any official documents but was shared with me in conversations on several occasions.
19   In other World Heritage sites where indigenous culture is part of the actual justification for inscription, such as Kakadu and Uluṟu-Kata Tjuṯa National Parks, traditional owners have majority representation on the management boards. This was something that the *samebys* pointed out when arguing for Sami control of the management of Laponia (c.f. *Mijá Ednam*, pp. 27-28).
20   *Mijá Ednam* 2000.

interests in the World Heritage site. In the *Mijá Ednam* proposal, the local Sami explained the reasons behind their determination to take a leading role in the future management of the area:

> "We Saami have managed Laponia for thousands of years. We have the knowledge, tradition and motivation to continue to manage Laponia without leaving major traces in the landscape – in spite of new times and modern technology. We are firmly determined to take our responsibility for the preservation of nature and the biological diversity and we think that we are particularly well suited to preserve the Saami culture in the area. We fully support the goals for the World Heritage site and want to formulate our own strategies in order to reach them. We also welcome an equal co-operation with other parties." [21]

The *Mijá Ednam* proposal shared many goals and objectives with the proposals from the other actors but was distinguished by one decisive factor: their demand to have majority representation on any future management board. Again, the other local actors did not agree, citing a concern that it was not possible within the framework of existing regulations.

After this followed several years of attempted talks, negotiations, stranded discussions, proposals and rounds of review statements.[22] The *samebys* persisted in their insistence on holding the majority of seats on the management board. They made it clear to the other local actors that they would not engage in any form of negotiations before this issue was addressed. This strategic choice was not understood by the others. Representatives from both the municipalities and the County Administration thought that it would be better to talk about the issues they agreed upon in order to get the development going and then save the difficult questions for later. But the *samebys* stood firm in their beliefs, and their representatives believed that it would serve their cause better to remain outside the negotiations. This emphasized the importance of their main objective: to be in a responsible position in the management organization.

During these years of disagreement among the local actors, there was a clear polarization between the local (reindeer herding) Sami and the authorities. Conflicts were acted out both on a personal and on a more structural level.[23] This was not the first time that the reindeer herding Sami in the area had been in disagreement with the local authorities and, in many ways, the argument over how to manage Laponia tapped into many of the matters that were already in focus.[24] What the World Heritage appointment did in this respect was very much to act as a vent for the many unresolved issues, issues that related to ownership of land and water, influence and control over the management of traditional land, and a wider goal of increasing Sami autonomy.

---

21 Ibid., p. 9. Translation in Dahlström 2003, p. 323.
22 I have described these events in detail in my doctoral thesis. See Green 2009.
23 For further details, see Dahlström 2003 and Green 2009.
24 Examples of such issues were predator politics in relation to reindeer herding, ownership/user's rights over traditional Sami land, tourism, Sami influence over nature conservation plans and policies, small game hunting in the mountain areas, the ongoing discussion as to whether or not Sweden should ratify ILO Convention 169 (on Indigenous and Tribal Peoples), and general questions related to the revitalization of Sami cultural heritage and language.

On a few occasions during this period in the process, national bodies were officially contacted. As a state agency, the County Administration had close contact with both government departments and the SEPA. Also in 2001, the *samebys* wrote an open letter to the government, seeking assistance going forward in the negotiations. However, the response from the government at the time was that this was a matter that should be resolved on a local level, and that it was the County Administration's responsibility to see that the negotiations continued in a satisfactory manner.[25]

Local influence in environmental protection, let alone Sami influence, has not been a reality in Swedish natural protection policy, in spite of the fact that this is something that is an aim in many of the conventions Sweden has ratified[26] and has been the objective of some reviews commissioned by the government.[27] Because Laponia had the potential to be of a precedential nature the wider Sami community showed an interest in the development of the Laponian process. The Sami Parliament was occasionally briefed about the situation, even though it did not have any official role or play any active part in the negotiations.[28] Different Sami politicians active on both national and international scenes also worked as advisory partners to the *samebys'* representatives.

UNESCO was not active either in the development of the Laponian process, even though representatives from Laponia approached UNESCO with their predicaments on a few occasions.[29] In Sweden's 2006 periodic report on the state of conservation of the Laponian Area,[30] it is noted that the site still lacks a functioning management plan but this document in itself did not lead to any further action on the part of the World Heritage Committee or on the part of the Swedish national authorities. The opinions of the *samebys* were not asked for in the periodic report. It was the Swedish National Heritage Board that was the authority responsible for submitting it and, in the work of producing it, only officials from the national and local authorities were asked to contribute. This led to some irritation among the *samebys'* representatives and was seen as a typical example of how the Sami were being left out of the process.

The table turns

In the fall of 2005, almost ten years after Laponia had been inscribed on the World Heritage list, the table suddenly turned. The representatives of the *samebys* were called to a meeting by the County Governor to resume the negotiations over the management issue. This time they were promised that the question of a Sami majority on a management board would indeed be brought into the discussion. The talks resulted in a proposal, signed by all three local actors, on how to go forward

---

25 Ministry of Agriculture 2001, Reg. No 2001/2594/SU.
26 For instance in the *Convention on Biological Diversity*.
27 Tunón 2004.
28 This is most probably due to the fact that the Sami Parliament in Sweden is both a publicly elected body and a state authority. This means that it is at times difficult for it to take a clear stance in certain matters that involve other governmental authorities and this restrains it somewhat from emphasizing Sami autonomy and self-governance.
29 Green 2009, pp. 135, 145ff.
30 UNESCO 2006.

The board of Laponiatjuottjudus, the management organization of the Laponian Area, in 2011.
Photo: Daniel Olausson

with the organization of Laponia's management and this was sent to the government in 2006.[31] This proposal entailed, among other things, plans for a Sami majority on the management board. The government this time gave the County Administration an official mandate that would allow for a strong Sami influence, and even control, of the management.

A new Laponia delegation was given three years to produce a management organization for the area and the work of forming a Sami-controlled management structure began for the three main local actors, together with SEPA. In June 2011, the government officially gave its blessing to the new management organization to be established. In the press release, the government said that the new proposal was in line with the government's view on the need for improved possibilities for local influence and responsibility on conservation management.[32]

With the new management structure, most of the Sami objectives, which they had struggled so hard to achieve for years, have in many respects been put into practice. In retrospect, it seems that the local disagreements and polarized positions that lasted for so long were overcome surprisingly effortlessly and suddenly. Many people with an insight into the process were both astonished and delighted to see this new turn of events. There is no simple explanation to the sudden change in

---

31   County Administration of Norrbotten 2006, p. 2, Reg. No. 11523-2006.
32   Ministry of Environment 2011.

attitude from the authorities' side but there are a few things that are worth pointing out as important in breaking the dead-locked position of the actors involved.

One important factor is that new people had come into the process. A new County Governor was appointed in 2003 who saw it as important to resolve the Laponian issue and get a proper management organization in place. Some of the involved individuals had been replaced (especially from the local authorities) and some of the old personal grievances therefore came to a natural halt. Another reason is to be found in the fact that the Laponian issue had become increasingly embarrassing for the Swedish government and there were signs of international pressure to include the indigenous population better in these kinds of ventures. Different varieties of joint management or cooperation projects between state authorities and indigenous peoples were becoming more common throughout the world and, in this respect, Sweden was lagging behind many other comparable nation states. Equally important for the positive turn of events was the fact that the representatives from the *samebys*, and the different Sami interest groups and political parties, managed to achieve relative unity on issues that related to Laponia. Needless to say there were differences of opinion, heated discussions and various aspirations and expectations linked to the World Heritage site but, in discussions with the other actors, they managed to go forward as a unified group with one major objective (Sami majority on the management board) rather than having many disparate aims. This was, in fact, a conscious strategy. The importance of 'speaking with one voice' was recognized as imperative in order to be better heard and recognized as a strong valid actor in relation to the local authorities.

Today, the management organization is characterized by local Sami viewpoints and principles. In the new management plan,[33] the protection of Sami cultural values and historical sites is emphasized and the reindeer herding industry is put into focus. The protection of natural values is no longer separated from the protection of a living cultural landscape that is open to development and sustainable change. There are also plans to strengthen the possibilities for developing tourism enterprises in the area, but in a manner that does not jeopardize the sustainability of the environment. The Sami language has been incorporated into the working documents and into the management structure itself. The new management organization is now called *Laponiatjuottjudus* (the Laponian management).

The board consists of nine members, five of whom are appointed by the local *samebys*. The other members comprise two representatives from the municipalities (of Jokkmokk and Gällivare), one from the regional County Administration office and one from SEPA. However, the issue of having majority representation of Sami on the management board has today been somewhat toned down. It is, nonetheless, an important statement that substantiates the leading Sami role in the process, but today the decision making process is guided by the principle of consensus, thus making the majority issue less significant. The board members are appointed on a two-year mandate. There is also an annual assembly, with representatives from all parties concerned. The annual assembly also has a Sami majority representation and one of their assignments is to appoint the Chairperson of the board.

---

33 Laponiatjuottjudus 2012.

In the new management plan, the *Laponiatjuottjudus* spells out the importance of respect, open communication and ongoing dialogue among all the actors involved and in relation to the broader local community. This is looked at as a way of achieving the practical implementation of local participation and the goal is that everybody can have an input and influence in the decision-making process. To ensure this, there will be a public deliberation – *rádedibme* – held at least twice a year. Here, local residents, concerned entrepreneurs and organizations, and other parties have the chance to meet, discuss and influence different issues related to the management of Laponia.

The *Laponiatjuottjudus* is of the opinion that a new, modernized management of the area means applying a holistic perspective in which ensuring the protection of the World Heritage values merges with a need to acknowledge the potential for sustainable development of the area. According to this vision, Laponia will be a place where new technology can be applied together with traditional knowledge in order to better monitor natural and cultural conservation efforts, and to improve communication and influence among the parties. Management is to be seen as a process in need of constant evaluation and renewal. In this process it is important to recognize that the task of managing Laponia is itself an arena for learning (*searvelatnja*) for all actors involved. It is also important to recognize and utilize Swedish administrative knowledge in combination with local knowledge in the practical everyday management.

The new management plan also points out the importance of protecting and developing not only the material heritage of the area but also the immaterial aspects. The intellectual and spiritual cultural heritage of the local Sami will have an important role in the new management of the area. This means that it is seen as important to protect and strengthen, for instance, narratives, memories, spiritual values, knowledge and attitudes that are intrinsically connected to the landscape. Again, care and reintegration of the Sami language is, in this respect, an essential component. It is equally important to safeguard and support relations among people, and between humans and landscape.

The official decree from the government took effect on January 1, 2012, making the *Laponiatjuottjudus* responsible and accountable for the management of the area. The sole mandate of the County Administration for the area's management is at an end and Laponia stands out as a shining example of how local influence over environmental conservation can be implemented in practice. A few, albeit important, concrete changes will come about in the area as a result of the new management regime. For instance, the local reindeer herding Sami will no longer have to seek permission from the County Administration to build huts or set up other constructions. From now on, they only have to report this to the *Laponiatjuottjudus.* Nevertheless, the major important change that is the result of the new management structure is the fact that the local Sami, together with the other local parties, will now be responsible for managing the area. There is a shift in influence and control from the national authorities toward a local and indigenous organization.[34]

From being a source of conflict and flawed communication, the World Heritage designation of Laponia has now turned into an arena for the very opposite: collaboration and renewed communication among local and national actors. Few would have guessed in the beginning of

---

34 I am deeply indebted to Michael Teilus, the Chairperson of *Laponiatjuottjudus,* for providing me with information on the latest occurrences regarding the management process.

the process that Laponia and its management organization would one day stand out as a role model for the international conservation community but, today, the story of the Laponian process is beginning to attract global attention. As a matter of fact, the *Laponiatjuottjudus* was recently presented with an award by the WWF for its progressive work on implementing local influence and emphasizing communication and collaboration in conservation management.[35]

This means that a new chapter in Swedish environmental protection management is being written. Laponia is the first area in which the indigenous Sami have gained an officially responsible role in the management of their traditional lands. Hopefully this will, as the *samebys*' representatives predicted all along, be a first step towards a more progressive and forward-looking political agenda in relation to the Sami in Sweden.

World Heritage and indigenous peoples – the Laponian example

One of UNESCO's official goals is to support indigenous peoples' culture and knowledge.[36] However, as with most international organizations, the intentions articulated and the rhetoric used in an international setting become generalized and malleable in order to unify as many different interests as possible. When implemented locally, these goals and intentions must be interpreted into the reality of the local context. For indigenous peoples, this often means that while the support for indigenous causes is very strong at an international level, it is still difficult to find the means to realize these intentions when relating to national and local authorities.[37]

The developments accounted for here in regard to Laponia can be said to reflect this situation. As can be seen, it was very difficult for the Sami involved to gain attention for their demands locally and nationally. On an international level, on the other hand, they did find support, first and foremost through the international conventions referring to indigenous peoples that Sweden has ratified.[38] One can conclude that even if there is strong support for the protection and development of indigenous cultural diversity, it is often difficult to implement practically and to support indigenous aspirations in the local setting. International support does not often translate into direct and practical encouragement or assistance on a local level. This 'double standard' also became visible in the early 2000s when indigenous peoples attempted to establish an

---

35 WWF 2011.
36 See, for instance, UNESCO Medium-Term Strategy for 2008-2013, in particular paragraphs 5 and 94. However, the support for indigenous claims on an international level can sometimes be a 'double edged sword' for indigenous peoples. Not only are their goals supported on this level, but there is also often a romanticized perception of them that reinforces stereotypes and cements perceptions of indigenous peoples as anti-modern or natural conservationists. I bring this up in my doctoral thesis, see Green 2009. It is also discussed by many other researchers, for instance Nash 1982; Redford 1990; Conklin 1997; Ellen et al. 2000.
37 Scott 1998, p. 13; Turtinen 2006, p. 58; Green 2009, p. 85
38 For the Laponian case, the *United Nations Declaration on the Rights of Indigenous Peoples* (UNDRIP) has not been of much significance, since it was not adopted by the UN General Assembly until 2007. It was above all the *Convention on Biological Diversity* that was referred to by the *samebys*. However, since 2007 the UNDRIP has also become essential for the Sami political establishment as a tool in the ongoing work to improve the situation for the Sami in Sweden.

advisory council of experts called the WHIPCOE (World Heritage Indigenous Peoples Council of Experts), which was to be directly linked to the World Heritage Committee. The goal was to increase indigenous influence over the implementation of the World Heritage Convention and safeguard indigenous rights and interests. However, in the end, states parties were not ready to meet the demands of the indigenous peoples on this issue. If WHIPCOE had been established as an advisory body of the World Heritage Committee, the problems faced by the local actors in the Laponian process may have developed differently. The *samebys* may then have come across more convincingly to the other actors.[39]

To conclude, one could say that the process of nominating the World Heritage site of Laponia comprised both negative and positive experiences and results for the local indigenous Sami community. In the work of preparing the application leading up to the inscription on the World Heritage list, the local Sami were partly included and informed about the work being done. However, their influence was not on an equal level with the local authorities, and they were not treated as a separate negotiating partner. When the site was nominated and gained its status in 1996, the local Sami decided to strengthen their position and demanded to be an actor in the process, equal to the local authorities. They also demanded to have a strong influence and even be in control of the site management. This was the start of a long and often frustrating process in which the local Sami often felt brushed aside and ignored. By applying a strategy whereby they refused to take part in negotiations until their main objective (to have the majority representation on a future management board) was taken seriously, they managed to achieve, in the end, most of what they had hoped for. Today, there is a management organization at work in the area, where the Sami hold a majority on the board and reindeer herding rights and the protection and development of the Sami cultural heritage are emphasized.

Many difficult issues still remain to be solved and there is an ongoing discussion among the different actors within the *Laponiatjuottjudus*. However, the greatest achievement is the fact that the parties are now involved in a positive communication on the future of the World Heritage site, in spite of the fact that they may have different interests and perceptions of how the area's interests should be protected and promoted. The process of forming a cohesive management plan for Laponia is an example of how a global intention is molded and interpreted in the local context and how a World Heritage site can prove to be a platform for both conflict and collaboration. In the end, Laponia became an arena for communication, in which longstanding problems and predicaments that the local Sami had in their relation to the authorities were vented and articulated. It was a process that showed the colonial structures still at work in Swedish society but also, in the end, may prove to be an important step on the path towards decolonization and increased self-governance. ○

---

39 Green 2009, pp. 97 ff.

References

Allard, C. 2006. *Two Sides of the Coin - Rights and Duties: The Interface Between Environmental Law and Saami Law Based on a Comparison With Aotearoa/New Zealand and Canada.* Luleå, Luleå University of Technology.

Beach, H. 1981. *Reindeer-Herd Management in Transition. The Case of Tuorpon Saameby in Northern Sweden.* Uppsala, Acta Universitatis Upsaliensis (Uppsala Studies in Cultural Anthropology, No. 3).

Conklin, B. A. 1997. Body Paint, Feathers and VCRs: Aesthetics and Authenticity in Amazonian Activism. *American Ethnologist*, Vol. 24, No. 4, pp. 711-737.

Cramér, T. 1966-2009. *Samernas vita bok.* Stockholm, The Author.

Dahlström, Å. N. 2003. *Negotiating Wilderness in a Cultural Landscape. Pred ors and Saami Reindeer Herding in the Laponian World Heritage Area.* Uppsala, Acta Universitatis Upsaliensis (Uppsala Studies in Cultural Anthropology, No. 32).

Ellen, R., Parkes, P. and Bicker, A. (eds.) 2000. *Indigenous Environmental Knowledge and its Transformations. Critical Anthropological Perspectives.* London, Routledge.

Green, C. 2009. *Managing Laponia. A World Heritage as Arena for Sami Ethno-Politics in Sweden.* Uppsala, Acta Universitatis Upsaliensis (Uppsala Studies in Cultural Anthropology, No. 47).

IUCN. 1990. *Re. Sjaunja World Heritage Nomination.* Letter from J. Thorsell, Senior Advisor at IUCN, to L. E. Esping, Assistant Director General at the SEPA.

Korpijaako-Labba, K. 1994. *Om samernas rättsliga ställning i Sverige-Finland: en rättshistorisk utredning av markanvändningsförhållanden och -rättigheter i Västerbottens lappmark före mitten av 1700-talet* (translation from Finnish by B-S. Nissén-Hyvärinen). Helsinki, Jusristförbundets förlag.

Laponiatjuottjudus. 2012. *Laponia, World Heritage in Swedish Lapland: Tjuottjudusplána/ Förvaltningsplan/ Management plan.* February 2012.

Lehtola, V.-P. 2004. *The Sámi People. Traditions in Transition* (translated from Finnish by L. W. Müller-Wille). Aanaar (Inari), Kustannus-Puntsi Publisher.

Lundmark, L. 1998. *Så länge vi har marker. Samerna och staten under sexhundra år.* Stockholm, Rabén Prisma.

Lundmark, L. 2002. *"Lappen är ombytlig, ostadig och obekväm..." Svenska statens samepolitik i rasismens tidevarv.* Umeå, Norrlands universitetsförlag.

Mijá Ednam. 2000. *Mijá Ednam – Samebyarnas Laponiaprogram.* Jokkmokk, Samebyarnas kansli.

Ministry of Environment. 2011. *Ny Förvaltningsorganisation för världsarvet Laponia.* Press Release, 16 June 2011. Available at: http://www.regeringen.se/sb/d/8149/a/170963.

Mörkenstam, U. 1999. *Om "Lapparnes privilegier": föreställningar om samiskhet i svensk samepolitik 1883-1997.* Stockholm, Acta Universitatis Stockholmiensis (Stockholm Studies in Politics No. 67).

Mörkenstam, U. 2002. The Power to Define: The Saami in Swedish Legislation. K. Karppi and J. Eriksson (eds.), *Conflict and Cooperation in the North.* Umeå, Norrlands Universitetsförlag.

Nash, R. 1982. *Wilderness and the American Mind.* New Haven, Yale University Press.

Redford, K. 1990. The Ecologically Noble Savage. *Orion Nature Quarterly*, Vol. 9, No. 3, pp. 25-29.

Rydving, H. 1993. *The End of Drum-time: Religious Change Among the Lule Saami 1670s-1740s.* Uppsala, Acta Universitatis Upsaliensis (Historia religionum, Vol. 12).

Sami Information Centre. 2006. *The Sami in figures.* www.eng.samer.se/servlet/GetDoc?meta_id=1536 (accessed 28 May 2011, last modified 17 August 2006).

Scott, J. 1998. *Seeing Like a State: How Certain Schemes to Improve the Human Condition Have Failed.* New Haven, Yale University Press.

Tunón, H. 2004. *Traditionell kunskap och lokalsamhällen: artikel 8j i Sverige.* Uppsala, Swedish Biodiversity Centre, Uppsala University.

Turtinen, J. 2006. *Världsarvets villkor. Intressen, förhandlingar och bruk i internationell politik.* Stockholm University, Stockholm Studies in Ethnology No. 1.

UNESCO. 1990. *Item 15 of the Provisional Agenda: Nominations of Natural Properties to the World Heritage List.* Doc. CC-90/CONF.004/10, 29 October 1990.

UNESCO. 2006. *Periodic Reporting, Europe, Cycle 1, Section II: Sweden, Laponian Area (Summary).* Available at: http://whc.unesco.org/en/list/774/documents.

UNESCO. 2007. *Medium-Term Strategy for 2008-2013.* Adopted by the General Conference at its 34th Session on 2 November 2007. UNESCO Doc. 34 C/4.

World Heritage Committee. 1996. Decision 20COM VIII.B - Inscription: The Laponian Area (Sweden). In Doc. WHC-96/CONF.201/21, 10 March 1997, p. 62.

WWF. 2011. *Föreningen Laponiatjuottjudus får WWFs naturvårdspris av kungen.* Press Release, 10 October 2011. Available at: http://www.wwf.se/press/pressrum/pressmeddelanden/1412303-freningen-laponiatjuottjudus-fr-ww-fs-naturvrdspris-av-kungen.

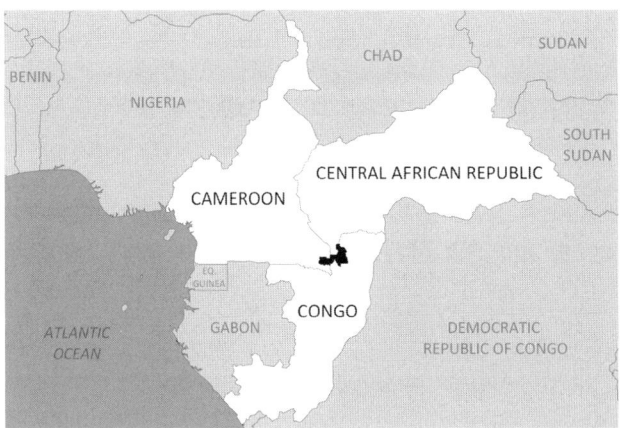

The Sangha Trinational World Heritage Site: The Experiences of Indigenous Peoples

Victor Amougou-Amougou and Olivia Woodburne

Introduction

The Sangha Trinational World Heritage site is located in the north-western Congo Basin where Cameroon, the Central African Republic (CAR) and the Republic of Congo (hereafter Congo) meet. It encompasses adjoining national parks in each of the three countries totalling an area of 746,309 hectares, collectively called the Sangha Trinational (TNS). These three national parks are Lobéké National Park in Cameroon, Dzanga-Ndoki National Park in the Central African Republic and Nouabalé-Ndoki National Park in Congo. The parks are set in a much larger forest landscape, referred to as the TNS landscape, which includes the World Heritage site's buffer zones totalling 1,787,950 hectares. The TNS was inscribed on the World Heritage List in 2012 for its outstanding natural values, with emphasis on the sheer size of this transboundary site and the "ongoing ecological and evolutionary processes in a mostly intact forest landscape at a very large scale".[1] The tropical forests of this region are home to many groups of people, including indigenous

---

1 World Heritage Committee Decision 36COM 8B.8 (2012).

Left: BaAka woman with her grandchild in a forest camp, Central African Republic. Photo: John Nelson

BaAka and Baka 'Pygmies'.[2] This chapter explores the inscription process for this large and complex site, and focuses on the consultation process in Cameroon, where direct research was conducted by one of the authors.

The peoples of the TNS

An estimated 18,000 people live in the buffer zones of the TNS,[3] a number that includes indigenous hunter-gatherers, their farming and fishing neighbours and many more recent immigrants. In Congo and CAR live the BaAka[4] Pygmies and a variety of other groups, including the Sangha-Sangha fisher people.[5] The Baka Pygmies and their farming neighbours the Bangando and Bakwele live in Cameroon. Although not without debate, most researchers consider the Pygmy hunter-gatherers to be long-standing inhabitants of the Central African forests, possibly for as long as 70,000 years.[6] At some point, maybe 4,000-5,000 years ago, farmers speaking Bantu, Adamawa-Ubangian and Central Sudanic languages encountered hunter-gatherers as they migrated into the forest regions.[7] Oral traditions suggest that the hunter-gatherers guided the immigrant farmers and showed them how to live in the forest, in return gaining access to cultivated foods, iron and salt.[8] Importantly, both the BaAka and the Baka are considered, by themselves and their farmer neighbours, to be first-comers to the area and indigenous to the forests.[9] Various farmer groups can also be considered indigenous to specific regions, in recognition of their long-standing occupancy relative to more recent immigrants, although they do not share the same kind of identity or historical relationship with the forest as Pygmies do. This includes the Bangando and Bakwele in Cameroon and the Sangha-Sangha fisher people in CAR.

The various Pygmy groups across the Congo Basin are enormously diverse, and yet there are remarkable similarities in language, relationship with the forest, social interactions and music. Whatever the historical links between hunter-gatherers in the region, all contemporary Pygmy groups living in the TNS landscape have strong and significant links with each other.

The long-standing relationship between Pygmy groups and their farmer neighbours is complex and has changed dramatically throughout history. There are generally two sides to this relationship.

---

2   The term 'Pygmy' refers to hunter-gatherers and former hunter-gatherers who are indigenous to the forests of Central Africa. They share many cultural characteristics and many groups have historical and contemporary links with each other. Although it is a contentious term that can have derogatory connotations, it is also used by Pygmy groups themselves as a collective term that easily distinguishes them from other indigenous and non-indigenous groups. We will therefore continue to use it here when more specific terms for individual groups are not appropriate.
3   Republic of Congo, Cameroon, Central African Republic 2012b, p. 74.
4   Also known as Bayaka and Bambinga as well as other locally specific names.
5   The Sangha-Sangha are specialist fishers, also practising agriculture, like other non-Pygmy groups.
6   Quintana-Murci et al. 2008.
7   Vansina 1990.
8   Lewis 2002.
9   For simplicity, we include all non-Pygmies in the category of 'farmer', although some - like the Sangha-Sangha - are historically specialist fisher people. Non-Pygmy groups are also often referred to as 'Bantu' people.

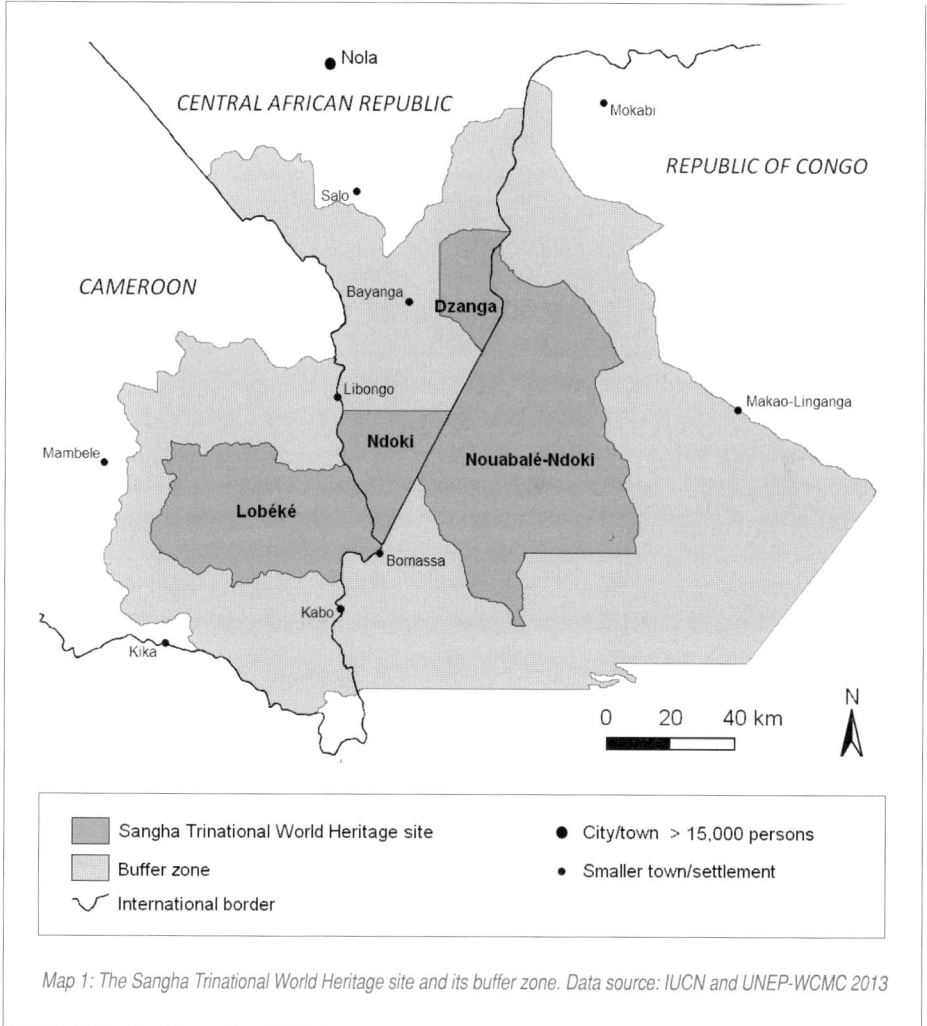

Map 1: The Sangha Trinational World Heritage site and its buffer zone. Data source: IUCN and UNEP-WCMC 2013

First, and most visible, is the extremely derogatory attitude farmers have towards Pygmies, manifested in oppressive relations. Some farmers consider that they 'own' a Pygmy family, often dating back generations, and treat 'their' Pygmies as slaves. The other side of the relationship is more positive, with hunter-gatherers recognised, through traditional stories, as teachers and saviours without whom life in the forest would not be possible. On a practical level, Pygmies are considered skilled hunters and (until recently) supplied much of the meat to farmers in exchange for agricultural products. Pygmies are often seen as possessing mystical powers vital for taming a wild and dangerous forest. For this reason, farmers often seek to participate in hunter-gatherer rituals to ensure their safety in the forest.[10]

---

10 Joiris 1998.

In addition to the indigenous peoples, there are also large numbers of immigrant families attracted by successive waves of industry, including coffee plantations, logging, diamond mining and conservation, who have made these forests their home. Many of these families have lived in well-established villages for generations and have formed their own relationships with indigenous farmer and hunter-gatherer groups.

In Lobéké National Park in Cameroon, the Baka traditionally lived in small nomadic groups dispersed throughout the forest and, as in other areas, are said to be the first inhabitants. Bangando farmers settled in the area some 200 years ago and live primarily in villages around the park. Baka now build semi-permanent settlements associated with these villages and periodically establish temporary forest camps.[11] The amount of time spent in forest camps versus the villages varies widely from place to place, and even between individuals of the same group. In 1986 it was estimated that Baka around Lobéké spent between five and six months a year in the forest, with two to three of those spent in remote areas.[12] This pattern is similar in CAR and Congo and, in all three countries, large areas customarily used by Pygmy communities have been included in national parks, where all access is prohibited.

The national parks

The tropical rainforests of this region are considered relatively intact and are home to an enormous diversity of animal and plant life. Mega-fauna including forest elephants, gorillas, chimpanzees and buffalo attract ecologists and tourists alike, as do the natural forest clearings characteristic of these forests, called 'bais', where large numbers of animals congregate. Lobéké National Park in Cameroon covers 217,850 ha of forests, with surrounding multiple-use zones consisting of six community hunting zones (487,600 ha), seven safari hunting zones (738,000 ha), six community forests (30,000 ha) and 14 forest management units owned by logging companies (911,454 ha), making the total area 1,470,799 ha.[13] Within these buffer zones there are an estimated 4,517 people, according to the World Heritage nomination document.[14] However, in the management plan for Lobéké – submitted as part of the proposal – it specifies that some 12,000 people live in the villages linked to the protected area, and a total of 30,000 in the region peripheral to the protected area, around half of whom are immigrants attracted by logging concessions and other employment opportunities.[15]

Lobéké was established in 2001 after a decade of activity by conservation agencies in the region, including the World Wide Fund for Nature (WWF) and the German development aid agency, GTZ. The park was created with the intention of integrating local communities and other stakeholders into the sustainable management of resources. This was partially achieved through the creation of committees to participate in the management of multiple-use zones. This participatory

---

11 Jell and Schmidt Machado 2002.
12 Joiris 1992.
13 Usongo and Dongmo 2010.
14 Republic of Congo, Cameroon, Central African Republic 2012b.
15 Ministère des Forêts et de la Faune Sauvage 2004.

approach has resulted in use rights for local communities and represents a move towards greater recognition of customary rights. However, the indigenous Baka who rely on the forest more than other groups were sidelined and marginalised throughout the entire process. The committees were dominated by local elites and, in one example, only 10% of participants were from the Baka majority, and even these appeared to have been chosen by non-Baka local people.[16] The committees were therefore not representative of the local communities, causing conflict as, for example, safari companies were given permission by the committee to use land relied upon by Baka.[17]

It is a similar story across the borders in CAR and Congo. The Dzanga-Sangha Protected Area Complex in CAR consists of two national park sectors (the Dzanga and Ndoki) and the Dzanga-Sangha reserve, where forest access and use is restricted but permitted.[18] In Congo, the Nouabalé-Ndoki National Park was established in 1993. The customary land rights of BaAka in these protected areas also remain unrecognised, and meaningful BaAka participation in protected area management is virtually non-existent.

Impacts of conservation policies on the indigenous peoples

Although most hunter-gatherer groups in the region today are settled in roadside villages, their relationship with the forest remains an enduring and essential component of their identity as forest people. While many hunter-gatherers now cultivate on a small scale, and some work for a wage in logging or conservation and development, most continue to rely primarily on the forest for their economic survival. Meat is obtained using traditional hunting methods including nets, spears, crossbows and dogs. A number of plant foods continue to be collected, such as various types of leaves, mushrooms, nuts, seeds, roots, tubers and honey. Meat and plant foods are used for both subsistence and to generate cash to purchase other essentials such as clothes, soap, salt and so on. The forest is also the source of building materials and medicine. It is generally acknowledged that such practices, when conducted primarily for subsistence, do not threaten conservation efforts.[19]

All three national parks of the TNS have had profound deleterious consequences on the ability of hunter-gatherers to continue their forest-related activities. Restrictions placed on where, when and with what technology people may use the forest have profound ramifications for forest-dependent communities. For example, a lack of access to plants and animals for subsistence and trade or for medicinal purposes not only contributes to poverty and poor health but also fuels illegal hunting practices as people have no other choice by which to obtain food, contributing to a decline in game near villages.[20] This also impacts on local social dynamics as Pygmies are no longer the

---

16 In the community hunting zone ZICGC 9 in November 2002. See Nelson 2003.
17 Ibid.
18 See Woodburne 2009.
19 Hunting and gathering practices cannot neatly be categorised as 'traditional' or 'modern', or easily defined as 'subsistence'. Nevertheless, the major threats facing Central African forests and wildlife come not from the activities of a relatively small number of hunter-gatherers but from large-scale commercial activities such as the bushmeat trade and logging. See Schmidt-Soltau 2003 p. 536; Lewis 2008; Jost 2012.

primary providers of forest products to their farmer neighbours. Cultural practices such as the Jengi dance,[21] common to all groups in the region, only make sense in the context of the forest and, as a result, religious practices have declined. Their way of life, such as their commitment to egalitarianism, is contingent on the forest. Their very identity and world view is intimately tied to the forest, which is often described as a 'mother'. Many pathways that connect distant parts of the forest are blocked by the national parks, meaning that journeys following traditional paths and lasting many months no longer take place,[22] contributing to sedentarism and compounding all the problems associated with the loss of forest access.

Among BaAka in CAR, traditional stories tell how they came to live in the forest and why farming peoples live in the villages. Through these stories, BaAka feel that their rightful place is the forest and that it was given to them by Komba (God) to live in. However, this does not constitute 'ownership' in a Western sense. BaAka believe that anyone can enter the forest and that no one has the right to prevent others from entering. Even though BaAka were given the forest by Komba, they do not believe this confers *exclusive* rights on them. When conservation policy gazettes areas of the forest and excludes all others from entering, BaAka perceive this as a violation of the principle of land ownership as they see it.

> "Komba left the forest for BaAka because we know the forest well. BaAka don't keep others out of the forest because Komba gave it – no one owns it. Komba does not keep others out of the forest. There is no problem if a [Farmer] walks in the forest, or a white person, because it is for everyone."
>
> BaAka man from Yandoumbe in CAR, 2009

In general, BaAka in CAR welcomed some aspects of conservation – such as limiting destructive practices to preserve the forest – but were angry at the way it was carried out. They felt they saw limited benefits from conservation and reported serious human rights abuses by eco-guards who patrol the forest. BaAka rights to access and use the forest, given to them by Komba, were undermined and ignored in the creation of the national parks. This in turn has a profound influence on how BaAka understand and interact with conservation projects.[23]

A landscape approach

In recent years, conservation in Central Africa has moved towards a 'landscape' approach in which large areas are managed with a view to incorporating multiple uses, including subsistence activities, tourism, logging and other commercial enterprises. This integrated approach claims to be inclusive of local needs while also protecting natural resources across an entire landscape.[24] The

---

20 Woodburne 2012.
21 Known as Ejengi in CAR and Congo, Jengi in Cameroon.
22 Louis Sarno, personal communication.
23 See Woodburne 2012.

reality on the ground in these countries right now, however, is that conservation organisations often use military style eco-guards to enforce the restrictions on hunting and gathering while industrial activities continue unchecked, causing huge ecological damage. Human rights abuses against local people perpetrated by eco-guards are common.[25] A fuller analysis of the landscape approach and its suitability for these countries is beyond the scope of this paper[26] but it is important to note that it is with this approach to conservation that the TNS was conceived and is managed.

The Central African World Heritage Forest Initiative (CAWHFI) is a collaborative undertaking between UNESCO's World Heritage Centre and various partners, including the Food and Agricultural Organization (FAO), international conservation NGOs (WWF, Wildlife Conservation Society, Conservation International) and national protected area authorities. CAWHFI supports clusters of protected areas that have potential to become World Heritage sites. Within this, there is a focus on policing the bushmeat trade and a major part of CAWHFI's funding goes to help national park authorities implement restrictions on hunting, often against local people practising subsistence hunting and gathering. The involvement of local communities in the initiative has been minimal from the outset. Even at CAWHFI's inception in 2004, it was criticised that "84% of funding is for enforcement activities and no funding is planned for community consultations, co-management initiatives or capacity building. Indeed no local NGOs were consulted in the elaboration of CAWHFI".[27] The TNS is one of the landscapes supported by CAWHFI since its creation in 2004, with the goal that the TNS would be inscribed as a World Heritage site. The World Heritage Centre has thus been actively pursuing the TNS inscription for many years – through CAWHFI – and was one of the primary driving forces behind it.[28] Given the abysmal record of this site in terms of meaningful consultations with indigenous peoples and local communities (discussed further below), the role of the World Heritage Centre in the development of this World Heritage site nomination is highly problematic, especially when viewed against UNESCO's responsibility and declared commitment to uphold and proactively seek to protect the rights outlined in the United Nations Declaration on the Rights of Indigenous Peoples (UNDRIP).[29]

Local participation in the nomination process

The development of the World Heritage nomination of the TNS has, from the very beginning, been characterised by an absence of meaningful consultation with indigenous peoples and local communities. The original nomination document, submitted to the World Heritage Committee in 2010, was developed with minimal and sub-standard participation of indigenous peoples and local communities, a fact recognised by the World Heritage Committee itself. At its 35th session in 2011, the

---

24 For a fuller discussion of the landscape approach to conservation, see Franklin 1993; Poiani et al. 2000; and Yanggen 2010.
25 Nelson and Hossack 2003.
26 See for example Lewis 2008.
27 Lewis 2004, p. 16.
28 UNESCO World Heritage Centre 2010.
29 See UNDRIP, Arts. 41 and 42. On UNESCO's declared commitment, see for example Matsuura 2007 (Message of UNESCO's Director-General on the occasion of the adoption of UNDRIP by the UN General Assembly).

Committee referred the nomination back to the State Parties to allow them to, among other things:

> "Increase further the involvement and representation of local and indigenous communities in the nomination process and future management, in line with stated commitments, in order to fully recognize the rich tapestry of cultural and spiritual values associated with the property, and in recognition of contributions by local and indigenous communities, such as local knowledge and adapted resource use practices..." [30]

The Committee also encouraged the three States Parties to "Evaluate the potential application of cultural criteria to the nominated property (i.e. nomination as a mixed property), taking into account the rich indigenous cultural heritage of the area".[31]

The Committee's decision to refer the TNS nomination was based on the observations of its IUCN Advisory Body in its technical evaluation of the nomination dossier.[32] IUCN had found that: "there is a rich cultural heritage associated with the nominated property, but this has not been strongly considered within the nomination and this has been noted as a concern regarding the appropriateness of the nomination" and that: "The importance of local knowledge does not feature prominently in the nomination but might deserve more consideration in wildlife management".[33] Moreover, IUCN had highlighted in its evaluation "that in two of the three nominating countries, indigenous resource use is entirely banned in the nominated property, while in the remaining country resource use is partially permitted raising questions of the involvement of local residents".[34]

As a result of the referral, each of the three States Parties undertook a consultation process with communities living in the buffer zones. According to a document submitted by the three States Parties to UNESCO in June 2012, the objectives of the consultations were that "indigenous peoples and local communities were informed about, have understood, and have given their approval to the possible World Heritage site inscription".[35] This was presumably meant to suggest that the consultation process was in line with the principle of free, prior and informed consent, as required by international human rights law, including UNDRIP.[36] However, there are a number of serious concerns as to how these consultations were conducted. The discussion of the consultations here will focus specifically on the actual experiences of communities in Cameroon, as direct field research was carried out in these communities.

---

30   Decision 35COM 8B.4.
31   Ibid. para. 2.d.
32   Note that IUCN had recommended a *deferral* rather than a *referral*. In the case of a deferral, "more in depth assessment or study, or a substantial revision" by the States Parties would have been necessary, followed by a new site evaluation (including field visit) by IUCN. The referral by the Committee meant that only some "additional information" was needed and that the nomination could be resubmitted to the following Committee session for examination. See the *Operational Guidelines for the Implementation of the World Heritage Convention*, paras. 159-160.
33   IUCN 2011, pp. 9, 10.
34   Ibid., p. 8.
35   Republic of Congo, Cameroon, Central African Republic 2012a, p. 1.
36   See, e.g., Art. 32(2) of the UNDRIP, according to which "States shall consult and cooperate in good faith with the indigenous peoples concerned through their own representative institutions in order to obtain their free and informed consent prior to the approval of any project affecting their lands or territories and other resources".

Baka women and children in Akambi village north of Lobéké National Park. Photo: CEFAID

In Cameroon, authorities responsible for Lobéké and the periphery conducted a consultation process with local communities in 13 different villages. In addition to indigenous Baka, the 13 consultation meetings included Bantu, employees of forest concessions, students and teachers. The overall percentage of Baka participants in the consultation meetings was around 37%.[37] This process took place with the financial and technical assistance of WWF between January 27th and February 1st, 2012 (6 days). This was the same period when the three States Parties and the Head of Conservation of Lobéké National Park were meeting with UNESCO officials in Yaoundé to finalise the nomination documents, which were then submitted on February 1st, before the consultations were completed and certainly before any results of the consultations could have been incorporated into the documents.[38] This raises the question as to how the concerns, wishes and views of the communities could have possibly been taken into consideration or reflected in a document that was being finalised and submitted at the very time that the consultations were taking place. Indeed, some of the communities were only visited after the application had been completed and submitted. Key decisions relating to the nomination were made without discussing them with the affected communities. For instance, the States Parties decided against re-nominating the

---

37 Republic of Congo, Cameroon, Central African Republic 2012a, p. 6.
38 See CEFAID 2012.

property as a mixed site, as the World Heritage Committee had suggested, without putting this option to the indigenous communities. Moreover, the nomination documents were not made publicly available for communities and organisations working with them to assess, and therefore informed consent was impossible.

Furthermore, a number of serious concerns were raised by local observers in Cameroon regarding the quality of the consultations that were carried out. These concerns were detailed in a report by local NGO, CEFAID, which was invited to follow the consultation process in Cameroon.[39] From the outset, it was clear that the planned consultations were inadequate. Very little time was allocated to each community and, even then, the schedule was unrealistic. This meant that, in reality, only brief meetings were held in each community, sometimes lasting less than 30 minutes. Unfortunately, even these short opportunities to engage with local people were not put to good use. In many cases, the authorities spoke to community members about unrelated issues such as security, poaching and hygiene. Furthermore, the large size of the visiting teams – more than seven people, including the mayor, gendarmes, police and others – was intimidating and alarmed community members. Coupled with the authoritarian nature of the speeches and the swift exit of the group, the community was left with no meaningful opportunity to ask questions, consider the implications of the project, discuss amongst themselves or share their concerns. This style of consultation – where powerful local authorities dictate to local communities – is wholly inappropriate for a participatory process that should genuinely engage local people on an equal footing, not only incorporating their views but making them equal partners in the process. In fact, in accordance with the UNDRIP, consultation with indigenous peoples should occur through indigenous peoples' own decision-making institutions and procedures. There is no indication (from the 'additional information' document discussed below or anywhere else) that any attempt was made to engage with such institutions or consider culturally-appropriate mechanisms for consultation. The CEFAID report concludes:

> "[T]he consultation process did not make it possible for the communities to gain sufficient information to provide their opinion on the nomination of their forest landscape as a World Heritage Site. Not only did the process fail to facilitate their understanding of the impacts of a concept which was completely new to them, but it also gave them no time to digest the information about the purpose of the consultation… [Q]uite simply, no-one in the villages visited was able to gain sufficient information or clarification about the proposal with a view to giving their opinion freely." [40]

An 'additional information' document was submitted by the States Parties to UNESCO in June 2012, in response to concerns raised at the UN Permanent Forum on Indigenous Issues about the consultation process in all three countries. This document, however, confirms that consultations across the three countries took place between the last week of January and March 2012, despite the proposal being submitted on February 1st, 2012.[41] Consultations in all three countries occurred

---

39 Ibid.
40 Ibid.

after the submission date – in Congo no consultations at all were carried out before late February[42] – clearly demonstrating that local views could not have influenced the nomination documents.

The 'additional information' document gives details of the participation process that are completely at odds with what CEFAID witnessed in Cameroon. For example, it specifies that *all* villages within the buffer zones of the nominated site were visited by the consultation teams. In the case of Cameroon, however, this is misleading. As detailed in the CEFAID report, there were a number of villages that were not visited, namely those along routes Mboy-Yokadouma and Yokadouma-Momboé, and those along the Ngoko River. Furthermore, some of the "villages" stated in the 'additional information' document in fact comprise a number of separate villages with separate leadership structures.[43] Yet others are very large – up to 4,000 people – and made up of a number of separate neighbourhoods extending for up to 25km along the road. The short consultation times of an hour or two cannot have hoped to adequately consult these large populations. The document also states that "potential risks and benefits of the proposed World Heritage site nomination were debated", and yet, as described above, this was far from the case in Cameroon. Furthermore, it claims that "all communities consulted approved of the World Heritage inscription". Again, it is hard to see how this was the case given that indigenous peoples' consent should be *free, prior* and *informed* and should be expressed through their own decision-making institutions. We have highlighted serious issues with all of these principles.[44] In CAR, the quality of the consultations was probably better since civil society organisations had a greater level of involvement in planning and implementation. Nevertheless, the fact remains that regardless of the quality of the consultations in the three countries, none of them can possibly have influenced the nomination document given the dates on which they were conducted, rendering them little more than an information-giving exercise.

What has happened since the inscription?

Despite these serious concerns regarding the consultation of local and indigenous peoples, which were brought to the World Heritage Committee's attention in a joint submission of over

---

41 See Republic of Congo, Cameroon, Central African Republic 2012a, pp. 4-6.
42 This despite the Republic of Congo's enactment in 2011 of *Act No. 5-2011 of 25 February 2011 On the Promotion and Protection of Indigenous Populations*, which requires the State to ensure that "indigenous populations are consulted before the formulation or establishment of any project having effect on the lands and resources which they possess and use traditionally", and that "indigenous populations are consulted every time the State considers the creation of protected areas likely to affect directly or indirectly their lifestyles" (Arts. 38, 39). The Act specifies that the consultations with the indigenous populations must be conducted: "In good faith, without pressure and threat with the aim of obtaining their free, prior and informed consent"; "Through institutions representing the indigenous populations or by representatives they have chosen"; "By appropriate procedures taking into account their modes of decision making"; and "By ensuring that all information about the proposed measures be provided to the indigenous populations, in terms that are understandable to them" (Art. 3).
43 For example, Mbangoy and Nguilili each comprise two villages, referred to as Mbangoy 1 and Mbangoy 2, Nguilili 1 and Nguilili 2.
44 On the elements of free, prior and informed consent, see United Nations Development Group 2008, p. 28; and UN Expert Mechanism on the Rights of Indigenous Peoples 2011, paras. 21-27.

70 indigenous organisations and NGOs,[45] the resubmitted nomination was approved by the World Heritage Committee at its 36th session in June 2012. Following the advice of IUCN, the Committee inscribed the TNS as a natural World Heritage site, losing the opportunity to celebrate both the natural and cultural aspects of the landscape. The result is that indigenous cultural values do not form part of the recognised outstanding universal value of the site, and the Pygmies' rights to hunt and gather are not part of the TNS World Heritage site philosophy and will thus always be considered secondary to the natural values.

In inscribing the TNS on the World Heritage List, the Committee followed the advice of IUCN, which recommended an inscription despite noting in its evaluation report that the rich cultural heritage associated with the nominated site had still not been strongly considered within the nomination and that concerns had been expressed regarding the adequacy of the consultations with local and indigenous communities. IUCN also noted that the establishment of the nominated national parks had excluded local communities from previously used land and resources, that in two of the three countries local resource use, including indigenous hunting and gathering, was not permitted in the proposed World Heritage site "thereby affecting local livelihoods and creating the potential for conflict", and that there was a need to consider the livelihood needs and rights of local and indigenous communities more thoroughly in the nominated areas.[46] The fact that IUCN nevertheless recommended that the nomination be approved, despite these serious shortcomings, is justified in the evaluation report with the "view that inscription on the World Heritage List would provide momentum to further and better consider these issues, and support the rights of the traditional communities within the existing protected areas that make up the nomination".[47] In line with this, the decision by which the TNS was inscribed (Decision 36COM 8B.8), drafted by IUCN and adopted by the Committee without changes, requests the States Parties to:

> "Increase further the involvement and representation of local and indigenous communities in the future conservation and management of the TNS landscape in recognition of the rich cultural heritage of the region, the legitimacy of their rights to maintain traditional resource use and their rich local knowledge, including through providing effective and enhanced mechanisms for consultation and collaboration..."

While this may appear to be a step in the right direction, there is, on closer inspection, nothing in the World Heritage Committee's decision that indicates that anything should be changed with regard to the prohibitions on indigenous resource use in the World Heritage site. Rather, the decision suggests that the livelihood needs of local and indigenous communities be addressed in the "surrounding landscape" of the World Heritage site (i.e. the buffer zone). In

---

45 "Joint Submission on the Lack of implementation of the UN Declaration on the Rights of Indigenous Peoples in the context of UNESCO's World Heritage Convention" (IWGIA et al. 2012). The joint submission was formally submitted to the World Heritage Committee by IWGIA on May 23rd, 2012.
46 IUCN 2012, pp. 45, 46, 48.
47 Ibid., p. 46.

fact, the decision even reinforces the prohibitions on indigenous hunting in the World Heritage site by making them part of the statement of integrity, which categorically states that: "Logging and hunting is banned in the national parks" (without there being an exception for indigenous hunting). Therefore, while highlighting the legitimacy of indigenous peoples' rights to maintain traditional resource use, Decision 36COM 8B.8 at the same time perpetuates and cements the exclusionary 'fortress conservation' approach that is in place in the national parks making up the World Heritage site.

Formal and informal discussions following the inscription, in particular at an expert workshop in Denmark in September 2012 organised by IWGIA, led to the partial recognition by some, such as the head of conservation of Lobéké and WWF staff, that the consultation procedures had been problematic, as identified in the CEFAID report.[48] Some of the same officials who had been responsible for these poor consultations were then charged with supporting a new local association to carry out participatory mapping with local farmer and Baka communities. Many of the previous problems have persisted, resulting in poor quality maps with many features missing, such as areas of the forest used by local communities, the activities carried out there and the times of year they are used.[49] Yet again, meaningful participation has not occurred.

This has compounded the continued lack of involvement in the management processes of conservation in Lobéké. Some local people remain opposed to the World Heritage site altogether, others are deeply hurt and angry that they remain marginalised from conservation activities more generally. This even led to violent outbreaks in Mambele on January 22nd, resulting in some WWF officials retreating to Yaoundé. Local people were angry over the lack of benefits such as employment, inadequate access to resources and the lack of local involvement.

Conclusion

Local people in all three TNS countries, particularly indigenous Pygmies who depend on the forest for their material and cultural survival, are furious that their rights to use the forest have been severely restricted by successive waves of conservation activities, of which the World Heritage inscription is the latest.[50] At the same time, they see destructive practices such as logging, mining and large-scale poaching destroying their forest largely unchecked.

> "You see, the park is bad because we are not allowed to go there. [Farmers] kill all the animals with guns. Where is the [conservation] project? So many [poached] animals pass here. That is the project's fault."
>
> BaAka man, Yandoumbe, CAR, 2009

---

48   CEFAID 2013.
49   Ibid.
50   See for example Woodburne 2009; or Lewis 2008.

"Some people don't like the [conservation project] because they have destroyed the forest with all the boundaries [the different zones]...What can I do? I don't have power to speak about this problem. I don't have the proper language...The [conservation project] came and took the forest so that BaAka couldn't stay there. They spoke to [farmers], not BaAka."

Elderly BaAka woman, Yandoumbe, CAR, 2009

For the future, it is clearly essential that consultation procedures are completely redesigned to enable the meaningful participation of all communities affected by the TNS. The brief consultations described in the 'additional information' document provided by the States Parties do not constitute meaningful participation as understood by indigenous peoples and required by agreements and standards such as the UNDRIP. It is worrying that the World Heritage Committee accepted this totally inadequate level of consultation, not only for the future of the TNS but also for other potential World Heritage sites.

We wish to make a number of recommendations to the World Heritage Committee. First, they should insist that the conservation authorities lift the restrictions on indigenous hunting and gathering in the national parks that make up the TNS site. The ecological role and traditional knowledge of the indigenous people – particularly the Pygmies – should form an integral part of the management philosophy of the site. Second, the World Heritage Committee should insist that indigenous and local people are included in a meaningful way in the decision making and management of the protected areas. Finally, the World Heritage Committee should continue to push for a re-nomination of the TNS as a mixed site so that the cultural values of the indigenous peoples will be an integral part of the World Heritage site on an equal footing with the natural values. The hunting and gathering way of life of Pygmy peoples includes unique forest-related knowledge and skills as well as a social and religious life that is intimately tied to the forest. As the World Heritage Committee has already indicated, this rich indigenous cultural heritage must be recognised as being of outstanding universal value.

References

CEFAID. 2012. *Proposal by the Conservation Authorities for the Inclusion of the Sangha Trinational on the UNESCO World Heritage List: Report on the consultation process undertaken with local and indigenous communities living around Lobeke National Park. 26th January to 2nd February 2012.* Yokadouma, CEFAID.

CEFAID. 2013. *The Sangha Trinational: the place and role of the actors involved following nomination as a World Heritage Site and development of the process in the field.* Yokadouma, CEFAID.

Franklin, J. 1993. Preserving biodiversity: species, ecosystems or landscapes? *Ecological Applications*, Vol. 3, pp. 202-205.

IUCN. 2011. *IUCN World Heritage Evaluations 2011.* Doc. WHC-11/35.COM/INF.8B2.

IUCN. 2012. *IUCN World Heritage Evaluations 2012.* Doc. WHC-12/36.COM/INF.8B2.

IWGIA et al. 2012. *Joint Submission on the Lack of implementation of the UN Declaration on the Rights of Indigenous Peoples in the context of UNESCO's World Heritage Convention.* May 2012. Available at: http://www.forestpeoples.org/sites/fpp/files/publication/2012/05/joint-submission-unpfii.pdf.

Jell, B. and Schmidt Machado, J. 2002. Collaborative Management in the Region of Lobéké, Cameroon: the Potentials and Constraints in Involving the Local Population in Protected Area Management. *Nomadic Peoples*, Vol. 6, No. 1, pp. 180-203.

Joiris, D. 1992. Entre le Village et la Forêt. Place des Femmes Bakola et Baka dans les Sociétés en Voie de Sédentarisation. F. Pinton and M. Lecarme (eds.), *Relations de genre et développement: femmes et sociétés*. Paris, Orstom, pp. 125-148.

Joiris, D. 1998. *La chasse, la chance, le chant: aspects du système rituel des Baka du Cameroun*. PhD thesis. Université Libre de Bruxelles.

Jost, C. 2012. *Beyond hunters and hunted: an integrative anthropology of human-wildlife dynamics and resource use in a central African forest*. PhD thesis, Purdue University, USA.

Lewis, J. 2002. *Forest Hunter-Gatherers and their World: A Study of the Mbendjele Yaka Pygmies of Congo-Brazzaville and their Secular and Religious Activities and Representations*. PhD thesis, University of London.

Lewis, J. 2004. *From Abundance to Scarcity. Indigenous resource management and the industrial extraction of forest resources. Some issues for conservation*. Available at: http://www.radicalanthropologygroup.org/old/pub_abundance_to_scarcity.pdf.

Lewis, J. 2008. Maintaining abundance, not chasing scarcity: the big challenge for the twenty-first century. *Radical Anthropology Group Journal*, No. 2, pp. 7-18.

Matsuura, K. 2007. *Message from Mr Koïchiro Matsuura, Director-General of UNESCO, on the occasion of the approval of the United Nations Declaration on the Rights of Indigenous Peoples by the UN General Assembly*. 24 September 2007.

Ministère des Forêts et de la Faune Sauvage. 2004. *Plan d'Aménagement du Parc National de Lobéké et de sa Zone Périphérique. Période d'exécution: 2006-2010*.

Nelson, J. 2003. Cameroon: Baka Losing Out to Lobeke and Boumba National Parks. *World Rainforest Movement Bulletin*, No. 67 (February 2003).

Nelson, J. and Hossack, L. 2003. Indigenous Peoples and Protected Areas in Africa: From Principles to Practice. Moreton-in-Marsh, Forest Peoples Programme.

Poiani, K. et al. 2000. Biodiversity conservation at multiple scales: functional sites, landscapes, and networks. *BioScience*, Vol. 50. No. 2, pp. 133-146.

Quintana-Murci, L. et al. 2008. Maternal traces of deep common ancestry and asymmetric gene flow between Pygmy hunter-gatherers and Bantu-speaking farmers. *Proceedings of the National Academy of Sciences of the United States of America*, Vol. 105, No. 5, pp. 1596-1601.

Republic of Congo, Cameroon, Central African Republic. 2012a. *Additional information: World Heritage Nomination – Sangha Tri-National*. Submitted by the State Parties to IUCN and the UNESCO World Heritage Centre on 9 June 2012. [Copy on file with the authors.]

Republic of Congo, Cameroon, Central African Republic. 2012b. *Proposition d'Inscription sur la Liste du Patrimoine Mondial 2012: Trinational de la Sangha* [World Heritage nomination]. Available at: http://whc.unesco.org/uploads/nominations/1380rev.pdf.

Schmidt-Soltau, K. 2003. Conservation related resettlement in Central Africa: environmental and social risks. *Development and Change*, Vol. 34, No. 3, pp. 525-550.

UNESCO World Heritage Centre. 2010. *World Heritage in the Congo Basin*. Paris, UNESCO.

UNESCO. 2012. *Operational Guidelines for the Implementation of the World Heritage Convention*. Doc. WHC. 12/01, July 2012.

UN Expert Mechanism on the Rights of Indigenous Peoples. 2011. *Expert mechanism advice No. 2 (2011): Indigenous peoples and the right to participate in decision-making*. UN Doc. A/HRC/18/42, Annex.

United Nations Development Group. 2008. *Guidelines on Indigenous Peoples' Issues*.

Usongo L. and Dongmo, Z. N. 2010. Lessons Learned in the Lobéké National Park, South-East Cameroon. D. Yanggenn, K. Angu and N. Tchamou (eds.), *Landscape Scale Conservation in the Congo Basin: Lessons Learnt from the Central African Regional Program for the Environment (CARPE)*. Gland, IUCN.

Vansina, J. 1990. *Paths in the Rainforest: Towards a History of Political Tradition in Equatorial Africa*. London, James Currey.

Woodburne, O. 2009. *Securing Indigenous Peoples' Rights in Conservation: a Review of Policy and Implementation in the Dzanga-Sangha Protected Area Complex*. Moreton-in-Marsh, Forest Peoples Programme.

Woodburne, O. 2012. *Navigating Moral Dilemmas: Participatory Conservation and Development among the Egalitarian BaAka of the Central African Republic*. PhD thesis, University of Kent, UK.

Yanggen, D., Angu, K. and Tchamou, N. 2010. *Landscape-scale conservation in the Congo Basin: lessons learnt from the Central African regional Program for the Environment (CARPE)*. Gland, IUCN.

'We are not Taken as People':
Ignoring the Indigenous Identities and History of Tsodilo Hills World Heritage Site, Botswana

Michael Taylor

Introduction

The Tsodilo Hills are an enigmatic outcrop of copper-coloured inselbergs that rise out of the Kalahari sands of north-western Botswana. The Male Hill reaches 400 metres above the sandy plain, and is the highest point in Botswana, standing like an imposing sentinel above a landscape that is otherwise almost flat for hundreds of kilometres in any direction. He is accompanied by the more extensive but not so high Female Hill, rich in wild foods and hosting the only permanent water sources in the Hills. Next is the smaller Child Hill, and then an outlying pile of rocks referred to as the Grandchild. Together, they cover an area of around ten square kilometres. They are among the last remnants of an ancient mountain range and have resisted erosion over 1,500 million years.

Beyond its geological uniqueness, Tsodilo is widely known for its 4,500 rock-art sites, representing one of the highest concentrations of rock art in the world. Despite their remoteness, the Hills have, for millennia, been a magnet for human use and habitation. The relative abundance of water, wild foods and grazing attracted Khoesan populations, for whom the Hills also became an important ritual site. The Hills also attracted Bantu speakers when they arrived in the subcontinent

Left: Gxao C'untae, elder of the Juc'hoansi village at Tsodilo, at the time of the preparation of the World Heritage nomination.
Photo: Michael Taylor

over the last millennium, for the same reasons, and in the early colonial period became an object of curiosity for intrepid explorers. It was declared a National Monument in 1934 by the British colonial administration but remained relatively unknown to the outside world until the second half of the twentieth century, when it was popularised by authors such as Francois Balsan (1953), who dubbed it the "Louvre of the Desert", and Sir Laurence van der Post, who made it a centrepiece of his book *Lost World of the Kalahari* in 1958.

Tsodilo has two villages today, about a kilometre apart from each other; one is a village of Juc'hoansi (Khoesan) with around 60 residents; the other is Hambukushu (Bantu-speaking) with around 140 residents.[1] Both of these were seasonal settlements until several decades ago. The extended families of both villages have an historical association with the Hills that stretches back to the late 1800s when the ancestors of the Hambukushu now living in Tsodilo migrated to the region from present-day Angola. Around this time, the ancestors of the Juc'hoansi, who had probably used the Hills as an occasional hunting and gathering ground for much longer, established their presence in the Hills more frequently. Preceding both groups was another Khoesan group known as NcaeKhoe, who no longer live in Tsodilo but whose names are still used for many areas in the Hills.

The Tsodilo Hills are iconic for the Khoesan, the first peoples of southern Africa, for reasons other than those most widely known or emphasised in the usual representations by UNESCO and others. This chapter will describe why they are so important to the history and identity of Khoesan, particularly Khoesan land rights, and how this has been affected by the designation of World Heritage status to Tsodilo in 1998. But first to contextualise; who are the Khoesan?

The Khoesan – genetically among the oldest human populations – inhabited the African subcontinent for many millennia before the arrival of Bantu speakers. They exist now – as many other Indigenous peoples also do – as scattered minorities: scattered across national borders (of a total population of 100,000, 50,000 live in Botswana), linguistically (in over 15 different language groups, several of which are spoken by only a handful of survivors), and in terms of access to power and influence, living on the edge of the societies that have dominated them. Their distinct cultural heritage and identity became a symbol of shame to their non-Khoesan neighbours and even to some Khoesan because of its association with poverty. Nonetheless, over the past two decades, with the birth of Khoesan cultural organisations and a new generation with access to education and an ability to link with wider Indigenous peoples' movements, many Khoesan have been working to claim a place of pride and dignity as equal citizens in the countries in which they live.

The marginalisation of the Khoesan, and their struggle for cultural identity and dignity, is most closely related to the loss of their lands. As Khoesan heritage and identity are closely tied to association with and use of land, the large-scale loss of their lands through appropriation by more powerful neighbouring groups, and the state (often in the name of nature conservation), has not only contributed to the impoverishment of Khoesan but has also undermined their identity and standing in wider society. Conversely, the struggle for recognition of their land rights has, over the last decades, become the spark that has galvanised collective action and an assertion of Khoesan identity.

---

1   Khoesan is the umbrella term for the First Peoples, or Indigenous peoples, of southern Africa. Each Khoesan language group has its own name, including Juc'hoansi and Ncaekhoe. Bantu-speakers, including Hambukushu and Batawana, are the majority population of the subcontinent, whose habitation of the subcontinent stretches back several millennia.

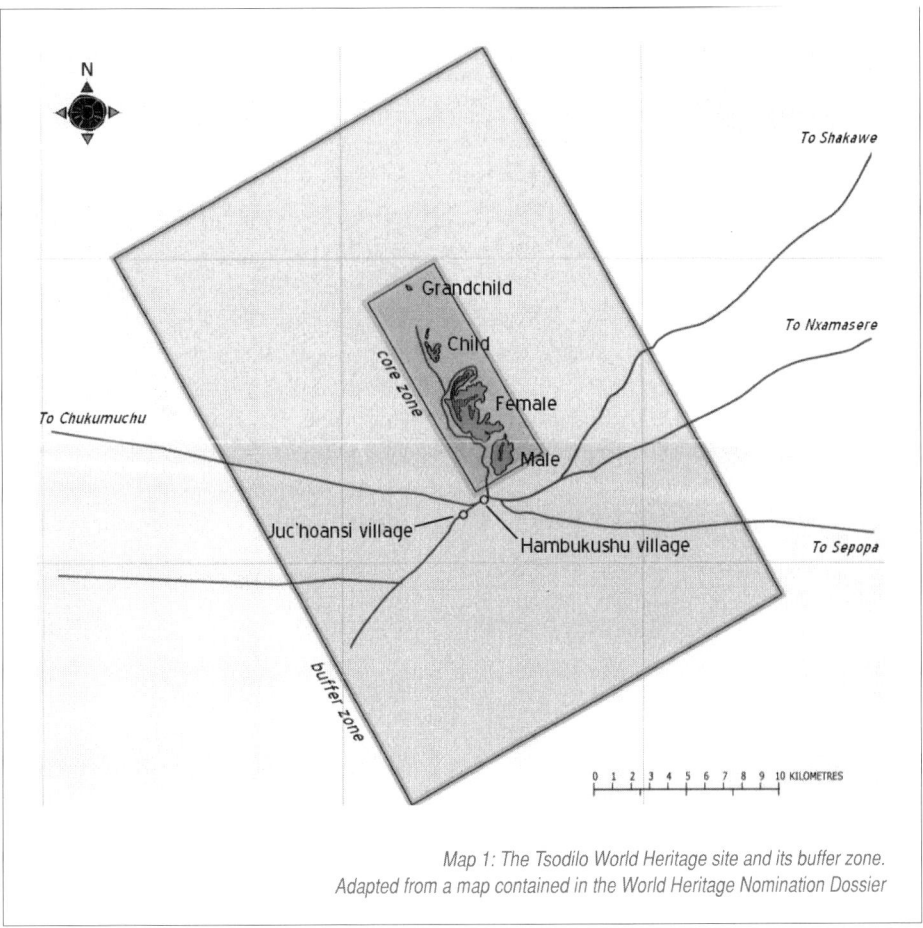

Map 1: The Tsodilo World Heritage site and its buffer zone.
Adapted from a map contained in the World Heritage Nomination Dossier

The significance of Tsodilo in the history of Khoesan

In the 1980s, the Department of National Museum, Monuments and Art Gallery (hereafter National Museum) initiated a series of archaeological expeditions that, over the next decade, began building a picture of the prehistory of the region that was to challenge many long-held assumptions of the peopling of southern Africa. Far from being the remote region of the Kalahari that it is today, the archaeological record revealed Tsodilo to be a trading hub in the last millennium, with some of the oldest remains of human habitation in the subcontinent, stretching back 100,000 years. The research at Tsodilo sparked a body of revisionist scholarship that reinterpreted long-held orthodoxies that Khoesan had always been hunter-gatherers. The archaeological record was interpreted as evidence that many had been livestock keepers and controlled trading routes in centuries past. Their status as purely hunter-gatherers is, from this perspective, a reputation gained in the wake of their dispossession during the rise of mercantile capitalism in the early-mid nineteenth century.

In other words, archaeological research at Tsodilo has caused major re-interpretations in understandings of the Khoesan peoples, and their position relative to the Bantu speakers in whose societies they now generally live as an underclass. It is now generally held that at least some Khoesan populations controlled land, livestock and trade. However, this began to change in the early 1800s when the Batawana (Bantu speakers) began forming a powerful centralised kingdom in what is now north-western Botswana. This involved subjugating the Khoesan into servitude and taking over their lands, as had happened elsewhere in the subcontinent. Over the course of a century, the Khoesan in Ngamiland were almost completely subjugated.

However, both oral history and the historical record of early explorers and the first colonial administrators in the final decades of the 19th century note a remarkable fact about Tsodilo: that it remained the recognised territory of Khoesan despite their political subjugation.[2] As such, it was the last known island of Khoesan territory in the Kalahari where ownership of the Indigenous inhabitants was recognised and respected. The appropriation of Khoesan territories in Ngamiland had been brutal, achieved through widespread forced servitude and killings. Of the many Khoesan groups who lived on the fringes of the Okavango Delta, the Ncaekhoe were the last to resist paying tribute to the growing Batawana kingdom, demanding instead that the Batawana, as latecomers, should recognise them as the original owners of the land. In a society that was becoming increasingly hierarchical, their stand did not last. In 1881, a regiment was detached by the Batawana king and the Ncaekhoe leader assassinated. Nonetheless, Tsodilo remained the recognised land of Ncaekhoe and Juc'hoansi until the end of the 19th century, when they finally capitulated. Part of Tsodilo's significance in recent history is as one of the last outposts of undisputed Khoesan ownership, an area of land that its Khoesan owners were able to protect as their own.

Tsodilo remains central to the contemporary identity of the Indigenous peoples living there, and nearby, as it is said to be the place where God created the first human, Kharac'umae, the progenitor of all Khoesan, and of the first wild animals. The marks they are believed to have left on the still soft rocks of the Female Hill are still visible today at a site called Gobekho. Most likely drawing on the myths of the Khoesan whom their ancestors encountered in the Hills, Hambukushu in the area talk of Tsodilo as the place where God let down the first people and cattle with a rope from the sky. To both the Juc'hoansi and Hambukushu, the Hills are a living terrain, containing sites that not only tell stories about their heritage and identity but also host Spirits capable of healing, assisting in hunting and providing rain.

The most tangible and widely-recognised association between Tsodilo and the Indigenous peoples of southern Africa, however, is the 4,500 or so rock-art sites that are scattered around the Hills. Painted almost entirely in the prehistoric period by the ancestors of the Khoesan, Tsodilo is one of the only rock-art sites – of the hundreds that exist in the subcontinent – where the descendants of Khoesan still live today.

---

2 For further references, see Campbell, Robbins and Taylor 2010.

View of the Male Hill, the tallest at Tsodilo. Photo: Mike Richardson / Sarah Winch (CC BY-NC-ND 2.0)

Designation as a World Heritage site

In December 2001, Tsodilo was inscribed as Botswana's first World Heritage site. The designation of World Heritage status was the result of a decade of planning and development by the National Museum, which oversaw the application in its capacity as custodian of Botswana's national monuments. In 1994, a management plan was prepared which proposed core and buffer zones and their uses. The core zone of 4,800 ha, including the Hills, was designated as being free from permanent human habitation. In addition, a buffer zone of an additional 65,600 ha was designated as a 'conservation zone'. This was intended to "preserve the wilderness experience of visiting Tsodilo" but with the intention that "management of the buffer zone will not interfere with the orderly and desirable development of local communities presently living within the buffer zone".[3] The Land Board granted the lease for the entire area to the National Museum in 2000. The lease explicitly recognised customary community use rights in the buffer zone, but not in the core zone.

In 2000, the sand track to Tsodilo was upgraded to a gravel road, greatly increasing the accessibility of the Hills to visitors. In 2001, a site museum was opened which offered visitors an interpretive experience of the Hills. A number of guides from the Hambukushu and Juc'hoansi villages

---

3   Department of National Museum, Monuments and Art Gallery 1994, p. 2

were trained by the National Museum as guides. A Tsodilo Liaison Committee was established, bringing together residents of the Hambukushu and Juc'hoansi villages to facilitate their participation; however, the management of Tsodilo remained fully in the hands of the National Museum. Additionally, no clear mechanisms were established to ensure that the particular interests of the Juc'hoansi – customarily subordinate to those of their Hambukushu neighbours – would be taken into account.

With its new status and easier access, the annual number of visitors to Tsodilo grew tremendously, passing the 10,000 mark in 2005. This has brought new opportunities for residents of both the Juc'hoansi and Hambukushu villages; a curio shop at the museum sells handicrafts, most of them made by residents of the Juc'hoansi village. All guides are local, as are some of the jobs at the site museum. For what was the poorest village in the District in the early 1990s, these opportunities have been significant. However, the changes have not come without a cost, and this cost has largely been borne by the Juc'hoansi.

While recognising the existence of community rights, the management plan explicitly places these, in cases of conflicting interest, as subordinate to the maintenance of Tsodilo as a Heritage area. The most immediate impact of this was on the Juc'hoansi village because it fell inside the core zone. Negotiations to move the settlement began in 1994 and, in 1997, the Juc'hoansi moved to a site they had chosen near the new borehole, provided by the National Museum several kilometres from the Hills. Procedures of the 1968 *Tribal Land Act* – which do not include the formal application of Free, Prior and Informed Consent procedures – were followed for the relocation, including the payment of compensation for rebuilding of dwellings. Despite the move being 'voluntary', many residents subsequently complained that their increased distance from the Hills and the main access route to Tsodilo curtailed their access, for example, to act as tourist guides, sell handicrafts or gather wild foods. Three years after their move, a researcher noted a significant decline in the use of the Hills by the Juc'hoansi.[4] Following the removal of the village, the site museum and dwellings for staff were built close to the original site of the Juc'hoansi village in the core zone.

The changes experienced by the two villages in Tsodilo have taken place in a context of diverse and competing priorities between the Hambukushu and Juc'hoansi residents. These challenges are not faced on a level playing field. The Hambukushu village has greater economic leverage (for example, at the time of the move they owned 600 cattle compared to the 34 owned by Juc'hoansi). More importantly, as external interests have become increasingly important in determining Tosdilo's future, the Juc'hoansi consider that the stigma they face as First Peoples has progressively marginalised them from decision-making. This was described as follows by Gxao Cuntae, a senior member of the Juc'hoansi village during the implementation of the 1994 management plan:

> "We used to be alone on this land. There were no black people. After meeting Batawana in the times of *Mmamosadinyana* [Queen Victoria] we met Hambukushu. They were not very powerful as they did not have guns. They tried to tell us this was their land. From there the government came in and Hambukushu told them this was their land, and the government agreed. Now when things are done we are not listened to. We are not taken as people.

---

4   Puskar 2000.

No-one listens to us. He [Samuchao, head of the Hambukushu village] is the chief, but that chief does not explain to anyone how he became chief, and he doesn't tell anything to those people he found on this land. He tells us we have no power, we have nothing, he must be the chief. About those he found here, he says, 'They are just *Basarwa* [Bushmen]' and has no respect for them." [5]

One response of the Juc'hoansi has been to protect their autonomy where possible. For example, when they relocated their village they declined Samuchao's invitation to join the Hambukushu village, choosing instead a site two kilometres away, even though this meant more difficult access to the Hills and tourist traffic.

Ignoring the 'Indigenous' in Tsodilo's ascension to Word Heritage status

Two parties were primarily involved in the process leading to Tsodilo's recognition as a World Heritage site: the National Museum as the responsible government department and UNESCO. The process followed and documents prepared by both these parties gave minimal recognition to the Juc'hoansi as Indigenous peoples and to the unequal context in which they live. They also placed little emphasis on the significance of the intangible heritage of Tsodilo as a cultural landscape shaped, in many different ways, by the people who have lived there, and who live there today. In particular, the significance of Tsodilo as the last bastion of recognised Khoesan land rights was ignored. The documents prepared by the National Museum and UNESCO instead focused more on the tangible heritage of Tsodilo in the archaeological record and paintings, and their contribution to scientific studies.

The World Heritage Nomination dossier prepared by the National Museum outlines the significance of Tsodilo in terms of its artistic, archaeological, cultural and natural heritage, its living traditions and research potential. Mention is made of the Khoesan and Hambukushu communities who live in Tsodilo, although the only reference implying a particular sense of belonging between Khoesan and the Hills is a quote from a Hambukushu resident of a village some distance from the Hills: "We were told that the first people at Tsodilo were the!Kung [Juc'hoansi]. We found them here and settled amongst them peacefully".[6] However, the dossier is then silent on the significance of this acknowledgement or the stories that it could provoke. Moreover, the significance of Tsodilo's cultural history is framed not in its importance to its residents but its importance to research and the wider world. The only reference to 'Indigenous peoples' is in their value to external researchers, stating that: "For the ethnologist, Tsodilo is an important data bank for the study of Indigenous peoples who continue to inhabit the site".[7]

That the dossier does not touch upon the significance of Tsodilo to Khoesan as the Indigenous peoples of Botswana was to be expected. Prepared by a government department, it followed the

---

5   Interview by author, 1995.
6   Department of National Museum, Monuments and Art Gallery 2000, p. 9.
7   Ibid., p. 12.

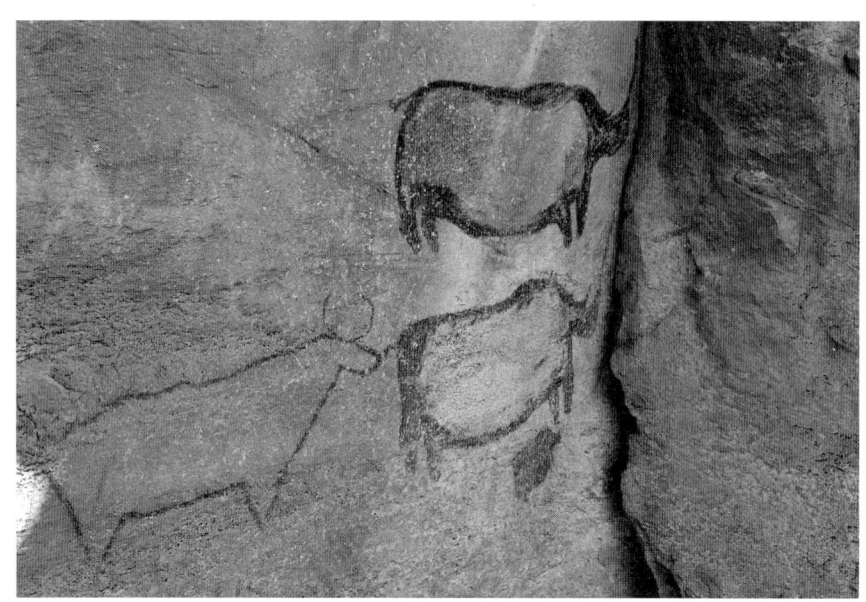
The Rhino Panel, one of 4,500 rock art paintings at Tsodilo. Photo: Joachim Huber (CC BY-SA 2.0)

official practices of not identifying Khoesan as Indigenous peoples or in any way as a distinct ethnic minority. Although not completely ignored, the choice not to give prominence to the intangible heritage of the Hills and their relevance to the identities and customs of those living there today could also be explained by the Government of Botswana's caution in giving any prominence to particular ethnic identities. This has prevailed despite the argument of at least one senior staff member at the Museum that the living cultural significance of Tsodilo should be given greater prominence in how it was managed by the Museum.[8]

Less explainable by the national policy context is the approach taken by the ICOMOS evaluation team following their visit to the site in January 2001. ICOMOS agreed that Tsodilo should be inscribed on the World Heritage List under cultural criterion (vi), alongside cultural criteria (i) and (iii). Criterion (vi) refers to sites directly or tangibly associated with events or living traditions, with ideas, or with beliefs, with artistic and literary works of outstanding universal significance. The report's justification for criterion (vi) was that: "The Tsodilo outcrops have immense symbolic and religious significance for the human communities who continue to survive in this hostile environment."[9] The evaluation report also notes, appropriately, that Tsodilo should be considered as an "associative cultural landscape" with "powerful religious, artistic, and cultural associations

---

8 Segadika 2006.
9 ICOMOS 2001, p. 65.

of the natural element" and an "organically evolved landscape" which retains "an active social role in contemporary society closely associated with the traditional way of life and in which the evolutionary process is still in progress".[10]

Despite its recognition of the continuing cultural significance of Tsodilo to the 'human communities' who live there, the report makes two fundamental errors. Firstly, it fails to recognise the Indigenous identity of the Juc'hoansi inhabitants. Secondly, it presents the people of Tsodilo (both Indigenous and non-Indigenous) as people whose significance is in terms of their interest to the outside world, as markers of humankind's evolutionary progress. This representation is not only ahistorical (ignoring the dispossession – and resistance to it – which are significant elements of the story that Tsodilo tells) but it also ignores the present by defining Tsodilo's inhabitants as people of the past, whose defining context is evolutionary rather than socio-economic or political. The cultural importance of Tsodilo today is interpreted narrowly through its spiritual significance and the archaeological and artistic record left by previous inhabitants. It places little emphasis on the wider values and meanings attached to Tsodilo by its residents and the relationship between these and the current socio-economic contexts in which they live. Rather than acknowledging Tsodilo as a landscape derived from, and protected by, its intimate relationship with its people, it ascribes "three basic long-term facts [that] contribute to Tsodilo's outstanding state of preservation: its remoteness, its low population density, and the high degree of resistance to erosion of its quartzitic rock."[11]

In sum, ICOMOS and the World Heritage Committee uncritically accepted and perpetuated the official narrative of Tsodilo and its peoples in the ascension of Tsodilo to World Heritage status. They failed to adequately recognise that Indigenous people live at Tsodilo, and the significance of the Hills to their heritage, identity and their status today as a marginalised and stigmatised minority. They failed to take into account how this status disables their ability to engage as equals in the changes associated with Tsodilo becoming a World Heritage site. They missed the opportunity to allow the story to be told of Tsodilo's significance through the eyes of those that live there – both Indigenous and non-Indigenous. They also failed to make any recommendations for particular measures that should be put in place to reverse exclusionary processes or to ensure the equal participation of Tsodilo's Indigenous residents in its representation to the outside world and in enjoying the benefits of heightened interest in the Hills.

Conclusion: lessons learnt from Tsodilo

The marginal position that the Juc'hoansi residents of Tsodilo occupy is characteristic of Indigenous peoples worldwide. The particular experiences evident from Tsodilo are similarly likely to be reflected in other contexts where decisions are made on World Heritage status, implying changes in land use, ownership and interpretation of landscapes belonging to Indigenous peoples. These include:

---

10 Ibid.
11 Ibid., p. 63.

- The likelihood that Indigenous peoples will not participate equally as decision makers, either with non-Indigenous populations who also have an interest in the landscape, or with national bodies involved in the process. Moreover, the risk is high that such changes will entrench their marginal position;
- The likelihood, particularly in Africa, that the particular situations of Indigenous peoples are not recognised or taken into account in the country-led processes that lead up to the nomination of the site for World Heritage status;
- Lack of recognition of the particular intangible heritage and meanings that the landscape – both historical, spiritual and cultural – has for its Indigenous residents;
- The opportunity that the explicit recognition of a cultural landscape may help overcome the marginalisation and voicelessness of Indigenous peoples and could allow them to take greater control of the landscape itself and how it is interpreted to the outside world.

In short, the challenge to UNESCO is how to manage a process of recognising the global value of a landscape which has belonged to Indigenous people for centuries in a manner that contributes to, rather than erodes, the recognition of that landscape belonging primarily to its inhabitants.

Meeting this challenge involves recognising and proactively managing both the risks and opportunities that are created by the ascension of a site to World Heritage status. Firstly, it should be recognised that this takes place in an historical context of dispossession and disenfranchisement. It also often takes place in national policy contexts of universal 'equality' which do not recognise the specificity, or even existence, of Indigenous peoples. This places an obligation on the World Heritage Committee not simply to follow dominant national representations and procedures in the nomination of potential World Heritage sites but to proactively ensure that it addresses inadequacies that may exist in these. Such measures could include:

- Ensuring that, where Indigenous peoples are associated with a potential World Heritage site, this is explicitly recognised in any documentation produced by UNESCO or the World Heritage Committee in the process towards a decision on World Heritage status;
- Making clear the expectation of UNESCO that the standards of the *UN Declaration on the Rights of Indigenous Peoples*, particularly on Free, Prior and Informed Consent, are followed in steps leading to the nomination of sites for World Heritage status, and in the implementation of management plans that follow. This will include putting in place safeguards that pay particular attention to the full participation of Indigenous peoples, and avoiding the assumption that providing equal opportunities for participation will automatically imply equal participation in reality;
- Encouraging the full recognition of the land and resource rights of Indigenous peoples in World Heritage sites, rather than as secondary rights on land under government custodianship;
- Encouraging particular measures to be put in place to ensure the meaningful participation of Indigenous residents in the management of World Heritage sites, rather than in merely consultative or advisory functions;

- Ensuring that the description of cultural landscapes of Indigenous peoples in documentation by UNESCO takes into account the full scope of factors contributing to the cultural and historical importance of the site, from the perspectives of Indigenous peoples themselves. UNESCO could provide assistance to facilitate such consultation and documentation.

The role of UNESCO in promoting recognition of the universal value of landscapes which may have had a long association with Indigenous peoples is an important one. The case of Tsodilo emphasises that UNESCO's neglect lies not so much in directly marginalising Indigenous populations but in uncritically giving assent to nationally-led and local processes that do not recognise the specificity of Indigenous residents. They thus fail to either provide important safeguards against further marginalisation or to take advantage of opportunities provided by the changes associated with World Heritage status to reverse this marginalisation. Although the management of World Heritage sites will, rightly, remain a national mandate, UNESCO's involvement demands that it plays a more proactive role in ensuring a more central role for Indigenous peoples.

References

Balsan, F. 1953. *Capricorn Road.* London, Arco Publishers.
Campbell, A., Robbins, L. and Taylor, M. (eds). 2010. *Tsodilo Hills: Copper Bracelet of the Kalahari.* Chicago, University of Michigan Press.
Department of National Museums, Monuments and Art Gallery. 1994. *Tsodilo Hills Management Plan, Scheme for Implementation.*
Department of National Museums, Monuments and Art Gallery. 2000. *Tsodilo, Mountain of the Gods: World Heritage Nomination Dossier,* 31 May 2000.
ICOMOS. 2001. *Evaluations of Cultural Properties Prepared by the International Council on Monuments and Sites (ICOMOS) 2001.* UNESCO Doc. WHC-01/CONF.208/INF.11 Rev.
Puskar, D. 2000. Impact assessment of the Management of Tsodilo Hills national Monument on the local Zhu and Hambukushu communities. Unpublished paper produced for the School for International Training.
Segadika, P. 2006. Managing Intangible Heritage at Tsodilo. *Museum International,* Vol. 58, No. 1-2, pp. 31-40.
Van der Post, L. 1958. *Lost World of the Kalahari.* London, Hogarth Press.

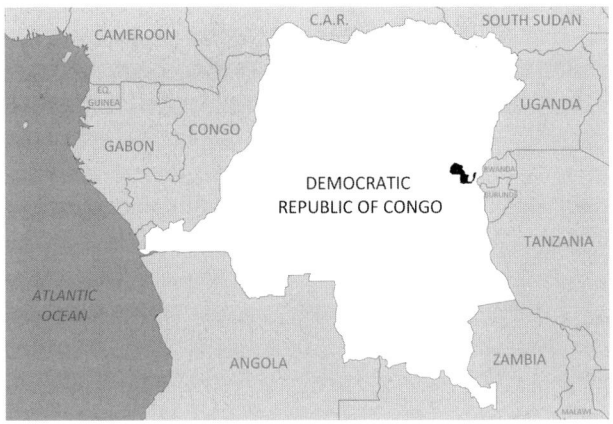

Kahuzi-Biega National Park: World Heritage Site versus the Indigenous Twa

Roger Muchuba Buhereko

"We have preserved these forests for thousands of years... It is because of our conservation methods that there are now several UNESCO World Heritage sites in the DRC."

Statement of Pygmy representatives from the DRC at the
UN Permanent Forum on Indigenous Issues, 2004[1]

Introduction

The Kahuzi-Biega National Park (KBNP) is situated in the eastern part of the Democratic Republic of Congo (DRC), not far from Lake Kivu and the Rwandan border, and covers an area of 600,000 ha in South Kivu, North Kivu and Maniema provinces. It is divided into two sections: a smaller highland area in the east (60,000 ha) and a much larger lowland area to the west, linked

---

1   AAPDMAC et al. 2004 (unofficial translation).

Left: Twa in the Chombo community on the outskirts of Kahuzi-Biega National Park. The Twa at Chombo were evicted from Kahuzi-Biega and now have even stopped collecting forest products from the Park for fear of the Park guards.
Photo: Dorothy Jackson

by a narrow environmental corridor. The eastern highland section is dominated by two spectacular extinct volcanoes, Kahuzi and Biega. It is the original section of the Park and, in biogeographical terms, its endemic centre. The low altitude section in the west is a later extension.

The Park consists largely of dense primary tropical forest, including species of bamboo which form the preferred food of the gorillas. It is extremely rich in biodiversity and home to an abundant and varied fauna, including mammals, birds, reptiles, amphibians, chimpanzees, gorilla, buffalo and many other animals. Between an altitude of 2,100 and 2,400 m above sea-level, it is inhabited by one of the last populations of eastern lowland gorillas in the Democratic Republic of Congo, numbering just 250 individuals or thereabouts.[2]

In addition to the flora and fauna, these spaces used to be home to around 40,000 indigenous people known as Twa, traditional hunter/gatherers whose existence alternated between periods spent moving from camp to camp in the Kahuzi-Biega forest and periods spent living near Bantu villages.

The Twa from Kahuzi-Biega believe that they form an integral part of the forest, which they perceive as their source of security and life. They have an intimate knowledge of the forest, and of the plants and animals living within it. Their practices and their way of life, their culture and their spirituality all revolved around it. Their traditional relations with farmers from other ethnic groups used to be based on bartering honey and medicinal substances for agricultural products, salt, iron tools and other goods. They would use the forest resources to treat their illnesses. Their ritual activities and religious rites, such as the initiation of boys, would take place in the forest, with which they had spiritual, cultural and material ties.[3]

Creation of the Park

The history of the Park began in 1937, when the Mount Kahuzi Zoological and Forest Reserve was created by Decree No. 81/AGRI of the Belgian colonial administration. The reserve covered an area of 75,000 ha and was regulated by the 1908 Colonial Charter and, more specifically, by a 1947 order and a 1949 decree. It formed part of the state domain and was managed by the Kivu National Committee. The establishment of the reserve had little effect on the Twa, who did not even know about its existence because they had not been informed or consulted about its establishment.[4] They continued to live inside the reserve and kept hunting and gathering within its boundaries.[5] Their rights to do so were, in fact, to some extent protected, as the reserve was *sous reserve de droits indigènes* according to a 1951 decree.[6]

This changed on 30 November 1970, when the reserve was reduced to 60,000 ha and gazetted as Kahuzi-Biega National Park by order of the President of the now independent Republic.[7] The

---

2   UNESCO 2012.
3   See Mutimanwa 2001, p. 90 ff.; Barume 2000, pp. 80-81.
4   Mutimanwa 2001, p. 94 (Testimony by Pilipili, Twa tracker in the KBNP).
5   Barume 2000, pp. 69-70; Mutimanwa 2001, p. 90 ff.
6   Barume 2000, pp. 68-69, 74.
7   *Ordonnance-loi* No. 70/316. Of the 75,000 ha of the Forest Reserve, 15,000 ha were distributed among 16 wealthy farmers (Mutimanwa 2001, p. 93).

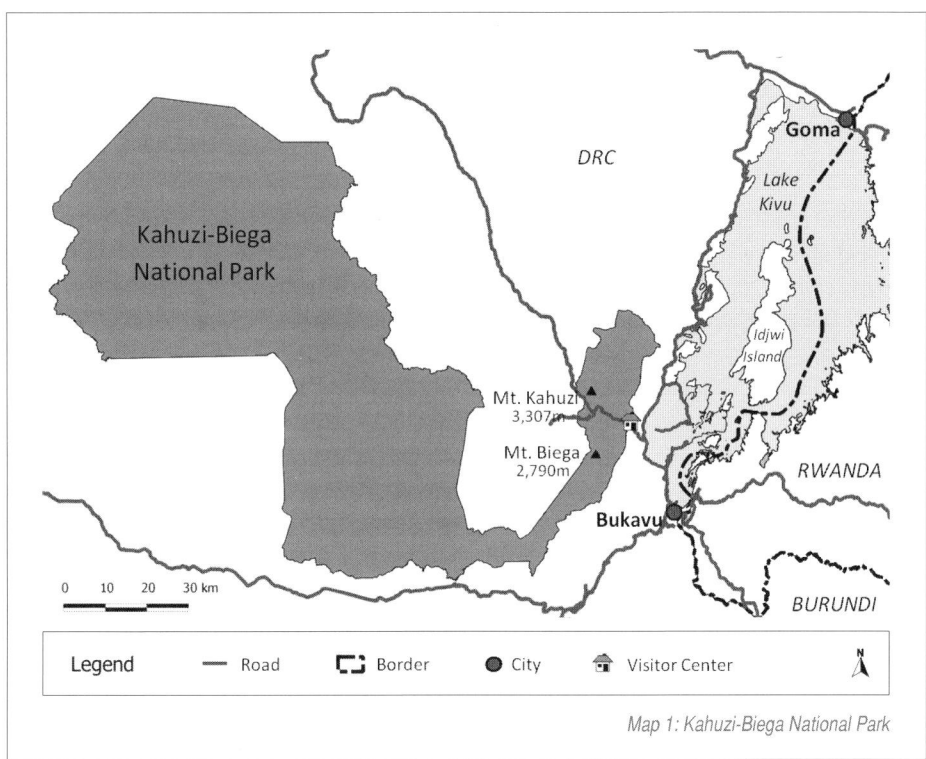

Map 1: Kahuzi-Biega National Park

main objective of the creation of the National Park was to protect the habitat and population of the endangered eastern lowland gorilla. The establishment of the National Park was, in part, the result of the lobbying efforts of international conservation organisations, including notably, the International Union for the Conservation of Nature (IUCN).[8] The local inhabitants of the area, including the indigenous Twa, were not consulted when the National Park was created.[9] The change in designation meant that human habitation, as well as hunting and gathering, was now prohibited within the boundaries of the Park.[10] An order dated 22 July 1975 extended the National Park into the lowlands to the west, increasing its area from 60,000 to 600,000 ha.[11] The lands of the local communities and indigenous peoples who lived in these lowland areas in proximity to the Park thus became annexed to the Park.

---

8   In 1966, the 9th General Assembly of IUCN (later renamed the 'World Conservation Congress') recommended "that the Congo Government should undertake without delay the establishment of a National Park in the Kahuzi-Biega region and the administrative measures necessary to ensure the immediate strengthening of protection..." (Res. 15). The recommendation was reiterated by the 10th General Assembly of IUCN in 1969 (Res. 6).
9   IUCN and UNEP-WCMC 2011, p. 4; Mutimanwa 2001.
10 Barume 2000, p. 70.
11 *Ordonnance-loi* No. 75/238.

The expulsion of the Twa from their forests had already begun before the establishment of the National Park, at the end of the 1960s, and was conducted by staff from the Congolese Institute for Nature Conservation (ICCN) with the support of the armed forces. Starting around 1967, the Twa who were living in what was the Kahuzi-Biega Reserve were forced out of the area on the orders of the provincial authorities (along with some Shi and Rwandese Tutsi refugees).[12] Although the evictions were carried out in the most brutal manner, they met little resistance from the Twa because they greatly feared coercive measures.[13] A Twa woman, a widow with five children, described her eviction as follows:

"We did not know they were coming. It was early in the morning. I heard people around my house. I looked through the door and saw people in uniforms with guns. Then suddenly one of them forced the door of our house and started shouting that we had to leave immediately because the park is not our land. I first did not understand what he was talking about because all my ancestors have lived on these lands. They were so violent that I left with my children." [14]

The Park authorities completed the evictions of the Twa from the highland areas of the Park in 1975. Twa inhabiting the lowland areas annexed to the Park in 1975 were affected by eviction pressures into the 1980s. All in all, around 580 Twa families and up to 6,000 individuals were thrown off lands on which the Twa had lived since time immemorial.[15] Today almost no Twa inhabit the Park, living instead in areas around the Park's borders.

Nothing was done to help the Twa evicted from the KBNP to find new land on which to settle. Each family or group was abandoned to its fate and they dispersed into various villages in Kalehe territory in South Kivu and Walikale territory in North Kivu.[16] The African Commission on Human and Peoples' Rights, the African Union body in charge of monitoring the implementation of the *African Charter on Human and Peoples' Rights*, has noted:

"Land should have been given in compensation to the Batwa, but this did not happen. Now the Batwa are forbidden to hunt in the park, and forbidden to collect park products. They have no food resources or medicinal plants, and the forest is no longer their place of worship. The Batwa have been culturally and psychologically shattered by the loss of their forests. The local authorities do not allow the Batwa to return to the forest of Kahuzi-Biega, as they claim they pose a high risk to the ecosystem. However, this is only a pretext, as traditionally the Batwa have never hunted gorillas, nor do they destroy the forest by cutting down trees…

---

12 Barume 2000, p. 74, 80 ff. Barume notes that, prior to the establishment of the National Park, the expulsion was illegal under domestic law as the reserve was still *sous reserve de droits indigenes*.
13 Muley, Sinafasi & Pacifique 2003, p. 17.
14 Cited in Barume 2000, p. 80.
15 Figures from the Twa NGO PIDP-Kivu and investigations by A. Barume. See Barume 2000, p. 80.
16 Ibid.

The entrance to Kahuzi-Biega National Park. Photo: Liz Williamson

The Batwa who were driven out of the Kahuzi – Biega forests are now extremely poor, even destitute. Most have no property, and it is very difficult for them to obtain their basic needs. To survive, some have learned from other non-Batwa how to make charcoal from wood to sell and this gives them around $10 every fortnight. Others who have plots of land try to cultivate them as best they can with potato and vegetables but, given that they are not used to farming, and that the rains have been extremely irregular in recent times, their situation remains one of extreme poverty. The Batwa in the north of the Kahuzi-Biega Park have settled on plots of land but these lands, officially unoccupied, may be allocated to someone else by the local authorities. The Batwa have no legal protection once neighbours from other ethnic groups decide to take their land or drive them out of their villages." [17]

While the evictions were felt heavily by the Twa, other communities continued to live on their lands.[18] It was only the weak, those with no voice and no legal protection, namely the Twa, who were evicted without any form of legal process. This is a serious form of discrimination that is

---

17 ACHPR 2003, p. 13.
18 For details, see Barume 2000, pp. 72-74.

inconsistent with the provisions of various international human rights treaties that the Democratic Republic of Congo has ratified, in particular the *International Convention on the Elimination of All Forms of Racial Discrimination* (ICERD).[19] The forced removal of indigenous peoples from their traditional lands is explicitly recognised as a serious violation of ICERD requiring immediate and urgent action.[20]

According to Congolese law, including the Constitution of 24 June 1967 which was in force both at the time of creating the KBNP and at the time of its expansion, as well as the Law of 20 July 1973[21] and the Law of 22 February 1977,[22] the expropriation of land for public use is conditional upon fair compensation being paid to the victims. Those who are deprived of their property for a compelling public interest reason must therefore obtain fair and prior compensation. The measures to evict the indigenous peoples from the KBNP were thus in violation of all legislation in force in this regard in the Democratic Republic of Congo.

It should be noted that no consultation or process for obtaining the consent of the indigenous peoples was implemented by either the Congolese government or its administrative departments in the procedure for creating the Kahuzi-Biega National Park, nor when the boundaries of the Park were extended in 1975. Furthermore, the Twa continue to be denied access to their resources and have been denied any share of benefits from the Park. As noted, they have also not received the compensation due to them under Congolese law. Although this occurred prior to DRC's accession to ICERD, the on-going and continued harm suffered by the Twa places the DRC in contravention of its international obligations under that Convention.[23] Moreover, Article 10 of the *UN Declaration on the Rights of Indigenous Peoples* (UNDRIP), adopted in 2007 by the UN General Assembly and endorsed by the DRC, explicitly forbids the forcible removal of indigenous peoples from their lands or territories in the future, and Article 32(3) establishes an obligation on States to provide "effective mechanisms for just and fair redress" where the lands and resources of indigenous peoples have previously been developed without their consent.

---

19 The international human rights treaty monitoring bodies have repeatedly expressed concern about the discrimination and marginalization of Pygmies, and the widespread violation of their rights, in the DRC. See, e.g. CERD 1996, para. 12 ("Grave concern is expressed at allegations of large-scale discrimination against the Pygmies (Batwa)"); HRC 2006, para. 26; or CESCR 2009, paras. 14, 17, 36. In 2007 CERD "note[d] with concern that the rights of the Pygmies (Bambuti, Batwa and Bacwa) to own, exploit, control and use their lands, their resources and their communal territories are not guaranteed and that concessions to the lands and territories of indigenous peoples are granted without prior consultation. The Committee recommend[ed] that the State party should take urgent and adequate measures to protect the rights of the Pygmies to land and: (a) make provision for the forest rights of indigenous peoples in domestic legislation; (b) register the ancestral lands of the Pygmies in the land registry; (c) proclaim a new moratorium on forest lands; (d) take the interests of the Pygmies and environmental conservation needs into account in matters of land use; (e) provide domestic remedies in the event that the rights of indigenous peoples are violated..." (CERD 2007a, para. 18). Also see UNGA 2006, para. 134 (report of the independent expert on the situation of human rights in the DRC to the UN General Assembly).

20 Committee on the Elimination of Racial Discrimination (CERD), *Guidelines for the Early Warning and Urgent Action Procedure* (CERD 2007b, para. 12 (h)).

21 *Loi* No. 73-021 *portant régime général des biens, régime foncier et immobilier et régime des sûretés* (General regime for real estate, land and guarantees). Modified and supplemented by Law No. 80-008 of 18 July 1980.

22 *Loi* No. 77-001 on expropriation for public use.

23 See, e.g., CERD 1997, *General Recommendation No. 23: Indigenous Peoples*, para. 5. Also see CAMV et al. 2006, p. 15.

Inscription of the World Heritage site

Despite widespread knowledge of the forced relocation of the Park's inhabitants, and explicit acknowledgement of the relocations in the World Heritage nomination sent to UNESCO,[24] the World Heritage Committee proceeded to declare the Kahuzi-Biega National Park a World Heritage site in 1980 because of its importance as a habitat for rare and endangered species, in particular the eastern gorilla.[25] The Twa who were evicted from the Park but continued to live in neighbouring villages were never consulted during the process of designating the Park a World Heritage site and, indeed, they do not even remember such a process. Neither the State Party's nomination document nor the Advisory Body Evaluation by IUCN or the relevant Decision of the World Heritage Committee contains any reference to the existence of the Twa.[26]

The suffering of the Twa, evicted from their property, was widely known and must have been clear to resident UN institutions, including UNESCO, which had a regional office in Kinshasa at the time. Corrective measures and reparation for all the harm suffered by the Twa should have been called for by the World Heritage Committee as a prior condition for inscribing the site on the World Heritage List, particularly since UNESCO is a UN institution supposed to "further universal respect for justice, for the rule of law and for the human rights and fundamental freedoms which are affirmed for the peoples of the world", according to its Constitution.[27] At the time the Park was being considered for World Heritage status, both of the International Human Rights Covenants as well as the *International Convention on the Elimination of All Forms of Racial Discrimination* had already been ratified by the DRC which thus had obligations in this regard. The country was not supposed to violate these international standards and yet, even now, with the adoption of the *UN Declaration on the Rights of Indigenous Peoples*, UNESCO has not sought any clarifications from the government with regard to the current situation and conflict between the indigenous peoples and the Park.

The World Heritage Committee has for years been very concerned, and rightfully so, about the occupation of the Park by armed militia, and in 1997 placed the site on the List of World Heritage in Danger, where it has remained ever since. It has obliged the government to use military force to safeguard the Park's integrity and outstanding universal value,[28] and thus spare the site from being removed from the World Heritage List. This threat of withdrawal of the UNESCO designation was taken very seriously by the Congolese government, and this begs the question as to why UNESCO's influence could not similarly be used to get the

---

24 IZCN 1979, p. 10: "When Kahuzi-Biega was given the status of a reserve, in 1960, and later of a national park, in 1970, the local populations were forced to leave the territory..." (unofficial translation).
25 See IUCN 1980.
26 IZCN 1979; IUCN 1980; WHC 1980.
27 *Constitution of the United Nations Educational, Scientific, and Cultural Organization*, Art. I, para. 1.
28 See, e.g., World Heritage Committee Decision 30COM 7A.6 (2006).

Congolese government to respect the rights of the indigenous Twa who were evicted from the area.[29]

In actual fact, these indigenous people are currently subject to the decisions of the World Heritage Committee without being able to have any influence over them. Although the Committee seeks "to enhance the role of communities in the implementation of the Convention"[30] and although it has examined KBNP annually since 1997, the Committee has never paid any attention to the existence of the Twa and they are not mentioned in any of its decisions.[31] The communities have little information on the process although, according to the *Operational Guidelines for the Implementation of the World Heritage Convention,* their participation in the protection of the site is to be ensured.[32] This lack of indigenous consultation and participation is becoming all the more conspicuous now that the Congolese authorities are just beginning to recognise the existence of indigenous peoples and the need for special measures to protect their interests and include them in decision-making processes.[33]

At the time the site was designated, however, conservation interests were placed over and above indigenous rights. The designation of the KBNP as a World Heritage site has led to an entrenched position on the part of the Congolese government and the ICCN, both of which firmly believe that they acted correctly by evicting the indigenous families, despite being in violation of both Congolese and international law.

Exclusion of the Twa from management

Following World Heritage designation, the Congolese authorities strengthened their protection measures with regard to the Park, and so the conservative and coercive 1969 Law on Nature Conservation, *Ordonnance-loi* No. 69-041 of 22 August 1969, was implemented to the letter. According to this law, no-one has the right to remove either non-timber forest products or dead wood from nature reserves, and the park police in KBNP are always sufficiently armed to deal not only with poachers but also with the indigenous communities, who are frequently punished for poaching, without any evidence.[34] The Congolese Institute for Nature Conservation, the government authority

---

29 According to the current (2013) *Operational Guidelines for the Implementation of the World Heritage Convention*, para. 192, a property can only be deleted from the World Heritage List when it has "deteriorated to the extent that it has lost those characteristics which determined its inclusion in the World Heritage List". As described above, the presence and culture of the Twa is not considered by the World Heritage Committee as part of those characteristics (i.e. the site's 'outstanding universal value'). However, the legitimacy of this assessment – if not of the World Heritage designation *per se* – is highly questionable given the blatant exclusion of the Twa from all decision-making processes regarding the World Heritage site.
30 Fifth Strategic Objective of the World Heritage Committee, see the Operational Guidelines (2013), para. 26.
31 This is also true for the "Statement of Outstanding Universal Value" adopted by the Committee in 2012 by Decision 36COM 8E.
32 Operational Guidelines (2013), paras. 12, 119.
33 See, for instance, Decree No. 09/40 of 26/11/2009 on the creation, composition and organisation of the structure for implementing the process for reducing emissions from deforestation and forest degradation ('REDD'), Art. 5; or the efforts to prepare a national development program for the indigenous peoples of the DRC (see World Bank 2009).
34 See, for instance, Barume 2000, p. 82 ff.

Settlement of Twa evicted from Kahuzi-Biega National Park, Chombo, DRC. Photo: Dorothy Jackson

in charge of the management of protected areas in the DRC, is prepared to go to great lengths to safeguard the integrity of a World Heritage site from which it hopes to obtain a great deal of funding and income from tourism.

Prior to the 1994 war in Rwanda, which destabilised the east of the DRC, and the successive wars, the mountain gorillas were a great attraction in this Park and tourism was booming.[35] However, none of the income found its way into the hands of the indigenous Twa, as the ICCN has almost absolute control over the Park and its income, and access and benefit-sharing mechanisms do not exist. The Twa are still landless and their situation continues to be one of extreme poverty. A few mini-projects are being implemented in villages close to the Park; however, they have no real impact on the lives of the Twa. The few schools that have been opened are attended mainly by Bantu children given that primary school is not free in the DRC and Twa families are unable to pay. An indigenous Twa chief evicted from the Park whom the author recently talked to was convinced that if the Twa were to receive aid from countries supporting the World Heritage site then the primary aim of this would be to keep them in poverty as the donors were more interested in the gorillas than in human beings.[36]

---

35   See UNESCO 2005, p. 117.
36   Interviews conducted in January 2012 by the author.

The management plans for the KBNP have always been completed by the ICCN without any Twa participation, including the current plan, the *General Management Plan 2009-2019*. Just a few NGOs that are somewhat supportive of the indigenous people were informed and participated in the discussions. The current plan does at least acknowledge that the Twa were removed from the Park at the time of its creation although they had coexisted with the forest for many generations and depend on it for hunting, fishing and gathering. It notes that they now live on the edges of the Park under very poor conditions and rely on hunting to supplement their livelihoods. However, the Twa continue to be treated as a major threat to the site in the management plan, which laments that they have not given up hunting and states that "the current method of illegal exploitation of the Park's resources by the Batwa represents a big risk for the future of the Park".[37] One positive aspect of the management plan is that the Twa ("Pygmées") are listed as one of the (many) stakeholder groups to be involved in programming workshops.[38] The plan also recognises the existence of Twa cultural sites inside the Park, and indicates that the communities will be able to access their cultural sites in the future.[39] Such recognition of cultural sites in the document is proof that the indigenous Twa communities have indeed been deprived of access to their sacred sites, something that is to their detriment. The management plan is unclear, however, as to when or how the Twa will concretely be able to enjoy such recognition.

In a conversation with a conservation worker, this latter felt that the communities understood nothing about the heritage site as their level of comprehension was too low, thus preventing them from being able to participate in this process. If this is the case, then why not provide them with information and capacity-building sessions?

When you visit the KBNP offices in Muhumba, the smartest district of Bukavu, the words "World Heritage Site" are inscribed on a board outside the building, a clear sign of the prestige that the UNESCO designation brings to the site and its administration. This position is in contrast to the situation of the indigenous Twa, who are abandoned and whose only privilege with regard to this world heritage is the possibility of being recruited as one of the few park guards on a salary of between US$50 and US$100 per month. There are no Twa in senior positions in the World Heritage site management team, which constitutes serious discrimination in employment terms and, in the absence of an educational policy for the indigenous Twa, means it will be difficult for them to play a substantial role in implementing the KBNP Management Plan in the future, or for an indigenous Twa to hold a management and decision-making position within the KBNP.

It should be noted that, in previous years, as now, various programmes and projects have been developed, the most visible being one financed by German development cooperation (GTZ/GIZ) and the WWF, the aim of which is to promote so-called participatory conservation in the Park, so-called because an evaluation of these projects and programmes to date shows little progress in terms of Twa rights. The KBNP *General Management Plan 2009-2019* seems

---

37 ICCN 2009, pp. 18-19, 22-23 (own translation).
38 Ibid., p. 109 (Annex 4).
39 Ibid., p. 29.

to recognise good principles; these are thus far no more than theories, however, and will need to be implemented in practice if we are to see any positive change. The donors and the government will also need to find out how provisions such as Article 8j of the *Convention on Biological Diversity* (CBD)[40] and the *Nagoya Protocol on Access and Benefit-sharing*[41] are being implemented in Kahuzi-Biega National Park, as there is no access and benefit-sharing initiative in place for the Twa.

As regards the profits from Park tourism, UNESCO has analysed the distribution of profits generated each year by tourists visiting the gorillas in the DRC. Local profits arising from the US$ 20.6 million each year only amount to US$ 0.7 million, or around 3.4% of the total.[42] Moreover, as Plumptre et al. have demonstrated, the benefits drawn from the conservation projects by indigenous peoples are less than those of others. While 7% of the population as a whole recollect having been able to benefit a little from the profits coming from tourism, not one Twa in the areas surrounding the Virunga and Kahuzi-Biega National Parks has ever experienced such a thing. The presence of these Parks has only negative consequences for them, such as restricted access, aggression during the harvesting of forest products, theft of harvests, and clashes with park guards.[43] The impoverishment of the indigenous peoples in the DRC through the establishment of national parks is thus evident, and the case of the KBNP is no exception.

Twa responses to their exclusion

It is abundantly clear that the indigenous people of the KBNP have suffered significant harm as they are now landless, unable to access their property, i.e. their lands and their forest, and unable to use or transmit to their children their traditional knowledge. The treatment they have been subjected to is not only discriminatory but also inhuman and degrading. Their various complaints calling for compensation to be paid by amicable arrangement have fallen on deaf ears and so they are now demanding justice through the Congolese courts, with a case aimed at obtaining compensation for the damage suffered and, indeed, still being suffered, as the extremely difficult living conditions

---

40 The CBD was ratified by the DRC in 1994. Art. 8 is on "*In-situ* conservation" and states in part: "Each Contracting Party shall, as far as possible and as appropriate: [...] (j) Subject to its national legislation, respect, preserve and maintain knowledge, innovations and practices of indigenous and local communities embodying traditional lifestyles relevant for the conservation and sustainable use of biological diversity and promote their wider application with the approval and involvement of the holders of such knowledge, innovations and practices and encourage the equitable sharing of the benefits arising from the utilization of such knowledge, innovations and practices..."
41 *Nagoya Protocol on Access to Genetic Resources and the Fair and Equitable Sharing of Benefits Arising from their Utilization to the Convention on Biological Diversity*. The Protocol was adopted by the Conference of Parties to the *Convention on Biological Diversity* in October 2010 and will enter into force 90 days after the date of deposit of the fiftieth instrument of ratification. The DRC has signed, but not ratified the Protocol (as of 14 January 2014).
42 UNESCO 2005, p. 132.
43 Plumptre et al. 2004, pp. 82 ff. Referenced in Schmidt-Soltau 2007, p. 23.

these people are experiencing make them a people "heading towards extinction".[44] The Twa are also demanding a return to their forest, as they have no land of their own on which to practise their way of life.[45]

The UN and state institutions are doing nothing for these people, despite this historic and flagrant injustice having been denounced for many years by national and international human rights NGOs, in writing and by other means. Failing any adequate response, and with the support of an NGO, the ERND Institute (Environment, Natural Resources and Development Institute), 66 of the Twa who were evicted from the KBNP have recently initiated legal action against the Congolese government and ICCN, seeking restitution of their ancestral lands, compensation for the harm suffered and guaranteed access to basic social services in the areas of education, health, employment and housing. In the first instance, the case was heard in the Kavumu District Court, in a village close to the Park, but this court ruled that the matter was outside its competence, without looking into the merits of the case.[46] The Bukavu Court of Appeal upheld this decision and again found the matter outside of its competence, ruling it a constitutional matter.[47] The case has now been submitted to the clerk of the Supreme Court in December 2013, where it awaits a hearing.[48]

The Democratic Republic of Congo has made a number of regional and global international commitments, including, for example, ratifying the *African Charter on Human and Peoples' Rights*. While the state is obliged to implement this important text, no results have as yet been forthcoming with regard to the situation of indigenous peoples in general and the Twa of the KBNP in particular.[49] The *UN Declaration on the Rights of Indigenous Peoples*, endorsed by the DRC at the time of its adoption in 2007, has as yet also not led to the government adopting concrete measures aimed at implementing its provisions.

ILO Convention 169 (*Indigenous and Tribal Peoples Convention, 1989*) is not even under consideration for ratification by the Congolese government. There are, however, internal discussions taking place with regard to the possibility of developing specific local texts on indigenous peoples' rights, prioritising the reality of each province with the adoption of local laws. These discussions are still informal, however, between locally-elected representatives and non-governmental organisations.[50]

The World Bank's *Strategic Framework for the Preparation of a Pygmy Development Program*,[51] proposed for adoption by the Congolese government, tries to establish a general framework for resolving indigenous issues; however a global solution will only come about through a jointly agreed

---

44 Barume 2000. Barume quotes a Twa man from Bishuleshule/Kalehe as follows: "...since we were expelled from our lands, death is following us. We bury people nearly every day. The village is becoming empty. We are heading towards extinction. Now all the old people have died. Our culture is dying too..." (Barume 2000, p. 87).
45 Interviews conducted in January 2012 by the author.
46 Case No. RC 4058, *Tribunal de Grande Instance* of Uvira.
47 Case No. RCA 4570, *Cour d'appel* of Bukavu.
48 Case No. RC 3817.
49 See ACHPR 2003.
50 ERND Institute 2009.
51 World Bank 2009.

framework taking into account the effects caused by the implementation of UNESCO processes related to World Heritage.

Conclusion

In terms of a conclusion and recommendations, it must be emphasised that the case of the KBNP and the indigenous Twa is an injustice that first and foremost has to be recognised, and then compensated, as amicable processes have not resulted in a solution. It is important that the Congolese authorities do not wait until convicted in this regard, particularly as the *UN Declaration on the Rights of Indigenous Peoples* anticipates that mechanisms be put in place to resolve conflicts involving indigenous peoples, and that a rapid solution is found.[52]

The case before the Congolese courts remains the only hope for the Twa who were evicted from Kahuzi-Biega National Park, as UNESCO seems oblivious to the victims of these inhuman acts, the consequences of which continue to be felt within the community, scattered as it is in the villages surrounding the Park and receiving no assistance. To cap it all, even access to justice remains a great challenge for the indigenous Twa. Without prejudice as to the outcome of this historic process for the Twa, the length of the proceedings and the threats against the activists behind the case - particularly indigenous leaders, the lawyers' collective and the ERND Institute - would seem to suggest that the case is being taken seriously. The independence of the Congolese justice system remains to be seen, however, in a young democracy that has just emerged from war. If, impossibly, the Twa do not win this domestic case then there is still the possibility of taking it to the international level, particularly the African Commission on Human and Peoples' Rights and the UN Human Rights Committee.[53] A wider demand is to also see the World Heritage Committee take this case on board and urge the government to respond to the indigenous concerns and put in place reparation and compensation measures in line with its international commitments.

After more than 30 years of World Heritage status, it is important that UNESCO finally conduct a serious evaluation of the way in which indigenous peoples are continuing to suffer serious harm at its site; to do nothing will be considered as being complicit with the Congolese government and ICCN, who are responsible for this situation. Those of us who believe in UNESCO's credibility want to see it committed to resolving this conflict, and to see justice done for the Twa victims of the Kahuzi-Biega National Park. ○

---

52 See UNDRIP, Arts. 8(2), 11(2), 32(3) and 40.
53 ERND Institute 2009.

References

AAPDMAC et al. 2004. Statement of Pygmy representatives from the DRC at the 3rd Session of the UN Permanent Forum on Indigenous Issues, 18 May 2004. Available at: www.docip.org/gsdl/collect/cendocdo/index/assoc/HASHdeac/67990c8f.dir/188_fs.pdf.

ACHPR 2003. *Report of the African Commission's Working Group on Indigenous Populations/Communities.* Doc. DOC/OS(XXXIV)/345. (The report, including its recommendations, was adopted by the African Commission on Human and Peoples' Rights on 20 November 2003 by Resolution 65(XXXIV)03).

Barume, A. K. 2000. *Heading Towards Extinction? Indigenous Rights in Africa: The Case of the Twa of the Kahuzi-Biega National Park, Democratic Republic of Congo.* Copenhagen, IWGIA/FPP.

CAMV and FPP. 2008. *The rights of indigenous "Pygmy" peoples in the Democratic Republic of Congo* (Supplementary Report on the DRC's 2007 Periodic Report to the African Commission on Human and Peoples' Rights). Bukavu, Centre d'Accompagnement des Autochtones Pygmées et Minoritaires Vulnérables/FPP.

CAMV et al. 2006. *Persistent and Pervasive Racial Discrimination against Indigenous Peoples in the Democratic Republic of Congo: Formal Request to Initiate an Urgent Action Procedure to Avoid Immediate and Irreparable Harm.* Document submitted to the UN Committee on the Elimination of Racial Discrimination. Available at: www.forestpeoples.org/sites/fpp/files/publication/2010/08/drccerdjun06eng.pdf.

CERD. 1996. *Concluding observations of the Committee on the Elimination of Racial Discrimination: Zaire.* UN Doc. CERD/C/304/Add.18, 27 September 1996.

CERD. 1997. *General Recommendation No. 23: Indigenous Peoples.* UN Doc. A/52/18, Annex V.

CERD. 2007a. *Concluding observations of the Committee on the Elimination of Racial Discrimination: Democratic Republic of the Congo.* UN Doc. CERD/C/COD/CO/15, 17 August 2007.

CERD. 2007b. *Guidelines for the Early Warning and Urgent Action Procedure* (adopted by the Committee on the Elimination of Racial Discrimination at its 71st Session in August 2007). UN Doc. A/62/18, Annex III, pp. 115-120.

CESCR. 2009. *Concluding Observations of the Committee on Economic, Social and Cultural Rights: Democratic Republic of the Congo.* UN Doc. E/C.12/COD/CO/4, 20 November 2009.

ERND Institute. 2009. *Les autochtones pygmées à la quête de la justice en RDC: Cas du procès PA du Parc Kahuzi Biega contre l'ICCN et Etat Congolais.* Bukavu, Environnement Ressources Naturelles et Développement Institute, June 2009.

HRC. 2006. *Concluding Observations of the Human Rights Committee: Democratic Republic of the Congo.* UN Doc. CCPR/C/COD/CO/3, 26 April 2006.

ICCN. 2009. *Plan Général de Gestion 2009 - 2019: Parc National de Kahuzi-Biega.* Kinshasa, Institut Congolais pour la Conservation de la Nature.

IUCN. 1980. *IUCN Review – World Heritage Nomination: Parc National de Kahuzi-Biega.*

IUCN and UNEP-WCMC. 2011. *Kahuzi-Biéga National Park, Democratic Republic of the Congo.* (Entry in the World Database on Protected Areas, as updated in May 2011). Cambridge, UNEP-WCMC.

IZCN. 1979. *Liste du patrimoine mondial: Parc National du Kahuzi-Biega, Zaïre* (World Heritage Nomination). Kinshasa, Institut Zaïrois pour la Conservation de la Nature.

Muley, A., Sinafasi, A. and Pacifique M. 2003. Forest Governance and Pygmy People Access of Pygmy Indigenes to Land: The Case of Pygmies Rejected from the Kahuzi-Biega National Park, South-Kivu, Eastern DRC. Center for Environment and Development, Rainforest Foundation and Forests Monitor (eds.), *Forest Management Transparency, Governance and the Law: Case studies from the Congo Basin*, pp. 15-21.

Mutimanwa, K. D. 2001. The Bambuti-Batwa and the Kahuzi-Biega National Park: the case of the Barhwa and Babuluko people. J. Nelson and L. Hossack (eds.), *From principles to practice: Indigenous Peoples and Protected Areas in Africa.* Moreton-in-Marsh, FPP, pp. 87-110.

Plumptre, A.J. et al. 2004. The socio-economic status of people living near protected areas in the Central Albertine Rift. *Albertine Rift Technical Reports*, Vol. 4.

Schmidt-Soltau, K. 2007. *Projet GEF/BM – Plan des Peuples Autochtones: Rapport Final.* Kinshasa, Institut Congolais pour la Conservation de la Nature (ICCN).

UNESCO. 2005. *Promoting and Preserving Congolese Heritage: Linking biological and cultural diversity* (Proceedings of a conference and workshops at UNESCO Headquarters, 13-17 September 2004). Paris, UNESCO (World Heritage Papers 17).

UNESCO. 2012. Kahuzi-Biega National Park, http://whc.unesco.org/en/list/137 (accessed 14 January 2014).

UNGA. 2006. *Progress report by the independent expert on the situation of human rights in the Democratic Republic of the Congo.* Doc. A/61/475.

WHC. 1980. *Report of the Rapporteur of the Fourth Session of the World Heritage Committee* (Paris, 1-5 September 1980), Doc. C-80/CONF.016/10.

World Bank. 2009. *Democratic Republic of Congo – Strategic Framework for the Preparation of a Pygmy Development Program.* World Bank Report No. 51108–ZR.

Bwindi Impenetrable National Park: The Case of the Batwa

Christopher Kidd [1]

The Batwa of Uganda

Historically, the Batwa were forest-dwelling hunter-gatherers, maintaining livelihoods within the high altitude forests around Lake Kivu and Lake Edward in the Great Lakes Region of Central and East Africa. The Batwa are widely regarded by their neighbours, and historians, as the first inhabitants of the region, who were later joined by incoming farmers and pastoralists approximately 1,000 years ago.[2] Today, the Batwa still live in Rwanda, Burundi, Uganda and eastern Democratic Republic of Congo. In each of these countries, they exist as a minority ethnic group living amongst the largely Bahutu and Batutsi populations. In Uganda, their dominant neighbours are the Bafumbira and Bakiga peoples.

While accurate figures are difficult to determine, as estimates vary between different sources, it is believed that approximately 6,700 Batwa now live within the present state boundaries of Uganda,

---

1   The findings of this chapter are based on a review of indigenous peoples' participation in protected area management conducted by Forest Peoples Programme in 2008. See Kidd and Zaninka 2008.
2   Taylor, Robertshaw and Marchant 2000.

Left: Bwindi Impenetrable National Park. Photo: Teseum (CC BY-NC 2.0)

with approximately half living in the south-west region of Uganda.³ The Batwa in this region are former inhabitants of the Bwindi, Mgahinga and Echuya forests, where they had lived since time immemorial in coexistence with the environment and in full reliance on the forest for their physical, economic, spiritual and social sustenance. Recently, however, they have suffered evictions and exclusions from their forests, primarily for the creation of protected areas that were established without their participation or their free, prior and informed consent.

As a result of their exclusion from their ancestral forests and the subsequent loss of their forest-based livelihoods, the majority of Ugandan Batwa suffer severe isolation, discrimination and socio-political exclusion. The Batwa's customary rights to land have not been recognized in Uganda and they have received little or no compensation for their losses, resulting in a situation where almost half of the Batwa remain landless and virtually all live in absolute poverty. Almost half of the Batwa continue to squat on other people's land whilst working for their non-Batwa masters in bonded labour agreements. Those who live on land that has been donated by charities still continue to suffer poorer levels of healthcare, education and employment than neighbouring ethnic groups. Today, the Batwa's political situation, on the margins of Ugandan society, is analogous to their physical existence in settlements on the edges of their ancestral forests.

A history of protection

The British colonial administration first established protected areas within the Batwa's forests in the 1930s, measures which probably served to protect the forests from complete destruction by the incoming cultivators and pastoralists who were eager to utilise the fertile lands. Nonetheless, despite this infringement of their land rights, the Batwa continued to consider the forests as theirs, to worship their ancestors there, and to use the forest to derive their livelihood and practise their culture. The chief objective of the conservation measures was the protection and preservation of the Mountain Gorilla and it seems that the initial colonial measures were contradicted by the conservation measures that were to follow. In 1930, one administrator's wife wrote that:

> "The danger to gorilla to be apprehended from local Africans is very little... a Swedish expedition offered the Kigezi mountain pygmies what to them was wealth to enlist their services as hunters for a museum specimen. They met with a blank refusal. The flesh, moreover, is considered by them as 'an abomination.' To suggest eating it is an insult. As regards the pelt, even the professional tanners will not touch it. They 'would as soon consent to flay a brother's skin'." ⁴

As such, the Batwa were not seen as a threat and their way of life went largely unhindered. Indeed, early colonial administrators even championed the Batwa's rights to live in these forests and demanded legal protection to secure the Batwa's continued well-being:

---

3 Uganda Bureau of Statistics 2002.
4 Phillipps 1930.

Former Twa hunter demonstrating use of spear near Echuya forest, Uganda. Photo: Dorothy Jackson

"The killing of animals is necessary for [the Batwa's] existence... The Batwa cannot be restricted in their habituation of the area nor can their hunting habits be interfered with. Fortunately they do not hunt the gorilla nor molest it in any way nor eat its flesh. Under such circumstances it will be necessary to modify the park regulations. Though maintaining the usual restrictions on visitors from outside, suitable modifications will be necessary in order to permit the Batwa to continue hunting." [5]

In 1964, Bwindi followed Mgahinga[6] in becoming gazetted as an animal sanctuary. At the time, the threats to the gorillas came from the great numbers of Batutsi and Bahutu who had entered the area from northern Rwanda, and habitat destruction became the greatest danger to the gorillas.[7] It is unclear how these earlier changes in protection affected the Batwa but, in 1964, Forest and Game Acts were introduced in Uganda which had serious effects on their access to their forest resources. Residing, hunting and farming were made illegal inside the park, as was the use of hunting dogs or the possession

---

5   Hingston 1931, p. 417.
6   Mgahinga was originally gazetted as a Gorilla Sanctuary in 1930.
7   Dart 1960, pp. 330-331.

of hunting weapons. Around this time, between 50 and 100 Batwa families were evicted from Bwindi.[8] Enforcement of these laws suffered during the post-colonial troubles which blighted Uganda, however, as government legislation was ignored. When the National Resistance Movement came to power in 1986, the stability it brought Uganda opened the door to various conservation interests, which took over the work that had stalled during the civil war period. As early as 1988, the Uganda National Parks department (UNP) presented a report to the Ugandan Cabinet proposing Bwindi as a National Park and, in 1989, the process began that led to the creation of Bwindi Impenetrable National Park (Bwindi) and Mgahinga Gorilla National Park (Mgahinga).[9] The establishment in 1991 of Bwindi and Mgahinga forests as national parks resulted in the permanent eviction and exclusion of the Batwa from their homeland. At this point in time, the previous infringement of their land rights was reinforced and their marginalisation completed by the removal of their use and access rights to the forests. It should also be noted that, at the very same time as these forests were being established as national parks, the Ugandan government was preparing its nomination of Bwindi as a World Heritage site. In neither case did the mechanisms employed to create Bwindi as a national park and a World Heritage site seek to include the Batwa's views, and the violation of their rights to their lands went unheard.

This path towards increasing levels of protection for these forests, and the corresponding restrictions on access that such protection entailed, did not go unnoticed by the communities surrounding these forests. In June 1990, a team comprising members of the UNP, Game Department and World Wide Fund for Nature (WWF) carried out a public enquiry to provide recommendations for the creation of a management plan for the proposed national park. The communities felt it vital that nobody should lose any land as a result of Bwindi becoming a national park; that financial benefits, particularly from employment, should accrue to the communities; that access should be given for communities to collect forest resources, and that local communities should be involved throughout the process.[10] The injustice felt by the people affected by the proposed restrictions led one community to ask: "Does the government care more about the gorillas than people?" and further: "Tourists come from countries where they have killed their own animals. Why shouldn't they go to see animals in zoos instead of coming to Bwindi?"[11] The Batwa's views were neither sampled nor represented anywhere in the public enquiry.

The creation of Bwindi as a national park in 1991 went ahead with the insistence of government officials and global conservation groups and, with the stroke of a pen, the Batwa became squatters on their own land. Initially, these groups' conservation method was firmly based on the 'Fortress Conservation' model. Communities were seen as being the cause of forest degradation and so the best way to conserve the forest was to exclude them from any contact. The Batwa and other local people were no longer allowed to enter BINP and attempts to collect water and firewood were repelled.

Despite this initial policy, the early 90s also saw Bwindi pilot a new form of conservation that positioned communities as an important component of conservation management. Whilst these new forms of conservation brought success to some local communities around Bwindi, the Batwa

---

8   IUCN 1994.
9   Hamilton, Baranga and Tindigarukayo 1990, p. 16.
10 Ibid., pp. 32-41.
11 Ibid., pp. 39-40.

were systematically excluded. Twenty years on since the creation of the national park, the Batwa remain marginalised from the management of Bwindi, from any forms of benefit deriving from the national park, and from the right to access and use the resources located inside the forests.

Batwa involvement in Bwindi Impenetrable National Park management

Social losses

At the time Bwindi was created, the Batwa – who were by far the people most heavily dependent on the forest for their sustenance, livelihood and culture – were recognized as having been particularly adversely affected, both socially, economically and culturally. The Global Environment Facility (GEF) provided funding to Uganda to support the management of these national parks, through the Mgahinga and Bwindi Impenetrable Forest Conservation Trust Fund, now known as the Bwindi Mgahinga Conservation Trust, BMCT (the 'Trust'). The 1995 Project Document for the Conservation Trust states:

> "When [Bwindi and Mgahinga] became Forest and Game Reserves in the 1930's, with human occupation and hunting formally banned, [the Batwa] began to shift out of the shrinking forest area and began spending more time as share-croppers and labourers on their neighbours' farms. However, they still had access to many forest resources and the forests continued to be economically and culturally important to them. The gazetting of the areas as national parks has virtually eliminated access to these opportunities for all local people, but the impact has been particularly harsh on the Batwa because they are landless and economically and socially disadvantaged, and have few other resources or options." [12]

A comprehensive socio-economic assessment and consultation was not completed until 1996, after the Trust had become fully operational. The resulting report recommended recognizing Batwa use rights to certain resources in the parks and the right to access sacred sites, the allocation of forest and farmland to evicted communities, capacity building, and educational, health and economic assistance. However, these recommendations were not fully implemented and it required the support of the Dutch government to provide funds for the Trust to acquire small parcels of land for a small minority of Batwa. Whilst this was a helpful initiative, the amount of land bought for each family was far below the recommended two acres per family and the land acquisition programme closed down before land had been bought for all affected communities. Even with the support of additional charity and church groups, around half of all Batwa are still landless. This places a large number of Batwa at the mercy of neighbouring ethnic groups, who continue to discriminate against them and who use the Batwa as farm labourers.

---

12 World Bank 1995.

Social benefits

Under the Wildlife Act, the UWA is obliged to allocate 20 percent of park entry fees paid by tourists to local community initiatives through Community Protected Area Institutes (CPAIs). However, virtually all projects funded by this revenue-sharing scheme are social infrastructure projects such as roads, schools and health facilities. These projects rarely benefit marginalised communities such as the Batwa. For example, Batwa children face particular hurdles in accessing and staying in school, and these obstacles have not been addressed by government. Further, in Bwindi, park entry fees are rather insignificant compared to revenues from gorilla tracking permits, which are currently around US$450 per person and likely to rise. Since 2004, a US$5 levy fee has been collected from gorilla tracking permits, in favour of community development. Additionally, a US$4 community levy is being 'set aside' for additional community developments. It is hoped that these funds will help to target Batwa communities but, on the evidence so far, the Batwa's claims to the benefits of this scheme are being marginalized by other sections of the community.

In 2011, after several years of negotiations and hard work, the UWA, Kisoro District Local Government and the Batwa's own NGO, the United Organisation for Batwa Development in Uganda, signed a memorandum of understanding to begin a joint tourism project in Mgahinga Gorilla National Park. This new project offers tourists the chance to visit the national park with Batwa guides and learn about the Batwa history and culture of the forest. This venture is a huge step forward in relations between the Batwa and the protected area managers and it is hoped that similar opportunities may open up in neighbouring Bwindi.

Customary use

In terms of national legislation, the Wildlife Statute (1996) allows local communities to access forests for traditional uses provided such uses are compatible with sustainable development. The Statute also recognises the historical rights of persons who used to reside inside conservation areas. These provisions, however, have yet to be implemented to a degree that benefits the Batwa.

Since 1993, the Government of Uganda has authorised a Multiple Use Programme (MUP) in Bwindi, through which neighbouring communities are permitted (under memoranda of understanding) to access medicinal plants, basketry materials and certain other non-timber forest products. This MUP is now operating in 12 of the 24 parishes bordering Bwindi and the Multiple Use Zones (MUZs) now cover approximately 20 percent of the forest area of Bwindi.

While these have, to some extent, been positive developments for some local communities, they remain flawed in their implementation and have provided few benefits for the Batwa. In practice, there has been no sustainable extraction of the Batwa's culturally-specific resources within Bwindi. Firstly, the Government of Uganda continues to operate under a power-relationship approach, with government officials holding all the knowledge, information and decision-making powers and communities having little understanding of their rights and virtually no real say in either process or outcomes. As one report notes:

"Rather than entering into open-ended negotiations, with compromises made on both sides, the quality of [the] process was limited by the willingness of park management to concede (or even discuss) access to resources of any significant value." [13]

Another author regards the MUP as:

"...another form of state control over resources...with the protected area management authority unwilling to trust resource users and subsequently to relinquish some of its responsibilities and authority." [14]

Resource use thus continues to be treated as a privilege rather than a right, and this privilege is, by most accounts, meagre at best.

Secondly, the small amount of resource use that does accrue to local communities is not adapted to Batwa needs, and they are thus once again excluded and marginalised by the MUP. The MUP has primarily helped local beekeepers and other local associations, which rarely include Batwa, to engage in activities that are considered beneficial by the dominant society. With the exception of wild yams, which are now being accessed by the Batwa in the last couple of years, the forest uses considered critical by the Batwa community – including collecting firewood and building materials, hunting small animals, fishing, collecting wild honey, mushrooms and fruit, and worshiping their ancestors – have not been addressed by these programmes, despite being widely known. Their forms of forest offtake are thus treated as illegal. A number of experts[15] have recommended that the Batwa, as the original inhabitants of the forest, the group with the greatest cultural dependence on the forest and the community most adversely affected by conservation programmes, be treated as a special group with special permission to access the forest in recognition of their rights. Additional studies have reported that the extraction of wild yams and wild honey could be sustainably managed; however, this advice has yet to be implemented.

The first comprehensive review of the memoranda of understanding (MoUs) since 1994 was carried out in 2008. Whilst wild yams are now included in the new MoUs, wild honey and other culturally-specific resources are still not included despite some resource extraction being supported by research from the scientific community.

Participation in management

Bwindi Impenetrable National Park continues to be managed and administered with a top-down approach by the Uganda Wildlife Authority (UWA), without any meaningful participation by the Batwa. UWA has attempted to engage local communities around both Bwindi and Mgahinga

---

13 Mutebi 2003, p. 7.
14 Namara 2006, p. 58.
15 See for instance Kabananukye and Wily 1996.

through the appointment of representatives to Local Environmental Committees (LECs). The selection process, however, which draws candidates from the local parish council committees in surrounding areas, has institutionalised the exclusion of the Batwa, who are not represented on these committees. The establishment of CPAIs has similarly failed to enhance community participation in general, since members feel they are simply surrogates of the protected area managers and government administrators as opposed to meaningful and equal participants. Further, these institutions have not involved the Batwa as the current mode of representation is based on local government structures and thus requires prior participation in leadership structures in which the Batwa are not represented.

World Heritage designation

The nomination of Bwindi as a World Heritage site was submitted to UNESCO by the Government of Uganda in 1992. In its Advisory Body Evaluation of the nomination, IUCN suggested that Bwindi:

> "...is the most important area in Uganda for species conservation due to an exceptional diversity that includes many Albertine Rift endemics. Bwindi has the highest diversity of tree and fern species in East Africa, and may be the most important forest in Africa for montane forest butterflies. Bwindi is also the home of nine globally threatened species, including almost one half of the world's population of mountain gorillas." [16]

In response, the World Heritage Committee in 1994 inscribed Bwindi as a World Heritage site with the following justification: "The Committee inscribed this site which has one of the richest faunal communities in East Africa, including almost half the population of the world's mountain gorillas, and one of Africa's most important forests for butterflies and bird diversity."[17]

It is not known if the Batwa were consulted at the time of nomination and, if any were, there is no evidence to confirm it. In IUCN's Advisory Body Evaluation there is only one mention of the Batwa, which damningly testifies to the Batwa's then situation and predicament,

> "The earliest evidence of forest clearance dates back 4,800 years, most likely due to the presence of the Batwa (hunter-gatherer) people manipulating vegetation with fire. This is the earliest evidence for cultivation anywhere in tropical Africa. It was not until approximately 2,000 years ago that Bantu agriculturalists arrived in the region. The extensive knowledge of wild animals and plants possessed by the Batwa people is threatened with disappearance unless their way of life is restored, or their knowledge condensed onto paper." [18]

---

16 IUCN 1994.
17 UNESCO 1995, p. 47. A retrospective Statement of Outstanding Universal Value was adopted by the Committee in June 2011. See Doc. WHC-11/35.COM/8E.
18 IUCN 1994.

The presence of the Batwa, and their inclusion in the nomination process, can best be inferred from the Government of Uganda's nomination document where, under the section outlining the justification for including Bwindi as a World Heritage site, it is stated: "Cultural Property: Not Applicable".[19] It seems, then, that the Batwa and their rich cultural heritage were not considered by the government at the time. Since Bwindi's inscription as a World Heritage site, there has also been no mention of the Batwa in any of the World Heritage Committee's reporting on Bwindi, which continues to suggest that the Batwa to this day are not included in the thoughts and actions of either the Government of Uganda or UNESCO.

As a result of their exclusion from both the nomination process and the continued management of Bwindi, it would be difficult to suggest that the Batwa have benefited from Bwindi's inclusion as a World Heritage site. If anything, the inclusion of Bwindi has only served to offer yet another example of their continued marginalisation from their ancestral territories and has added another layer of management which they were not consulted on and did not consent to.

Discussion

Importantly, the concepts of indigeneity, management, participation and rights are proving difficult to define in south-west Uganda and this is a cause of the continued gulf between policy and practice. If the Batwa are to gain any benefits from World Heritage status, it is important that these concepts are acknowledged and discussed, with their full participation.

Indigeneity

One of the crucial obstacles preventing the realisation of the rights of the Batwa is the definition of indigeneity as understood by the Government of Uganda and protected area (PA) managers in Uganda. In Ugandan law, the definition of an indigenous person is outlined in the constitution of Uganda as anyone existing and residing within the borders of Uganda before 1926. As a result, indigenous people in Uganda are both everyone - there are 56 different ethnic groups listed in the constitution as indigenous in 1926 - and no-one in particular at the same time.

In the case of the Batwa, this failure to acknowledge their internationally recognised indigenous status[20] has dramatic effects. On the one hand, when challenged to justify their support to indigenous

---

19 Government of Uganda 1992.
20 See, e.g., the *Concluding Observations of the African Commission on Human and Peoples' Rights on the 3rd Periodic Report of the Republic of Uganda*, in which the African Commission expresses its concern about "The apparent lack of political will to take measures to realize the rights of indigenous populations especially the BATWA people as guaranteed under the [African] Charter [on Human and Peoples' Rights]" and "the exploitation, the discrimination and the marginalization of indigenous populations, in particular the BATWA people of Uganda, who are deprived of their ancestral lands and live without any land titles" (ACHPR 2009, paras. 21, 39). Also see the 2010 *Report by the Special Rapporteur on the situation of human rights and fundamental freedoms of indigenous people, James Anaya to the UN Human Rights Council,* Chapter XXX ("Uganda: Situation of the Batwa people of southwest Uganda"), which specifically addresses the situation in Bwindi; and CERD 2003, para. 14.

peoples in Uganda, the government and other agencies are able to highlight their support for local communities surrounding Bwindi despite the fact that the internationally recognised indigenous Batwa are not specifically targeted in any of the measures and are typically excluded. From the government's perspective, as all Ugandans are indigenous, their work with any Ugandan local communities constitutes work with indigenous communities. A prime example is the case of the CPAIs, which currently have no Batwa participating in their structures. Because of the constitutionally understood definition of indigeneity, the CPAIs are often quoted as being one way in which indigenous people are involved in park management, despite the fact that no Batwa are involved in the process.

On the other hand, the government is able to refuse to specifically focus on or target the Batwa because, by law, the Batwa are not the only indigenous people in Uganda and do not deserve the particular attention they should otherwise receive as internationally recognised indigenous people.

Management

The next issue that prevents the effective participation of the Batwa in the management of Bwindi is the way in which the term 'management' is understood by the government, PA managers and civil society groups. The meaning of management may vary in terms of the degree of participation being offered to communities. At one extreme is a community-centred approach that "transfers all management responsibilities and full property rights over natural resources to communities at the local level".[21] At the other lies an approach that sees communities "not as proprietors of the nation's conservation estate but merely as its neighbours".[22] For many groups and agencies working in and around Bwindi, management is rarely understood in terms other than benefit sharing or consultation.

Participation

This next issue follows on from the discussion above. Importantly, the question asked here is: what does effective and meaningful participation actually mean? Some examples of 'participation' around Bwindi include the consultations of local communities before the creation of the management plans, the various benefit mechanisms and the MUP, whereby local communities identify the resources to be harvested, agree the offtake amount and then manage the sustainable extraction of the resource.

In practice, however, while the communities may identify the desired resources it is the UWA that takes the ultimate decision as to which resources are harvested and, despite the UWA claiming that the local communities agree on the offtake quotas, the actual amounts of harvestable resources are decided by scientific research into sustainable extraction amounts.

It is therefore doubtful whether these measures constitute effective and meaningful participation, and instead constitute token handouts that do not go far enough to actively engage the Batwa in meaningful participation. As Hulme and Murphree note of conservation policy more generally:

---

21 Hulme and Murphree 1999, pp. 278 ff.
22 Ibid.

"While the labels of community conservation and community-based conservation have become widely used this is, to a significant degree, because of the positive image generated by the idea of 'community' rather than because of their accuracy." [23]

Rights vs. privileges

The participation of the Batwa and local communities is often called into question by the continued research being conducted into whether benefit sharing and collaborative management have been able to decrease the illegal resource use of local communities around Bwindi. Many agencies and actors working in and around Bwindi only acknowledge the need to specifically target the Batwa because they see the Batwa as the biggest threat to biodiversity and not because of any inherent right the Batwa may have. This understanding of participation begs the question of what is 'appropriate' and who gets to decide? This further suggests that what constitutes the effective and meaningful participation of indigenous peoples in PA management is a subjective decision that is most often made by PA managers and conservationists. From the experience of the Batwa around Bwindi, the involvement of indigenous people is seen by most PA managers as a privilege that is facilitated by the PA managers rather than a right which the Batwa have that does not require the privilege of others.

Recommendations

The Batwa must be included in the decision-making processes of Bwindi as a World Heritage site so that they can help to shape and inform Bwindi's future direction. Ultimately, such involvement requires fundamental changes in the way in which the Batwa are involved in protected area management across the board. These changes include the following:

- A commitment must be promoted at all levels of government to view communities as equal partners in development and conservation. Stronger mechanisms are needed for their participation, including the direct involvement of indigenous Batwa people in project design and implementation and the administration of funds.
- Batwa communities should be recognized by government as a special group whose rights to access and use of their ancestral lands must be protected when establishing and implementing national legislation and policy. Where rights are being violated, legal action should be considered.
- Building on the numerous existing studies, government should develop and implement, in consultation with the Batwa, a targeted 'Batwa and Protected Areas programme' that recognises and addresses Batwa needs and realities, including:
  - Their unique historical land and resource rights in respect of their ancestral lands, with reference to international human rights law;

---

23 Ibid., p. 283.

- Their particular cultural and socio-economic needs in respect of forest resource use and access.
- Government should urgently implement a targeted and long-term programme, developed in consultation with the Batwa, to increase the Batwa's capacity to participate in decision-making bodies and processes, including:
Culturally-appropriate initiatives to improve Batwa access to education;
  - Adult literacy programmes;
  - Batwa community sensitisation and consultations on collaborative park management;
  - Improved access to information for Batwa on protected area management in appropriate languages and formats;
  - Training and support for Batwa communities to strongly and independently represent themselves;
  - In tandem with the above measures, the adoption or creation of PA management structures which are more inclusive and sensitive to the capacity of the Batwa.
- In partnership with the Ugandan government and the Uganda Wildlife Authority, the World Heritage Committee should immediately carry out a review of Bwindi Impenetrable National Park to ensure that the rights of the Batwa are being upheld and enshrined in its World Heritage status. Where these rights are being violated, immediate steps should be taken to redress the situation.
- Again in full collaboration with the Ugandan state, and in order to recognize the unique culture of the Batwa, the World Heritage Committee should review Bwindi's status as a site of natural importance and seek to have Bwindi relisted as a site of both cultural and natural importance.

While certain frameworks exist, and there is growing recognition of community rights in relation to protected areas, the genuine participation of the Batwa, based on a position of equality, remains illusory in Uganda. Government authorities continue to act in a paternalistic manner and merely pass on a few responsibilities to communities rather than empowering the Batwa to be active partners in decision-making and implementation.

The Batwa, in particular, continue to suffer multiple layers of marginalisation in protected area management. Not only were they arbitrarily evicted from their homeland, thereby suffering the greatest injustice, they also now receive the least attention from government in the ongoing efforts to make protected area management more socially responsible. From the example of Bwindi, it is clear that despite the call for a new conservation paradigm, and a new set of standards that reflect such a call,[24] in practice, protected area managers still perceive the Batwa as external to the conservation agenda.

Despite this, in 2011 two important opportunities have opened up which will hopefully provide a new framework for relationships between the Batwa and protected area managers. Firstly, the joint tourism venture in neighbouring Mgahinga offers a chance for the Batwa's unique cultural

---

24 See in particular IUCN World Parks Congress 2003 (*Durban Action Plan*); CBD 2004 (*Programme of Work on Protected Areas*); and the resolutions on indigenous peoples adopted at the 4th IUCN World Conservation Congress in Barcelona, 2008 (Resolutions 4.049-4.056).

Batwa cultural mapping of important sites in Bwindi.
Photo: United Organisation for Batwa Development in Uganda

knowledge and heritage to be included in the ongoing conservation of these forests. If this venture proves successful, it could lead to broader relationships that go beyond tourism revenue and allow for meaningful participation in the management and future of Bwindi.

Secondly, the Batwa's own NGO in Uganda, the United Organisation for Batwa Development in Uganda, supported Batwa communities to carry out a month long cultural mapping of Bwindi Impenetrable National Park. For the first time, the mapping process allowed over 100 Batwa from the ten communities neighbouring Bwindi to apply their traditional knowledge and heritage to a three-dimensional model of their ancestral lands. Some of the information documented included the location of sacred sites and burial sites within the national park as well as the locations of some of the Batwa's most cherished resources, such as wild honey, wild yams and medicinal herbs. The completed model stands as testimony to their extensive knowledge and attachment to Bwindi forest and offers a real chance for protected area managers to finally include such knowledge in the future management of Bwindi. The Batwa hope that this model will, among other things, help them access employment and resources within the park and help them develop a more meaningful role in its continued management. It is opportunities such as these that need to be grasped by protected area managers so that the injustices of the past can be redressed in significant and meaningful ways. If this can be done, the potential is there for a new and more equitable future to be realized whereby the Batwa are acknowledged as essential to the conservation of the heritage contained in Bwindi Impenetrable National Park. ○

References

ACHPR. 2009. *Concluding Observations of the African Commission on Human and Peoples' Rights on the 3rd Periodic Report of the Republic of Uganda* (presented at the 45th Ordinary Session of the African Commission in Banjul, May 2009.

Anaya, J. 2010. *Report by the Special Rapporteur on the situation of human rights and fundamental freedoms of indigenous people, James Anaya to the UN Human Rights Council.* UN Doc. A/HRC/15/37/Add.1, 15 September 2010.

CBD. 2004. *Programme of Work on Protected Areas* (adopted by the Conference of the Parties to the Convention on Biological Diversity at its Seventh Meeting). Doc. UNEP/CBD/COP/DEC/VII/28, 13 April 2004, Annex.

CERD. 2003. *Concluding Observations of the Committee on the Elimination of Racial Discrimination: Uganda*, UN Doc. CERD/C/62/CO/11, 2 June 2003.

Dart, R. A. 1960. Can the Mountain Gorillas be Saved? *Current Anthropology*, Vol. 1, No. 4, pp. 330-333.

Government of Uganda. 1992. *Bwindi Impenetrable National Park: World Heritage Site Proposal.* Uganda National Parks.

Hamilton, A., Baranga, J. and Tindigarukayo, J. 1990. *Proposed Bwindi (Impenetrable) Forest National Park: Results of Public Enquiry and Recommendations for Establishment* (Draft Report). Kampala, Uganda National Parks, p. 16.

Hingston, R. 1931. Proposed British National Parks for Africa. *The Geographical Journal*, Vol. 77, No. 5, pp. 401-422.

Hulme, D. and Murphree, M. 1999. Communities, Wildlife and the 'New Conservation' in Africa. *Journal of International Development*, Vol. 11, No. 2, pp. 277-286.

IUCN. 1994. *Advisory Body Evaluation – Bwindi World Heritage Nomination – IUCN Summary.*

IUCN. 2009. *Resolutions and Recommendations, World Conservation Congress, Barcelona, Spain, 5-14 October 2008.* Gland, IUCN.

IUCN World Parks Congress. 2003. *Durban Action Plan.* Adopted at the 5th IUCN World Parks Congress, March 2004.

Kabananukye, K. and Wily, L. 1996. *Report on a Study of the Abayanda Pygmies of South Western Uganda.* Kabale, Mgahinga and Bwindi Impenetrable Forest Conservation Trust.

Kidd, C. and Zaninka, P. 2008. *Securing Indigenous Peoples' Rights in Conservation: A review of south-west Uganda.* Moreton-in-Marsh, Forest Peoples Programme.

Mutebi, J. 2003. *Co-managed Protected Areas: from conflict to collaboration. Experience in Bwindi Impenetrable National Park, Uganda.* Kampala, CARE Uganda.

Namara, A. 2006. From paternalism to real partnership with local communities? Experiences from Bwindi Impenetrable National Park (Uganda). *Africa Development*, Vol. XXXI, No. 2, pp. 39-68.

Phillipps, T. 1930. Gorillas at home. *The Times*, 8 February 1930, p. 13.

Taylor, D., Robertshaw, P. and Marchant, R. 2000. Environmental change and political economic upheaval in pre-colonial western Uganda. *The Holocene*, Vol. 10, No. 4, pp. 527-536.

Uganda Bureau of Statistics. 2002. *2002 Uganda Population and Housing Census.* Available at http://www.ubos.org.

UNESCO. 1995. *World Heritage Committee, Eighteenth Session, Phuket, Thailand, 12-17 December 1994: Report.* Doc. WHC-94/CONF.003/16, 31 January 1995.

UNESCO. 2011. *Adoption of retrospective Statements of Outstanding Universal Value.* Doc. WHC-11/35.COM/8E, 27 May 2011.

World Bank. 1995. *Uganda: Bwindi Impenetrable National Park and Mgahinga Gorilla National Park Conservation.* Washington DC, World Bank (Global Environment Facility, Project Document 12430 – UG), Annex 6.

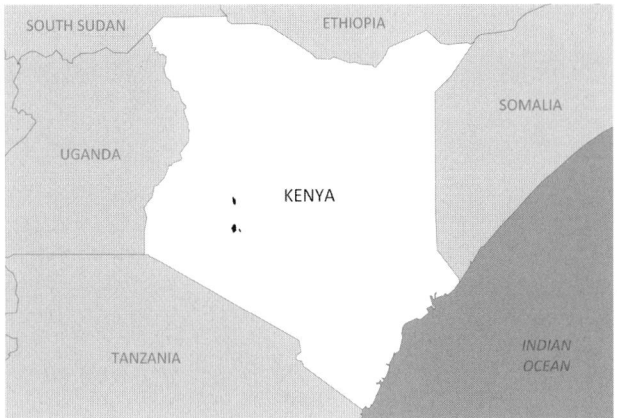

Ignoring Indigenous Peoples' Rights: The Case of Lake Bogoria's Designation as a UNESCO World Heritage Site

Korir Sing'Oei Abraham

Introduction

The 'Kenya Lake System in the Great Rift Valley' was added to UNESCO's World Heritage List in June 2011 during the World Heritage Committee's 35th ordinary session at UNESCO Headquarters in Paris. The 'serial' World Heritage site[1] covers a total area of 32,034 hectares and comprises three alkaline lakes, together with their surrounding territories, on the floor of the Great Rift Valley in Kenya: Lake Bogoria (10,700 ha), Lake Nakuru (18,800 ha) and Lake Elementaita (2,534 ha). The focus of this chapter is Lake Bogoria, located some 100 km to the north of the other two lakes.

---

1   'Serial' sites are those World Heritage sites that consist of two or more geographically separate component parts.

Left: Endorois men celebrating the 2010 ruling of the African Commission on Human and Peoples' Rights calling for the restitution of Endorois ancestral lands around Lake Bogoria. Photo: Lewis Davies

The three lakes are home to an exceptional diversity of birds, including enormous flocks of Lesser Flamingos, and contain important populations of numerous threatened bird as well as mammal species. They are surrounded by hot springs, geysers and the steep escarpment of the Rift Valley with its volcanic outcrops. Because of its exceptional scenery and geological, ecological and biological features, the serial site was inscribed on the World Heritage List as a natural site with reference to criteria (vii), (ix) and (x).[2] The three lakes have also each been internationally recognized as wetlands of international importance under the 1971 Ramsar Convention on Wetlands.

Under national law, Lake Elementaita is protected as a National Wildlife Sanctuary, while Lake Nakuru is a National Park and Lake Bogoria a National Reserve. Geographically, the Kenya Lake System lies within the former Rift Valley Province. Under the new administrative set-up provided by the 2010 Kenyan Constitution, the Lake System straddles two counties, with both Lake Elementaita and Lake Nakuru located within Nakuru County and Lake Bogoria lying within Baringo County.[3]

The area is occupied by several ethnic groups, including two distinct indigenous groups: the Endorois and the Maasai. The other ethnic groups who live in this region are the Agikuyu, Kipsigis, Tugen and Pokot, as well as a sprinkling of other ethnic groups, especially within the cosmopolitan Nakuru town.[4] The focus of this chapter shall be exclusively confined to the indigenous Endorois community, who live around Lake Bogoria within Baringo County.

The Endorois number approximately 60,000 people. The community is, and always has been, largely pastoralist with a strong sense of communal access to natural resources. Its leadership is entrusted to elders. The communal lifestyle and social cohesion of the Endorois is illustrated by the way in which they rely on a representative organization, the Endorois Welfare Council (founded in 1996), as the medium through which they channel their grievances. The Endorois' communal lifestyle is quite resilient and has weathered many storms over the years. This resilience was particularly evident in the face of adversity visited upon the community when the Government of Kenya forcefully evicted them from their area of habitation on the shores of Lake Bogoria after the Lake Bogoria Game Reserve was created in 1973. The eviction rapidly forced the community into abject poverty, from which they have yet to recover. Beginning in the 1990s, the Endorois began to challenge the legality of their eviction in the courts, first at the domestic level and later at the African Commission on Human and Peoples' Rights (ACHPR), which in 2009 issued a landmark ruling in the community's favour, laying new ground for the defence of the traditional and customary land rights of indigenous peoples throughout Africa.[5]

The area around Lake Bogoria is of great social, economic and cultural significance to the Endorois community. From an economic standpoint, the lake provides water and the area's fertile soil provides green pasture as well as medicinal salt lick for the community's livestock, keeping the

---

2 World Heritage Committee Decision 35 COM 8B.6 (2011).
3 See the First Schedule of the new Kenyan Constitution, promulgated on 27 August 2010. The counties envisioned by the 2010 Constitution are supposed to become fully operational after the 2012 general elections.
4 Koigi wa Wamwere 2010.
5 ACHPR 2009, Decision on Communication 276/2003, *Centre for Minority Rights Development (CEMIRIDE) and Minority Rights Group International (MRG) on behalf of Endorois Welfare Council v Kenya*.

Flamingos and zebras on the shores of Lake Bogoria. The massed congregations of flamingos on the shores of Lake Bogoria are one of the main reasons for the lake's listing as a World Heritage site and a significant attraction drawing tourists to the park. Photo: Geoffroy Mauvais, IUCN (CC BY-NC-SA 2.0)

cattle healthy and the community's pastoralist enterprise alive. Further, from a social perspective, the lake epitomizes the community's religious and other traditional practices, given that the areas contiguous to the lake provide the community with sacred prayer sites, venues for initiation rites such as circumcision rituals, and grounds for hosting the periodic assembly of the community, where norms are enacted and given force. The spirits of every dead member of the community are believed to repose within the lake, irrespective of where the person was buried.[6] In addition to the lake itself, members of the community also regard the neighbouring Mochongoi Forest as sacred ground, which they consider as their birthplace.[7] Thus, the landscape upon which the community's livelihood derives is important for their social, cultural as well as spiritual needs.

The eviction of the Endorois from Lake Bogoria Game Reserve

While all three lakes are protected under national law, this paper shall confine itself to the Lake Bogoria Game Reserve. This is because, out of the three lakes, Lake Bogoria is the one whose protection efforts have had the most far-reaching effects upon the Endorois indigenous community. Lake Bogoria Game Reserve was established in 1973, through the declaration of Legal Notice

---

6 World Wildlife Federation 2004, p.16, para. 2.1.10.2.
7 Ibid.

Number 239, as "Lake Hannington National Reserve". The name of the reserve was changed one year later, through another Legal Notice, to Lake Bogoria Game Reserve.[8]

The establishment of the Reserve was not without controversy; a controversy that persists to this day. During the colonial period, the land around Lake Bogoria was part of the *Suk-Kamasia* 'native reserve' and was reserved for the sole use of the native community in the area, the Endorois. At Kenyan independence, in 1963, native reserves were converted into Trust Lands. Such lands were vested upon the respective local authorities (county councils) in trust for the people 'ordinarily resident' (a term of art meaning the native community of the area).[9] The particular local authorities in which the land around Lake Bogoria was vested were the County Councils of Baringo and Koibatek. These two county councils were thus entrusted to manage the land and its attendant resources for the benefit and on behalf of the members of the Endorois community as well as the other communities who ordinarily resided within the area in question.[10]

The process by which the government extinguished the proprietary interests within Trust Lands was known as 'setting apart'. This process was provided for by section 117 of the old Constitution[11] as read together with the Trust Land Act.[12] The process of setting apart could be initiated by the local authority under which the land in question was situated or the President of the Republic.

Beginning in 1973, the government designated the most important of Endorois lands as a game reserve. This decision was not preceded by consultation in good faith through the representative institutions of the affected community, in line with today's international standards affirming the right of indigenous peoples to effectively participate in decisions that affect them.[13] All that happened was unilateral and undocumented promises made by the government ostensibly to ameliorate the resulting vulnerabilities arising from the group's impending displacement. Unfettered access to Lake Bogoria, construction of cattle dips, building of schools and, most importantly, relocation to land of equal value, constituted the most significant promises made by state officials to the community leadership.[14] The state did not extend any real choice to the community, and did not extend an invitation to it to reject, amend or accept the proposed development intervention. The removal of the community from Lake Bogoria in this context of unequal bargaining power and

---

8   No. 270 of 1974.
9   Section 115, Constitution of Kenya (repealed in 2010).
10 These two county councils have since been combined into a single entity, the Baringo County Government, which has absorbed their responsibilities and authorities.
11 The effect of 'setting apart' in law was clear: "Where a county council has set apart an area of land in pursuance of this section, any rights, interests or other benefits in respect of that land that were previously vested in a tribe, group, family or individual under African customary law shall be extinguished." Section 117(2) Constitution of Kenya (repealed in 2010).
12 Chapter 288, Laws of Kenya.
13 See e.g., *UN Declaration on the Rights of Indigenous Peoples* (2007), Art. 18; *ILO Convention (No. 169) concerning Indigenous and Tribal Peoples in Independent Countries* (1989), Art. 6; Committee on the Elimination of Racial Discrimination, *General Recommendation No. 23: Indigenous Peoples* (1997), para. 4(d); and UN Expert Mechanism on the Rights of Indigenous Peoples, *Expert Mechanism Advice No. 2 (2011): Indigenous peoples and the right to participate in decision-making*.
14 See Witness Statement of Richard Arap Yegon, dated 15 August 2005 (on file with author) submitted in support of the Endorois Communication before the African Commission.

coercion was neither consensual nor based on an informed appreciation of the scope of the state's intrusion into the community's livelihood.

The establishment of the game reserve within the area inhabited by the Endorois community marked a turning point in the rhythm of their lives and livelihoods. This is because the game reserve is a protected area where access of people and livestock is restricted. Consequently, the members of the community and their livestock were denied access to the lake and the surrounding areas. This meant the community's livelihood, heavily dependent on mobile livestock keeping, was directly and seriously threatened. The lack of access to their lands and resources, on which they relied to sustain their livelihoods, formed the basis upon which the community instituted the legal action both at the Kenyan High Court and at the African Commission on Human and Peoples' Rights (see below).

The marginalization of the Endorois in the management of Lake Bogoria Game Reserve

Background

The management of wildlife protected areas is generally the preserve of the state, through a parastatal organization, the Kenya Wildlife Service (KWS). The Kenya Wildlife Service is a creation of the *Wildlife (Conservation and Management) Act*.[15] Under this law, there are three regimes of wildlife protection, namely: National Parks, National Reserves and Local Sanctuaries. National Parks are under the direct management of the KWS while National Reserves are managed and controlled by the local authorities within whose jurisdictions they are located (although according to national policy set by the KWS). Local sanctuaries are privately-owned ranches. The role of indigenous communities, and indeed any communities, in the decision-making over the management of protected areas in Kenya is thus very restricted. This is because the exclusive role of either the KWS or the local authorities is imposed by the operation of the law. Local authorities (recently reformed into county governments) are sub-national units with their own governance structures, which provide social services within their area of jurisdiction and also manage certain natural resources on behalf of the residents who are ordinarily resident within the area in question, operating under the laws of the state.

Lake Bogoria Game Reserve, the establishment of which displaced the Endorois indigenous community, is a National Reserve. Consequently, its management and control falls within the jurisdiction of the relevant local authority or county government. During its creation, this was the County Council of Baringo, and is now the Baringo County Government.[16]

---

15 Chapter 376, Laws of Kenya.
16 In the late 20th century Baringo was divided into two separate Councils, the Baringo and Koibatek County Councils, although this division has been reversed back and the local authority is now the recombined Baringo County Government.

The Endorois community lacks direct participation in and control over the management of this protected area. Instead, the community has to contend with an indirect role in the decision-making over the management, through their elected representatives in the county councils (the county councils are controlled by councillors elected during General Elections). The role of the Endorois community in decision-making regarding the Game Reserve is therefore very limited and their input is predicated only upon the role of the county councillors. This indirect role of the Endorois community is premised upon the fallacy that democratic elections ensure an effective participation of indigenous communities in the management of protected areas in Kenya.[17] Even though the democratic process does allow for some form of participation, international standards on effective representation require that indigenous peoples themselves be allowed to determine the procedures for choosing their own representatives in the state's governing bodies (whether traditional or otherwise).[18]

Further, two fallacies regarding the indirect representation of indigenous peoples emerge. Firstly, most of the indigenous communities are numerically disadvantaged and not able to make an electoral impact within their areas.[19] As a consequence, such communities are usually under-represented and hence unable to influence the management and decision-making within the councils. This means that they are excluded from playing the active roles that one would expect them to play as major stakeholders and rights holders within the respective protected sites. Secondly, there is simply no guarantee that the decisions to be made or taken by the elected representatives will always be in tandem with the requirements of the community. Processes such as the elaboration of management plans are usually devoid of consultations between the county councils (and/or the KWS) on the one hand and the local communities on the other. Elected councillors, even those with the support of the community, are not mandated to represent the Endorois specifically but rather to fulfil the usual democratic mandate of representing their constituency as a whole. This does not provide the Endorois with representative participation in the county councils, nor does it enable enjoyment of the right to effective participation in decision-making as outlined in the *UN Declaration on the Rights of Indigenous Peoples*. In a nutshell, then, the present governance structures do not ensure the adequate, informed and effective participation of indigenous peoples.

---

17 For instance, in the context of the *African Commission on Human and Peoples' Rights*, the Government of Kenya has argued "that the community is represented in the Country Council by its elected councillors, therefore presenting the community the opportunity to always be represented in the forum where decisions are made pertaining to development" (ACHPR 2009, para 276).

18 See *United Nations Declaration on the Rights of Indigenous Peoples*, Art. 18: "Indigenous peoples have the right to participate in decision-making in matters which would affect their rights, through representatives chosen by themselves in accordance with their own procedures, as well as to maintain and develop their own indigenous decision-making institutions."

19 For instance, the population of the Endorois community is estimated as being just about 60,000 people. Political and administrative boundaries have been created in such a way as to fracture the community into several constituencies, thereby making it difficult for the community to be represented by one of their own in parliament.

Non-recognition of the Endorois' own decision-making institutions

The Endorois community is strongly communal. The community's decision-making structures revolve around an institution known as the Endorois Welfare Council (EWC). Its decision-making process is a deliberative process that takes place under the auspices of the EWC. However, like the rest of the ethnic-based institutions in Kenya, the EWC was denied registration by the Kenyan government during the 24 long years of President Moi's rule between 1979 and 2003. This left the Endorois community without any recognized avenue through which it could deliberate on, make or communicate community decisions to the government.

The government's refusal to register the Endorois Welfare Council was also one of the reasons that informed the community's decision to seek legal redress. Numerous attempts by the community to have the EWC registered were unsuccessful. The African Commission on Human and Peoples' Rights has noted that the lack of registration for the EWC has denied the community the right to fair and legitimate consultation:

"The EWC, the representative body of the Endorois community, have been refused registration, thus denying the right of the Endorois to fair and legitimate consultation. The Complainants further allege that the failure to register the EWC has often led to illegitimate consultations taking place, with the authorities selecting particular individuals to lend their consent 'on behalf' of the community." [20]

Taking cognizance of this shortcoming, the African Commission recommended that the Government of Kenya grant registration to the EWC so as to enable the community to effectively participate in decisions and development processes affecting their territory.[21]

While the EWC has enjoyed, and continues to enjoy, great authority and credibility as the community's decision-making organization, negotiating group and mouthpiece, some dissenting voices have emerged.[22] The dissenting voices, receiving tacit encouragement from the state,[23] have objected to the validity of the EWC as the community's sole interlocutor vis-à-vis the state. Consequent upon this, the effectiveness of the EWC's engagement has been severely tested. The apparent divisions, while not effectively weakening the community's ability to mount advocacy initiatives and engage the authorities on matters relating to their economic welfare, have been used as an excuse by the state and its agencies to do less than would otherwise be expected. This especially relates to Lake Bogoria Game Reserve.[24]

---

20 ACHPR 2009, Decision on Communication 276/2003, para. 280.
21 Recommendation 1(e) of the African Commission on p. 178.
22 Okoth 2011.
23 The Kenyan government sponsored some members of the Endorois community to denounce the community's efforts at the African Commission and to present a documentary that was designed to portray the community as either having fully embraced modernity or having been well integrated into national development.
24 Okoth 2011.

Lack of recognition of Endorois land, resource and usage rights

For most indigenous communities in Kenya, both the use of and access to land and land-based resources was, and remains, customary. The customary mode of such access has usually been what is sometimes termed 'the communal type'.[25] Under this mode of access, each member of the community has the right to use the land in perpetuity on the condition that proper land-use practices that ensure inter-generational equity are pursued. This is the form of land tenure that the Endorois community practices.[26]

Under the old Constitution, private (individual) land tenure was considered superior to other forms of land tenure, such as the communal title. This was largely due to the fact that private tenure accorded the rights holder an indefeasible registered title.[27] In contrast, the communal (customary) tenure did not offer registered title to the users. In fact, the communal form of land tenure was largely practised within the Trust Lands as set out in section 114-118 of the old Constitution.

One of the most important recent achievements precipitated by the country's new Constitution, adopted in 2010, has been the elevation of communal (customary) tenure to the same level as private (individual) tenure. The 2010 Constitution categorizes land into public, private and community land.[28] The entry point for communal land tenure is through the category of community land. Based on this elevated status of communal tenure, the customary land and resource rights and the land-use systems of indigenous communities stand a real chance of being respected if enabling legislation is enacted. However, legislation to give effect to these constitutional provisions has not yet been enacted by parliament due to vested interests in land. Consequently during this transitional period – which could stretch to five years if political commitment is lacking – many institutions continue to deal with land that could potentially be protected as community land as if such lands were still solely under the complete legal authority of the county councils, deliberately forgetting or de-emphasizing the need for community consultations. For instance, in the course of seeking the designation of Lake Bogoria as a World Heritage site, KWS relied entirely on the Lake Bogoria National Reserve Integrated Management Plan 2007-2012, and did not factor in the effects of the new Constitution on this strategy.

In this Management Plan, the only hint of the existence of the Endorois is a reference to the community's Cultural Centre, which is only mentioned because it "has traditional artifacts and resident traditional dancers' troupes" that may be of interest to visitors.[29] The Management Plan sees no role for the Endorois' communal organizations and structures in developing consensus around the implementation and formulation of conservation and management measures, instead proposing a reliance on "inter-sectoral" and "interdisciplinary teams".[30] Assuming that this

---

25 Garner 2004.
26 See ACHPR 2009, para. 16.
27 Section 28 of *The Registered Land Act*, Chapter 300, Laws of Kenya.
28 See Articles 61-64 of Constitution of Kenya, 2010.
29 Baringo County Council and Koibatek County Council 2007, p. 19.
30 Ibid., p. 23.

Management Plan will form the basis for securing compliance with the UNESCO World Heritage Convention, it will no doubt result in the exclusion or, at most, the marginal participation of the Endorois in the decision-making regarding the World Heritage site.

More disconcertingly, Kenya appears to be using the designation of Lake Bogoria as a World Heritage site merely as a political cover to further deprive the community of its rights to the land. The acts of the Kenyan State, if properly examined, are incompatible with the professed intent to protect the natural beauty of the Kenya Lake System. For instance, the state, through its geothermal energy generation company, KENGEN, has invited bids for investment in electricity generating plants using steam within the Bogoria-Silali area (again without the consent of the Endorois).[31] This action by the state is worrying, considering that it not only violates the land and resource rights of the Endorois community but also threatens the objectives of conserving the Kenya Lake System's natural beauty, both flora and fauna. This action may be interpreted in two ways. First, that it is a poignant indication that the state has not fully appreciated the need to fully co-operate with indigenous communities as rights holders. In the state's view, the community is just like any other stakeholder, whose rights and interests can be conveniently dispensed with. Second, that the state's action is an indication that national development interests (i.e. geothermal energy production) will always trump community rights or environmental concerns. From a sustainable development perspective, these remain worrying conclusions.

At the same time as Endorois land is being tacitly licensed for the production of alternative energy needed for national development, grazing easements and other access rights of the Endorois, which the government is obligated to ensure according to the African Commission's decision,[32] continue to be severely restricted, discretionary and uncertain. The Endorois continue to face the grave situation described by the Commission as constituting "limited access to Lake Bogoria for grazing their cattle, for religious purposes, and for collecting traditional herbs... [T]he lack of legal certainty surrounding access rights and rights of usage renders the Endorois completely dependent on the Game Reserve authority's discretion to grant these rights on an ad hoc basis."[33] One positive development, however, was the permission granted to the Endorois in February 2010 to host a high-profile cultural festival to formally receive the decision of the African Commission and celebrate their victory. The ceremony of returning to their land "was full of elaborate rituals", as *The Standard* reported. "The community's elders – old men with grey hair, others with countable strands of hair – led the community into reconciling and reuniting with their ancestors at the shores of the lake." Old women who had become alienated from their soil and community life courtesy of the forced displacement, "reconnected by brushing and braiding their hair – perhaps a ritual in the past as they collected firewood along the shores of the lake..." [34]

---

31 Okoth 2011; Senelwa 2011.
32 ACHPR 2009, Decision on Communication 276/2003, para. 298 and Recommendation 1(b) on p. 178.
33 Ibid., para. 15.
34 Kiprotich 2010.

Lack of benefit-sharing

Kenya is renowned for its great wildlife and biodiversity, hence its position as a top international tourist destination. Most of the wildlife is conserved within the country's National Parks, Game Reserves and the Local Sanctuaries established within the *Wildlife (Conservation and Management) Act*.[35] Tourism has, over the years, shot up to become one of the country's topmost foreign exchange earners. In fact, according to Central Bank figures from 2008, tourism ranked as the second most important foreign exchange earner after the horticulture industry, with a net income of Kshs 65.4 billion (US $1.04 billion).[36]

While it cannot be denied that the protected areas have been an economic boon to the national government, it is equally true that the economic benefits generated have not been equitably shared. In particular, there have long been murmurs among the indigenous people within the Kenya Lake System area, especially the Endorois community, regarding the lack of a benefit-sharing mechanism. During the establishment of the Lake Bogoria Game Reserve, the Kenyan government promised members of the community that they would benefit from jobs and other social amenities. The government did not keep its promise to the indigenous community. Consequently, the members of the community have contested their eviction and the lack of direct economic benefits to their kinsmen.

The lack of benefit sharing from the economic activities within the Lake Bogoria Game Reserve became a constant source of irritation in the relationship between the government and the indigenous community. In fact, among the legal claims raised by the community before the High Court of Kenya, it stood out more prominently than the rest. In dismissing the community's quest for benefit sharing, the court observed that "the law did not allow individuals to benefit from such a resource simply because they happen to be born close to the natural resource."[37] The reasoning here is clear: there was no legal obligation on the state to ensure that communities directly benefit from revenue accruing from protected areas in their locality. In contrast, and cognizant of the failure of government revenue redistribution systems, the African Commission directed that the Government of Kenya pay royalties to members of the community from the economic activities (read: tourism and ruby mining) that derive from the Game Reserve.[38]

Lack of training and capacity building for the indigenous community

The management of wildlife protected areas in Kenya is a preserve of the Kenya Wildlife Service, local authorities and private individuals. More often than not, training in management of the protected

---

35 Chapter 376, Laws of Kenya.
36 Kimathi 2008.
37 *William Ngasia and Others v Baringo County Council and Others*, High Court Miscellaneous Civil Case No. 159 of 1999.
38 See recommendation 1(d) of the Endorois decision (ACHPR 2009, p.178).

areas is a preserve of the officers of the KWS and local authorities. There is very little evidence of support and training for the local communities, especially not the indigenous communities. As a matter of course, therefore, the roles that such communities play in the management of the protected areas, if any, remains largely peripheral since their own expertise and potential remain largely untapped.

However, where private partnerships between communities and investors have led to the development of wildlife conservancies, community members are often beneficiaries of conservation-related training. For instance, the Northern Rangeland Trust (NRT), active in Isiolo, Samburu and Laikipia districts, recruits "skilled management staff with high standards of training" while availing "further education... to Community Conservancy staff." For the most part, staff employed by NRT are from the local population, mainly Samburu and Borana communities.[39] In contrast, few if any initiatives to increase the skills of the Endorois in wildlife conservation specifically, or in the hospitality industry generally, have been witnessed. Indeed, the community has watched with dismay as the main hotel in the reserve, the Lake Bogoria Hotel and Spa, has continued to pass over the community when it comes to employment opportunities, instead preferring dominant groups from the district on the grounds that these latter are better educated.

The landmark ruling of the African Commission on Human and Peoples' Rights (2010)

The forceful eviction of the Endorois from Lake Bogoria caused much suffering to the community and threatened its cultural integrity and economic survival due to the deaths of thousands of livestock as a result of the loss of grazing grounds. Consequently, the creation of the Lake Bogoria Game Reserve is a phenomenon that has become the subject of numerous political and legal battles both within the Kenyan court system as well as at the African Commission on Human and Peoples' Rights. On the domestic front, the community was unsuccessful in challenging the government's decision to evict them to pave way for the establishment of the Lake Bogoria Game Reserve. This was the reality the community had to grapple with through the outcome of the case of *William Yatich Sitetalia & others v. Baringo County Council & others.*[40] The unfavourable result in this case impelled the community to turn to the African Commission, whose decision, delivered in November 2009 (and adopted by the African Union on 2 February 2010), was in the community's favour.

The Commission found that the Endorois' forced eviction from their ancestral lands and the failure to adequately involve them in the management, benefit sharing and decision making of the reserve had violated their right to practise their religion, their right to property, their right to culture, their rights to free disposition of natural resources and their right to development (Articles 1, 8, 14, 17, 21 and 22 of the *African Charter on Human and Peoples' Rights*). It recommended that the government:

---

39 Northern Rangelands Trust 2012.
40 High Court Civil Case No.183 of 2000.

"a) Recognise rights of ownership to the Endorois and Restitute Endorois ancestral land.
b) Ensure that the Endorois community has unrestricted access to Lake Bogoria and surrounding sites for religious and cultural rites and for grazing their cattle.
c) Pay adequate compensation to the community for all the loss suffered.
d) Pay royalties to the Endorois from existing economic activities and ensure that they benefit from employment possibilities within the Reserve.
e) Grant registration to the Endorois Welfare Committee.
f) Engage in dialogue with the Complainants for the effective implementation of these recommendations.
g) Report on the implementation of these recommendations within three months from the date of notification." [41]

In finding against the Government of Kenya, and that the Endorois community had suffered a violation of its right to development, the African Commission stressed that the Government of Kenya "is obligated to ensure that the Endorois are not left out of the development process or benefits" and that "[c]losely allied with the right to development is the issue of participation".[42] Development should result in the empowerment of the Endorois and an improvement in their capabilities and choices, the Commission noted, in order for their right to development to be realized.[43] If, therefore, the Government of Kenya had "allowed conditions to facilitate the right to development as in the African Charter, the development of the Game Reserve would have increased the capabilities of the Endorois, as they would have had a possibility to benefit from the Game Reserve." However, the African Commission is convinced that the Endorois "have faced substantive losses" as a result of the establishment of the Reserve, including "the actual loss in well-being and the denial of benefits accruing from the Game Reserve. Furthermore, the Endorois have faced a significant loss in choice since their eviction from the land." In particular, "the forced evictions eliminated any choice as to where they would live".[44] On the issue of participation, the Commission agreed with

---

41 ACHPR 2009, Decision on Communication 276/2003, p. 178, Recommendations. The legal effect of the Commission's recommendations can be derived from Article 27 of the Vienna Convention on the Law of Treaties (VCLT), 11155 U.N.T.S. 331(1980). In *International Pen and Others (on behalf of Saro Wiwa) v Nigeria*, Communication 154/96, the Commission noted that non-compliance with provisional measures issued under Article 111 of the Commission's Rules of Procedure constituted a violation of Article 1 of the African Charter (see para 122 of the decision). In reflecting on this failure, the Commission echoes the VCLT thus: "The Nigeria government itself recognizes that human rights are no longer solely a matter of domestic concern… once ratified, state parties to the Charter are legally bound to its provisions…" (para. 116). In 2010, the Commission adopted new rules of procedure that provide both a comprehensive follow-up process for the recommendations it makes, and establish a process to refer cases to the African Court where implementation does not result. Under Rule 115 of the Commission's new rules, there are specific timelines for states to respond to the Commission on matters of implementation. Previously, at its 40th session (November 2006), the Commission had adopted a *Resolution on the Importance of the Implementation of the Recommendations of the African Commission on Human and Peoples' Rights* obliging states to report on measures taken and constraints encountered within 90 days of notification of decision.
42 Ibid., paras. 289, 298.
43 Ibid., para. 283.
44 Ibid., paras. 279, 297.

Lake Bogoria is surrounded by hot springs and geysers representing important sacred sites for the Endorois. The ACHPR has held that the forced eviction of the Endorois from their ancestral lands "removed them from the sacred grounds essential to the practice of their religion, and rendered it virtually impossible for the Community to maintain religious practices central to their culture and religion". Photo: Corrado Mostacchi (CC BY-NC-ND 2.0)

the Endorois "that the consultations that the Respondent State did undertake with the community [regarding the development of the Game Reserve] were inadequate and cannot be considered effective participation", as "community members were informed of the impending project as a *fait accompli*, and not given an opportunity to shape the policies or their role in the Game Reserve... [T]he Respondent State did not obtain the prior, informed consent of all the Endorois before designating their land as a Game Reserve and commencing their eviction".[45]

The Commission underlined that, in the case of "any development or investment projects that would have a major impact within the Endorois territory, the State has a duty not only to consult with the community, but also to obtain their free, prior, and informed consent, according to their customs and traditions."[46] The question of whether a proposed development constitutes a "major impact" can only be determined on a case-by-case basis, taking into account, among other things, the extent to which an intervention may impede the practise of traditional livelihood and culture. There can be no doubt that the designation of Lake Bogoria as a World Heritage site falls within this category, as World Heritage status can potentially have far-reaching consequences for indigenous

---

45   Ibid., paras. 281, 290.
46   Ibid. para. 291.

peoples and their ways of life.[47] As will be further discussed below, this is also the view held by the African Commission, which in the context of reviewing Kenya's implementation of its recommendations in the Endorois case has expressed deep concern about the lack of consultation with the Endorois in the process of designating Lake Bogoria as a World Heritage site.

Despite various promises to implement the African Commission's ruling, the Kenyan government is thus far continuing to act as if the ruling did not exist.[48] In November 2011, the Endorois Welfare Council noted in a statement at the 50th Ordinary Session of the African Commission:

> "Your ruling recognized Endorois' rights over our ancestral land, and offered justice to the Endorois people, who have struggled for over 40 years in an effort to make the Government uphold our rights, and respect our livelihood and security. This landmark decision was expected to bring back hope and life not only to the indigenous populations in Kenya, but in Africa as a whole... However, despite... the clear directive from the Honourable Commission, the state party has refused to implement the ruling or negotiate with the Endorois indigenous community... The Kenyan Government promised implementation to this Commission in the 48th session... Despite these promises, the Government has been taking steps which don't respect the ruling, for example the Government earlier this year went ahead to propose Lake Bogoria National Reserve a UNESCO World Heritage Designation, without Endorois consultation." [49]

The World Heritage designation and its effects on the indigenous people

Exclusion of the Endorois from the nomination process

The nomination of the Kenya Lake System as a World Heritage site is a good example of the limited role that the Endorois community continues to play in decision making related to the Lake Bogoria National Reserve, despite the ruling of the African Commission on Human and Peoples' Rights. The nomination process was a unilateral one that excluded rights holders such as the indigenous communities who reside within the area or who have been displaced from it. Apparently, the whole idea was conceived and the process put into motion by the KWS. There is no indication of any noteworthy consultations regarding the nomination of Lake Bogoria as a World Heritage site between the KWS (or the Kenyan government for that matter) and the affected communities.[50]

---

47 For instance, the changed protection status (which subjects the management of a site to the overall goal of preserving its 'outstanding universal value') may result in additional restrictions on land-use practices and limit the options for indigenous peoples' self-determined development. World Heritage designation also often leads to a rapid increase in tourism, which can have major impacts on indigenous peoples' lives and cultures.
48 See Okoth 2011; Kavilu 2011.
49 Endorois Welfare Council and Minority Rights Group International 2011.
50 The nomination documentation merely indicates that in October 2009, three months before the nomination was submitted to UNESCO, a consultative workshop was held for stakeholders of the Greater Lake Elmenteita Conservation Area to get "updated on status of the Kenya Rift Valley Lakes Systems world heritage nomination" (National Museums of Kenya and Kenya Wildlife Service 2010, pp. 238, 296).

Endorois representative Christine Kandie delivering a statement to the 50th Ordinary Session of the African Commission on Human and Peoples' Rights, October 2011, highlighting the lack of consent from the Endorois in the listing of Lake Bogoria as a Word Heritage site.
Photo: Minority Rights Group International

In particular, the Endorois Welfare Council, as the representative organization of the Endorois community, was not consulted. Considering this, it is evident that the concerns of the community, such as their values, were not adequately taken into account. In fact, the Endorois community is not even mentioned in the nomination document submitted to UNESCO[51] and is not included in the list of major stakeholders contained in the submitted management plan for Lake Bogoria National Reserve.[52] It thus appears that the Kenyan government opted to pursue the route it took in the early 1970s during the establishment of the Lake Bogoria Game Reserve.

Endorois leaders decried their community's marginalization in the processes leading to the World Heritage nomination of Lake Bogoria on several occasions. For instance, in June 2009, the

---

51 With the exception of a note in the management plan for Lake Bogoria Game Reserve (attached to the nomination document), which mentions the existence of an Endorois Community Cultural Centre that "has traditional artifacts and resident traditional dancers' troupes" (p. 19).
52 Baringo County Council and Koibatek County Council 2007, p. 24.

following message from Endorois leader Wilson Kipkazi was published by Minority Rights Group International (MRG):

> "It is with shock and dismay for me and the general members of Endorois Community, to learn through the press that the Kenya Wildlife Service and National Museums of Kenya are campaigning to have Lake Bogoria in the Rift valley declared a world heritage site.
>
> As you are aware, Lake Bogoria is under dispute for having been converted by the Government of Kenya in 1973 into a game reserve without consulting the Endorois community of their intentions, hence resulting in the eviction of the members of our community without compensation nor given alternative land to settle. According to us this is another scandal in the offing since what is happening is similar to what happened in 1973 - the Government is doing things without consulting the community.
>
> The Government has been holding seminars among themselves ignoring the community and expecting us to embrace what is illegitimate arrangements. We would appreciate Lake Bogoria becoming an international heritage, but with community consent and also knowledge of the benefits for all." [53]

In May 2011, the Endorois Welfare Council (on behalf of the Endorois community), together with over 70 indigenous organizations and NGOs from around the world, submitted a joint statement to the UN Permanent Forum on Indigenous Issues protesting against the fact that the World Heritage nominations of the Kenya Lake System and two other sites had been prepared and submitted to UNESCO without obtaining the free, prior and informed consent of the indigenous peoples concerned. The indigenous organizations urged the World Heritage Committee to defer these nominations and to "call on the respective State parties to consult and collaborate with the Indigenous peoples concerned, in order to ensure that their values and needs are reflected in the nomination documents and management plans and to obtain their free, prior and informed consent".[54] The statement was subsequently submitted to both the Bureau of the World Heritage Committee and the World Heritage Centre, with a request to be brought to the attention of all Committee members. The statement was also brought to the attention of the Committee's Advisory Bodies.

In June and August 2009, MRG and CEMIRIDE had already written to UNESCO to inform the World Heritage Committee about the legal contestation over Lake Bogoria, pitting the Endorois community on the one hand against the Kenyan government on the other. The letters noted that the Endorois had not been consulted on the World Heritage nomination and stressed the need for them to be included in the UNESCO designation process.[55] While the Endorois did not receive a

---

53 See Minority Rights Group International 2009.
54 Endorois Welfare Council et al. 2011.
55 Letters on behalf of the Endorois community dated 19 June 2009 and 3 August 2009, addressed to the Director of the World Heritage Centre (on file with author). A follow-up letter was sent to the World Heritage Centre on 6 April 2010, informing UNESCO that the African Commission had ruled in the Endorois' favour.

direct response from UNESCO, the Director of the World Heritage Centre forwarded the community's concerns to KWS, which also happened to be the national focal point for UNESCO's World Heritage Natural Sites. In dismissing the Endorois' complaint regarding non-consultation, KWS submitted that a "Management Plan ha[d] already been developed with the involvement of the local communities including the Endorois" and that designation of Lake Bogoria as a World Heritage site would "confer greater involvement of the local communities in its management and use."[56] The KWS has also claimed, through a Dr. Njogu, that the entire nomination process was highly consultative and included community sensitization.[57] The organization intimates that the sensitization involved meetings between the KWS and all the stakeholders, the Endorois community included. However, civil society organizations working with indigenous peoples contest this view.[58] The community's objection to their exclusion from the nomination process has been loudly proclaimed to the world through statements at international forums and in letters addressed to UNESCO. Moreover, the KWS, by stating that the Endorois were involved only within the wider rubric of 'local communities', demonstrates that it has not appropriately consulted with or involved the Endorois community in its nomination processes. No evidence of consultation with the Endorois has been presented by KWS, nor that such consultation, if any, was 'informed'.

In spite of the objections of the Endorois community, which were reiterated in an oral statement of an Observer NGO during the World Heritage Committee's session on the day before the vote,[59] the Committee followed the recommendation of its Advisory Body IUCN and inscribed the "Kenya Lake System in the Great Rift Valley" on the World Heritage List. The concerns raised by the Endorois Welfare Council and the other indigenous organizations and NGOs were neither discussed nor mentioned by the Committee before it adopted its decision. In doing so, the Committee also disregarded a plea of the UN Permanent Forum on Indigenous Issues "that the UNESCO World Heritage Committee, and the advisory bodies IUCN, ICOMOS and ICCROM, scrutinize current World Heritage nominations to ensure they comply with international norms and standards of free, prior and informed consent".[60] The Kenyan delegation claimed during the World Heritage Committee's discussions that the site was co-managed by the KWS and the local communities and promised that listing would place management in the hands of the local communities.[61]

Response of the African Commission

The inscription of Lake Bogoria on the World Heritage List without consulting the Endorois was brought to the attention of the African Commission on Human and Peoples' Rights at its 50th

---

56 Letter from KWS Director dated 31 August 2009, addressed to MRG and copied to UNESCO (on file with author).
57 Njoroge and Omanga 2011.
58 See IWGIA, CEMIRIDE, MRG and Endorois Welfare Council 2011.
59 UNESCO 2011, p. 150.
60 UN Permanent Forum on Indigenous Issues 2011, para. 42. The same plea was also made in an oral statement by UNPFII Representative Kanyinke Sena at the World Heritage Committee's session on 22 June 2011, two days before the decision regarding the inscription of the Kenya Lake System was adopted.
61 Information from IWGIA observer Stefan Disko (pers. comm.). Also see UNESCO 2011, p. 162.

Ordinary Session in October 2011. As a result, the Commission adopted a resolution in which it recalled its Endorois Decision and expressed its deep concern that the World Heritage Committee had inscribed Lake Bogoria National Reserve on the World Heritage List "without obtaining the free, prior and informed consent of the Endorois through their own representative institutions, and despite the fact that the Endorois Welfare Council had urged the Committee to defer the nomination because of the lack of meaningful involvement and consultation with the Endorois".[62] In the resolution, the Commission:

> "**Emphasizes** that the inscription of Lake Bogoria on the World Heritage List without involving the Endorois in the decision-making process and without obtaining their free, prior and informed consent contravenes the African Commission's Endorois Decision and constitutes a violation of the Endorois' right to development under Article 22 of the African Charter..."

The resolution urges the World Heritage Committee, UNESCO and IUCN to review and revise their current procedures for evaluating World Heritage nominations and for overseeing the implementation of the World Heritage Convention, with a view to ensuring that indigenous peoples are fully involved in these processes and that their rights are respected, protected and fulfilled in these processes. It also calls on the World Heritage Committee to "consider establishing an appropriate mechanism through which indigenous peoples can provide advice to the World Heritage Committee and effectively participate in its decision-making processes". The Government of Kenya is urged to ensure the full and effective participation of the Endorois, through their own representative institutions, in the decision-making regarding the World Heritage site.[63]

At its 54th Ordinary Session, on 5 November 2013, the African Commission adopted a resolution in which it expressed its concern regarding "the lack of feedback from the Government of Kenya on the measures it has taken to implement the Endorois decision", and called on the Government of Kenya "to inform the Commission of the measures proposed to implement the Endorois decision, and more particularly, the concrete steps taken to engage all the players and stakeholders, including the victims, with a view to giving full effect to the decision."[64] The African Commission also sent a letter to the Director of the World Heritage Centre in which it underlined the need for the World Heritage Committee to "collaborate with the Government of Kenya, UNESCO and IUCN to ensure the effective participation of the Endorois in the management and decision-making of the

---

62 ACHPR Res.197 (L)2011 ("Resolution on the protection of indigenous peoples' rights in the context of the World Heritage Convention and the designation of Lake Bogoria as a World Heritage site"). See Appendix 1 at the end of this volume.
63 Similarly, the World Conservation Congress at its session in Jeju, Republic of Korea (2012) adopted a resolution which "URGES the Government of Kenya to ensure the full and effective participation of the Endorois in the management and decision making of the 'Kenya Lake System' World Heritage area, through their own representative institutions, and to ensure the implementation of the African Commission's Endorois Decision" (Res. 047, *Implementation of the United Nations Declaration on the Rights of Indigenous Peoples in the context of the UNESCO World Heritage Convention*).
64 ACHPR Res. 257 (LIV) 2013: *Resolution Calling on the Republic of Kenya to Implement the Endorois Decision*.

'Kenya Lake System' World Heritage area through their own representative institutions".[65] The World Heritage Centre responded to this letter by saying that it was "discussing with IUCN, the advisory body concerned, on the possibility to address the issue through the *State of Conservation* (SoC) processes with the State Party of Kenya".[66]

Outstanding Universal Value vis-à-vis indigenous values

The Outstanding Universal Value of the Kenya Lake System as adopted by the World Heritage Committee does not readily coincide with or reflect the indigenous values of the area. This is because the processes for nominating the site (including the 'tentative listing') were not done in consultation with the indigenous community. The IUCN evaluators of the nomination, too, failed to consult with the Endorois during their field visit in October 2010 and neither the Endorois community nor the landmark ruling of the African Commission are mentioned in IUCN's Advisory Body Evaluation.[67] As a result, the Statement of Outstanding Universal Value, as drafted by IUCN and adopted by the World Heritage Committee, only represents the wildlife management and conservation values as appreciated by the nominating body, the State Party, Kenya, through its KWS agent. The universality of value of the designated sites is therefore called into question by the failure of the consultation mechanism used by the Kenyan government and its agencies.

The disparity between the values comes as a result of the fact that, for the KWS (and the World Heritage Committee), the primary concern seems to be the management and conservation of the wildlife within the site. However, for the indigenous community, the main concern is on the conservation of resources for the sustenance of the human population. The conflict between these two sets of values can clearly be seen in the clash of interests between the two groups: from the government's point of view, establishing wildlife conservation areas requires the eviction of the community members. For their part, the indigenous community members continually resist such attempts and seek to find ways through which they can mutually co-exist with, as well as exploit, the wildlife for their benefit.

One real challenge that has beset the conservation efforts within the Kenya Lake System area, especially in the region occupied by the indigenous community, is this clash of values. It emanates from the fact that the government's conservation efforts are not usually customized to take into account the unique cultural community values found within the areas where the protected areas are situated. Rather, cultural values may be co-opted at the corporate body's discretion. This is because its mandate is national and is supposed to take care of the country's national or 'universal' values and interests, at the expense of individual community values. Consequently, indigenous

---

65 Letter signed by Commissioner Soyata Maiga, dated 5 November 2013 (on file with author).
66 Response letter from Kishore Rao, Director of the World Heritage Centre dated 3 December 2013 (on file with author).
67 See IUCN 2011, p. 77. According to the Evaluation Report, the field mission only met with representatives of the National Museum of Kenya, KWS, Kenya Forest Service, Baringo and Koibatek Councils, Soysambu Conservancy, Ututu Wildlife Conservation Trust, WWF in Nakuru, local Water Users' Associations, local Conservation Forest associations and representatives of Nakuru town.

community values become compromised as the KWS struggles to put national and international wildlife conservation and management values in place.

Effects of the World Heritage designation on the Endorois

The World Heritage designation of Lake Bogoria occurred so recently that the effects of the listing may not yet be fully apparent. However, considering the adopted Statement of Outstanding Universal Value, it can be speculated that greater efforts will now be geared towards wildlife management and conservation at the expense of indigenous rights and interests. According to the OUV Statement, the Committee considers cattle grazing as one of the main threats to the outstanding universal value of the site: "Surrounded by an area of rapidly growing population, the property is under considerable threat from surrounding pressures. These threats include... [inter alia] overgrazing... Management authorities must be vigilant in continuing to address these issues through effective multi-sector and participatory planning processes." [68] Unless the outstanding universal value is redefined so as to put a blend of natural and cultural World Heritage values in place, it is highly likely that the indigenous community will benefit little from the designation.

One aspect of the nomination that is being emphasized is the likelihood of improved economic activities from a possible increase in tourism. The KWS has stressed that the community's economic well-being is likely to be greatly boosted by the listing. For instance, KWS representative, Dr. James Njogu, has been quoted as saying that the community "stands to benefit from the lakes' new found status as more tourists will visit the sites and provide increased business opportunities".[69] Similar sentiments were expressed by the KWS Chief Warden for Lake Bogoria National Reserve, Mr. William Kimosop, who noted that the publicity generated by the endorsement would lead to more tourists visiting the lakes and that this would spur economic activities in adjacent areas.[70]

However, whether or not any long-term benefits will be achieved by the indigenous community is a question for which an answer is predicated on a number of issues. For instance, with the designation already approved, and depending on how the KWS conducts its marketing of the site, tourism and other related activities may increase substantially. Increased tourism may be a double-edged sword for the indigenous community's economic interests. On the one hand, it may boost the community's economic income if the government implements a suitable benefit-sharing strategy with the community as rights holders. In the absence of such benefit-sharing strategies, however, communities may lose out economically due to the denial of access to pasture for their livestock which translates into a weakened herd that cannot fetch optimal prices at the market.

In any case, the World Heritage designation may be detrimental to the community's economic interests due to the fact that World Heritage status may require an increased level of protection and

---

68 Decision 35 COM 8B.6 (2011), para. 3. In the same decision, the Committee also encourages the State Party to "upgrade the protection of Lake Elementaita through... prohibition of cattle grazing so that it is afforded a similar standard of protection as the other components of the property" (para. 6).
69 Njoroge and Omanga 2011.
70 Ibid.

conservation which, in turn, could lead to the three lakes being upgraded into National Parks. Notably, IUCN has stated in its Advisory Body Evaluation that "National Park designation for all three lakes would provide a more desirable level of protection".[71] This kind of development would sound a death knell for the community's livelihoods as this would mean they would be banished from the parks. As a result of such a decision therefore, the economic interests of the community would become adversely affected, as they were during the years when the government displaced the Endorois to create the Lake Bogoria Game Reserve.

Critical evaluation, conclusions and recommendations

At the moment, we can but guess what lies in store for the people living within the Kenya Lake System area in the future. The inscription of the area as a World Heritage site will bring with it certain challenges whose full effects may simply not be fully fathomable at present. On the one hand, there is a glimmer of hope that the local people may have an enhanced economic status given that the site may witness an increase in tourist activities. This comes with increased foreign exchange earnings for the country. With increased earnings, the local inhabitants should stand to benefit from such resources through a well-planned benefit-sharing strategy by the government.

On the other hand, if the government opts to raise the conservation bar within the site so as to make the lakes National Parks, then the community stands to lose. This is because the people and their livelihoods would be excluded from the protected areas. Consequent upon this, the people's economic prospects would dwindle as their very source of livelihoods would be threatened. This directly contravenes the decision of the ACHPR in the Endorois case, whereby the Commission was emphatic that unless development expanded the "capabilities and choices of the Endorois" it ran counter to the African Charter's right to development.[72]

The hopes and expectations of the people within the World Heritage area, including the Endorois, are presently pervaded by dark clouds of doubt, doubts that emanate from the shroud of mystery that engulfed the KWS' nomination processes for the site in question. The bitter memories of the community's eviction from the land along the shores of Lake Bogoria to pave the way for the establishment of the world famous Lake Bogoria Game Reserve between 1973 and 1986 were no doubt re-awakened by Kenya's unilateral World Heritage nomination, barely a year after the Endorois' legal success in the African Commission. The lack of consultation with the various stakeholders and rights holders during the nomination and inscription, despite the recent landmark ruling of the African Commission, bodes ill for such an important international wildlife management and conservation exercise.

In order for the process to proceed smoothly and with the blessing, particularly, of the Endorois, there is a need for the full engagement, through dialogue, of everyone who is deemed a stakeholder

---

71 IUCN 2011, p. 80.
72 ACHPR 2009 (Endorois decision), para 283.

or rights holder. While the indigenous community has emphasized this in several communications sent to UNESCO, the relevant UN agency responsible for this very important process, no effective action has been taken to date.[73]

In proceeding to inscribe Kenya's great lakes as a World Heritage site without first obtaining the consent of the Endorois, the World Heritage Committee has committed an egregious error. However, this unsatisfactory outcome must serve as a lesson to UNESCO and the World Heritage Committee in their future dealings. They need to ensure that indigenous peoples and communities are fully involved during the nomination and designation processes, in accordance with their rights under international law, as urged by the African Commission at its 50th session. The entire attendant processes need to be consultative, transparent and all-inclusive. An important first step in this direction was taken by the World Heritage Committee at its 35th session in 2011, when it adopted a decision in which it encourages States Parties to "Involve indigenous peoples and local communities in decision making, monitoring and evaluation of the state of conservation of the properties and their Outstanding Universal Value" and to "Respect the rights of indigenous peoples when nominating, managing and reporting on World Heritage sites in indigenous peoples' territories".[74]

The Kenyan government, through KWS and other state organizations such as KENGEN, must stop the cavalier manner in which they treat indigenous rights holders. The indigenous communities must now be engaged as true partners in decision-making processes, and not as the 'inconsequential other' whose needs and interests can be dispensed with at will. In addition, UNESCO and the World Heritage Committee must find ways to ensure that World Heritage nominations are consultative processes and not unilateral ones whose pace and content are determined only by the government, as happened with the Kenya Lake System. The World Heritage Committee may, for instance, make it a requirement that all future nomination documents are accompanied by statements of prior informed consent from the affected communities, whether indigenous or not.

With regard to the Kenya Lake System, UNESCO and the World Heritage Committee still have a very central role to play. Of utmost urgency, they need to insist that the Government of Kenya fully implement the African Commission's Endorois decision without further delay, and ensure the effective participation of the Endorois in the management and decision-making of the Lake Bogoria World Heritage area, through their own representative institutions. They also need to insist on the need for suitable mechanisms to be put in place by the Government of Kenya to ensure that the Endorois community receives appropriate economic benefits from the activities within the World Heritage area. The Committee should also promote the re-listing of the Kenya Lake System as a mixed cultural/natural site. The universal wildlife conservation values espoused by the government

---

73 More recently, the Endorois Welfare Council and some of its partners sent a letter to the World Heritage Centre on 18 November 2013 (on file with author) requesting that UNESCO and IUCN raise the Endorois' concerns with the World Heritage Committee in the form of a State of Conservation (SOC) report on the Kenya Lake System. The Centre did send a response to this letter (with a copy to the Kenyan authorities), saying that they would discuss this possibility with IUCN. At the same time, the Centre "encourage[d] the Endorois, their representative institutions and the Kenyan national authorities ... for dialogue in order to seek resolution to the situation, including strengthened involvement of the Endorois through the Endorois' representative institutions in the management and decision-making processes of the property". Letter from the Director of the World Heritage Centre, dated 3 December 2013 (on file with author).
74 Decision 35 COM 12E (2011), para. 15.

agency, KWS, could in this way be infused with cultural ones stemming from the indigenous community. If this were done, then the hard-line positions adopted by both players would thaw considerably, ensuring that every player in the conservation process is brought on board.   ○

Postscript by the editors

On 16 May 2014 the World Heritage Centre and IUCN submitted a report on the state of conservation (SOC) of the Kenya Lake System to the World Heritage Committee, noting that the Centre had been "informed by the African Commission on Human and Peoples' Rights (ACHPR) about the lack of free, prior and informed consent from the Endorois community for the inscription of Lake Bogoria on the World Heritage List, and concerns on the lack of participation of the Endorois in management and decision making". The report drew attention to the resolutions of the ACHPR with regard to the recognition of rights of the Endorois in relation to Lake Bogoria and recommended that the World Heritage Committee at its 38th Session in Doha, Qatar in June 2014 adopt a decision "urg[ing] the State Party to respond to the ACHPR regarding these resolutions and to ensure full and effective participation of the Endorois in the management and decision-making of the property, and in particular the Lake Bogoria component, through their own representative institutions".[75] The report also contained a corresponding draft decision which was adopted by the Committee on 18 June 2014 without changes.[76]

Already before the Committee meeting, on 26 May 2014, representatives of the Endorois Welfare Council and the various Kenyan Government agencies involved in the management of Lake Bogoria signed a Memorandum of Understanding (MoU) entitled *Kabarnet Declaration on Lake Bogoria National Reserve as a World Heritage Site* which appears to have been facilitated by the intervention of UNESCO and IUCN through the SOC process. The MoU recognizes in its Preamble the creation of Lake Bogoria National Reserve and its listing as a World Heritage site. At the same time it recognizes that "Lake Bogoria is part of the Endorois Community ancestral land" and that "their involvement in the management is paramount". It then goes on to establish that Lake Bogoria National Reserve is to be managed through a Management Committee comprising "Baringo County Government, Endorois Welfare Council, Kenya Wildlife Service and National Museums of Kenya and any other entity that shall be deemed relevant", which would deal among other things with issues relating to the conservation and management of the reserve as a Ramsar and World Heritage site; revenue allocation and benefit sharing; and resolution of management conflicts. The MoU explicitly states that "[t]he Endorois people are formally recognized as a community and any decision making concerning them must have free, prior and informed consent (FPIC)" and that "Endorois Welfare Council shall be the officially recognized organization of Endorois community in the management of the Lake Bogoria National Reserve". The MoU also affirms that "[c]ommunity sites (e.g. sacred sites) within the Reserve and its catchment areas will remain accessible to the community…"

---

75 UNESCO 2014, pp. 112-113.
76 Decision 38 COM 7B.91.

This MoU provides a basis for the development of an improved management framework for Lake Bogoria National Reserve and the recognition of the need to obtain the free, prior and informed consent of the Endorois in any decision-making concerning them is a highly positive step. However, the extent to which the new Management Committee will give the Endorois a real voice and decision-making power in the management of the Reserve, and ensure an equitable sharing of the benefits arising from the Reserve, remains to be seen.

References

ACHPR. 2009. *Communication 276/2003 – Centre for Minority Rights Development (Kenya) and Minority Rights Group International on behalf of Endorois Welfare Council v Kenya*. Decision of the African Commission on Human and Peoples' Rights, adopted in November 2009, endorsed by the African Union on 2 February 2010. 27th Activity Report of the ACHPR (2009), Annex 5.

ACHPR. 2011. *Resolution on the protection of indigenous peoples' rights in the context of the World Heritage Convention and the designation of Lake Bogoria as a World Heritage site*. ACHPR Res.197 (L)2011. Adopted by the African Commission on Human and Peoples' Rights at its 50th Ordinary Session, on 5 November 2011.

ACHPR. 2013. *Resolution Calling on the Republic of Kenya to Implement the Endorois Decision*. ACHPR Res. 257 (LIV) 2013. Adopted by the African Commission on Human and Peoples' Rights at its 54th Ordinary Session, on 5 November 2013.

CEMIRIDE. 2003. *Centre for Minority Rights Development (CEMIRIDE) on behalf of the Endorois Community v. Kenya* (Communication No. 276/2003 to the African Commission on Human and Peoples' Rights).

Committee on the Elimination of Racial Discrimination. 1997. *General Recommendation No. 23: Indigenous Peoples* (1997), UN Doc. A/52/18, Annex V.

County Council of Baringo and County Council of Koibatek. 2007. *Lake Bogoria National Reserve Integrated Management Plan 2007 – 2012.*

Endorois Welfare Council and Minority Rights Group International. 2011. *Statement at the 50th Ordinary Session of the African Commission on Human and Peoples' Rights, 24th October 2011 to 7th November 2011, Sheraton Hotel, Banjul, The Gambia*. Available at: http://www.iwgia.org/images/stories/int-processes-eng/achpr/docs/sessions/50/statement%20mrg%20ewc.pdf.

Endorois Welfare Council et al. 2011. *Joint statement on continuous violations of the principle of free, prior and informed consent in the context of UNESCO's World Heritage Convention*. UN Permanent Forum on Indigenous Issues, Tenth Session, 17 May 2011. Available at: http://www.docip.org/gsdl/collect/cendocdo/index/assoc/HASH018c/e07e9861.dir/PF11miliani080.pdf.

Garner, A. B. (ed.). 2004. *Black's Law Dictionary*. St. Paul: Thomson West Publishing Co.

High Court of Kenya. 1999. *William Ngasia and Others v Baringo County Council and Others*, High Court Miscellaneous Civil Case No. 159 of 1999 (ruling of June 12, 1999).

High Court of Kenya. 2000. *William Yatich Sitetalia & others v. Baringo County Council & others*, High Court Civil Case No.183 of 2000 (judgement of 19 April 2002).

IUCN. 2011. *World Heritage Nomination – IUCN Technical Evaluation: Kenya Lakes System in the Great Rift Valley (Kenya)*, UNESCO Doc. WHC-11/35.COM/INF.8B2, pp. 75-85.

IWGIA, CEMIRIDE, MRG and Endorois Welfare Council. 2011. *Joint Submission on the right of indigenous peoples to participate in decision-making in the context of UNESCO's 1972 World Heritage Convention*, UN Expert Mechanism on the Rights of Indigenous Peoples, Fourth Session, 12 July 2011. Available at: www.docip.org/gsdl/collect/cendocdo/index/assoc/HASH7f9e/b4476744.dir/EM11stefan078.pdf.

Kavilu, S. 2011. Indigenous Endorois Call for Implementation of African Commission Ruling on Their Ancestral Land. *Gáldu*, 24 January 2011. http://www.galdu.org/web/index.php?odas=5087&giella1=eng (accessed 10 January 2012).

Kimathi, N. 2008. Kenya: Horticulture Takes Lead as Foreign Exchange Earner. *The Standard.*, 26 March 2008. http://allafrica.com/stories/200803251162.html (accessed 10 January 2012).

Kiprotich, A. 2010. Endorois finally return to their family land. *The Standard*, 21 March 2010. http://www.standardmedia.co.ke/archives/education/InsidePage.php?id=2000006093&cid=4& (accessed 10 January 2012).

Koigi wa Wamwere. 2010. Why Nakuru can never become a county for one ethnic community. *Daily Nation*, 8 September 2010. http://www.nation.co.ke/oped/Opinion/Why%20Nakuru%20can%20never%20become%20a%20county%20for%20one%20ethnic%20community%20/-/440808/1006536/-/2nskgc/-/index.html (accessed 10 January 2012).

Minority Rights Group International. 2009. *Kenyan authorities bid for Lake Bogoria heritage status without consulting true custodians of land.* Website news item, 6 June 2009. http://www.minorityrights.org/6780/trouble-in-paradise/whats-new.html (accessed 10 January 2012).

National Museums of Kenya and Kenya Wildlife Service. 2010. *Greater Lake Elmenteita Conservation Area Management Plan 2010-2020.*

Njoroge, K. and Omanga, B. 2011. At last, Kenyan Lakes get Global Protection. *The Standard*, 3 July 2011. http://www.standardmedia.co.ke/InsidePage.php?id=2000038321&cid=4& (accessed 10 January 2012).

Northern Rangelands Trust. 2012. Community Institutional Development (website text). http://www.nrt-kenya.org/institutional.html (accessed 10 January 2012).

Okoth, D. 2011. Cheers turn to tears for Endorois waiting for land. *The Standard*, 17 June 2011. http://www.standardmedia.co.ke/specialreports/InsidePage.php?id=2000037356&cid=259& (accessed 10 January 2012).

Republic of Kenya. 2010. *Nomination Proposal – Kenya Lakes System in the Great Rift Valley (Elementaita, Nakuru and Bogoria).* Available at http://whc.unesco.org/en/list/1060/documents/.

Senelwa, K. 2011. Govt invites bids for steam power plants at the Bogoria-Silali block. *The East African*, 28 March 2011. http://www.theeastafrican.co.ke/business/-/2560/1133308/-/bukqamz/-/index.html (accessed 10 January 2012).

UNESCO. 2011. *World Heritage Committee, Thirty-fifth Session, Paris, UNESCO Headquarters, 19-29 June 2011: Summary Record.* Doc. WHC-11/35.COM.INF.20.

UNESCO. 2014. *Item 7B of the Provisional Agenda: State of conservation of World Heritage properties inscribed on the World Heritage List* (World Heritage Committee, 38th Session). UNESCO Doc. WHC-14/38.COM/7B.Add.

UN Expert Mechanism on the Rights of Indigenous Peoples. 2011. *Expert Mechanism advice No. 2 (2011): Indigenous peoples and the right to participate in decision-making.* UN Doc. A/HRC/18/42, 17 August 2011, Annex.

UN Permanent Forum on Indigenous Issues. 2011. *Report on the tenth session (16-27 May 2011).* UN Doc. E/C.19/2011/14.

World Heritage Committee. 2011a. Decision 35 COM 8B.6 (Inscription: Kenya Lake System in the Great Rift Valley). Doc. WHC-11/35.COM/20, 7 July 2011, p. 171 ff.

World Heritage Committee. 2011b. Decision 35 COM 12E (Global state of conservation challenges of World Heritage properties). Doc. WHC-11/35.COM/20, p. 270 ff.

World Heritage Committee. 2014. Decision 38 COM 7B.91 (Kenya Lake System in the Great Rift Valley). Doc. WHC-14/38.COM/16, p. 143 f.

World Wildlife Federation. 2004. *Lake Bogoria National Reserve Draft Management Plan*, July 2004.

A World Heritage Site in the Ngorongoro Conservation Area: Whose World? Whose Heritage?

William Olenasha

Introduction

The Ngorongoro Conservation Area (NCA) is a multiple land-use area in the north of Tanzania that was excised from Serengeti National Park in 1959 as a compromise deal between the resident Maasai pastoralists and the British colonial administration. While the Maasai pastoralists were forced to vacate Serengeti National Park following years of campaigning by international conservation organizations, they were guaranteed the right to continue to use and occupy the adjacent NCA, where wildlife conservation was to be reconciled with the rights of the Maasai in a multiple land-use context.[1] Specifically, the NCA was conceived as a "special conservation unit, administered by Government, with the object of conserving water supplies, forest and pasture – primarily in the interests of man, but with due regard for the preservation of wild animal life".[2] It did not appear to the Maasai at the time that life in their newly-created home in Ngorongoro would soon be as restricted as if it were another national park.

---

1   See Shetler 2007, pp. 209 f.; Dowie 2009, p. 24 ff.
2   Parliament of Tanganyika 1959.

Left: Maasai boy driving a cattle herd through Ngorongoro Crater. Photo: Nicor (CC BY-SA 3.0)

The designation of the area as a World Natural Heritage site two decades later in 1979 did not serve to make life better for the Maasai but, on the contrary, led to fresh conservation standards being added to the burden of human development. The human rights situation of the resident pastoralists and hunter-gatherers in the area has deteriorated in parallel with the extra-conservation standards accorded to their land.

In a 1998 study on Maasai rights in Ngorongoro, law professors Issa Shivji and Wilbert Kapinga emphasized that:

> "The problems and predicament of the Maasai residents in the Area relate to the special, internationally significant conservation and tourist status accorded to their home. The Conservation Area is on UNESCO's World Heritage List and is a Biosphere Reserve. It is probably the most important tourist attraction, yielding the highest foreign-exchange income, in the tourism sector. These virtues of their homeland have not necessarily been a boon to the human rights of the residents... It is with this as a backdrop, that the human rights of the Maasai residents, both as a community, as individuals and as citizens, have come under severe stress." [3]

In 2010, another conservation standard was added to the area when the NCA was inscribed on the World Heritage List as a cultural site on account of its rich historical, palaeontological and archaeological characteristics. While this extra conservation 'medal' may work to draw additional tourists to see rock paintings at Nasera Rock and to hear stories of our ancestors who once lived a million years ago in Olduvai Gorge, it also means an extra burden for pastoralists who, once again, have to observe additional restrictions on their activities in their lands. Like the original World Heritage designation, the inscription as a cultural site was done without the free, prior and informed consent of the local communities, in contravention of the requirements stated in regional and international human rights law. Simultaneous recognition of the cultural significance of the Maasai cultural landscape in Ngorongoro was explicitly rejected by the World Heritage Committee.[4]

The World Heritage listings have led to a rearrangement of management priorities and have undermined the multiple land-use philosophy of the Conservation Area at the expense of the Maasai residents. While this has clearly not helped to address the complexity of issues in Ngorongoro in a balanced and sustainable manner, factors such as human population growth,[5] wild

---

3 Shivji and Kapinga 1998, p. 5.
4 ICOMOS 2010.
5 Since the World Heritage inscription in 1979, the human population of the NCA has risen from around 20,000 to over 80,000. It is important to note, however, that in spite of this population increase, the number of cattle has remained more or less the same, resulting in a substantial decrease in livestock per capita (UNESCO and IUCN 2009, p. 11).

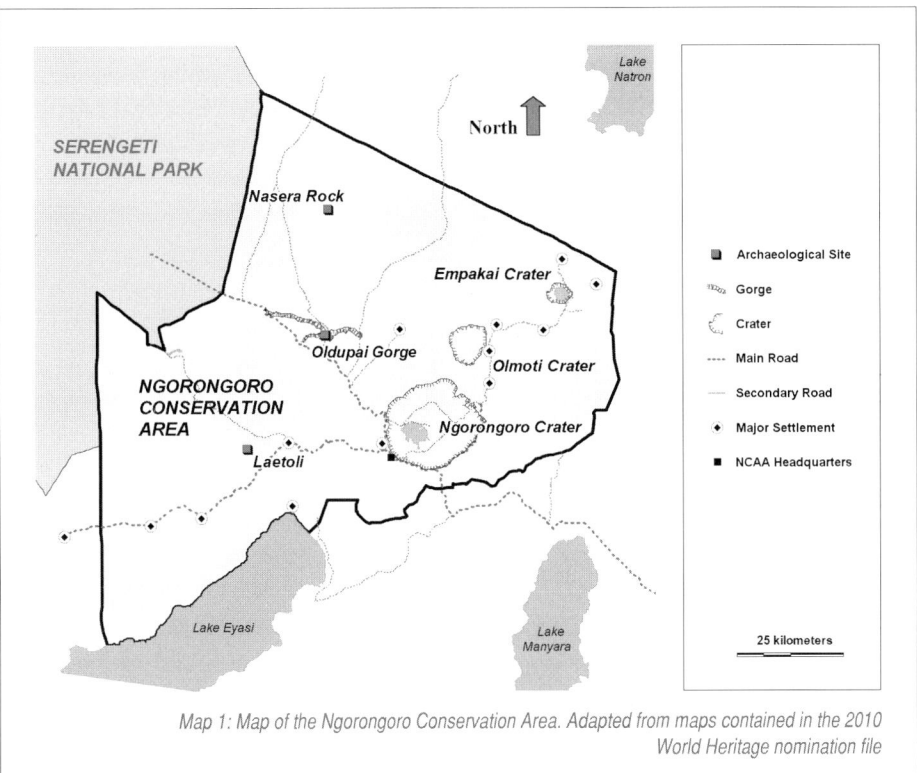

Map 1: Map of the Ngorongoro Conservation Area. Adapted from maps contained in the 2010 World Heritage nomination file

animal numbers[6] and the huge increase in tourists[7] are imposing serious management challenges on the conservation area. The involvement and participation of local people in finding workable solutions to these challenges has been and continues to be totally insufficient.

This article is therefore an account of the Ngorongoro Conservation Area as both a home for the local people and for wildlife, and as a 'World Heritage site'. The article begins with a brief historical account of the area as a home for pastoralists, agro-pastoralists and hunter-gatherers. It then evaluates the situation of the indigenous people following the inscription of the area on the World Heritage List, detailing their level of participation in different decision-making processes. Finally, a few recommendations are given as to what could be a feasible solution to the present

---

6 The NCA is home to a population of some 25,000 large animals and also supports one of the largest animal migrations on earth, including well over 1 million wildebeest, 72,000 zebras and 350,000 Thompson and Grant gazelles. Wildebeest numbers expanded from approximately 240,000 to 1,600,000 following the creation of the NCA, due to the removal of Maasai cattle from the Serengeti and the eradication of rinderpest. The huge increase in wildebeest numbers has brought serious problems for the pastoralists, as wildebeest carry a virus which transmits a disease that kills cattle, and less grazing is available for Maasai cattle in the dry season (McCabe 2002, p. 69f.; Homewood and Rodgers 1991).

7 Since the designation of the NCA as a World Heritage site in 1979, visitor numbers have risen steadily, from about 20,000 per year in 1979 to more than 500,000 in 2008 (UNESCO and IUCN 2007, p. 12 and 2009, p. 13).

problems, complexities and challenges in the NCA. A central question will be whose world and whose heritage it is that matters.

The peoples of the area

The history of indigenous peoples in the area now covered by the Ngorongoro Conservation Area predates the modern era. The interaction between people and wildlife has been ongoing for thousands of years. From palaeontological and archaeological discoveries, it is believed that pre-human hominids lived in the area at least 3.5 million years ago.[8] The first peoples to inhabit the area were hunter-gatherers, probably ancestors of the present-day Hadza who live in the Mangola area of the NCA. Peoples following a pastoral lifestyle are very recent occupiers of the area but there is concrete evidence to suggest that they have been there for at least 2,000 years.[9] According to one source, a rough date of 2,000-2,500 years ago seems to be appropriate for the emergence of pastoralism in Ngorongoro.[10] The Barbaig (Datog) are said to have inhabited the Ngorongoro Crater Highlands by 1000-1500 AD.[11] The long occupation by the Datog is even acknowledged by the Maasai, who still refer to Ngorongoro Highlands as the 'Oldoinyo Laltatua' (the Mountain of the Datog). The Maasai are more recent occupiers, having moved into the area around 1830-1850, displacing the Datog.

As a home for pastoralists, the NCA must be discussed in connection with Serengeti National Park. Both these areas used to form part of a wider landscape within which pastoralism thrived. The plains in the Serengeti and highlands in Ngorongoro collectively provided a perfect environment for practicing pastoralism, balancing the potential of each landscape at different seasons of the year. Maasai pastoralists would graze in the dry season in the Western Serengeti but retreat to the highlands and low grass plains during the rainy season, and especially during the calving of the wildebeest. The Western Serengeti, and especially the area near Moru Kopjes, provided a good grazing environment in the dry season with the availability of permanent rivers and springs. This was the livelihood of Maasai pastoralists in Ngorongoro before an agreement to alter this arrangement was arrived at in 1958.

The Anglo-Maasai Agreement to vacate the Serengeti in 1958

The process which saw the eventual eviction of the Maasai from the Serengeti began with the creation of Serengeti National Park in 1940.[12] When Serengeti National Park was created, certain restrictions were imposed on human activities but they did not affect the customary land rights of the Maasai significantly. While hunting was prohibited and entry by persons not ordinarily resident in the Park was restricted, the

---

8   Homewood and Rodgers 1991, p. 34.
9   Ibid., p. 33-34.
10   Ibid., p. 57.
11   Ibid., p. 59.
12   Under the *Game Ordinance* of 1940.

Maasai pastoralists' rights to grazing, cultivation and residence were not touched.[13] However, despite the recognition of these rights by the subsequent *National Parks Act*,[14] pressure mounted from different angles[15] to restrict human activities in Serengeti National Park. At the beginning of the 1950s, efforts by the Trustees of Serengeti National Park to persuade pastoralists to vacate the Park met with stiff resistance as people did not want to relinquish their critical grazing and water sources in the Park.

The colonial government itself was divided as to whether the Maasai should leave the Park or not. For some officers, the Maasai were not destructive to the Park as they did not farm or hunt. Others felt that the presence of the Maasai was important for tourism purposes in the Park. The latter, it appears, considered that the Maasai should only be allowed to live in the Park as long as international visitors wanted to view them alongside the wildlife. The Governor of Tanganyika espoused this position and is recorded as saying that, for the Maasai to remain in the Serengeti, they had to be prepared to become a "museum exhibit, living in a kind of human national park".[16] Similarly, the Commissioner of the Northern Province wanted the Maasai in Ngorongoro badly since "they are the most interesting feature of the crater for tourists to photograph".[17] After a long debate between the Maasai and the functionaries of the colonial government at different levels, it was finally agreed that the bigger Serengeti-Ngorongoro area would be divided into two parts. While the Serengeti would be kept for exclusive wildlife protection, Ngorongoro would be excised from the National Park and developed in the interests of both nature conservation and the people who lived there. The agreement was made on 21 April 1958 between 12 representatives of the Maasai and the representatives of the British colonial government. In this agreement, the Maasai renounced their claims and rights to Serengeti National Park in exchange for a solemn pledge by the government that they would be "permitted to continue to follow or modify their traditional way of life subject only to close control of hunting" in the Ngorongoro Conservation Area.[18]

Under this agreement, the Maasai were expected to have moved out of Serengeti National Park by 31 December 1959 and in the main they had moved by the deadline. Some force was used against those who remained past the deadline, and all were considered gone by the end of 1960.[19] It is the practice in literature today to regard the occasion a negotiated settlement between the Maasai and the British, and a relocation that was consented to by the Maasai. However it is important to note the context of the negotiations and the fact that the Maasai did not have many options at their disposal when pitted against the will of the strong colonial administrators supported by a sustained international conservation campaign that wanted the Serengeti free of people. The fact that it took almost eight

---

13 Shivji and Kapinga 1998, pp. 7-8.
14 No. 7 of 1948.
15 Especially from the wildlife lobby in Europe and Africa, such as IUCN, the Wildlife Societies of Kenya and Tanganyika, the Fauna Preservation Society, the Frankfurt Zoological Society, the Nature Conservancy, etc.
16 Quoted in Shetler 2007, p. 208.
17 Quoted in Shetler 2007, p. 208.
18 Tanganyika *Government Paper No. 5 of 1958: Proposals for Reconstituting the Serengeti National Park.* Quoted in Shivji and Kapinga 1998, p. 9.
19 According to the late Lazaro Moringe Parkipuny, physical force was only used to remove people who did not move by the agreed deadline. By some accounts, the people were only completely out of the Serengeti by 1960 (Shetler 2007, p. 210).

years for any settlement to be recorded stands as testimony to the resistance that the indigenous people put up against being removed from their land. In the end, they did not have much choice, they had to sign the agreement because otherwise they risked losing everything, they risked being kicked out of the Serengeti in exchange for nothing or for some token financial compensation. In any case the terms of the compromise agreement were unbalanced, considering that the Maasai had to leave the rich resources in Moru Kopjes and the central Serengeti Plains in exchange for limited pastoral resources in the Ngorongoro Highlands and, even there, they were not completely free from restrictions. For the Maasai, this meant relinquishing a very important part of their pastoral resources, which had serious effects on the pastoralist grazing rhythm.

New lives in Ngorongoro

Vacating Serengeti National Park meant that the Maasai pastoralists were living in a much smaller area in the Ngorongoro Conservation Area, and had lost critical pastures and water sources in the Serengeti. In anticipation of this, and in compensation for their lost access to the Serengeti, the colonial government promised rights and services within the Ngorongoro Conservation Area, including water and veterinary services. Although this promise was not captured in the written version of the agreement, it is clear from available literature and from various pronouncements of officers of the colonial government.[20]

A 1959 speech of the Governor of Tanganyika to the Maasai Federal Council is often cited as the most authoritative when it comes to said compensation schemes:

> "Another matter which closely concerns the Masai is the new scheme for the protection of the Ngorongoro Crater. I should like to make it clear to you all that it is the intention of the Government to develop the Crater in the interests of the people who use it. At the same time the Government intends to protect the game animals of the area, *but should there be any conflict between the interests of the game and the human inhabitants, those of the latter must take precedence.* The Government is ready to start work on increasing the waters and improving the grazing ranges of the Crater and the country around it; for your part you must take care to fulfil the agreements into which you have entered to keep the countryside in good heart. You must not destroy the forests, nor may you graze your cattle in areas which have been closed under any controlled grazing scheme; at the same time you must be certain to follow veterinary instructions designed to prevent disease." [21]

The above proclamation of the Governor formed the basis of the first management plan for the NCA, the 1960 Management Plan, which sought to integrate the development needs of the Maasai and

---

20 Homewood and Rodgers 1991, p. 71; Parkipuny 1991, p. 22; Shivji and Kapinga 1998, pp. 9-10. For the written version of the agreement, see Shivji and Kapinga 1998, p. 74.
21 Quoted in Homewood and Rodgers 1991, p. 72 (emphasis added).

the requirements of conservation. In what looks like a departure from the agreement of 1958, the Governor's proclamation introduced a very important caveat, that pastoralists also had to respect environmental laws and regulations. If these restrictions had been discussed at the time of the negotiations, they would have certainly made the negotiations between the colonial government and pastoralists difficult, but such discussions are absent from the record. This U-turn had a significant and lasting impact on the character of the NCA. While pastoralists and other resident communities could still live in the area, they could only do so if they did not interfere in any significant way with the conservation of wild animals and the environment. It is not surprising, therefore, that when a law was passed to govern Ngorongoro in 1959, the long title to the law was purely about conservation:

> "An ordinance to control entry into and residence within the Ngorongoro Crater Highlands Area, to make provision for the conservation and development of natural resources therein and for purposes connected therewith." [22]

As will become evident in the coming pages, the conflict between conservation and human development characterises the better part of the 50-year history of the Conservation Area and, indeed, is even threatening the very existence of the multiple land-use concept. In fact, it can be said that this land-use concept has failed in Ngorongoro.

Designation of Ngorongoro as a World Heritage site

The history and present situation of Ngorongoro cannot be understood without reference to the international status that has been accorded to it by being designated a UNESCO World Heritage site and a UNESCO biosphere reserve.

Ngorongoro became a natural World Heritage site in 1979 when it was inscribed on the World Heritage List under criteria (vii), (viii), (ix) and (x). In 2010, the area was additionally inscribed under cultural criterion (iv) in recognition of its palaeontological and archaeological significance, thus becoming a 'mixed' site. Although the Government of Tanzania had applied for simultaneous recognition of the NCA's significance as a Maasai cultural landscape, this was wholly rejected by the World Heritage Committee following a negative and highly biased assessment of its advisory body for cultural sites, ICOMOS.[23]

The justification for inscription contained in the Statement of Outstanding Universal Value adopted by the World Heritage Committee in 2010 is reproduced in Box 1 below.

---

22 The *Ngorongoro Conservation Area Act, 1959* (Cap 413).
23 See ICOMOS 2010. In addition to criticizing the low quality of the information on the Maasai cultural landscape provided by the Tanzanian government in the nomination dossier, ICOMOS found fault with the fact that "pastoralism within the Conservation area has now been significantly changed into agro-pastoralism through the impact of population growth and other factors", that the "largely settled communities now rely for food on agricultural produce as well as on resources from their animals", and that the Maasai "have recently begun keeping camels, although this is not traditional". Hence, the conclusion was that the 'Maasai pastoral landscape' did not satisfy the conditions of integrity and authenticity and that the Maasai in Ngorongoro were "neither a unique nor an exceptional testimony to… pastoralist traditions".

Criterion (iv): Ngorongoro Conservation Area has yielded an exceptionally long sequence of crucial evidence related to human evolution and human-environment dynamics, collectively extending from four million years ago to the beginning of this era, including physical evidence of the most important benchmarks in human evolutionary development. Although the interpretation of many of the assemblages of Olduvai Gorge is still debatable, their extent and density are remarkable. Several of the type fossils in the hominin lineage come from this site. Furthermore, future research in the property is likely to reveal much more evidence concerning the rise of anatomically modern humans, modern behavior and human ecology.

Criterion (vii): The stunning landscape of Ngorongoro Crater combined with its spectacular concentration of wildlife is one of the greatest natural wonders of the planet. Spectacular wildebeest numbers (well over 1 million animals) pass through the property as part of the annual migration of wildebeest across the Serengeti ecosystem and calve in the short grass plains which straddle the Ngorongoro Conservation Area/Serengeti National Park boundary. This constitutes a truly superb natural phenomenon.

Criterion (viii): Ngorongoro crater is the largest unbroken caldera in the world. The crater, together with the Olmoti and Empakaai craters are part of the eastern Rift Valley, whose volcanism dates back to the late Mesozoic / early Tertiary periods and is famous for its geology. The property also includes Laetoli and Olduvai Gorge, which contain an important palaeontological record related to human evolution.

Criterion (ix): The variations in climate, landforms and altitude have resulted in several overlapping ecosystems and distinct habitats, with short grass plains, highland catchment forests, savanna woodlands, montane long grass plains and high open moorlands. The property is part of the Serengeti ecosystem, one of the last intact ecosystems in the world which harbours large and spectacular animal migrations.

Criterion (x): Ngorongoro Conservation Area is home to a population of some 25,000 large animals, mostly ungulates, alongside the highest density of mammalian predators in Africa including the densest known population of lion (estimated 68 in 1987). The property harbours a range of endangered species, such as the Black Rhino, Wild hunting dog and Golden Cat and 500 species of birds. It also supports one of the largest animal migrations on earth, including over 1 million wildebeest, 72,000 zebras and c.350,000 Thompson and Grant gazelles.[24]

Box 1: Justification for inscription of the NCA as a World Heritage site

---

24 Statement of Outstanding Universal Value, in World Heritage Committee Decision 34COM 8B.13 (2010).

Zebras and wildebeest in Ngorongoro Crater. The NCA supports one of the largest annual animal migrations on earth, including well over 1 million wildebeest. Photo: Philip Sheldrake (CC BY-SA 2.0)

The inscription of the NCA as a World Heritage site under such a diversity of natural and cultural criteria makes the area very special and it stands out as one of the few 'mixed' World Heritage areas in the world. However, being a World Heritage site does not come without a price; it usually means that stricter standards of conservation and care must be put in place with a view to maintaining this status. For a multiple land-use area such as the NCA, where people are supposed to be a part of the conservation equation, it means that the people's development and livelihoods must be carried out with the World Heritage site status in mind. More restrictions have therefore been imposed on human activities in the conservation area, justified on the grounds of it being a World Heritage site. In particular, human activities have been restricted so that no major alteration to the 'naturalness' of the area will occur. Moreover, there are clear indications that the designation as a cultural World Heritage site in 2010 will lead to further restrictions (discussed below). This is problematic because the additional conservation status of 'World Heritage site' and the corresponding degrees of care and resulting restrictions were not contemplated when the NCA was created as a multiple land-use area in 1959.

To make things worse, the resident population were not consulted in any way in the processes leading to the World Heritage inscriptions, either in 1979 or in 2010. Perhaps in both cases, the lack of involvement was deliberate as the government knew that the residents would have strongly resisted the inscriptions since, for them, agreeing would have amounted to welcoming new restrictions on the pastoral and human activities in the Conservation Area.

The lack of consultation with the Maasai is particularly striking in the case of the 2010 nomination, which included a bid for the living culture of the Maasai to be recognized as an integral part of the NCA's outstanding universal value (albeit a very half-hearted bid, as also observed by IUCN in its evaluation of the proposal: "The nomination document notes the interaction of the Maasai with the landscape of Ngorongoro, but this appears to be very much a secondary consideration, relative to the palaeontological sites related to human evolution."[25]) The lack of involvement of the Maasai in the preparation of the nomination had significant effects on the quality and accuracy of the sections on the culture and role of the Maasai. Overall, these sections are marked by misrepresentations and omissions, a fact that may well have affected the outcome of the World Heritage Committee's decision. ICOMOS lamented in its evaluation that: "Details on history are only provided in the nomination dossier for the archaeological sites – no material is provided for the Maasai pastoral landscape or on the history of the Ngorongoro Conservation Area", that "No information is provided on the organization of grazing grounds, on the traditional or more modern grazing arrangements, or on how numbers of livestock are managed", and that "no substantial details or justification has been put forward to show that a robust pastoral system still exists or indeed is fostered".[26] Had the Maasai been effectively involved in the elaboration of the proposal, this important information could have easily been included.

While the inscription in 1979 was done at a time when the rights of indigenous peoples were only just beginning to be recognized in international law, and consulting indigenous peoples was not a matter of legal obligation for international organizations like UNESCO, the inscription in 2010 was done three years after the United Nations had adopted the *UN Declaration on the Rights of Indigenous Peoples* (UNDRIP). This Declaration requires, among other things, that governments and international organizations involve indigenous peoples in decision-making processes on issues that affect their lives. The African Commission on Human and Peoples' Rights (ACHPR) has recently passed an important resolution in which it recalls the UNDRIP and objects to the 2011 inscription of Lake Bogoria in Kenya on the World Heritage List without the involvement of the indigenous peoples of the area. In this resolution, the African Commission:

> "**Not[es] with concern** that there are numerous World Heritage sites in Africa that have been inscribed without the free, prior and informed consent of the indigenous peoples in whose territories they are located and whose management frameworks are not consistent with the principles of the UN Declaration on the Rights of Indigenous Peoples; ... [and]
>
> **Emphasizes** that the inscription of Lake Bogoria on the World Heritage List without involving the Endorois in the decision-making process and without obtaining their free, prior and informed consent... constitutes a violation of the Endorois' right to development under Article 22 of the African Charter [on Human and Peoples' Rights]" [27]

---

25 IUCN 2010, p. 189.
26 ICOMOS 2010, pp. 65, 68.
27 *Resolution on the Protection of Indigenous Peoples' Rights in the Context of the World Heritage Convention and the Designation of Lake Bogoria as a World Heritage Site*, adopted on 5 November 2011.

Undoubtedly, these same concerns also apply to the World Heritage designations of the Ngorongoro Conservation Area. In the case of the listing as a cultural site in 2010, the lack of involvement of the Maasai in the nomination process and the absence of their free, prior and informed consent was even noted by IUCN in its technical evaluation of the nomination,[28] however, this was clearly not seen as a concern by the World Heritage Committee and ICOMOS and had no effect on the Committee's decision.

The potential impacts of a failure to appropriately involve indigenous peoples in inscription processes are significant, as Stefan Disko underscores:

> "the justification for inscription... affects management priorities and frameworks, and if the indigenous peoples' own values are not properly taken into account, this can have major implications for them... For example, if a site is inscribed and protected as a natural site, without recognizing the existence and role of the indigenous inhabitants, this can lead to all kinds of restrictions on their land-use practices and undermine their ways of life. It can lead to a loss of control over their lands and can have significant consequences for their ability to maintain and strengthen their cultures and traditions and develop their societies in accordance with their own aspirations and needs." [29]

The new inscription of the NCA as a cultural World Heritage site without the involvement and participation of the local indigenous people, and without due consideration of their cultural values and priorities, can have a range of adverse impacts on their livelihoods.

Impacts of the World Heritage designation on the Maasai

The inscription of Ngorongoro on the World Heritage List, which - as described - occurred without the appropriate consultation, involvement or participation of the local people either in 1979 or 2010, is having real and significant impacts on the enjoyment of rights for the people living in the Conservation Area. The following are just some of the impacts:

Limitation of grazing resources

The worst impact to be felt so far by residents as a result of their lands being inscribed on the World Heritage List is the reduction in grazing resources that they are allowed to use. In the name

---

28 IUCN 2010, p. 189: "Reviewers noted that there is little or no information presented in the nomination regarding consultation with the Maasai as key stakeholder in Ngorongoro. It is suggested important to confirm that the nomination was prepared with free prior and informed consent from the Maasai." Additionally, in a 2009 report of a UNESCO/IUCN monitoring mission to Ngorongoro it was noted that a "re-nomination under cultural criteria... was submitted by the State Party on 1 February 2009 and will be reviewed by the Committee at its 34th session in 2010. The mission was surprised to learn that the representatives of the Maasai were not aware of this nomination." (UNESCO and IUCN 2009, p. 19)
29 Disko 2010, p. 169.

of conservation, access to grazing resources has gradually been decreased over time. Critical resources have been taken and still more may be taken yet. Some of the most significant incidences of alienation of pastoralists' resources and limitations of grazing rights are:

Restrictions on accessing Ngorongoro Crater

Ngorongoro Crater has traditionally been an important refuge for the pastoralists who live near it. The crater is the only source of salt for the cattle of pastoralists who live near the crater rim. It is also an important source of water in the dry season. Pastoralists were living in the crater until they were removed in 1975. Due to their prior residence there, pastoralists have enjoyed grazing rights even though, over time, restrictions have been imposed to control the number of cattle for environmental reasons. In recent years, the Ngorongoro Conservation Area Authority (NCAA), the management and governing body of the NCA, has been offering alternative sources of salt by providing salt from Lake Babati in grazing areas outside the crater; however, this is a practice which has proved costly and unsustainable. UNESCO and IUCN have recently initiated moves "to limit or remove cattle grazing in the crater" (supposedly to avoid soil erosion in the crater), in total disregard of the importance of the crater for pastoral livelihoods and the rights that pastoralists have enjoyed traditionally.[30] There is no explanation as to why a few hundred head of cattle accessing the crater periodically should be more harmful to it than the thousands of wild animals who live there permanently.

New threats: restrictions in Olduvai Gorge and Nasera Rock

The recent inscription of the NCA as a cultural World Heritage site in recognition of its archaeological and palaeontological significance appears to mean that further restrictions must be imposed on the use of land and other resources by pastoralists. The fact that pastoralists were not consulted when making the decision will have a strong bearing on their acceptance of any new restrictions. It would have made a considerable difference if they had been consulted since they are the ones who are best placed to know the land-use patterns of their grazing areas. Besides, they are the ones who stand to be affected by any further restrictions imposed on grazing.

The Statement of Outstanding Universal Value adopted by the World Heritage Committee when it inscribed the NCA as a cultural site makes it clear that the Committee considers the land use by the Maasai pastoralists as a threat not only to the natural but also to the cultural values of the NCA:

"Further growth of the Maasai population and the number of cattle should remain within the capacity of the property, and increasing sedentarisation, local overgrazing and agricultural

---

30 UNESCO and IUCN 2007.

encroachment are threats to both the natural and cultural values of the property... The property encompasses not only the known archaeological remains but also areas of high archaeo-anthropological potential where related finds might be made. However the integrity of specific paleo-archaeological attributes and the overall sensitive landscape are to an extent under threat and thus vulnerable due to the lack of enforcement of protection arrangements related to grazing regimes..." [31]

In order to mitigate these threats, the World Heritage Committee proposed the development of a pastoralism strategy for the NCA, not appreciating the fact that pastoralists in Ngorongoro have, over the years, developed workable strategies by which to best utilise the available resources without any significant impacts on the environment.[32]

Following the inscription of the NCA under cultural criteria, UNESCO and ICOMOS undertook a reactive monitoring mission to the area to assess the state of the historical, archaeological and palaeontological sites. As can easily be seen from the report of this mission, they did not meet with representatives of the Maasai during their visit.[33] They claimed after their visit that Olduvai Gorge had been overgrazed and issued recommendations that measures should be taken to arrest this, which read in part:

"Mitigate and limit the impacts of livestock at the Olduvai Gorge through a renewed participatory approach in collaboration with the pastoral communities..." [34]

While it may seem a positive thing to recommend consulting pastoralists with regard to any intention to limit the impacts of livestock on the Gorge, it would have made more sense if they had been consulted before the area was inscribed for cultural values to begin with.

Olduvai Gorge provides important riverine grazing areas and water during the dry season and the beginning of the rainy season. The gorge lies between the highlands and the low grasses of the Serengeti and provides palatable grass for goats and sheep, a mainstay of many pastoralists who are now almost entirely dependent on these animals for their survival. The gorge also contains the highly nutritious, salty grass species known in Maasai as *erikaru* and *embokui,* which are not easily available in the highlands. According to traditional leader Francis Ole Siapa, who lived and grazed his livestock in the area for many years, no other place in the NCA can match Olduvai Gorge in terms of its diversity of pastoral resources. According to him, the gorge is always the first place to get the critical early rains in November/December and hence the first rescue for weak animals after a long dry season.[35] Another traditional leader, Godfrey Lelya, underscored the importance of the

---

31 Decision 34COM 8B.13 (2010), para. 4.
32 Ibid., para. 7. The proposal to develop a pastoralism strategy was based on recommendations by ICOMOS in its Advisory Body Evaluation. It was reiterated by the World Heritage Committee in 2011 and 2012, as well as by the UNESCO/ICOMOS Reactive Monitoring Mission in 2011.
33 For the itinerary and programme of the monitoring mission, see UNESCO and ICOMOS 2011, p. 53.
34 UNESCO and ICOMOS 2011.
35 Personal Communication, 3rd October 2013.

gorge for pastoralists by saying that it is not only a reserve grazing area for cattle when the wildebeest have migrated to other areas but also a major source of water for pastoralists during the dry season because of the wells dug along the entire bed of the Olduvai River.[36] Any limitations on grazing in this area would cause further disruption of the grazing rhythm and further reduce options available to pastoralists in the NCA. While UNESCO is calling for further measures to limit grazing activities in the gorge, pastoralists already face restrictions placed on their grazing in the gorge by the government.

UNESCO and ICOMOS have also called for control of pastoralists' activities at Nasera Rock.[37] The 2011 reactive monitoring mission was of the opinion that pastoralists' activities were having impacts on the rock and should therefore be restricted. However, no evidence was given to show that the effects were actually caused by livestock. Wild animals do frequent the area as well and, very recently, tourists were regularly camping near the rock. In any case, what is absent from the monitoring mission's report is a more realistic danger to the Nasera Rock and its immediate surroundings, namely a major road that is currently being constructed from the Ngorongoro Conservation Area to Loliondo and which will have much more far reaching consequences than pastoral activities which have been going on for generations.

Cultivation

Cultivation was at the heart of land-use conflict in the NCA even before the area was made a multiple land-use area. It is believed that cultivation has been practiced in the Ngorongoro Highlands for over a million years. The history of cultivation in the area is complex but, for our purposes, it is sufficient to simply say that cultivation has been present for a long time.

When Ngorongoro was made an independent conservation area in 1959, cultivation was one of the activities that the Maasai were allowed to continue to practice. However, owing to concerns about a perceived deterioration of the environment in the NCA, cultivation was prohibited and phased out in 1975 through amendments to the *Ngorongoro Conservation Area Act*. The decline of the pastoral economy and challenges to food security for the Maasai prompted the government to temporarily lift the ban on cultivation in 1992 while measures were worked out to find solutions to these problems.[38] To address these challenges, the NCAA partnered with the Danish International Development Agency, DANIDA, and local residents to undertake a major pastoralism improvement project which focused on restocking destitute communities and building the necessary livestock infrastructure (water, health) capable of sustaining a pastoral economy.[39] While significant improvements were noticed during the eleven-year-life of the project (1998-2009), it proved difficult to sustain and poverty ensued in the following years.

---

36 Personal Communication, 3rd October 2013.
37 UNESCO and ICOMOS 2011, p. 6.
38 Olenasha 2006.
39 Ereto, Ngorongoro Pastoralist Project. For more information, see http://www.ereto-npp.org/.

During the same period, in 2007 and 2008, the UNESCO World Heritage Centre and IUCN conducted two reactive monitoring missions to Ngorongoro to assess the state of conservation of the NCA.[40] They considered that cultivation was widespread and negatively impacting on the integrity of the World Heritage property. For instance, the December 2008 mission noted in its report:

> "[T]here has been an increasing area of the NCA that is used for subsistence agriculture... While cultivation is still regarded as an illegal activity in the property, the GMP [General Management Plan] foresees no interventions to curb it or manage it. This means that while it is officially prohibited, cultivation is in reality tolerated without restrictions in the development zone, without any measures in place to manage these pressures. [...] On the basis of the information gathered during the mission, the mission concludes that the Outstanding Universal Value of the Property is increasingly threatened by the impact of resident human populations and unsustainable land use practices linked to subsistence agriculture..."[41]

The mission stated in strong terms that the issue needed to be addressed urgently and current degradation patterns stopped in order to avoid an eventual loss of the NCA's Outstanding Universal Value. Noting in passing that the Maasai community had "argued" in a document submitted to the mission team that subsistence agriculture was an absolute necessity for the survival of people in the area, the mission recommended that a "dialogue should be started between NCAA, Maasai community leaders and other stakeholders to develop a joint strategy".[42]

In May 2009, when the Tanzanian Parliamentary Committee on Land and Natural Resources and Environment visited Ngorongoro, the Board of the NCAA, through its chairperson Pius Msekwa, alerted the Committee to the fact that UNESCO had threatened to withdraw Ngorongoro from the World Heritage List because of perceived threats to its integrity caused by cultivation and other problems in the area.[43] After visiting a few areas carefully selected for their intensity of cultivation, the Committee decided that the ban on cultivation had to be re-imposed. The reasons for this were not difficult to understand. The Deputy Minister for Tourism and Natural Resources at the time,

---

40 UNESCO and IUCN 2007; UNESCO and IUCN 2008.
41 UNESCO and IUCN 2008, pp. 11 and 22.
42 Ibid. For the document prepared by the Maasai community, see www.tnrf.org/files/E-INFO-UNESCO-IUCN_Ngorongoro_Residents_Statement_dec_2008.pdf.
43 Mr. Msekwa presented the Committee with a memo (on file with the author) which the NCAA had submitted to the Minister of Natural Resources and Tourism and which reads in part: "...the permission that the Government gave residents to continue subsistence cultivation is very pleasing to the residents and has brought calm and tranquillity to them. However, because of the strong position of international stakeholders, I am obliged to caution the Government as follows: That the decision to allow cultivation to continue in NCA is opposed strongly by international stakeholders led by UNESCO, together with many other environmentalists/ conservationists such as the World Heritage Centre and IUCN... [L]ast year the main message of IUCN was... that cultivation and encroachment were among the threats facing NCA... In short, to continue allowing cultivation in the conservation area could lead to NCA being withdrawn from the World Heritage List, which could lead to the loss of many tourism-related advantages that come with World Heritage site status..." (NCAA, undated. Unofficial translation from the Swahili original).

Ezekiel Maige, said the financial benefits from being on the UNESCO World Heritage List outweighed the local benefits of cultivation. In his own words:

> "NCA being a World Heritage site and a major tourist allure, generates revenues amounting to USD 30million annually. Now tell me, can our subsistence farming earn us such amount?" [44]

The Deputy Minister seemed sympathetic to the plight of the Maasai, saying that the government was caught in a difficult situation, trying to balance the food needs of its hungry population in the NCA while at the same trying to appease UNESCO so that the NCA would not lose its World Heritage status. Any sympathy from the Deputy Minister did not, however, stop the government from re-imposing the ban on cultivation later in 2009, although it was careful to place blame on pressure from UNESCO for the re-introduction of the ban. The words of the then Chairman of the Parliamentary Committee on Land, Environment and Natural Resources make this clear:

> "If UNESCO removes the NCA from the list of the World Heritage sites, no tourists will come to visit the place. So it is important to comply with their guidelines..." [45]

When the media reported that UNESCO was responsible for pressuring the government to take brutal measures against its people,[46] UNESCO was quick to move and deny any involvement. In a press release written by the Director of the UNESCO Office in Dar es Salaam, the organization denied that there was any threat to withdraw Ngorongoro from the World Heritage List, noting that: "For a property to be deleted from the World Heritage List, its Outstanding Universal Value must be irremediably lost, which is not the case with the Ngorongoro" and that "Ngorongoro is not even inscribed on the List of World Heritage sites in Danger". While it admitted that the World Heritage Committee had expressed concerns about threats to the integrity of the property, including from cultivation, UNESCO noted that the Committee had urged Tanzania to engage in a dialogue with the Maasai community and ensure their active participation in decision-making. In closing, the press release declared that: "UNESCO works closely on various issues related to indigenous communities and encourages in all its programmes the enhancement of their cultural identity and living conditions". [47]

While UNESCO thus denied liability for the ban on cultivation, the report of its monitoring mission the following year was very telling:

> "In regard to the banning of cultivation practices within the NCA, the mission noted positive progress by the State Party; areas/plots previously farmed by the Maasai communities are no longer under active cultivation and are actually going through a natural rehabilitation process... Therefore, farming has been deterred through enforcement, awareness

---

44 Quoted in Ihucha 2009a.
45 Quoted in Ihucha 2009b.
46 Ihucha 2010; Peter 2010.
47 Jensen 2010.

programmes among the pastoral communities and the continuous monitoring being undertaken by the NCAA... The effective removal of agriculture from the NCA is particularly important in that it has potential to limit possible human population densities *and encourages the expanding resident populations to move outside the conservation area boundaries.*

Recommendations:

– Continue monitoring and enforcing the ban on agriculture within the NCA." [48]

The re-imposition of the ban on cultivation was done without providing any alternatives to the poverty-stricken and food-insecure communities in the NCA. Following the ban, the residents of the NCA were officially listed in the records of the National Grain Reserve as people permanently in need of emergency food support. In July 2011 alone, NCAA had to procure 278 tonnes of maize as relief food for hungry residents.[49] A respected elder in Ngorongoro, Francis Ole Siapa, was quoted by the press as saying, "We are not allowed to engage in any farming activities in this area. So, famine has been a constant threat to us since 2009 when the government banned farming in this area".[50] Agnes Sandai, a Special Seats Councillor from Oloirobi ward and an active member of the Pastoral Council, pleaded for women, urging the authorities to at least allow them to cultivate potatoes and vegetables, because "people here are not sure of what to eat tomorrow".[51]

The second half of 2012 and much of 2013 witnessed intense struggles by the communities in the NCA to achieve food security and avoid famine, and also to demand their broader human rights, which they see as having been denied as a direct result of their living inside a World Heritage site. In 2012, a coalition of NGOs that support pastoralists made the hunger situation in the NCA public. In a press release, they highlighted the fact that there was an undeniably serious hunger situation in Ngorongoro, so severe that children and adults had died of hunger and malnutrition, and so widespread that a huge majority of the estimated 70,000 residents were facing acute hunger and starvation. The NGO statement pointed out that:

"Food [in]security and human rights violations are unfortunately also linked to the international significance that has been attached to Ngorongoro Conservation Area. The present hunger situation can, in the immediate be attributed to a harsh and hurriedly made decision by the Government in 2009 to re-impose the ban on cultivation without coming with an alternative means of livelihood and food security for the local community in the Conservation Area. International conservation actors such as UNESCO and IUCN cannot deny culpability in the present hunger situation since they are known to have pressurized

---

48 UNESCO and ICOMOS 2011, p. 28 (emphasis added).
49 Juma 2011.
50 Quoted in Philemon 2011.
51 Quoted in Philemon 2011.

the Government to re-impose the ban on cultivation owing to a perceived deterioration of the integrity of the Ngorongoro Conservation Area as World Heritage Site." [52]

Threats of eviction

Another pressing issue is the continuous threat of eviction of local residents from the Ngorongoro Conservation Area. The possible relocation of pastoralists from the conservation area is something that seems to have gained ground since Ngorongoro was made a World Natural Heritage site in 1979. To remain a World Natural Heritage site, the NCA must retain the outstanding natural values for which it was inscribed, which means that people's development activities must be kept within limits. When it comes to striking a balance between conservation and development, one of these has to give and, in conservation areas, it is the people who have to go!

An intention to evict indigenous peoples from the area has been clear from decisions taken from time to time by UNESCO and the Government of Tanzania. Just a few years after the NCA was inscribed on the World Heritage List, the threat of eviction was knocking at the door. In the 1980s, UNESCO and the Government of Tanzania were openly discussing this possibility but wanted scientific findings to support any policy. According to Homewood and Rodgers:

> "The management in Ngorongoro Conservation Area... have for decades perceived a conflict between wildlife values and pastoralist activities. By 1980 the conflict was seen as severe enough to warrant expulsion of the pastoralists, but the Ngorongoro Conservation Area Authority needed objective documentation to back up action. UNESCO was to fund a management plan and we were commissioned to produce background information on the ecological facts. Our input was expected to be a standard environmental impact assessment: *In what way do pastoralists affect the wildlife? Is this a major problem? If so, recommend pastoralist relocation.*" [53]

Homewood and Rodgers found that "pastoralist land use presents no threat to wildlife populations or the environment in NCA" and instead found that pastoralism actually complements and reinforces wildlife conservation. They concluded that "there is no justification on conservation or other grounds for expelling the Maasai".[54] As a result, no relocation of pastoralists was carried out at the time; however, the threat of eviction never ceased to exist for the Maasai in the NCA.

---

52 PINGO's Forum et al. 2012.
53 Homewood and Rodgers 1991, p. xi (emphasis added).
54 Ibid., pp. 247, 265.

Maasai homesteads ('boma') in the Ngorongoro Conservation Area. Photo: Dongyi Liu (CC BY-NC-ND 2.0)

In recent years, fears of a possible eviction of pastoralists from the area have grown mostly as a result of UNESCO's interventions in the area. The UNESCO/IUCN monitoring mission to Ngorongoro in 2008 made it clear that it considered human population pressure one of the key factors threatening the universal values of the property and called strongly on the Government of Tanzania to take urgent measures:

"The mission team is extremely concerned by the increased numbers of resident populations and their impact on the natural resources through agriculture and overgrazing on the integrity of the property. The mission team is of the opinion that these impacts constitute the most important and growing threat to the Outstanding Universal value of the property... Populations have increased beyond the carrying capacity of the property... **Therefore the mission considers that the issue of the impact of resident populations on the values of the property needs to be addressed urgently...**" [55]

Either in sheer panic or simply to suit some hidden agenda, the government began taking rushed measures against the residents of the conservation area after receiving this report, including a re-introduction of the ban on cultivation, prohibiting access to the Ngorongoro crater and evicting so-

---

55 UNESCO and IUCN 2008, pp. 11-12 (emphasis in original).

called 'illegal immigrants'.[56] Amid these rushed decisions, panic ensued, with some media outlets reporting that people were going to be evicted from Ngorongoro.[57]

The reported threats of eviction received the strongest of condemnations from the local people, local NGOs and international NGOs, most notably the International Work Group for Indigenous Affairs (IWGIA) and the International Land Alliance. IWGIA, for one, wrote a letter to UNESCO expressing its concern and opposition to the threats of eviction and other violations of human rights of the indigenous people of the Conservation Area.[58] UNESCO was swift to deny liability and involvement in any attempts to evict people from the conservation area. In a letter to the Director of Antiquities of Tanzania, the organization demanded an explanation of the reported threats of eviction, making it clear that UNESCO would not support such a move since "as a UN agency [it] fully subscribes to the Declaration on the Rights of Indigenous Peoples and is against any eviction of indigenous peoples be it from cultural sites or protected areas". UNESCO "emphasize[d] that technical issues pertaining to the conservation of heritage should not be used to justify any decision to evict indigenous peoples".[59]

Carrying Capacity Study: In search of scientific evidence to support eviction?

The recommendations of UNESCO's monitoring missions cast doubt on the above assertions, however, and play well into the hands of those who would like to evict pastoralists from the NCA. UNESCO has not only called for an effective removal of agriculture from the NCA in order to "encourage" residents to move outside the conservation area[60] but has, for years, pressured the Tanzanian government to undertake a study of the human "carrying capacity" of the area. Recent monitoring missions from UNESCO and IUCN have consistently emphasized that the present human and livestock numbers are among the factors threatening the integrity of Ngorongoro as a World Heritage site, a claim that is vigorously contested by the Maasai.[61] UNESCO has supported the conducting of a carrying capacity study to ascertain how real the threat is:

> "The Mission team notes and commends the process of undertaking a systematic study of carrying capacity within the conservation area. It is important that such a study is credible and, in particular, is undertaken by an objective and competent person/institution. This study should be based on both social and environmental considerations and should provide the

---

56 The term 'illegal immigrants' is frequently used by the government to refer to NCA residents other than those who were already present in the NCA when the conservation area was established in 1959 and their descendants. The term is also applied to people who were paid to re-settle in 1975 who have since returned.
57 See Ihucha 2010; Peter 2010.
58 Letter from IWGIA to UNESCO dated 13 April 2010 (on file with author).
59 Letter from the Director of the World Heritage Centre, dated 21 April 2010 (on file with author).
60 UNESCO and ICOMOS 2011, p. 28.
61 See e.g. the joint statement that was submitted by the indigenous residents of the NCA to the 2008 UNESCO/IUCN monitoring mission (Ngorongoro Pastoral Council et al. 2008): "There are no signs and no significant ecological damage to the area from overuse of the areas by the local communities although there has been above 50.000 people in the area for decades."

Maasai men cultivating land following heavy rain, in Endulen, Ngorongoro Conservation Area. Especially in times of drought, subsistence agriculture is essential for the survival of people in the area. However cultivation was prohibited in the NCA in 2009, a decision that has seriously undermined the food security of residents.
Photo: Geoff Sayer/Oxfam

opportunity for adequate and effective input from the Maasai populations, including through the Maasai Pastoral Council and its Chairman. Based on professional judgement, the Mission Team assumes that *such a study would result in the identification of a carrying capacity figure significantly less than the current population within the conservation area.*" [62]

The prospect of a carrying capacity study is causing a great deal of stress among the residents of the NCA, who fear that the findings of such a study would be used to evict them from the NCA. This fear appears justified by UNESCO's own pre-determined conclusion that the carrying capacity has already been surpassed and that the study would identify a carrying capacity figure which is far less than the NCA's current population of 60,000 people. The fear is compounded by a litany of other threats that resident pastoralists have been receiving from many quarters, including government. UNESCO recently reported that: "The State Party report notes that the WH property does not have the capacity to sustain the current Maasai population of 60,000 people and 360,000 cattle".[63]

---

62 UNESCO and IUCN 2007, p. 6 (emphasis added).
63 UNESCO 2006, p. 5. The figure of 360,000 cattle is wrong and has never been reached in the entire history of the NCA. The highest recorded figure is 200,000 heads of cattle, recorded in 1987.

The Government of Tanzania has itself made clear on several occasions that it views eviction as a potential solution to resolving what it sees as a long existing conflict between people and wildlife in Ngorongoro. As explained by the 1990 Ad Hoc Ministerial Commission on Ngorongoro:

> "The possibility of resettling the NCA's pastoralists in lightly populated areas, such as the Loliondo Division of Ngorongoro District or the Simanjiro Plains has been considered at various times in the past. This approach would help ensure the maintenance of the NCA's conservation and archaeological values, and would make the management of the Area considerably more simple; resettlement would also enable the Maasai to pursue their development interests free of restrictions. However, the Commission recognised that resettlement would be a contravention of the assurances which have been given to the Maasai people, and would lead to resentment, upheaval and human suffering. Resettlement would also be difficult from a logistical point of view, costly in economic terms, and at risk of evoking both national and international criticism. Lastly, the areas which are proposed for resettlement are already experiencing some of the highest rates of immigration in the nation, and are the focus of considerable controversy over land allocation; and additional and large influx of people from the Conservation Area could only intensify these conflicts." [64]

In sum, the threat of eviction has been there for many years but the Government of Tanzania fears the logistical implications of undertaking an eviction of this magnitude, as well as the expected resistance from the affected people themselves and human rights activists all over the world.

When a UNESCO monitoring mission visited the Pastoral Council and elders of Ngorongoro in April 2012, pastoralists made it abundantly clear that they were certain that the proposed study on the carrying capacity would be used as a management tool to evict them from Ngorongoro, not seeing what other purpose it could serve. And, indeed, the question is: if such a study was carried out and did conclude that the human population in Ngorongoro exceeds the carrying capacity of the area, what would happen to the 'excess' population?

The 2012 monitoring mission responded to the pastoralists' concerns by noting in its report that the idea of a carrying capacity study "has had the unfortunate and unhelpful side effect of heightening tension between management and pastoralists, by keeping the possibility of involuntary relocation alive in people's minds". The mission therefore recommended "that a study of carrying capacity should no longer be envisaged as it is impracticable, unnecessary and could lead to serious conflict with the Maasai pastoralist groups". However, the mission at the same time reaffirmed "that the number of livestock almost certainly exceeds the carrying capacity of the areas set aside for pastoralism (although understandably most Maasai choose to be in denial about it)" and underlined the importance of "a reduction in the number of people" in the Conservation Area.[65] While the mission noted that "the relocation of people out of the NCA can only take place voluntarily, and certainly *bona fide* residents need have no fear of the sort of large scale, forcible eviction that

---

64 Tanzania 1990, p. 15.
65 UNESCO, ICOMOS and IUCN 2012, pp. 23-26.

would be needed to bring the pastoral system below carrying capacity", the mission's notion of a 'bona fide resident' is hardly reassuring to the pastoralists:

> "[The pastoral community should be reassured that] while no *bona fide* residents will be evicted, those remaining have firstly to respect the legally valid livelihood constraints peculiar to the NCA, and secondly to accept that because of them the best interests of the community and the management authority are actually almost identical. The *quid pro quo* for those electing to stay, respect the law and collaborate with the NCAA and share responsibility for sustaining their pastoral way of life, is that the latter will continue to provide them with all the familiar benefits..." [66]

Participation of the residents in management and decision-making processes

Ngorongoro Conservation Area was created for three objectives, the development of Maasai pastoralists being one of them. It is only reasonable that the Maasai should be able to participate fully in the management of the area. Unfortunately, this has not been the case, as their participation in management and decision-making has not been commensurate with the attention that should be attached to their development. This has been decried by Maasai representatives and organizations for many years[67] and has recently also begun to be criticized by UNESCO and the World Heritage Committee.[68]

Management decisions in the area are made at two levels: at the level of the board of directors and the level of management. At both levels, the participation of indigenous peoples is not legally guaranteed.

According to the *Ngorongoro Conservation Area Act* (Section 5), the overall manager of the affairs of the Conservation Area is the Board of Directors of the NCAA. The law contains no mechanism to ensure that resident communities can participate in the management of the Conservation Area through this important body. The Chairperson of the Board is appointed by the President of Tanzania while the additional 6-11 members of the Board are appointed by the Minister responsible for Natural Resources and Tourism.[69] While representatives of the resident communities have, at times, been appointed to the Board, this was not due to a legal requirement but simply at the discretion of the appointing authority. For many years, the Chairperson of Ngorongoro District Council and the Member of Parliament (MP) from Ngorongoro Constituency have been serving on the Board as *de facto* representatives of local communities but no attempts have been undertaken

---

66   Ibid., pp. 24, 35.
67   See e.g. the statement of the NCA's indigenous residents submitted to the 2008 UNESCO/IUCN monitoring mission (Ngorongoro Pastoral Council et al. 2008): "Participation in NCAA decision making bodies of local communities and local authorities is highly insufficient. People of NCA are not enjoying the same rights as other citizens of Tanzania."
68   See in particular World Heritage Committee Decision 33COM 7B.9 (2009); UNESCO and IUCN 2009; UNESCO and ICOMOS 2011.
69   Section 5 of the *Ngorongoro Conservation Area Act* and section 2 of the fourth schedule to the *Act*.

to make this a legal requirement. With the instigation of the Pastoral Council in 1994, the Chairman of the Pastoral Council seems to have replaced the Chairperson of the District Council as the *de facto* representative of communities. Interestingly, in the most recent re-constitution of the Board in December 2009, the local MP was dropped. There have been repeated calls from different people and institutions (governmental and non-governmental) to increase the number of representatives of the local communities on the Board. The Ad Hoc Ministerial Commission in 1990 recommended that residents should, as a minimum, be allocated two places on the Board for representatives chosen by the residents themselves.

At the level of management, where important decisions are taken and implemented, there is not a single representative of local residents in the top management team. In the present structure of the NCAA, there are three directors and, below them, are eight divisional managers. Overall, the total number of local residents who are employed in the conservation area is less than a hundred out of a total workforce of nearly five hundred persons.[70] A precise figure is difficult to establish as the estimates provided by the conservation authorities tend to overstate the employment of local residents by counting all Maasai people as local residents, whether they are from the NCA or not. Confusion also stems from the tendency of the authorities to include temporary casual labour and short contracts in the definition of employment. Not one local person is currently employed in a management position. In the past, the excuse for not having community representatives in these positions was that members of these communities lacked education and the required technical skills. Today, there are many local residents who would be qualified to fulfil these positions but the system continues to exclude them from employment.

The Ngorongoro Pastoral Council is so far the only space that can even remotely be said to be providing for some degree of community participation in the management of the NCA. The Pastoral Council has played a very large role in the provision of education services to the resident communities. However, the way it is structured and the powers given to it by law make it incapable of enabling effective community participation as it cannot pass binding decisions. Moreover, while the Pastoral Council was initially intended to be an autonomous body of local people contributing to the management of the NCA, this has not been achieved as the Pastoral Council was set up as a branch of the NCAA. It is therefore often perceived as an arm of the NCAA rather than an independent organ safeguarding the interests of local communities.

The idea to create the Pastoral Council was first introduced in a draft management plan prepared in 1966.[71] Concretely, however, the structure of the present Pastoral Council goes back to proposals made by the Ad Hoc Ministerial Commission on Ngorongoro in 1990. The position of the Commission was very clear on Ngorongoro:

> "It is the Commission's view that the long-term success of the Conservation Area will rely upon the active involvement and participation of local communities in all aspects of

---

70 In 2008, the number of local residents employed was put at 70 out of a total workforce of 420 employees, See Parliament of the United Republic of Tanzania 2008, p. 8.
71 Tanzania 1990, p. 55.

the NCA's management. In this regard, it is vitally important that residents of the NCA be provided with a much greater voice in the affairs of the Conservation Area than is the case at the present time..." [72]

The Commission also made recommendations as to how the participation of local communities in the affairs of the Conservation Area should be achieved in practice. The Commission recommended the establishment of what it called a 'local community council' as a forum for discussion between the NCAA and residents and a space through which the residents could channel concerns to the Board of the NCAA. The Commission proposed that the council should be composed of elected ward councillors for the area, the chairperson from each of the registered villages in the NCA, additional representatives elected by the communities from among the permanent residents of the area, and the conservator and senior staff from the NCAA.

When the Ngorongoro Pastoral Council was established, almost all of the recommendations of the Ad Hoc Ministerial Commission were taken on board. The Pastoral Council has been in existence informally since 1994 although it was legalised only in 2000.[73] The subsidiary legislation establishing the Pastoral Council also contains a scheduled constitution governing the activities of the Council. According to this constitution, one of the functions of the Pastoral Council is to advise the Board of the NCAA on all policies relevant to the implementation of the Pastoral Council's constitution.[74] The Council is also empowered to plan and implement development projects for the benefit of local communities.[75] However, the decisions of the Pastoral Council must gain the approval of the Board of the NCAA before they are implemented. The Pastoral Council may also amend its constitution but, again, only with the approval of the NCAA Board and the Minister responsible for the Conservation Area.

The composition of the Pastoral Council closely reflects the recommendations that were made by the Ad Hoc Ministerial Commission on Ngorongoro. The Pastoral Council is composed of all Councillors in the NCA, the Chairpersons of all registered villages in the NCA, six traditional leaders (one from each ward), six representatives of women (one from each ward), six representatives of youth (again one from each ward) and the Conservator of the NCAA.[76]

While the present configuration of the Pastoral Council is largely in accordance with the recommendations of the Ad Hoc Ministerial Commission, the fact that the Conservator of the NCAA is part of the council is problematic because it compromises its independence. When local communities were consulted on the composition of the local community council, their recommendation, which was not taken on board, was that the council should be an autonomous body which is not part of the NCAA and that it should be fully constituted by representatives of the

---

72 Tanzania 1990, p. 55.
73 *Ngorongoro Conservation Area (Establishment of Ngorongoro Pastoral Council) Rules, 2000* (Government Notice No. 234 of 23rd June, 2000). The rules were made under section 24 of the NCA Ordinance.
74 Article 2.03(a) of the Constitution of the Pastoral Council.
75 Section 8(1) of the Rules.
76 Article 5.01 of the Constitution of the Pastoral Council.

local communities without involving ex-officio members from the communities, let alone people from the Conservation Area Authority.[77]

Benefit-sharing

Benefit-sharing is another important way of ensuring that the local people participate in the affairs of the conservation area. It has been observed on many occasions by UNESCO and IUCN that equitable benefit-sharing in the NCA will help to make local residents appreciate the importance of conserving the natural environment. Accordingly, the World Heritage Committee has repeatedly requested that the Government of Tanzania take deliberate measures to improve participation and benefit-sharing in the NCA. For instance, in 2009, the Committee adopted the following recommendation:

> "Requests the State Party to ensure the active participation of resident communities in decision-making processes and develop benefit-sharing mechanisms to encourage a sense of ownership of, and responsibility for, the conservation and sustainable use of the property's natural resources…" [78]

While implementation of this vital recommendation could have been better, it is worth mentioning that benefit-sharing is an area where some light can be seen at the end of the tunnel. NCAA receives around 30 million USD a year from tourism. The Ngorongoro Pastoral Council receives a direct grant from this of approximately 2-3% annually for the development of local communities.[79] This amount has been critical in enabling the Pastoral Council to undertake important social services, especially in the area of education. With this money, the Pastoral Council has been able to send many residents to schools. For the entire period of its existence, the Pastoral Council has directly supported the education of around a thousand students in different secondary schools and colleges.[80] Through this support, the Pastoral Council has also been able to construct a very good secondary school in Ngorongoro, the Embarway Secondary School, and is currently (2014) completing another secondary school in Nainokanoka. In addition to the direct grant, other development support is also given through the NCAA's Department of Community Development.

---

77 Lazaro Moringe Parkipuny, pers. communication. L. Parkipuny was the Hon Member of Parliament of Ngorongoro Constituency from 1980 to 1990 and a member of the Ad Hoc Ministerial Commission on Ngorongoro.
78 Decision 33COM 7B.9, para. 7.
79 The exact proportion given is not fixed and varies from year to year. In 2010/2011 the contribution for the direct grant was 1.25 billion Shillings, in 2011/2012 it went slightly up to 1.35 billion Shillings and in 2012/2013 it was 1.4 billion Shillings. In 2013/2014 the direct grant increased suddenly to 2 billion Shillings in response to the serious food shortages that hit the area and some of the direct grant was used to purchase grain. Jamhuri ya Muungano wa Tanzania, Ofisi ya Waziri Mkuu 2013.
80 In the past, the Pastoral Council used to sponsor students up to Master's degree level; however, this privilege was removed by the NCAA Board allegedly to make the bursary available for more students at the lower levels of education. The Pastoral Council resisted this saying, among other things, that it amounted to interference in their decision-making.

Safari vehicles in Ngorongoro Crater. Being a major tourist destination, the NCA attracts more than 500,000 visitors per year, generating revenues of around 30 million USD annually. Only 2-3 percent of that revenue goes to the local communities. Photo: Paulo Cunha

While the 2-3% direct grant to local people's development is an attempt to implement benefit-sharing arrangements, it is clearly not an equitable arrangement, especially considering that the development of local residents in Ngorongoro is among the three key objectives for which the conservation area was established. If equity in benefit-sharing is to be realised, then at least 30% of the income of the NCAA should be set aside for people's development. This is among the recommendations that local residents are making towards a new law for the conservation area.[81] In December 2012, pastoralist organizations from the NCA released a joint statement calling on the Government of Tanzania to "repeal and re-enact Ngorongoro Conservation Area Act, a draconian piece of legislation which denies local community an opportunity to co-manage the conservation area as well as getting equitable benefits from the income accrued from tourism". They urged the government to "make sure that the income accruing from Tourism is distributed equally amongst the three objectives for which the area was established" and "to make sure that at least 30% of the income [is] allocated to the Pastoral Council".[82]

Recent developments

In the first quarter of 2013, the people of Ngorongoro themselves started a movement in response to the problems of the NCA that quickly proved too strong for the government to ignore. They began

---

81 Olenasha 2010.
82 PINGO's Forum et al. 2012.

mounting pressure in April and May threatening to close the main gate to the NCA and Serengeti National Park if the government did not respond to the situation facing them. This strategy worked because, however difficult implementing that threat would have been, the government took the threat seriously and responded quickly.

The Prime Minister of Tanzania, the Honourable Peter Kayanza Pinda, made a quick trip to Arusha in June to talk to members of the Pastoral Council, select traditional leaders and a few educated youths. After listening to the voices of the people of Ngorongoro, he ordered an assessment of income status and food security in Ngorongoro, which was conducted immediately afterwards in July/August 2013. The assessment, done in close consultation with the Pastoral Council, revealed that the economic situation of the people of the NCA was shocking. According to the assessment report, the population of the NCA was 87,851 people. The number of cattle was found to be 131,509, while goats numbered 163,207 and sheep 166,872. The assessment revealed that 3% of the population of the NCA owned 80% of all the cattle, leaving only 20% of the cattle in the hands of the remaining 97%.[83] At least 74% of the people of the NCA would be categorised as poor, very poor or destitute, all categories meaning they face food insecurity. The survey also revealed a shocking situation in terms of access to and provision of social services, with 73.4% of the people of the NCA never having seen inside the doors of formal education. Significantly, the survey admits that poverty in the area is directly related to the status of the area as a conservation area.[84]

Following the release of the report, the Prime Minister went to Ngorongoro on 19 September to speak directly to the people of Ngorongoro. The people hoped at the time that the Prime Minister would lift the ban on cultivation, as one of his predecessors had done in 1992. However, the Prime Minister did not do this, instead promising free food for everybody in the area while seeking more durable solutions. According to press reports, he said:

> "There are about 20,000 households in the Ngorongoro Conservation Area, my office offers to give each household ten sacks of grain (One tonne of maize) every year, free of charge to supplement food requirements as we work to find other means of sustaining the population here."[85]

Just as the government is slowly responding to pressure from the local community in Ngorongoro, there are signs that UNESCO is doing the same. Heightened criticism of UNESCO and other international conservation players as being the reason behind the re-imposition of the ban on cultivation and other conservation policies in Ngorongoro so unfavourable to the local communities

---

83 Jamhuri ya Muungano wa Tanzania, Ofisi ya Waziri Mkuu 2013.
84 "The assessment has revealed several challenges facing the citizens of Ngorongoro Division, including income poverty resulting from dependence on pastoralism and livestock keeping as the main economic activity in a conservation area (NCA) where the relevant authority has not taken enough measures to improve and protect the interests of the residents as required by law [Section 6 of the *Ngorongoro Conservation Area Act*]". Jamhuri ya Muungano wa Tanzania, Ofisi ya Waziri Mkuu 2013 (unofficial translation from the Swahili original by the author).
85 Nkwame 2013.

has prompted UNESCO to play some clever diplomacy. Human rights organizations and pastoralists' organizations from Tanzania have repeatedly pointed to UNESCO's responsibilities, and the representatives of UNESCO who visited Ngorongoro in April 2012 were told very clearly that UNESCO was part of the problem. When UNESCO met with representatives of local communities in 2012, it promised that it would organize a workshop to discuss the problems of Ngorongoro and find a new way forward. UNESCO has fulfilled this promise by initiating a project entitled "People and Wildlife; Past, Present and Future: Connecting wildlife management to the sustainable development of communities". The objectives of this project include reviewing the successes and challenges of the NCA as a multiple land-use area; developing a relationship of trust and a common understanding of values, management and benefit-sharing among all stakeholders; and working towards an equitable balance between the needs and aspirations of the Maasai community and the goals of ecosystem management, wildlife conservation, tourism and the protection of archaeological sites. The project intends to review the governance framework and management of the NCA in order to try to better address the challenges facing the area.[86]

These objectives closely reflect the objectives for which the conservation area was originally established, as well as the recent emphasis on the protection of archaeological sites. While it is too early to pass any verdict on this project, it is good that UNESCO is encouraging changes in the governance framework of the NCA. However, it is important to note that the response is limited to this particular site, and nothing appears to have changed in terms of UNESCO's overall policy framework for the governance of World Heritage sites. It is questionable as to whether a change in the governance of the NCA in favour of the local communities will be sustained or effective, or will be supported by UNESCO over the long-term, when the policies of UNESCO, which plays such a decisive role in the management of the site, have not changed.

Conclusion and recommendations

It is becoming an increasing challenge to balance the interests of conservation and tourism with those of human development in the NCA. Reasons for this include, among others, the more than six-fold increase in the human population in the last 50 years, the rapid increase in tourist numbers, and increasing conservation activities that place evermore restrictions on human activities.

The future of Ngorongoro as a multiple land-use area is unpredictable. One thing that is certain, however, is that the current lack of involvement of local people in decision-making processes and threats of evictions from the area are not part of the winning formula. This is particularly stark considering the 'World Heritage' status of the area. The local communities' disenfranchisement and marginalization from decision-making processes begs the questions of whose world and whose heritage are being safeguarded and protected under this label, and whether the concept of 'mankind as a whole' that is embedded in the World Heritage Convention includes the pastoralists living in the Ngorongoro Conservation Area.

---

86   UNESCO 2013.

There are a number of steps that urgently need to be taken to establish a better balance between conservation interests and the livelihood needs of the local communities. Key among these are strengthening the local authority and self-determination of the local communities, and ensuring that they are able to effectively participate in all decision-making processes relating to the conservation area. This should include not only decisions relating to the daily management of the area but also more high-level decisions such as those that are periodically passed by UNESCO and other international conservation actors. An opportunity exists in the current attempt by UNESCO to initiate a dialogue to chart out a new governance structure for the conservation area. A central question in this context must be how to ensure that local communities can fully participate in the governance and management of the NCA. A prerequisite for this is the repeal of the *Ngorongoro Conservation Area Act*, a draconian piece of legislation which denies the local communities the opportunity to co-manage the conservation area or to equitably access tourism benefits.

Second, in order to ensure that pastoralists feel that they are full participants in and co-owners of the heritage in Ngorongoro, renewed attempts should be made to ensure that Maasai cultural values are officially recognized as part of the outstanding universal value of the site. To this end, a re-nomination of the site should urgently be developed in collaboration with the pastoralists. This would also facilitate the establishment of a more balanced management framework that is in line with the multiple land-use concept. If UNESCO is sincere in championing a better balance between the needs and aspirations of the Maasai and the interests of conservation then it must lead by example, by supporting a re-nomination process so that such a balance is achieved at the World Heritage Convention level.

Third, as part of establishing a better management framework, it is essential that all stakeholders work towards finding an equitable benefit-sharing arrangement that would scale up the extent to which the income from tourism contributes to the livelihoods of the local communities, who are increasingly finding it difficult to live by pastoralism alone.

Fourth, the government should consider setting aside lands in or near the NCA for the local communities to farm. Livelihood diversification is urgent due to the restrictions on pastoralism in the NCA, coupled with factors such as the increase in population and climate change. To further boost food security in the area, the government should also consider making it mandatory for the NCAA and businesses operating in the area to give priority to the employment of local people who have the required qualifications. Income from employment will greatly help to boost household income and increase the food security of NCA residents.

Finally, the international governance framework for World Heritage sites such as the NCA needs to be revamped to reflect the requirements of international law and ensure that indigenous peoples fully participate in the inscription and management of World Heritage sites that incorporate or affect their lands, territories or resources. ○

References

Disko, S. 2010. World Heritage Sites in Indigenous Peoples' Territories: Ways of Ensuring Respect for Indigenous Cultures, Values and Human Rights. D. Offenhäußer, W. Zimmerli and M.-T. Albert (eds.), *World Heritage and Cultural Diversity.* Bonn, German Commission for UNESCO, pp. 167-177.

Dowie, M. 2009. *Conservation Refugees – The Hundred-Year Conflict between Global Conservation and Native Peoples.* Cambridge, MIT Press.

Homewood, K. and Rodgers, W. 1991. *Maasailand Ecology: Pastoralist development and wildlife conservation in Ngorongoro, Tanzania.* Cambridge, Cambridge University Press.

ICOMOS. 2010. *Evaluations of Cultural Properties - Ngorongoro Conservation Area (Tanzania).* UNESCO Doc. WHC-10/34.COM/INF.8B1, pp. 62-81.

Ihucha, A. 2009a. Ngorongoro crater issue tough – govt. *The Guardian*, 5 May 2009.

Ihucha, A. 2009b. Ngorongoro on Unesco's axing list? *The Guardian*, 4 May 2009.

Ihucha, A. 2010. Pressure mounts to move Maasai from Ngorongoro crater. *The Guardian*, 25 February 2010.

Jamhuri ya Muungano wa Tanzania, Ofisi ya Waziri Mkuu Tawala za Mikoa na Serikali za Mitaa. 2013. *Taarifa ya Tathmini ya Watu na Hali ya Uchumi Tarafa ya Ngorongoro.* Dar es Salaam, Prime Minister's Office.

Jensen, V. 2010. Ngorongoro still listed as World Heritage site. *The Guardian*, 11 March 2010. (Letter to the Editor by the Director of the UNESCO Dar es Salaam Cluster Office.)

Juma, M. 2011. Pastoralists facing acute food shortage in Ngorongoro. *The Arusha Times*, Issue 00673, 16 July 2011.

McCabe, J. 1991. Giving Conservation a Human Face? Lessons from Forty Years of Conservation and Development in the Ngorongoro Conservation Area, Tanzania. D. Chatty and M. Colchester (eds.). *Conservation and Mobile Indigenous Peoples: Displacement, Forced Settlement, and Sustainable Development.* New York, Berghahn, pp. 61-76.

NCAA. (undated). *Memo Kutoka Mwenyekit wa Bodi kwenda kwa Waziri wa Maliasili na Utalii kuhusu Kilimo Ndani ya Hifadhi ya Ngorongoro* (Memo submitted to the Minister of Natural Resources and Tourism).

Ngorongoro Pastoral Council et al. 2008. *Statement, findings and recommendations from the indigenous residents and stakeholders of Ngorongoro Conservation Area to decision makers, national and international organizations.* 4 December 2008. Available at: www.tnrf.org/files/E-INFO-UNESCO-IUCN_Ngorongoro_Residents_Statement_dec_2008.pdf.

Nkwame, M. 2013. Ngorongoro: Conservation area is for wildlife not farming. *Daily News*, 23 September 2013.

Olenasha, W. 2006. *Parks Without People: A Case Study of the Ngorongoro Conservation Area, Tanzania.* Chiang Mai, International Alliance of Indigenous and Tribal Peoples of Tropical Forests.

Olenasha, W. 2010. *In search of a New Legal Dispensation on Ngorongoro: Residents' Ideas for a New Law* (unpublished manuscript).

Parkipuny, M. S. 1991. *Pastoralism, Conservation and Development in the Greater Serengeti Region.* London, International Institute for Environment and Development.

Parliament of Tanganyika. 1959. *Ngorongoro Conservation Area: Objects and Reasons* (Introduction to the Bill for the NCA Act, 1959, by Attorney-General J.S.R. Cole, 21 March 1959). Dar es Salaam: Government Printer. FAOLEX No: LEX-FAOC017716.

Parliament of the United Republic of Tanzania. 2008. *Hansard*, 31 October 2008. Available at http://polis.parliament.go.tz/PAMS/docs/HS-13-4-2008.pdf.

Peter, F. 2010. Maasai must give wildlife freedom, insists UNESCO. *The Guardian*, 27 February 2010.

Philemon, L. 2011. Ban on farming in Ngorongoro crater rim intact, says minister. *The Guardian*, 12 July 2011.

PINGO's Forum et al. 2012. *Hunger in a World Heritage Site. Where is the World?* Press Release by pastoralists' civil society organizations on state of hunger and starvation in the NCA, 21 December 2012. Available at http://www.iwgia.org/news/search-news?news_id=732.

Shetler, J. 2007. *Imagining Serengeti: A History of Landscape Memory in Tanzania from Earliest Times to the Present.* Athens, Ohio University Press.

Shivji, I. and Kapinga, W. 1998. *Maasai rights in Ngorongoro, Tanzania.* Dar es Salaam, IIED/HAKIARDHI.

Tanzania, United Republic of. 1978. *World Heritage List Nomination submitted by Tanzania: Ngorongoro Conservation Area.* 6 July 1978.

Tanzania, United Republic of. 1990. *Report of the Ad Hoc Ministerial Commission on Ngorongoro: A Conservation and Development Strategy for the Ngorongoro Conservation Area.* Dar es Salaam, Ministry of Tourism, Natural Resources and Environment.

Tanzania, United Republic of. 2009. *Ngorongoro Conservation Area (Mixed World Heritage Site) – Nomination File for Ngorongoro Conservation Area to be submitted to UNESCO, February 2009.*

UNESCO. 2006. *State of conservation reports of properties inscribed on the World Heritage List: Ngorongoro Conservation Area (United Republic of Tanzania).* UNESCO Doc. WHC-06/30.COM/7B, 9 June 2006, pp. 4-7.

UNESCO. 2013. *People and Wildlife; Past, Present and Future: Connecting wildlife management to the sustainable development of communities in Ngorongoro Conservation Area World Heritage Property, Tanzania* (Project Proposal).

UNESCO and ICOMOS. 2011. *Report on the joint UNESCO/ICOMOS Reactive Monitoring Mission to Ngorongoro Conservation Area (United Republic of Tanzania), 6 to 12 February 2011.* Paris, World Heritage Centre.

UNESCO and IUCN. 2007. *Ngorongoro Conservation Area (United Republic of Tanzania): Report of the Reactive Monitoring Mission, 29 April to 5 May 2007.* Paris, World Heritage Centre.

UNESCO and IUCN. 2009. *Mission Report: Reactive Monitoring Mission, Ngorongoro Conservation Area (United Republic of Tanzania), 1-6 December 2008.* Paris, World Heritage Centre.

UNESCO, ICOMOS and IUCN. 2012. *Report on the Joint WHC/ICOMOS/IUCN Mission to Ngorongoro Conservation Area, Republic of Tanzania, 10th-13th April 2012.* Paris, World Heritage Centre.

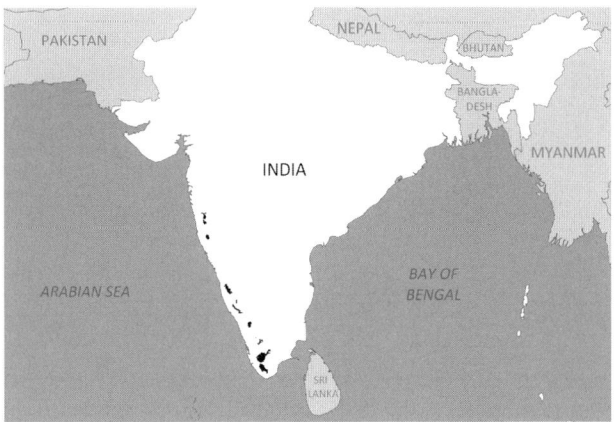

Western Ghats of India: A Natural Heritage Enclosure?

C.R. Bijoy

Introduction

Of the 981 properties inscribed on UNESCO's World Heritage List as of July 2013, 24 cultural sites and six natural sites are in India.[1] One of the natural World Heritage sites in India is the Western Ghats, inscribed at the 36th Session of the World Heritage Committee in Saint Petersburg, Russian Federation (24 June – 6 July 2012).

The Government of India's Ministry of Environment and Forests (MoEF) took responsibility for identifying potential sites in the Western Ghats, Eastern Himalaya and Terai Ecoregions in 2002 jointly with the Wildlife Institute of India (WII), Dehradun (a scientific institution), and two civil society organizations, Ashoka Trust for Research in Ecology and Environment, Bangalore (ATREE), and Nature Conservation Foundation, Mysore. The results of the assessment were discussed in a National Seminar on World Heritage Properties organized by WII on 23 September 2004. In 2006,

---

1 Another 33 properties have been included on India's tentative list of potential World Heritage sites, a prerequisite for inscription on the World Heritage List.

Left: Huts of Malappandaaram tribal people, Pathanam Thitta District, Kerala (Periyar Sub-cluster). Photo: Riyas

the Western Ghats Cluster was entered on India's tentative list as a potential 'serial' World Heritage site nomination.[2]

The seven Sub-clusters of the Western Ghats (see Figure 1) were then formally nominated as a serial natural site in January 2010 and first considered by the World Heritage Committee at its 35th session in June 2011. However, the nomination was 'referred' back to the State Party – which means that India had to provide additional information and meet some recommendations of the Committee for approval to be granted. The decision to refer was accompanied by a range of actions suggested to India, largely focused on ensuring that the size, complexity and scope of the proposed site were suitable and that appropriate management arrangements for the site would be formed. The decision also referenced, tangentially, a need for "participatory governance approaches", "increased engagement with all stakeholders", and greater "community membership and input" into the management of the site.[3]

The World Heritage Committee's lack of reference to local communities and indigenous peoples directly dependent on and living within the proposed sites was in contrast to local-level activism against the declaration of the site as World Heritage. The preparation of the nomination of the Western Ghats was met with protests from local inhabitants in various of the 39 component parts of the serial site – a population of approximately 100 000+ people is directly dependent on the 7,953.15 km^2 that was included in the proposed site. The tribal peoples living in these areas argued that they had not been involved in the preparation of the nomination of their lands, nor were they represented in the management structures that would take overall control of the sites. They also expressed concern that a World Heritage inscription would restrict their access to the lands and resources on which they depend.

Western Ghats: Adivasi homelands

The Western Ghats, a chain of mountains, runs parallel to India's western coast, about 30-50 km inland, and traverses the states of Kerala, Tamil Nadu, Karnataka, Goa, Maharashtra and Gujarat. Spread over 140,000 km^2 in a 1,609 km long stretch, it is interrupted by the Goa Gap, Palghat Gap and Shencotta Gap. It is the source of at least 60 rivers, including three major ones (the Krishna, Cauvery and Godavari) and is a lifeline for over 300 million people. It influences the entire Indian peninsula.

The Western Ghats is the abode and homelands of Adivasis in southern and western India. The term 'Adivasis' is the more socially acceptable and recognized term of reference and translates to the literal meaning of 'indigenous peoples'; however, the officially recognized term 'Scheduled Tribes' is often used instead and has a very specific legal

---

2   A serial nomination is any nomination that consists of two or more geographically unconnected areas.
3   Decision 35 COM 8B.9.

meaning.[4] Scheduled Tribes are notified by the President of India in relation to a particular state or union territory. The states of Kerala, Tamil Nadu, Karnataka and Maharashtra together have a total of 121 Scheduled Tribe communities.[5] Of these, 14 are also categorized as 'Particularly Vulnerable Tribal Groups' (earlier called 'Primitive Tribal Groups') as they are considered as the most marginalised among the Scheduled Tribes. At the time of the 2001 Census, the southern region consisting of Kerala, Tamil Nadu and Karnataka together had an Adivasi population of 4,479,496 with a share of 5.31% of the total ST population of the country and Maharashtra with 8,577,276 had a share of another 10.17%.[6] An overwhelming majority of Scheduled Tribes in Kerala and Karnataka inhabit the Western Ghats while in Tamil Nadu and Maharashtra a significant section of Scheduled Tribes dwell in the Western Ghats.

Over 300 hamlets with about 75,000 to 100,000 tribals, and over 4,000 non-tribals are located within the sites in Western Ghats now conferred with World Heritage status. Another 100,000+ people live in areas bordering these sites. These are the minimum estimates as no clear figures are available.[7] There are at least 29 tribal communities inhabiting these sites, of whom four are categorized as Particularly Vulnerable Tribal Groups, namely Cholanaicken (semi-nomadic cave dwellers 'discovered' by the outside world about four decades ago), Jenu Kuruba (honey gatherers), Koraga ('untouchables' forced to do the most menial and dirty jobs) and Paniya (mostly landless agricultural workers and forest produce gatherers). There are also subsistence farmers such as Mannan, Muthuvan, Kurichiar and Hallaki Gouda. Forest-dependent nomadic hunter-gatherers, foragers, forest produce collectors, agricultural workers and cultivators include the Paliya, Ulladan, Hill Pulaya, Urali, Irula and Siddi. The Siddis are the descendants of African slaves who were brought to India mainly by Arabs, the Portuguese and the Dutch. Adiya and Paniya, former bonded laborers working on plantations, are mostly landless. The Betta Kuruba produce household items such as baskets and sieves from bamboo and other forest produce. Only the three sites in Maharashtra do not have any tribal population. The Western Ghats therefore contains a significant array of cultural diversity and a diversity of relationships between the different indigenous and tribal peoples and the lands on which they depend. Altering the protected status of the Western Ghats impacts on each of these peoples in distinct ways; however, this was not considered in the World Heritage nomination process.

---

4   '*Scheduled Tribe*' is defined under Article 366 (25) of the Constitution of India as "such tribes or tribal communities or parts of, or groups within such tribes, or tribal communities as are deemed under Article 342 to be Scheduled Tribes for the purposes of this Constitution". This status, conferred on the basis of birth of a person into a Scheduled Tribe, offers certain specific constitutional privileges, protection and benefits. Although not all Scheduled Tribes are Adivasand vice versa, by and large, the Scheduled Tribes as a category covers most of the Adivasi communities. Moreover, a community recognized as Scheduled Tribe in one state need not be recognized similarly in another.
5   Kerala state has 36 Scheduled Tribes, Tamil Nadu 36, Karnataka 50 and Maharashtra 45. A number of their inhabited areas are divided between states and so they find themselves listed in more than one state as STs. Taken together, there are 121 ST communities.
6   Census of India 2001.
7   The calculations are based on a variety of sources, incl. Government of India 2009, National Tiger Conservation Authority 2011, Johnsingh 2000, data of the Forest Department, Kerala (maintained by the Chief Conservator of Forests and as per working/management plans) and personal communications.

Environmentally, the area is a rich store of biodiversity. An estimated 23% (43,611 km^2) of the original extent of forests (189,611 km^2) remains intact.[8] The Western Ghats is home to around 5,000 species of flowering plants (of which 1,700 are unique to the area), 58 endemic plant genera, 267 species of orchids, nearly 650 tree species, about 139 mammal species, 508 bird species, 179 species of amphibians, 157 species of reptiles, 218 species of fish and 330 species of butterflies. It has the world's largest population of endangered 'landscape' species such as the Asian elephant, with around 11,000 elephants, gaur and tigers. At least 325 globally threatened (IUCN Red Data List) species live in the Western Ghats. It is ranked, together with Sri Lanka, as one of the most important biodiversity hotspots globally, and is one of the Global 200 most important ecoregions.[9]

Whose land is it?

Spread throughout the states of Kerala, Tamil Nadu, Karnataka and Maharashtra, the Western Ghats serial sites total an area of 7,953.15 km^2. All of the 39 sites are forest areas administered by the Forest Department under the jurisdiction of the Ministry of Environment and Forests and the respective state governments. Within this designation, however, there is a wide range of legal frameworks that apply to the various sites in the Ghats, which makes a singular analysis of the legal situation of the lands problematic. Twenty-two of the sites fall within the Protected Area (PA) regime of either national parks or wildlife sanctuaries (2,028.76 km^2 and 3,064.39 km^2 respectively). Of these, two are notified as Critical Tiger Habitats in Tiger Reserves (with one more likely to be notified) while five more sites are part of three other Critical Tiger Habitats (totaling 1,954.35 km^2 under Critical Tiger Habitat status). The remaining sites are classed as either reserve forests (2,144 km^2) or forest divisions (716 km^2). There are therefore five different legal classifications of protected status currently active in the 39 component sites, each with different restrictions and permitted activities.

The legal status of the lands involved and the complexity therein reflects a wider situation in India. The appropriation of forested lands by the state has a long history, beginning when large tracts of Adivasi homelands were declared forest under the *Indian Forest Act, 1927*.[10] This law is a piece of central legislation and, together with the respective state laws patterned on the central law, represents a colonial regime that treats the area and its inhabitants as 'conquered'. The law stipulates that the rights of the inhabitants are to be recognized while declaring the areas as 'forest'. Many areas in the Western Ghats were notified as forest during British rule and have continued to be classified that way since India's independence. However, the legal rights of their inhabitants remained largely denied, unrecognized or unsettled, which means that they are treated as though they are encroachers and criminals.

The *Wildlife (Protection) Act, 1972* provides for the demarcation and notification of sections of forest for wildlife protection either by restricting human activity via Wildlife Sanctuaries or totally prohibiting it via National Parks.[11] However, in a study of Protected Areas, it was found that 69%

---

8   Of this, 140 000 km^2 are mountainous.
9   Government of India 2009, pp. 1-13.
10 Act No. 16 of 1927 [21 September 1927].
11 Act No. 53 of 1972 [9 September 1972]. For details on the procedures and restrictions imposed, see Chapter IV of the Act.

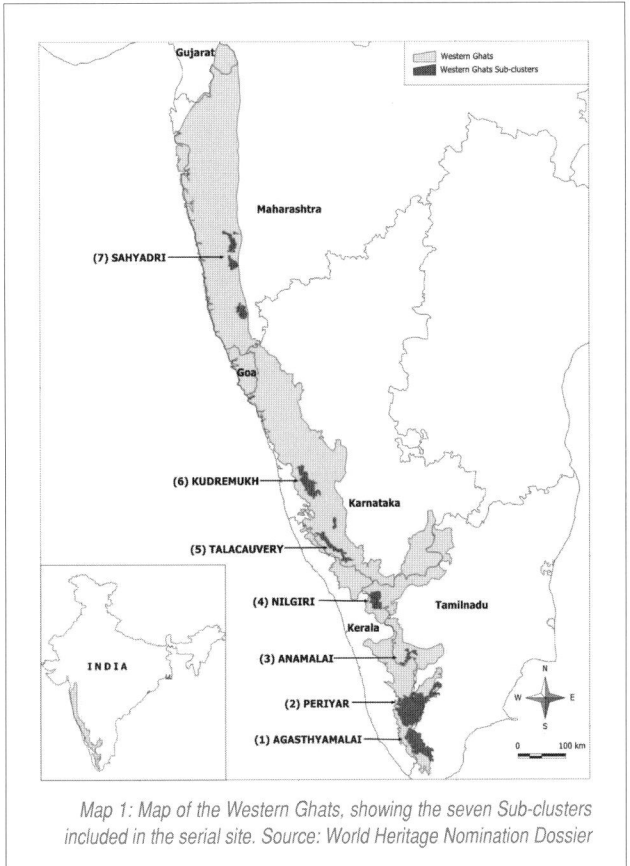

Map 1: Map of the Western Ghats, showing the seven Sub-clusters included in the serial site. Source: World Heritage Nomination Dossier

of PAs surveyed had human populations living inside the declared area and 64% had community rights, leases or other customary concessions.[12] Consultative processes involving local people during the declaration of the PAs and subsequent regulation and restriction of resource use were generally found to be lacking.

The *Forest (Conservation) Act, 1980* marked a shift in three important ways: by introducing the element of conservation to the previous approach of maximizing revenue through forest extraction; by prohibiting encroachment into the forests since 1980 and regulating the diversion of forest for non-forestry activities; and by making control over the forests a joint management responsibility with the central government whereas forests had previously been

---

12 Kothari et al. 1989.

the exclusive domain of the respective state governments.[13] The result was disastrous for the Adivasis. The slow process of settlement of rights of the traditional forest dwellers, an issue of persistent struggle since independence, came to an absolute halt, intensifying the crisis faced by Adivasis.

In 1990, the central government and the state governments jointly decided to settle some of the claims of these peoples and recognize a limited number of their rights;[14] however, the implementation of this joint decision never got off the ground and state governments ignored the relevant directives of the central government. The crisis of survival for Adivasis only deepened.

Forest governance: from a colonial to a democratic regime

The widespread illegal evictions that were taking place across the country in 2002 under the guise of reversing encroachment into the forests, and the consequent state violence, led to a nationwide struggle of Adivasis asserting their traditional and customary rights, insisting that 'historic injustice' be rectified through the recognition of their rights to their lands and resources.[15] The rapid spread of the Maoists and their armed struggle – predominantly in forested regions – simultaneously brought forested areas to the attention of both central and state governments.

The result of these pressures was the enactment of what is now popularly known as the 'Forest Rights Act' in 2006, which became operational on 1 January 2008.[16] The Act was drafted amidst a heated and bitterly contested national debate, both in the media and in the corridors of power.[17] The Act seeks "to recognise and vest the forest rights and occupation in forest land in forest dwelling Scheduled Tribes and other traditional forest dwellers who have been residing in such forests for generations but whose rights could not be recorded; to provide for a framework for recording the forest rights so vested and the nature of evidence required for such recognition and vesting in respect of forest land". It recognizes that "forest rights on ancestral lands and their habitat were not adequately recognised in the consolidation of state forests during the colonial period as well as in independent India resulting in *historical injustice* to the forest dwelling Scheduled Tribes and other traditional forest dwellers who are integral to the very survival and sustainability of the forest ecosystem".[18] The passage of this Act was a significant victory for recognition of the inherent rights of Adivasis to their traditional and customary lands and resources.

---

13 Act No. 69 of 1980 [27 December 1980].
14 This process was to include: a review of the claims of inhabitants who had contended that their claims to lands were not enquired into or commuted before notifying these lands as forests, the regularization of 'encroachment' prior to 1980, and the restoration of titles, grants and leases of lands that were illegally cancelled at the time of notification of forests and conversion of forest settlement into revenue settlement.
15 Led by the Campaign for Survival and Dignity, a coalition of over a hundred Adivasi mass organizations from 11 states; for details see www.forestrightsact.com.
16 *The Scheduled Tribes and Other Traditional Forest Dwellers (Recognition of Forest Rights) Act, 2006.* Act No. 2 of 2007 [29 December 2006].
17 For a detailed account of this, see Bijoy 2008.
18 Extracted from the preamble to the Forest Rights Act (emphasis added).

Arrayed against the interests and rights of Adivasi peoples in the passage of this Act were the powerful elite conservationists and environmentalists who not only angrily opposed any attempt at recognizing the rights of forest dwellers but blamed them squarely for the rapid decimation of forests and wildlife and demanded that they be forcibly evicted. This elite also targets those conservationists who show any support for community conservation.[19] This is despite the fact that conservation science itself has increasingly exposed the fallacy and myth of pristine inviolate wilderness while moving towards conservation with and by the people, especially indigenous peoples and forest dwellers.[20]

This period of heightened tension also occurred when the proposal to nominate the Western Ghats for World Heritage listing was first mooted. It is notable, however, that mention of the Forest Rights Act could be found neither in the 2009 proposal for nomination nor in the Supplementary Information submitted by MoEF at the request of IUCN in February 2011.[21] This is despite the fact that a significant part of the proposed sites fell within the customary and traditional boundary of Adivasi villages and the responsibility for conservation, including of the cultural and natural heritage in these areas, was legally vested in the *Gram Sabhas* or village assemblies (see below). For the MoEF, the Forest Rights Act (under which it is the *Gram Sabhas* who now have the power to protect and conserve forests falling under their jurisdiction) and its implementing agency, the Ministry of Tribal Affairs, simply did not figure in the proposed protection and management structure for the site. Neither did the IUCN evaluation see fit to point out this major flaw in the proposal.[22]

There was pushback against the rights recognized under the Forest Rights Act. In 2006, the *Wildlife Protection Act* was amended to provide for the establishment of a National Tiger Conservation Authority (NTCA) and the elevation of 'Tiger Reserves' from an administrative category to a legal category consisting of 'Critical Tiger Habitat', to be kept 'inviolate' from all human interference, and buffer zones where human activities were restricted.[23] Since the amendment was passed, there has been a rapid expansion in the number of areas declared protected and in which all human interference is banned. Assessment and recognition of the rights of the inhabitants was not carried out prior to a declaration of 'Critical Tiger Habitat', as legally required. The state governments did not follow the procedures for consulting and obtaining the informed consent of local communities legally mandated under the above

---

19 Sethi 2011.
20 Dowie 2009.
21 Government of India 2011.
22 IUCN's Advisory Body Evaluation mentions the Forest Rights Act only in the following context: "A number of sites have had their protection status and/or their boundaries altered since the nomination and this may have implications for management. In most cases this has strengthened protection, however, there are likely to be implications for ... relationships with local human populations. For example Tiger Reserves require core 'no go' areas which, in the past, required relocating people into buffer zones. The *Scheduled Tribes and Other Traditional Forest Dwellers (Recognition of Forest Rights) Act*, is leading to a redefined understanding of 'core', as property rights of forest dwellers have been recognised and forced relocation is banned. The implications of these changes need to be carefully weighed. The State Party did not provide detailed supplementary information on the changed protection status of component parts of the nomination." (IUCN 2011, p. 42).
23 *Wild Life (Protection) Amendment Act, 2006*, No. 39 of 2006 [3 September 2006].

Adivasis at the gate of the Periyar Tiger Reserve, Kerala, one of the 39 sites included in the Western Ghats 'serial' World Heritage site. Photo: Ashish Kothari

mentioned amendment to the *Wildlife Protection Act* nor did they negotiate the required resettlement packages with secure livelihoods prior to the identification and notification of a Critical Tiger Habitat.[24] Despite such criticisms and complaints, and despite active resistance by forest-dwelling communities, the MoEF and its National Tiger Conservation Authority have continued to demarcate Critical Tiger Habitat and relocate inhabitants through compensation packages that are not legally defensible.

Perpetuating historical injustice

The Forest Rights Act acknowledges a set of 13 rights, both individual and collective, and prescribes a democratic and transparent process for determining the rights of the communities through their *Gram Sabhas,* to be subsequently recognized by the state governments. This, in effect, recognizes not only the prior failure of the state governments to protect such rights but also the need for full and effective participation of the communities in rectifying the historic injustice to which they have been subjected. One key change brought about by the law is the recognition granted to 'community

---

24 For a detailed discussion on the law and practice, see Bijoy 2011.

forest resources', the "customary common forest land within the traditional or customary boundaries of the village" (Sec.2.a) where the communities were vested with the "right to protect, regenerate or conserve or manage any community forest resource which they have been traditionally protecting and conserving for sustainable use" (Sec.3.1.i). This right is to be exercised through the powers vested in the *Gram Sabha* for protecting wildlife, forest and biodiversity from "destructive practices affecting their cultural and natural heritage" (Sec.5).[25]

Expectations for change after the passage of the law were, however, disappointed. Even the official government Committee on Forest Rights Act concluded that "with notable exceptions, the implementation of the Forest Rights Act has been poor, and therefore its potential to achieve livelihood security and changes in forest governance along with strengthening of forest conservation, has hardly been achieved".[26] There has been a uniform reluctance to consider claims to community rights, particularly the most significant Community Forest Resource rights, across the country. At best, partial recognition to individual rights of occupation has taken place in some instances but rejection rates remain exceptionally high at over 50%.[27] One major impediment to the implementation of the Forest Rights Act has been the active resistance of the forest bureaucracy at all levels, with even numerous challenges to the Act itself being filed in a number of High Courts by retired forestry officers and in the Supreme Court by conservation non-government organizations, e.g. the Bombay Natural History Society,[28] Wildlife Trust of India, Wildlife Society of Orissa, All Assam Tribal Youth League, Wildlife First, Nature Conservation Society and Tiger Research and Conservation Trust.[29] MoEF has also been granting clearance, in violation of its own 30 July 2009 order, to hundreds of projects diverting the forest for non-forestry purposes without the consent of, and despite resolutions to the contrary by, the concerned *Gram Sabhas*.

In the case of Kerala and Karnataka, the implementation process has been particularly abysmal, and no titles have been issued at all in Tamil Nadu. Invariably, claims are not even considered in

---

25 In full, Section 5 of the Act ('Duties of holders of forest rights') states:
    "The holders of any forest right, Gram Sabha and village level institutions in areas where there are holders of any forest right under this Act are empowered to—
    a) protect the wild life, forest and biodiversity;
    b) ensure that adjoining catchments area, water sources and other ecological sensitive areas adequately protected;
    c) ensure that the habitat of forest dwelling Scheduled Tribes and other traditional forest dwellers is preserved from any form of destructive practices affecting their cultural and natural heritage;
    d) ensure that the decisions taken in the Gram Sabha to regulate access to community forest resources and stop any activity which adversely affects the wild animals, forest and the biodiversity are complied with."
26 National Committee on Forest Rights Act 2010.
27 As of 30 September 2013, out of 3.54 million claims filed (3.47 million individual and 71,154 community), 3.08 million were disposed of, of which about 1.41 million titles have been distributed. Updated data, including data for the individual States, are available at http://tribal.nic.in/Content/ForestRightActOtherLinks.aspx.
28 The Bombay Natural History Society withdrew from the case under pressure in April 2012. It is still the petitioner in a legal challenge to the provisions of the 2006 amendment to the Wildlife Protection Act 1972, however, which provides for a consultative and democratic process with local communities in the determination of Tiger Reserves and stipulates that Scheduled Tribes or other forest dwellers shall not be relocated from Critical Tiger Habitats unless their prior and informed consent has been obtained and their livelihoods have been secured.
29 For a brief on the court cases, see http://www.forestrightsact.com/court-cases.

protected areas, which is in violation of the law. Adivasis await settlement of their claims and continue to wait despite the clear law now in place guaranteeing them protection of their rights to forest lands and resources. Outside the forest area, the story is no different.

Unlike in central India and in the north-eastern region, in southern India no tribal area has been brought under the Fifth or Sixth Schedules of the Indian Constitution, which provide for a certain degree of self-management.[30] The *Panchayats (Extension to the Scheduled Areas) Act* (PESA 1996) formally recognized the primacy of the *Gram Sabha* (the village assembly) over key areas of community life in the Fifth Schedule Areas.[31] Kerala, Tamil Nadu and Karnataka have not brought Adivasi settlements under the Fifth Schedule despite the recommendation of the Dilip Singh Bhuria Committee, which was constituted by the central government to recommend the framework for PESA 1996.[32] This has also been criticized by the National Advisory Council of the Government of India, which has recommended, as recently as 2012, that tribal areas in these states be brought under the Fifth Schedule.[33] In Kerala, such autonomy is a demand of the Adivasis, and forms one of the terms of the agreement of 16 October 2001 between the Kerala government and the leaders of the Adivasi struggle. In Tamil Nadu, too, the official recommendation of the Tribal Welfare Department in 2002 was that "All tribal habitations (hamlets/villages) should be declared as 'Scheduled Area' under article 244(1) of the Constitution", yet this recommendation remains unattended.[34] Article 244 also mandates the state to enact legislation to protect the Adivasis from alienation of their lands and to restore illegally alienated land. While such laws have been enacted in a number of states, both Tamil Nadu and Karnataka have no such legislation. In the case of Kerala, although a law was enacted as far back as 1975, this was not implemented and the law was instead repealed in 1999 and alternative land proposed.[35] The impoverishment resulting from this denial of land rights led to an uprising in 2003 that was brutally suppressed.[36] Land rights, limited mostly to homestead or residence, are conferred usually only as a result of the persistent struggles of the Adivasi.

---

30   There is also one area in western India that is a Fifth Schedule Area: Maharashtra.
31   Act No. 40 of 1996 [24th December, 1996]. The *Gram Sabha* was recognized as having, inter alia: the competence to safeguard and preserve the traditions and customs of the people, their cultural identity and community resources; the power to prevent alienation of land in the Scheduled Areas and to take appropriate action to restore any unlawfully alienated land of a Scheduled Tribe; the ownership of minor forest produce; the planning and management of minor water bodies; the right to be consulted on matters of land acquisition for development projects and before resettling persons affected by such projects in the Scheduled Areas; the power to exercise control over institutions and functionaries in all social sectors; the power to control local plans and resources for such plans, including tribal sub-plans; and the power to issue utilization certificates for government works undertaken in their village.
32   See Bhuria Committee 1995, para. 7(2): "The process of scheduling was commenced in the fifties and was resumed in the seventies as a part of making the tribal sub-plan and scheduled areas co-terminus. But somehow it has remained incomplete. It is necessary that the remaining tribal sub-plan and MADA [Modified Area Development Approach] areas as well as similar pockets in West Bengal, Tamil Nadu, Kerala and Karnataka should be covered by scheduled areas notification."
33   National Advisory Council 2012, p. 16.
34   Adi Dravida and Tribal Welfare Department 2002.
35   For details see Bijoy 1999.
36   Bijoy and Raman 2003.

Gram Sabha meeting in Yelavali village, Bhimashankar Sanctuary, Maharashtra, in the process of claiming community forest rights under the Forest Rights Act. Photo: Ashish Kothari

All these are consistent with what a recent study of constitutional, legislative and administrative provisions concerning indigenous and tribal peoples in India and their relation to international law on indigenous peoples summarizes as follows: "The seemingly impressive range of legal and policy instruments that exist in Indian law for indigenous peoples' rights are vitiated by one fundamental flaw – the Indian state's reluctance to respect the political rights of indigenous peoples and the subsequent widespread violations".[37] Tamil Nadu and Karnataka, and to a slightly lesser extent Kerala, have failed to put in place the appropriate mechanisms to implement many of these impressive legal instruments and thus effectively denied recognition of the rights they protect.

Nomination of the Western Ghats

In January 2010, the Government of India submitted a nomination to UNESCO for the Western Ghats to be listed as a 'serial' natural World Heritage site. The nomination was prepared by MoEF and based on criterion (vii) ("contains superlative natural phenomena or areas of exceptional natural beauty and aesthetic importance") and criterion (x) ("contains the most important and significant

---

37 Bijoy, Gopalakrishnan and Khanna 2010, p.10.

natural habitats for in-situ conservation of biological diversity, including those containing threatened species of outstanding universal value from the point of view of science or conservation") of the World Heritage Convention's Operational Guidelines.[38] MoEF constituted a Western Ghats Natural Heritage Management Committee on 31 August 2010 for the purpose of "deal[ing] with matters relating to the inscription and management of the Western Ghats Serial Sites".[39] This Committee had 13 members but did not include any representatives of tribal peoples. It met in September of that year to review itinerary and logistics for the two-member IUCN team visiting to assess the scientific, technical and administrative aspects of the proposal through site visits and interactions with scientists, conservationists and government officials. From the report of the evaluation mission, it is evident that no meetings were scheduled with representatives of the Adivasis living in the 39 nominated sites.[40] The team travelled to the four states of Kerala, Tamil Nadu, Karnataka and Maharashtra, where the component sites are located, from 10-23 October 2010. Significantly, the team was confronted by various sections of the local population, including Adivasis, in some locations.[41] The local inhabitants were irked at the secrecy maintained by the forest officials and conservationists around the team's visit. The secrecy seemed to give credence to the suspicion that the whole exercise had a sinister objective of depriving the local inhabitants of whatever little rights they had, and that local inhabitants would be displaced or evicted as a result of the World Heritage designation.[42]

Following the evaluation mission, IUCN sent a request for supplementary information to the Government of India, stating, among other things, the following:

> "IUCN notes that evidence of a lack of community support for the nomination was witnessed by the evaluation mission through a demonstration that prevented the access of the mission to one of the nominated components of the property. Such a scale of protest by a local community is unusual in relation to IUCN's experience and would seem to imply the need for further stakeholder consultation in relation to at least some parts of the nomination. IUCN would be grateful for the State Party's advice on the nature and extent of community consultation it has carried out with regard to each of the nominated components of the property, and the degree to which there is presently community support for the nomination in each case... IUCN would also welcome the provision of more detailed advice by the State

---

38 While the original submission cited criteria (vii) and (x), IUCN considered that the property did not meet criterion (vii). It suggested that it instead be nominated under criteria (ix) and (x). The WH Committee in 2011 referred the nomination back to the State Party, noting its potential to meet criteria (ix) and (x), without mentioning criterion (vii). In 2012, the nomination was resubmitted under criteria (ix) and (x).
39 Government of India 2011, Appendix III ('Constitution of Western Ghats Natural Heritage Management Committee', 31 August 2010).
40 See IUCN 2011, p. 37, para 1d (Consultations).
41 See, for instance, *The Hindu* 2010. The Advisory Body Evaluation by IUCN states that the IUCN mission "witnessed strident opposition to NGOs, Government and the nomination in some places such as Kodagu and Karnataka" (IUCN 2011, p. 42).
42 See *Deccan Herald* 2010; *The Hindu* 2011b.

Party regarding the participation of local people foreseen in the proposed management system for the property, at both local levels and within the overall management system." [43]

In its response to IUCN's request for supplementary information, the Government of India asserted that "extensive stakeholder consultations" had been carried out both during the process of including the Western Ghats in India's tentative list and also during the preparation of the World Heritage nomination dossier. The protests against the nomination were dismissed by the Indian government as follows: "The '*one-off*' demonstration witnessed by the IUCN Evaluation Mission in one of 39 serial elements is no way a reflection of the lack of community support for this nomination. It was simply a manifestation of a local rivalry for seeking attention of the media and government."[44] The government further claimed "that the incident at Kodagu in which some local residents demonstrated their '*wrath*' to the IUCN Evaluation Mission against the proposed world heritage designation is basically a reflection of one vested interest group of people working against another group and cannot be considered as a generalized and popular view across the Western Ghats landscape… It is globally accepted that the world heritage designation to a site '*per se*' does not lead to any economic hardships/loss of livelihoods to the local communities. In view of the above, it is our considered view that not much credence should be given to the said petition [sent by the protesters to the Director-General of UNESCO]".[45]

The government acknowledged that "[t]he local communities including indigenous people living in and around these sites depend on a variety of resources mainly to sustain their livelihood needs" and that "[l]egal restrictions on the extraction of resources from the protected areas do affect the local communities and give rise to conflicts with the management". However, the government maintained that "involvement of local communities and securing their support" was already a focus of current management plans for the sites and that "processes of Joint Forest Management in managed forest areas and eco-development in protected areas are being focused and pursued in all sites" in order to "address the issues of local communities participating in the conservation initiatives and to categorically understand the quantum, nature and seasonality of resource dependency from these areas and to strategically address the issues". Although the government acknowledged that "[i]n some areas, the efforts being made are in the initial stages", it promised that "these will improve as the process evolves".[46]

It can be assumed that at least some of the indigenous peoples and organizations from the Western Ghats would not have been satisfied with these explanations and assurances by the Indian government had they been asked for their opinion and views. However, neither the original nomination document nor the supplementary information submitted at the request of IUCN was made public by the Indian government, or UNESCO, prior to the 35th session of the

---

43 IUCN Evaluation of Western Ghats (India) – Request for Supplementary Information', 6 January 2010. Contained in Government of India 2011, Appendix I.
44 Government of India 2011, p. 19.
45 Ibid., Appendix II (Letter from the Inspector General of Forests).
46 Ibid., p. 23.

World Heritage Committee at which the nomination was considered. Indigenous organizations from Western Ghats were therefore not informed about the content of these documents and the various explanations and claims presented by the Indian government.

On 17 May 2011, a joint statement was delivered at the United Nations Permanent Forum on Indigenous Issues, endorsed by a number of Adivasi organizations from the Western Ghats,[47] in which they denounced the fact that the World Heritage nomination of the Western Ghats was "prepared without meaningful involvement and consultation of the Indigenous peoples concerned and without obtaining their free, prior and informed consent" and that insufficient consideration had been given to the indigenous cultural values connected to the nominated sites. The joint statement urged the World Heritage Committee to defer the nomination and call on the Indian government "to consult and collaborate with the Indigenous peoples concerned, in order to ensure that their values and needs are reflected in the nomination documents and management plans and to obtain their free, prior and informed consent".[48] After being delivered to the UN Permanent Forum, the statement was submitted to the Bureau of the World Heritage Committee, the World Heritage Centre, the Director-General of UNESCO as well as the three Advisory Bodies, IUCN, ICOMOS and ICCROM, prior to the World Heritage Committee's session.[49] In addition, the UN Permanent Forum called on the World Heritage Committee to "scrutinize current World Heritage nominations to ensure they comply with international norms and standards of free, prior and informed consent".[50] It should also be noted that the government of Karnataka officially opposed the nomination of the 10 component parts within Karnataka, expressing concern, among other things, at the implications for the rights of the tribal peoples living within the forest areas.[51]

IUCN's technical evaluation of the nomination (which was not made public until after the World Heritage Committee's session) noted that "there are obvious concerns in some locations over what listing would mean" and that the IUCN mission "witnessed strident opposition to NGOs, Government and the nomination in some places such as Kodagu and Karnataka".[52] While the IUCN evaluation

---

47 Budakattu Krishikara Sangha (Karnataka), Pothigaimalai Adivasi Kanikkaran Samuthaya Munnetra Sangam (Tamil Nadu), Adivasi Gothrajaan Sabha (Kerala), Adivasi Gothra Mahasabha (Kerala) and Kerala Girivarga Kanikkar Sangham (Kerala). Taken together, these organizations represent indigenous peoples from 20 of the 39 sites included in the serial nomination.

48 Endorois Welfare Council et al. 2011. 'Joint Statement on continuous violations of the principle of free, prior and informed consent in the context of UNESCO's World Heritage Convention'.

49 Additionally, the main concerns expressed in the joint statement were reiterated in an oral intervention of the International Work Group for Indigenous Affairs (IWGIA) during the World Heritage Committee's session, on 23 June 2011 (the day before the vote on Western Ghats was taken).

50 Permanent Forum on Indigenous Issues 2011, para. 42. The same recommendation was repeated in an oral statement to the World Heritage Committee by Permanent Forum member Paul Kanyinke Sena on 22 June 2011.

51 See, e.g., The Hindu 2011a; The Hindu 2011c.

52 IUCN 2011, p. 42.

Forest-dwelling community in southwest Karnataka. Photo: Kai Vara

considered the local inhabitants of the nominated sites mainly in the context of discussing threats to the natural values of the sites,[53] it recognized that "property rights of forest dwellers have been recognized" through the Forest Rights Act and criticized the fact that the implications of this had not been sufficiently taken into account in the proposal.[54] The technical evaluation also noted that "there are some unclear land tenure issues", due to the fact that parts of the property are private land or community-controlled land, making it "difficult to effectively evaluate adequate protection".[55] IUCN therefore concluded, for these and other reasons, that "the management of the nominated property does not meet the requirements set out in the Operational Guidelines" and that "the protection status of at least parts of the nominated property does not meet the requirements set out in the Operational Guidelines".[56] IUCN recommended that the Committee *defer* examination of the nomination to allow the State Party to address the various issues.

On 24 June 2011, the Committee instead decided to *refer* the nomination of Western Ghats back to the State Party, which meant that India needed to provide some additional information but could resubmit the nomination to the following Committee session for examination. (In contrast,

---

53 For instance, the evaluation observed that "many of the natural areas have been disturbed... with different types of cultivation... as well as human habitation" and that "[i]nevitably the presence of human settlements [within or in close proximity to the nominated sites] poses a threat to the natural values of the property components through issues such as encroachment, livestock grazing, fodder and fuel wood collection, illegal hunting and increasing interest in tourism-related activity among others". Pilgrimage sites within some components of the property were also mentioned as a threat, due to the "resultant periodic heavy use and impact" (ibid., pp. 38-39).
54 Ibid., p. 42.
55 Ibid., p. 40.
56 Ibid. p. 41-42.

a deferral would have required substantial revisions or more in-depth research by the State Party and necessitated a complete re-evaluation and an additional site visit by IUCN.) The Committee's decision stated that the nomination was referred, among other things, in order to allow the State Party to "facilitate increased engagement with all stakeholders to build awareness and support, foster participatory governance approaches, and ensure equitable sharing of benefits" and to "strengthen community membership and input" in the management of the component sites. The decision further called on the Indian government to "harmonize arrangements between the 'Western Ghats Natural Heritage [Management] Committee' and the 'Western Ghats Ecology Expert Panel'", and to "review the scope and composition of the current serial nomination to take account of any recommendations of the 'Western Ghats Ecology Expert Panel'… to further enhance the protection of the values of the nominated property".[57]

The Western Ghats Ecology Expert Panel (WGEEP) was set up by MoEF in 2010 to "assess the current status of ecology of the Western Ghats region", "demarcate areas which need to be notified as ecologically sensitive" and "make recommendations for the conservation, protection and rejuvenation of the Western Ghats Region following a comprehensive consultation process involving people and Governments of all the concerned States".[58] The final report of the WGEEP was issued in August 2011, while MoEF was preparing the additional information requested by the World Heritage Committee.[59] The report stressed that "The Forest Rights Act (FRA) 2006 has yet to be implemented in its true spirit and the State Forest Departments to be alerted to the fact that implementation of this act is needed for future forestry governance".[60] In regard to the World Heritage nomination, the WGEEP concluded that there was "a need for greater participation of local people and communities in formulation and implementation of the Western Ghats National Heritage proposal", adding that the "objections raised at the UN Permanent Forum on Indigenous Issues to the Indian proposals on 17 May 2011" were "serious and quite genuine".[61] The Panel also noted that it was "inappropriate to depend exclusively on Government agencies for constitution and management of Ecologically Sensitive Zones". The Panel suggested that instead "the final demarcation of the Zones (…also in context of the UNESCO Heritage Site proposal)…, and fine-tuning of the regulatory as well as promotional regimes, must be based on extensive inputs from local communities and local bodies" and that the "process of fine-tuning the limits of the various zones, deciding on management regimes and the implementation be a participatory process going right down to gram sabhas". Such an approach, the WGEEP remarked, "would more effectively serve the objectives of the UNESCO Heritage Programme, than the proposals currently submitted by the Government of India".[62]

---

57   Decision 35 COM 8B.9.
58   Ministry of Environment and Forests 2010
59   The WGEEP's report was only made public by MoEF in May 2012 following a court directive, and with a disclaimer that it had not been formally accepted by the Ministry and was being analyzed and considered by the Ministry. See Dhar 2012; Garg 2012.
60   WGEEP 2011, Part II, p. 66
61   Ibid., Part II, pp. 121, 322.
62   Ibid., Part I, p. 40; Part II, p. 121.

Despite these recommendations of the WGEEP, the Government of India went ahead and resubmitted the Western Ghats World Heritage nomination to UNESCO in January 2012. The additional information submitted by India[63] continued to ignore the Forest Rights Act and the statutory authority of the *Gram Sabhas*, and the Government did not "strengthen community membership and input" as requested by the World Heritage Committee, nor did it "facilitate increased engagement with all stakeholders to build awareness and support, foster participatory governance approaches, and ensure equitable sharing of benefits". In response to the Committee's request that India review the scope and composition of the serial nomination taking into account the recommendations of the WGEEP, the government claimed that: "The matter of determining the inclusion/exclusion of sites in the serial nomination has not been dealt by the Western Ghats Ecology Expert Panel and accordingly there are no recommendations on this issue".[64] In fact, however, the report of the WGEEP did deal with the subject, as outlined above.

IUCN evaluated the additional information submitted by India and recommended, once again, that the nomination be deferred. Among other things, IUCN saw a need for the State Party to "undertake a further consultation to facilitate increased engagement to ensure the views of all stakeholders, including local indigenous groups are considered, in order to ensure and demonstrate broad-based support for the nomination". IUCN also recommended that the Indian government "review and refine the scope and composition of the current serial nomination to take into account the recommendations of the WGEEP noting the Panel was tasked to... define ecologically sensitive areas through consultation".[65]

In the meantime, Adivasi organizations in the Western Ghats again submitted a joint statement to the 2012 Session of the UN Permanent Forum on Indigenous Issues, to UNESCO and to the World Heritage Committee urging the Committee not to approve the nomination of Western Ghats "or any other nominations of sites in Indigenous peoples' territories, until it has been ensured that the Indigenous peoples concerned have been adequately consulted and involved and that their free, prior and informed consent has been obtained". The statement noted:

"The Government of India has resubmitted a revised nomination in January 2012, however, there still has not been any meaningful involvement and consultation of the affected Indigenous peoples and their free, prior and informed consent has not been attained. This is underscored by the fact that the revised nomination documents have not been made public by the Indian Government and are also kept secret by UNESCO. It is clear then that the concerns raised in last year's joint statement have not been adequately addressed... We are deeply troubled by the lack of transparency and the secrecy of the procedures.

It is noteworthy that the concerns raised in last year's joint statement have been corroborated in the final report of the Western Ghats Ecology Expert Panel (WGEEP)... We

---

63 Government of India 2012.
64 Ibid., pp. 10-11.
65 IUCN 2012.

are deeply concerned that the revised nomination..., which could only be obtained through unofficial sources, conceals the conclusions of the WGEEP regarding the World Heritage nomination. We are also concerned that the nomination documents still do not acknowledge nor recognize the Forest Rights Act according to which the village assemblies (gram sabhas) have statutory authority over the management and protection of significant parts of the nominated areas." [66]

The statement was sent to all members of the World Heritage Committee on 23 May 2012 and receipt was acknowledged by the Chairperson during the Committee's 36th session in Saint Petersburg.[67] However, the Committee – of which India was a member – resolved to inscribe the Western Ghats on the World Heritage List on the basis of criteria (ix) and (x), rejecting the assessment of IUCN and ignoring the objections of the Adivasi organizations.[68] The concerns regarding the lack of consultation of indigenous peoples were not discussed by the Committee, except for the fact that the Indian representative, Ambassador Vinay Sheel Oberoi, declared that India was a democracy and that each of the indigenous communities in the Western Ghats had been "a part and a party to the process". He also maintained that the nomination had "gone through a process of community consultation mandated by law" and that the boundaries of the World Heritage site had been defined with "the greatest possible consultation".[69] In essence, being a member of the Committee, India lobbied hard to make sure its nomination was approved and the Committee meeting was just a formality, a farce devoid of facts or science.

The Statement of Outstanding Universal Value (OUV) adopted by the World Heritage Committee states that all component parts of the serial site are "owned by the State and are subject to stringent protection under laws including the Wildlife (Protection) Act of 1972, the Indian Forest Act of 1927, and the Forest Conservation Act (1980). Through these laws the components are under the control of the Forestry Department and the Chief Wildlife Warden, thus the legal status is adequate." [70] The OUV Statement fails to mention the Forest Rights Act, although this law overrides all the other forest laws, substantively and qualitatively changing the forest governance in most parts of the forests in the country.[71] What is thus being denied is the legal reality that the forest communities are now the statutory authority to govern and manage those forests under their traditional and customary usage, qualifying as 'Community Forest Resource' under the Forest Rights Act. Instead MoEF is projecting the so-called 'Village Eco-development Committees' as the sole effective instrument for community participation,[72] which, unlike the *Gram Sabhas*, are controlled by the forest bureaucracy and created

---

66 For the complete statement, which also contains a summary of the relevant recommendations of the WGEEP, see IWGIA et al. 2012.
67 See UNESCO 2012, p. 130.
68 See ibid., p. 193 ff. and World Heritage Committee Decision 36COM 8B.10.
69 A recording of the debate is available at http://whc.unesco.org/en/sessions/36COM/records (See July 1, 2012, at 6:49 PM – 6:53 PM).
70 Decision 36COM 8B.10, para. 3.
71 It should be noted that IUCN, too, failed to list the Forest Rights Act among the laws governing the protection of the serial site (see IUCN 2011; 2012).
72 See Government of India 2012, pp. 23-24.

by administrative fiat. This reflects a disrespect for the law and a desire for hegemonic control over the forests, relegating conservation to the periphery. MoEF also refuses to acknowledge the existence of *Panchayat Raj* institutions (locally-elected governance bodies), or the elected members of the relevant state legislatures and of the Parliament, in its desperation to keep everything exclusively within the confines of the forest bureaucracy. In inscribing the Western Ghats on the World Heritage List, the World Heritage Committee therefore neither upheld the principles of the *UN Declaration on the Rights of Indigenous Peoples* nor Indian laws but instead provided prestige and legitimacy to something that is patently illegal and unjust with regard to indigenous peoples.

Conclusion and recommendation

The designation of Western Ghats as a natural World Heritage site has to be contextualized and placed in the reality of its traditional inhabitants, the Adivasis or Scheduled Tribes, including the widespread violations of their rights both historically and to the present day. There is a fear, which was expressed by local peoples during the IUCN evaluation and afterwards, that the inscription of the Western Ghats on the World Heritage List will precipitate a survival crisis. Union Environment Minister, Jayanthi Natarajan, has tried to allay these fears by stating that "tribal communities living in and around the 39 serial sites will not be adversely affected by the World Heritage designation" and that listing would "in no way affect the present management regime of the sites, which would be managed… under the legal provisions of the Wildlife Protection Act, Indian Forest Act and the Forest Rights Act".[73]

Such promises are hardly reassuring to the traditional inhabitants, considering that the Forest Rights Act was not even mentioned in the nomination documents and is routinely violated in India and Western Ghats. Moreover, the Forest Rights Act was violated during the World Heritage nomination itself, which was prepared without the full and effective participation of the *Gram Sabhas* concerned and submitted without obtaining their free, prior and informed consent. The decision of the World Heritage Committee to inscribe the Western Ghats without insisting on a substantial revision of the nomination that takes adequate account of the implications of the Forest Rights Act compounds the gross illegality of the Indian government agencies. This made the World Heritage Committee a collaborator in the violation of the traditional inhabitants' rights. The added prestige brought to the site by international recognition and the pressure that inscription entails are likely to perpetuate injustices. World Heritage inscription in ignorance and violation of existing rights and without the consent of the traditional inhabitants delays the recognition of rights and is an incentive to continue denying those rights.

---

73 Cited in Gandhi 2011. Similarly, the previous Environment Minister, Jairam Ramesh, stated in June 2011 that "these sites would continue to be managed under national laws and will not be subject to any additional legal provisions imposed by UNESCO. I would like to reiterate that the World Heritage designation will in no way affect the tribal and other local communities living in and around these sites" (*The Economic Times* 2011).

The World Heritage Committee is aware of these concerns. At its 35th Session in June 2011, the Committee adopted a decision that explicitly "encourages States Parties to... Respect the rights of indigenous peoples when nominating, managing and reporting on World Heritage sites in indigenous peoples' territories".[74] However, this decision was not reflected in the instructions given to India at the 35th and 36th Sessions regarding the Western Ghats nomination.

This situation can be redeemed only by ensuring that the rights of indigenous peoples are respected in the Western Ghats through a series of actions. First, there should be a complete and satisfactory implementation of the Forest Rights Act in the listed sites prior to any further action by MoEF to develop or implement new management and governance mechanisms for the World Heritage site. Any new management systems for these sites should incorporate the relevant *Gram Sabhas* as the authority with power to protect wildlife, forest and biodiversity from 'destructive practices affecting their cultural and natural heritage' in the customary and traditional boundary of Adivasi villages recognized as a 'community forest resource'. As part of this, the free, prior and informed consent of the relevant *Gram Sabhas* must be obtained before any new governance or management mechanisms are introduced, not just as a matter of principle but as an implicit legal requirement under the Forest Rights Act. Finally, the Ministry of Tribal Affairs should be included on a par with the Ministry of Environment and Forests as the agency responsible for the sites. ○

References

Adi Dravida and Tribal Welfare Department, Government of Tamilnadu. 2002. *Report on Tenth Five Year Plan 2002-2007*. Chennai, Adi Dravida and Tribal Welfare Department.

Bhuria Committee. 1995. *Report of MPs and Experts to make recommendations on the salient features of the law for extending provisions of the Constitution (73rd) Amendment Act, 1992, to Scheduled Areas*. 17 January 1995.

Bijoy, C.R. 1999. Adivasis Betrayed: Adivasi Land Rights in Kerala. *Economic and Political Weekly*, Vol. XXXIV, No. 22, pp.1329-35.

Bijoy, C.R. 2008. Forest Rights Struggle: The Adivasis Now Await a Settlement. *American Behavioral Scientist*, Vol.51, No. 12, August 2008, pp.1755-73.

Bijoy, C.R. 2011. The Great Indian Tiger Show. *Economic & Political Weekly*, Vol. XLVI, No. 4, pp.36-41.

Bijoy, C.R. and Raman, R. 2003. Muthanga: The Real Story – Adivasi Movement to Recover Land. *Economic & Political Weekly*, Vol. XXXVIII, No. 20, pp.1975-82.

Bijoy, C.R., Gopalakrishnan, S. and Khanna, S. 2010. *India and the Rights of Indigenous Peoples: Constitutional, Legislative and Administrative Provisions Concerning Indigenous and Tribal Peoples in India and their Relation to International Law on Indigenous peoples*. Asia Indigenous Peoples Pact (AIPP), Thailand.

Campaign for Survival and Dignity. 2009. *Court Cases Against the Forest Rights Act*. http://www.forestrightsact.com/court-cases (Accessed 17 October 2013).

Deccan Herald News Service. 2010. World heritage tag proposal for Western Ghat opposed. *Deccan Herald*, 18 October 2010.

Dhar, A. 2012. Western Ghats expert panel report out in public domain. *The Hindu*, 25 May 2012.

Dowie, M. 2009. *Conservation Refugees: The Hundred-Year Conflict between Global Conservation and Native Peoples*. Cambridge, MIT Press.

Endorois Welfare Council et al. 2011. *Joint Statement on continuous violations of the principle of free, prior and informed consent in the context of UNESCO's World Heritage Convention* (Joint statement of indigenous organizations and NGOs from around the world). Available at: www.forestpeoples.org/sites/fpp/files/publication/2012/04/joint-statement-indigenous-organizations-unesco-2.pdf.

---

74 Decision 35 COM 12E, para. 15.f.

Gandhi, D. 2011. Western Ghats panel report on Wednesday. *The Hindu*, 17 September 2011.

Garg, A. 2012. Release Western Ghats report, Delhi high court tells environment ministry. *The Times of India*, 20 May 2012.

Government of India. 2009. *Serial Nomination of The Western Ghats of India: Its Natural Heritage For Inscription on the World Natural Heritage List Submitted by State Party: India, 2009.*

Government of India. 2011. *Serial Nomination of the Western Ghats, India on the UNESCO Natural World Heritage List – Supplementary Information Submitted by State Party: India to IUCN and UNESCO World Heritage Centre, February 2011.*

Government of India. 2012. *Serial Nomination of the Western Ghats, India on the UNESCO Natural World Heritage List: Response to the World Heritage Committee Decision 35 COM 8B.9, Submitted by State Party: India to UNESCO World Heritage Centre, Paris, January, 2012.*

IUCN. 2011. *World Heritage Nomination – IUCN Technical Evaluation: Western Ghats (India).* UNESCO Doc. WHC-11/35.COM/INF.8B2, pp. 35-47.

IUCN. 2012. *World Heritage Nomination – IUCN Technical Evaluation: Western Ghats (India).* UNESCO Doc. WHC-12/36.COM/INF.8B2, pp. 51-61.

IWGIA et al. 2012. *Joint Submission on the Lack of implementation of the UN Declaration on the Rights of Indigenous Peoples in the context of UNESCO's World Heritage Convention* (Joint submission of indigenous organizations and NGOs from around the world). Available at: http://www.forestpeoples.org/sites/fpp/files/publication/2012/05/joint-submission-unpfii.pdf.

Johnsingh, A.J.T. 2000. Neyyar Wildlife Sanctuary. *Wildlife Institute of India Newsletter*, Vol. 7, Nos. 3 and 4, 2000.

Kothari, A. et al. 1989. *Management of National Parks and Sanctuaries in India: A Status Report.* New Delhi, Indian Institute of Public Administration.

Ministry of Environment and Forests. 2010. *Office Order: Constitution of Western Ghats Ecology Expert Panel.* No.1/1/2010- RE (ESZ), 4 March 2010. Available at http://moef.nic.in/downloads/public-information/OO-const-westernghats.pdf.

National Advisory Council. 2012. *Recommendations on Panchayat (Extension to the Scheduled Areas) Act, 1996.* 31 December 2012. Available at: http://nac.nic.in/pdf/pesa_31dec.pdf.

National Committee on Forest Rights Act. 2010. *Manthan: Report by the National Committee on Forest Rights Act.* A joint committee of Ministry of Environment and Forests and Ministry of Tribal Affairs, Government of India. Available at http://www.cgforest.com/English/Reports.htm.

National Tiger Conservation Authority. 2011. Kalakad – Mundanthurai Tiger Reserve. http://projecttiger.nic.in/kalakad.htm (Accessed 17 October 2013).

Permanent Forum on Indigenous Issues. 2011. *Report on the tenth session (16-27 May 2011).* UN Doc. E/2011/43-E/C.19/2011/14.

WGEEP. 2011. *Report of the Western Ghats Ecology Expert Panel*, 31 August 2011 (two Parts and Summary). Government of India, MoEF. Available at: http://cat.org.in/index.php/article/western-ghats-ecology-expert-panel-wgeep-report/.

Sethi, N. 2011. Scientist Sacked for Supporting Tribal Rights. *The Times Of India*, 22 May 2011.

The Economist Times. 2011. Heritage tag to Western Ghat sites to benefit local populace: Ramesh. *The Economist Times*, 21 June 2011 (ET Bureau).

The Hindu. 2010. IUCN team heckled in Madikeri. *The Hindu*, 20 October 2010 (anonymous Staff Correspondent).

The Hindu. 2011a. Fear of eviction unfounded. *The Hindu*, 18 June 2011 (anonymous Staff Reporter).

The Hindu. 2011b. People of Kodagu oppose World Heritage tag for Western Ghats. *The Hindu*, 28 June 2011 (anonymous Staff Correspondent).

The Hindu. 2011c. State declines heritage tag for sites in Western Ghats. *The Hindu*, 15 June 2011 (anonymous Special Correspondent).

UNESCO. 2012. *World Heritage Committee, Thirty-sixth session, Saint Petersburg, Russian Federation 24 June – 6 July 2012: Summary Record.* Doc. WHC-12/36.COM.INF.19.

Indigenous Peoples and Modern Liabilities in the Thung Yai Naresuan Wildlife Sanctuary, Thailand: A Conflict over Biocultural Diversity

Reiner Buergin

Introduction

Since the 1970s, a global environmental and developmental crisis has been conceptualized and negotiated in controversial modern discourses about nature conservation, sustainable development and globalization. The need to protect endangered 'natural forests', 'wilderness areas' and 'biodiversity hotspots' as global heritage and assets figures prominently in academic arguments and conservation strategies of non-governmental organizations, as well as in the policies of national and international administrative bodies.

In this context, conflicts have emerged between culturally diverse local communities, particularly indigenous peoples, who derive their livelihoods and identity from their lands and resources, and external modern actors and institutions who claim rights and control over these areas and resources, invoking national and global interests in nature conservation and modernization. These conflicts represent an historically specific expression of competing claims at the fringes of expanding modern societies, framed in current discourses which increasingly propose, at the same time, the preservation of biological as well as cultural diversity.

Left: A Karen house in Gosadeng village in the Thung Yai Naresuan Wildlife Sanctuary. Photo: Reiner Buergin

This article is concerned with these widespread conflicts over bio-cultural diversity, focusing on the particular case of the Karen indigenous communities living in the Thung Yai Naresuan Wildlife Sanctuary in Western Thailand. Together with the adjoining Huai Kha Khaeng Wildlife Sanctuary, their living place was declared a UNESCO World Heritage site in December 1991. The two sanctuaries encompass more than 6 200 km² and are the core area of the so-called Western Forest Complex, constituting Thailand's largest remaining forest area. Based on an extensive study of the history and current situation of the Karen communities in Thung Yai, the paper will refer to the relationship between the local communities and their natural and social environments, their interaction with the Thai state and the World Heritage nomination and management systems, recount changing ideological and legal views of the conflict, and explore approaches to solving the problems.

History, identity and livelihood of Karen people in Thung Yai

At the beginning of the 21st century, some 3 500 people are living in the Thung Yai Naresuan Wildlife Sanctuary. Most of them are Pwo Karen and were born in Thailand, predominantly within the sanctuary itself. They generally grow rice as subsistence farmers on swidden and paddy fields.[1] According to Karen oral history, their ancestors came to the area fleeing political and religious suppression in Burma after the Burmese had conquered the Mon kingdoms of Lower Burma in the 18th century. The first written historic references to their residence in Siam's[2] western border area can be found in chronicles of the late 18th century. In the early 19th century, they received formal settlement rights from the Governor of Kanchanaburi, and the rank of Siamese nobility *Khun Suwan* was conferred on their leader. When the status of the border area was raised to that of a *muang* or principality – between 1827 and 1839 – the Karen leader of the *muang* was awarded the title of *Phra Si Suwannakhiri* by King Rama III. Since 1873 at the latest, *Phra Si Suwannakhiri* has resided in Sanepong, which became the centre of the *muang* and is now one of the Karen villages lying within the Wildlife Sanctuary. During the second half of the 19th century this *muang* was of considerable importance to the Siamese kings, guarding part of their western border with British Burma. Karen living there were consulted regarding the delineation of the border between Siam and Burma under King Rama V.[3] It was only at the beginning of the 20th century, after the establishment of the modern Thai nation state, that the Karen in Thung Yai lost their former status, reappearing on the national political agenda as forest encroachers and illegal immigrants towards the end of the 20th century.

The Thai name *Thung Yai* (big field) refers to a savannah in the centre of the sanctuary. For the Karen, the savannah is a place of deep spiritual significance, referred to in Karen as *pia aethala aethae*, which can be translated as 'place of the knowing sage'. The Karen term

---

1   The survey data on which this article is based is accessible in Buergin 2002a, 2004, see also note 6.
2   The Kingdom of Siam was renamed Thailand in 1939.
3   See Buergin 2004, pp. 83-100; regarding the history of the western border areas see also Renard 1980; Thongchai 1994.

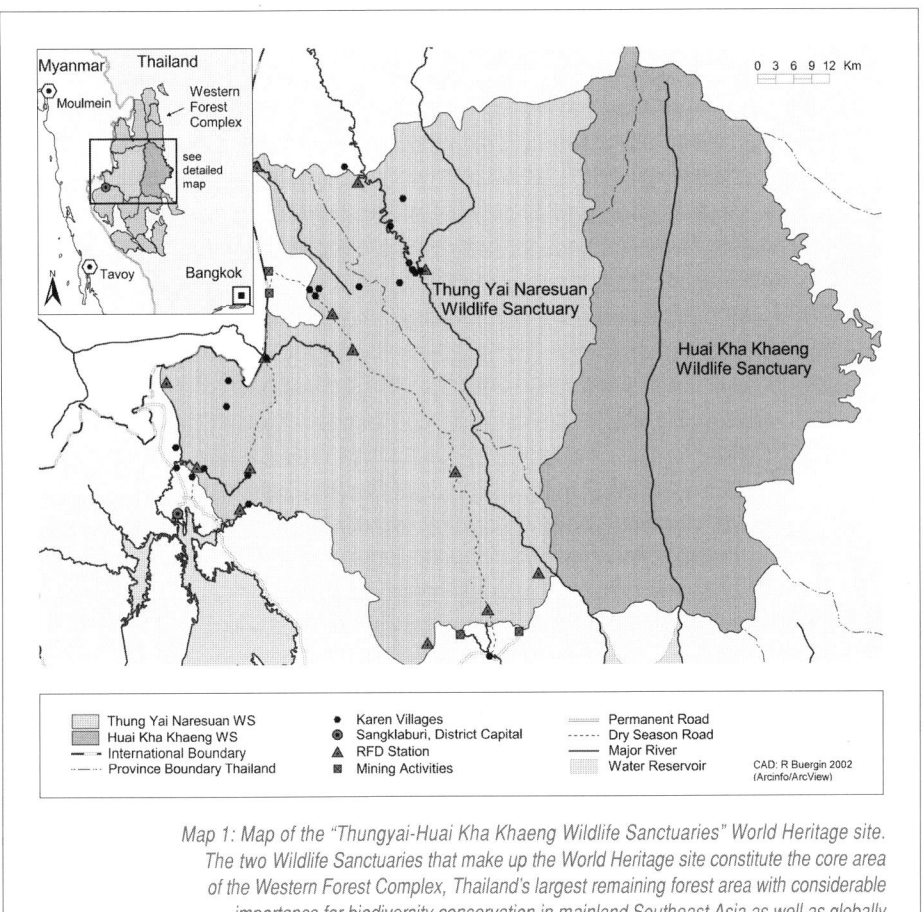

Map 1: Map of the "Thungyai-Huai Kha Khaeng Wildlife Sanctuaries" World Heritage site. The two Wildlife Sanctuaries that make up the World Heritage site constitute the core area of the Western Forest Complex, Thailand's largest remaining forest area with considerable importance for biodiversity conservation in mainland Southeast Asia as well as globally

aethae refers to mythological hermits who, according to Karen lore, lived and meditated in the savannah. The story of these hermits is important for the identity of the Karen in Thung Yai and they are honoured. Karen seeking spiritual development still retreat to this place for meditation. To refer to their community and homeland, the Karen in Thung Yai use the term *thong bou tai*. The term refers to a specific way of life and values, focusing on the control of greed and spiritual development. These conceptions are related to the Telakho sect, a millenarian Buddhist sect originating in the middle of the 19th century, possibly in or close to the present-day sanctuary, and which is still influential in Thung Yai.[4] All the villages in the sanctuary, as well as some Karen villages at the edge of the sanctuary, are included in this culturally and geographically determined community.

---

4   See Stern 1968; Ewers Andersen 1976; Buergin 2004.

Karen ceremony for the guardian of the forest 'rukkhajue', part of a big festival in the 'Thung Yai' savannah to honour the mythological hermits 'aethae'. Photo: Reiner Buergin

The Karen in Thung Yai conceive of themselves as people living in and of the forest, as part of a very complex community of plants, animals, humans and spiritual beings. Within this community, the Karen do not feel superior but rather as highly dependent on the various other beings and forces. Living in this community requires adaptation as well as specific knowledge about the interdependencies and rules of the community. Fostering relations with the various caretaker spirits of this 'forest community' is an important part of Karen life in the sanctuary. Their permission and support has to be sought continuously in order to live in and use the forest and land. From a modern perspective, many of these rules and traditions could be labelled 'ecological knowledge'. In these rules and norms, as well as in their daily livelihood practices, passed on and transformed from generation to generation, a very rich and specific knowledge has been conserved about the environment of the Karen.

The Karen's relations with the outside world, specifically the 'Thai world', have changed frequently. During the first half of the 20th century, the Karen communities were largely autonomous, even though the villages in Thung Yai were formally integrated into the Thai nation state. It was not until the 1960s, in the wake of the growing interest of the state in its peripheral areas, that state institutions became increasingly relevant in Thung Yai: stations of the Border Patrol Police (BPP) were established in the 1960s, followed by various state offices supporting 'development', as well as the Royal Forest Department (RFD) and the military since the 1980s.

The permanent presence of Thai people in Karen villages since the 1960s, as well as the activities of government institutions aimed at assimilating the Karen into the Thai nation state, resulted in changes in the social, political and religious organization of Karen communities in Thung Yai. These include the decreasing importance of the traditional Karen matrifocal kinship groups and the emergence of a more household-centred and patrifocal ritual system at the village level, the clash of a rather egalitarian and consensus-oriented political organization at the village level with a more authoritarian and hierarchical external political system, and the obstruction of the transmission of Karen identity to the younger generations due to the introduction of the Thai education system in the villages.[5]

The economic organization of most of the households remained relatively unchanged until the late 1980s and early 1990s when restrictions on their land-use system began to threaten the subsistence economy and material wellbeing of the Karen in Thung Yai. Even today, most of the households in Thung Yai practise subsistence farming, predominantly growing rice in swidden fields and some paddy fields. Within a territory 'supervised' by the village community, every year each household selects a swidden field according to household size and work capacity. The secondary vegetation of a fallow area – predominantly bamboo forest – is cut, and burnt after a period of drying. After being used to grow hill rice, generally for one year, the field is once again left fallow for several years, while numerous plants growing in the fallow are used continuously. The traditionally long fallow periods of 5-15 years or more are currently prohibited by the Thai Royal Forest Department (RFD), which considers land uncultivated for that length of time to be reforested, and therefore land that cannot be cleared or used for cultivation. In swidden fields, gardens and forests, a great variety of other plants are grown and collected. Fishing is important for protein. Small supplementary cash incomes are obtained in most households by way of selling chillies, tobacco and various other fruits grown within the traditional land-use system. Wage labour is of little importance to most households. The mean annual per capita income in 1996 was less than US$ 50.[6]

Deforestation, protected areas and 'hill tribes' in Thailand

Throughout the second half of the 20th century, the relationship of the Karen in Thung Yai with the Thai state was predominantly defined by the state categorizing them as 'hill tribes' and declaring their living place a national forest. Profound changes to their economic organization began in the

---

5   Regarding the complex dynamics of these changes see Buergin 2002b, 2004, pp. 269-322.
6   To date, the data collected in 1996/97 (see Buergin 2002a, pp. 219-278) is the most detailed and reliable data available. More recent demographic and economic data regarding the Western Forest Complex (WEFCOM) was collected in 2003/2004 by public authorities in rapid socio-economic surveys and were compiled in the context of the GMS Biodiversity Conservation Corridors Initiative of the Asian Development Bank (see ADB 2005, pp.8-11). According to this data, the mean annual income in Sub-district Lai Wo (which comprises most of the Karen communities in Thung Yai) was around US$ 263 per household or US$ 53 per person, while the figures for Lai Wo in my survey in 1996/97 were US$ 271 per household and US$ 57 per person. Population data for 2004 giving a total of 3,319 Karen people living in the Thung Yai Naresuan Wildlife Sanctuary likewise indicates that basic socio-economic data such as population size and incomes has not changed significantly.

1980s and were closely related to the follow-on effects of the declaration of Thung Yai as a Wildlife Sanctuary in 1974. The case of Thung Yai is only one example of a broader controversy on people and forests in Thailand (and globally), rooted in conflicting interests involving the resources of peripheral forest areas in the context of changing forest, development and conservation policies.[7]

Forest and biodiversity conservation in Thailand has focused on the establishment of protected areas that are controlled by the government. This modern approach to nature conservation gained strength in Thailand in the 1950s, during a period of pronounced nationalism, and was based on a prevailing international trend of presupposing an inherent incompatibility between nature conservation and resource use by local communities. Legal provisions for protected areas were created in the 1960s, and the RFD was made responsible for their creation and management.[8] Prior to this approach that emerged in the 1950s, the main concern of the RFD was the allocation of concessions for teak extraction, a lucrative business. After World War II, however, tropical forests were increasingly seen as important and swidden cultivation was stigmatized as inefficient and detrimental to tropical forest resources. By the mid-1960s, almost 40% of Thailand's total land area had been assigned to concession areas, and swidden cultivation was prohibited. At the same time, the demarcation of protected areas was beginning, although this proceeded slowly at first. The global spread of modernization and the expanding world market was also influencing national agricultural policies: Thailand's rapid economic growth during the 1960s and 1970s was based on the state-propagated extension of agricultural areas for the cultivation of cash crops for the world market. Alongside a fast growing population, this policy resulted in rapid deforestation.

Despite the emergence of protected areas' legislation from 1950 through to the early 1980s, the forest cover in Thailand decreased from almost two-thirds to less than one-third of the total land area, and deforestation was increasingly perceived as a problem. The RFD then had to explain this rapid deforestation to a conservation-sensitive urban public with growing political power. It also had to deal with some 10 million rural people – about one-fifth of the total population – who were living 'illegally' in areas declared as forest reserves. Of these 'forest areas', more than one-third were being used for agriculture, constituting at least one-third of Thailand's entire agricultural area. In this situation of contested competence and growing resistance, the RFD concentrated on implementing a Protected Area System (PAS) that was to encompass 28% of the total land area of Thailand.[9]

The issue of people living in forest areas became an important societal controversy, including issues of justice, resource control, land rights and democratization. On the one hand, the RFD –

---

7   See for example Sato 2002; Buergin 2003b; Vandergeest and Peluso 2011. For a more comprehensive account see Buergin 2004, pp. 101-200.
8   On the history and policies of the RFD see Usher 2009.
9   See Buergin 2003a. The PAS was devised in detail in the Thai Forestry Sector Master Plan 1993 (TFSMP) without a stated timeline. While the TFSMP as a whole was never approved by the Thai government, the objective to designate 27.5% of Thailand's terrestrial area as 'protected areas' had already been adopted in 1992. In 2008, almost 19% of the land area was legally designated 'protected areas' with another 4% currently in preparation according to the National Parks, Wildlife and Plant Conservation Department (Usher 2009, p. 174). Furthermore, around 10% are designated as Class 1A and 1B Watershed Forests, which are not categorized as 'protected areas' but are subject to 'conservation' objectives. The most recent official forest policy statement (in the 10th Social and Economic Development Plan 2007) targets a minimum forest cover of 33%, incorporating both protected areas and watershed forests.

together with primarily conservation-oriented NGOs and academics – concentrated on conservation issues. For them 'people and forests cannot co-exist' and forest protection required the removal of human settlements from the forests. On the other, peasant movement groups, socially concerned academics and people-oriented NGOs focused on the interests and problems of rural communities and the rights and interests of long-standing forest communities. They presupposed a vital interest of local communities in protecting their forests as a source of livelihood, as well as for ecological and cultural functions, and pointed to a history of community conservation in the remaining forested areas.[10] This controversy led in part to the drafting of the Community Forest Bill (CFB), which was fiercely disputed throughout the 1990s and finally approved in 2007. The final passage of the bill did not, however, resolve the long-running conflict and the status of communities and community forests in protected areas remains problematic and controversial.[11]

The particularly problematic issue of ethnic discrimination is rarely addressed in the debate on forest legislation: most of the people living in areas designated for the PAS are members of the 'hill tribes', or *chao khao* in Thai. This term came into use in the 1950s as a generic name for various non-Tai ethnic groups living predominantly in the uplands of northern and western Thailand, and does not differentiate between those who have lived on their customary lands for generations, pre-dating the Thai state, and those who migrated into the Thai state at a later date. Officially it covers nine distinct tribal peoples, the Karen, Hmong, Lisu, Lahu, Akha, Mien, Khamu, Lua' and H'tin, each with its distinct language and culture. The term implies a negative stereotype associated with destruction of the forest, the cultivation of opium, and dangerous non-Thai troublemakers. During the 1960s and 1970s, the move to eradicate opium cultivation and the on-going communist insurgency dominated the government's attitude towards highland peoples. By the mid-1980s, both of these issues had lost their urgency, and forest conservation had risen to replace them in the public interest. Although the settlement areas of hill tribes were those areas where most of the remaining forests were to be found, the hill tribes were conceived of as being the main 'problem group' regarding deforestation and resettlement was the preferred solution.[12] Members of the highland groups dislike the term hill tribes and prefer either Thai Mountain peoples (*chao Thai phu khao*), more commonly used within Thailand, or indigenous peoples (*chon pao puen muang*), more often used internationally.

At the local level as well, conflicts between ethnic Tai and hill tribe groups arose during the 1980s. Resource conflicts over land, forests and water occurred as ethnic Tai farmers spread into the uplands, and as the populations of hill tribes grew and many of them took up cash cropping. Increasingly in the late 1990s, ethnic minority groups in the uplands were arbitrarily arrested, forcibly resettled and terrorized.[13]

---

10   For example Santasombat 1992; Ganjanapan 1998; Buergin and Kessler 2000; Laungaramsri 2000.
11   Brenner et al. 1999; Weatherby and Somying; 2007; Usher 2009.
12   Buergin 2000.
13   McKinnon and Vienne 1989.

Nature conservation, oppression and eviction in Thung Yai

The idea to protect forests and wildlife in western Thailand by establishing two wildlife sanctuaries arose in the mid-1960s among conservation-oriented officials of the RFD. At the same time, Western biologists had drawn attention to the zoological importance of the region. By then, deforestation was already increasing considerably in other parts of the country, although it was generally not perceived as a problem at that time but rather as supporting national development and security. Due to strong logging and mining interests in the area, it was not until 1972 that the first of the two sanctuaries, Huai Kha Khaeng, was established. Commercial interests in Thung Yai Naresuan were even stronger. However, after a military helicopter crashed in Thung Yai in April 1973, revealing an illegal hunting party of senior military officers, businessmen, family members and a film star – attracting nationwide public outrage – the area was finally declared a Wildlife Sanctuary in 1974.[14]

During the 1960s, not only timber and ore were of interest for commercial profit and national development but also the waters of the western forests, as a hydroelectric power resource. Four major dams were planned in the upper Mae Klong River, incorporating both the major tributaries, Khwae Yai and Khwae Noi. Three of these were completed: Sri Nakharin was finished in 1980, Tha Thung Na 1981 and Khao Laem (later renamed Vajiralongkorn) in 1984. The fourth planned dam, the Nam Choan Dam, was supposed to flood a forest area of about 223 km^2 within the Thung Yai Naresuan Wildlife Sanctuary, and sparked a widespread public debate. The public dispute lasted for more than six years, dominating national politics and public debate in early 1988 until the project was shelved in April of that year with little prospect of being revived. Pointing to the area's high value for nature conservation and biodiversity, national and international opponents to the dam raised the possibility of declaring the area a World Heritage site. This prestigious option would have been lost with a huge dam and reservoir in the middle of the two wildlife sanctuaries judged most promising for fulfilling the requirements for nomination as global heritage.[15] The success of

---

14 In a time of great political unrest, the poaching incident had become a focal point for the prevailing discontent with the military rule, triggering public protest and demonstrations that finally led to the fall of the Thanom-Prapas Regime after the uprising of October 14, 1973 and the establishment of a new democratic government. After the military had taken power once again in October 1976, many of the leaders and activists of the democracy movement fled into the peripheral regions of the country that were under control of the Communist Party of Thailand. Many of them sought refuge in the western forests and among the Karen people living in the sanctuaries. For commercial hunters, logging companies and state authorities, vast areas of the western forests became inaccessible until the beginning of the 1980s, one of the reasons why they have remained largely undisturbed until today.

15 Most outspoken in this regard were Veeravat Thiraprasat, then chief of the Thung Yai Naresuan Wildlife Sanctuary and supportive of the Karen in Thung Yai, and Prince Bernhard of the Netherlands, founder and former president of the WWF. Just before the Nam Choan Controversy reached its peak, Thailand had ratified the World Heritage Convention in December 1987. During a visit to Thailand in February 1988, Prince Bernhard had raised his concerns about the dam project in the wildlife sanctuary, emphasizing particularly the interest of the WWF in having the area declared a World Heritage site, which would require giving up the dam project. After the project had been shelved, student groups, NGOs and academics again pushed the idea, fearing the dam project might be revived – something which seemed to be less probable in a World Heritage site.

the anti-dam movement was not only a remarkable victory for conservation in Thailand but also a milestone for the development of Thailand's civil society and the process of democratization.[16]

However the Karen people living in the area to be flooded by the Nam Choan Dam never had a voice of their own in the debate. For the so-called Thienchai Committee, which was established by the government to decide on the project and predominantly included proponents of the dam, their existence was irrelevant. Their interests were partly brought to the debate by NGOs and journalists but hardly appeared as an important argument, very much in contrast to the forests and wildlife, which finally emerged as the crucial factors.

On behalf of the Royal Forest Department, the proposal for the nomination of Thailand's first natural World Heritage site to UNESCO was written by two people who had been outspoken opponents of the dam in the Nam Choan controversy: Seub Nakhasathien, chief of the Huai Kha Khaeng Wildlife Sanctuary, and Belinda Stewart-Cox, who had done research as a biologist in Huai Kha Khaeng.[17] Quite predictably, the Karen in Thung Yai were not included in the processes of elaborating the proposal. When the two wildlife sanctuaries of Huai Kha Khaeng and Thung Yai Naresuan were nominated together and subsequently inscribed as a Natural World Heritage site in December 1991, the 'outstanding universal value' was justified by the extraordinarily high biodiversity due to its unique location at the junction of four biogeographic zones, as well as its size and "the undisturbed nature of its habitats". Despite this "undisturbed nature", the nomination document defined the people living in Thung Yai and Huai Kha Khaeng as a threat to the sanctuaries and announced the resettlement of the remaining villages in the near future.[18]

The lead-up to the nomination had already seen a considerable amount of coerced resettlement of communities from both Huai Kha Khaeng and Thung Yai Naresuan. Karen villages in Huai Kha Khaeng had been removed in the 1970s when the Wildlife Sanctuary was established and when the Sri Nakarin Dam was built and later flooded their settlement areas.[19] During the 1980s, most villages of the Hmong ethnic group were removed from the Huai Kha Khaeng and Thung Yai Naresuan wildlife sanctuaries.[20] The resettlement of all remaining villages was stipulated in the management plans for the sanctuaries, drafted in the late 1980s[21] and adopted by the RFD in 1990, following an established policy of relocation of settlements from protected areas. When the nomination for a World Heritage site was prepared in 1990, there remained four Hmong villages in the north-east of the proposed site, some Thai villages which had only recently moved into the proposed buffer zone along the eastern border of Huai Kha Khaeng, and around 16 Karen villages in Thung Yai.

---

16 Buergin and Kessler 2000.
17 Seub committed suicide on September 1, 1991. Belinda Stewart-Cox commented on his death by reproaching his superiors at the RFD: "Seub's death was suicide – an act of despair – but it might as well have been murder. When he needed the support of his superiors to do the job they had asked him to do – stop the hunting and logging that was rampant in Huai Kha Khaeng at that time, master-minded by police and military officials – it was withheld. A terrible betrayal." (Stewart-Cox 1998).
18 Nakhasathien and Stewart-Cox 1990, pp. 44-45.
19 Jørgensen 1996.
20 Eudey 1989; MIDAS 1993.
21 Kutintara and Bhumpakhapun 1988, 1989.

The imminent relocation of all these communities was announced in the nomination documents.[22] This was noted – but not criticized – in IUCN's evaluation of the nomination,[23] and accepted by the World Heritage Committee without comment when it decided to inscribe the property on the World Heritage List.[24] While the relocation of the Hmong and Thai villages was accomplished in the early 1990s, the plans to remove the Karen from Thung Yai provoked strong public criticism and forced the RFD to reverse its resettlement scheme for the time being. Nevertheless, the objective to drive the Karen out of the sanctuary remained strong within the agency.[25]

Guarding a global heritage not only brought prestige to the Nation and the Royal Forest Department but also the prospect of economic assets as well as increasing political importance for the sanctuaries. Immediately after the declaration, international organizations, in cooperation with national partners, began to plan projects in and around the sanctuaries. The most prominent and most important in terms of 'economic weight' was a joint project of the World Bank and the Ministry of Agriculture, designed to improve biodiversity conservation and protected areas management in Thailand. The pre-investment study for the project was criticized by NGOs in Thailand who disliked its narrow conservation perspective, its top-down approach and the high costs of the project.[26] The negotiations between World Bank, state agencies and NGOs focused on the controversial issue of resettlement.[27] The study cautiously argued against resettlement in the specific case of the Karen villages in Thung Yai, although the option for resettlement was kept open and a whole chapter of the study devoted to its implementation. The negotiations only gradually led to limited agreement, and the NGOs refused to cooperate on a project based on the pre-investment study.[28] Even though the affected Karen people did not have a voice of their own in this debate, their interests were considered for the first time.

As resource conflicts between Thai lowlanders and 'hill tribes' heated up in the late 1990s, the RFD, under its new Director General, took up the offensive again in Thung Yai. On April 13, 1999,

---

22 Nakhasathien and Stewart-Cox 1990, p. 45; Thailand 1991.
23 IUCN's Advisory Body Evaluation notes that, "There is a policy to remove the remaining illegal settlements in the reserve and several have been relocated to date" (IUCN 1991, p. 70). The WCMC datasheet from March 1991, which is attached to the IUCN Evaluation, states: "Some 3,800 tribal people live within the sanctuary. There are still four Hmong villages... Since 1987, 2-3 Hmong villages have been moved each year... By 1991 all villages will have been closed. Sixteen Karen villages (1,826 people) are still resident [in the sanctuary complex], but there are plans to resettle them.".
24 UNESCO 1991, p. 29.
25 Buergin 2004, pp. 175-186.
26 MIDAS 1993. The proposed project was to have a timeframe of five years, beginning in 1994. The total project cost was estimated at US$ 96 million to be covered by a grant of US$ 20 million from the Global Environment Facility (GEF), a US$ 40 million loan from the World Bank, and funds from bilateral aid donors and the Royal Thai Government.
27 The study had argued against resettlement in the specific case of the Karen villages in Thung Yai Naresuan Wildlife Sanctuary, albeit in a rather ambivalent way and under strict conservation reservations. The detrimental effects of the villages and risks to the sanctuary were assessed as relatively low, while their resettlement would supposedly cause high costs and considerable difficulties.
28 The project was halted after grant funds from the GEF were made conditional on ratification of the *Convention on Biological Diversity* (CBD) in July 1994, which Thailand had not yet ratified. In the controversy about the project the representative of the Bank had tried to exert moderate pressure, indicating that the limited funds of the GEF may go to other countries if the ratification of the CBD were delayed.

the Director General himself flew into the wildlife sanctuary, landing with his helicopter at the place where the Karen had just started to celebrate an important annual religious festival supposed to last for three days. The Director General demanded an end to the ceremonies. Soon after, soldiers burned down religious shrines of the Karen. From April 18 to May 12, soldiers and forest rangers went to the Karen villages, demanded that they stop growing rice, demolished huts and personal belongings, and burnt down a rice barn.[29] Throughout the following months, efforts to convince the Karen people to resettle 'voluntarily' continued. Military officials prohibited agricultural activities and prevented villagers from using their fields. They allegedly even confiscated identity cards and house registration papers while they raided villages, arresting people without warrants and holding them for days, and removing families without Thai identity cards. Even though the Senate Human Rights Panel criticized the incidents, RFD and the military continued their joint resettlement programme in November 2000, announcing further relocations of families as well as the preparation of the resettlement area for all the villages.[30] The Karen oppose any relocation from their lands, a position expressed in detail during a comprehensive household survey conducted in 1996/97 in which they almost unanimously expressed their wish to stay in Thung Yai in the face of ongoing efforts to evict them from their homeland.[31]

Since the RFD had to delay its resettlement plans regarding the remaining Karen villages in Thung Yai in the early 1990s due to public pressure, it concentrated on the elimination of the traditional land-use system of the Karen by prohibiting the use of fallow areas older than three years.[32] In the longer term, these restrictions will lead to the breakdown of the traditional land-use system, as the soils under constant use rapidly lose their productivity. In the villages where control on the part of the RFD and the military has been most effective, people were already reporting decreasing yields in the second half of the 1990s. In 2002, the RFD also began planting tree seedlings on swidden fields in some villages,[33] at the same time announcing in Thailand's periodic report to UNESCO that: "If Karen villages inside the WH zone exert increasing demands on natural resources in the park, relocation will be conducted".[34]

The human rights implications of the resettlement programme were overlooked by both the World Heritage Committee and IUCN during their examination of the nomination proposal in 1991, as well as during their review of Thailand's periodic report on the state of conservation of the sanctuaries in 2003. This happened even though the Thai government has never been reticent in explaining to IUCN and the World Heritage Committee that the involuntary resettlement of long-settled communities is part of its management strategy for the sanctuaries. The Committee has

---

29 When these events became public, the Director General of the RFD downplayed his role in the incidents, at first denying any military actions at all. In contrast to the Director General, the commander of the military troops involved seemed rather proud of the achievements. He declared the operation a 'pilot project' of the new alliance between the military and the RFD agreed upon in May 1998, and exemplary in their joint efforts to prevent forest destruction.
30 For details and references regarding evictions and oppressions in Thung Yai see Buergin 2004, pp. 159-200.
31 Buergin 2002a, pp. 290-293.
32 Even from an external utilitarian conservation perspective, the resettlement of the Karen and the prohibition of their subsistence-oriented swidden system is unreasonable. Assuming a mean fallow period of 10 years, the total agricultural area in the sanctuary, including fallow areas, only accounts for about 1% of its area.
33 Steinmetz, personal communication February 2002.
34 Thailand 2003, p. 234.

never questioned this although it is demonstrable that the Karen in Thung Yai – far from being a threat to its continued existence – have long been an integral part of a complex eco-social system in which they shape and manage their environment in Thung Yai.[35]

Local resistance and transnational alliances

Forced to choose between being charged with being forest destroyers 'provoking' relocation or facing severe subsistence problems, the only possibility for the Karen to adapt to the restrictions on their swidden system – apart from trying to conceal their fields – seems to be 'modernization'. They can either try to increase the productivity of the fields, using fertilizers and pesticides (which most of them cannot afford), or turn to cash cropping in, or wage labour outside, of the sanctuary. Intensification of agriculture and cash cropping is already supported by some of the government institutions and NGOs working in the sanctuary. Most of the Karen in Thung Yai reject these efforts, however, and are trying to carry on with their subsistence farming. Furthermore, intensification of land use, cash cropping and increasing market orientation – that is, 'modernization' – jeopardizes their reputation as 'forest people living in harmony with nature' on which their claim to remain in the sanctuary is based.

A concept of 'benign environmentalists' has gained strength in international debates on environment, development and human rights since the 1980s, which conceives of traditional or indigenous people rather as partners in biodiversity conservation than as culprits or foes. In Thailand, such an alternative image, in contrast to the still prevailing stereotype of the forest-destroying hill tribes, has come to be assigned to at least some of the ethnic groups in the uplands – prominent among them the Karen. Here, this image emerged in rising conflicts towards the end of the 1980s when an emerging peasant movement, concerned academics and NGOs – resisting resettlement policies in forest reserves, eucalyptus plantations, illegal logging and corruption – developed a community forest concept as an alternative perspective and a counter model to the conservation concept and commercial reforestation approach of the RFD and big agribusiness companies. In Thailand, as well as on an international level, this alternative stereotype meets with reproaches from various sides as being partly fictional, over-generalizing, or in violation of people's right to development.[36] However, far from being 'comfortable' for the Karen, this positive image of 'benign environmentalists', attributed to the Karen in Thung Yai in parts of national and international public discourse, is presently the only position in these disputes to which they can relate at least to some degree. As long as their inherent land rights to the area are not acknowledged and the legal basis for their continuing settlement in national Thai law is ambiguous, this seems to be their most important asset in the debates that will decide the future of their villages.

So far, the Karen in Thung Yai have had no chance to participate directly in the national and international discourse and decision-making regarding their homeland, including its declaration as part of a wildlife sanctuary and a World Heritage site. In their encounters with state agencies, they

---

35 Boonpinon 1997; Steinmetz 1999; Buergin 2002a, 2004; Delang and Wong 2006.
36 Regarding the ambiguities of this stereotyping, see e.g. Buergin 2003a; Forsyth and Walker 2008.

frequently feel powerless and without any rights. Open resistance to continuous repression and acts of violence on the part of the RFD and military officials is difficult for the Karen, not least due to specific cultural frames of behaviour and historically grounded inter-ethnic relations between Karen and Thai. They have the impression that their rights and concerns are not relevant in the national and international discourses about their homeland. A strong feeling prevails among them that they cannot communicate their own view, that they have to use words, arguments and ideas that are not really their own while trying to justify their claims, even with their Thai allies among the peasant movement, NGOs and activists. The Karen conceive of these 'communication problems' not predominantly as language problems, even though many of the elder Karen have only limited competence in the Thai language, but attribute them to different cultural contexts.

Almost all of the Karen in Thung Yai believe that resettlement is neither justified nor desirable but they do take different positions towards the external influences and the resettlement threat. There is a rather small group, including most of the Phu Yai Ban (the village heads in the context of the state administrative system) which is open to 'moderate modernization' while trying to retain a Karen identity. The vast majority is rather more reluctant to engage in 'development' and 'modernization, preferring to 'live like our grandparents did' as a common saying goes. Among them there are marked differences in their reactions to the external influences. A rather large group, who could be labelled 'extroverted traditionalists', including many influential elders as well as young people, is trying to shape the change and resist the threats. They are doing so by trying to strengthen and revitalize Karen culture and identity as well as seeking support and advocacy outside of Thung Yai. Another group of more 'introverted traditionalists' is likewise focusing on strengthening 'traditional' Karen culture but invoking millenarian and more 'exclusive' frames of Karen culture to a higher degree, avoiding transcultural exchange and support.

Despite these differences in position and strategy, all these groups wish to remain in their villages as well as to protect their homeland and way of life. Furthermore, they all refer to the same specific cultural frame of values and objectives regarding a 'decent' life appropriate to a Karen living in Thung Yai. Sharpened – but not created – in the clashes with external actors and influences, this conception of specific Karen values and objectives focuses on the concepts of 'modesty' as opposed to 'greed', 'harmony' in contrast to conflict, as well as 'spiritual development' versus 'material development'. The counterpart to these concepts is quite obvious and explicitly named by the Karen as such. It is primarily the 'modern' Thai society which is increasingly 'intruding' into their traditional living places and spaces, threatening their cultural particularity and physical existence in Thung Yai.

Modern legacies, national liabilities and indigenous peoples

This article has tried to give a rough idea of the complexity of the conflicts over Thung Yai, where the local, national and international levels are highly interdependent as well as asymmetric in power. Transformations on a national and international level involving shifting framings of the 'problem' of the Karen in Thung Yai have significantly determined the changing circumstances of the local communities. In the second half of the 19th century, the economic and political interests of colonial and regional powers in Southeast Asia brought about the demarcation of territorial nation-states according to Western models. In the context of this national territorialization, Thung Yai and the Karen living there were enclosed in the 'geo-body' of the Siamese nation-state, which at the same time became part of an international community of states primarily defined in terms of territory and economic relations, while heterogeneous social and physical spaces were merged in the modern nation-state.

In the first half of the 20th century, the development of a specific national identity of this state focused on a common language, Buddhism and the monarchy. The Karen in Thung Yai, who had been incorporated into the state spatially, were now excluded from its 'people-body' in the context of this nationalization process and disappeared from the political agenda. Since the middle of the 20th century, growing international and national interests in the resources and people of the peripheral areas of the state – in the context of modernization objectives and the fight against communism – have resulted in the extension of state institutions into these areas as well as their exploitation for national economic development. The people living there were now predominantly conceived of as backward problem groups or alien troublemakers in conflict with national interests, which had to be controlled and modernized. After the environmental costs of this economic development became obvious in the 1980s, the forests of these peripheral areas were declared precious wilderness and biodiversity assets of global significance, which had to be protected against encroachments from local people in the context of a global 'ecologization' of peripheral areas of modernity. In this frame, the Karen in Thung Yai became a disruptive factor in a natural global heritage, requiring strict monitoring as long as their removal was not feasible. When Thung Yai was declared a natural World Heritage site in 1991, the Karen were seen as a 'disruptive factor'. In contrast, the studies done there since then clearly indicate that the Karen are an integral part of Thung Yai. With their sustainable land-use system, they have shaped the sanctuary considerably over a long time and even increased its biodiversity. In their culture, they keep a unique body of knowledge about their natural environment with which they maintain a specific and deep spiritual relationship. As noted earlier, the Karen have unanimously expressed their desire to remain on their lands and reject continuing efforts to relocate them.

Pressure to exclude or assimilate highland peoples, including their removal from protected areas, is still strong in Thailand. Over the last 30 years, however, Thailand has undergone a remarkable process of democratization and enacted a constitution in 1997 that explicitly recognizes the rights of local communities to cultural self-determination as well as to the use of local resources.[37] This may provide political space for the Karen to seek a greater level of control over their future. Unfortunately, these commitments are not always easily realizable. Furthermore, their interpretation is often contested and subject to social bargaining, whereby weaker social groups may be at a disadvantage. The Community Forest Bill and conservation policies are a case in point, where these problematic asymmetries urgently need to be reconsidered and amended, specifically regarding the vulnerable position of highland peoples.

---

37 Thailand 1997. Section 46 states: "Persons so assembling as to be a traditional community shall have the right to conserve or restore their customs, local knowledge, arts or good culture of their community and of the nation and participate in the management, maintenance, preservation and exploitation of natural resources and the environment in a balanced fashion and persistently as provided by law."

A recent positive step was the approval of the government project "Recovering the Karen Livelihood in Thailand", proposed by the Ministry of Culture and adopted via a cabinet resolution of the Royal Thai Government in August 2010. The resolution recognizes the particular ethnic identity and culture of the Karen people, and seeks to actively support them in perpetuating this culture, including their rotational farming system and traditional land management, while deploring "the arrest and detention of the Karen people who are part of local traditional communities settled on disputed land which is traditional land used for making a living".[38] For the Karen communities in Thung Yai specifically, the resolution recommends the implementation of a "special cultural zone" intended to support the transmission of cultural heritage.[39] The resolution also recommends the "promotion of the Karen rotational farming system to become a world cultural heritage" (presumably under UNESCO's 2003 *Convention for the Safeguarding of Intangible Cultural Heritage*).[40] The recommendations of the cabinet resolution reveal a new sensitivity to the problems and indicate a sincere intention to approach them; however, it remains to be seen how the project will be realised.[41] The case of the Karen in Thung Yai, as well as the more general problem of integrating the 'hill tribes' into Thai society, remains a controversial challenge for democratic forces in Thailand.[42]

In this type of globally widespread conflict between the livelihood interests of local people and national or global interests in nature conservation and 'modernization' – which may be

---

38 The cabinet resolution further made the following recommendations: "Repeal the declarations concerning protected areas, reserve forests and settlements of Karen people which already have the capability to prove that their settlement, living on and use of these lands has continued for a long time or since before the declaration of laws or policies that now cover these areas"; "Support and recognize the rotational farming systems which belong to the Karen ways of life and livelihood, and which support the sustainable use of natural resources and self-sufficiency"; "Support self-sufficiency or alternative agriculture instead of cash crop production or industrial agriculture"; and "Support and recognize the ways of using the land and the management of local traditional communities, e.g. through issuing communal land titles" (see Thailand 2010).

39 The Lai Wo Sub-district (Sangkhla Buri District, Kanchanaburi Province) has been designated as one of four pilot areas. Most of the villages which constitute this Sub-district are located within the Thung Yai Wildlife Sanctuary where they comprise about 64% of the Karen population in Thung Yai. Considering the close relationship of these villages to the other Karen villages in the eastern part of the sanctuary (Sub-district Mae Chan, Umphang District, Tak Province) it seems desirable to include all the Karen villages in Thung Yai into this 'cultural zone'. Furthermore, the villages in the eastern part of Thung Yai are closely related to the Karen village Le Taung Hkoo in the Umphang Wildlife Sanctuary, which is also recommended as a 'special cultural zone'. Together, these villages constitute what the Karen in Thung Yai identify as '*thoung bou tai*', their homeland and cultural community (see text above).

40 The 2003 Convention explicitly recognizes the "deep-seated interdependence between the intangible cultural heritage and the tangible cultural and natural heritage" and was adopted "Considering that existing international agreements, recommendations and resolutions concerning the cultural and natural heritage [such as the 1972 World Heritage Convention] need to be effectively enriched and supplemented by means of new provisions relating to the intangible cultural heritage" (Preamble). If the Karen rotational farming system is indeed recognized under the 2003 Convention, Thung Yai could potentially become a 'model' World Heritage site, illustrating the interaction between the two (1972 and 2003) Conventions.

41 Recent violations by the National Park staff and the Thai military against Karen people living in the Kaeng Krachan National Park in 2011 indicate that at least some state authorities are ignoring the resolution and still following more familiar repression and resettlement policies (see AIPP 2011).

42 Evident, supposed or assigned differences between social groups are frequently highlighted and exploited in these struggles over resources, redistribution, identity, social status and power. Not least, these struggles are significantly framed and negotiated in discourses about national identities and cultural diversity, which unavoidably invoke disputed conceptualizations of modernity. (See e.g. Keyes 2002; Connors 2005.)

termed conflicts over biocultural diversity[43] – not only livelihoods and homelands are at stake but also issues of local identity and self-determination as well as cultural diversity and self-conceptualizations of modern societies. The ideological and legal framings of these conflicts over biocultural diversity are predominantly negotiated in very heterogeneous discursive and political spheres at the national and international level.[44] It is here that local people's chances of resisting transgressions and defending their rights are determined, even though these people frequently have no access to the discourses and institutions that are framing their circumstances and chances. Very often, they are not even represented in any appropriate way in political processes and decisions regarding their living places. However, these discourses also provide new chances for them to defend claims to local resources and particular identities.

In particular, the concept of 'indigenous peoples' has become a powerful idea, adopted as a legal concept or operational category by important international institutions such as the United Nations, ILO, the World Bank and the Asian Development Bank, and increasingly acknowledged by many nation states. It emphasizes indigenous rights to lands, territories, resources and self-determination[45] and provides an appealing reference point regarding identification, compensation and action for many marginalized peoples at the fringes of modern societies. However, the concept often provokes considerable caveats at the national level, particularly among Asian governments where – in Southeast and East Asia – only the Philippines and Japan accept the use of the term to describe parts of their populations.[46]

The Thai state emphasizes its 'un-colonized' history[47] and, until recently, pursued an ambiguous policy towards the 'hill tribes', conceiving of them either as illegal immigrants to be expelled or proclaiming their total assimilation if eligible for naturalization.[48] It is hardly interested in recognizing any indigenous peoples in its own territory. In a reply to the UN Special Rapporteur on the situation of human rights and fundamental freedoms of indigenous peoples in February 2003, the Government of Thailand noted that the highland peoples were not considered indigenous

---

43 Buergin 2009, 2010.
44 Interrelations between biological and cultural diversity – increasingly labelled biocultural diversity – have come into the focus of academic, political and economic interests and discourses since the late 1980s. In this context, the protection of cultural diversity is often conceived of as a promising means for the conservation of biological diversity. Furthermore, the worldwide loss of cultural diversity is causing increasing concern among scholars and activists and even provoking commitments on the part of international organizations such as UNESCO (2010) or global environmental organizations such as WWF (e.g. Oviedo et al. 2000) and IUCN (IUCN and WCPA 2003) with regard to the protection of cultural diversity.
45 See, for instance, the 2007 United Nations Declaration on the Rights of Indigenous Peoples.
46 See e.g. Kingsbury 1998; Erni 2008.
47 In Asia, European colonialism only rarely took the form of territorial conquest but rather resulted in radical transformations of regional societies by promoting or enforcing the formation of territorial nation-states and inducing modernization processes adopted and pursued by regional elites. Even though the pre-colonial Tai states never became European colonies, the formation of the modern Thai state was deeply influenced by European colonialism, which is equally true for the situation of the diverse Karen groups in mainland Southeast Asia from the first half of the 19th to the middle of the 20th century. In the case of the Karen in Thung Yai, evictions, repression and marginalization cannot be directly traced back to territorial occupations by European colonial powers but were predominantly caused by regional powers in the wake of colonial hegemony in mainland Southeast Asia as well as the spreading of a 'culture of modernity' deeply rooted in European and colonial history.
48 See Buergin 2000.

peoples under domestic law,[49] and when the World Heritage Committee considered a proposal to establish a "World Heritage Indigenous Peoples Council of Experts" as an advisory body to the Committee in 2001, Thailand's representative disapproved of the idea arguing that "indigenous issues are a domestic, national question, and are best handled on that level".[50]

However, United Nations human rights bodies and mechanisms, such as the UN Special Rapporteur on the Rights of Indigenous Peoples or the Committee on the Rights of the Child, clearly conceive of the so-called hill tribes or ethnic minority groups of Thailand as indigenous peoples.[51] Moreover, in Thailand, Karen increasingly identify themselves as 'indigenous' and participate in international organizations and networking in support of indigenous rights. Several of the associations of ethnic minority groups in Thailand are members of the Asia Indigenous Peoples Pact (AIPP), including the Assembly of Indigenous and Tribal Peoples of Thailand, the Hmong Association for Development in Thailand, the Inter Mountain Peoples Education and Culture in Thailand Association (IMPECT), and the Karen Network for Culture and Environment. Based on distinct ethnic identities, they share common experiences of discrimination and marginalization within nation-states and try to assert their rights to self-determination as well as land, territories and resources which, since the 1980s, are being increasingly challenged by national and global claims for nature conservation.

National conservation policies and laws worldwide have long been considerably influenced by modern ideas about nature conservation and protected area management, focusing on 'fortress-conservation' approaches. The rights and interests of local people in or close to protected areas have only recently been acknowledged, and these revisions are still contested. However, in international environmental discourses and institutions, principles of free, prior and informed consent as well as participation and cooperative resource management approaches are now approved standards regarding people in protected areas.[52] Protected areas for nature conservation are increasingly subject to international and transnational regulations regarding stakeholders and rights-holders – World Heritage sites being a particularly prominent example. This provides new opportunities for local people by appealing to international standards and advocacy. International standards clearly support the right of the Karen to live in their traditional and customary lands (in Thung Yai) and their forced resettlement is not a legitimate option. Having adopted Thung Yai as a global heritage, concerned international organizations (including UNESCO, the World Heritage Committee and its Advisory Bodies) should disapprove of the pressures and violence towards the Karen in Thung Yai and insist on their full and effective participation in decision-making processes, in accordance with their rights under international law.

Unfortunately, these international standards are often only hesitantly adopted on the national level, frequently encounter considerable national reservations and are open to interpretation and negotiation.[53] Furthermore, regulations regarding UNESCO natural World Heritage sites in parts

---

49 See Commission on Human Rights 2004, p. 18.
50 World Heritage Centre 2001, p. 2.
51 See e.g. Commission on Human Rights 2003, para. 22; Human Rights Council 2008, para. 464 ff.; or Committee on the Rights of the Child 2006. Also see UN DESA 2008, pp. 8, 28.
52 See for instance *Convention on Biological Diversity*, Art. 8(j); IUCN et al. 1999; CBD COP7 2004.
53 For example, when the World Heritage Committee voted to support customary law and customary management by 'traditional' or indigenous peoples as a sufficient basis to guarantee the protection of natural World Heritage sites, Thailand disassociated itself from the decision (UNESCO 1999, pp. 26, 56).

still fall short of these standards and evoke approaches to nature conservation that assume an inherent antagonism between 'man and nature'. However, these conceptualizations and provisions are debated and there are strong arguments for a revision acknowledging and supporting rights of local people living in and close to natural World Heritage sites in the light of UN commitments to universal human rights and the rights of indigenous peoples, as well as the significance of cultural diversity for the protection of biodiversity.[54] The establishment of the so-called Cultural Landscapes category by the World Heritage Committee reflects an awareness of some of these problems as well as a new attentiveness to interrelations between 'nature' and 'culture'.[55] The history of the Karen in Thung Yai and their relationship with their homeland suggests the need for a reconsideration of the status of Thung Yai, which may be better conceived of as a Cultural Landscape World Heritage site.

Conclusions

The Karen in Thung Yai not only have to face the threat of eviction from their homeland but also the destruction of their 'culture', their local identity and their particular way of life in Thung Yai. They have consistently asserted their desire to remain in Thung Yai and to pursue a particular way of life there as Karen people but their legitimate interests and rights are largely disregarded and they have never been given the possibility of defending these rights on their own terms.

This paper cannot provide a 'Karen view' of the conflicts over Thung Yai. It is rather the perspective of a scholar who, whilst having some first-hand experience, is looking at the problem from the outside, based on a concern for the protection of human rights as well as cultural and biological diversity. His viewpoint is that of his own 'culture of modernity', which he is interested in critically exploring. From such a perspective, the case of the Karen in Thung Yai – as well as the situation of other 'local', 'traditional', 'tribal', 'native' or 'indigenous' peoples at the periphery of modern societies – is essentially interrelated with issues of modern identity and hegemony. To enable them to maintain a particular self-determined way of life, perpetuating global cultural diversity requires, not least, a culture of modernity which is attentive to its hegemonic and violating relations with non-modern groups, supportive of ways of life different from its own, and able to reconsider universalistic claims to modernity.

The moral and legal obligations of modern societies and international organizations already provide standards by which to assess infringements in the case of the Karen in Thung Yai and reason to call for changes in the approach of the government to the management of this area. Due to both their history in Thung Yai as well as national and international commitments to human rights and conservation ethics, the right of the Karen to remain in Thung Yai has to be acknowledged without reservation. The Thai government has taken some steps towards such a realization in the cabinet resolution "Recovering the Karen Livelihood in Thailand" (August 2010). This resolution should be implemented in cooperation with the Karen people as soon as possible and its objectives should be extended to all indigenous groups in Thailand.

---

54 Disko 2010; Hay-Edie et al. 2011.
55 For example World Heritage Centre 2003; Taylor and Lennon 2011.

Participatory mapping of Karen land use areas in the Thung Yai Naresuan Wildlife Sanctuary, together with Wildlife Fund Thailand (WFT). Photo: Reiner Buergin

With specific regard to the situation in Thung Yai, the Karen should be integrated into the management and decision-making processes concerning the sanctuary as well as the reporting to UNESCO. It is important to enable the Karen to participate in these processes and tasks through their own political institutions and in accordance with their own customs, which are adapted to their way of life in Thung Yai but which are not currently acknowledged in their interactions with the administrative agencies. As part of this, already existing interests and activities in participatory research, monitoring and environmental education in the sanctuary should be supported and expanded.[56]

More broadly, and external to the situation in Thailand, the monitoring of the World Heritage sites conducted by the responsible international organizations urgently needs to be improved to conform to their own standards and regulations. Regulations concerning the implementation and monitoring of World Heritage sites have to be reviewed to take account of international commitments, principles and declarations regarding the rights of indigenous peoples and the conservation of cultural diversity.[57]

56　Steinmetz et al. 2006.
57　Disko 2010.

References

ADB 2005. *The Tenasserim Biodiversity Conservation Corridor: Western Forest Complex – Kaeng Krachan Complex, Thailand*, GMS Biodiversity Conservation Corridors Initiative, Manila, Asian Development Bank.

AIPP 2011. Statement from the Karen Network for Culture and Environment, AIPP and NGOs, government networks and academic institutions – Case of Human Rights Violations by the Head of the Kaeng-Krachan National Park against Ethnic Karen Villagers. Asia Indigenous Peoples' Pact.

Boonpinon, K. 1997. *Institutional arrangements in communal resource management: A case study of a Karen village in a protected area*. M.Sc. Thesis. Bangkok, Mahidol University, Faculty of Graduate Studies.

Brenner, V. et al. 1999. *Thailand's community forest bill: U-turn or roundabout*. Freiburg, Albert-Ludwigs-Universität.

Buergin, R. 2000. *'Hill tribes' and forests: Minority policies and resource conflicts in Thailand*. Freiburg, Albert-Ludwigs-Universität, Working Group Socio-Economics of Forest Use in the Tropics.

Buergin, R. 2002a. *Lokaler Wandel und kulturelle Identität im Spannungsfeld nationaler Modernisierung und globaler Umweltdiskurse*. Ph.D. Dissertation. Freiburg, Albert-Ludwigs-Universität, Institute for Ethnology.

Buergin, R. 2002b. *Change and identity in Pwo Karen communities in Thung Yai Naresuan Wildlife Sanctuary, a 'global heritage' in Western Thailand*. Freiburg, Albert-Ludwigs-Universität.

Buergin, R. 2003a. Trapped in environmental discourses and politics of exclusion. C. O. Delang (ed.). *Living at the Edge of Thai Society*. London, Routledge Curzon, pp. 43-63.

Buergin, R. 2003b. Shifting frames for local people and forests in a global heritage. *Geoforum*, Vol. 34, No. 3, pp. 375-393.

Buergin, R. 2004. *Umweltverhältnisse jenseits von Tradition und Moderne*. Stuttgart, Ibidem-Verlag.

Buergin, R. 2009. Konflikte um biokulturelle Diversität in Thailand: Moderne Herausforderungen an Karen-Gemeinschaften im Weltnaturerbe Thung Yai. *Asien*, Vol. 2009, No. 112-113, pp. 9-30.

Buergin, R. 2010. Conflicts about biocultural diversity in Thailand. K. Walker Painemilla et al. (eds.), *Indigenous Peoples and Conservation*. Arlington, VA, Conservation International, pp. 17-26.

Buergin, R. and Kessler, C. 2000. Intrusions and exclusions: Democratization in Thailand in the context of environmental discourses and resource conflicts. *GeoJournal*, Vol. 52, No. 1, pp. 71-80.

CBD COP7. 2004. *Decision VII/16F, Annex: Akwé: Kon Guidelines*. Seventh Meeting of the Conference of Parties to the Convention on Biological Diversity, Kuala Lumpur, Malaysia, 9-20 February 2004.

Commission on Human Rights. 2003. *Human rights and indigenous issues Report of the Special Rapporteur on the situation of human rights and fundamental freedoms of indigenous people, Rodolfo Stavenhagen, submitted in accordance with Commission resolution 2001/65*, UN Doc. E/CN.4/2003/90, 21 January 2003.

Commission on Human Rights. 2004. *Human rights and indigenous issues: Report of the Special Rapporteur on the situation of human rights and fundamental freedoms of indigenous people, Rodolfo Stavenhagen*, UN Doc. E/CN.4/2004/80/Add.1, 6 February 2004.

Committee on the Rights of the Child. 2006. *Consideration of reports submitted by states parties under article 44 of the convention: Concluding observations: Thailand*, UN Doc. CRC/C/THA/CO/2, 17 March 2006.

Connors, M. K. 2005. Ministering culture: Hegemony and the politics of culture and identity in Thailand. *Critical Asian Studies*, Vol. 37, No. 4, pp. 523-551.

Delang, C. O. and Wong, T. 2006. The livelihood-based forest classification system of the Pwo Karen in Western Thailand. *Mountain Research and Development*, Vol. 26, No. 2, pp. 138-145.

Disko, S. 2010. World Heritage Sites in Indigenous Peoples' Territories: Ways of Ensuring Respect for Indigenous Cultures, Values and Human Rights. D. Offenhäußer et al. (eds.), *World Heritage and Cultural Diversity*. Bonn, German Commission for UNESCO, pp. 167-177.

Erni, C. 2008 (ed.). *The concept of indigenous peoples in Asia*. Copenhagen, IWGIA.

Eudey, A. A. 1989. Eviction orders to the Hmong of Huai Yew Yee village, Huai Kha Khaeng Wildlife Sanctuary, Thailand. J. M. McKinnon and B. Vienne (eds.), *Hill tribes today*. Bangkok, Golden Lotus, pp. 249-259.

Ewers Andersen, K. 1976. *The Karens and the Dhamma-raja*. Thesis. Copenhagen, University of Copenhagen.

Forsyth, T. J. and Walker, A. 2008. *Forest Guardians, Forest Destroyers: The Politics of Environmental Knowledge in Northern Thailand*. Washington DC, University of Washington Press.

Ganjanapan, A.1998. The politics of conservation and the complexity of local control of forests in the Northern Thai highlands. *Mountain Research and Development*, Vol. 18, No. 1, pp. 71-82.

Hay-Edie, T. et al. 2011. The roles of local, national and international designations in conserving biocultural diversity on a landscape scale. *International Journal of Heritage Studies*, Vol. 17, No. 6, pp. 527–536.

Human Rights Council. 2008. *Report of the Special Rapporteur on the situation of human rights and fundamental freedoms of indigenous people, S. James Anaya, Addendum: Summary of cases transmitted to Governments and replies received*, UN Doc. A/HRC/9/9/Add.1, 15 August 2008.

IUCN 1991. *World Heritage Nomination – IUCN Technical Evaluation 591: Thung Yai – Huai Kha Khaeng Wildlife Sanctuary (Thailand)*. Gland, IUCN.

IUCN and WCPA 2003. *Recommendations of the Vth IUCN World Parks Congress*. Durban, IUCN and WCPA.

IUCN, WCPA and WWF 1999. *Principles and guidelines on indigenous and traditional peoples and protected areas*. Gland, IUCN.

Jørgensen, A. B. 1996. *Elephants or people: The debate on the Huai Kha Khaeng and Thung Yai Naresuan World Heritage Site*. Honolulu, Hawaii.

Keyes, C. F. 2002. Presidential Address: 'The Peoples of Asia' – Science and politics in the classification of ethnic groups in Thailand, China, and Vietnam. *Journal of Asian Studies*, Vol. 61, No. 4, pp. 1163-1203.

Kingsbury, B. 1998. 'Indigenous peoples' in international law: A constructivist approach to the Asian controversy. *American Journal of International Law*, Vol. 92, No. 3, pp. 414-457.

Kutintara, U. and Bhumpakhapun, N. 1988. [Draft management plan for the Huai Kha Khaeng Wildlife Sanctuary] (in Thai). Bangkok, Kasetsart University, Department of Forest Biology.

Kutintara, U. and Bhumpakhapun, N. 1989. [Draft management plan for the Thung Yai Wildlife Sanctuary] (in Thai). Bangkok, Kasetsart University, Department of Forest Biology.

Laungaramsri, P., 2000. The ambiguity of 'watershed': The politics of people and conservation in Northern Thailand. *Sojourn*, Vol. 15, No. 1, pp. 52-75.

McKinnon, J. M. and Vienne, B. 1989. Introduction: Critical words for critical days. J. M. McKinnon and B. Vienne (eds.), *Hill tribes today*. Bangkok, Golden Lotus, pp. xix-xxvii.

MIDAS Agronomics Company and CIRAD-Forêt 1993. *Conservation forest area protection, management, and development project: Pre-investment study*. Bangkok, MIDAS Agronomics Company.

Nakhasathien, S. and Stewart-Cox, B. 1990. *Nomination of the Thung Yai - Huai Kha Khaeng Wildlife Sanctuary to be a U.N.E.S.C.O. World Heritage Site: Submitted by the Wildlife Conservation Division, Royal Forest Department*. Bangkok, Thailand, Royal Forest Department.

Oviedo, G. T., Maffi, L. and Larsen, P. B. 2000. *Indigenous and traditional peoples of the world and ecoregion conservation*. Gland, WWF and Terralingua.

Renard, R. D. 1980. The role of the Karens in Thai society during the Early Bangkok Period, 1782-1873. *Contributions to Asian Studies*, Vol. 15, pp. 16-28.

Santasombat, Y. 1992. Community-based natural resource management in Thailand. *Asian Review*, Vol. 6, pp. 78-124.

Sato, J. 2002. Karen and the Land in Between: Public and Private Enclosure of Forests in Thailand. In D. Chatty and M. Colchester (eds.), *Conservation and Mobile Indigenous Peoples – Displacement, Forced Settlement, and Sustainable Development*. New York, Berghahn Books, pp. 277-295.

Steinmetz, R. 1999. The ecological science of the Karen in Thung Yai Naresuan Wildlife Sanctuary, Western Thailand. M. Colchester and C. Erni (eds.), *From principles to practice*. Copenhagen, IWGIA, pp. 84-107.

Steinmetz, R., Chutipong, W. and Seuaturien, N. 2006. Collaborating to conserve large mammals in Southeast Asia. *Conservation Biology*, Vol. 20, No. 5, pp. 1391-1401.

Stern, T. 1968. Ariya and the Golden Book. *Journal of Asian Studies*, Vol. 27, No. 2, pp. 297-328.

Stewart-Cox, B. 1998. Forests too precious for Seub legacy to be lost. *The Nation*, 23 September 1998.

Taylor, K. and Lennon, J. 2011. Cultural landscapes: A bridge between culture and nature? *International Journal of Heritage Studies*, Vol. 17, No. 6, pp. 537–554.

Thailand. 1991. *Nomination of natural property to the World Heritage List submitted by Thailand: ThungYai - Huaikhakhaeng Wildlife Sanctuary*. Bangkok, Government of Thailand (Royal Forest Department).

Thailand. 1997. *Constitution of the Kingdom of Thailand*. Bangkok, Government of Thailand.

Thailand. 2003. Thailand: Thungyai - Huai Kha Khaeng Wildlife Sanctuaries. UNESCO World Heritage Centre (ed.). *Summaries of Periodic Reports Submitted by States Parties*. Paris, UNESCO, pp. 232-235.

Thailand. 2010. *Recovering the Karen Livelihood in Thailand: Cabinet Resolution of the Royal Thai Government, August 3rd, 2010*. Bangkok, Ministry of Culture, Government of Thailand. Available at: www.ikap-mmsea.org/thailand.htm.

UN DESA. 2008. *Resource Kit on Indigenous Peoples' Issues* (prepared by the Secretariat of the UN Permanent Forum on Indigenous Issues). New York, United Nations Department of Economic and Social Affairs.

UNESCO. 1991. *World Heritage Committee, Fifteenth Session (Carthage, 9-13 December 1991)*. Doc. SC-91/CONF.002/15, 12 December 1991.

UNESCO. 1999. *World Heritage Committee, Twenty-second session (Kyoto, Japan, 30 November - 5 December 1998)*. Doc. WHC-98/CONF.203/18, 29 January 1999.

UNESCO. 2010. *A proposed joint programme of work on biological and cultural diversity lead by the Secretariat of the Convention on Biodiversity and UNESCO*. Montreal, UNESCO and CBD.

Usher, A. D. 2009. *Thai forestry: A critical history*. Chiang Mai, Silkworm Books.

Vandergeest, P. and Peluso, N. L. 2011. Political violence and scientific forestry: Emergencies, insurgencies, and counterinsurgencies in Southeast Asia. M. J. Goldman, M. D. Turner and P. Nadasdy (eds.), *Knowing Nature*. Chicago, University of Chicago Press, pp. 152-166.

Weatherby, M. and Soonthornwong, S. 2007. The Thailand Community Forest Bill. *RECOFTC Community Forestry E-News*, December 2007.

Winichakul, T. 1994. *Siam mapped*. Honolulu, University of Hawaii Press.

World Heritage Centre. 2001. WHIPCOE on Stage. *World Heritage Newsletter*, Vol. 31, July-September 2001.

World Heritage Centre. 2003. *Cultural Landscapes: The challenges of conservation*. World Heritage Papers 7. Paris, UNESCO.

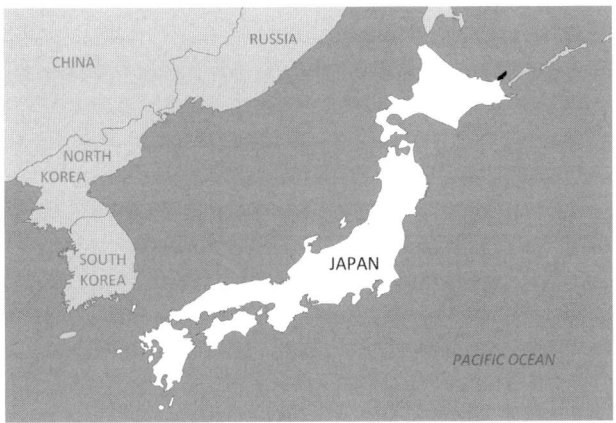

Shiretoko Natural World Heritage Area and the Ainu People

Ono Yugo[1]

Introduction

The Shiretoko peninsula, stretching out to the north-east of Hokkaido, the northernmost island in the Japanese archipelago, is the ancestral home of the Ainu people. In 2005 it was inscribed on the World Heritage List as a natural site of outstanding universal value. This inscription process took place largely without consultation with, or participation from, the Ainu people in Japan. This article examines the reasons for this lack of consultation, including the historic marginalization that the Ainu have faced in Japan and the contemporary situation whereby the Ainu people are beginning to claim back their rights as indigenous people in the islands.

It is not simply the nomination and inscription process in which the Ainu have been largely ignored, but the continuing management arrangements used to preserve this place of natural

---

1   In accordance with Japanese convention, all the Japanese names are given with the family names first followed by the given names.

Left: A ritual calling out to all of nature (fire, land, water and forest – collectively called 'Kamuy' in Ainu) conducted in Shiretoko by Ainu leader Yuki Koji in an ecotour organized by SIPETRU. Photo: SIPETRU

beauty and sacred areas. This article will look at the existing management arrangements and provide some recommendations as to how these arrangements could be changed to better include the Ainu in the management of their ancestral places.

The Ainu people: a brief history

The Ainu are an indigenous people living in Japan. Ainu means 'human' or 'people' in their language. Although now settled entirely in Japan, the Ainu previously inhabited a wider area of north-east Asia, including Kamchatka, the southern part of Sakhalin, Hokkaido (*Ainu Mosir* in the Ainu language) and the northern part of Tohoku (the north-eastern area of mainland Japan). Some anthropological studies have pointed out similarities between the Ainu and the Neolithic Jomon people who first settled the Japanese archipelago between 14,000-12,000 BC. However, while the Jomon culture was found throughout the archipelago, the Ainu appear to have emerged from a wave of migration into the north of Japan by a people called the Okhotsk, who mingled with the existing settlements.[2] Since the Okhotsk people (migrants from northern Sakhalin or Siberia) invaded Hokkaido and lived there between the third and twelfth centuries, archaeologists believe that the Ainu originated in this period. However, the distribution of place names in the Ainu language in the northern part of Tohoku overlaps with that of a special type of earthenware that appeared both in Hokkaido and Tohoku in the third and fourth centuries. This fact suggests the Ainu-speaking people migrated from Hokkaido to Tohoku with their earthenware technique during that period.

The origin of the Ainu-speaking people can be dated to around this period, and most possibly with earlier links to the Jomon period. The earliest Ainu cultures were dependent on subsistence activities, predominantly salmon fishing, hunting and plant gathering. Ainu culture was modified by contact through trade and war with the Okhotsk people, the Wajin (non-Ainu ethnic Japanese of the main island), neighboring North Asian peoples and the Chinese. The main trade materials were natural resources such as fur, brown bear gallbladder, sea tangle and eagle feathers. The Ainu traded these materials for rice, tobacco, alcohol, silk clothes and lacquer-ware. The trade nourished the Ainu people and several different tribes of Ainu occupied different regions all over Hokkaido between the twelfth and seventeenth centuries. In the fourteenth century, they invaded northern Sakhalin and into the mainland Asian continent, fighting against Mongolia in a war that lasted for more than forty years (1264-1308) before they were finally defeated.

With the invasion of southern Hokkaido by the Japanese in the fifteenth century, the independence of the Ainu began to erode. Losing the battle of Koshamain in 1457 weakened the force of the Ainu although they retained their independence. In 1604, the Japanese (*Wajin*) established the Matsumae Domainal Government on the south-western margin of Hokkaido. This

---

2   Recent DNA analysis shows that the DNA composition of the Ainu can be explained as a hybrid of the Jomon and Okhotsk peoples' DNA. See Adachi et al. 2007; Sato et al. 2007. In comparison, the modern Japanese of the main island share genetic stock with the Jomon and Yayoi peoples (migrants from the Asian continent from 400-300 BC). See Hanihara 1991.

increased conflict between the Ainu people and Wajin settler populations. A turning point in relations between the Wajin and the Ainu was the Shakushain battle of 1669. After defeat in that battle, the Ainu were forced to obey the Matsumae Domainal Government, and they began to lose their political and economic autonomy. The Shogun government in Edo (today's Tokyo) supported this trend. The Ainu lost their independent right of trading, and their economy was brought under the control of the Japanese. The Kunashiri-Menashi war of 1789 was the final war between the Ainu and the Wajin and took place close to Shiretoko. Their defeat in this war led to the loss of their power in the Shiretoko peninsular. Since the Shiretoko area is rich in salmon, the Wajin monopolized the catching of salmon and this was one of the reasons why the Ainu inhabitants disappeared from what is now the World Heritage Area of Shiretoko. Continued economic dependency caused the Ainu to become far poorer during the two-hundred-year period from the seventeenth to the nineteenth century.[3]

The Ainu completely lost their own governance after Japan colonized Hokkaido under the rule of the Meiji Emperor in 1868. Over the following 30 years, the Ainu lost all of their rights without any treaties being concluded between the Ainu and the occupiers. In 1899, a discriminative law called the *Hokkaido Former Aborigines Protection Act* was promulgated, and with it came a government policy that was strongly assimilative, designed to weaken the Ainu language and culture.

Present situation of the Ainu in Japanese society

According to government figures from 2006, the Ainu population in Hokkaido was roughly 24,000. In addition to this population in Hokkaido, several thousand Ainu lived in the Tokyo area.[4] Actual Ainu population numbers may be more than ten times larger, however, as many Ainu hide their identity because of the discrimination against the Ainu people which continues today. The Ainu are still under tremendous pressure to assimilate into the majority Japanese population, and any recovery of their indigenous rights, language and culture is obstructed by government policy. Since being invaded by the Japanese, the Ainu have lost their basic rights, including their rights to land and the free use of natural resources. They lost their economic base under the rule of the Japanese Empire and the decline of the Japanese Empire in 1945 did not change this basic situation.

An organization called the Hokkaido Ainu Association was established in 1945 as the first ethnic alliance of the Ainu people, but it was not a politically or economically independent association. Rather, it was established under the control of the Hokkaido prefectural government and its main objective was to distribute welfare from the government to the Ainu people.[5] This created a new system of economic dependency on the part of the Ainu on the government. The Hokkaido Ainu Association changed its name to Hokkaido Utari Association in 1961. *Utari* means 'fellow Ainu' in the Ainu language. One of the reasons for the name change was that many Ainu disliked using the word Ainu, because this word evoked a bad feeling of discrimination.

---

3   Walker 2001.
4   2006 Survey of Ainu Livelihood conducted by the Hokkaido prefectural government (cited in IWGIA 2013, p. 222).
5   Emori 2007.

In 1984, the Hokkaido Utari Association proposed that a new law concerning the Ainu people be adopted by the Japanese government. This marked the first attempt by the Ainu to legally recover their indigenous rights. The Japanese government did establish a committee to draft a new law but failed to appoint any Ainu members to the committee. In consequence, although the *Hokkaido Former Aborigines Protection Act* was abolished and a new law was enacted in 1997, the new law - called the 'Ainu Culture Promotion Act'[6] - does not acknowledge the indigenous status of the Ainu nor their rights over their natural resources, including their rights to traditional livelihoods such as salmon fishing and wildlife hunting. It can therefore be said that even with the new law the Ainu people continue to live under the conditions of the 19th century policies aimed at colonization and assimilation.[7]

The Ainu Culture Promotion Act did have some positive as well as negative impacts on Ainu society. Positive impacts included an increase in budget support to Ainu affairs and the creation of a Foundation for Research and Promotion of Ainu Culture, which financially supports various projects of the Ainu, including the activities of the Ainu language schools. One of the negative effects was the increased economic dependency of the Ainu on the government. This was particularly true of the Hokkaido Ainu Association (having changed its name back in 2008), which became much more attached to the government in order to obtain more funding and to easily implement projects supported by the government. The government also continued to treat the Association as the only representative body for all of the Ainu, a position that is highly problematic given the close governmental relations maintained by the Association. It is clear that the Hokkaido Ainu Association is not a representative body for all of the Ainu people, most simply due to the fact that it has only 4,000 members, a small fraction of the total Ainu population. It also continues to define itself geographically, as the 'Hokkaido' Ainu Association, and this means that Ainu living outside of Hokkaido cannot hold membership of the Association.[8]

In response, Ainu living in the Tokyo area have established their own organizations to demand the recovery of indigenous rights more explicitly than the Hokkaido Ainu Association has done. The creation of many other Ainu organizations and groups suggests criticism of the Hokkaido Ainu Association, and several Ainu have left the Hokkaido Ainu Association and joined some of these other groups. However, these newer groups are not regarded as formal partners in negotiations with the government. While some of these groups have recently attained NPO (Non-Profit Organization) status and are now much more empowered than before, in 2004-2005 (at the time of the World Heritage nomination), these groups were still weak, and most of the information regarding the nomination was concentrated in the Hokkaido Ainu Association.[9]

---

6   *Act for the Promotion of Ainu Culture, the Spread of Knowledge Relevant to Ainu Traditions, and an Education Campaign* (Law No. 52, 1997).
7   Ono 1999b.
8   This is closely related to the fact that the Association was established in 1945 so that the Hokkaido prefectural government could distribute welfare to the Ainu inhabitants of Hokkaido. The Hokkaido prefecture still uses the Association for this purpose and since it cannot offer welfare to Ainu living outside of Hokkaido, it does not want the Association to change its name or its membership rules. This is supported by the national government, which does not want Ainu affairs to be nationalized but rather localized in Hokkaido.
9   Ono 2006.

In 2008, Ainu activists achieved a great step forward when the House of Representatives in Japan (the Diet) recognized the Ainu as an indigenous people. This was an important turning point in the history of relations between the Ainu and the Japanese government. However, it has not appeared to accelerate the process of the recovery of Ainu rights. In fact, the "Expert Meeting Concerning Ainu Affairs", a council created in 2008 by the Japanese government, had no Ainu members at first. After receiving strong objections from the Ainu, the government finally included Kato Tadashi, a director of the Hokkaido Ainu Association, although he was still the only Ainu among eight committee members.

The World Indigenous Peoples Network: Ainu (WIN-Ainu), an organization established in 2009 by the organizers of the Indigenous Peoples Summit held just before the G8 Summit in 2008,[10] sent a message to the Japanese government requesting the creation of a permanent committee for the recovery of indigenous rights with an equal number of Ainu and non-Ainu members;[11] such a committee has not, however, yet been established.

Shiretoko Peninsula and the World Natural Heritage Area

Shiretoko is a peninsula that protrudes into the Sea of Okhotsk in north-eastern Hokkaido, the northernmost island of Japan. Severe winters in which thick ice covers the sea from December to March and ragged volcanic landforms have prevented agricultural development and preserved the natural ecosystem in its wild state. The dense mixed forest offers good habitat for the brown bear and Blakiston's fish owl, two important Ainu gods that are now endangered species.[12] The coastline of the peninsula is rich in globally rare mammals and birds such as Hawker's least shrew, Steller's sea lion, Steller's sea eagle and the white-tailed eagle.

The peninsula runs from south-west to north-east, following a line of active volcanoes that extends into the Kuril Islands. Many of these volcanoes exceed 1,500 m and the highest one is Mt. Rausu at 1,611 m. As the peninsula is less than 20 km wide in most parts, lava rock exposed to the sea and eroded by wave action has formed steep cliffs that surround the entire peninsula, while short rivers with steep gradients and many waterfalls flow into the sea. This topography gives the Shiretoko peninsula a special ecosystem with intimate connections between mountains, rivers and the sea. These unique natural features were the main reasons why Shiretoko was inscribed as a World Natural Heritage Area at the World Heritage Committee's 29th Session in Durban, South Africa in July 2005.[13] The site was inscribed as a 'natural site' only, without reference to the cultural heritage contained within the Shiretoko Peninsula.

The World Heritage Area, including the buffer zone, covers 71,000 ha (48,700 ha of land and 22,300 ha of the surrounding seas) and falls within the jurisdiction of Shari and Rausu towns. It

---

10 Indigenous Peoples Summit in Ainu Mosir Steering Committee 2008.
11 Kayano and Akibe 2009.
12 Ono 1999a.
13 See UNESCO 2005, pp. 114-115.

contains several partially overlapping protected areas, including the Onnebetsudake Wilderness Area, the Shiretoko National Park, the Shiretoko Forest Ecosystem Reserve and parts of the Shiretoko National Wildlife Protection Area. Most of the land within the World Heritage Area (38,636 ha) corresponds to Shiretoko National Park, first established in 1964. Human occupation is limited to only two towns on the inland side of the peninsula: Utoro and Rausu. There are no permanent inhabitants in any other area of Shiretoko, demonstrating how pristine the peninsula is.

At the domestic level, the World Heritage Area is protected through a number of national laws and regulations, including the Nature Conservation Law (1972), the Natural Parks Law (1957), the Law on Administration and Management of National Forests (1951) and the Law for Conservation of Endangered Species of Wild Fauna and Flora (1992). It is managed by the Ministry of the Environment, the Forestry Agency, the Agency for Cultural Affairs and the Hokkaido prefectural government, which are responsible for implementing the various laws and regulations relevant to the conservation and administration of the heritage site.[14] In terms of land ownership, 95 percent of the land within the World Heritage Area is National Forest, which is administered by the Forestry Agency.[15] In 2009, an integrated management plan for the World Heritage site was adopted which attempts to simplify the management of the area through better coordination between the many involved government agencies.[16]

None of the mentioned laws on national parks or national forests refer to the Ainu people or mention their rights or roles. The introduction of the Ainu Culture Promotion Act (1997) did not change anything in this regard because this law aims only to promote the "Ainu culture" as defined by the government. For example, any modern or contemporary Ainu arts are not regarded as "Ainu culture" but only their traditional dance, music and embroidery. The Act carefully avoids any reference to their indigenous rights, land rights and rights of natural resources use. In such a situation, it is not surprising that the nomination of the Shiretoko World Heritage Area was written without any involvement of the Ainu people.

Despite such legal blindness, the connection between the Ainu and Shiretoko is a long one. Not only the name of the peninsula but all the place names in Shiretoko are derived from the Ainu language. Shiretoko means 'cape' (*Shir*: 'land', *etoko*: 'end') in the Ainu language. The place names illustrate the fact that Ainu people inhabited the entire peninsula in the past. They lived off the rich natural resources of the peninsula, such as the autumn salmon migration, abundant sea

---

14 The Agency for Cultural Affairs is involved because of its responsibilities under the Law for the Protection of Cultural Properties, by which some of the species found on the World Heritage site have been designated as Natural Monuments because of their significant scientific value to the country.

15 The Japanese National Park system differs from the Western model. The landowner is usually not the Ministry of the Environment, although they are responsible for the designation and management of the parks (the same is true for wilderness areas and wildlife protection areas). The biggest landowner is normally the Forestry Agency or, in some cases, even private paper companies. In such a situation, conflicts can easily occur between the management office and the landowners. In Shiretoko, a serious conflict took place in 1986-87 on the issue of logging a forest area of 1,700 ha within the National Park. In spite of strong opposition and a campaign against logging, the forest was felled by the Forestry Agency in 1987. The Ministry of Environment in this case agreed with the logging, based on the result of an environmental assessment that suggested that there would be no damage to the fish owl, the most important endangered species living in the Park area.

16 Ministry of the Environment et al. 2009.

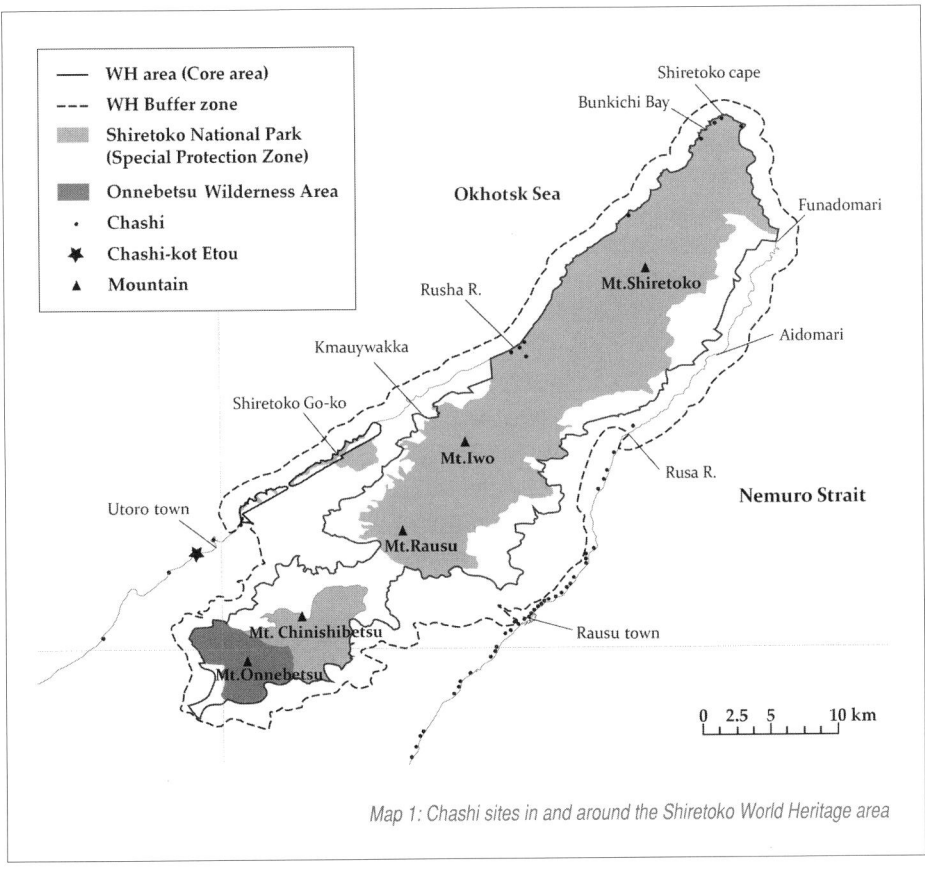

Map 1: Chashi sites in and around the Shiretoko World Heritage area

mammals, eagles, fish owls, brown bears and deer as well as many different kinds of native plants. The tail feathers of the Steller's sea eagle were important trade materials for the Ainu during the Edo era (1603-1868). Conflicts over the exclusive possession of these natural resources occurred between Wajin and the Ainu and also within Ainu society, mainly in the eastern part of Hokkaido, including Shiretoko.[17]

This history explains the abundance of Chashi sites (Chashi-kot) found along the coast of the peninsula (Map 1). A Chashi-kot is an archaeological site that was originally used by the Ainu in the early–modern era (mainly between the sixteenth and eighteenth centuries).[18] Chashi are believed to have been fortified villages, although they may have originated as holy places used for communicating with the gods. As the wooden buildings and walls of Chashi no longer exist, only defensive ditches and pits (kot in the Ainu language) used as house foundations remain for archaeologists to study today (hence the name, Chashi-kot, which is often used in the names of

---

17 Walker 2001.
18 Kato 2008, 2009; Udagawa 2003.

places on the peninsula). Some Ainu people regard the *Chashi-kot* as sacred sites and wish to protect them from destruction, although many of them have already been destroyed through the construction of roads, dams and other public infrastructure.

Neglect of the Ainu people in the nomination process of the Shiretoko World Heritage Area

On the basis of its wildness and the abundant presence of endangered species, Shiretoko was nominated to become a World Natural Heritage site in 2004 by the Japanese government. However, the government completely neglected the Ainu in the process of promoting Shiretoko as a World Natural Heritage Area. They tried to legitimize this attitude by emphasizing the fact that there were no Ainu inhabitants in the heritage area at present. They also failed to refer to the existence of the large number of *Chashi* in Shiretoko, including those in the World Heritage site itself, although the Hokkaido prefectural government had a list of *Chashi* that were excavated or recognized by archaeologists.

The government's nomination document and management plan for Shiretoko as a World Natural Heritage site did not mention the possibility of Ainu cooperation in the management of the site, despite recognizing the historical relationship that the Ainu have with the site.[19] This was raised in a meeting of the Sapporo Branch of the Hokkaido Ainu Association in 2004, which appears to have been the first time that the Ainu people recognized the Shiretoko World Heritage nomination as an issue.

The nomination was prepared by the Japanese Ministry of the Environment, which asked the Hokkaido prefectural government for cooperation in the nomination process. This is notable as the Hokkaido prefectural government has a close relationship with the Hokkaido Ainu Association, exercising some control through funding and project direction.[20] The government controlled the information about the nomination very tightly, and the fact of nominating Shiretoko was not known among Ainu people generally until a very late stage in the nomination process. It is possible that some core members of the Hokkaido Ainu Association were in a position to know about the nomination but it did not become a public issue until Ainu NPOs criticized the neglect of the Ainu in the nomination process.

---

19 See Government of Japan 2004; Ministry of Environment et al. 2004. This lack of inclusion of the Ainu notably contrasts with the following observation in the management plan: "Instead of damaging the nature, the people living in the peninsula adapted their lives to realize sustainable use of the nature's bounties and created a unique local lifestyle, industry and culture. It is essential to study the culture of the Ainu people and the traditional wisdom and skills of the local residents in order to determine the methods to preserve, manage and realize sustainable use of the natural environment." (Ibid., p. 214).

20 In fact, when the Association was first established the secretary general of the Hokkaido Ainu Association was an officer sent from the Hokkaido prefectural government and this has only recently changed. Now, the secretary general is a person selected by the Association, although there has not yet been an Ainu in the job.

View of the Shiretoko Mountains from Lake Ichiko, Shiretoko National Park. Photo: Martyn Steiner

Ainu NPOs' efforts to be involved in managing the Shiretoko World Heritage site

Following the Sapporo branch meeting in 2004, Abe Yupo, a leader of Uhanokka-no-kai, an Ainu NPO, and an executive member of the Hokkaido Ainu Association, sent a personal letter (not representing the Hokkaido Ainu Association) to IUCN and presented a statement at the UN Permanent Forum on Indigenous Issues in May 2004 criticizing the injustice of neglecting the Ainu in the nomination process.[21] These actions brought the connection between the Ainu and the Shiretoko World Heritage site to the attention of IUCN. As a result, when David Sheppard, Head of the IUCN Protected Areas Programme, visited Shiretoko in July 2004 to examine its natural values and management planning (as part of IUCN's Advisory Body Evaluation of the World Heritage nomination), he expressed a wish to meet with the Ainu people.

However, the Ministry of the Environment and the Hokkaido prefectural government refused to allow Sheppard to meet with any Ainu people who were criticizing the neglect of the Ainu in the application process. Instead, the government arranged an informal meeting with a director of the Hokkaido Ainu Association who told Sheppard that the Ainu welcomed the World Heritage nomination and denied the existence of sacred sites within the nominated area. A request for a

---

21 See IWGIA 2005, pp. 280-281.

formal meeting between Sheppard and all interested Ainu groups was refused by the Hokkaido prefectural government and the Ministry of Environment, who did not want the effective participation of a variety of Ainu groups. The Hokkaido Ainu Association complied with this decision. An informal meeting did take place but only through standing and chatting during the welcome party.

Subsequently, the Ainu elder and activist for indigenous rights, Ogawa Ryukichi, challenged the declaration of the director of Hokkaido Ainu Association that there were no Ainu sacred sites within the heritage area, stressing the importance of *Chashi* as sacred sites and of preserving Ainu cultural heritage in Shiretoko. His wife, Ogawa Sanae, a leader of the Ainu NPO Etekekanba-no-kai, sent a letter to David Sheppard in September 2004 reporting on the matter of the *Chashi* and asking about the involvement of the Ainu in the future management of the Shiretoko World Heritage site. Abe Yupo not only sent a letter to David Sheppard but also visited him in November 2004 at his IUCN office in Switzerland, again emphasizing the need for Ainu involvement in managing the site.

Since there are no Ainu living in the Shiretoko World Heritage Area, the Ainu groups and activists demanding Ainu involvement in managing the Shiretoko World Heritage Area decided to develop a business plan to provide an entry into the management of the World Heritage site. Ainu ecotourism in the World Heritage Area was chosen as a measure to recover indigenous rights, especially the right to natural resource use such as salmon fishing.[22] SIPETRU (Shiretoko Indigenous Eco-Tourism Research Union)[23] was created for this purpose in April 2004 and began eco-tours guided by Ainu people on July 1st of that year. At that time, SIPETRU sent a message to IUCN emphasizing the importance of Ainu involvement in managing the Shiretoko World Heritage Area through indigenous ecotourism.

IUCN did take note of these requests, highlighting in their technical evaluation of the site:

"It is important, as reinforced in the management plan (page 214 of the nomination document) to 'study the culture of the Ainu people and the traditional wisdom and skills of the local residents in order to determine the methods to preserve, manage and realize sustainable use of the natural environment.' Accordingly it is considered important that representatives of the Ainu people, such as through the Hokkaido Utari (Ainu) Association, have the opportunity to be involved in the future management of the property, including in relation to the development of appropriate ecotourism activities which celebrate the traditional customs and uses of the nominated property." [24]

However, despite this recommendation by IUCN, the World Heritage Committee made no mention of the Ainu in its decision to inscribe Shiretoko on the World Heritage List later in 2005.[25]

---

22 Ono 2006.
23 The abbreviation 'SIPETRU' means 'main or big (*si*) river (*pet*) way (*ru*)' in the Ainu language. It is an allusion to the idea that the activity of SIPETRU will be a main way of recovering indigenous rights. *Pet* (river) is traditionally the most important route for the transfer of natural resources for the Ainu, and regarded as divine by the Ainu.
24 IUCN 2005, p. 31.
25 Decision 29 COM 8B.6.

Nevertheless, the IUCN evaluation was important, for it clearly indicated a process that would allow the Ainu people to be involved in managing the Shiretoko World Heritage site even though the Japanese government did not mention Ainu participation in their application. The IUCN document is also remarkable from the viewpoint of indigenous rights since the recommendation is included in a section entitled "Involvement of Indigenous Peoples", which means that the IUCN document recognized the Ainu as an indigenous people three years before the Japanese Parliament (Diet) officially recognized the indigenous status of Ainu, in June 2008, just before the Hokkaido-Toyako G8 Summit.[26]

However, the IUCN evaluation uses wording that is conciliatory to the government: "It is considered important that representatives of the Ainu people, such as through the Hokkaido Utari (Ainu) Association, have the opportunity to be involved in the future management…" It leaves room to defer implementation of the recommendation to 'the future', and mentions only the Hokkaido Utari (Ainu) Association, not the other Ainu organizations that actually brought the Ainu issue to the attention of IUCN. This reflects the actual balance of power between the Hokkaido Ainu Association and other Ainu organizations in relation to the Japanese government, which only recognizes the former group as representative of the Ainu people even though its membership makes up only a fraction of Ainu society.

The management system for the World Heritage Area

The current management system for the Shiretoko World Heritage site does allow for some involvement of Ainu individuals and organizations, although it is very limited. To understand where their influence is possible, it is necessary to review the management system as a whole. The current management plan for the Shiretoko World Heritage site dates from 2009 and consolidates earlier management processes that were considered by the World Heritage Committee to be too complex.[27] The large number of laws applied to the lands and seas of the Shiretoko site (see above) requires the involvement of a similarly large number of government agencies. Agencies with legal responsibilities over part of the site include the Forestry Agency, the Ministry of the Environment, the Ministry of Education, Culture, Sports, Science and Technology and the regional fisheries agency of Hokkaido, all with specific laws that they are tasked to oversee.

---

26 "Resolution calling for the Recognition of the Ainu People as an Indigenous People of Japan", adopted by both houses of the National Diet of Japan on June 6, 2008. For details, see IWGIA 2009, p. 280. Note that UN human rights treaty bodies had for years been calling on Japan to take steps to promote the rights of the Ainu as an indigenous people (see e.g., Committee on the Elimination of Racial Discrimination, *Concluding Observations: Japan*, 27 April 2001, Doc. CERD/C/304/Add.114, paras. 4, 5, 17). Shortly before the Diet resolution, the following recommendations had been made to Japan during the UN Human Rights Council's Universal Periodic Review: "Review, inter alia, the land rights and other rights of the Ainu population and harmonize them with the United Nations Declaration on the Rights of Indigenous Peoples. (Algeria); Urge Japan to seek ways to initiating a dialogue with its indigenous peoples so that it can implement the United Nations Declaration on the Rights of Indigenous Peoples (Guatemala)" (UN Doc. A/HRC/8/44, 30 May 2008, Recommendation 19).

27 This was the conclusion of a 2008 UNESCO/IUCN reactive monitoring mission, which issued a number of recommendations as to how the management system could be simplified (see UNESCO 2008).

In order to facilitate this process, there is a 'Shiretoko World Natural Heritage Regional Liaison Committee', the body responsible for coordinating the various bodies involved in the site management and for building consensus among these agencies. In addition, a 'Shiretoko World Natural Heritage Scientific Council' was established to provide independent and scientific advice and inform government agencies in their management choices. In practice, the three main agencies now actively managing the site are the Kushiro Nature Conservation Office (Hokkaido Regional Environment Office, under the Ministry of the Environment), the Hokkaido Regional Forestry Office (under the Forestry Agency) and the Hokkaido government, together with the local administrations of Rausu Town and Shari Town. All their roles are undertaken within the framework agreed in the Shiretoko Management Plan.

The agreed framework for management focuses on a division of the area into two broad categories of protection, Areas A and B. The former refers to areas under strict environmental conservation with no human intervention allowed, and comprises lands under a range of different legal classifications (Wilderness Area, Special Protection Zone, etc.). This land is managed predominantly by rangers under the employ of the Ministry of Environment and the Forestry Agency. Area B refers to lands and resources in which human interaction is allowed, and includes all areas in which tourism is allowed, in addition to all of the marine resources included in the park in which sustainable and managed fisheries are allowed. There are a larger number of actors involved in these 'Area B' parts of the site, as these can be used for various purposes.

To assist in the management of the Area B parts of the site, which can be used, there are two further advisory bodies, the 'Committee on the Proper Use of the Shiretoko World Natural Heritage Site' and the 'Shiretoko Ecotourism Association'. The Proper Use Committee advises on the formulation of rules for the use of the site, and is expected to incorporate scientific research into its recommendations. The Shiretoko Ecotourism Association is tasked with "tak[ing] the lead in spreading efforts based on the concept of ecotourism" in order to allow conservation of the natural environment to take place alongside tourism, a critical industry in the area.[28] It is in the Shiretoko Ecotourism Committee that Ainu people have managed to find a small role in the management of the Shiretoko area.

The core members of the Shiretoko Ecotourism Association are the tourism, tour-guide, hotel and hot spring associations, and the Shiretoko Foundation, which is financially supported by Shari and Rausu towns. Other members, such as the association of commerce and industry, the fishermen's association, as well as associations of transportation, agriculture and dairy farming, are ranked as working members who can give advice to the committee. The Shari and Rausu branches of the Hokkaido Ainu Association are also involved as working members.

The structure and name of the Shiretoko Ecotourism Association clearly illustrates the nature tourism-oriented character of this committee. Its main interest is to promote tourism that preserves the natural resources of Shiretoko and the outstanding natural values of the World Heritage site. The Association was established in 2004 following a Ministry of Environment initiative to promote ecotourism, with Shiretoko serving as a model. These circumstances led

---

28 Ministry of the Environment et al. 2009, p. 9.

the Shiretoko Ecotourism Association to stress nature tourism and neglect the cultural aspects of Shiretoko, based on a perception of Shiretoko as a 'cultureless wilderness area'.

SIPETRU sends a representative and a vice-representative to the Shiretoko Ecotourism Association. The representative, Umezawa Toshio, is also a representative of the Shari branch of the Ainu Association, while the vice-representative is a representative of the Rausu branch. They therefore have a dual representative function in the Shiretoko Ecotourism Association. These two representatives are, however, a tiny minority within the association.

There are no Ainu participants in any of the other advisory committees mentioned, the Proper Use Committee, the Scientific Committee or the overall Regional Liaison Committee. There is also no representation of the Hokkaido Ainu Association within any of these. This means that Ainu involvement in Shiretoko is restricted purely to two representatives within one of the advisory committees dealing only with 'Area B' of the site.

A significant problem for the Ainu people is that only a very small number of inhabitants around the World Heritage Area, in Utoro and Rausu towns, publicly identify as Ainu. There seem to be many other Ainu inhabitants but they choose to hide their identity to avoid suffering discrimination. The Shari branch of the Ainu Association actually comprises only the Umezawa family, while the Rausu branch has about thirty members. The Ainu members of SIPETRU come mainly from Sapporo, although one member, Hayasaka Masayoshi, relocated to Utoro from Sapporo. Ainu eco-tours in Shiretoko are operated by Hayasaka, who works as a guide, and the Umezawa family, who run an inn at Utoro. They represent only a small portion of all the eco-tours conducted in the Shiretoko World Heritage Area.

Ecotourism activities in the Shiretoko World Heritage Area

As is clear from the description of the Shiretoko management arrangements, one area in which the management system has allowed Ainu involvement is the area of ecotourism on the site. This emerged from the persistent efforts of Ainu and non-Ainu supporters in Hokkaido to develop Ainu ecotourism on the peninsula.

When SIPETRU began its Ainu eco-tours in 2004, it chose *Chashi-kot Etou* as a tour site (Map 1) because it was regarded as a sacred site by some Ainu and had not been visited by tourists even though it was quite close to Utoro, one of the entry points to the World Heritage Area. SIPETRU modeled this first attempt to introduce Ainu ecotourism to Japan on studies of Maori ecotourism in Aotearoa (New Zealand), developing three- and five-hour eco-tour programs. Each tour begins with a traditional Ainu salutation to the gods (*On-kami*), and includes a visit to the *Chashi-kot*, an explanation of plant resources traditionally used by the Ainu, along with a taste of traditional Ainu tea and a performance of traditional musical instruments such as the *mukkuri* and *tonkori*. Some tours also include a traditional *Kamuy-nomi* ceremony.

The Ainu eco-tours created by SIPETRU are designed to facilitate a communicative, participation-oriented experience in which non-Ainu participants have opportunities to play traditional instruments, taste traditional tea and pray to the gods together with the Ainu. Tourists also have the opportunity to work on a traditional Ainu boat (*Itaomachip*) by helping to hollow out a tree trunk with a hammer and chisel. They can then create a pendant from one of the shavings with the help of an Ainu woodcutting artist. Some Ainu eco-tour participants stay at the inn run by the Umezawa family in Utoro where they can enjoy Ainu-style cooking and embroidery, especially on rainy days not suitable for the outside program.

SIPETRU sees the development of ecotourism as one part of a recovery of Ainu rights more generally and defines its five core goals as ecotourism, research, employment for Ainu youth, sharing the Ainu spirit and indigenous rights activism. These five points are interconnected and together contribute to the recovery of indigenous rights through ecotourism.

SIPETRU research is already bearing fruit. Studies conducted together with the Hokkaido University Centre for Ainu and Indigenous Studies (HUCAIS) have revealed a dwelling pit at *Chashi-kot Etou* originally created by the Okhotsk people. The Okhotsk were seafarers who migrated to the Okhotsk and Japan Sea coasts of Hokkaido from coastal regions of Siberia, Sakhalin and Kamchatka between the third and thirteenth centuries.[29] The dwelling pit at *Chashi-kot Etou* was formed around the twelfth or thirteenth century in the final stage of the Okhotsk culture. Also known as the Tobinitai culture, it had features of both Okhotsk and Satsumon-Ainu cultures.[30]

Sharing the Ainu spirit with participants is an important task for Ainu ecotourism. Spiritual aspects of Ainu culture are shared with the participants through ceremonies as well as on various occasions during the eco-tours. The tours emphasize respect for the forest, rivers and ocean, as well as a general sense of living in harmony with nature conveyed through music, chanting and story-telling. They further include a discussion of the present situation of the Ainu in Japanese society. Ainu eco-tours in Shiretoko also provide an important opportunity for Ainu youth to study traditional knowledge of natural resource use as well as Ainu ceremonies and spiritualism. Because Ainu youth have few chances to study these traditions, participation in an eco-tour guided by an Ainu elder can be a valuable educational experience.[31]

The employment of Ainu youth in ecotourism is one of the most important goals of SIPETRU's activities. There is still a big gap between Ainu and non-Ainu youth in levels of employment and education due to the economic realities of Ainu society. Job creation is urgently needed for Ainu youth, and Ainu ecotourism has strong potential in this area. The fee for a three-hour Ainu eco-tour in Shiretoko is set at 5,000 yen per person, with a maximum of ten participants to ensure an intimate experience and reduce the ecological impact of the tour. If there are enough tourists, Ainu youth can potentially make a living from the ecotourism business.

Since the establishment of SIPETRU, one Ainu, Hayasaka Masayoshi, has been employed by SINRA, an ecotourism company in Shiretoko that supports the activities of SIPETRU. He now works partly as an independent Ainu eco-tour guide. However, although he led more than sixty Ainu eco-tours in 2010 and eighty in 2011, he still cannot make a living solely from conducting tours. When there is no demand for Ainu eco-tours, he continues to work as a nature guide for SINRA,

---

29 Amano 2008.
30 Onishi 2009; Ono 2010.
31 Ono et al. 2007.

Ainu crane dance. "Traditional Ainu Dance" was inscribed on UNESCO's Representative List of the Intangible Cultural Heritage of Humanity in 2009. Believing that deities can be found in their surroundings, the Ainu frequently use dance to worship and give thanks to nature. Photo: Cactusbeetroot (CC BY-NC 2.0)

and sell his woodcarvings at a small shop that benefits from his activity as a tour guide. Hayasaka's wider family is also involved in Ainu tourism. His mother opened a small souvenir shop in one of the larger hotels that sells Ainu art and craft items, such as Hayasaka's woodcarvings, his brother's paintings and his sister's embroidery. This approach to ecotourism as a family business is common in Maori eco-tours in Aotearoa. Members of SIPETRU were also involved in the establishment of the non-profit organization 'World Indigenous Peoples Network, Ainu (Win-Ainu)' which was legally admitted in October 2012. This organization will facilitate and support future ecotourism activities in Shiretoko. The successes achieved to date in developing Ainu ecotourism in Shiretoko are due in part to the value of the Shiretoko World Heritage designation. They are also due to the Ainu movement demanding involvement in the management of the site.

Conclusion

As can be seen from this paper, the involvement of the Ainu in the nomination and inscription process for Shiretoko was nearly non-existent, despite continual efforts by Ainu to reach out to the Japanese government and to IUCN to highlight their desire to be engaged in the process. The management system in place now similarly does not provide adequate space for the Ainu to have any form of political or representative presence. The Shiretoko Ecotourism Association has proved the only avenue through which the Ainu have been able to get themselves involved in the management of their ancestral home in any role more significant than as a subject of study and research.

Unfortunately, the efforts of the Ainu to recover their indigenous rights, including the efforts of Ainu organizations to be involved in managing the Shiretoko World Heritage Area, are being stymied by the recent tendency of the Hokkaido Ainu Association to cooperate ever more closely with the Japanese government (largely to access more funding). A drastic policy change is urgently needed on the part of the Hokkaido Ainu Association if the Ainu are to recover their indigenous rights, both in Shiretoko and in Hokkaido generally.

Given the difficult situation, Ainu ecotourism is assuming an increasingly important role. Although the Hokkaido Ainu Association has not contributed to the development of Ainu ecotourism, since 2005 Ainu eco-tours have been launched in various parts of Hokkaido, including Akan, Sapporo, Noboribetsu and Shiraoi, creating jobs for Ainu youth, albeit on a limited scale for the time being.[32] In Shiretoko, SIPETRU's ecotourism activities have had a considerable effect, although increasing local Ainu membership remains an important challenge. Rights recovery through ecotourism has a long way to go but participation in managing the Shiretoko World Heritage Area will be enhanced by continued efforts to develop Ainu ecotourism in the area.

To support these (limited) signs of progress at the national level, there is also a need for the World Heritage Committee and IUCN to remain appraised of, and monitor, the situation of the Ainu at the Shiretoko site. IUCN, as the Committee's key advisory body for natural heritage sites, made early references to the Ainu in its technical evaluation of the original nomination of Shiretoko in 2005. In this evaluation, IUCN specifically recommended that management of the site be adjusted to ensure that the Ainu had opportunities to participate:

> "... it is considered important that representatives of the Ainu people... have the opportunity to be involved in the future management of the property..." [33]

However the Government of Japan did not act on this 2005 recommendation, as demonstrated in this paper. Despite this, IUCN and UNESCO failed to return to the issue in the report of their monitoring mission to Shiretoko and subsequent State of Conservation Reports, wherein they issued a series of recommendations related to the management of the site without ever mentioning the Ainu.[34] Indeed in a document annexed to the report of the 2008 monitoring mission, the Ainu are again relegated to symbolic language, with local government, including the Governor of Hokkaido, declaring that "we will maintain the wisdom and skills that the region's ancestors, the Ainu, have passed on through the generations as well as conserve the valuable history and remember what the land has provided us".[35]

---

32 Akibe 2011; Ono 2010.
33 IUCN 2005, p. 31.
34 IUCN and UNESCO 2008; UNESCO 2008; UNESCO 2012, p. 33 ff.
35 See IUCN and UNESCO 2008, Annex C: 'Shiretoko World Treasure Declaration signed by the Governor of Hokkaido and the Mayors of Shari and Rausu, in October 2005'.

Apart from this, the Ainu do not merit a single further mention. IUCN and the World Heritage Committee should keep the pressure on the Government of Japan to ensure that the original 2005 recommendation is followed, and that the Ainu are provided with the opportunity of being meaningfully involved in the management of Shiretoko.

This would also be in accordance with the 'Kyoto Vision' adopted on 8 November 2012 at the Closing Event of the Celebrations of the World Heritage Convention's 40th Anniversary in Kyoto, Japan, which stresses the important role of indigenous peoples in the implementation of the World Heritage Convention and appeals to the international community to ensure effective involvement of indigenous peoples in conservation "from the preparatory phase of the World Heritage nomination process, so that heritage conservation contributes to the sustainable development of the whole society".[36] ○

References

Adachi, N. et al. 2008. Mitochondrial DNA analysis of Jomon skeletons from the Funadomari site, Hokkaido, and its implication for the origin of Native American. *American Journal of Physical Anthropology*, Vol. 138, pp. 255-265.

Akibe, H. 2011. Akan Ainu no Eco-tourism. *Maukopirka*, No. 3/4, pp. 87-89.

Amano, T. 2009. *Kodai no Kaiyoumin Okhotsk-jin no Sekai - Ainu Bunka wo sakanoboru*. Tokyo, Yuzankaku.

Committee on the Elimination of Racial Discrimination. 2001. *Concluding Observations of the Committee on the Elimination of Racial Discrimination: Japan*, Doc. CERD/C/304/Add.114.

Government of Japan. 2004. *Shiretoko World Heritage List Nomination 2004*. Tokyo, Ministry of Environment.

Emori, S. 2007. *Ainu Minzoku no Rekishi*. Tokyo, Sofukan.

Indigenous Peoples Summit in Ainu Mosir Steering Committee. 2008. *Indigenous Peoples Summit in Ainu Mosir 2008*.

IUCN. 2005. World Heritage Nomination-IUCN Technical Evaluation: Shiretoko (Japan). *IUCN Evaluation of Nominations of Natural and Mixed Properties to the World Heritage List*, UNESCO Doc. WHC-05/29.COM/INF.8B.2.ADD, pp. 25-34.

IUCN and UNESCO. 2008. *Shiretoko Natural World Heritage Site, Japan: Report of the reactive monitoring mission, 18-22 February 2008*. Paris, UNESCO.

IWGIA. 2005. *The Indigenous World 2005*. Copenhagen, IWGIA.

IWGIA. 2009. *The Indigenous World 2009*. Copenhagen, IWGIA.

Kato, H. 2008. *World Heritage and Indigenous archaeology in Hokkaido Island* (Paper prepared for the 6th World Archaeological Congress, Dublin, Ireland). Sapporo, Center for Ainu and Indigenous Studies, Hokkaido University.

Kato, H. 2009. Whose Archaeology?: Decolonizing Archaeological Perspective in Hokkaido Island. *Journal of the Graduate School of Letters, Hokkaido University*, Vol. 4 (March 2009), pp. 47-55.

Kayano, S. and Akibe, H. 2009. [Ainu no Seisaku no arikata ni kansuru Yushikisha Kondankai] Hokokusho ni tsuite. *Maukopirka*, No.1/2, p. 30.

Ministry of Environment, Forestry Agency, Agency for Cultural Affairs and Hokkaido Prefectural Government. 2004. *Management Plan for the Shiretoko World Natural Heritage Nominated Site*.

Ministry of the Environment, Forestry Agency, Agency for Cultural Affairs and Hokkaido Government. 2009. *Management Plan for the Shiretoko World Natural Heritage Site*. December 2009.

Onishi, H. 2009. *Tobinitai Bunka karano Ainu Bunka-shi*. Tokyo, Doseisha.

Ono, Y. 1999a. Ainu homelands: natural history from ice age to modern times. W. Fitzhugh and C. Dubreuil (eds.), *Ainu: Spirit of a Northern People*, Washington, University of Washington Press, pp. 32-38.

Ono, Y. 1999b. Ainu- go Chimei no Heiki wo kangaeru. *Kotoba to Shakai*, No.1, pp. 78-86.

---

36 Reproduced in UNESCO 2013, p. 11.

Ono, Y. 2006. The participation of the Ainu people in the management of Shiretoko World Natural Heritage and the role of researchers. *Kankyo Shakaigaku Kenkyu*, Vol. 12, pp. 41-56 (Japanese with English abstract).

Ono, Y. 2010. Ainu Eco-tourism ni yoru Kenri Kaihuku. *Maukopirka*, No.1/2, pp. 23-24.

Ono, Y., Umezawa, M., Ponpe, I., Yuuki, K., Nishihara, Sh. and Fujisaki, T. 2007. *Recovering Ainu governance in the Shiretoko World Natural Heritage area in Japan through education and training for the Development of Indigenous Ecotourism* (Paper for the Proceedings of the 7th World Indigenous Peoples' Conference on Education, Hamilton, Aotearoa, 2005).

Sato, T. et al. 2007. Origins and genetic features of the Okhotsk people, revealed by ancient mitochondrial DNA analysis. *Journal of Human Genetics*, Vol. 52, pp. 618-627.

SIPETRU. 2006. *Shiretoko Indigenous Peoples' Eco-Tourism Research Union* (leaflet).

Udagawa, H. 2003. Chashi. S. Erori (ed.), *Ainu no Rekishi to Bunka*. Sendai-shi, Sodosha, pp. 94-103.

UNESCO. 2005. *Decisions of the 29th Session of the World Heritage Committee (Durban, 2005)*. Doc. WHC-05/29.COM/22.

UNESCO. 2008. *State of conservation of World Heritage properties inscribed on the World Heritage List: Shiretoko (Japan) (N 1193)*. Doc. WHC-08/32.COM/7B.Corr.

UNESCO. 2012. *State of conservation of World Heritage properties inscribed on the World Heritage List*. Doc. WHC-12/36.COM/7B.

UNESCO. 2013. *Looking Forward: Report on the 40th Anniversary of the World Heritage Convention – A Worldwide Celebration*. Paris, UNESCO World Heritage Centre.

UN Human Rights Council. 2008. *Report of the Working Group on the Universal Periodic Review – Japan*. Doc. A/HRC/8/44, 30 May 2008.

Walker, B. L. 2001. *The Conquest of Ainu Lands. Ecology and Culture in Japanese Expansion, 1590-1800*. Berkeley, University of California Press.

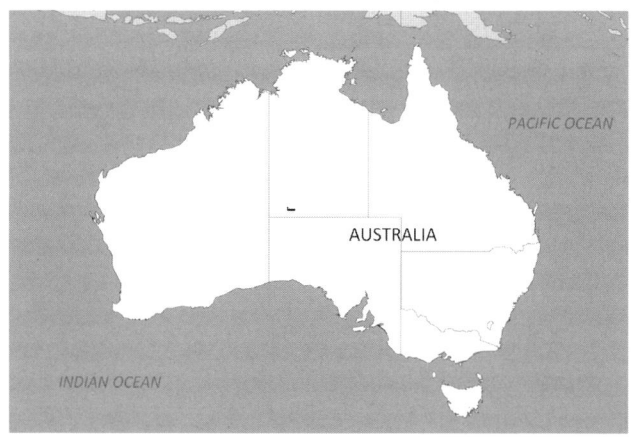

Pukulpa pitjama Ananguku ngurakutu – Welcome to Anangu land: World Heritage at Uluru-Kata Tjuta National Park

Michael Adams[1]

Introduction

Ananguku Tjukurpa kunpu pulka alatjitu ngaranyi. Inma pulka ngaranyi munu Tjukurpa pulka ngaranyi ka palula tjana-languru kulini munu uti nganana kunpu mulapa kanyinma. Miil-miilpa ngaranyi munu Ananguku Tjukurpa nyanga pulka mulapa. Tjukurpa panya tjamulu, kamilu, mamalu, ngunytjulu ngananaynya ungu, kurunpangka munu katangka kanyintjaku.

"There is strong and powerful Aboriginal Law in this Place. There are important songs and stories that we hear from our elders, and we must protect and support this important Law. There are sacred things here, and this sacred Law is very important. It was given to us by our grandfathers and grandmothers, our fathers and mothers, to hold onto in our heads and in our hearts."

Tony Tjamiwa[2]

---

1 Written in consultation with an Anangu Working Group of the Uluru-Kata Tjuta National Park Board of Management, the Central Land Council Joint Management Officer and Parks Australia staff.
2 All italicised quotes in section introductions are from: Director of National Parks 2010a.

Left: A view of the Kata Tjuta domes. Photo: Pierre Lesage (CC BY-NC-ND 3.0)

Located in the centre of Australia, the Uluru-Kata Tjuta National Park and World Heritage site is centred on the huge sandstone monolith Uluru, arguably the best known natural symbol of Australia and a major focus of the tourism industry. The Pitjantjatjara and Yankunytjatjara-speaking Indigenous people of this Western Desert region of the Northern Territory call themselves Anangu. The landscape of the Park includes ecological zones typical of the Central Australian arid ecosystems, as well as the monoliths of Uluru and Kata Tjuta themselves, which have been recognised in Anangu culture and practices for millennia.

In Anangu terms, this landscape was created at the beginning of time by ancestral beings who are the direct ancestors of contemporary Anangu. For Anangu, all relationships with each other and with their homeland are governed by *Tjukurpa*, the law. In Western terms, Anangu have lived in the region that now contains Uluru-Kata Tjuta National Park for thousands of years. The landscape bears the marks of their presence in an ecology determined by culturally-specific fire regimes and hundreds of archaeological and art sites. As indicated in the quote above, *Tjukurpa* determines the responsibilities that present-day Anangu have for continuing to care for the country created by their ancestors. These relationships and responsibilities intersect with modern conservation regimes imposed on the region since 1958.

Since 1985, Uluru-Kata Tjuta National Park has been jointly managed by the Anangu people and Parks Australia, an Australian government conservation bureaucracy.

World Heritage values

Nintiringkula kamila tjamula tjanalanguru. Wirurala nintiringu munula watarkurinytja wiya. Nintiringkula tjilpi munu pampa nguraritja tjutanguru, munula rawangku tjukurpa kututungka munu katangka kanyilku. Ngura nyangakula ninti – nganana ninti.

"We learnt from our grandmothers and grandfathers and their generation. We learnt well and we have not forgotten. We've learnt from the old people of this place, and we'll always keep the Tjukurpa in our hearts and minds. We know this place – we are ninti, knowledgeable."

Barbara Tjikatu

Tjurkulytju kulintjaku kuranyu nguru pinangku munu utira ngukunytja tjura titutjaraku witira kanyintjikitjaku kututungku kulira.

"Clear listening, which starts with the ears, then moves to the mind, and ultimately settles in the heart as knowledge."

Tony Tjamiwa

Uluṟu-Kata Tjuṯa National Park has been inscribed twice on the World Heritage List. It was first nominated in 1986 by the Australian government for inclusion on the World Heritage List as both a 'cultural' and a 'natural' site.[3] However, the nomination was processed by UNESCO as a natural site rather than a mixed site, and only considered under the natural heritage criteria.[4] In 1987, two years after the Handback (see below) and initiation of joint management arrangements, the Park was listed as a natural World Heritage site only, although IUCN's evaluation of the nomination recognised (within the terms of the then natural heritage criterion iii) that there was an "exceptional combination of natural and cultural elements" and that the "overlay of the aboriginal occupation adds a fascinating cultural aspect to the site".[5]

The natural values for which Uluṟu-Kata Tjuṯa National Park is inscribed on the World Heritage List include, among other values:

- the remarkable and unique natural geological and landform features formed by the huge monoliths of Uluṟu and Kata Tjuṯa set in a contrasting sand plain environment;
- the immense size and structural integrity of Uluṟu, which is emphasised by its sheer, steep sides rising abruptly from the surrounding plain;
- the exceptional natural beauty of the view fields in which the contrasts and the scenic grandeur of the monoliths create a landscape of outstanding beauty of symbolic importance to both Aṉangu and European cultures;
- tectonic, geochemical and geomorphic processes associated with the inselbergs of Uluṟu and Kata Tjuṯa, which result in the different composition of these two relatively close outcroppings, their differing extent of block tilting and types of erosion, the spalling of the arkose sediments of Uluṟu and massive 'off loading' of conglomerate at Kata Tjuṯa.[6]

The listing of Uluṟu-Kata Tjuṯa National Park as only a 'natural' World Heritage site, and the lack of international recognition of the ongoing relationship between Aṉangu and their country, was met with concern by Aṉangu Traditional Owners, the Park's Board of Management, as well as heritage professionals. This criticism contributed to the decision by the World Heritage Committee to develop the World Heritage Convention's Operational Guidelines and revise the cultural heritage criteria in order to accommodate the inclusion of 'cultural landscapes' on the World Heritage List.[7] In 1992, the Committee adopted revisions to the cultural heritage criteria along with new

---

3   Commonwealth of Australia 1986.
4   The reasons for this are somewhat obscure. While IUCN's evaluation of the nomination noted that "Cultural values of the area are being reviewed by ICOMOS" (IUCN 1987, p. 8), such a review did not occur. All working documents from the 11th session of the World Heritage Committee (1987), including the Bureau session, treat the park as a natural site. See http://whc.unesco.org/en/sessions/11COM/documents; and http://whc.unesco.org/en/sessions/11BUR/documents.
5   IUCN 1987, p. 12. Natural heritage criterion (iii) at the time inter alia referred to sites containing "superlative natural phenomena, formations or features, for instance... exceptional combinations of natural and cultural elements". The reference to "cultural elements" was removed from the text of natural criterion (iii) in December 1992 (see Layton and Titchen 1995, p. 176).
6   Director of National Parks 2010a, pp. 151-152.
7   Layton and Titchen 1995; McBryde 1990; Harrison 2013, p. 122.

interpretive paragraphs recognising three distinct categories of outstanding cultural landscape.[8] These changes to the cultural heritage criteria, through which the significance of Uluṟu-Kata Tjuṯa to the Aṉangu people could be better acknowledged, revived the debate in Australia concerning the international recognition of the cultural values of the Park.[9]

In 1994, Barbara Tjikatu and Tony Tjamiwa, the Aṉangu Traditional Owners quoted above, were part of a group who travelled to Phuket, Thailand, to present a renomination by the Australian government to the World Heritage Committee for Uluṟu-Kata Tjuṯa National Park to be listed as a 'cultural landscape' in addition to the natural heritage listing.[10] The proposal was accepted and the Park listed as a cultural landscape under cultural criteria (v) and (vi) in the same year.[11] Under cultural criterion (v) recognised values include:

- the continuing cultural landscape of the Aṉangu *Tjukurpa* that constitutes the landscape of Uluṟu-Kata Tjuṯa National Park and which:
    - is an outstanding example of a traditional human type of settlement and land-use, namely hunting and gathering, that dominated the entire Australian continent up to modern times;
    - shows the interactions between humans and their environment;
    - is in large part the outcome of millennia of management using traditional Aṉangu methods governed by the *Tjukurpa*;
    - is one of relatively few places in Australia where landscapes are actively managed by Aboriginal communities on a substantial scale using traditional practices and knowledge that include:
        - particular types of social organisation, ceremonies and rituals, which form an adaptation to the fragile and unpredictable ecosystems of the arid landscape;
        - detailed systems of ecological knowledge that closely parallel, yet differ from, the Western scientific classification;
        - management techniques to conserve biodiversity such as the use of fire and the creation and maintenance of water sources such as wells and rockholes.[12]

Under cultural criterion (vi) recognised values include:

- the continuing cultural landscape which is imbued with the values of creative powers of cultural history through the *Tjukurpa* and the phenomenon of sacred sites;
- the associated powerful religious, artistic and cultural qualities of this cultural landscape;

---

8   See Layton and Titchen 1995, p. 176.
9   Ibid. Layton and Titchen also note that due to the removal of the reference to 'exceptional combinations of natural and cultural elements' from natural criterion (iii), which also occurred in 1992 and which they strongly criticise, the "continuing relationship between Aṉangu and their land at Uluṟu [was] even less well recognized than at the time of Uluṟu's original inclusion on the World Heritage List".
10 Commonwealth of Australia 1994.
11 The park was inscribed under the categories of 'organically evolved landscape; continuing cultural landscape' and 'associative cultural landscape'. For details, see Calma and Liddle 2003.
12 Director of National Parks 2010a, p. 150.

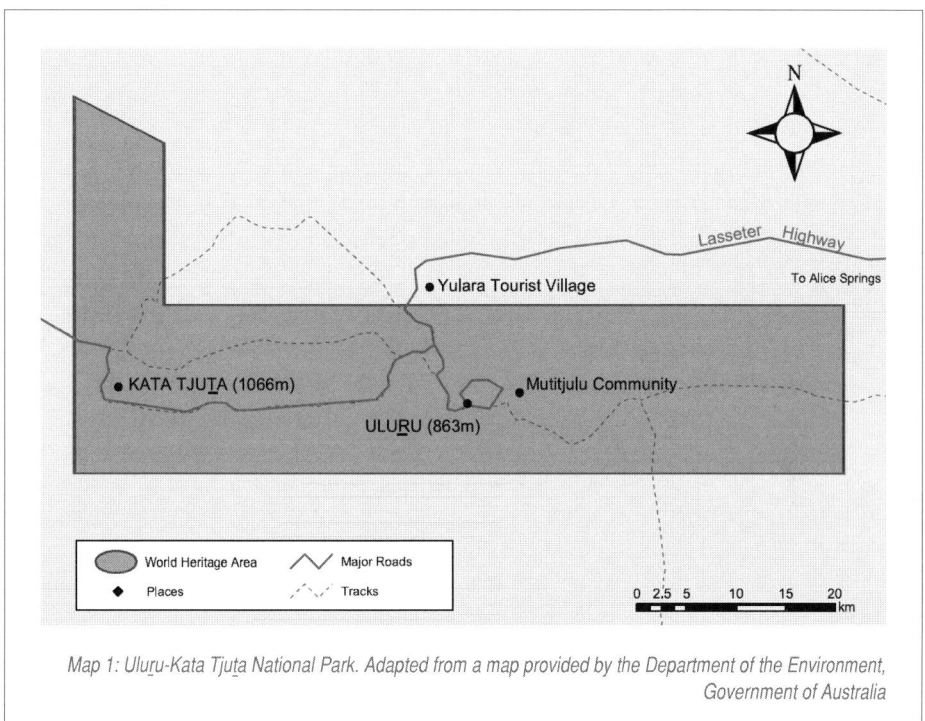

Map 1: Uluṟu-Kata Tjuṯa National Park. Adapted from a map provided by the Department of the Environment, Government of Australia

- the network of ancestral tracks established during the *Tjukurpa* in which Uluṟu and Kata Tjuṯa are meeting points.[13]

The World Heritage recognition of the Park's cultural values clearly acknowledges both ancient Aṉangu occupation and interaction with the landscapes and ecosystems, and the continuity of this into the present, including the necessity of maintaining Aṉangu practices and cultural structures. It also acknowledges the significance and primacy of *Tjukurpa*. This recognition establishes a very strong basis for requiring the managing authority to integrate Aṉangu practices and *Tjukurpa* into the management of the World Heritage site.

The listing of the natural values, in contrast, recognises Western scientific explanations for the geological origins of the site, as well as acknowledging that the monoliths are of "symbolic importance to both Aṉangu and European cultures".[14] This symbolic importance to non-Aṉangu people is central to the tourism interest in the site, and has clear implications for the activity known as 'the climb' (discussed later). The 1986 nomination stated that "Australian tourists perhaps feel more Australian after visiting the park",[15] an observation borne out by subsequent research discussed later.

---

13 Director of National Parks 2010a, p. 151.
14 Director of National Parks 2010a, p. 151.
15 Commonwealth of Australia 1986, p. 4.

World Heritage issues in Australia are managed through several policy levels. Day-to-day management is generally the responsibility of one of the state or federal government agencies delivering protected area management. In the case of Uluru-Kata Tjuta National Park, this is Parks Australia. Coordination at a national level is achieved through the Australian World Heritage Advisory Council (made up of representatives of all Australian World Heritage sites), which makes recommendations to the Environment Protection and Heritage Advisory Council, a council of elected government ministers. On Indigenous issues, the Australian World Heritage Advisory Council is advised by a group comprising Indigenous representatives from relevant World Heritage Areas, the Australian World Heritage Indigenous Network (AWHIN). While the Council fully supports AHWIN, in recent years no funding has been supplied by government to support the operations of AWHIN, limiting its ability to provide effective input. Periodic reporting to UNESCO is done by the Commonwealth Department of the Environment, as part of its responsibilities under the *Environment Protection and Biodiversity Conservation Act* 1999.

Historical background

Park-angka unngu munu park-angka urilta Tjukurpa palunyatu ngaranyi kutjupa wiya. Ngura miil-miilpa tjuta park –angka ngaranyi – uwankara kutju ngaranyi, Tjukurpangka.

"It is one Tjukurpa inside the park and outside the park, not different. There are many sacred places in the park that are part of the whole cultural landscape—one line. Everything is one Tjukurpa."

Tony Tjamiwa

Pitjantjatjara and Yankunytjatjara-speaking people first encountered non-Aboriginal people when the explorers Ernest Giles and William Gosse crossed the region in the 1870s, following the initial British arrival in Australia in 1788. Attempts from the 1920s to isolate the region's Aboriginal people from contact with European society included the creation of the Petermann Aboriginal Reserve, which included Uluru, and was intended as a 'refuge' so "the Aboriginal may here continue his normal existence until the time is ripe for his further development" [sic].[16] The creation of government reserves, as well as religious-based missions, was in part a response to the violence of the colonial frontier's pastoralists and police towards Aboriginal people. The development of pastoralism also had an impact on water sources and animals traditionally hunted for food, with significant environmental changes due to the introduction of cattle. These pressures contributed to forcing many local people away from their traditional country, sometimes onto nearby pastoral stations, sometimes to the fringes of towns like Alice Springs, and sometimes to the reserves and missions. Since the 1940s, the focus from government has been conservation and tourism, in addition to Aboriginal welfare issues. From 1936, tourists started to come to Uluru and, as interest increased, ad hoc accommodation facilities were built at the base of Uluru and Aboriginal people were actively discouraged from visiting or

---

16 Layton 1986, p. 73.

staying. In 1958, the area including Uluru and Kata Tjuta was excised from the Peterman Aboriginal Reserve, and gazetted as Ayers Rock-Mount Olga National Park, using the European names given to Uluru and Kata Tjuta by Giles and Gosse. Once excised from the Aboriginal Reserve, Aboriginal people had no right to enter the area. Instead, tourists "freely entered sites to which Aboriginal women and children had never been allowed access" in accordance with Aboriginal law.[17]

Following the massive alienation of land from Indigenous peoples in Australia which took place during the colonial period, Aboriginal leaders were active in campaigning to regain rights to land from at least the 1850s on. During the late 1960s and early 1970s, those struggles intersected with changing political conditions, and led eventually to the passing of the *Aboriginal Land Rights (Northern Territory) Act* by the federal (Commonwealth) government in 1976. The legislation was the first attempt by an Australian government to legally recognise the Aboriginal system of land ownership and put into law the concept of inalienable freehold title: successfully claimed lands are communally held, and cannot be sold or traded. The only land able to be claimed was unalienated Crown land or land already wholly owned by Aboriginal people. A successful land claim under this legislation required the Aboriginal landowners to prove their traditional relationship to the land under claim. The Northern Territory government of the time vigorously opposed the *Land Rights Act* and formally opposed every land claim, leading to very extensive delays. However, the Act eventually led to the return of very significant amounts of land to Aboriginal peoples across the Northern Territory.

In 1978, a claim was lodged under this Act for an area that included Uluru-Kata Tjuta National Park. While the Aboriginal Land Commissioner found that there were verifiable traditional owners for the Park, the Park itself could not be claimed due to the constraints of the legislation (as a national park, it was not 'unalienated Crown land'). Other land surrounding the Park was granted as Aboriginal land held by the Katiti and Petermann Land Trusts. Anangu successfully lobbied the government to amend the Act to allow the claim over the Park and, on 26th October 1985, at a large ceremonial 'Handback' event, title to Uluru-Kata Tjuta National Park was returned to the traditional owners. However, the Handback took place under imposed conditions, including the simultaneous leasing of the land back to the Commonwealth Government as a national park managed by the Commonwealth agency, Parks Australia, and with the continuation of tourist climbs on the rock. Soon after the Handback, the first Board of Management was declared, with Anangu man Yami Lester, a seasoned land rights campaigner, as the inaugural Chair.

Joint management

Ngaranyi manta park-angka urilta kulu-kulu manage-amilantjaku. Atunymankunytjaku ngura park-angka urilta ngarantja tjuta.

"The land both within and outside the park needs to be managed. There are many significant places to protect outside the park."

Barbara Tjikatu

---

17 Layton 1986, p. 76.

With the 1985 Handback, Uluṟu-Kata Tjuṯa National Park became the second national park in Australia to be jointly managed by Aboriginal owners and a government conservation agency.[18] While the Aṉangu Traditional Owners hold inalienable freehold title (via a Land Trust), the land is leased back to the Australian government to continue to be managed as a national park. The staff of the Park are employed as officers of the Department of the Environment, under Australian Public Service conditions. The Park is entirely surrounded by the extensive lands of the Petermann and Katiti Aboriginal Land Trusts, with the exception of the small areas of Yulara township and airport.

Variations of this joint management model have been adopted in all conservation jurisdictions in Australia as a way of resolving competing claims and interests from Indigenous peoples, on the one hand, and conservation interests on the other. Over the last 30 years, there has been a very significant increase in such arrangements. Coupled with the creation of Indigenous Protected Areas (which are conservation agreements over existing Aboriginal freehold, without a leaseback arrangement, discussed later), the formally recognised Aboriginal conservation estate comprises around 50 Aboriginal-owned reserves and more than 150 jointly-managed reserves, currently more than 30% of the protected area estate of Australia.[19]

The diversity of approaches to co-management in Australia is in part a response to the existence of the Commonwealth (federal) and six state governments, as well as two territory governments, all with responsibilities for creating and managing protected areas. While a number of generally applicable legislative models are emerging, in the past special legislation has been used to put specific co-management arrangements in place. For instance, the Northern Territory government enacted the *Cobourg Peninsula Land and Sanctuary Act* 1981 to create and provide for co-management of Gurig National Park (now Garig Gunak Barlu National Park). This example is distinctive because although negotiations were conducted under the cloud of an unresolved land rights claim, ownership was granted to a land trust to hold on behalf of the traditional owners without any requirement for a leaseback to the protected areas agency.[20]

At Uluṟu-Kata Tjuṯa National Park, a majority of the Board of Management must be Indigenous persons nominated by the Traditional Owners, so Aṉangu are nominated to eight of the twelve positions on the Board. They typically hold these positions for around five years. The Board is responsible for making decisions relating to Park management that are consistent with the Plan of Management. In conjunction with the Director of National Parks, it is also the Board's responsibility to prepare Park management plans; monitor Park management; and advise the Minister on all aspects of the future development of the Park. Board meetings are held several times each year, and are conducted simultaneously in English and Pitjantjatjara and/or Yankunytjatjara. Plans of Management have been prepared five times, with the current plan covering the period 2010-2020.

The Lease Agreement, first signed in 1985 and continuing for a period of 99 years, sets out the obligations of Parks Australia. These include a specified rent payment to the Traditional Owners as

---

18 While Stage 1 of Kakadu National Park was declared in 1979, effective joint management commenced around 1990 (see Lawrence 2000). Gurig National Park (now Garig Gunak Barlu National Park) was established as a jointly managed park under its own legislation in 1981. Both of these are also in the Northern Territory.

19 Smyth 2001; http://www.environment.gov.au/parks/nrs/about/ownership.html#table.

20 Smyth 2001; Foster 1997.

The traditional owners Mr. Peter Bulla, Mr. Peter Kanari, Mr. Nipper Winmarti and his wife, Barbara Tjirkadu, with Australian Government representatives Sir Ninian Stephen, Mr. Holding and Mr. Cohen (left to right) during the 1985 Handback ceremony. Photo: Department of Aboriginal Affairs, Government of Australia

well as 25% of receipts in respect of entry fees and other charges, fees or fines received arising out of the operation of the legislation. The Lease also commits Parks Australia to a suite of tasks, including the maintenance of Anangu tradition through protection of sacred sites and other areas of significance; maximising Anangu involvement in Park administration and management, and providing necessary training; maximising Anangu employment in the Park by accommodating Anangu needs and cultural obligations with flexible working conditions; and using Anangu traditional skills in Park management. The Lease includes provision for a five-yearly review.

It could reasonably be argued that Australia has been a global leader in the concept and implementation of joint management of protected areas with Indigenous peoples. The many versions of joint management operating in Australia in part reflect the diversity of Aboriginal peoples, local cultures and landscapes, as well as the diversity of policy situations, and while there are challenges and disagreements in probably every case, there are also generally continuing attempts to work towards better outcomes. This is sometimes achieved by Indigenous litigation and political advocacy challenging entrenched government structures, and sometimes by committed individuals, both Aboriginal and non-Aboriginal, working towards solutions. For non-Indigenous individuals working within the various parks agencies, it can be a frustrating paradox to be responsible for implementing

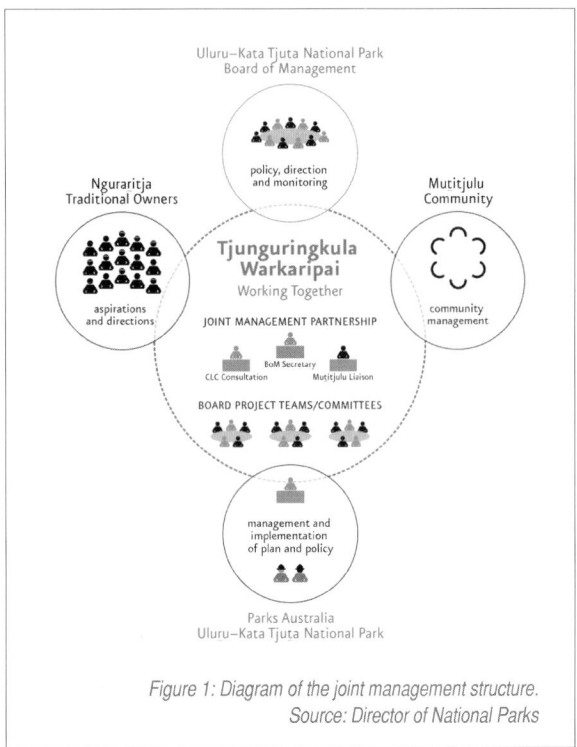

Figure 1: Diagram of the joint management structure.
Source: Director of National Parks

public service regulations which are clearly at odds with the practice of Indigenous culture. For Indigenous owners, it can be disheartening and frustrating to hear a repeated set of commitments to an ideal while watching the failure of those ideals in practice. While some of the difficulties are due to individuals, much is a product of ineffective and contradictory legislation and policy.

As well as jointly-managed reserves, there are also now more than 50 Indigenous Protected Areas declared across Australia, covering more than 36 million hectares, and with an ambitious program for expansion. Indigenous Protected Areas differ in general from joint-management arrangements in that they are voluntarily requested by Indigenous owners over land owned by them.[21] They are recognised as part of Australia's national system of protected areas, and Indigenous owners are able to access funds to assist with management and planning. Within Indigenous Protected Areas, Indigenous owners maintain autonomy over their land and cultural practices, choosing whether or not to collaborate with non-Indigenous institutions. Recent developments include multi-tenure Indigenous Protected Areas,[22] providing a further vehicle for collaboration between government protected areas and Indigenous landowners.

Anangu Traditional Owners have been working with the Central Land Council to develop an Indigenous Protected Area on the Katiti and Petermann Aboriginal freehold land that surrounds Uluru-

---

21 Bauman and Smyth 2007.
22 E.g., Mandingalbay Yidinji Indigenous Protected Area: http://www.environment.gov.au/indigenous/ipa/declared/mandingalbay.html.

Kata Tjuta National Park. This has the potential for very positive outcomes, with clear Anangu control and the opportunity to coordinate conservation and cultural activities across a very large area.

The role of *Tjukurpa* and Anangu traditional knowledge in the management of the Park

Manta atunymananyi, kuka tjuta atunymananyi munu mai tjuta atunymananyi. Kaltja atunymananyi munu Tjukurpa kulu-kulu. Park atunymananyi. Kumuniti atunymananyi.

"Looking after land. Looking after animals, and bush tucker. Looking after culture and Tjukurpa. Looking after park. Looking after community."

Judy Trigger

At Uluru-Kata Tjuta National Park, the joint management framework and philosophy are central to the successful protection of World Heritage values. Prioritising *Tjukurpa* and Anangu traditional knowledge is the only way that some World Heritage values can be maintained, for example:

"...landscapes are actively managed by Aboriginal communities on a substantial scale using traditional practices and knowledge that include: particular types of social organisation, ceremonies and rituals which form an adaptation to the fragile and unpredictable ecosystems of the arid landscape; detailed systems of ecological knowledge that closely parallel, et differ from, the Western scientific classification; [and] management techniques to conserve biodiversity such as the use of fire..."[23]

This section examines examples of management to investigate the effectiveness of these processes. It shows an embedded and ongoing tension in the differences between Western scientific and bureaucratic structures and assumptions, and Anangu society and beliefs, which is expressed in the detail of management operations and policy decisions.

Mala

Australia has the worst record of mammal extinctions in recent times of any country in the world, with arid and semi-arid ecosystems having the highest rates of extinctions and decline.[24] Three key factors have been identified as causing these extinctions: habitat clearing, introduction of non-native animals, and changes to fire regimes. Among the mammals that have become regionally extinct in the area is the rufous hare-wallaby (*Lagorchestes hirsutus*). This small animal is known

---

23 Director of National Parks 2010a, p. 150.
24 McKenzie et al. 2007.

to Anangu as *mala*, and *Mala Tjukurpa* (the Mala Law) is central to Anangu culture. One of the creation stories for Uluru tells of the journey of the *Mala* ancestors, who travelled to Uluru from the north. This *Mala Tjukurpa* connects Uluru to places to the north, south and south-east, embedding Anangu cultural meaning across the landscapes, including areas far outside the Park.

At a 1999 cross-cultural workshop, Anangu identified *mala* as one of the priority species for reintroduction to the Park's ecosystems. Since 2005, the Mala Project has successfully bred, from an initial group of 24, a population of more than 200 *mala* in a 170 hectare predator-proof enclosure. Anangu also support the reintroduction of a number of other locally extinct species, including *mitika*, the burrowing bettong (*Bettongia lesueur*), *wayuta*, the common brushtail possum, (*Trichosurus vulpecula*), *ninu*, the bilby (*Macrotis lagotis*) and *waru*, the black-footed rock wallaby (*Petrogale lateralis*).[25] Like all management at Uluru-Kata Tjuta, the Mala Project attempts to navigate a path through Western scientific perspectives and Anangu cultural tradition. How successful this is depends on the commitment and involvement of both Anangu and Park management.

All extant *mala* derive from 24 animals captured in the Tanami Desert in 1998. One of the challenges this creates is to avoid inbreeding within the captive populations, which Anangu recognise in terms of Anangu marriage laws. These laws specify protocols for choosing appropriate marriage partners within Anangu society. Uluru's population of around 200 *mala* is extremely important nationally, as only about 300 exist in total.

Mala ecology is like that of many central Australian species, with its close link to fire. *Mala* prefer a particular mosaic of burnt and unburnt patches of habitat.[26] Park management has determined a ratio of 50% recently burnt to 50% regenerating spinifex areas as the optimum habitat for the captive *mala*. To ensure that the *mala* in the enclosure are not accidentally burnt in these habitat fires, burning is conducted at night when mala are active and can react to the approaching fire. Although burning at night is not Anangu practice, Anangu have so far accepted this approach.

Similarly, while Anangu are very keen to use the presence of *mala* to teach their children and grandchildren *mala* law, constraints around Western animal ethics procedures, occupational health and safety, and other bureaucratic processes make it increasingly difficult for Anangu to do this. During interviews, the Working Group indicated that some young Anangu are assisting in the annual population surveys and the Aboriginal 'Junior Rangers' are occasionally taken to the *mala* enclosure, but they are concerned that most children remain *ngurpa*/unfamiliar with *mala* and their ways. Anangu continue to teach *mala inma*, the dances and song narratives associated with the *mala* at Uluru. Anangu aspire to see more opportunity to directly teach about *mala* with the support of the non- Anangu Rangers, while some of the older people who grew up with these animals are still alive. Support may include such things as providing vehicles and time to accompany groups to track by day, observe within the enclosure at night, produce and show films about *mala* as well as access to *ara irititja* [a multi-media cultural heritage database], and to the Park's database, including recordings of cultural stories.

---

25   *Waru* has been reintroduced to an enclosure on Anangu-controlled lands in South Australia, under Anangu control and in collaboration with Western scientists (see Muhic et al. 2012).
26   Lundie-Jenkins 1993.

Fire

Tjilpi tjutangku waru tilintjaku ngurkantara tjunkupai ngura uwankaraku atunymankupai wirura pukulpa ngaranytjaku munu wati yangupala tjuta nintilpai ka tjana nyakula mula-mularingkula nintiringkupai. Tjilpingku kutju tjukurpa palunya miil-miilpa tilintjaku tawara tjukarurungku atunymara wati yangupala tjukarurulpai ka kuwari nganana palumpa waru tilintjikitja mukuringanyi ukiri wiru pakantjaku mai tjuta kampurarpa tjuta kutjupa kutjupa winki.

"The senior men select the areas for burning, look after all the places and teach the young men. They watch and really learn about the proper way to do things well. The senior men are the ones that ensure sacred places are not burnt and look after the young men so burning is done correctly according to traditional law. Presently we want to use it, fire, to get good green regrowth in grasses and regenerate bush foods like the desert raisins and the various other plants."

Jim Nukiti

Traditional burning of the Uluru area ceased when Anangu were forced away from the area in the 1930s, resulting in large wildfires through the Park in 1950 and 1976, and *mala* became extinct in the wild soon after that. Anangu were able to begin burning appropriately again when joint management commenced. The use of fire is a clear recognition of the significance of Anangu knowledge and management in preserving World Heritage values. This reintroduction of Anangu burning has increased protection from wildfire[27] and there is significant scientific literature demonstrating the positive biodiversity outcomes of northern Australian Aboriginal fire regimes.[28]

Anangu fire knowledge is held by particular Elders and transmitted orally and experientially to younger people over time. The early years of joint management were a period of Anangu teaching non-Aboriginal people about the correct way to burn Country. The Western science of fire is comparatively recent, with most research in Australia being developed over the last few decades. There is now a general level of dialogue between Indigenous burning practices and Western approaches to fire management.[29]

While regular burning has been a feature of Park management since Handback, the level of Anangu control over and involvement in burning has fluctuated. With increasing bureaucratic regulation of activities in the Park, Anangu face a number of challenges to the level of their involvement. These regulations, for example, exclude the involvement of children. To continue the tradition of teaching grandchildren, Anangu are having to go off-park, into the Petermannn and Katiti Land Trust areas, to burn in ways which are culturally appropriate and under their control. There are also quite tight prescriptions, identified from a Western perspective, on when and how burning can be done, which are not necessarily reflective of Anangu cultural tradition or knowledge. Anangu decision-making processes do not always mesh well with increasingly regulative planning

---

27   See Reid et al 1993, Director of National Parks 2010a
28   See Woinarski et al. 2007; Gammage 2011; Bliege Bird et al. 2012.
29   Murphy and Bowman 2007; Vigilante et al. 2009.

processes, and limits on the resources available within the organisational structure restrict both the range and number of burns planned. If there is less flexibility or fewer resources available within the organisational structure with which to involve and incorporate casual employees in the adaptive planning and conduct of burning throughout the season, then there will be less Anangu involvement in the Park's fire management program. One of the Anangu strengths is the ability to make and adapt fire plans in response to changing environmental circumstances throughout the year.

The current Plan of Management says that "fire management is integral to *Tjukurpa* and there are expectations that skills and knowledge will be passed through generations of Anangu and practised in day-to-day management".[30] However, in interviews, Anangu described the fire management in the Park as being about essentially protective burns planned by Park staff in the winter, when they cautiously burn spinifex *Kutju-kutju tilira nyanganyi/*one by one watching *Kapitjara kutju/*with water tanks available. They try not to burn within mulga areas or near Mulgara (a small marsupial carnivore) or *tjakura* (Great Desert Skink). Anangu would like to see more direct teaching of the creative Anangu way within the Park, and to be asked/*altinyi* to plan and do these type of burns more often. It was said that elder Reggie Uluru and the young fellas go to Patji, look at the grasses drying and, when the time is right, they can burn within mulga areas to create grass for animals, and on the sand plains to produce bushfoods for Anangu. Anangu light fires '*putingka kutju'/*in the bush, outside the Park for these purposes, as well as to communicate: the quote at the beginning of this section reflects some of these Anangu aspirations.

The climb

Ananguku ngura nyangatja ka pukulpa pitjama. Nyakula munu nintiringkula Anangu kulintjikitjangku munu kulinma Ananguku ara kunpu munu pulka mulapa ngaranyi. Nganana malikitja tjutaku mukuringanyi nganampa ngura nintiringkunytjikitja munu Anangu kulintjikitja. Kuwari malikitja tjuta tjintu tjarpantjala nyakula kutju munu puli tatilpai. Puli nyangatja miil-miilpa alatjitu. Uti nyura tatintja wiya! Tatintjala ara mulapa wiya.

"This is Anangu land and we welcome you. Look around and learn so that you can know something about Anangu and understand that Anangu culture is strong and really important. We want our visitors to learn about our place and listen to us Anangu. Now a lot of visitors are only looking at sunset and climbing Uluru. That rock is really important and sacred. You shouldn't climb it! Climbing is not a proper tradition for this place."

Tony Tjamiwa

Many tourists visit Uluru specifically to climb the monolith. The route used by tourists in climbing the rock is the traditional route taken by the ancestral *Mala* men on their arrival at Uluru. It is consequently of great significance to Anangu, and Anangu have long been opposed to the climb. *Tjukurpa* requires Anangu to look after visitors to their country – when visitors are killed or injured

---

30 Director of National Parks 2010a, p. 78.

on the climb, Anangu participate in the grieving. So far, more than 30 people have died and many more have been injured on the climb.

"That's a really important sacred thing that you are climbing... You shouldn't climb. It's not the real thing about this place. The real thing is listening to everything. And maybe that makes you a bit sad. But anyway that's what we have to say. We are obliged by Tjukurpa to say. And all the tourists will brighten up and say, 'Oh I see. This is the right way. This is the thing that's right. This is the proper way: no climbing."

Kunmanara, Nguraritja[31]

The inappropriateness of the climb has been formally acknowledged since at least 1991 (3rd Plan of Management) and discussed in consecutive management plans.[32] The climb has nevertheless continued to be available to tourists through the strong lobbying activities of the tourist industry. Research has started to identify what particular segment of visitors choose to climb, and to investigate how the creation of alternatives may reduce the interest of visitors in this. The centrality of Uluru as an Australian icon has also been extensively analysed by researchers, including its contested 'ownership'.[33] The 5th Plan of Management (2010-2020) is significant in that it, for the first time, identifies the permanent closure of the climb as an objective and sets out conditions to enable this. These conditions include minimising the impact on the tourism industry and meeting the following criteria:

- the Board, in consultation with the tourism industry, is satisfied that adequate new visitor experiences have been successfully established, or
- the proportion of visitors climbing falls below 20 per cent, or
- the cultural and natural experiences on offer are the critical factors when visitors make their decision to visit the Park.[34]

While the existence of the climb has, for several decades, clearly been contrary to Anangu wishes, and Anangu have expressed disappointment that the climb continues, the explicit objective of permanent closure is a very positive step. However, the wording of the criteria to be met for closure continues to create uncertainty. The move towards closure of the climb will, however, also support the aspirations of some Anangu to develop new tourism experiences.[35]

Kata Tjuta

Kata Tjuta (Pitjantjatjara for 'many heads') is the other distinctive landscape feature in the Park, about 30 kilometres west of Uluru and also a focus of tourist attention. The multiple monoliths

---

31 Quoted in Director of National Parks 2010a, p. 90.
32 Director of National Parks 1991, p. 61; 2000, p. 119; and 2010a, p. 92.
33 For example: Hill 1994; James 2007; Hueneke and Baker 2009; Robinson et al 2003; Waitt et al. 2007.
34 Director of National Parks 2010a, p. 92.
35 Director of National Parks 2010b, p. 8.

of Kata Tjuta are, however, treated quite differently to Uluru. Kata Tjuta is sacred under Anangu men's law: it is at the intersection of two of the most sacred ancestral routes of the Western Desert. Details of the special stories of this place cannot be revealed to non-Anangu, and access to some places is restricted. Climbing of any of the 36 domes is expressly forbidden. Because Uluru was already being accessed by tourists, in order to reassert control Anangu needed to identify which sites they wanted closed for cultural reasons, and why. As no information is divulged about Kata Tjuta, Anangu were able to simply indicate which areas were available for access.

The tourism industry

Ngura pulka Uluru-nya tjamulu munu kamilu iriti atunytju kanyintja tjukurpa pulkatjara. Iniwai putukaramilantja wiya. Anangu munu piranpa tjungu ngarama. Nyuntu nyanganyi puli wiru mulapa palu tjukurpa nyuntu putu nyanganyi munu kulini.

"Uluru is a very significant place with significant law that has been looked after and protected by our grandfathers and grandmothers for a long time. Do not photograph it without regard for the proper way to do this. This applies to both Anangu and non-Anangu alike. You are seeing a really beautiful rock but you might not be seeing and considering its cultural significance."

Rene Kulitja

It has been argued that World Heritage designation "acts as an international top brand" for tourism.[36] At Uluru-Kata Tjuta National Park, the recent *Tourism Directions: Stage 1* strategy refers to "the Uluru brand" as being nationally and internationally significant.[37] An economic analysis completed in 2008 found that Uluru-Kata Tjuta National Park was "the largest contributor of economic activity to the Northern Territory economy, followed by Kakadu National Park".[38] This demonstrates the dominance of nature tourism, culture tourism and World Heritage in the economy of the Northern Territory. Tourism is Australia's largest service export industry, with significant expenditure in many regional areas.

Over the last decade, visitor numbers at Uluru-Kata Tjuta National Park have averaged around 350,000-400,000 people annually, half of whom are overseas visitors. While the monolith itself is the focus of much tourist interest there is also significant interest, particularly from international visitors, in engaging with Anangu culture. However, the tourism industry in the region is dominated by non-Indigenous enterprises, with Aboriginal tourism enterprises forming a tiny fraction of these.

The Working Group said it was good that tourists came: on the whole tourists respected *Tjukurpa* and enjoyed learning about it. The group said Anangu wanted visitors to learn about their land and their law from Anangu. This was the proper way. Visitors are seen as wanting to understand the relationship Anangu have with their country and how they look after it. They also felt a strong

---

36 Buckley 2004, p. 70.
37 Director of National Parks 2010b, p. 3.
38 Gillespie 2008, p. 50.

sense of responsibility to *Kanyintjikitja*/look after visitors properly and said that this was done best by following *Tjukurpa* as well as government law. The challenge for joint management is to find a balance between enabling tourism while maintaining cultural traditions. For example, Anangu mentioned that, over time, it had become more difficult to access some sites at Uluru and teach the younger people in the proper way. The number of tourists and their proximity to sacred sites made Anangu anxious about conducting activities there. Tourism is a key revenue source for both the Park and the Traditional Owners, and maintaining a balance between tourism numbers and income, and appropriate privacy and space for normal life as well as cultural activities, is a key challenge.

Aboriginal/Anangu employment

Anangu yangupala tjuta warkaku mukuringanyi panya tjukurpa wiru nintiringkunytjaku uwankara. Munu warka wiru putitja, Tjukurpa, paluru tjananya uwankara. Tjutangku yangupala nintiringkula kungka kulu-kulu park wiru palyantjaku. Nyaa Putitja tjuta nintintjaku putjikata tjuta tjina wanara nyakunytjaku, paluru tjanampa ka palulangnuru tjana nintiringanyi computerku – ngapartji ngapartji nintiringkunytjaku.

"Many young Anangu want to work and to learn about the proper way to do everything; good land management, provide information, all the different aspects of park work. The young men and as well as young women are learning to maintain the park well. In land management, they are showing them, for example, how to track feral cats and then they are learning to use computers–to learn in turn."

Andrew Taylor

In Western nations such as Australia, employment is central to social institutions and identity. However, this is not necessarily the case for Aboriginal people in remote communities, who often have many cultural commitments and aspirations, as well as a desire to engage with both the cash economy and opportunities to 'work on Country'.[39] Negotiating the relationship between a Western work culture and Indigenous cultural frameworks is one of the many challenges at Uluru-Kata Tjuta National Park, and there is an ongoing spectrum of approaches to this. There are essentially three sources of employment for Anangu at Uluru-Kata Tjuta: the Park itself, the tourism industry (including Indigenous-owned enterprises), and Indigenous organisations and enterprises.

Discussions with current Uluru-Kata Tjuta staff and those from earlier periods of the Park's history indicate particular changes in the relationships between Anangu and Park management over 28 years. After the Handback, there was a very clear sense of the development of a 'new way' of managing the Park, with strong acknowledgement of Anangu expertise and practical strategies to incorporate this knowledge into the Park operations. This was seen as an effective response to an entirely new kind of relationship, based on highly exploratory approaches. Many non-Aboriginal

---

39 McRae-Williams and Gerritsen 2010.

staff from the period of the Handback consider themselves very privileged to have been a part of that process. Since then, however, there continues to be a high turnover of non-Aboriginal staff, including in senior management positions. In many respects, there are limited opportunities for non-Aboriginal and Anangu staff to develop effective and collaborative long-term relationships.

Since the late 1990s, changes in the legislation governing Australian Public Service activities, including employment and procurement, have increasingly proscribed local, adaptive responses. Employment must be 'merit-based' and there are requirements regarding proficiency in the English language. As many Anangu are fluent in several Indigenous languages before English, and older Anangu are often not literate in English, this creates clear barriers to Anangu employment in some positions. The occupational health and safety requirements discussed earlier are standard government regulations but clearly have the potential to affect the practice and teaching of culture in a number of ways. A recent IUCN analysis of Booderee National Park, another Commonwealth administered joint-managed park in south-east Australia also indicated the impact of these regulatory and competitive environments.[40]

In interviews, Anangu said that a lot of *Ananguku work wiyaringu*/work for Anangu had finished and non-Anangu *Tjana piranpa ma paturingu*/were a long way ahead in terms of employment. They feel that what work there is for Anangu in the Park is sporadic, casual work. A higher value is put on writing and computer literacy than on Anangu understanding of the land. It was often said there was *mani wiya*/no money to be able to do more work or employ more staff to do land and cultural heritage management work. This made it hard to play a strong role in the management of the Park. The group said a higher priority could be placed on cultural heritage management work in order to help keep *Tjukurpa* strong. This would lead to more resources being provided to get the work of protecting and looking after/*atunmara kanyintjaku* the Park done by Anangu and to be able to teach younger Anangu about this more effectively. In 2012, the Park Manager advised that five positions in the Park were held by Anangu: the Cultural Heritage Officer, the Interpretation Officer (job-shared by two people) and two Operations Rangers. There are also Indigenous staff from other areas of Australia employed in the Park. In addition to permanent positions, there is a flexible casual work program that regularly employs Anangu in a variety of areas. Typically, the permanent positions are largely protected from budget fluctuations whereas the casual positions, which often facilitate 'working on Country', are subject to cuts; the casual budget has, however, been retained at the same amount for a number of years now while permanent positions have reduced.

Increasing centralisation of administrative control and regulation within state structures reduces flexibility and innovation at Uluru itself, a situation recognised by current management. The Park and World Heritage Area are now beginning to transition to a new generation of Anangu Traditional Owners, with only a few of the Anangu involved in the World Heritage nomination still alive. This new generation has indicated growing dissatisfaction with government structures and ways of operating, prompting recent and ongoing discussions around 'rethinking management' that might lead to new approaches.[41]

---

40 Farrier and Adams 2011.
41 Director of Parks Australia 201

Since 1984, 'Ayers Rock Resort', located outside and adjacent to the national park, has been the sole provider of accommodation for visitors to the Park. Aboriginal representation among the resort's nearly 600 employees was almost non-existent until recently, with only two Aboriginal employees in 2010. However, in 2011, the resort and its company, Voyages, was purchased by the Indigenous Land Corporation,[42] with an ambitious plan to create an Indigenous tourism training academy integrated with the resort.[43] By late 2013, more than 200 Aboriginal people, including 60 trainees, had been employed and it is planned to create 350 hospitality jobs for Indigenous workers at Uluru and elsewhere in Australia. This is clearly a major development and, while many of the proposed positions will be for Aboriginal people from other parts of Australia, there will likely be significant benefits for Anangu both in direct employment and training and in increasing the acceptance of Indigenous tourism workers in the region.

There is also an active process to develop a Memorandum of Understanding between the resort and the Park aimed at guiding more formal collaboration. This formalised approach to collaboration, combined with the purchase of the resort by the Indigenous Land Corporation and the potential development of activities on the Katiti and Petermann Land Trust areas, is a very positive indication of significantly increased Anangu involvement and benefit from the tourism industry. In interviews, Anangu said they hoped to be more meaningfully involved in the tourist industry and to benefit more from tourism activity in the Park in the future.

Mutitjulu

Nganana wirura councilangka warkaripai Mutitjulula parka kulu-kulu atunymara kanyilpai munula tjukaruru kanyinma ngura nganampa.

"We do good work on the Council, both at Mutitjulu and also protecting and looking after the park. We must look after our place properly."

Judy Trigger

Anangu, recognised as the Traditional Owners of Uluru-Kata Tjuta National Park, live within the Park in Mutitjulu community as well as a number of other communities in the region, including Kaltuktjara (Docker River), Pukatju (Ernabella), Utju (Areyonga), Imanpa and Amata. Increasingly, individuals are living in Alice Springs (the regional centre) in order to access health services that are relatively limited in Mutitjulu and other small communities. Families continue to move between places as the need arises. They have a corporation called the Yangkuntjatjarra Kutu Aboriginal

---

42 The Indigenous Land Corporation is a statutory authority established in 1995 with the purpose of assisting Indigenous people with land acquisition and land management to achieve economic, environmental, social and cultural benefits. See http://www.ilc.gov.au/.

43 See http://www.voyages.com.au/corporate/. Voyages was purchased by the Indigenous Land Corporation on behalf of Wana Ungkunytja, which represents the business interests of the nearby communities of Mutijulu, Imanpa and Docker River.

Corporation the role of which is to distribute Park rent and entry gate income to the Traditional Owners.

One of the historic idiosyncrasies of the establishment of Uluru-Kata Tjuta National Park is that the Park management inherited the responsibility for providing essential services (power, water, sewage disposal) to Mutitjulu. This costs around 1 million Australian dollars, from an annual operating budget of about 13 million, and is clearly outside normal national park management activities. Mutitjulu has a troubled social history, reflecting that of many small and remote Indigenous communities in Australia. It is nevertheless a key place for contemporary Anangu.

Two decades of World Heritage

Nguraritja tjuta tjana mantu, tjana ma pamparinganyi tjilpiringanyi ka tjana mukuringanyi tjitji malatja tjutangku runamilentjaku ngulaku munu tjanampa tjitji ku.

"Naturally the traditional owners, the senior women and men are growing older, and they want their children to be able to run the park in the future, and their children in turn."

Nyinku Jingo

The World Heritage listing for Uluru-Kata Tjuta National Park's cultural values is quite specific: "The continuing cultural landscape of the Anangu Tjukurpa that constitutes the landscape of Uluru-Kata Tjuta National Park and which... is in large part the outcome of millennia of management using traditional Anangu methods governed by the *Tjukurpa*;...[and] is one of relatively few places in Australia where landscapes are actively managed by Aboriginal communities on a substantial scale using traditional practices and knowledge..." [44]

After 28 years of joint management, it is clear that there are many successes, but also ongoing challenges. While there are fluctuating numbers of Anangu staff within the Park, there has never been an Anangu Park Manager and Anangu continue to be very poorly represented in the tourism industry. The monolith of Uluru itself is an internationally recognised symbol of Australia and Aboriginality but its recognition as a site of sacred significance has been compromised by the continuing presence of the climb. Western science is successfully bringing back *mala* but with limited Anangu control and involvement. While Anangu have had a majority of members on the Board of Management since Handback, this does not necessarily mean that Anangu are in control. Powerful external influences such as the tourism industry, and powerful internal influences such as Australian government politics and processes, exert significant pressure. Anangu have often accommodated these pressures rather than create disharmony and conflict by challenging how these affect cultural practices.

---

44 Director of National Parks 2010a, p. 150.

In the interviews, Anangu in the Working Group felt the listing was just as relevant now because they continue to live on and look after their land today. The government understood that Uluru was a significant place/*tjukurpa pulkatjara* that Anangu continued to look after. The group reaffirmed that they *Tjukurpa Kanyini*/still hold to the Anangu law and that this works, together with the government laws, to run the Park. When there is enough money, things are equal and running properly according to both laws. They said a key to finding the balance between the two sets of law in joint management was to *Wanganara kulintjaku*/listen responsively to each other/*ngapartji-ngapartji*. From the Anangu perspective, it seemed that when resources were reduced/*mani wiya* it was the non-Aboriginal/*Piranpa* priorities and law that took precedence because the government knew those laws well and saw them as essential. They underlined the fact that Anangu were equally responsible and accountable under *Tjukurpa*. When things do not happen according to *Tjukurpa*, there is trouble for Anangu. When people work closely together, things work well and joint management is strong. The challenge is to maintain the balance and strength in joint management. When this does not happen, things become *Kali kali kuwari*/not straight or *lipula*/level.

Anangu want to work in the Park to *atunymankunytjikitjangu*/look after the *Tjukurpa*/the cultural landscape and the law associated with the Park, in a way that allows their children to *rawangku atunmara kanyintjaku*/continue to protect and look after it properly, according to the law, when they are gone. In the Working Group, there is a real sense of urgency about this, as 'only two are left' of the generation of senior men present in the lead up to Handback. This makes teaching a crucial priority. Senior members of the group spoke of their aging, *punu piltiringu*/a metaphor for the amount of time that had passed since they began talking about this and how important it is that people listen properly to their concerns about the future. They want their children to be able to play a strong role in the management of the Park, as they do. They would like to see more opportunities for younger Anangu to learn about park management and work in the Park to help keep *Tjukurpa* strong.

The values underpinning Western and Anangu societies differ in many fundamental aspects. These differences are evident in on-the-ground management activities. Institutional change in Australian society and government, reflected in a greater concern for the regulation of risk management and increasing economic and bureaucratic efficiency, can interact negatively with Anangu cultural tradition. While at least some of these impacts are well outside the control of park management agencies and Anangu, this incommensurability is reflected in joint management tensions at World Heritage sites and other protected areas across Australia and, while often acknowledged by management, they continue to be unresolved.

World Heritage designation at Uluru-Kata Tjuta National Park is a point of pride for Anangu people: their cultural traditions are acknowledged as being internationally significant, and *Anangu Tjukurpa* is explicitly recognised as the appropriate way to care for this Country. A central challenge for the future is whether Western science and management can facilitate, or even allow, a process that supports the meaningful practice of Anangu traditions of caring for country and the passing on of this knowledge and skill to subsequent generations.

Acknowledgements

The information in this chapter was derived from four sources. An Anangu Working Group of the Uluru-Kata Tjuta National Park Board of Management comprising eight Anangu Traditional Owners held discussions with the Joint Management Officer, responding to a set of questions about World Heritage. These people were: Anangu men (Jim Nukuti, Johnny Tjingo, Malya Teamay), Anangu women (Barbara Tjikatu, Yvonne Yiparti, Judy Trigger, Millie Okai, Rene Kulitja) and Joint Management Officer Patrick Hookey. Patrick collated and translated the responses. The author interviewed several non-Indigenous Uluru-Kata Tjuta National Park staff, including the current Manager, Acting Manager, Training Officer and others, as well as previous Uluru-Kata Tjuta National Park staff. Two key Uluru-Kata Tjuta National Park documents were consulted for additional statements by Anangu Traditional Owners: the 2011 *Visitor Guide* and the *Plan of Management 2010-2020*. Both published and unpublished research and management documents were sourced.

References

Adams, M. 2011. Arctic to outback: Indigenous rights, conservation and tourism. G. Minnerup and P. Solberg (eds.), *First World First Nations*. East Sussex, Sussex Academic Press.

Aplin, G. 2007. World Heritage cultural landscapes. *International Journal of Heritage Studies*, Vol. 13, No. 6, pp. 427-446.

Bauman, T. and Smyth, D. 2007. *Indigenous Partnerships in Protected Area Management in Australia: Three Case Studies*. Canberra, Australian Institute of Aboriginal and Torres Strait Islander Studies.

Bliege Bird, R. et al. 2012. Aboriginal hunting buffers climate-driven fire-size variability in Australia's spinifex grasslands. *Proceedings of the National Academy of Sciences of the United States of America* no. 109 (26), pp. 10287-10292.

Buckley, R. 2004. The effects of World Heritage listing on tourism to Australian national parks. *Journal of Sustainable Tourism*, Vol. 12, No. 1, pp. 70-84.

Calma, G. and Liddle, L. 2003. Uluru-Kata Tjuta National Park: Sustainable Management and Development. *World Heritage Papers*, Vol. 7 ("Cultural Landscapes: the Challenges of Conservation"), pp. 104-119.

Commonwealth of Australia. 1986. *Nomination of Uluru (Ayers Rock-Mount Olga) National Park for Inclusion on the World Heritage List*. Canberra, Australian National Parks and Wildlife Service.

Commonwealth of Australia. 1986. *Renomination of Uluru-Kata Tjuta National Park for Inscription on the World Heritage List*. Canberra, Department of the Environment, Sport and Territories.

Director of National Parks. 2012. *Kakadu and Uluru-Kata Tjuta World Heritage Areas*. Paper presented to the Symposium "Keeping the Outstanding Exceptional: the Future of Australia's World Heritage", Cairns, 9-10 August 2012.

Director of National Parks. 1991. *Third Uluru (Ayers Rock-Mount Olga) National Park Management Plan*. Canberra, Australian National Parks and Wildlife Service.

Director of National Parks. 2000. *Fourth Uluru-Kata Tjuta National Park Management Plan 2010-2020*. Canberra, Parks Australia.

Director of National Parks. 2010a. *Fifth Uluru-Kata Tjuta National Park Management Plan 2010-2020*. Canberra, Parks Australia.

Director of National Parks. 2010b. *Uluru-Kata Tjuta National Park Tourism Directions: Stage 1*. Canberra, Department of Sustainability, Environment, Water, Population and Communities.

Director of National Parks. 2011. *Palya! Welcome to Anangu land: Uluru-Kata Tjuta National Park Visitor Guide*. Canberra, Department of Sustainability, Environment, Water, Population and Communities.

Director of National Parks. nd. *Uluṟu-Kata Tjuṯa National Park Note: Fire Management.* Canberra, Parks Australia.
Farrier, D. and Adams, M. 2011. Indigenous–Government Co-Management of Protected Areas: Booderee National Park and the National Framework in Australia. B. Lausche (ed.), *Guidelines for Protected Area Legislation.* Gland, IUCN.
Gammage, B. 2011. *The Biggest Estate on Earth: How Aborigines Made Australia.* Sydney, Allen and Unwin.
Harrison, R. 2013. *Heritage: Critical Approaches.* New York, Routledge.
Hill, B. 1994. *The Rock: Travelling to Uluru.* St. Leonards, Allen and Unwin.
Hueneke, H. and Baker, R. 2009. Tourist behavior, local values, and interpretation at Uluṟu: 'the sacred deed at Australia's mighty heart'. *GeoJournal,* Vol. 74, pp. 477-490.
IUCN. 1987. World Heritage Nomination – IUCN Summary and Technical Evaluation: 447 Uluru National Park (Australia). Available at http://whc.unesco.org/en/list/447/documents/.
James, S. 2007. Constructing the climb: visitor decision-making at Uluṟu. *Geographical Research,* Vol. 45, No. 4, pp. 398-407.
Lawrence, D. 2000. *Kakadu: The Making of a National Park.* Melbourne, Melbourne University Press.
Layton, R. 1986. *Uluru: An Aboriginal History of Ayers Rock.* Canberra, Australian Institute of Aboriginal Studies.
Layton, R. and Titchen, S. 1995. Uluru: An Outstanding Australian Aboriginal Cultural Landscape. B. von Droste, H. Plachter and M. Rössler (eds.), *Cultural Landscapes of Universal Value.* Jena, G. Fischer, pp. 174-181.
Lundie-Jenkins, G. 1993. Ecology of the Rufous Hare-wallaby, Largorchestes hirsutus in the Tanami Desert, Northern Territory. *Wildlife Research,* Vol. 20, pp. 457-476.
McBryde, I. 1990. 'Those truly outstanding examples...': Kakadu in the Context of Australia's World Heritage Properties – A Response. J. and S. Domicelj (eds.), *A Sense of Place? A Conversation in Three Cultures.* Canberra, Australian Govt. Pub. Service, pp. 15-19.
McKenzie, N.L. et al. 2007. Analysis of factors implicated in the recent decline of Australia's mammal fauna. *Journal of Biogeography,* Vol. 34, pp. 597-611.
McRae-Williams, E. and Gerritsen, R. 2010. Mutual incomprehension: the cross cultural domain of work in a remote Australian Aboriginal community. *The International Indigenous Policy Journal,* Vol. 1 (2).
Muhic, J., Abbott, E. and Ward, M. 2012. The *warru (Petrogale lateralis* MacDonnell Ranges Race) reintroduction project on the Aṉangu Pitjantjatjara Yankunytjatjara Lands, South Australia. *Ecological Management and Restoration,* Vol. 13, No. 1, pp. 89-92.
Murphy, B and Bowman, D. 2007. The interdependence of fire, grass, kangaroos and Australian Aborigines: a case study from central Arnhem Land, northern Australia. *Journal of Biogeography,* Vol. 34, pp. 237-250.
Reid, J.R.W., Kerle, J.A., Morton, S.R. 1993. *Uluṟu Fauna,* Canberra, Australian National Parks and Wildlife Service.
Robinson, C., Baker, R. and Liddle, L. 2003. Journeys through an Australia sacred landscape. *Museum International,* Vol. 55, pp. 74-77.
Smyth, D. 2001. Joint management of national parks. R. Baker, J. Davies and E. Young (eds.), *Working on Country: Contemporary Indigenous Management of Australia's Land and Coastal Regions.* South Melbourne, Oxford University Press.
Vigilante, T., Murphy, B. and Bowman, D. 2009. Aboriginal fire use in Australian tropical savannas: Ecological effects and management lessons. M. Cochrane (ed.), *Tropical Fire Ecology: Climate Change, Land Use, and Ecosystem Dynamics.* Chichester, Springer-Praxis.
Waitt, G., Figueroa, R., and McGee, L. 2007. Fissures in the rock: rethinking pride and shame in the moral terrains of Uluṟu. *Transactions of the Institute of British Geographers,* Vol. 32, Issue 2, pp. 248-263.
Woinarski, J. et al. 2007. *The Nature of Northern Australia.* Canberra, ANU EPress.

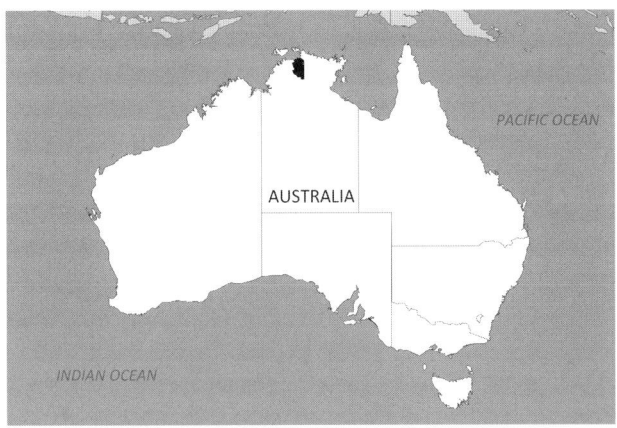

No Straight Thing: Experiences of the Mirarr Traditional Owners of Kakadu National Park with the World Heritage Convention

Justin O'Brien[1]

Aus so krummen Holze, als woraus der Mensch gemacht ist, kann nichts ganz Gerades gezimmert werden.[2]

Introduction

Since the mid-1990s, the Mirarr people of Kakadu National Park and Western Arnhem Land in Australia have actively fought against the expansion of uranium mining on their traditional

---

1 The author acknowledges, along with Alon Confino, that, 'memory is a malleable understanding of the past that is different from history because its construction is not bounded by a set of limiting disciplinary rules' (Confino 2006, p. 75). He has, nevertheless sought in his research and writing to arrive at an objective view of these events, particularly by drawing on sources other than his own or the Corporation's, but acknowledges that a degree of political bias in interpreting key events and the motivations of particular actors is unavoidable. The author thanks his friend and colleague Dr James Warden whose advice and assistance with this paper was both valuable and appreciated.
2 The quote, "Out of the crooked timber of humanity no straight thing can ever be made", derives from Immanuel Kant's "Idea for a Universal History with a Cosmopolitan Purpose".

Left: Mirarr senior traditional owner Yvonne Margarula on country with her nephew Marty Liddy. Photo: Dominic O'Brien

lands at Jabiluka.³ From 1997 to 1999, a major focus of their campaign was in the deliberations of the UNESCO World Heritage Committee (the Committee), during which the community sought Kakadu's inscription on the List of World Heritage in Danger on the grounds of environmental and cultural threats posed by the mine proposal. This paper explores the political experience of the Mirarr with the World Heritage Convention, which, they argued, "must be seen as protecting one of the few remaining islands of traditional culture from the relentless forces of development".[4] In opposition to the State Party, Australia (itself a Committee member at the time) but strongly supported by NGOs and the Committee's expert advisory bodies, IUCN and ICOMOS, the Mirarr brought a forceful and media-focussed campaign against Jabiluka into UNESCO, placing hitherto unprecedented public scrutiny on the standing of Indigenous peoples and the effectiveness of the World Heritage Convention to protect World Heritage.

No other single Indigenous group has lobbied the World Heritage Committee so intensely, networked so effectively or so challenged the Convention and its administration. The Mirarr led an unprecedented public examination of the Committee's decision-making and the role of its expert advisory bodies with "an intricate set of alliances with environmental NGOs, anti-nuclear activists, and influential organizations".[5] The Committee was unaccustomed to and unprepared for such scrutiny and initially scrambled for an effective response, deciding in 1998 to send a special mission to Kakadu to directly investigate the matter. In contrast was the Australian government's speedy reaction to what it regarded as a threat to its state sovereignty, marked by cynical and clandestine lobbying of other State Parties and Committee members. Ultimately, the consensus among Committee members was not to directly intervene in Australia's management of Kakadu, revealing the true extent to which the Committee was willing to protect heritage when a State Party was intent on destroying it. Critical questions raised by the Kakadu debate remain unanswered, as was highlighted in a recent summary of the debate.[6] This continuing uncertainty and the all-important role of the expert advisory bodies and staff of the World Heritage Centre, who often played a critical mediating role during the debate, may serve as an important guide to other Indigenous groups seeking redress in the Convention for similar challenges to their traditional lands, cultural rights and political integrity.

Kakadu National Park

The area that would ultimately become Kakadu National Park had been earmarked for such a future as early as 1965, when the Northern Territory Reserves Board sought approval for a

---

3 The Ranger uranium mine and Jabiluka deposit are today under the ownership of Rio Tinto subsidiary Energy Resources of Australia (ERA). Rio acquired a controlling interest in ERA in August 2000.
4 GAC 1998, p. 15. Focussing as it does on the processes undertaken by the Mirarr, relevant policies of the World Heritage Committee itself are not addressed in any detail in this piece.
5 Altman 2012, p. 71.
6 Cameron and Rössler 2013. See also Logan 2013.

Rock art at Burrunggui (Nourlangie Rock), Kakadu National Park.
Photo: Hansjoerg Morandell (CC BY-NC-SA 2.0)

declaration from the Northern Territory Administrator.[7] The park was ultimately declared under the federal *National Parks and Wildlife Conservation Act 1975* in three stages between 1979 and 1991.[8] World Heritage inscriptions of the declared areas duly followed in 1981, 1987 and 1992. From the beginning, Kakadu was inscribed on the World Heritage List for both its natural and cultural values.

Kakadu covers approximately 19,800 square kilometres of the so-called 'Top End' of Australia's Northern Territory. It is some 150 kilometres north to south and 120 east to west, and Australia's largest national park. Darwin, the capital of the Northern Territory, is some 250 kilometres to the west and, to the east, lies the vast Arnhem Land plateau.[9] Climatically, Balanda (European Australians) think of three tropical seasons, namely, the monsoonal 'wet', the 'dry' and the (humid)

---

7   Lawrence 2000, p. 45.
8   Director of National Parks 2007, p. 6.
9   In 1931 the massive Arnhem Land region, close to 100,000 km^2 in size, was gazetted an Aboriginal reserve. The reserve lies immediately east of Kakadu, from which it is divided in the north by the East Alligator River.

'build-up'.[10] Local Indigenous people, Bininj,[11] see six distinct seasons marked by sometimes quite subtle natural signs.[12] Kakadu's varied landscape comprises tidal flats and mangrove forests, floodplains and billabongs, savannah woodland, monsoon forests, hills and ridges and, to the east, the dominant sandstone escarpment. The speciation and biodiversity is rich with 77 mammals (one quarter of the Australian total), 132 reptiles, 27 frogs, 346 fish, over 2,000 plants, 10,000 described insects and 271 birds (a third of the national total).[13]

Kakadu is, however, first and foremost a living cultural landscape in the truest sense of that phrase (although it is not inscribed by the World Heritage Committee as such). It is host to a rich, ancient and abiding Indigenous cultural heritage, evidenced by hundreds of thousands of prehistoric rock art paintings, dreaming tracks and sites of cultural significance, whose age-old stories have been handed down from tens of thousands of years ago to the present day. Inextricably linked to their land via complex totemic and kinship obligations, Bininj landowners have two leading responsibilities – looking after country (*gunred*) and looking after people (*guhpleddi*). These obligations are intrinsically linked and encompass a complex set of relationships and cultural obligations between landowners, their country and other Bininj.[14]

The Indigenous occupancy of the region stretches back some 60,000 years, as evidenced by one of Australia's oldest human occupation sites, traditionally known to archaeologists as Malakunanja II and to the Kakadu Indigenous community as Madjedbebe.[15] The site, located at the base of a sandstone outlier and replete with traditional rock art covering a wide range of styles and time periods, is within the Jabiluka mineral lease, itself entirely surrounded by the national park.

Kakadu has always, it seems, courted controversy. Even its very inscription as a World Heritage site was caught up in debate when, outside the World Heritage Committee's fifth session at the Sydney Opera House in 1981, "a massive demonstration by Australia's Aboriginal people" decried the listing as "the traditional landowners of Kakadu ... felt that they had not been properly respected".[16] Aboriginal observers were allowed into the meeting and during the Kakadu debate lifted placards, some of which read "Where are the Aboriginal delegates?", "We can't proclaim uranium mines World Heritage areas" and "Our heritage, no uranium mining in Kakadu".[17] Later stages of the Park's declaration were similarly controversial, with the opposition of the Northern Territory Government especially strident. In the late 1990s, attention on proposed uranium mining

---

10 The term 'Balanda' derives from 'Hollander' and stems from the Dutch colonisation of the Indonesian archipelago, from people (the Macassans) who traded with Bininj for centuries prior to the European conquest of the Australian landmass.
11 The term 'Bininj' is a local term used to refer to Aboriginal people generally. Bininj (denoting 1. person, human being; 2. Aboriginal person; and 3. man) is pronounced 'bi-niny' or 'binning', or in the International Phonetic Alphabet 'bini ʔ'. See Bininj Gunwok Project 2013, entry for 'Bininj'.
12 Within each of the six seasons there are more subtly defined sub-seasons, namely, the beginning, middle and end of each season.
13 Unfortunately, feral animals and invasive plants have also arrived in considerable numbers and present significant ongoing difficulties for park management.
14 Masterson 2010, p. 17.
15 Roberts, Jones and Smith 1990, pp. 153-156.
16 von Droste 2009, p. 8.
17 von Droste 2009, p. 11.

meant Kakadu again openly challenged the integrity of the World Heritage Committee, perhaps like no other site has done, as the then Director of the World Heritage Centre has described:

> "In the history of UNESCO's World Heritage Convention no other mining case has been so complex, controversial and of worldwide public attention than the intended uranium mining on Aboriginal land in the Jabiluka enclave of Kakadu National Park in the Northern Territory of Australia..." [18]

Uranium mining

Mining was unilaterally imposed upon the Aboriginal community of what would become Kakadu National Park via measures undertaken by successive federal governments over a decade, eventuating in a mining agreement for the Ranger uranium mine signed by the Northern Land Council (NLC) in 1978.[19] Ranger was, by any reckoning, a done deal well ahead of any reference to the traditional landowners, with export contracts to at least Japan issued in 1972, federal ownership of 50% of the mine secured in 1974, repeated supply commitments to overseas purchasers throughout the 1970s and the denial in 1976 of the otherwise customary Aboriginal capacity to veto the development.[20] The move to proclaim the surrounding Kakadu National Park was concurrent with the push for mining at Ranger and, notably, the government purposefully stalled the former until the latter was secured.[21] Following the execution of the mining agreement and national park lease on 3 November 1978, authorities and miners were free to turn their attention to the next prospect, the proposed Jabiluka uranium mine, a deposit some 20km north of the Ranger deposit discovered in June 1971 and which dwarfed Ranger in both volume and grade of uranium.[22] In the wake of the Ranger agreement, a sober and ultimately accurate assessment of Kakadu was made by Friends of the Earth, Australia:

---

18 von Droste 2009, p. 2.
19 The NLC is a statutory authority of the federal government established by the *Aboriginal Land Rights (Northern Territory) Act* 1976 to represent Indigenous landowners in transactions regarding their land, including land claims and mining and other land use negotiations. The historical aspect of the debate over uranium mining in the Kakadu region has been extensively dealt with elsewhere, including O'Brien 2003; Trebeck 2009; and Scambary 2013. For the present purposes it should be recognised that as a territory of the federal government with low political exposure (the entire current population of the Northern Territory today is a mere 230,000), it was feasible for the government to implement Aboriginal land rights there. Due to decisions aimed at administrative expediency, land rights sadly became the vehicle through which the government pursued and executed its mining agenda in Kakadu.
20 The capacity under the *Aboriginal Land Rights (Northern Territory) Act 1976* (Commonwealth statute) to veto proposed development on Aboriginal land was and remains enjoyed by all other Aboriginal groups in the Northern Territory except the Mirarr people in the case of the Ranger mine proposal, their veto powers over this proposal being denied via express provision within the Act.
21 Anthony 1978. The Cabinet submission, which was adopted, bluntly rejected Indigenous aspirations for the national park agreement to be concluded separately to that for the Ranger mine, applying pressure for the speedy conclusion of negotiations over mining.
22 Grey 1994, p. 37. The Jabiluka deposit also contains a considerable amount of gold.

"Since the setting up of the Ranger Inquiry which heard their land claim, the Aboriginal people have received only part of the land they claim, a National park whose benefit to them is largely a matter for the discretion of a Commonwealth Government official, and the prospect of a number of uranium mines in what should then be called a controlled disaster zone rather than a National park." [23]

Negotiations over Jabiluka were initially frustrated and yet ultimately facilitated by a second land claim in the region, with talks commencing in January 1981 at a meeting where Bininj were told that the Northern Land Council would discuss *only* the land claim with Jabiluka's prospective mining company, Pancontinental Mining. On the very evening of the meeting, notwithstanding this express commitment, the NLC sent a telegram to Pancontinental triggering negotiations for the proposed Jabiluka uranium mine. In June 1982, amid extreme duress culminating in an intense 10-day 'bargaining session', the Northern Land Council (purporting to represent local Indigenous interests) entered into a mining agreement with Pancontinental Mining for the development of Jabiluka.[24]

The Mirarr oppose Jabiluka on environmental and cultural grounds and reject the 1982 agreement, and have consistently claimed that Jabiluka's development "will destroy the unique source of Mirarr language, culture, sacred sites and living tradition".[25] The foremost cultural concern is the protection of the Boyweg-Almudj Sacred Site Complex within the mineral lease.[26] Jabiluka's development was thwarted, however, the following month when the national conference of the Australian Labor Party arrived at a new national policy on uranium mining. After a bitter and divisive debate, the final position, among other things, precluded the development of new uranium mines, in effect permitting existing mines (including the Ranger mine, although it was not named) to continue but preventing the development of the Jabiluka deposit.[27] The fundamentals of what became known as the 'three mine uranium policy' remained intact throughout the 13 years of the Labor Party's tenure in government from 1983 to 1996, ensuring Jabiluka was not developed during this time. In March 1996, a Liberal-National conservative coalition led by John Howard formed a new federal government and promptly announced the scrapping of the restrictive uranium policy. With this, the battle to prevent mining at Jabiluka recommenced for the Mirarr and their civil society campaign colleagues across Australia and the globe.

Within four months of the election of the Howard government, the new Environment Minister, Senator Robert Hill, was proudly taking credit for advancing the Jabiluka mine proposal.[28] Toward

---

23 Lawrence 2000, p. 105.
24 In the early 1990s Pancontinental sold its mining lease to Jabiluka to Energy Resources of Australia, a company which already owned and ran the nearby Ranger mine.
25 GAC 1999, p. 8.
26 GAC 1998, pp. 12-13. The Mirarr contest the validity of the 1982 Jabiluka agreement on the grounds that it was negotiated under extreme duress and involved unconscionable conduct on the part of the federal government and the Northern Land Council. See GAC 1997b, p. 19 ff.
27 Panter 1991, p. 7. The federal executive's control over the issuing of export permits was the mechanism by which it controlled the number of operational uranium mines.
28 Hill 1996.

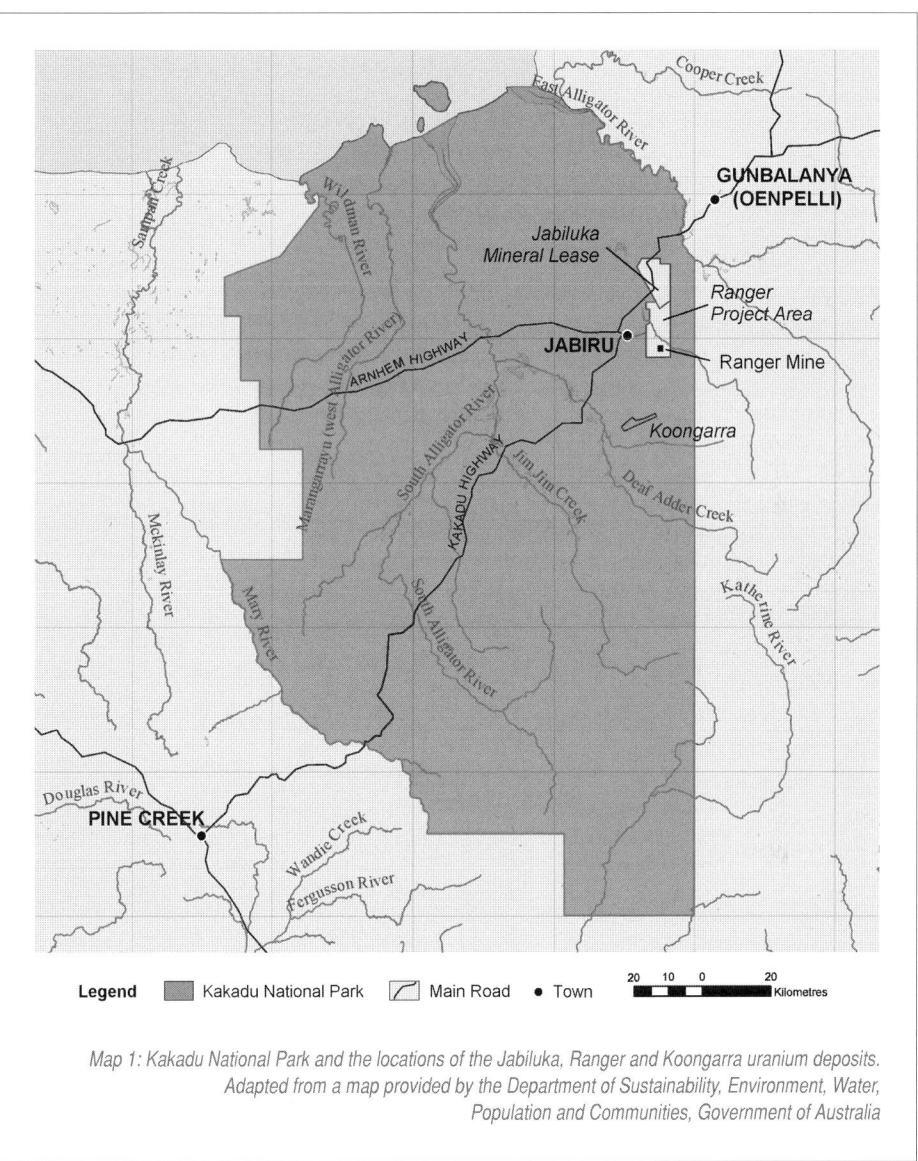

Map 1: Kakadu National Park and the locations of the Jabiluka, Ranger and Koongarra uranium deposits. Adapted from a map provided by the Department of Sustainability, Environment, Water, Population and Communities, Government of Australia

the end of 1997 the Resources Minister, Senator Warwick Parer, announced he had "cleared the way for the Jabiluka uranium project to proceed".[29] The renewed threat to Mirarr country roughly coincided with the establishment of a new local representative body for the Mirarr. In July 1995, frustrated at the recurrent waste (on, inter alia, bad debt and exorbitant management costs) of

---

29 Parer 1997.

mining royalty income from the Ranger mine by the then royalty receiving entity, the Gagudju Association, the Northern Land Council incorporated a new Aboriginal corporation to represent Mirarr interests. Unlike Gagudju, the membership of which comprised over a dozen clans, the Gundjeihmi Aboriginal Corporation or GAC (so named after the traditional language of the Mirarr) was comprised solely of and directly accountable to Mirarr traditional owners.[30] The new corporation quickly found itself pitted in a struggle to protect Jabiluka's sacred lands from uranium mining. By the end of the year, Mirarr senior traditional owner, Yvonne Margarula, had appointed a new executive officer to the corporation, the outspoken and compelling Jacqui Katona.[31] With a forthright and gifted radicalism, coupled with a great capacity to network across traditional cultural and organisational divides, Katona perfectly complemented the understated but discerning traditional Aboriginal mien of Yvonne Margarula. Supported by GAC staff and NGO campaign colleagues, they led an unprecedentedly high-profile campaign to protect Jabiluka from mining, travelling Australia and the world and securing numerous prestigious awards and widespread civil society support. With a national speaking tour, protest actions in the Northern Territory and Australia's major cities, significant media coverage and the strong support of civil society, they literally made 'Jabiluka' a household name in Australia.

Throughout 1997 and 1998, other domestic and international campaign initiatives against Jabiluka were carried out and secured significant media coverage and political concessions for the Mirarr in their bid to prevent the development. In 1997 a coordinated national campaign instigated by Mirarr via the Gundjeihmi Corporation and major national environmental NGOs, primarily the Australian Conservation Foundation, The Wilderness Society and Friends of the Earth, was bearing significant fruit.[32] Minor political parties, the Australian Democrats and the Australian Greens, had joined the public opposition to the Jabiluka proposal in its early days and were to remain strong supporters throughout the years ahead.[33] A well-coordinated blockade of the Jabiluka mine site from March to October 1998 drew over 5,000 protesters from across Australia and the world to join the Mirarr in their struggle. Over 530 protesters were arrested during the eight-month peaceful blockade of the mining site.[34] With its mix of Indigenous rights, environmental and anti-nuclear activism, the Jabiluka blockade quickly became a lightning rod for the progressive left in Australian

---

30 The spelling of the corporation's name was formally altered in 2002 from 'Gundjehmi' to 'Gundjeihmi', in line with the standard orthography developed for the Gundjeihmi language. The spelling of the clan name Mirarr was similarly altered (from Mirrar to Mirarr) to reflect standard orthography. The contemporary spellings are used throughout.

31 An Indigenous woman of Kakadu heritage (Djok clan) with family connections to the Mirarr, Katona had previously worked on the two seminal Indigenous political milestones in the latter part of the twentieth century, the Royal Commission into Aboriginal Deaths in Custody (1987-91) and the 'Bringing Them Home' National Inquiry into the Separation of Aboriginal and Torres Strait Islander Children from Their Families (1995-97).

32 Mirarr received support from a wide variety of NGOs and professional representative bodies internationally, encompassing the medical profession, unions, universities, anti-nuclear groups, Indigenous rights organisations, peace and a large number of environmental groups.

33 The 1999 Senate inquiry into Jabiluka was a prime example of this political support.

34 The blockade was operated by a central committee of NGO representatives and protestors acting on the instructions of the Gundjeihmi Aboriginal Corporation. The campaign brought the issue of uranium mining in Kakadu into the headlines and swayed public opinion such that, by 1998, a Newspoll survey found that 67% of Australians opposed the mining proposal.

Yvonne Margarula and Jacqui Katona lead a Jabiluka blockade march through Kakadu National Park in 1998.
Photo: Clive Hyde

politics, particularly given the vexation among the left at the obstinacy of the Howard government on environmental issues and over recognising the rights of Indigenous Australians. Indeed, the government's approach to the Jabiluka controversy was considered, by at least one prominent commentator, to be "an unmistakable test of the new Government's commitment to reconciliation with Aboriginal people".[35] For many, the government failed that test.

From its inception, the Mirarr campaign focussed on cultural, social and environmental protection in the context of the Kakadu's World Heritage status. Publicly restating her opposition to Jabiluka in June 1997, Yvonne Margarula requested that an assessment of the social impact of mining be completed "independently of government, land council and mining interests", underlining the Mirarr lack of faith in the jurisdictional arrangements determined by government.[36] The campaign differentiated itself from previous major Australian environmental campaigns with its extensive and vociferous emphasis on the cultural rights of Kakadu's original owners. These rights, it was argued, had been ignored, misrepresented or impaired by what Mirarr regarded as discriminatory decisions by government and corporate agencies whose authority was deemed illegitimate. A GAC media statement from 1997 entitled 'This is bullshit', in which Ms Margarula questioned the authority of

---

35 Hamilton 1996, p. 17.
36 GAC 1996.

the Alligator Rivers Region Advisory Committee, is a prime example of this emphasis.[37] She told committee members:

> "You treat me like an animal. That is my Country, I have dreaming for that Country. What do you have, what do you know?" [38]

The GAC were responding to the marginalisation of Indigenous people from decision-making over their traditional lands, a distinct feature of the imposition of uranium mining development on Kakadu. This negative dynamic of depriving meaningful Indigenous agency and relegating Mirarr to the role of observer-stakeholder was already recognised and had been considered by the 1984 'Consolidated Report on the Social Impact of Uranium Mining on the Aborigines of the Northern Territory', prepared by the Australian Institute of Aboriginal Studies after an intensive and expert six-year study.[39]

The Mirarr campaign had a particularly strong international focus, drawing significant overseas civil society support and the active interest of several key intergovernmental agencies. In January 1998, the European Parliament passed a resolution calling on the Australian government to "respect the status of the Kakadu National Park as a World Heritage site", "respect the land rights of the Aboriginal Peoples" and "not to proceed with the [Jabiluka] project".[40] By April 1998, protest organisers in Melbourne, Sydney and Brisbane had mustered over 7,000 people to march against the Jabiluka proposal.[41] In July, Yvonne Margarula was awarded the inaugural Nuclear Free Future Award by an international panel of prominent authors, physicians and civil rights activists, in recognition of her tireless grassroots campaigning.[42]

It was against this backdrop that the campaign of the Mirarr people and their supporters in (primarily) environmental NGOs turned to the World Heritage Committee, calling on the Committee to inscribe Kakadu on the List of World Heritage in Danger on the basis of threats posed by Jabiluka's proposed development. Given the renowned standing of the World Heritage Convention and the Australian government's pride in Australia's long-standing role in the Convention, no other single initiative during the Jabiluka campaign stirred as much government attention and activity as the World Heritage debate. Senator Robert Hill told an Estimates hearing of the Senate in February 1999 that around one million dollars had been dedicated to preventing an 'In Danger' listing for Kakadu.[43]

---

37 The Alligator Rivers Region Advisory Committee is a statutory forum of government, industry and NGOs addressing the environmental issues associated with uranium mining in Kakadu and is established under Part III of the *Environment Protection (Alligator Rivers Region) Act* 1978 (Commonwealth statute).
38 GAC 1997a.
39 Australian Institute of Aboriginal Studies. Uranium Impact Project Steering Committee 1985, p. 130. Comprised of eminent Australian and international experts, the committee's work was insightful. Sadly, its recommendations were largely unheeded.
40 European Parliament 1998.
41 Ceresa 1998.
42 Ryan 1998.
43 Australian Parliament 1999a. The Howard government ultimately downplayed the extent of the financial cost of defending its position on Jabiluka, later scaling down this figure substantially.

UNESCO

The first obstacle confronting the Mirarr in their bid to bring the Jabiluka dispute before the UNESCO World Heritage Committee was that they simply had no standing. The Committee is comprised solely of State Parties. At the time it also included Australia which was clearly acting against the interests of the Indigenous landowners in the Kakadu debate. From early 1997, using a Sydney-based legal representative, Bruce Donald, the GAC commenced a process of, firstly, having their independent submissions considered by the Committee and, secondly, securing observer status at Committee meetings via correspondence directly to the World Heritage Centre and to the Convention's expert advisory bodies, particularly IUCN and ICOMOS. The first reply from the World Heritage Centre, in February 1997, underscored the fact that State Parties were responsible for reporting on the state of conservation of World Heritage properties and therefore urged that future Mirarr communications be sent "directly to the relevant authorities within the Government of Australia", although it was recommended that copies be forwarded to the Centre, IUCN and ICOMOS.[44] Earlier considerations by IUCN of the dangers to Kakadu's status posed by Jabiluka's development proved to be invaluable to the Mirarr campaign. IUCN's initial interest had been prompted by the October 1996 session of the World Conservation Congress, during which a formal recommendation was passed noting that "mining in Jabiluka ... has the potential to damage the natural and cultural values of Kakadu" and urging "the Government of Australia to prevent the development of Jabiluka ... should it be shown that such mining would threaten the Park's World Heritage values".[45]

Meanwhile, in Australia in August 1997, the federal government's environmental impact assessment had concluded that "there does not appear to be any environmental issue which would prevent the preferred Jabiluka proposal from proceeding", and Senator Hill issued 77 "strict and stringent" conditions on the mine's development. The conditions were largely technical and related to mining operations, although a number directly addressed matters of cultural concern, including the need for a cultural heritage management plan to be completed.[46]

In the December 1997 World Heritage Bureau and Committee meetings in Naples, the IUCN formally conveyed its concerns regarding Jabiluka and tabled the World Conservation Congress resolution. IUCN reported that 'Australian groups' were proposing that the site be considered for the List of World Heritage in Danger.[47] Not considered at the meetings, however, was the submission on the matter from the GAC, the direct representative body of the Mirarr. In a subsequent explanation to Bruce Donald, the then World Heritage Coordinator of ICOMOS, Dr Henry Cleere, made it plain that Australian government intervention had thwarted consideration of the GAC submission. Dr Cleere explained that the Secretary General of ICOMOS, Jean-Louis Luxen, had met with the Australian delegation, the World Heritage Centre and representatives of IUCN and that Luxen had

---

44   Ishwaran 1997.
45   Recommendation No. 1.104, "Conservation of Kakadu World Heritage Site, Australia". See IUCN 1997.
46   Hill 1997.
47   UNESCO 1997, p. 13.

informed him "that it had been decided not to bring this before the Bureau, since it was the subject of a public enquiry and no decisions had yet been made." [48]

The manner in which the World Heritage Committee declined to consider GAC's submission in 1997 was not lost on the Corporation and its campaign colleagues. The following year, in the lead up to the twenty-second session of the Bureau in June 1998, the GAC and various NGOs mounted a persistent and ultimately successful lobbying effort to secure accredited observer status. Notable among the supporters of the GAC was former Australian Prime Minister, Gough Whitlam, who wrote directly to the World Heritage Centre requesting that the GAC delegation be granted status.[49] Alongside this, environmental NGOs across Australia were individually writing to the Director of the Centre requesting the same.[50] Finally, the delegation, comprising Yvonne Margarula, Jacqui Katona and GAC staffer Christine Christophersen and Alec Marr of The Wilderness Society, was granted observer status, notwithstanding concerns raised at the meeting from the Japanese delegation that a precedent should not be set by allowing such access.[51]

Observer status came at a crucial time in the debate, enabling Mirarr representatives and their supporters to maximise the support of the advisory bodies in direct lobbying of State Parties at the June 1998 Bureau meeting. The Bureau was informed of correspondence from "the lawyer for the Mirarr Aboriginal people" (Bruce Donald) which referred to the Bureau and Committee responses on the state of conservation of Kakadu at the twenty-first sessions as "entirely unsatisfactory" and of a submission from four eminent Australian scientists highly critical of the quality and process of Jabiluka's environmental impact assessment and calling for a new assessment.[52] The support of the distinguished Australian pre-historian, John Mulvaney, with his long association with both the international heritage community and the convention itself, as well as the respect he commanded at the World Heritage Committee, was also important at this time.[53] The secretariat and chairperson also referred to the "many letters they had received which expressed concern about the state of conservation of Kakadu National Park and called for the inclusion of Kakadu on the List of World Heritage in Danger".[54] IUCN presented a statement to the Bureau in which it reminded State Parties of the 1996 World Conservation Congress resolution, referred to a June 1998 draft policy on "mining and associated activities in relation to protected areas" adopted by

---

48 Cleere 1997.
49 Whitlam 1998.
50 The Wilderness Society 1998.
51 UNESCO 1998a, p. 2. The Chairman replied to these Japanese concerns "by stressing that the decision of the Bureau would not constitute a binding precedent as the Rules of Procedure clearly allow the World Heritage Committee and its Bureau to decide on the participation at each meeting".
52 Ibid., p. 14. The four scientists, Professor R. J. Wasson, Professor I. White, Dr B. Mackey (all of the Australian National University) and Mr M. Fleming (consulting eco-hydrologist), originally wrote to the World Heritage Committee on 22 June 1998. Their correspondence was ultimately incorporated into a formal submission to the 1998 UNESCO Mission to Kakadu (Wasson et al. 1998).
53 Mulvaney would later provide additional important assistance to the Mirarr in their efforts, releasing previously unpublished rainfall data (critical to the accurate prediction and impact of severe weather events) from the community of Gunbalanya (or Oenpelli) in the vicinity of the Jabiluka site in his submission to the 1998 Mission to Kakadu. See also Mulvaney 1998.
54 UNESCO 1998a, p. 14.

IUCN's World Commission on Protected Areas, and stated that IUCN was "not in possession of information on the 77 conditions set by the Australian Government" on the Jabiluka's development and was therefore "unable to make any assessment of their adequacy or otherwise".[55] Critically, the IUCN statement concluded: "if invited to do so and provided with the necessary information and resources to support a multi-disciplinary team, IUCN would participate in a mission to assess the situation and report to the Bureau/Committee".[56]

In response, the Australian delegation argued, inter alia, that the mine would not be within or impact upon the World Heritage area, that the Mirarr traditional owners' opposition to the mine's development was a minority position among local Aboriginal people, that the 77 conditions set on Jabiluka's development would protect the park's World Heritage values in terms of environmental impact, and that the social impacts of the development were catered for in the (government-controlled) Kakadu Region Social Impact Study (KRSIS) then underway.[57] Seeking to downplay the significance of the Boyweg-Almudj sacred site complex, the Australians were also somewhat mischievous in their interpretation of the findings of an Aboriginal Areas Protection Authority (AAPA) investigation into whether the site complex should be formally registered as a sacred site, stating that the Authority had "examined the site and has concluded that there is insufficient evidence about this site to register it as a sacred site".[58] Firstly, it was plainly misleading to focus on a single site when the Mirarr contention and the AAPA investigation related to a complex of sites focussed on the Boyweg (knob-tailed gecko) and Almudj (rainbow serpent) sacred sites and the dreaming track that connects them. Secondly, insufficiency of evidence was not the reason AAPA had declined to register the site, as was made plain in correspondence at the time, and later confirmed in evidence to the 1999 Australian Senate inquiry into Jabiluka. During that evidence, AAPA's Chief Executive Officer, David Ritchie, told the Committee that the Authority had declined to register the site because of disagreement over the extent of the site and features and stories associated with it, adding that the Authority's finding "in no way was a statement that the area was not a sacred site".[59]

Despite the ardour of the Australian delegation, the Bureau, citing the "importance, complexity and sensitivity of the issue", proposed that a mission to Kakadu be undertaken, headed by the Chairperson of the World Heritage Committee, Francesco Francioni, with participation from the Director of the World Heritage Centre, Bernd von Droste, IUCN and ICOMOS.[60] In a concession

---

55 IUCN 1998, p. 2.
56 Ibid.
57 UNESCO 1998a, Annex VII. The GAC had, by this time, largely dissociated itself from the KRSIS process, arguing that it was overly influenced by a pro-development agenda, that its make-up and administration unfairly precluded Mirarr and inadequately addressed the likely social impacts specifically associated with Jabiluka's development.
58 Ibid.
59 Australian Parliament 1999b. AAPA is a statutory authority of the Northern Territory Government.
60 The mission comprised Professor Francesco Francioni (Chairperson of the World Heritage Committee and leader of the mission), Dr Bernd von Droste (Director, UNESCO World Heritage Centre), Dr Patrick Dugan (IUCN), Dr Patricia Parker (ICOMOS), Dr John Cook (US National Park Service) and two Australian government appointees – Professor Jon Altman and Dr Roy Green. The mission was also ultimately accompanied by two State Party Observers, namely the then Supervising Scientist, Dr Peter Bridgewater, and the First Assistant Secretary Australian and World Heritage Group of the Environment Department, Sharon Sullivan.

to the Australians, it was ultimately (later) agreed that two Australian nationals would be "invited to be permanent member[s] of the team", with attributes including "perceived impartiality by the Australian community in relation to the public debate about uranium extraction at the Jabiluka site".[61] The mission would examine the situation, hold discussions with Aboriginal groups, including the Mirarr, officials, NGOs and Energy Resources of Australia (ERA) and report to the Bureau and Committee at their November-December 1998 sessions.[62] Publicly, Senator Hill downplayed the significance of the mission by portraying it as "standard practice".[63] Notwithstanding this modulated analysis, the World Heritage Centre proceeded with what would ultimately be "the largest-scale, most expensive mission in the history of the World Heritage process".[64] Preparation was not trouble free, with the Australian government, via Senator Hill, successfully delaying the mission on the pretext of the announcement of a federal election, something that the mission head and Committee chairperson later said made "the preparation of the report much more difficult time-wise".[65]

Ultimately, the mission visited Australia and conducted its business from 26 October to 1 November 1998, holding meetings in both the Northern Territory and in Canberra.[66] The two Australians appointed to the mission were geologist, Dr Roy Green, and social scientist, Dr Jon Altman, notwithstanding correspondence from the GAC to the World Heritage Centre stating that Dr Altman should not be appointed given his "perceived bias towards the development of the Jabiluka uranium mine".[67] The then Director of the World Heritage Centre, Bernd von Droste, has subsequently described his task of organising the mission ("for which the Australian government showed no enthusiasm") as "quite an undertaking".

> "The tactic the government employed was to delay the mission to the furthest extent possible despite the fact that the Committee members had underlined its urgency. Another move was to submerge the international participants of the mission by government appointed Australian participants." [68]

The mission visited Kakadu and met with Mirarr and the Kakadu Board of Management, government officials and representatives of the mining company Energy Resources of Australia. In Darwin, the mission met with the Northern Territory government and in Canberra it met with a wide variety of senior government representatives, environment groups, industry representatives and eminent academics. Despite initial resistance from the Australian government, the Gundjeihmi Aboriginal Corporation was afforded an additional opportunity of addressing the mission in Canberra.[69]

---

61 Wardrop 1998.
62 UNESCO 1998a, p. 14.
63 ABC 1998.
64 Aplin 2004, pp. 152–174.
65 Francioni 1998.
66 The Mission itinerary, it should be noted, was hotly debated in correspondence between the GAC, the World Heritage Centre and the Australian government, with the GAC eventually securing independent status with the Mission.
67 Katona 1998.
68 von Droste 2009, p. 22.
69 UNESCO 1998c.

The Mirarr presented a 20,000-word submission to the mission team, detailing the cultural desecration caused by the Ranger mine and the threat of a complete loss of cultural identity posed by Jabiluka's proposed development. They were allocated four hours to show the mission cultural sites on the Jabiluka Mineral Lease and their living conditions within Kakadu National Park. In their submission "the Mirarr argued that the actual and potential threats to their living tradition and culture posed by further mining on their land required that Kakadu be inscribed on the List of World Heritage In Danger".[70] During the mission's visit to the Mirarr and Gundjeihmi Corporation in Kakadu, the Australian members and observers were not permitted to attend, at the express wish of the Mirarr, leaving the Director of the Centre, Bernd von Droste, to later note that "no doubt the government and the Mirarr people were not on speaking terms." [71] Archaeologist John Mulvaney has described the Australian government's management of the mission:

"It disparaged the expertise of the prestigious committee, having ensured that during its visit to Kakadu the committee's contact with critics was minimal. As a person giving evidence to that committee I can vouch for the contrivances employed by the host department to achieve that end. Nations on the World Heritage executive committee were extensively lobbied while taxpayers funded a three-week visit to Paris by the minister and several senior staffers. They secured a reversal of the recommendation." [72]

The final report of the mission was sent to the Australian authorities on 24 November, just days ahead of the twenty-second extraordinary session of the Bureau, in Kyoto. The report provided 16 recommendations addressing the cultural, social and environmental threats posed by Jabiluka's imminent development. The first recommendation stated that the mission had "noted severe ascertained and potential dangers to the cultural and natural values of Kakadu National Park posed primarily by the proposal for uranium mining and milling at Jabiluka [and] ... therefore recommends that the proposal to mine and mill uranium at Jabiluka should not proceed".[73] Noting that some of Australia's "most eminent scientists" had given information as to "the unacceptably high degree of scientific uncertainties relating to the Jabiluka mine design, tailings disposal and possible impacts on catchment ecosystems", the mission applied the application of the precautionary principle, "which requires that mining operations at Jabiluka be ceased".[74] The Australian appointees to the Mission, in correspondence from Dr Jon Altman, dissented from the key Mission recommendations, including that the Jabiluka development be halted.[75] Opposed to the "no-mining statement" of the Mission report, the letter from Dr Altman argued that the Ranger mine had existed "adjacent to the

---

70 Fagan 1999b. Matthew Fagan, an employee of the Gundjeihmi Aboriginal Corporation, was a former adviser to the Australian Greens.
71 von Droste 2009, p. 23.
72 Mulvaney 2007, p. 159.
73 UNESCO 1998c, p. v.
74 Ibid.
75 Altman 1998.

World Heritage Area, for nearly twenty years", that "world-class work" had been carried out there and that mining and World Heritage need not be considered as mutually exclusive.[76]

There was significant jockeying by the GAC and its civil society campaign colleagues ahead of the Kyoto meetings of the Bureau and Committee, which were again attended by GAC. During his presentation on the mission to the Bureau, chairperson Francioni described how the Australian Government, in correspondence from both the Environment Minister Robert Hill and Foreign Affairs Minister Alexander Downer, had sought to have the Kakadu mission report withdrawn from the meeting's agenda on the grounds that the government had been given insufficient time to properly consider the report.[77] Stressing that it was imperative for the mission to fulfil its mandate by presenting the report to the twenty-second session, the chairperson noted that "the Australian Government ha[d] been privy to the work of the mission since its inception" and that the mission had met with the Minister and the Secretary of Environment Australia in Canberra and expressed "in an open and candid manner what trends were emerging from the hearings and briefings". The Chairperson said that he was of the opinion that as chairman of the Committee, he should fulfil the mandate provided at the last session of the Bureau, adding that the Bureau "is faced with an urgent situation as the construction of the mine at Jabiluka, located within an enclave excised from the World Heritage property, is proceeding."[78] On this basis, the Bureau went on to consider the mission report.

Privately, Francioni had become "livid with anger" on hearing of the Australians' request and "threatened to step down as World Heritage chair if Kakadu would be deleted from the agenda."[79] Bernd von Droste later conceded that Australia had undertaken "a lobbying campaign of a magnitude never before experienced in the World Heritage Committee".[80] In addition to its diplomatic efforts to have the mission report withdrawn from the Bureau session, the Australian Government separately wrote to von Droste arguing that the Mirarr viewpoint was a minority one that contradicted earlier (allegedly 1982) consents for mining, that mining operations would "not directly affect sites with cultural heritage values within the lease area", and that an assessment of the "one natural site of significance" and of the social impact of the proposed development were subject to domestic processes.[81]

In addressing the Bureau IUCN indicated its strong support for the mission report, stating its firm belief "that the conditions exist for inscribing Kakadu on the List of World Heritage in Danger" and that a "failure to recognise the dangers would seriously undermine the standards [of] the World Heritage Convention".[82] ICOMOS joined IUCN in endorsing the recommendations of the mission

---

76   Ibid., p. 2. Dr Altman's actions during this episode of the Jabiluka debate, incongruent with his career generally, clearly escaped his attention in his recent summary of the debate. See Altman 2012, p. 60.
77   UNESCO 1998b, p. 28. See also Hill 1998, and Downer 1998.
78   UNESCO 1998b, p. 28.
79   von Droste 2009, p. 32. Von Droste considered the Australian request as a "delaying technique".
80   Ibid. Elsewhere, Australia's actions have been described as a "diplomatic offensive in the foreign capitals of Committee members to gain support for its position." Cameron and Rössler 2013, p. 230.
81   Sullivan 1998b. This "one site of significance" was the Boyweg site, repeatedly and somewhat misleadingly referred to as 'natural' rather than cultural. There are, of course, several sites of great significance at Jabiluka and literally hundreds of other important archaeological sites.
82   UNESCO 1998b, Annex II.

report. The Australian delegation argued that Australia had been given insufficient time to respond to the mission report, that an initial reading suggested it contained errors of law, fact and analysis and that its recommendations were therefore "flawed and unacceptable to the Australian government". The Australians asked the Bureau to recommend to the committee that Australia be given more time to provide a more considered response on the mission report ahead of the next Bureau session.[83]

Chairperson Francioni referred to the responsibility of the Bureau to "implement the Convention as an instrument of international cooperation not through narrow national interpretations" and "pleaded... for reinforcement of the spirit of cooperation and fiduciary responsibilities".[84] Following this, recommendations were drafted in closed sessions by Bureau members prior to returning to the full session of the Bureau. This was, after some two years of dialogue, decision time for the members of the Bureau, who found themselves in the middle of a particularly public and passionate debate on the extent to which international obligation could inform actions against the wishes of a sovereign government.

After a relatively brief debate the Bureau determined to provide the Australians with additional time to respond to the mission report and to grant the following Bureau meeting (the 23rd) the mandate to inscribe Kakadu on the List of World Heritage in Danger if it deemed such action necessary. The Bureau also noted "with concern that in spite of the dangers to the World Heritage values, construction of the mine at Jabiluka began in June 1998 and is currently progressing" and that "there is significant difference of opinion concerning the degree of certainty of the science used to assess the impact of the mine on the World Heritage values of Kakadu". The Bureau recommended that the Australian authorities be given until 15 April 1999 to provide a detailed report on "their efforts to prevent further damage and to mitigate all the threats identified in the UNESCO mission report, to the World Heritage cultural and natural values of Kakadu". Significantly, the Bureau also recommended that the Australians "be requested to direct the Australian Supervising Scientist Group to conduct a full review of the scientific issues" and that the review be submitted "to peer review by an independent scientific panel composed of scientists selected by UNESCO in consultation with the International Council of Scientific Unions and the Chairperson of the World Heritage Committee".[85]

The Committee meeting immediately following the Bureau session, under the new chairmanship of Koïchiro Matsuura of Japan, as expected, endorsed all of the Bureau's recommendations and added two more. Firstly, an extraordinary session of the Committee would be conducted following the next Bureau meeting to consider the Australian Government's response and determine whether or not to inscribe Kakadu on the List of World Heritage in Danger due to Jabiluka's development. Secondly, the Committee "urged the Australian authorities and Energy Resources Australia to immediately undertake ... the voluntary suspension of construction of the mine".[86] Several months after the Kyoto meetings a blunter, realpolitik summary of the

---

83 Ibid., p. 29.
84 Ibid., p. 30.
85 Ibid., pp. 31-32. The last recommendation was especially significant as it effectively dissociated the Mirarr from what would become a strictly scientific debate among 'peers'. The full significance of this would only be realised at a later time.
86 UNESCO 1998d, p. 19.

proceedings was revealed with the leaking by the then Australian Labor Party Shadow Foreign Minister, Laurie Brereton, of "highly protected" documents showing that the government had "embarked on a $1 million lobbying campaign to pressure key nations on the United Nations World Heritage Committee to back Australia's right to mine at Jabiluka".[87]

The documents, which included confidential cables from the Australian Embassy in Tokyo, provided an insight into the extent of Australia's politicisation of the World Heritage Committee, the extent of its efforts to prevent an 'In Danger' listing and the range of other nations involved in and/or targeted by its diplomatic effort.[88] The primary document, correspondence from the then Environment Department Secretary, Roger Beale, to his Minister, shows a government under siege from a coordinated NGO and diplomatic campaign, and determined to develop Jabiluka at all costs. Describing the need for a "coordinated, resource-intensive effort across a range of portfolios both domestically and internationally", the correspondence outlined a comprehensive strategy to secure Australia's objective of avoiding "a listing of Kakadu as World Heritage in Danger, while securing arrangements for ... development of the Jabiluka mine".[89] An international lobbying strategy beyond the Committee members and "dealing with IUCN, ICOMOS and ICCROM and World Heritage Secretariat" would be developed. The Embassy cables were particularly revealing, highlighting the extent to which Australia was secretly joined by the United States in securing its diplomatic objectives, and the perceived threats to Australia's position posed by the advisory bodies.

Third extraordinary session

The third extraordinary session of the World Heritage Committee in Paris in July 1999 was the first session in the history of the Committee "exclusively devoted to a single conservation issue".[90] This underscored both the significance of Kakadu as a World Heritage site and the need to address long-standing unresolved issues raised by mining in or adjacent to World Heritage areas and the inscription of sites on the List of World Heritage in Danger against the wishes of the State Party.

Throughout the entire debate the Australian Government underscored the importance of its sovereign right to determine what it regarded as the appropriate response to the challenges presented by Mirarr resistance to Jabiluka. On the eve of the Committee's consideration of the Mission report, the government went a little further with an especially baleful letter. Writing on behalf of the government to all delegates at the 22nd session of the Committee in Kyoto in November 1998, Sharon Sullivan stated that an 'In Danger' listing "would not be an act of respect for Australia's sovereignty" and that to do so "may also unfortunately prevent a negotiated settlement to these complex issues".[91]

---

87 MacDonald 1999.
88 Beale 1998.
89 Ibid., p. 1.
90 Cameron and Rössler 2013, p. 145.
91 Sullivan 1998a.

In April 1999, just months prior to the third extraordinary session of the Committee, the Mirarr public campaign was boosted when Yvonne Margarula and Jacqui Katona were jointly awarded the prestigious Goldman Environmental Award for Excellence in Protecting the Environment.[92] Also on the eve of the extraordinary session, the Australian Senate delivered a report on the mine proposal, finding (inter alia) that Jabiluka threatened the natural and cultural World Heritage values of Kakadu and recommending that the project not proceed.[93] Underscoring the political utility of the World Heritage Convention, the Senate report also found that a 'World Heritage in Danger' listing "may be the only way of changing the Government's present support for mining at Jabiluka." [94]

April 1999 also saw the Australian Government present its detailed response to the Kakadu Mission report. In a transparent assertion of its sovereign status, the government entitled the report "Australia's Kakadu" and delivered it on 15 April following a presentation at the Australian Embassy in Paris to World Heritage Committee members, advisory body representatives and staff of the World Heritage Centre. The 140-page report was highly critical of the Mission and its findings and, across eight chapters, sought to discredit the Mirarr position on Jabiluka with, inter alia, the mischievous reinterpretation of the anthropological record to the favour of the government's mining agenda, a highly selective account of the history of uranium development at Kakadu, false and misleading interpretations of Aboriginal culture favourable to the government's position and the selective use of its own government reports on social impact.[95]

The GAC responded with its own submission, detailing the extent to which the Australian Government would go in advancing its agenda, arguing that the Government had abandoned the role of independent assessor and clearly become a mining advocate.[96] The submission stressed that "the only reason the Mirarr are opposed to the development of Jabiluka is because they know it will destroy the unique source of Mirarr language, culture, sacred sites and living tradition".[97] The GAC argued that Australia misrepresented the findings of the Ranger Uranium Environmental Inquiry, denied key aspects of the history of uranium development in Kakadu, made "false and misleading" claims about Jabiluka's cultural heritage, and ignored findings of its own Kakadu Region Social Impact Study that argued against the official pro-mining government view.[98]

In a setting described by the former Director of the World Heritage Centre as "the most dramatic I have seen in World Heritage", the World Heritage Committee set to work on 12 July 1999 to consider Australia's response to the Mission report, the Mirarr response to the Australian position, hundreds of pages of scientific reports and voluminous correspondence from NGOs

---

92 For this they travelled to the US, meeting dignitaries such as Hillary Clinton and the Kennedy family.
93 Australian Parliament 1999b.
94 Australian Parliament 1999b, p. viii.
95 Environment Australia 1999.
96 GAC 1999.
97 Ibid., p. 8.
98 Ibid., pp. 8-17.

across the globe.⁹⁹ The meeting heard from Senator Robert Hill on behalf of the Australian Government and, in a world first, from Yvonne Margarula on behalf of her country and the Mirarr people. In his address Senator Hill effectively divided cultural and scientific matters into distinct spheres, addressing them separately from within the one technical rational framework. Senator Hill emphasised that Australia fully supported the recommendations of the Independent Scientific Panel (convened by the Bureau in 1998) and would work toward consensus on agreed outstanding matters of science.¹⁰⁰ In relation to cultural concerns, Senator Hill argued that internal processes and dialogue were more appropriate than any international intervention from UNESCO.¹⁰¹ Importantly, Australia also outlined that it had managed to negotiate, in addition to the sequencing of the Ranger mine and Jabiluka project, "a pause that would allow the building of a better environment in which to carry out the cultural assessments".¹⁰²

All three advisory bodies to the Committee, IUCN, ICOMOS and ICCROM, "called for Kakadu National Park to be inscribed on the List of World Heritage in Danger." In their statements the advisory bodies reiterated the final conclusion of the UNESCO mission and referenced "continuing scientific uncertainties relating to the water management and retention system and disposal of tailings at the Jabiluka mine, visual encroachment on the integrity of Kakadu and threats to the tangible and associative cultural values of the Park".¹⁰³

In her historic address Yvonne Margarula, speaking in her traditional Gundjeihmi language, addressed the question of sacred sites, noting that "Aboriginal people do not invent stories about our culture and our sacred sites. Our law is true."¹⁰⁴ Underlining that any discussion about sacred sites was very intense, Ms Margarula said Aboriginal people "must speak with the truth when we talk about these things" and that she hoped Senator Hill would listen to Mirarr concerns. She was especially eloquent on the appropriateness of the 'In Danger' proposal before the Committee.

> "Some of the information presented today casts aspersions on our traditional beliefs about the location of sacred sites. We feel that still we are not believed and trusted about these issues. The label in-Danger is an appropriate way to describe the situation we find ourselves in. This is a dangerous issue for us. And, so that is what I would wish to see placed is this description." ¹⁰⁵

---

99 Audio interview of Bernd von Droste by Christina Cameron and Mechtild Rössler, Paris, 5 April 2007, cited in Cameron and Rössler 2013, p. 172.
100 UNESCO 1999, p. 7. It is noteworthy that the technical rationality of the 'administered world' (as described in Horkheimer and Adorno 2002), with its separation of the universe into the discrete spheres of 'nature' and 'culture', underpins the World Heritage Convention itself and, naturally enough, well served the Australian Government in its management of the Kakadu debate.
101 UNESCO 1999, p. 8.
102 UNESCO 1999, p. 9.
103 UNESCO 1999.
104 Ibid., p. 54.
105 Ibid.

As delegates, in turn, addressed the question as to whether Kakadu should be listed as 'In Danger' the efficacy of Australia's lobbying efforts and the reluctance of Committee members to intervene into the affairs of an otherwise widely respected State Party became evident. A grouping of States opposed to the listing quickly emerged and emphasised that it was "not appropriate to include Kakadu on the List of World Heritage in Danger at this time" and that "the development of a program of corrective measures in cooperation with the State Party" should be undertaken.[106] The strong support Australia enjoyed from the United States was critical in the closing moments of the debate, with the US stating that "out of respect for Australia's sovereignty", the "concerns raised here today can be addressed adequately without placing Kakadu on the List in Danger".[107] In supporting the move to not list Kakadu as 'In Danger', Zimbabwe – which as an African country had experienced "similar violations of its cultural values by Europeans settlers" – appealed to the Australian Government "to respect the values, the sacred values of the Mirarr people and to increase its dialogue with those people".[108]

In the end, the extraordinary session decided against inscribing Kakadu on the List of World Heritage in Danger and instead held that the Australian Government should submit a progress report on cultural mapping, social and welfare benefits, and details of the output and scale of any parallel activities at Ranger and Jabiluka by 15 April 2000. The decision also expressed concern "about the lack of progress with the preparation of a cultural heritage management plan for Jabiluka", establishing the focus of its future interest in the matter.[109] Supporters of the Mirarr were divided in their response to the decision, with some environment groups mistakenly interpreting confidential meetings between the Australian Government and the Mirarr delegation as signalling that a 'deal' had been done whereby the Mirarr capitulated on their request for an 'In Danger' listing. In turn, the GAC defended the final outcome on the basis of gains secured and the ongoing delay of Jabiluka's development.[110] For his part, the former World Heritage Committee chairperson Francioni was disappointed:

"I would have liked to see more courage, a bolder Committee ... Kakadu was a very important case because of the ... natural value but also because of the local communities ... That was a decision I would have liked to see on the part of a treaty body like the World Heritage Committee that unfortunately was not made." [111]

Subsequent meetings of the Bureau and Committee saw a steady scaling down of interest and activity on the part of the Centre and UNESCO in general. If the foundations for this more 'hands-off' approach were laid in Paris in July 1999 they were no more clearly demonstrated

---

106 Ibid., p. 11.
107 Ibid., p. 86.
108 Ibid., p. 87.
109 Ibid., p. 23.
110 Fagan 1999a.
111 Cameron and Rössler 2013, p. 230.

than at the Cairns 2000 Committee meetings. Here it was no longer a case of direct dialogue between Mirarr and Committee members but of negotiations between Australia and the Mirarr. The deft dissection by the Australian Government of the natural and cultural aspects of the debate effectively rendered a cornerstone of the Mirarr argument (that the inseparability of the physical and cultural in the Indigenous worldview constitutes the need for a significantly higher threshold of environmental protection and that the effects of physical damage have widespread social ramifications, well beyond the mining 'footprint') null and void. The cultural supremacy of Western science within UNESCO (embodied in the work of the Independent Scientific Panel) served to demonstrate that Australia was genuinely addressing outstanding environmental matters. Meanwhile, attention on 'cultural concerns' was relegated to a focus on the dispute between Australia and the Mirarr on the development of a cultural heritage management plan for the proposed mine site, with inordinate attention paid to the voluminous correspondence between the parties.[112] Fortunately for the Mirarr the significance of the Kakadu World Heritage debate for their broader struggle to prevent Jabiluka's development was lessened with the new campaign opportunities afforded by Rio Tinto's acquisition of the property in August 2000.

Conclusion

The Jabiluka matter was somewhat more satisfactorily 'settled' (to the extent that it can be in the present) outside both Australian land rights and environmental law and the World Heritage Convention via a direct contract between the Mirarr People and the mining company ERA under the agreement of its parent company Rio Tinto. It is unfortunate that the agency of the Mirarr and the GAC in successfully negotiating the so-called Jabiluka Long Term Care and Maintenance Agreement with Rio Tinto (following commitments by the company's chairperson, Sir Robert Wilson, in 2002 that Jabiluka would not be developed without community support) is downplayed by most commentators.[113] Implicit in such analyses is that the Jabiluka settlement derived from the good grace of Rio Tinto. They place the company's decisions within a discourse of increasing international corporate social responsibility, effectively and unfortunately casting the Mirarr in a distinctly passive role as the recipients of industrial beneficence.[114]

The confidence of the Mirarr traditional owners that they might one day finally end the Jabiluka dispute was boosted in recent times with the decision by the Australian Government that the Koongarra uranium deposit in Kakadu would not be mined but instead incorporated into the national park.[115] This action resulted from the long-standing opposition of the Djok traditional owner of the Koongarra area, Jeffrey Lee, to uranium mining on his land and a commitment

---

112 See UNESCO 2000.
113 In addition to statements in reply to questions at both the UK and Australian annual general meetings of Rio Tinto, the chairman explicitly committed to no mining at Jabiluka without Mirarr consent on the BBC, see Sebastian 2002. The GAC played a pivotal, although undisclosed, role in both the AGM questions and the BBC interview.
114 See especially Trebeck (2009) and Altman (2012). For a more even-handed summary see Scambary 2013.
115 Mining is prohibited in federal national parks. The Djok clan, in whose land the Koongarra uranium deposit is located, are clan neighbours to the Mirarr people and are in a so-called 'company clan' relationship with the Mirarr.

Jeffrey Lee and Stewart Gangali outside the UNESCO building in Paris after the World Heritage Committee added Koongarra to the Kakadu World Heritage area. Photo: Justin O'Brien

by the federal Australian Labor Party that Koongarra would not be mined.[116] Mr Lee, who was awarded the Order of Australia in 2012 for his efforts to protect his traditional land and offer it for inclusion in Kakadu National Park, has publicly acknowledged the inspiration and support he has received over the years from the Mirarr people and particularly from Yvonne Margarula. A small delegation of the Gundjeihmi Aboriginal Corporation accompanied Mr Lee to Paris in 2011 to facilitate a minor boundary modification to the Kakadu World Heritage area to include the Koongarra area.[117] In February 2013 the Australian Government legislated to incorporate Koongarra into Kakadu National Park, thereby ruling out any mining of the site.

It is without doubt that the international prominence of the Kakadu World Heritage debate delivered the Mirarr significant leverage in their negotiations with Rio Tinto. The World Heritage Committee proved an effective international stage to highlight the impacts of the imminent destruction of country and culture in a remote but significant corner of the globe. That the Committee and the Convention itself were arguably not able to adequately protect Kakadu but deferred instead to the State Party intent on mining is an enduring disappointment. It should be remembered, however, that the Jabiluka debate is not ended but merely in a lull.

---

116 See Murdoch 2007. The federal branch of the Liberal Party, Australia's conservative party, largely concurred with the Labor Party's view on Koongarra.
117 UNESCO 2011, pp. 248-249. Ms Margarula has to date sadly received no official government recognition for her decades-long struggle to protect her land in Kakadu from mining.

References

ABC. 1998. Environment Minister dismisses concerns that the Kakadu National Park is under threat from the Jabiluka uranium mine. *Radio National: Breakfast*, 25 June 1998.

Altman, J. 1998. *Statement received from Professor Jon Altman, prepared jointly with Dr Roy Green (24 November 1998)*. UNESCO Doc. WHC-99/CONF.204/INF.9A, Annex I.

Altman, J. 2012. Indigenous Rights, Mining Corporations, and the Australian State. S. Sawyer and E. T. Gomez (eds.), *The Politics of Resource Extraction: Indigenous Peoples, Multinational Corporations, and the State*. London, Palgrave Macmillan, pp. 46-74.

Anthony, J.D. 1978. *Ranger Uranium - Agreement with the NLC: Options for early conclusion*. Cabinet Submission by J .D. Anthony, Chairman, Ad Hoc Committee (Uranium) and Minister for Trade and Resources, Canberra, 17 October 1978.

Aplin, G. 2004. Kakadu National Park World Heritage Site: Deconstructing the Debate, 1997–2003. *Australian Geographical Studies*, Vol. 42(2), pp. 152–174.

Australian Institute of Aboriginal Studies. Uranium Impact Project Steering Committee. 1985. *Aborigines and Uranium: Consolidated Report on the Social Impact of Uranium Mining on the Aborigines of the Northern Territory*. Canberra, Australian Government Publishing Service.

Australian Parliament. 1999a. *ECITA Legislation Committee Estimates Hansard*. Canberra, Government Printer, 10 February 1999.

Australian Parliament. 1999b. *Jabiluka: The Undermining of Process - Inquiry into the Jabiluka Uranium Mine Project*, by the Senate Environment, Communications, Information Technology and the Arts References Committee. Canberra, Government Printer.

Beale, R. 1998. Confidential letter to Minister for the Environment and Heritage entitled "Kakadu World Heritage Issues: Planning". Environment Australia, 23 December 1998 (on file with author).

Bininj Gunwok Project. 2013. Karri-borlbme Kun-wok ('learning language'): entry 'Bininj'. http://words.bininjgunwok.org.au/words/bininj (Retrieved 3 March 2013).

Cameron, C. and Rössler, M. 2013. *Many voices, one vision: the early years of the World Heritage Convention*. Farnham, Ashgate.

Ceresa, M. 1998. Digging in for a fight. *The Weekend Australian*, 18 April 1998, p. 23.

Cleere, H. 1997. Letter to Bruce Donald, ICOMOS, 4 July 1997 (on file with author).

Confino, A. 2006. *Germany as a culture of remembrance: promises and limits of writing history*. Chapel Hill, University of North Carolina Press.

Director of National Parks. 2007. *Kakadu National Park: Management Plan 2007 - 2014*. Darwin, Parks Australia North.

Downer, A. (Minister for Foreign Affairs). 1998. Letter to His Excellency Mr Federico Mayor Zaragoza, Director-General UNESCO, 24 November 1998 (on file with author).

Environment Australia. 1999. *Australia's Kakadu – Protecting World Heritage: Response by the Government of Australia to the UNESCO World Heritage Committee regarding Kakadu National Park*. Canberra, Commonwealth of Australia.

European Parliament. 1998. *Uranium Mining Urgency Resolution* (on the proposed Jabiluka Uranium Mine). Adopted on 15 January 1998.

Fagan, M. 1999a. *Aboriginal Self-Determination within the United Nations*. Jabiru, Gundjeihmi Aboriginal Corporation.

Fagan, M. 1999b. UNESCO Special Mission to Kakadu National Park. *Indigenous Law Bulletin*, Vol. 4, Issue 17, p. 16.

Francioni, F. (World Heritage Committee Chairperson). 1998. Letter to Australian Minister for the Environment, Senator Robert Hill, 25 November 1998 (on file with author).

GAC. 1996. *Senior Traditional Owner of Jabiluka announces opposition to proposed mine*. Media release by Gundjeihmi Aboriginal Corporation, 17 June 1996.

GAC. 1997a. *This is bullshit*. Media release by Gundjeihmi Aboriginal Corporation, 9 December 1997.

GAC. 1997b. *"We are not talking about mining": The history of duress and the Jabiluka Project*. Jabiru, Gundjeihmi Aboriginal Corporation.

GAC. 1998. *Mirarr Living Tradition In Danger, World Heritage In Danger: Submission to the World Heritage Committee Mission to Kakadu*. Jabiru, Gundjeihmi Aboriginal Corporation, October 1998.

GAC. 1999. *Submission from the Mirrar People to the UNESCO World Heritage Committee, ICCROM and ICOMOS in relation to the Australian Government's report "Australia's Kakadu: Protecting World Heritage"*. Jabiru, Gundjeihmi Aboriginal Corporation. May 1999.

Grey, T. 1994. *Jabiluka: The Battle to Mine Australia's Uranium.* Melbourne, Text Publishing Company.

Hamilton, C. 1996. *Mining in Kakadu: Lessons from Coronation Hill.* Lecture to the Parliamentary Library 'Vital Issues' Seminar Series Parliament House, Canberra, 19 June 1996. Canberra, The Australia Institute.

Hill, R. 1996. *Hill delivers on Jabiluka commitment.* Media release by Leader of the Government in the Senate and Minister for the Environment, Senator Robert Hill. 28 June 1996.

Hill, R. 1997. Letter to Senator the Hon Warwick Parer, Minister for Resources and Energy, from the leader of the Government in the Senate and Minister for the Environment, 22 August 1997 (on file with author).

Hill, R. 1998. Letter to Professor Francesco Francioni, Chairperson of the World Heritage Committee, from the Leader of the Government in the Senate and Minister for the Environment, 24 November 1998 (on file with author).

Horkheimer, M. and Adorno, T.W. 2002. *Dialectic of enlightenment: Philosophical fragments* (E. Jephcott, Trans.). Stanford, Stanford University Press.

Ishwaran, N. (UNESCO World Heritage Centre). 1997. Letter to Bruce Donald re Kakadu National Park - proposed uranium mine at Jabiluka, 18 February 1997 (on file with author).

IUCN. 1997. *Resolutions and Recommendations, World Conservation Congress, Montreal, Canada 13–23 October 1996.* Gland, International Union for Conservation of Nature and Natural Resources.

IUCN. 1998. Statement on the State of Conservation of Australian World Heritage sites and specifically relating to Kakadu National Park (Bureau of the World Heritage Committee, Twenty-Second Session). UNESCO Doc. WHC-98/CONF.202/INF.2, Annex VI.

Katona, J. 1998. Letter to Dr Bernd von Droste. Gundjeihmi Aboriginal Corporation, 13 October 1998 (on file with author).

Lawrence, D. 2000. *Kakadu: the making of a national park.* Melbourne, The Miegenyah Press/ Melbourne University Press.

Logan, W. 2013. Australia, Indigenous peoples and World Heritage from Kakadu to Cape York: State Party behaviour under the World Heritage Convention. *Journal of Social Archaeology*, Vol. 13, No. 2, pp. 153–176.

MacDonald, J. 1999. Dirty tricks claim over Kakadu. *The Age*, 17 February 1999.

Masterson, A. 2010. *The Mirarr: yesterday, today and tomorrow: a socioeconomic update.* Jabiru, Gundjeihmi Aboriginal Corporation.

Mulvaney, D. J. 1998. The Landscape of the Aboriginal Imagination and its Heritage Significance: some observations to introduce World Heritage experts to Australian Cultural Landscapes. Unpublished paper.

Mulvaney, D.J. 2007. *'The Axe Had Never Sounded': Place, People and Heritage of Recherche Bay, Tasmania.* Canberra, ANU E Press and Aboriginal Heritage Incorporated.

Murdoch, L. 2007. Sole survivor sitting on a $5b fortune. *Sydney Morning Herald*, 14 July 2007.

O'Brien, J. 2003. Canberra yellowcake: the politics of uranium and how Aboriginal land rights failed the Mirarr people. *Journal of Northern Territory History*, Vol. 14, pp. 79-91.

Panter, R. A. 1991. *Uranium Policies of the ALP, 1950-1990.* Background Papers (Science, Technology and Environment Group). Canberra, Parliamentary Library.

Parer, W. 1997. *Parer clears Jabiluka to proceed.* Media release by Federal Minister for Resources and Energy, Senator Warwick Parer. 8 October 1997.

Roberts, R., Jones, R. and Smith, M.A. 1990. Thermoluminescence dating of a 50,000-year-old human occupation site in northern Australia. *Nature*, Vol. 345, pp. 153-156.

Ryan, C. 1998. Mining the memory to save her people's land. *The Age* 5.

Scambary, B. 2013. *My Country, Mine Country: Indigenous people, mining and development contestation in remote Australia.* Canberra, ANU Press.

Sebastian, T. 2002. The business of caring: BBC Hardtalk interview with Sir Robert Wilson. London, BBC World.

Sullivan, S. 1998a. Letter from First Assistant Secretary Australian and World Heritage Group, Sharon Sullivan, to Delegates of the Twenty-second session of the World Heritage Committee meeting in Kyoto. Environment Australia, 20 November 1998 (on file with author).

Sullivan, S. 1998b. Letter to Mr Bernd von Droste, Director World Heritage Centre re State of Conservation of a Selected Number of Australian World Heritage sites. Environment Australia, World Heritage Unit, 19 June 1998 (on file with author).

The Wilderness Society. 1998. Urgent fax regarding accreditation at World Heritage Committee (on file with author).

Trebeck, K. 2009. Corporate responsibility and social sustainability: Is there any connection? J. Altman and D. Martin (eds.), *Power, Culture, Economy: Indigenous Australians and Mining.* Canberra, ANU E Press, pp. 127-148.

UNESCO. 1997. *Report of the Rapporteur of the Extraordinary session of the Bureau of the World Heritage Committee (Naples, 28 – 29 November 1997).* Doc. WHC-97/CONF.208/4B.

UNESCO. 1998a. *Report of the Rapporteur of the twenty-second session of the Bureau of the World Heritage Committee (Paris, 22-27 June 1998)*. Doc. WHC-98/CONF.202/INF.2.

UNESCO. 1998b. *Report of the Rapporteur on the twenty-second extraordinary session of the Bureau of the World Heritage Committee (Kyoto, 27-28 November 1998)*. Doc. WHC-98/CONF.203/5.

UNESCO. 1998c. *Report on the Mission to Kakadu National Park, Australia, 26 October to 1 November 1998*. Doc. WHC-98/CONF.202/INF.3 Rev. / WHC-98/CONF.203/INF. 18.

UNESCO. 1998d. *World Heritage Committee, Twenty-second session, Kyoto, Japan, 30 November – 5 December 1998: Report*. Doc. WHC-98/CONF.203/18.

UNESCO. 1999. *World Heritage Committee, Third extraordinary session, Paris, UNESCO Headquarters, 12 July 1999: Report of the Rapporteur*. Doc. WHC-99/CONF.205/5Rev.

UNESCO. 2000. *World Heritage Committee, Twenty-fourth session, Cairns, Australia, 27 November – 2 December 2000: Report*. Doc. WHC-2000/CONF.204/21.

UNESCO. 2011. *World Heritage Committee, Thirty-fifth Session, Paris, UNESCO Headquarters, 19-29 June 2011: Summary Record*. Doc. WHC-11/35.COM.INF.20.

von Droste, B. 2009. The Uranium Mining Controversy in Kakadu. Unpublished paper (on file with author).

Wardrop, M. 1998. Letter from Martin Wardrop, Assistant Secretary World Heritage and Wilderness Branch to Jacqui Katona. 4 September 1998 (on file with author).

Wasson, R. J. et al. 1998. *The Jabiluka Project: Environmental Issues that Threaten Kakadu National Park: Submission to UNESCO World Heritage Committee Delegation to Australia*. October 1998.

Whitlam, G. 1998. Facsimile letter to Anne Siwicki of Australian Embassy, Paris. 19 June 1998 (on file with author).

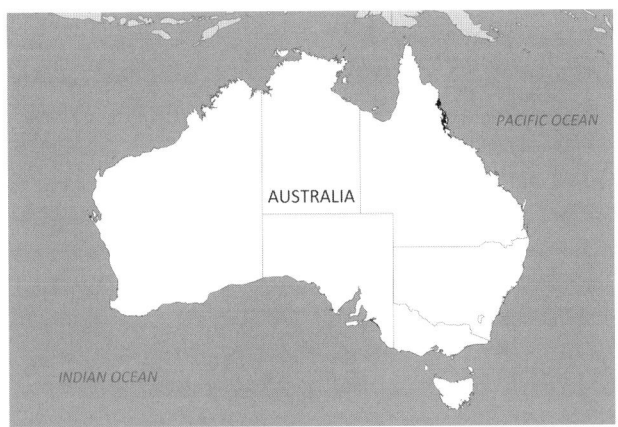

Rainforest Aboriginal Peoples and the Wet Tropics of Queensland World Heritage Area: The Role of Indigenous Activism in Achieving Effective Involvement in Management and Recognition of the Cultural Values

Henrietta Marrie and Adrian Marrie

"Over the past 20 years, I have seen the World Heritage listing raise the wider community's appreciation of our country to that which it deserves. The listing seemed to formalise what we, as Traditional Owners, already felt toward the land and we are now working hard to have our land formally recognised for its cultural values."

Phil Rist, Nywaigi Traditional Owner and CEO, Girringun Aboriginal Corporation[1]

---

1   WTMA 2009, p. 53.

Left: A Gimuy Walubarra Yidinji Elder, Gudju-Gudju Fourmile, gathering bush tucker (wild macadamia nuts) in the rainforest.
Photo: Adrian Marrie

Marginalised in the initial World Heritage listing processes, this chapter outlines the struggles of the Rainforest Aboriginal peoples and the processes they engaged in to gain a seat at the table as partners in the cooperative management of the Wet Tropics of Queensland World Heritage Area, and their continuing quest to have the cultural values of the World Heritage Area recognised on a par with its natural values.

Introduction

The Wet Tropics of Queensland World Heritage Area (WTWHA), covering 894,420 hectares, is located within and covers slightly less than half of the Wet Tropics Bioregion (1,967,000 hectares). It extends in a narrow band for approximately 600 kms along the northeast Queensland coastline from Cooktown in the north to Townsville in the south (Map 1). It is the traditional home of 18 distinct rainforest Aboriginal peoples[2] who have inhabited the region continuously for up to 100,000 years.

To the 18 hunter-gatherer Aboriginal peoples of these rainforests, the Wet Tropics Bioregion is a series of cultural landscapes which identify their place in their country and reinforces their ongoing customary laws and connections to country, and their obligations to care for and manage it – traditional obligations that are generally expressed throughout Indigenous Australia in the words 'Caring for Country'.

The Rainforest Aboriginal peoples' experience of the WHA is complex and its impacts are felt differently among the various peoples. Their experiences are fashioned more by over-riding issues concerning land tenure, particularly with regard to recognition of their native title, and dealing with a plethora of government agencies that have actual day-to-day management responsibilities in the WHA and adjacent lands, than issues raised directly as a consequence of parts of their traditional estates falling within the WHA. They are also shaped by Rainforest Aboriginal peoples' own struggles to overcome welfare dependency, and to find a place within mainstream Australian society. As native title claims are determined, the WHA is starting to provide more business and employment opportunities for them and thus could play a significant role in alleviating Aboriginal poverty and enhancing life opportunities.

In the context of this chapter, it also needs to be understood that the status of the Indigenous peoples of Australia, as First Nations peoples, is not recognised in the Australian Constitution, which came into effect in 1901 with the establishment of the Commonwealth of Australia. Further, no treaty was ever concluded between the British colonisers and the Indigenous peoples and, accordingly, Indigenous peoples in Australia have no treaty rights

---

2   The 18 Aboriginal peoples signatory to the Wet Tropics of Queensland World Heritage Area Regional Agreement are the Bandjin, Djabugay, Djiru, Girramay, Gugu Badhun, Gulgnay, Gunggandji, Jirrbal, Koko Muluridji, Kuku Yalanji, Ma:Mu, Ngadjon-Jii, Nywaigi, Warrgamay, Warungnu, Wulgurukaba, Yidinji and Yirrganydji peoples (WTMA 2005a, pp. iii-iv). There are also several named clan groups within these peoples.

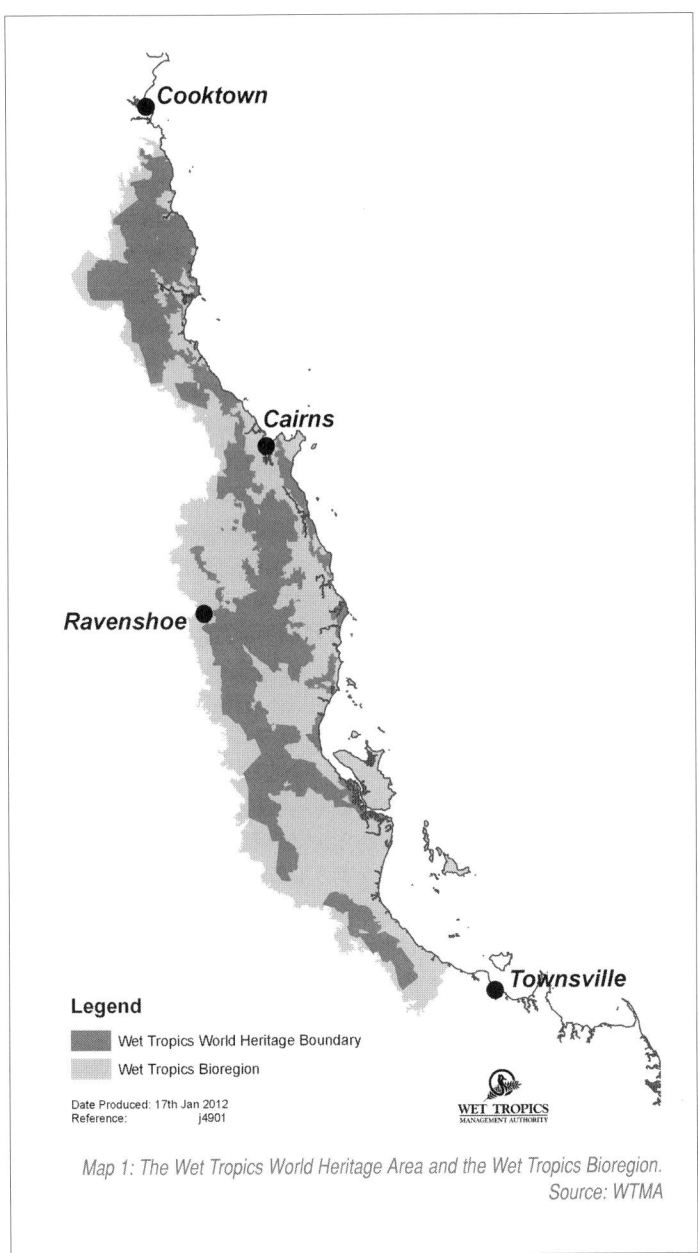

Map 1: The Wet Tropics World Heritage Area and the Wet Tropics Bioregion.
Source: WTMA

which would recognise or guarantee ownership of land and natural resources and continued enjoyment of their cultures and lifestyles. Under the Australian Constitution, Indigenous people have the same rights and responsibilities as all Australians, and have no special status. None of their rights as First Nations peoples constitutionally recognised or protected.[3] Until the 1967 Constitutional Referendum, responsibility for Indigenous peoples was solely a state matter.[4] The referendum enabled the Commonwealth Government to take overall responsibility for Indigenous affairs, although the states and territories have continued to make and amend laws in relation to Indigenous peoples, and to maintain responsibilities for Indigenous peoples within their own jurisdictions. Without recognition of any specific political, civil, social, cultural or economic rights, Indigenous peoples are subject to the same laws as other Australians, and laws and policies that are implemented with regard to or for the benefit of Indigenous people, such as state and territory Aboriginal land rights and cultural heritage protection laws, exist within the bounds of what is politically acceptable to the wider society. The only major source of protection for Indigenous peoples in Australia is the Commonwealth's *Racial Discrimination Act 1975*, which gives effect to Australia's obligations under the *International Convention on the Elimination of All Forms of Racial Discrimination*. Without constitutional recognition of Indigenous rights, Indigenous peoples in Australia exist in a state of perpetual legislative insecurity – what one government (federal or state) grants, another can take away depending on the electoral climate. Under Section 51(xxvi) of the Constitution – the so-called 'race power' – racist policies were entrenched in what was generally referred to as the White Australia Policy[5] which effectively existed within the separate states pre-federation and continued post-federation until the 1960s. While this policy effectively barred non-Caucasian people from migrating to and settling in Australia, it also rationalised the protective segregation policies with regard to Aboriginal peoples, particularly across northern Australia.

History of the WTWHA

European settlement of the region began in the 1870s. Land was gradually cleared along the coastal strip between the sea and the Great Dividing Range and on tablelands suitable for agriculture and cattle grazing. For Aboriginal peoples, the colonization process was brutal. Many Rainforest Aboriginal people were massacred or succumbed to introduced diseases. In 1897, the Queensland Government implemented the *Aborigines Protection and Restriction of the Sale of Opium Act* and established the office of the Chief Protector of Aborigines to try to stem the abuse of Aboriginal people and offer a measure of protection by setting up a number of Aboriginal reserves for their

---

3   Although some national-level laws (notably the Native Title Act) do recognise rights that are inherent to indigenous peoples in Australia, the lack of constitutional protection means that such recognition is always at the mercy of changing political circumstance.
4   In the 1967 Constitutional Referendum, 90.77 per cent of Australians voted in favour of two amendments to the Australian Constitution removing the provisions that (i) excluded Aboriginal Australians from the census and (ii) prevented the Commonwealth Government from enacting laws affecting Aboriginal peoples, a power that had previously been the preserve of the states.
5   The *Immigration Act 1901* (Cwth) was the legislative basis for this policy. Section 51 (xxvi) allows the Commonwealth to legislate in regard to "any race for whom it is deemed necessary to make special laws". This clause is still in force although there is some hope that it will be removed in the future.

protective segregation from mainstream society. By the 1920s, most Aboriginal people in northeast Queensland had been rounded up off their traditional lands and placed on reserves run by Christian missionaries at Yarrabah, Wujal Wujal (formerly the Bloomfield River Mission), Daintree River, Mossman Gorge, Mona Mona, Murray Upper and Palm Island. Many small government reserves were also established on the fringes of small rural townships such as Ravenshoe, Malanda, Mareeba, Atherton, Tully and Ingham where small groups of Aboriginal people remained until these township reserves were largely disbanded in the 1960s. Thus Aboriginal peoples in Queensland, from 1897 until the mid-1970s, were 'managed peoples' – effectively 'wards of the state' – subjected to the wide-ranging discretionary powers of the Chief Protector and the Reserve Superintendents. These officials administered a series of restrictive laws[6] which governed the movement of Aboriginal people on and off reserves, their employment (including working conditions and wages), education, financial affairs (with powers to manage their personal bank accounts) and, of course, their right to own property. They also restricted who they could associate with and who they could marry. And, until 1965, Aboriginal people in Queensland could not vote in state elections. Aboriginal people speak of this time as 'living under the Act', although they could apply for exemption certificates which enabled them to live and work in mainstream society subject to strict conditions.[7] Under mission regimes, Aboriginal people were generally forbidden to speak their languages or practice their ceremonies. The missionaries enforced this through the dormitory system whereby children were taken from their parents and placed in special dormitories where they were given a basic education and taught how to behave like 'white-fellas'. In some communities, such as Palm Island, this system remained in force until the mid-1970s.[8]

Following the 1967 Constitutional Referendum and the passage of the *Race Discrimination Act 1975* (Cwth), the situation regarding Aboriginal peoples in Australia began to change quite rapidly. In Queensland, the *Community Services (Aborigines) Act 1984* vested secure title to land in the form of a deed-of-grant-in-trust in a number of reserve communities, including Yarrabah, Wujal Wujal and Palm Island, administered by Aboriginal community councils elected by community members to run their communities and administer their lands. Such communities generally became known as 'DOGIT communities'. This Act enabled these communities to enjoy a measure of self-government patterned on mainstream structures of governance. For members of the Rainforest Aboriginal communities generally, employment was found in the agricultural, timber and cattle industries, and as domestic workers; however, in the 1960s, with the mechanisation of the sugar industry and the introduction of equal wages in the cattle industry, many Aboriginal people became unemployed and welfare dependent. This situation has continued to the present, although Aboriginal people who gained exemption certificates and

---

6   After the passage of the *Aborigines Protection and Restriction of the Sale of Opium Act 1897* (Qld) followed the *Aborigines Preservation and Protection Act 1939* (Qld) amended in 1946; *Aborigines' and Torres Strait Islanders' Affairs Act 1965* and *1967* (Qld); and the *Aborigines Act 1971* (Qld) and *Regulations 1972* which were repealed by the *Community Services (Aborigines) Act 1984* (Qld). The Commonwealth Government's *Racial Discrimination Act 1975* forced state governments to repeal the discriminatory clauses in their laws dealing with Indigenous Australians and revise their administrative practices or face possible challenges in the High Court of Australia.

7   The regulations regarding exemption certificates were in force from 1939 to 1965.

8   For an account of life 'under the act', read Bill Rosser's *This Is Palm Island* (1978) and *Return to Palm Island* (1994).

Cape Tribulation in Daintree National Park, Wet Tropics World Heritage Area.
Photo: Courtesy of Tourism and Events Queensland

moved off the reserve communities to live in the mainstream, or who managed to avoid being removed to such communities, have generally fared better than their DOGIT community counterparts on all socio-economic indicators.

By the 1980s, nearly all the arable and pastoral lands on the coastal side of the Great Dividing Range within the Wet Tropics Bioregion and on the Atherton Tablelands had been cleared save the lowland forests of the region generally known as 'the Daintree'. In effect, what remained were a few large areas of mountain forests and some smaller isolated patches, sometimes connected by narrow corridors of rainforest vegetation. This meant that some tribal groups and their clans had lost all or most of their land to rural land-holders and urban settlement, with the only remaining remnants of their lands still covered by natural forests being in mountainous areas. Other tribal groups, like the Eastern Kuku Yalanji in the northern areas of the Wet Tropics Bioregion, remained relatively undisturbed on their traditional lands and were consequently able to maintain their languages and retain most of their cultural practices. Most of the remaining forest lands in the central and southern areas of the Wet Tropics Bioregion were under government tenure as National Park, State Forest and Timber Reserve to which public access was officially restricted.[9]

---

9   Despite restrictions, Rainforest Aboriginal people still continued to hunt, gather and fish using traditional means – all low impact activities. Authorities tended to 'turn a blind eye' because, if Aboriginal people were helping to support themselves, then this meant less expense to government for their rations.

Consequently, by the time of listing in 1988, the Wet Tropics of Queensland World Heritage Area comprised slightly less than half of the Wet Tropics Bioregion. The listing of the remaining areas of wet tropical rainforests as a World Heritage site was achieved largely through a desperate rear-guard action by the conservation movement to save what was left of the Wet Tropics Bioregion from further destruction. While the focus from the early 1980s was on the Daintree, with the scientific realisation at the time that the Wet Tropics rainforests were in fact the world's oldest living rainforests estimated to be over 100 million years old,[10] efforts were extended to preserve what was left of these forests within the Wet Tropics Bioregion. The World Heritage nomination of the forests was strenuously opposed by the National Party-led Queensland Government, most local government councils in the region and by the timber industry. However, the federal Labour Government was committed to the nomination and conducted wide consultations within the mainstream Wet Tropics community, including offering compensation packages to the timber industry. Rainforest Aboriginal peoples were marginalized during the consultation process, and Aboriginal communities such as Yarrabah, Wujal Wujal, Mona Mona and Mossman Gorge opposed the nomination due to the lack of consultation and because it appeared that World Heritage listing would subject them to an overall management plan and affect their rights to self-determination and self-management[11] and place further restrictions on their already limited enjoyment of the remaining rainforests. In particular, they were concerned that listing would affect their ability to access the forests and forest resources for traditional hunting and gathering, for cutting timber to build houses and for other domestic and commercial purposes.[12] Furthermore, there was no assurance that the Rainforest Aboriginal peoples would play an adequate role in the future management of the WHA.

The fact that the Rainforest Aboriginal peoples had been sidelined in the nomination process, and that several Aboriginal communities were opposed to the World Heritage listing of their lands,

---

10 Their age is now estimated at 180 million years – tens of millions of years older than the Amazon rainforest in South America (see www.tq.com.au).

11 Self-determination as government policy rhetoric in the 1970s and '80s was clearly articulated within the framework of Australian law and did not have the same meaning as the term that was evolving in the development of the *UN Declaration on the Rights of Indigenous Peoples*. It was about Indigenous Australians having the right to develop their own governance institutions (such as community councils, and health, housing and legal organisations), and to take control of and manage their own affairs, i.e., it was really about self-management. The Commonwealth Government's policy of self-determination was often cynically described as 'self-management without funds'.

12 For instance, in October 1987, the Chairman of Yarrabah Aboriginal Council, Fr Lloyd Fourmile, wrote to the Commonwealth Minister of the Environment: "The proposed boundary and the process of the proposal show no regard for the Yarrabah community's land rights and entitlements to self-management and self-determination. It seems that your Government is not prepared to trust the Aboriginal community with the conservation of its own land". In November 1988, Fourmile's successor Peter Noble wrote to the Minister: "you have offered us nothing but the assurance that we will still be able to use our land as we do presently, if all goes well… We thought you would do more to consult with us. We thought you would have more regard for our land rights and self-management… Yet you have never been here… We finally met with you on October 18, 1988, only to find that our inclusion in World Heritage Listing was non-negotiable… We as an Aboriginal community are sick of outside interference in our affairs… we oppose the listing of our land. If listed, it will be without our consent." (Quoted in Brennan 1988).

was well known to both the World Heritage Committee and IUCN.[13] The nomination dossier contains no evidence that Rainforest Aboriginal peoples had been consulted during its elaboration and no information regarding their agreement to the inclusion of their lands. In fact, the Advisory Body Evaluation of the nomination by IUCN explicitly notes that "the position of the aboriginal owners on the question of inclusion of their land within this nomination has not yet been formally presented." However, IUCN considered this as a "secondary issue" and recommended that the nomination should nevertheless be approved:

"...it is the opinion of IUCN that the nomination should be approved and that the management authority proceed with its work to institute an effective management regime for the site. Secondary issues such as... aboriginal lands can subsequently be addressed through the detailed management planning process set to begin once the site has been inscribed."[14]

The Committee followed the advice of IUCN and, in December 1988, inscribed the area on the World Heritage List, ignoring the concerns about the lack of consultation with traditional owners and merely recommending "that an appropriate management regime be established".[15]

The 1980s saw the establishment of a number of Aboriginal representative bodies within the region: the statutory Aboriginal community councils in Yarrabah, Wujal Wujal and Palm Island; the Cape York, North Queensland and Central Queensland Aboriginal Land Councils; and then, with the establishment of the Commonwealth Aboriginal and Torres Strait Islander Commission (ATSIC) in 1988, three ATSIC regional councils (Cape York, Cairns and District, and Townsville).[16] Funding through the ATSIC regional councils also enabled a number of smaller Traditional Owner-based community organisations to be established during the 1990s. All these bodies relied on federal and/or state grants for their existence and to carry out their functions. When the federal government abolished ATSIC in 2005 and mainstreamed its funding responsibilities, many of these small community-based Indigenous organisations folded, and the Rainforest Aboriginal peoples' voice was seriously compromised. In addition to the Aboriginal representative bodies, there were also federal and state government ministries and departments with responsibilities for Indigenous affairs, as well as sections within other government agencies with responsibilities for Indigenous health, housing, education, employment and training, the protection of Indigenous cultural heritage, the funding and promotion of Indigenous arts, and the issuing of permits for traditional hunting.

---

13 In June 1988, a large delegation of the Queensland Government, including two Aboriginal representatives, travelled to Paris to bring their opposition to the World Heritage listing to the attention of the Bureau of the World Heritage Committee (WTMA 2007). According to Brennan (1988), IUCN and the Bureau "were not happy at the idea of including Aboriginal land unless the owners were involved in and fully endorsed the aims of the Convention in their area as at Uluru and Kakadu". The Bureau "requested the Australian authorities to provide clarifications and further information on... land ownership by Aboriginal peoples..." before the 12th session of the Committee, at which the decision regarding the listing of the Wet Tropics was to be taken (UNESCO 1988, p. 4).
14 IUCN 1988, pp. 11, 13.
15 UNESCO 1988b, p. 14.
16 Initially there were four: Yarrabah and Palm Island had their own ATSIC Regional Council, but it was decided in the mid-1990s that it should be disbanded in favour of Yarrabah amalgamating with the Cairns and District Regional Council and Palm Island becoming part of the Townsville Regional Council.

Yidinji rangers on Lake Morris within the Wet Tropics World Heritage Area. Photo: Jenny Lynch

The current Rainforest Aboriginal population with direct connections to the WHA is about 20,000, while the total population of the Wet Tropics Bioregion (including Indigenous people with no traditional connection to the WHA) is around 260,000. About a third of the Rainforest Aboriginal population lives in the DOGIT communities of Yarrabah and Wujal Wujal, and former Aboriginal reserve communities at Mossman Gorge, Murray Upper, and around Kuranda – all within or adjacent to the boundaries of the WHA. These are the communities that are generally most directly impacted by the WHA. The bulk of the Rainforest Aboriginal population, however, live in the two regional cities of Cairns and Townsville and in the smaller rural townships of Mossman, Gordonvale, Babinda, Mareeba, Innisfail, Tully, Malanda, Ravenshoe, Millaa Millaa, Cardwell and Ingham. Cairns, with its international airport, is the major tourist hub for the region, providing easy access to prime tourist sites within the northern and central sections of the WHA, such as Mossman Gorge, the Daintree and Barron Gorge.

In the DOGIT communities unemployment is high, often around 70-80% of the able-bodied work-force, and most of the jobs that are there are provided through the community councils. Welfare-dependency is very high, with most families and individuals relying on various forms of social security benefits. Lacking a viable rate base, their local community councils rely heavily on state and federal funds to carry out their day-to-day responsibilities. A major source of funds for over 20 years has been the federal government's Community Development Employment Program

(CDEP) – essentially a 'work-for-the-dole' scheme – which generally enabled councils to employ community residents to undertake community maintenance and infrastructure work, and operate such services as the community ranger programs.[17] CDEP was also available to regional Rainforest Aboriginal community organisations operating in local towns, enabling Traditional Owner groups to fund caring for country activities within the WHA, and on adjacent tribal lands. In a move aimed at lessening welfare-dependency by forcing Aboriginal people to look for work, the federal government no longer made CDEP available within the region in 2008, and consequently ranger and caring for country activities were initially severely curtailed. However, realising the importance of such programs, funds became available under the federal government's new 'Caring for Country' initiative.

In the years leading up to World Heritage listing, and using the (developing) *Draft United Nations Declaration on the Rights of Indigenous Peoples* as a reference point, the focus of Rainforest Aboriginal peoples' concerns was primarily on the recognition of cultural values, access to and protection of sacred and other sites of significance, access to flora and fauna for traditional purposes, protection of intellectual and cultural property, involvement in decision-making and on-ground management, creating employment, and community ranger and training programs. While these earlier concerns still remained on their agenda, from the mid-1990s, particularly after the passage of the *Aboriginal Land Act 1991* (Qld) and the *Native Title Act 1993* (Cwth), reaching agreement about tenure, land use and management regimes has become the key focus for Rainforest Aboriginal people in their struggle to maintain the vitality of their cultural values and to achieve social and economic benefits from their traditional lands.

Spiritual	Ecological	Social	Economic
- creations stories	- bush tucker (animals and plants)	- language	- hunting and gathering
- sacred sites		- living areas and camps	- tools
- burial grounds	- bush medicine		- food preparation
- bora grounds	- knowledge of ecological relationships	- walking tracks	- shelter building
- ceremony		- kinship systems	- harvesting resources
- responsibility for country	- fire management	- clans	- art and craft
- totems	- seasonal calendar	- cultural identity	
		- traditional law	

Figure 1: Some Rainforest Aboriginal cultural values relating to land use in the WHA[18]

---

17 These community ranger services work in conjunction with Queensland Parks and Wildlife Service (QPWS), the Great Barrier Reef Marine Park Authority and the Department of Primary Industry & Fisheries, but their jurisdiction is limited to their DOGIT lands and they have no powers of enforcement. They perform important work with regard to issuing hunting permits for dugong and turtle to community members, monitoring hunting activities, supervising traditional forest management activities such as seasonal burning, and carrying out weed and invasive species control.
18 WTMA 2005b, p. 88. See also Leo et al. 2011.

Governance of the WTWHA

The Wet Tropics of Queensland was inscribed on the World Heritage list on 9 December 1988 as a property that fulfilled all four criteria regarding natural values. The broad structural and funding arrangements for the management of the WHA are set out in the Wet Tropics World Heritage Area Management Scheme, an intergovernmental agreement signed by the Prime Minister and Premier of Queensland in 1990.[19] The *Wet Tropics World Heritage Protection and Management Act 1993* (Qld) (herein 'the Queensland Act') was proclaimed on 1 November 1993 and the *Wet Tropics of Queensland World Heritage Area Conservation Act 1994* (Cwth) (herein 'the Commonwealth Act') on 15 March 1994. The intergovernmental agreement is scheduled in the Queensland Act and given effect by section 3 of the Commonwealth Act. The Commonwealth Act provides the legal basis for the Australian Government to meet its obligations under the World Heritage Convention.

The special association of Rainforest Aboriginal people with the land in the WHA is recognised in both the Queensland and Commonwealth Acts. The preamble to the Queensland Act states: "It is also the intention of the Parliament to acknowledge the significant contribution Aboriginal people can make to the future management of cultural and natural heritage within the Area, particularly through joint management agreements".

The Queensland Act provides the legal basis for the *Wet Tropics Management Plan 1998* which regulates land-use activities in the WHA through a zoning and permit system. The implementation of the plan is the primary responsibility of the Wet Tropics Management Authority.

The Wet Tropics Management Authority (WTMA)

WTMA, which has managed the area since 1991 as a partnership between the Commonwealth and Queensland governments, was set up to ensure that Australia's obligations under the World Heritage Convention are met in relation to the WHA. The Authority is a body corporate, with statutory powers defined under the Queensland Act. WTMA's functions, as defined under section 10 of the Queensland Act, are, inter alia, to:

- develop and implement policies and programs for the management of the Wet Tropics Area, including management plans;
- facilitate and enter into Cooperative Management Agreements;
- rehabilitate and restore the Area;
- develop public and community education programs;

---

19 Commonwealth and Queensland Ministers revised the agreement in 1995 with a second review initiated in late 2005. This review took place in the context of an examination of governance and funding arrangements for all Queensland World Heritage properties.

- liaise with the Queensland and Australian Governments, agencies and international organisations;
- monitor the state of the Area; and
- advise and report to the Minister and the Ministerial Council on the state of the Area.

In performing its functions, the Authority "must, as far as practicable – (a) have regard to the Aboriginal tradition of Aboriginal people particularly concerned with land in the wet tropics area; and (b) liaise, and cooperate with, Aboriginal people particularly concerned with land in the wet tropics area" (section 10, para. 5).[20]

The Authority is a small organisation that works in partnership with other agencies and stakeholder interest groups. It has produced a range of strategic policy and planning documents which guide management of the WHA, consistent with its statutory responsibilities, such as the *Wet Tropics Conservation Strategy (2004)*.[21]

Management structure

The intergovernmental agreement provides for a Wet Tropics Ministerial Council comprising two Commonwealth and two Queensland Government Ministers. Its function is to coordinate policy and funding for the WHA between the Commonwealth Government and the Queensland Government. The Queensland Minister for Environment chairs the Council.

The Board of Directors of the WTMA is set up under the Queensland Act and originally consisted of six directors: the Executive Director of the WTMA (as a non-voting board member), two directors appointed by the Commonwealth Government, two directors appointed by the Queensland Government, and a chairperson appointed by the Ministerial Council. According to the Commonwealth Act (Section 6), the Minister may, on behalf of the Commonwealth, make nominations of members to the WTMA Board, such nominees "must include... one or more Aboriginal representatives who have appropriate knowledge of, and experience in, the protection of cultural and natural heritage."

Indigenous representation on the Board, subject to the Commonwealth Minister's discretion,[22] was thus guaranteed from the beginning, and Board meetings since 1994 have generally included one Indigenous representative nominated by the Commonwealth Government.[23]

---

20 Aboriginal people are "particularly concerned with land", according to section 5 of the Act, "if – (a) they are members of a group that has a particular connection with the land under Aboriginal tradition; or (b) they live on or use the land or neighbouring land".
21 WTMA and QPWS 2004.
22 The distinction between the words 'may' and 'must' has proved critical in the exercise of Ministerial powers with regard to the WTWHA.
23 Initially there were a couple of occasions when the Commonwealth Minister failed to make such nominations in time for WTMA Board meetings. His nominees during the first few years were also Aboriginal people from outside the region and with little involvement in the issues affecting the Rainforest Peoples at the time – hence their agitation for the review.

However, in 1998 a review of Aboriginal involvement in the management of the WHA (see below) found that "Rainforest Aboriginal people feel alienated from the nomination process and wish to be actively involved in deciding the Commonwealth's nominee". It was recommended that "WTWHA Rainforest people be requested through a peak representative body... to provide the Commonwealth with a nominee or set of nominees to take up the position", in a manner that is "transparent, open and accountable to Rainforest Aboriginal people." The review also noted that Rainforest Aboriginal peoples "wish to see a second Aboriginal representative on the Board".[24]

These aspirations were realized following the *Wet Tropics World Heritage Area Regional Agreement* negotiated in 2005 (herein 'the Wet Tropics Regional Agreement') (see below). A seventh director was added to the Board, who must be an "Aboriginal person... particularly concerned with land in the wet tropics area" and is appointed on the nomination of the Ministerial Council (Section 14, Queensland Act). Additionally, a statutory advisory committee of the WTMA, the Rainforest Aboriginal Advisory Committee (RAAC), was established to represent the views of Aboriginal peoples within the World Heritage Area, to "enhance the meaningful and beneficial participation of Rainforest Aboriginal people in management of the WTWHA" and to "form the basis for cooperative management of the WTWHA".[25] State and Commonwealth are required to consult with the advisory committee regarding the selection and appointment process of Aboriginal people as Board directors and to seek its advice on the appropriate Aboriginal people to assist in recruitment processes, which have to be open, transparent and accountable.[26]

WTMA itself is a unit within the Queensland Government's environment portfolio and is accountable to the Director-General of the Queensland Environment Protection Agency. WTMA is responsible to the Director-General regarding compliance with state government administrative and financial standards and, as part of the Queensland public sector, it is also subject to established public sector legislation, regulations, standards and guidelines governing administrative functions and arrangements.

WTMA began with two statutory committees appointed by the Board under the Queensland Act, the Scientific Advisory Committee and the Community Consultative Committee, to advise the Authority on its research, policies and programs. Under the processes leading up to the signing of the Wet Tropics Regional Agreement, a third – the Rainforest Aboriginal Advisory Committee – was added in 2004. However, at the request of its members, this committee was disbanded in 2011 in favour of establishing a new body, the Rainforest Aboriginal Peoples Alliance (see below).

WTMA also supports two liaison groups, the Conservation Sector Liaison Group and the Tourism Industry Liaison Group. Liaison Groups are chaired by a Board director and meet quarterly prior to Board meetings, thus providing a valuable two-way information exchange about important and emerging conservation and tourism issues. Currently both Liaison Groups (each with 19 members) have two members representing Rainforest Aboriginal organisations.[27]

---

24 Review Steering Committee 1998, pp. 67-68.
25 Wet Tropics Regional Agreement, Section 4.2.4.
26 Ibid., Section 4.2.6.
27 WTMA 2011a, pp. 18-19.

While the Authority is the lead agency responsible for policy, planning, developing standards and the co-ordination of on-the-ground management activities in the WHA, it is not responsible for day-to-day operational issues such as infrastructure construction and maintenance, or pest and weed control. These are the responsibility of the respective land managers, which include the Queensland Parks and Wildlife Service (QPWS), local government authorities (including the Yarrabah and Wujal Wujal Aboriginal shire councils), the Queensland Departments responsible for the environment, natural resources and mines, and relevant infrastructure service providers for power, water and roads.

A Principal Agencies Forum meets every six weeks to ensure that management activities are coordinated between WTMA, QPWS and the Queensland Department of Environment and Resource Management. To prioritise and coordinate management activities in the protected area estate within the WHA, a Service Agreement is developed each year between the Authority and QPWS. The Service Agreement outlines products and services to be delivered by QPWS under funding provided by the Queensland Government for WHA management.[28]

In addition to WTMA, many of the mainstream management and research agencies that are involved in some way with Aboriginal affairs in the Wet Tropics Bioregion/WTWHA, such as Far North Queensland Natural Resources Management Ltd (FNQNRM Ltd) and the Rainforest Cooperative Research Centre (Rainforest CRC) based at James Cook University, also have special Indigenous units and advisory bodies within their organisation and employ Aboriginal people.

Rainforest Aboriginal inclusion in the WTMA administrative structure

From the mid-1990s, as part of its administrative structure, WTMA maintained the Aboriginal Resource Management program, which was responsible for Aboriginal community liaison, policy and protocol development, cultural heritage management and the implementation of the Wet Tropics Regional Agreement (see below). Over the years, the program has worked closely with peak Rainforest Aboriginal bodies such as the Rainforest Aboriginal Network, Bama Wabu, the Aboriginal Rainforest Council and now the Rainforest Aboriginal Peoples Alliance, and with native title holders and the three land councils (as native title representative bodies). It has also worked closely with the Indigenous Coordination Centre (for Commonwealth Government departments), which has replaced the ATSIC Regional Councils, Aboriginal local governments at Yarrabah and Wujal Wujal, local Aboriginal corporations, and other bodies dealing with Rainforest Aboriginal matters, such as negotiating teams, and reference and working groups.

The program usually worked through a staff of five: a manager, project officer and three Aboriginal Community Liaison Officers (ACLOs) assigned to the northern, central and southern regions of the WHA. The ACLOs, however, are usually employees of the North Queensland Aboriginal Land Council and the Girringun Aboriginal Corporation and are contracted to WTMA to provide liaison services. Employment of the ACLOs as permanent staff of WTMA has been an

---

28 WTMA 2005, pp. 14-15.

ongoing issue with Rainforest Aboriginal organisations since the program's inception. The ACLOs play a vital role in engaging Rainforest Aboriginal peoples in WHA management. Their key objectives are to inform Rainforest Aboriginal peoples and their peak organisation about WTMA's role and processes, to inform WTMA about Rainforest Aboriginal views and to raise community awareness of Rainforest Aboriginal peoples' aspirations regarding management of the WHA.

More recently, in line with the Queensland Government's general policy across all departments on Indigenous engagement through the establishment of partnerships with Aboriginal and Torres Strait islander communities and organisations, WTMA ended the Aboriginal Resource Management Program as a separate management entity in favour of redefining its role in relation to the Rainforest Aboriginal peoples. To this end, it created two projects within the newly established Communities and Partnerships Program. The Program includes four main projects:

- Community Engagement;
- Indigenous Partnerships;
- Eastern Kuku Yalanji Indigenous Land Use Agreement Implementation; and
- Tourism and Visitor Services.[29]

The Indigenous Partnerships project has involved, inter alia, a review of the Rainforest Aboriginal Advisory Committee (RAAC) (completed in March 2011), which led to the request by the RAAC members to the WTMA Board of Directors to dissolve in favour of establishing the Rainforest Aboriginal Peoples' Alliance (RAPA); supporting the establishment of RAPA; support for the Australian World Heritage Indigenous Network (see below); production and distribution of the 12th edition of *Rainforest Aboriginal News*; liaising with native title holders in the development of Indigenous Land Use Agreements (ILUAS – see below) that involve lands within the WTWHA; and carrying out community liaison work with regional Aboriginal organisations, the land councils and relevant government agencies.[30]

In 2007, the Eastern Kuku Yalanji had their native title recognised over 230,000 ha in the northern sector of the WTWHA. A suite of 15 Indigenous Land Use Agreements established a cooperative approach to land ownership, use and management and community development involving WTMA, QPWS, relevant local governments (the Cairns Regional Council and the Cook Shire Council) and other land-holders and government agencies. The core objective of this project is the protection of World Heritage values and Yalanji peoples' improved well-being and sustainable livelihoods through the establishment of environmentally, culturally, socially and economically sustainable Community Development Plans and Activity Guidelines. These will assist Yalanji people to move back onto and care for country in a sustainable fashion in accordance with their Native Title rights and interests.[31] An important part of the implementation of the Yalanji ILUAs is WTMA's engagement of local government planning scheme experts to

---

29 WTMA 2011a, p. 35.
30 Ibid., p. 38.
31 Ibid., p. 39-40.

assist in developing master plans to inform the development of a *Bush Living Code* or other mechanism to incorporate Aboriginal Community Development Plans into Local Government planning schemes. It is envisaged that these outcomes may also assist in framing a broader *Bush Living Code* for Aboriginal Land to be adopted as State Planning Policy.[32]

Current situation: Rainforest Aboriginal peoples and governance of the WHA

At the time of nomination, Rainforest Aboriginal groups generally opposed the proposed WHA on several grounds, including: lack of consultation; failure to recognise the Aboriginal cultural values in the nomination; major concerns over access to native flora and fauna for food and other cultural purposes; access to and protection of sacred and other significant sites; and failure to provide for statutory involvement of Rainforest Aboriginal peoples in the administration, planning and management of the WHA. In the early years following listing in December 1988, Rainforest Aboriginal issues were generally addressed through the advocacy of the Rainforest Aboriginal Network (RAN). RAN, a volunteer organisation, was formed to lobby federal and state governments and other WHA stakeholders (e.g., the tourism industry, academic institutions) during the legislative drafting process to ensure that the concerns and interests of Rainforest Aboriginal peoples were not overlooked either within the administrative structures or in the management of the WHA. RAN was successful in lobbying for statutory representation on the WTMA Board of Directors (via the Commonwealth Act) and for having Rainforest Aboriginal representation on the Scientific Advisory and Community Consultative Committees. It also lobbied for an all-Rainforest Aboriginal committee of the Board to be established. RAN convened important meetings and conferences, such as the Julayinbul Conference on Aboriginal Intellectual and Cultural Property in the Daintree in 1993.[33] Its members also carried out important research, particularly regarding regional agreement and co-management models between Indigenous peoples and mainstream authorities over protected areas and pushed for a review of Indigenous involvement in the WTWHA. In 1992, when the World Heritage Convention provided for inclusion of cultural landscapes of outstanding universal value within the World Heritage list, RAN began the long and arduous process of presenting the case for re-listing the WTWHA as a cultural landscape to properly take account of the Rainforest cultural values of the WHA.[34]

In the mid-1990s, RAN decided to disband as many in the Rainforest Aboriginal community felt that a new organisation that was incorporated and therefore eligible to receive funding from ATSIC and other agencies would better serve their interests. The Rainforest Bama Aboriginal Corporation – known as Bama Wabu – was therefore formed in 1996 as the peak organisation to represent the 18 Rainforest Aboriginal communities to deal with Indigenous matters in the WHA. Bama Wabu also played a coordinating role between the other peak Indigenous bodies representing Indigenous interests in the WHA (the three land councils, the DOGIT community

---

32 Ibid.
33 Rainforest Aboriginal Network 1993.
34 Fourmile, Schnierer and Smith 1995.

councils, and the ATSIC regional councils) and generally represented them in dealing with WTMA and other government departments with management responsibilities within the WHA as well as with other stakeholder groups. Bama Wabu was able to liaise directly with WTMA, oversee the review process (see below), provide input into the drafting of the statutory WTWHA Management Plan, and begin the important task of drafting a regional agreement between WTMA and the Rainforest Aboriginal peoples until this responsibility was taken over by the Aboriginal Negotiating Team within the Interim Negotiating Forum process initiated in 2001 (see below).

Review of Aboriginal involvement in the management of the Wet Tropics World Heritage Area

After continuous lobbying by Rainforest Aboriginal peoples, through RAN and other avenues, a review of Aboriginal involvement in the management of the WTWHA was commissioned by the Wet Tropics Ministerial Council in 1995. Work on the Review started in 1996 and was completed in April 1998. An all-Aboriginal Steering Committee guided the Review process. The Review was entitled *Which Way Our Cultural Survival?* to reflect the views of Rainforest Aboriginal peoples that their cultures were likely to be threatened unless changes to the management of the WHA could be achieved.[35]

The Review:

- identified that Rainforest Aboriginal peoples were very passionate about meeting their land management and religious obligations as defined under traditional lore and custom;
- presented a commentary on current approaches to Aboriginal involvement in the WTWHA;
- identified issues of concern to Aboriginal peoples in the way the WTWHA was being managed;
- provided a series of recommendations regarding ways of more effectively meeting land management needs and the rights and aspirations of Rainforest Aboriginal peoples;
- focused on various tenures within the WTWHA which were managed by QPWS and WTMA.[36]

A key recommendation of the Review was the negotiation of a Wet Tropics Regional Agreement between Rainforest Aboriginal peoples from throughout the WHA, on the one hand, and WTMA and the other government departments primarily responsible for managing the WHA, on the other. Such an agreement was seen as the best way to resolve all the issues highlighted in the Review. The Wet Tropics Ministerial Council agreed with a key recommendation to establish an Interim Negotiating Forum to facilitate the regional agreement process and to negotiate solutions to difficult management issues identified in the Review.

---

35 Aboriginal Negotiating Team Secretariat 2003.
36 Review Steering Committee 1998.

The Interim Negotiating Forum process comprised an Aboriginal Negotiating Team and a Government Negotiating Team. The Aboriginal Negotiating Team membership included four representatives of Rainforest Aboriginal communities: one representative each from the three land councils and one representative from the Queensland Indigenous Working Group (established to provide input into the drafting of a new Aboriginal Cultural Heritage Act). The Government Negotiating Team's membership comprised one representative each from WTMA, Environment Australia, QPWS, the Queensland Department of Natural Resources and Mines, and the Queensland Department of the Premier and Cabinet. The Wet Tropics Ministerial Council also appointed a 'high profile' independent facilitator to ensure that the negotiations would be fair and that the process moved towards meaningful and equitable outcomes for all parties. The purpose of the Interim Negotiating Forum was to:

- Set up a negotiating process. Set a time limit for how long the final Wet Tropics Regional Agreement would take to get finished. Set rules for the two negotiating teams to follow to make sure that the negotiations were fair and would not get bogged down.
- Find answers to the management issues identified by the Review by clarifying and resolving specific issues for potential legislative, policy and administrative change (e.g. protecting culture, fire management, managing permits, building tourist ventures, employment and training) in such a way that would meet the needs of the parties.
- Put in place a short term way of fixing up management and cultural heritage problems that would fill the gap until the final Agreement was developed.
- Develop the final Wet Tropics Regional Agreement for government agencies and Rainforest Aboriginal peoples to sign. This agreement would specify the mechanisms and guidelines on how Aboriginal peoples and government will work together to cooperatively manage the WTWHA.

The key issues discussed within the Interim Negotiating Forum were:

1. Recognition of cultural values;
2. Native Title and WTWHA management;
3. Aboriginal involvement in developing policy, planning and management;
4. The development of meaningful management agreements;
5. Traditional natural resource use and the use of traditional ecological knowledge.[37]

The Wet Tropics World Heritage Area Regional Agreement 2005

The Interim Negotiating Forum process between Rainforest Aboriginal and WHA Government representatives was completed in June 2004. The process resulted in the *Wet Tropics World*

---

37 Aboriginal Negotiating Team Secretariat 2003.

Heritage Area Regional Agreement 2005 between the 18 Rainforest Aboriginal tribal groups and the Queensland and Commonwealth Government WHA management agencies.[38] This agreement was endorsed by the Ministerial Council in September 2004 and signed by Elders representing all the tribal groups, Ministers representing the Commonwealth and Queensland Governments, and the Chairperson of WTMA's Board of Directors at Innisfail in April 2005. The Agreement sets out principles, guidelines and protocols for the meaningful involvement of Aboriginal peoples in the management of the WTWHA. Key outcomes of the Wet Tropics Regional Agreement included:

- the establishment of the Aboriginal Rainforest Council, recognised by WTWHA management agencies as the peak organisation for land and cultural heritage matters in the WHA, including its recognition as a statutory advisory committee to the WTMA Board;
- support to seek listing of the WHA on the National Heritage List, for both its cultural and natural values, as a precursor to potential nomination of cultural values for World Heritage listing;
- the appointment of a second Aboriginal Board Director to the Wet Tropics Management Authority;
- the development of detailed protocols and guidelines outlining how Rainforest Aboriginal peoples are to be involved in the range of management activities, using such instruments as Management Agreements,[39] Cooperative Management Agreements[40] and Indigenous Land Use Agreements (ILUAs);
- support for improved training and employment opportunities for Rainforest Aboriginal people;
- support for long term contracts for the Authority's ACLOs; and
- recognition and protection of intellectual and cultural property rights and involvement in research.

The Regional Agreement reconfirms the WTMA's statutory obligations and commitment to cooperatively manage the WHA with Rainforest Aboriginal peoples. Implementation of the Agreement began with the establishment of the Aboriginal Rainforest Council (ARC) in September 2004. The WTMA Board then established the Rainforest Aboriginal Advisory Committee (RAAC)

---

38 WTMA 2005a.
39 A Management Agreement (MA) is a voluntary, negotiated, cooperative agreement under s.42 of the Wet Tropics Management Plan 1998 between Aboriginal people, land-holders and WTMA for carrying out activities in the WTWHA which are normally prohibited under the Wet Tropics Management Plan 1998. This usually entails an amendment to the application of the Wet Tropics Management Plan, and must also contribute to the primary goal of the WTWHA (Wet Tropics Regional Agreement 2005).
40 A Cooperative Management Agreement (CMA) is a voluntary agreement under s.41 of the Wet Tropics Management Plan 1998 between the WTMA and the land-holder or land manager, setting out how a piece of land on or neighbouring the WTWHA should be managed. This usually entails an amendment to the application of the Wet Tropics Management Plan. However, it must also contribute towards the primary goal of the WTWHA (Wet Tropics Regional Agreement 2005).

in November 2004. The ARC functioned as the peak body for Rainforest Aboriginal involvement in land and cultural heritage matters in the WHA, while the RAAC dealt with issues specific to WTMA. Each of the 18 Rainforest Aboriginal peoples with a connection to country within the WHA nominated a member for appointment by the Board. The membership of the ARC and the RAAC was the same.

While the ARC was shortly thereafter disbanded, the RAAC continued for 6 years. In 2011 its members decided to recommend to the WTMA Board that it be dissolved in favour of establishing the Rainforest Aboriginal People's Alliance (RAPA).[41] The Alliance is an incorporated peak Indigenous body for land and sea management in the Wet Tropics under a skills-based Board with membership including sub-regional and local level Aboriginal cultural and natural resource management organisations. RAPA is seeking to provide greater efficiencies in service delivery and more effective streamlined governance to matters that require a strategic voice in the Wet Tropics, including advising the WTMA Board on Rainforest Aboriginal cultural issues.[42]

The decision to dissolve RAAC and establish RAPA highlights the difficulties for Rainforest Aboriginal peoples in finding a workable model for an effective peak body to represent their interests. For over 15 years, the members of RAN, Bama Wabu and then ARC argued strongly for a statutory Aboriginal committee such as RAAC to be established because statutory committees are guaranteed the secretariat services and financial support of the WTMA and the outcomes of their meetings tabled at meetings of the WTMA Board of Directors. RAAC had an important statutory function regarding the selection and appointment of Aboriginal people as Board Directors.[43] It also had an important role in nominating Aboriginal people to represent the Rainforest Aboriginal community on both the Scientific Advisory and the Community Consultative Committees, and the Conservation Sector Liaison and the Tourism Industry Liaison Groups. RAPA has sacrificed this statutory status for an uncertain future in which funding and other kinds of support are not guaranteed. While the WTMA has a statutory obligation "to liaise and cooperate with Aboriginal people particularly concerned with land in the wet tropics area",[44] it no longer has to give the same weight to the advice of RAPA as it would have had to RAAC. Nevertheless, the WTMA provided financial and in-kind resources, including executive support, to Rainforest Aboriginal peoples in their aspirations to establish RAPA.[45] In commenting on the disbanding of RAAC, the WTMA Chair stressed that "this in no way represents any reduction in commitment to the effective engagement of Rainforest Aboriginal people in the management of the Wet Tropics World Heritage Area".[46]

---

41   This decision was related in part to difficulties in achieving adequate representation from all the involved tribal and clan groups.With each tribal group comprising between 3 to 5 clans, a fully representative body would contain over 70 members, which is unworkable. RAPA, like its predecessors, Bama Wabu and ARC/RAAC, is trying to address this issue by finding a way to provide adequate representation.
42   Rainforest Aboriginal News 2011, p. 4; WTMA 2011a, pp. 18, 37.
43   Section 4.2.6 of the Wet Tropics Regional Agreement.
44   Section 10, para. 5 of the Queensland Act.
45   WTMA 2011a, p. 37.
46   Ibid., p. 9.

Millstream Falls on the Atherton Tablelands near Ravenshoe. Photo: Rob and Stephanie Levy (CC BY 2.0)

Wet Tropics Aboriginal Cultural and Natural Resource Management Plan (FNQNRM Ltd and Rainforest CRC)

Recognising the limitation of the Wet Tropics Regional Agreement, in that it only effectively applies to the WTWHA, the Rainforest Aboriginal peoples have sought to create a plan that could be applied to manage activities over the whole of their traditional estates within the Wet Tropics Bioregion, including their 'sea country', much of which falls within the adjacent sections of the Great Barrier Reef Marine Park / World Heritage Area. The Aboriginal Traditional Owners of the Wet Tropics Area, with the support of the FNQNRM Ltd's Indigenous Technical Support Group (ITSG), therefore decided that they would develop their own plan for looking after country to address the reality that, while the reef and rainforest World Heritage Areas generate enormous wealth for non-Aboriginal people in Far North Queensland, many Traditional Owners live in poverty. The resulting *Wet Tropics Aboriginal Cultural and Natural Resource Management Plan*, based on sound cultural and natural resource management strategies, is one avenue for addressing the economic, social and cultural issues that Rainforest Aboriginal peoples face on a daily basis.[47]

The plan provides a comprehensive and detailed set of guidelines and blueprints covering a number of different enterprises (tourism, fisheries and aquaculture, forestry, etc.). In the context of managing the WTWHA, the Wet Tropics Regional Agreement could be considered as a

---

47 Foley in Wet Tropics Aboriginal Plan Project Team 2005, p. 5.

framework agreement within which the more detailed elements of the *Wet Tropics Aboriginal Cultural and Natural Resource Management Plan* can be exercised.

Native title and other land tenure issues

The WTWHA includes within its 3,125 km boundary over 700 separate parcels of land under a variety of land tenures: National Park (32%), Forest Reserve (29%), State Forest (10%), Timber Reserve (7%), Unallocated State Land (7%), Freehold and Leasehold (2%), various reserves and dams (1%) and rivers, roads and esplanades (1%). Included also are the DOGIT lands of Yarrabah and Wujal Wujal, and Aboriginal community lands at Mossman Gorge and Mona Mona. A corresponding range of government agencies and private land-holders have responsibilities for managing these tenures under an extraordinary range of legislative arrangements, including leasehold, freehold, protected areas, mining leases, local government lands, recreational reserves, DOGIT, Aboriginal Land Act holding and coastal and marine areas – all of which Aboriginal Traditional Owners must negotiate. Although World Heritage listing does not affect land ownership,[48] the *Wet Tropics Management Plan 1998* does regulate activities in the WHA across all tenures.[49]

The *Aboriginal Land Act 1991* (Qld) (herein 'the ALA')[50] has enabled Aboriginal people by virtue of either traditional or historical association, to claim back areas of state-owned land that had been set aside, for example, on the fringes of many townships to enable them to establish housing and community facilities, and establish businesses. Successfully claimed areas are generally referred to as ALA freehold. In 1993, the federal government passed the *Native Title Act 1993* (Cwth) that, inter alia, established a claim process by which Traditional Owners could seek recognition of their native title over traditional lands that had not been alienated by a prior government act (such as making land available for acquisition under freehold title). As more than half of the Wet Tropics Bioregion had already been effectively alienated as freehold land, the only significant areas of claimable land remaining were within the WTWHA, where it was estimated that at least 80% of the land was potentially claimable.[51]

Native title rights have been recognised by the government as existing in two forms: exclusive and non-exclusive. The former enable the holders to exclusively occupy, possess and use the lands over which their native title has been determined by the Federal Court to exist. Non-exclusive rights enable the native title holder(s) to exercise a bundle of rights on lands owned by

---

48 See Art. 6 of the World Heritage Convention.
49 WTMA 2005b, pp. 62-63.
50 The ALA recognises both traditional and historical associations as a basis for claiming back land under the Act. The Act recognises that, in the past, Aboriginal people were forcibly removed from their traditional lands and placed on specially created reserves, thereby creating historical associations that were not necessarily traditional. In 1938, while conducting the Adelaide – Harvard Universities Anthropological Expedition 1938-1939, Norman Tindale and Joseph Birdsell found representatives of 48 different tribes in Yarrabah. On Palm Island, there were 60 tribes represented (Tindale and Birdsell 1941).
51 WTMA 2005b, p. 88.

someone else, usually the government in the form of national parks, state forests and timber reserves – hence the reason why so much of the WHA is potentially claimable under native title. Such rights, which are usually exercised through an Indigenous Land Use Agreement (ILUA)[52] with the land owner(s) and other stakeholders, and depending on the determination, may include rights to access, camp, hunt, gather, fish, conduct ceremonies, tend sites, exercise management responsibilities, be buried, and be included in any decisions and decision-making processes affecting their native title lands.

Native Title

'Native Title' refers to the recognition in Australian law that Aboriginal and Torres Strait Islander peoples had systems of law and land ownership before European settlement. Under the *Native Title Act 1993* (Cwth) native title comprises the rights and interests in relation to land or waters (that are capable of recognition by the common law) possessed by Aboriginal and Torres Strait Islander people under their traditional laws/lores and customs. Native title rights and interests are vulnerable to extinguishment and may no longer exist because of competing interests that have been validly created in the land. The native title rights and interests of a particular Traditional Owner group will depend on the traditional laws and customs of those people. In determination of Native Title, the way that native title rights are recognised may vary from group to group depending on what native title rights continue to exist and also the negotiated outcomes between all of the people and organisations that claim an interest in that area. In Aboriginal customary law/lore, people with rights to use land and natural resources also have corresponding obligations and responsibilities for caring for country. Thus traditional land ownership and existing native title rights and interests frequently have a close relationship with management of natural resources. Native title may exist in areas such as unallocated state land (vacant crown land), national parks, forests, public reserves, pastoral leases, land held for the benefit of Aboriginal people, beaches, oceans, seas, reefs, lakes, rivers, creeks, swamps and other waters. Native title holders have a right to continue to practice their law/lore and customs. These rights and interests can include: accessing Country, hunting, gathering, collecting, visiting Country to protect important places and making decisions about the future use of their land or waters.[53]

Box 1 : Native Title

---

52 An ILUA is a voluntary agreement made between one or more native title groups and other groups such as miners, pastoralists or governments. ILUAs can be made with regard to the use and management of an area of land or water. An ILUA may be entered into as part of a native title determination or can be made independently of a native title application. A registered ILUA is legally-binding on the native title holders and all parties to the Agreement (Wet Tropics Aboriginal Plan Project Team 2005, p. 13).
53 Wet Tropics Aboriginal Plan Project Team 2005, p. 14 (referencing information from the National Native Title Tribunal website, www.nntt.gov.au).

The Aboriginal land claims process in Queensland, both under the ALA and the *Native Title Act*, has generally been difficult and at times extremely divisive between peoples, clans, and sometimes within families. It can affect whole communities, as it has done in Yarrabah. The land claims process, as one of the causes of lateral violence in Indigenous communities, has been addressed by the Aboriginal & Torres Strait Islander Social Justice Commissioner in his two recent reports on native title and social justice.[54] Aboriginal people have often likened it to a process whereby "governments give you crumbs, then expect you to fight over them". After several generations of intermarriage between tribes on reserves such as Yarrabah and Palm Island, how can traditional and historical claims be sorted out? Or, after most of the Elders who understand traditional lineages and connections to country have passed on, how can native title claims be settled, or how can the rightful claimants be identified? The process is highly legalistic, with claimants and parties engaging lawyers and anthropologists to prepare their claims and counter claims, can involve many parties (government agencies, utilities, and other land-holders/users with interests in the area subject to claim), and can take a decade or more to reach a determination. The land councils, as statutory native title representative bodies, are supposed to supervise and administer the claims processes, but they can also become seats of Indigenous political power and intrigue. Native title enmities play out in the politics of representation with regard to the creation of organisations such as Bama Wabu, ARC and RAPA whose purpose is to represent, in this case, the interests of Rainforest Aboriginal peoples to WTMA and other government bodies and stakeholder groups. Increasingly, and perhaps more appropriately, government agencies and other organisations are choosing to deal directly with native title holders through such mechanisms as, for example, Indigenous Land Use Agreements.

Favourable native title determinations can become the basis of economic development, enabling holders to proceed with a number of activities, such as establish tourism enterprises, and ranger services to care for country (usually in conjunction with QPWS and WTMA). Protracted native title negotiations have held back such development for many claimants.

Currently there are 16 native title claims that have been lodged with the National Native Title Tribunal for land in the WHA, some of which have been determined.[55] The determinations themselves reflect the differing impacts of colonisation on the Rainforest Aboriginal peoples of the region. In 2007, the Eastern Kuku Yalanji people had their native title recognised to more than 230,000 ha covering most of their traditional estates (although within the Eastern Kuku Yalanji some clans fared better than others) – including exclusive native title rights over some 30,000 ha of unallocated state land. By contrast, the Ngadjon-Jii, also in 2007, had their native title recognised to 13,287 ha of land and waters, with exclusive native title rights only over a 2.4 ha island in the

---

54 Aboriginal & Torres Strait Islander Social Justice Commissioner 2011a; 2011b.
55 Rainforest Aboriginal peoples to have received native title determinations include the Djabugay, Girramay, Dulabed and Malanbarra Yidinji, Jirrbal, Eastern Kuku Yalanji, Ngadjon-Jii, Mandingalbay Yidinji. Some of these determinations only concern the traditional estates of particular clans of the 18 Rainforest Aboriginal tribes. The determinations also involve the signing of ILUAs between the other parties to each claim who have interests in the areas for which native title has been determined. These parties include the Queensland Government, government agencies (such as WTMA and QPWS), power and water utilities, local government(s), and other land-holders/users (see, for example, North Queensland Land Council 2011).

middle of the Russell River. The balance of the determination was over land falling within the WHA for which they could only exercise non-exclusive native title rights.

Following lodgement of a native title claim, and during the native title determination process, ILUAs are the principal instruments by which native title claimants/holders can exercise their rights and responsibilities to use, care for and engage in economic development on their lands which fall within the WTWHA. In addition to the suite of 15 Yalanji ILUAs entered into with WTMA and the State of Queensland mentioned above, a number of other ILUAs have been established with, among others, the Jirrbal, Djiru, Wanyurr Majay (Yidinji), and Gunggandji peoples. These ILUAs aim to appropriately balance World Heritage values with the well-being of Rainforest Aboriginal peoples, their cultural obligations to protect and manage lands, and their aspirations for land use, community development and socio-economic recovery.[56]

The complexity of land tenure regimes both within the WHA and the greater Wet Tropics Bioregion deeply affects Rainforest Aboriginal traditional owners. Even where Rainforest Aboriginal peoples have exclusive native title to traditional lands or have received lands back under ALA freehold title, their access to, use and enjoyment of their lands, including plans for economic development, settlement/occupation, access to significant sites, or establishing their own community ranger programs to care for country, are subject to a mass of laws and regulations, policies, impact assessments, and development and management plans administered by all three tiers of government. This situation afflicts all landowners/leaseholders, Indigenous and non-Indigenous alike, irrespective of whether their lands fall within the WHA. A recent headline in *The Cairns Post*, "Layers of regulations imposed on Indigenous people all over Cape York blocking economic opportunity with intimidating paperwork and costs"[57] aptly sums up the frustrations felt by many Rainforest Aboriginal peoples, who, after fighting for years to get their land back, find they are effectively restricted in what they can do with it.

Recognising the Aboriginal cultural values of the WTWHA

Virtually since the inscription of the remaining Wet Tropical rainforests within the Wet Tropics Bioregion on the World Heritage List in December 1988 for their natural values, the Rainforest Aboriginal peoples have fought for similar recognition of the World Heritage Area's Indigenous cultural values. The already mentioned 1998 Review of Aboriginal involvement in the management of the WTWHA noted:

> "Rainforest Aboriginal people (and, in fact, indigenous Australians generally) see the trend by western managers to manage a region's values according to two distinct categories (i.e. Natural and cultural values) as artificial and inadequate. Rainforest Aboriginal people adopt a holistic view of the landscape, asserting that a region's natural and cultural values are

---

56 WTMA 2011a, p. 38.
57 Beck 2011.

in fact inseparably interwoven within the social, cultural, economic, and legal framework of Bama custom and tradition. They are also concerned at the tendency, particularly at the day-to-day level of management, by western managers to treat cultural heritage considerations as secondary to those afforded to natural values." [58]

In its 2002 Periodic Report on the state of conservation of the WTWHA, the Australian Government therefore wrote:

"Rainforest Aboriginal people have indicated they wish to have the Property recognised as a living cultural landscape. The Aboriginal view is that the natural values and cultural values cannot be separated. Cultural values include the living, continuous traditions of the Aboriginal peoples who are associated with the Wet Tropics. For this reason, Aboriginal people see their involvement in land management as essential to maintaining their culture." [59]

Already in 2000, the Australian Committee of IUCN had reported to the World Heritage Committee that "there is a widely held view that the Aboriginal cultural landscape of the region is undoubtedly of world heritage significance" and recommended "that the area be re-nominated for its cultural values".[60]

As pointed out above, the WTWHA was also listed on the National Heritage List in May 2007 for its natural values. In 2008, after receiving a nomination from the ARC,[61] the Australian Heritage Council began an assessment to consider whether the WTWHA had nationally significant Indigenous heritage values that should be included on the National Heritage List. This process culminated in the amendment of the National Heritage Listing for the Wet Tropics in November 2012 to include the Indigenous heritage values.[62] The listing is widely seen as a precursor to the Australian Government's application for such values to be inscribed on the World Heritage List and vindicates the stance taken by the Rainforest Aboriginal peoples for over two decades. It justifies Rainforest Aboriginal peoples having the same level of protection for their cultural values as afforded to the Area's natural values and therefore a more equitable and integrated role in the overall administration and management of the WHA. It also justifies their obtaining a greater share of resources to carry out their management responsibilities to protect and enhance those values.

---

58 Review Steering Committee 1998, p. 12.
59 Government of Australia 2002, p. 8. The Periodic Report also states: "Although the Property was not listed for its cultural values the area between Cooktown and Cardwell contains the only recognised existing Australian Aboriginal rainforest culture. The oral pre-history of the surviving Aboriginal rainforest culture is the oldest known for any indigenous people without a written language... The Rainforest CRC is presently collating information and undertaking research into whether there is a substantive case for a re-nomination of the Property, in whole or part, on cultural grounds".
60 ACIUCN 2000, pp. 11, 24.
61 Aboriginal Rainforest Council 2007. For a comprehensive account of this process, undertaken by ARC in conjunction with a number of partners, see Hill et al. 2011.
62 See Commonwealth of Australia Gazette notices No. S168 and S169 of 12 November 2012, available at http://www.environment.gov.au/heritage/places/world/wet-tropics/index.html.

The preparation of the nomination was overseen by ARC and its Indigenous Intellectual Property Sub-committee, which guided the nomination process. The preparation of the evidence and documentation required by the listing process, substantially based on cultural mapping projects undertaken by Traditional Owner groups with both philanthropic and government funding support, was also in itself an empowering process. As Hill et al. report:

> "The resultant heritage nomination process empowered community efforts to reverse the loss of biocultural diversity. The conditions that enabled this empowerment included: Rainforest Aboriginal peoples' governance of the process; their shaping of the heritage discourse to incorporate biocultural diversity; and their control of interaction with their knowledge systems to identify the links that have created the region's biocultural diversity." [63]

WTMA is providing on-going support for the listing process, and assistance to the Commonwealth Government for their public consultation to ensure Rainforest Aboriginal peoples are involved in the listing decision and its implication for the WTWHA.[64]

Australia has 17 World Heritage properties, of which 12 have traditional owners involved in their management. Some of these, such as Kakadu National Park, Uluru-Kata Tjuta and the Willandra Lakes Region, have been listed for both their natural and cultural values, while others are listed only for natural values. Regardless of this, traditional owners from all of the 12 World Heritage Areas have formed the Australian World Heritage Indigenous Network (AWHIN) to enable them to share experiences and lobby governments, the World Heritage Committee and its Advisory Bodies, and to network with other similarly placed Indigenous peoples internationally. WTMA has facilitated the involvement of Rainforest Aboriginal peoples in the AWHIN, enabling Wet Tropics Traditional Owners to meet with and develop strategies and ideas with Traditional Owners from other Australian World Heritage Areas. A former Indigenous WTMA Board Director was also successful in being appointed to fill the female Aboriginal position on the Australian World Heritage Advisory Committee.[65]

World Heritage designation and its effects on employment and business opportunities for Rainforest Aboriginal peoples

A main effect that World Heritage listing has had on the Rainforest Aboriginal peoples has been to create economic and employment opportunities, particularly in relation to tourism and hospitality, land care and management, and in administration.

---

63 Hill et al. 2011, pp. 571, 577ff.
64 WTMA 2011a, p. 36.
65 WTMA 2011a, p. 37.

Tourism

In May 2011, an article under the headline "Future of tourism lies in indigenous culture" appeared in *The Cairns Post*.[66] In the article, the Chairman of the Australian Tourism Export Council argued that "As the world becomes more homogenous, people all over the world are going to be looking for authentic experiences which help differentiate one country from another. ... One of the most significant ways we can do this is to bring indigenous culture and experiences to the core of Australia's essential experiences." Tourism is one of the Wet Tropic region's key economic drivers. Nearly 2 million domestic visitors and 1 million international visitors come to the region each year. Tourism is by far the major source of revenue contributing nearly $2 billion[67] to the regional economy. Total visitor expenditure in the WTWHA is estimated to generate around $750 million per year, while that in the adjacent section of the Great Barrier Reef World Heritage Area is $770 million.[68] A more recent study conducted by the Commonwealth Government in 2008 estimated that the WTWHA generates just over $3 billion in annual direct and indirect national output or business turnover within Queensland and supports around 18,000 jobs.[69] However, whilst tourism and recreation are providing significant economic benefits to the region, few benefits flow to traditional owners, despite the fact that their lands and cultures are important for the tourism industry. Aboriginal involvement in the mainstream tourism industry is very limited and there are few Aboriginal tourism enterprises in the region.[70]

Traditional owners of the region have identified tourism as an economic development opportunity, as a vehicle for cultural education and maintenance, and as a means to gain recognition of their culture.[71] Economic opportunities in the tourism industry identified by Traditional Owners include:

- employment;
- training and skills development for young people in the tourism and hospitality industries;
- stand-alone Traditional Owner (TO) cultural tourism enterprises;
- cultural tourism services attached to mainstream and other enterprises; and
- joint ventures between Traditional Owners and mainstream tourism enterprises.

Many Traditional Owners have stressed the importance of Traditional Owners actually owning and operating tourism ventures in the region. Tourism is also seen as a means to achieve cultural and social aspirations such as facilitating Traditional Owners getting back into and maintaining

---

66 Dalton 2011.
67 All amounts are given in Australian dollars (AUD). Currently 1 AUD is roughly equivalent to 1 USD.
68 Wet Tropics Aboriginal Plan Project Team 2005, p. 93.
69 WTMA 2011a, p. 40.
70 Wet Tropics Aboriginal Plan Project Team, 2005, p. 93, citing McDonald and Weston 2004.
71 Wet Tropics Aboriginal Plan Project Team, 2005, p. 93, citing Ignic 2001.

Signage at the Crystal Cascades in the traditional land of the Gimuy Walubarra Yidinji people. The place is a sacred story site of the rainbow serpent, Gudju-Gudju, who made the many rivers in Yidinji country and formed the mountains and mountain streams. Photo: Jenny Lynch

contact with Country. It is also seen as a vehicle for increasing the cultural awareness of the wider Australian community and overseas visitors about Aboriginal culture.[72]

While still a fledgling industry, the Indigenous tourism experience in the Wet Tropics extends from Indigenous festivals and fairs to cultural entertainment, personalised cultural tours and walks, art galleries, and experiencing Aboriginal-owned cattle properties. Important new Indigenous tourism infrastructure has also been built, such as the Mamu Rainforest Canopy Walkway, and the Mossman Gorge Visitor and Training Centre.[73] Many enterprises have received national and state industry awards, such as the Tjapukai Aboriginal Cultural Park, and coverage in local, state and national media, and have even formed part of the Qantas in-flight entertainment service promoting Australia to the rest of the world. A number of national, state and regional Indigenous tourism organisations have been formed over the years to help promote and facilitate Indigenous tourism, such as the North Queensland Aboriginal Torres Strait Tourism Alliance established in 2009, which WTMA is also supporting by facilitating its establishment.[74] Aboriginal Tourism Australia also

---

72 Wet Tropics Aboriginal Plan Project Team, 2005, p. 93.
73 See Environmental Protection Agency 2008 and Pinnacle Tourism Marketing n.d.
74 See Rainforest Aboriginal News 2011, p. 11 and WTMA 2011a, p. 43.

published a *Financial Management Guide: The Business of Indigenous Tourism* in 2002.[75] As more native title claims are decided and more ILUAs established, it is anticipated that the Rainforest Aboriginal tourism sector will grow more rapidly.

However, tourism is not enthusiastically welcomed by all Rainforest Aboriginal peoples and communities. Yarrabah, an hour's drive from Cairns, has not seriously sought to develop tourism as an economic activity, despite having a community museum and an arts centre. Community residents generally prefer privacy over the intrusion of outsiders visiting their community. Local Yarrabah artists instead generally sell their work through a variety of shops and galleries in Cairns. Other Rainforest Aboriginal communities, although interested in exploring tourism opportunities, are disadvantaged by distance from the major tourist routes and market venues. Failure to resolve native title issues within the community is also a factor discouraging tourism initiatives.

Concerns have also been expressed by Rainforest Aboriginal Traditional Owners about the impacts that tourists are having on sacred and other sites of significance. Problems can arise because of the sheer weight of numbers of tourists visiting particular areas, inhibiting Traditional Owner observance of a site. Other common problems include: direct interference with a site (for example, by stealing objects associated with a site); littering; visiting sites without the relevant Traditional Owners' permission or unaccompanied by a Traditional Custodian; inappropriate visitation (male tourists disrespecting and visiting sacred women's sites); and tourists disregarding and/or defacing signage pertaining to sites of significance. The problem is not so much with the larger established professional tour operators and guides, many of whom work in conjunction with and promote Rainforest Aboriginal tourism initiatives as part of their tourism packages, but with individual tourists who tour the region independently. As more Rainforest Aboriginal tourist enterprises emerge, many of these issues can be resolved. There is also strong support within the regional tourism industry for the concept of a World Heritage-based guide certification program, operating in the context of a national accreditation system to ensure that rainforest tour guides maintain international best standards in environmental and cultural interpretation.[76] Such a certification program will presumably address issues related to engaging with Traditional Owners and visiting Rainforest Aboriginal cultural sites.

Caring for Country

The other major source of employment is through 'Caring for Country' programs. While the QPWS employs some Rainforest Aboriginal people as rangers, a number of local Rainforest Aboriginal organisations/native title holders also maintain their own community ranger services, usually with the support of federal funding. Such services are often contracted by QPWS and other land management agencies to undertake specific land management

---

75 Aboriginal Tourism Australia and Department of Industry, Tourism and Resources 2002.
76 WTMA 2011a, 41.

activities such as pest eradication, controlled burning (based on traditional practices)[77] and infrastructure maintenance on their native title lands. However, Aboriginal community rangers do not enjoy the same levels of responsibility or have the same powers of enforcement as do the QPWS rangers. Such community ranger services perform important community work within the region, particularly with regard to recovery efforts after severe cyclone activity. For example, the Girringun Aboriginal Corporation received a federal grant of $1.5 million to employ 60 Aboriginal people from within the southern WTWHA to help the recovery effort after Cyclone Yasi devastated the region in February 2011.

Conclusions

While the right sentiments were expressed in the preambles to both the Commonwealth and Queensland Acts governing the WTWHA,[78] it took the sustained activism of the Rainforest Aboriginal peoples to give effect to those sentiments through direct lobbying of politicians to ensure they were given statutory representation on the WTMA Board of Directors and the Scientific Advisory and Community Consultative Committees. They demanded that a review of their involvement in the management of the WHA be carried out according to Terms of Reference negotiated with the Wet Tropics Ministerial Council.[79] This review influenced the re-drafting of the Wet Tropics Management Plan 1998, the first draft of which was publicly burnt outside the WTMA office as it did not satisfy the demands of the Rainforest Aboriginal peoples. It paved the way for the Wet Tropics Regional Agreement, which finally enabled Rainforest Aboriginal traditional owners to have an effective role in the day-to-day management of their traditional estates lying within the WHA. The native title process has also been a powerful tool as it has required federal, state and local government authorities, including WTMA, to factor native title into their planning and permit regimes and to negotiate ILUAs over native title lands both within and outside the WHA. The resulting ILUAs have usually required that the native title holders have a direct role in the management of their native title lands.

While the push by the Rainforest Aboriginal peoples for recognition of their cultural values through the listing of the WTWHA as Cultural Landscape – begun by RAN in 1992, and pursued by Bama Wabu, ARC and now RAPA – has yet to achieve its ultimate goal, this process has nevertheless been empowering for Rainforest Aboriginal Traditional Owners.

In assessing the positives and negatives of World Heritage listing, it is necessary also to contemplate what the situation might have been without such a listing. By 1980, when the fight to

---

77 See, for example, Hill et al. 2004 with regard to Eastern Kuku Yalanji traditional fire management practices.
78 The Preamble to the Commonwealth Act reads, inter alia: "Aboriginal people have occupied, used, and enjoyed land in the Area since time immemorial. The Area is part of the cultural landscape of Rainforest Aboriginal peoples and is important spiritually, socially, historically and culturally to aboriginal people particularly concerned with the land. It is, therefore, the intention of the Parliament to recognise a role for Aboriginal peoples particularly concerned with land and waters in the Area, and give Aboriginal peoples a role to play in its management." For the Preamble of the Queensland Act, see Section 3 above.
79 Review Steering Committee 1998.

save the Daintree began, the area under natural vegetation within the Wet Tropics Bioregion had already been reduced by half. Under the then National Party-led Queensland Government, no doubt more forests would have been logged, more land would have been cleared for agriculture and cattle grazing, and more land alienated as freehold title for private ownership, occupation and usage. World Heritage listing put an end to all that, and has instead enabled more of the Wet Tropics Bioregion to be protected through rehabilitation of strategic conservation areas by adding to the protected area estate, creating corridors to link otherwise isolated areas of natural bushland, and re-vegetating waterways to create further wildlife corridors and stop riparian erosion, without necessarily adding to the WHA estate but yet benefiting it.

For the Rainforest Aboriginal peoples, the creation of the WTMA has enabled them, through their own representative organisations, to deal more directly with a single organisation, rather than several, to have their concerns and interests addressed – at least in regard to the World Heritage Area. However, one is sensing that the dynamics of this relationship are starting to change. Difficulties among Rainforest Aboriginal peoples in trying to find an effective model for a peak body to represent their interests with regard to their involvement in the management of the WHA and within the Wet Tropics Bioregion generally have seen WTMA preferring to deal more directly with the Traditional Owner/Native Title holder groups and their prescribed body cooperates through such mechanisms as ILUAs and Cooperative Management Agreements rather than with Aboriginal Rainforest peoples more generally through any particular body set up to represent them. This is also reflected in changes to the WTMA management structure. Whereas in 2005, for example, the Aboriginal Resource Management program constituted one of four programs in its own right (the others concerned Conservation, Research, and Presentation),[80] the Rainforest Aboriginal portfolio is now placed within the Communities and Partnerships Program along with public relations, community engagement, education, communications, tourism presentation and community development and planning.[81] The former Aboriginal Resource Management Program generally employed five people. The WTMA Indigenous Partnerships Team within the new Communities and Partnerships Program employs three people.

World Heritage listing has also been a huge boost to the tourist industry although impacts and benefits of tourism have been uneven across the WHA, and for Indigenous tourism businesses. The Daintree and areas close to Cairns are favoured destinations (areas within a 1-2 hour drive from Cairns or Port Douglas). The Daintree receives some 500,000 visitors a year, while tourism sites within the southern Wet Tropics (generally a 3 to 4 hour drive from Cairns) receive but a fraction of that. This volume of tourists provides many business opportunities for local Kuku Yalanji tour guides and artists in and near the Daintree. It also requires more tourism infrastructure and supervision. WTMA and QPWS are working with Aboriginal Traditional Owners/Native Title holders to open more sites and construct tourism facilities within the southern regions of the WHA to spread the tourism load. A recent example of this is the construction of the Mamu Rainforest Canopy Walkway near Innisfail.[82]

80   WTMA 2005b, p. 13.
81   WTMA 2011a, p. 21.
82   Environmental Protection Agency 2008.

Despite the positives, however, the creation of the World Heritage Area has failed to address and, indeed, has exacerbated one of the main problems facing Rainforest Aboriginal peoples: the large number of federal, state and local government agencies, laws, stakeholders, interest groups and funding bodies they must deal with in order to pursue their way of life and enjoy their country. This situation stifles initiatives many of which are aimed at developing business and employment opportunities as a means to overcome poverty. Although it would be unfair to attribute this situation entirely to the existence of the WHA and its management agency WTMA, its existence does create yet another layer of bureaucracy for Rainforest Aboriginal peoples to deal with.

Funding also remains a critical issue. Rainforest Aboriginal organisations and programs generally rely on a basket of federal and state funds, awarded competitively and often as 'one-offs', both to maintain their organisations and their services (such as the Aboriginal community ranger services), and to carry out specific land management programs and projects. As Hill et al. point out: "The slow response by governments to these resourcing needs is testimony to the ongoing marginalisation of Indigenous peoples from the [natural resource management] arrangements of the Australian nation-state".[83] The funding situation affects organisations such as WTMA (regarding the employment/engagement of ACLOs) as well as organisations like the Girringun Aboriginal Corporation, which oversees a number of caring for country projects and maintains a community ranger service, and the DOGIT community councils.

While much has been achieved regarding the involvement of the Rainforest Aboriginal peoples in the WTWHA, and much has been improved, the ultimate goal still remains: the listing of the WTWHA also for its Indigenous cultural values. That so much has been achieved is a credit to those Rainforest Aboriginal activists and their supporters who have doggedly pursued their goals for over two decades to obtain the right of Traditional Owners to be directly involved in decision-making and management of the WTWHA, and for their cultural values to be properly recognised.

References

Aboriginal Rainforest Council Inc. 2007. Nomination of the Wet Tropics of Queensland World Heritage Area (home of Rainforest Aboriginal People) for inclusion on the National Heritage List. Cairns, ARC.

Aboriginal & Torres Strait Islander Social Justice Commissioner. 2011a. *Native Title Report 2011*. Sydney, Australian Human Rights Commission. Available at: http://www.humanrights.gov.au/social_justice/nt_report/ntreport11.

Aboriginal & Torres Strait Islander Social Justice Commissioner. 2011b. *Social Justice Report 2011*. Australian Human Rights Commission, Sydney. Available at: http://www.humanrights.gov.au/social_justice/sj_report/sjreport11.

Aboriginal Negotiating Team Secretariat. 2003. *Minutes of the Bama INF Workshop: Clump Mountain Wilderness Camp, Mission Beach Queensland, 21- 23 March, 2003*. Cairns, North Queensland Land Council.

Aboriginal Tourism Australia and the Department of Industry, Tourism and Resources. 2002. *Financial Management Guide: The Business of Indigenous Tourism*. Canberra.

ACIUCN. 2000. *Report on the state of conservation of the Wet Tropics of Queensland World Heritage Area, Australia*. Prepared by the Australian Committee of IUCN. UNESCO Doc. WHC-2000/CONF.203/INF.6.

Australian Human Rights Commission. 2010. *The Community Guide to the UN Declaration on the Rights of Indigenous Peoples*. Sydney.

---

83 Hill et al. 2011, p. 576.

Beck, H. 2011. When bureaucratic blockages threaten to send... A noble vision down the drain. *The Cairns Post*, May 17, p. 6.

Brennan, F. 1988. Yarrabah fights Heritage Listing. *Catholic Leader*, 4 December 1988, p. 1, 5.

Dalton, N. 2011. Future of tourism lies in indigenous culture. *The Cairns Post*, May 20, p. 5.

Department of Environment and Resource Management. 2011. *World Heritage Nomination for Areas of Cape York Peninsula*. (Queensland Government pamphlet). www.derm.qld.gov.au

Elks, S. 2011. Elders stymie Cape York heritage plans. *The Australian*, April 21, pp. 1 and 4.

Environmental Protection Agency, Queensland Government. 2008. *Mamu Rainforest Canopy Walkway: A rainforest walk with altitude!* (Pamphlet). www.epa.qld.gov.au/mamu

Fourmile, H.L., Schnierer, S. and Smith, A. (eds). 1995. *An identification of problems and potential for future Rainforest Aboriginal Cultural Survival and Self-Determination in the Wet Tropics: Report to the Wet Tropics Management Authority*. Townsville, James Cook University.

Fourmile, H.L. 1996. "Making Things Work: Aboriginal and Torres Strait Islander Involvement in Bioregional Planning." *Approaches to bioregional planning. Part 2. Background papers to the conference, 30 Oct-1 Nov 1995, Melbourne*. Canberra, Department of the Environment, Sport and Territories, pp. 145 – 274.

Garrett, P. (Commonwealth Minister for Environment Protection, Heritage and the Arts). 2010. Extension of periods for assessment of nominations for the National Heritage List. Ministerial Notification, 18 June 2010. Canberra, Department of Environment and Heritage.

Government of Australia. 2002. *Australian National Periodic Report, Section II, Report on the State of Conservation of the Wet Tropics of Queensland*.

Hill, R. et al. 2004. *Yalanji-Warranga Kaban: Yalanji People of the Rainforest Fire Management Book*. Cairns, Little Ramsay Press.

Hill, R. et al. 2011. Empowering Indigenous peoples' biocultural diversity through World Heritage cultural landscapes: a case study from the Australian humid tropical forests. *International Journal of Heritage Studies*, Vol. 17:6, pp. 571-591.

Ignic, S. 2001. *Cultural Tourism in the Wet Tropics World Heritage Area – A Strategic Overview for Rainforest Bama*. Unpublished Report. Cairns, Rainforest CRC.

IUCN. 1988. *World Heritage Nomination – IUCN Technical Evaluation – Wet Tropical Rainforests of North-East Australia*. October 1988.

Karvelas, P. 2011. Historic push to give Aborigines 'new power'. *The Australian*, December 9, pp. 1, 8.

Larson, L. and Pannell, S. (eds.) 2006. *Developing the Wet Tropics Aboriginal Cultural and Natural Resource Management Plan: Workshop Proceedings*. Cairns, Cooperative Research Centre for Tropical Rainforest Ecology and Management, James Cook University.

Leo, D., Pentecost, L. and Nywaigi Elders. 2011. *Nywaigi Country: Our Plants & Their Cultural Uses*. Cardwell, Girringun Aboriginal Corporation and Nywaigi Land Corporation.

McDonald, G. and Weston, N. 2004. *Sustaining the Wet Tropics: A Regional Plan for Natural resources Management Volume 1 – Background to the Plan*. Cairns, Rainforest CRC and FNQNRM Ltd.

National Native Title Tribunal. 2000. *Short guide to native title*. Canberra, Commonwealth of Australia.

North Queensland Land Council. 2011. *Message Stick*. December. Also visit: http://www.nqlc.com.au.

Pinnacle Tourism Marketing. n.d. *Mossman Gorge Visitor and Training Centre* (pamphlet). Brisbane, Indigenous Land Corporation.

Rainforest Aboriginal Network. 1993. *Proceedings of the Julayinbul Conference on Aboriginal Intellectual and Cultural Property: Definitions, Ownership and Strategies for Protection in the Wet Tropics World Heritage Area, 25-27 November, 1993*. Unpublished. Cairns.

Rainforest CRC. 2003. *Annual Report 2002-2003*. Cairns, James Cook University.

Review Steering Committee. 1998. *Which Way Our Cultural Survival? The Review of Aboriginal Involvement in the Management of the Wet Tropics World Heritage Area. Volume 1 Report* (prepared for the Wet Tropics Board of Management). Cairns, WTMA.

Rosser, B. 1978. *This Is Palm Island*. Canberra, Australian Institute of Aboriginal Studies.

Rosser, B. 1994. *Return To Palm Island*. Canberra, Aboriginal Studies Press.

Schmider, J. 2011. Eastern Kuku Yalanji ILUA update. *Rainforest Aboriginal News*, No. 12, May, p. 5.

Smyth, D. 1994. *Understanding Country: The importance of Land and Sea in Aboriginal and Torres Strait Islander Societies*. Council for Aboriginal Reconciliation Australia. Australian Government Publishing Service.

Tindale, N.B. and Birdsell, J. 1941. Results of the Harvard-Adelaide Universities Anthropological Expedition, 1938-39. Tasmanoid Tribes in North Queensland. *Records of the South Australian Museum*. Vol. VII, No. 1, pp. 1-9.

UNESCO. 1988a. *Bureau of the World Heritage Committee, Twelfth Session, Unesco Headquarters, Paris, 14-17 June 1988, Report of the Rapporteur.* Doc. SC-88/CONF.007/13, 10 August 1988.
UNESCO. 1988b. *Report of the World Heritage Committee, Twelfth Session, Brasilia, Brazil, 5-9 December 1988.* Doc. SC-88/CONF.001/13, 23 December 1988.
Wet Tropics Aboriginal Plan Project Team. 2005. *Caring for Country and Culture – The Wet Tropics Aboriginal Cultural and Natural Resource Management Plan.* Cairns, Rainforest CRC and FNQNRM Ltd.
WTMA. 2004. *Wet Tropics Conservation Strategy: the conservation, rehabilitation and transmission to future generations of the Wet Tropics World Heritage Area.* Cairns, WTMA.
WTMA. 2005a. *Wet Tropics of Queensland World Heritage Area Regional Agreement.* Cairns, WTMA.
WTMA. 2005b. *Annual Report, 2004-2005.* Cairns, WTMA.
WTMA. 2007. *A chronology of the protection and management of the Wet Tropics of Queensland World Heritage Area.* Cairns, WTMA. Available at: www.wettropics.gov.au/mwha/mwha_pdf/history/chronology.pdf.
WTMA. 2009. *From the Heart: Celebrating 20 years of the Wet Tropics of Queensland World Heritage Area.* Cairns, WTMA.
WTMA. 2011a. *Annual Report, 2010-2011.* Cairns, WTMA.
WTMA. 2011b. *The Australian World Heritage Gateway* (Information pamphlet). Cairns, WTMA.

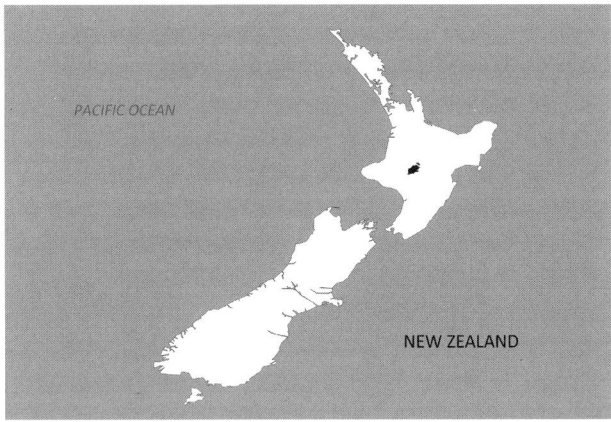

The Tangible and Intangible Heritage of Tongariro National Park: A Ngāti Tūwharetoa Perspective and Reflection

George Asher

Introduction

This chapter provides an account of the relationship of Ngāti Tūwharetoa, a New Zealand indigenous (Māori) group, with their ancestral landscape, which now comprises the World Heritage-listed Tongariro National Park (the Park). The chapter is a commentary on the ongoing challenge to appropriately reflect this relationship within the framework of the Tongariro National Park's governance and management structures and processes. Meeting this challenge is long overdue considering the fact that over 20 years have passed since the Māori cultural and spiritual associations with the Park's landscape were recognized as being of outstanding universal value under the UNESCO World Heritage Convention.

Tongariro National Park was listed as a natural World Heritage site in 1990 in recognition of its outstanding geological and ecological values. In 1993, it was also listed as a cultural site when it became the first site to be inscribed on the World Heritage List under the newly created category of 'cultural landscape'. This was done in recognition of the outstanding significance of the living traditions, beliefs and artistic works of the Māori people associated with the site. Despite

Left: Mount Ruapehu and lakes. Photo: Lee ter Wal Design

this international recognition, however, very little substantive progress has been achieved in recognizing, understanding and protecting the Park's cultural and spiritual values.

Physical description, flora and fauna

Centrally located in the North Island of New Zealand, the landscape of the 80,000 ha Tongariro National Park is dominated by the volcanoes of Mount Ruapehu, Mount Ngāuruhoe and Mount Tongariro. The volcanoes, which lie at the heart of the Taupō volcanic zone, form one of the most spectacular, diverse and active volcanic complexes in the south-west Pacific.[1] The rhyolitic explosions of this complex were among the largest to have occurred on the planet over the last two million years. Volcanism is manifested in many forms, including violent volcanic eruptions, ash showers, lava and debris flows, hot springs, fumaroles and crater lakes. Streams and rivers radiating from the mountains form the major river systems of the North Island.

The Park's remarkable biodiversity is represented in over 50 bird species, including rare endemic species of blue duck, North Island brown kiwi, fern bird and kaka, and more than 500 species of indigenous plants.[2] New Zealand has only two native mammal species, the short and long tailed bat, and both are found within the Park.

Indigenous peoples associated with the Park

The Māori, the indigenous people of New Zealand, call themselves *tangata whenua* (literally 'people of the land'), signifying their ancestral and spiritual affinity to the land. A person's *whakapapa* (genealogy) is very important in demonstrating one's ancestral connection to the land. Māori traditional social units are called *iwi* (tribes) and *hapū* (the social and political unit that makes up the *iwi*). Each *hapū* unit is made up of *whanau* (extended family units).

There are several *iwi* with ancestral associations in the Park. This report will focus solely on the issues from a Ngāti Tūwharetoa perspective because this is the tribe to which the author belongs. It is important, however, to acknowledge that the focus on Ngāti Tūwharetoa should not detract from or diminish the ancestral associations of other *iwi* groups with the Park's landscape and its natural and customary attributes.

Ngāti Tūwharetoa history and occupation of the Taupō/Tongariro region

Ngāti Tūwharetoa's presence in the central North Island was first established by Ngātoroirangi, the *tohunga* (high priest) and navigator of the Te Arawa *waka* (canoe), who journeyed from the Pacific

---

1   Department of Conservation 2006, pp. 4, 31.
2   Ibid., p. 60.

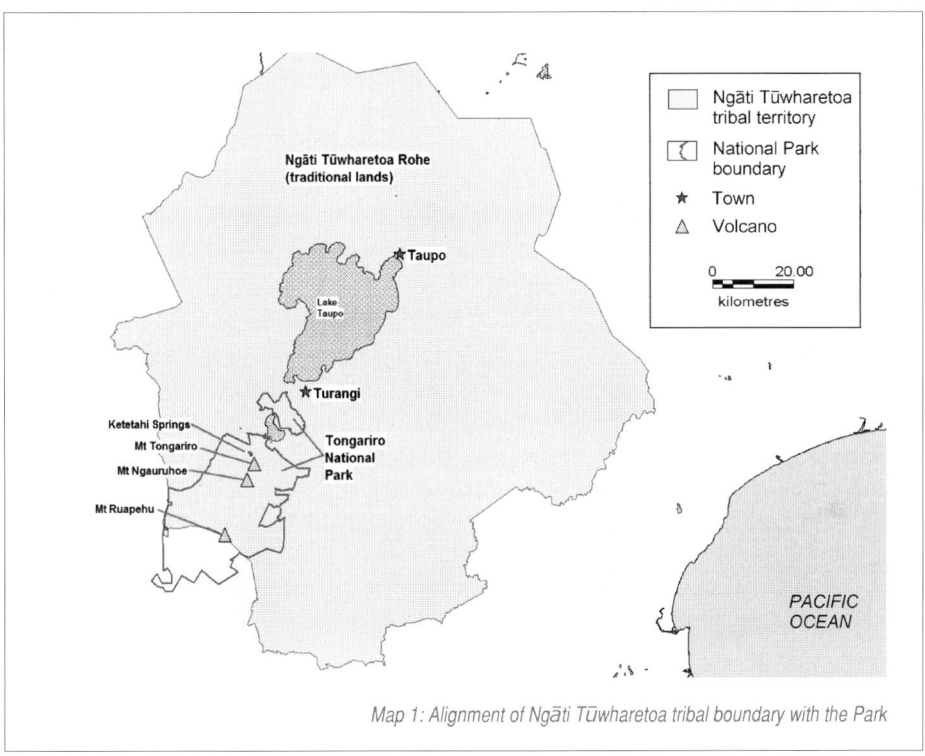

Map 1: Alignment of Ngāti Tūwharetoa tribal boundary with the Park

to the coasts of New Zealand. The Ngāti Tūwharetoa tribe directly descends from Ngātoroirangi and the ancestors of this canoe.

Around eight generations after Ngātoroirangi's journey to the Taupō district, his direct descendant, Tūwharetoa, arrived in the Central North Island followed by his sons and grandsons. The purpose of the latter was to fulfill their ancestor Ngātoroirangi's claim to and compact with the lands, including the sacred mountains and the waters flowing from these mountains. The history of Ngāti Tūwharetoa records that Ngāti Tūwharetoa successfully fought to reclaim and maintain their rights of occupation over the above-mentioned land areas.[3] The following traditional statement affirms the extent of the occupation of Ngāti Tūwharetoa in the hinterland of the North Island:

Ko Te Arawa te Waka
Mai i Maketu ki Tongariro
Mai i Tongariro ki Maketu
(The bow of the Arawa canoe rests at Maketu and the stern at Tongariro)

---

3 Grace 1959.

Ngāti Tūwharetoa's inextricable links with their lands and waters, their unity and leadership are expressed in the following proverb:

Ko Tongariro te maunga
Ko Taupō te moana
Ko Ngāti Tūwharetoa te iwi
Ko te Heuheu te tangata.

(Tongariro is the sacred, ancestral mountain
Taupō is the ancestral inland sea
Ngāti Tūwharetoa is the tribal entity affiliated with the surrounding lands
Te Heuheu is our venerated leader.)[4]

Today, the population of Ngāti Tūwharetoa numbers over 34,000.[5] In line with recent trends, only about 20% of the tribe is estimated as residing within their traditional tribal territory, the remainder having migrated to urban or other locations within New Zealand or overseas.[6] The Park's regulations prohibit permanent residential occupation for everyone within the boundary of the Park; however, semi-permanent occupation is allowed for visitors and the Park's workforce.

A summary of important Ngāti Tūwharetoa cultural and spiritual values associated with Tongariro National Park

The following is a summary account of the intimate and intrinsic relationship of Ngāti Tūwharetoa with the landscape of the Park. It is mainly based on information that exists within tribal oral tradition, although there are limited written accounts that are not readily available or known outside of the tribal precincts and which have also been drawn on for this account. While over 20 years have passed since the Park was inscribed on the World Heritage List as an 'associative cultural landscape' of outstanding universal value, very little progress has been made in the substantive recognition, understanding and protection of the Park's cultural and spiritual values.

Connections to the Sky and the Earth

In Ngāti Tūwharetoa's worldview, the Park constitutes a complex network of interrelationships. The airspace represents celestial entities and clusters, including named planets, stars, the sun and the moon, which form part of the genealogical record of Ngāti Tūwharetoa. This is the realm

---

4   Tūwharetoa lore.
5   Te Puni Kōkiri 2012.
6   Statistics New Zealand 2004, pp. 18-19.

of Ranginui (the Sky Father), while that of Papatūānuku (the Earth Mother) comprises all earthly entities.

The links that connect Tūwharetoa to all of the elements and ancestors in this 'world' are referred to as *whakapapa* (genealogy or kinship). *Whakapapa* connects Māori to every entity in the universe, animate or inanimate. Ngāti Tūwharetoa's linkage with every entity of the Park is timeless and connects the tangible with the intangible, the physical with the metaphysical. The connections between human and non-human are seamless and encompass a holistic and meaningful network of relationships. Oral and artistic traditions of song, dance, carving and rich oratory express over 800 years of intimate interaction with the Park's environment.

> "The Rautawhiri tree shows me how to plait the rope that binds me from the land to the sky,
> the sky to the land, to my family, my sub-tribe, my tribe, my world;
> Indeed, my lineage is the binding rope." [7]

Whānaungatanga is the linkage or relationship that exists between entities in the genealogy. It provides the context of the relationship. The following narrative provides an insight into Ngāti Tūwharetoa's relationship with key natural attributes of the Park.

Values of the sacred mountains (Kāhui Maunga)

The mountains of the Park are physical attributes of extraordinary significance to the *iwi* of the central part of the North Island. The most physically distinct of the mountains of the National Park are Mount Tongariro, Mount Pīhanga, Mount Ngāuruhoe and Mount Ruapehu. For Ngāti Tūwharetoa they are also important symbols of our powerful, sacred connection with our ancestral lands.

Within the history of Ngati Tuwharetoa, the names of the three mountains of Tongariro, Ngāuruhoe and Ruapehu are associated directly with the actions of Ngāti Tūwharetoa's famous ancestor, Ngātoroirangi. He was a priest of the highest order of esoteric knowledge and wisdom. When he ascended the peak of Mount Tongariro, his claim to the land was undeniably confirmed to other aspiring explorers and tribal leaders. His status, deep knowledge and genealogical connections enabled him to engage the highest metaphysical authorities to seal the compact between Ngāti Tūwharetoa and these mountain landscapes.

During his ascent of Tongariro, Ngātoroirangi was overcome by a great blizzard. He summoned his ancestors, Te Pupu and Te Hoata, the elders of the fire tribe of Hine Tapeka, to assist him. His sisters, Kuiwai and Haungaroa, also conjured up their fire ancestors to help. Te Pupu and Te Hoata travelled underground with three kits of sacred fire and emerged at the summit of Tongariro in time to save Ngātoroirangi. The actions of Ngātoroirangi in summoning his ancestors from Hawaiiki

---

7   Tūwharetoa lore.

(the traditional place of origin of Māori tribes before they embarked on their ocean journey to Aotearoa/New Zealand) confirm the close connections of Ngāti Tūwharetoa with our ancestors of the Pacific and emphasize Ngāti Tūwharetoa's intimate relationship with the southern geothermal resources that comprise the Pacific Rim of Fire.

Ngātoroirangi's ascent of Tongariro remains the most powerful demonstration of Ngāti Tūwharetoa's compact with the spiritual guardians (*kaitiaki*) of the mountains and Parklands.

> "Tongariro is the spiritual fount of Tūwharetoa. The name Tongariro encapsulates the state of Ngātoroirangi's body, cold to the touch, as he contemplated the pathway of Io. Tongariro's peak is the most sacred because his head is unseen – the lore of Io is unseen."

> "Ngāuruhoe is the second height of Ngātoroirangi. His pointed cone represents the rapid journey of Ngātoroirangi through the skies of understanding. Ngāuruhoe means 'The Binding of the Path to the Zenith'. Its peak is sacred because it binds the path of Ngātoroirangi's non-physical journey to the physical face of the earth."

> "Ruapehu is the third height of Ngātoroirangi. His outspread sprawl represents the sharing of the wisdom gained by Ngātoroirangi. Ruapehu means 'The Resounding Pit'. Its peak is sacred because it holds the pit, the mouthpiece that would resound and spread the message."

> "The wānanga lore as laid down here is crucial to any understanding of the cultural value of the Tongariro mountains to Tūwharetoa. They are physical representations of spiritual understanding. Our cultural lore, etched as it is from the rock of spirituality, is the final bastion for us. Our land might be taken, our language might be stymied, our customs may be ridiculed, but what cannot be changed is the essence of who we are, enshrined in the very land that we live upon." [8]

The compact between Ngātoroirangi and the spiritual *kaitiaki* of the mountains confirmed the requisite spiritual authority between Ngāti Tūwharetoa and their ancestral lands. The mountains are therefore viewed as inspiring symbols of identity and kinship not only with the terrestrial world of Papatūānuku but also with the heavenly and celestial world of Ranginui and the spiritual world of Māori lore. Mount Tongariro is also regarded as a symbol of strength and leadership by Ngāti Tūwharetoa. It has become synonymous with Te Heuheu, the lineage of Paramount Chiefs and the legacy that continues to provide protection for the *mauri* (life essence) of the land and the people of Ngāti Tūwharetoa.

Mountains are powerful symbols of tribal identity and strength throughout New Zealand. All tribal affiliations with ancestral mountains are acknowledged in the engagement between tribal groups. The term 'Kāhui Maunga' (descendants of the sacred mountains) is an acknowledgement of the symbolic relationships between the mountains of the North Island and the tribal groups that affiliate with them.

---

8 Brief of evidence of Chris Winitana, 20 April 2005. Waitangi Tribunal 2005a.

Values associated with earthquakes, volcanic and geothermal activity

Indigenous worldviews often highlight the cause and effect phenomenon of natural disasters. The constant and sometimes violent seismic, volcanic and geothermal activities occurring within the Park were observed and articulated as an important part of Ngāti Tūwharetoa's oral tradition. The ancestor Ruaumoko is the central figure in this history. In myth, he is the vengeful, younger child of Ranginui and Papatūānuku whose tantrums cause violent earthquakes. Oral tradition conveys the story of another brother named Rakahore who imbued the sacred *ahi tamou* (intense heat) into the bedrock of Papatūānuku. It is said that Ruaumoko's violent outbursts weakened the earth's crust, allowing the sacred fires of Hine Tapeka to burst forth and escape in the form of volcanic eruptions and other geothermal manifestations.

Ngāti Tūwharetoa's relationships with the geothermal manifestations of the Pacific were already discussed briefly in the narrative on Ngātoroirangi. Ngāti Tūwharetoa has developed a benign connection with the geothermal elements over eight centuries of occupation of the Central North Island area. The hot springs and pools are used for warmth, cooking, bathing and healing. Heated water was also used to irrigate and warm the soil, to extend the growing periods and increase crop production. All geothermal manifestations have names that often relate to tribal cosmological and ancestral history.

Values associated with the plant and animal resources of the Park

In our folklore, Tane Mahuta was the eldest son of Ranginui and Papatūānuku. Tane's domain comprises all flora, birds, insects and animals. The natural landscape provided food, shelter, transport, clothing and medicine – the basis for human survival. Parts of the barren landscape of the Park were too desolate for sustaining most species but the lower altitude forests and the mountain slopes of Ruapehu and Tongariro contained abundant seasonal supply of birdlife. The latter was a seasonal source of *iwi* protein. Obtaining spiritual permissions was an important prerequisite to the sustainable harvest of natural resources. Ngātoroirangi's compact for the subsequent occupation of these lands by Ngāti Tūwharetoa included obtaining the assurances of powerful, local guardians called *kaitiaki patupaiarehe* to ensure the sustainable use of the local resources.[9]

Kaitiakitanga is the Māori concept of guardianship. It is an holistic and integrated system of sustainable management of natural resources. Within this system, human interaction with their natural environment is based on both generational observations and respect for their genealogical relationship with the natural world. In addition, Māori traditional management systems are guided by the lore of the *maramataka* (nature's celestial calendar) which specifies the optimal periods and conditions for planting crops, harvesting, fishing and extracting natural resources and food species.

---

9   Wai 575 Cluster Steering Committee 2006, p. 50.

The history of human activity within the Park is an important aspect of Ngāti Tūwharetoa's cultural heritage. Hunting and harvesting locations and the paths that people were permitted to traverse are recorded in oral history. Reciprocal food gathering and harvesting agreements within the tribe and with other tribal groups further enforced important genealogical connections and alliances. Many important sites and events are mapped and referenced within the private records of Ngāti Tūwharetoa.[10]

Kaitiakitanga exemplifies the remarkable creation of a people that enables them to co-exist with relative certainty within a changing, challenging and sometimes hostile environment. The knowledge accumulated through many generations by indigenous experts is comparable to that of modern day scientists. Indigenous experts have developed an in-depth knowledge of each species but maintain a totally holistic awareness and working knowledge of all aspects of their physical and metaphysical world.

Values relating to the freshwater resources of the Park

Iwi respect for their relationship with water is paramount. Water is the life-giving gift of Io (the creator). In the Māori worldview, the guardian of water is Tangaroa and its regulator is his older brother Tāwhirimātea, who are both sons of Ranginui and Papatūānuku. In Māori custom, water assumes myriad forms and functions in the context of ecosystems, physical, social, cultural and spiritual well-being. All these elements were carefully nurtured and actively managed within the holistic Māori custom.

The fresh water resources of the Park are a vital source of Ngāti Tūwharetoa's livelihood. In addition, Ngāti Tūwharetoa maintain a significant *kaitiaki* (guardian) obligation to ensure that the freshwater that flows through the Park's water bodies and into other tribal areas retains its quality to sustain their well-being.

The myth of the 'noble gift'

The catalyst for the formation of the Park was the 1887 'gift' by the Ngāti Tūwharetoa *Ariki* (Paramount Chief) Horonuku Te Heuheu Tukino IV (Horonuku) to the Crown of the peaks of the three mountains of Tongariro, Ruapehu and Ngāuruhoe. While the 'gift' area comprised 2,640 hectares, large-scale Crown land acquisitions subsequently took place and, when the *Tongariro National Park Act* was passed in October 1894, the Park had expanded to about 25,000 hectares. Currently, it covers nearly 80,000 hectares.[11]

The notion of the 'gift' and the various interpretations of this notion by the Crown and Ngāti Tūwharetoa require careful consideration. During Waitangi Tribunal[12] hearings in 2006, Ngāti

---

10   Wai 575 Cluster Steering Committee 2006, p. 50.
11   Department of Conservation 2006, pp. 21, 23.
12   The Waitangi Tribunal is a permanent commission of inquiry established under the *Treaty of Waitangi Act 1975*. The Tribunal is charged with investigating and making recommendations on claims brought by Māori relating to actions or

Portrait of Horonuku Te Heuheu Tukino IV

Tūwharetoa's account of the 'gift' differed markedly from the official Crown version, indicating that there was not a meeting of minds due to conflicting cultural, legal and linguistic assumptions between the two cultures. The official notion that Horonuku's 'gift' was a freely initiated, noble gesture is at odds wiNgāti Tūwharetoa's historical and cultural reality. Ngāti Tūwharetoa's thinking is governed by its cultural belief that land is not owned in the Western sense, and nor can it be given away.

Horonuku was born into a proud and honourable legacy. His grandfather Te Heuheu Tukino I refused to sign the *Treaty of Waitangi* and have his *mana* (customary chiefly and decision-making authority) usurped by the Queen of England. Both his father (Tukino II) and uncle (Tukino III) demonstrated exceptional leadership directed at retaining tribal *mana whenua* (authority over the

---

omissions of the Crown that constitute breaches of the *Treaty of Waitangi*. Signed in 1840 between the Crown and Māori tribes, the *Treaty of Waitangi* recognises the customary rights of Māori and the position of the Crown in New Zealand.

land) by entering into historical compacts that are now a significant part of New Zealand history. Horonuku inherited this unconditional obligation to protect the *mana* of the land and, above all, to never put at risk the *tino tapu* (extreme sacredness) of the mountains.

Horonuku knew that the sacred mountains were under threat from the wave of colonisation advancing into the interior of the North Island. He was determined to act to protect them. Underpinning his thinking was the Ngāti Tūwharetoa *tikanga* (customary law) surrounding the concept of a *tuku whenua*. Although this was translated into English as a 'gift', philosophically it is quite different. In Western culture, a gift means a voluntary transfer of property from one person to another completely free of payment and without 'strings attached'. The Māori meaning of a *tuku* has been explained in evidence submitted to the Waitangi Tribunal as follows:

> "Intrinsic to the Māori notion of gifting is reciprocity. Something received means something to be given. Amongst the nobility in particular this reciprocal approach was not only a matter of common courtesy but a social requirement. This maintained balance, equality of the mana/prestige of the giver and the recipient. A one sided gifting equated to being out of balance. This required utu (revenge), or rebalance, normally paid for in blood." [13]

And hence we can glean that, in making the *tuku*, Horonuku was not giving the peaks away as many believe. Instead, he wanted to create a partnership arrangement with the Crown to protect the sacred tribal heritage. Any notion that Horonuku could give away the Kāhui Maunga is completely at odds with his conceptual framework. The Kāhui Maunga were a legacy that he, as Paramount Chief of Ngāti Tūwharetoa, was bound to protect because they symbolised the strength and authority of Ngāti Tūwharetoa. In 1920, his son Tūreiti Te Heuheu explained:

> "The prestige of my people depends upon our holding those Mountains for all time, or an interest in them… I would not give the prestige which is contained in those Mountains. It is my mana." [14]

This is particularly true in the case of Mount Tongariro, which is clearly understood to be the physical embodiment of the sacred head of Horonuku's father (Mananui).[15]

Horonuku's expressed intention that the land be put into a joint trusteeship with him and the Queen of England was never acted upon. He died in 1888, several years before the passing of the 1894 legislation that constituted the Park. Horonuku's son, Te Heuheu Tureiti, was assigned a position as member on the inaugural Park Board, an inferior and ineffective position compared with shared trusteeship.

---

13 Brief of evidence of Chris Winitana, 20 April 2005. Waitangi Tribunal 2005a, p. 9.
14 Notes of an interview between Te Heuheu Tukino and the Minister for Tourist and Health Resorts, William Nosworthy, 13 November 1920 (doc. A56(a), p. 313). Cited in Waitangi Tribunal 2013, sect. 7.6.2(3).
15 Wai 575 Claims Cluster Steering Committee 2006, p. 277; Waitangi Tribunal 2013, sect. 7.6.2(3

The effect of the 1894 Act was to negate the *mana* (authority) of Ngāti Tūwharetoa over their most sacred lands and it failed to provide a framework for recognition of the vital ancestral bond between Ngāti Tūwharetoa and their sacred land that Horonuku envisioned and wished to safeguard. The following paragraph by his great-great grandson Sir Tumu te Heuheu expresses the perpetual nature of this bond:

> "Although Te Heuheu Tukino had gifted the area as a national park, the relationship with the donor tribes did not automatically cease. Māori perspectives on land tenure are not unlike those of other indigenous peoples and recognise that the bond between tribe and territory is a perpetual bond that does not cease when the land is gifted or even when it is sold. Underlying this perspective is a worldview that links tribal identity with tribal land. The people and the land form an inseparable whole that transcends legal title or for that matter any other form of alienation." [16]

The Waitangi Tribunal has agreed with the argument advanced by Ngāti Tūwharetoa, concluding that:

> "… we are of the view that the phrase 'noble gift' is not suitable to describe Te Heuheu's tuku of the mountain peaks in 1887. The tuku was not, as the Native Minister believed, an English-style gift of the mountains to the Crown. From the evidence we received, we found that Te Heuheu intended to accept the Queen as partner or co-trustee of the mountains. He was inviting her to share with him the rangatiratanga ['chieftainship' or 'authority'] and kaitiakitanga ['guardianship'] of the maunga. Te Heuheu considered that this partnership would ensure that his tribe would never lose their association with the mountains, and that the mountains would be protected for the benefit of Māori and Pākehā forever." [17]

Furthermore, the Tribunal supported the tribal call for the Crown to honour the spirit of the *tuku*:

> "…we recommend that the Crown honour its obligations and restore the partnership intended by the 1887 tuku." [18]

The Tribunal recommended that the national park be taken out of Department of Conservation control and held jointly by the Crown and the *iwi* of the Kāhui Maunga under a new 'Treaty of Waitangi' title. Exactly how that should happen has yet to be determined through negotiations between the Crown and the *iwi* associated with the Kāhui Maunga.

For now, Ngāti Tūwharetoa can take solace in the Tribunal's conclusion "that the story of the 'Noble Gift'… is indeed a myth that can now finally be put to rest".[19]

---

16 Te Heuheu, Sir Tumu 2010.
17 Waitangi Tribunal 2012.
18 Waitangi Tribunal 2012.
19 Waitangi Tribunal 2013, p. 523.

Nomination and inscription of Tongariro National Park as a World Heritage cultural site

Tongariro National Park was nominated for World Heritage status in 1986 as a joint natural and cultural site. The late Sir Hepi Te Heuheu, the Paramount Chief of Ngāti Tūwharetoa, supported the notion of the Park as a World Heritage site on the understanding that the new arrangements would provide much needed protection for the cultural heritage associated with the sacred Kāhui Maunga:

> "The mountains of the south wind have spoken to us for centuries. Now we wish them to speak to all who come in peace and in respect of their tapu." [20]

In 1990, the Park was inscribed on the World Heritage List under natural criteria only, while the cultural aspect of the nomination was deferred because the Park did not fit the then existing criteria for cultural sites. However, the World Heritage Committee at the same time initiated a process of revision of the cultural heritage criteria that led to the introduction of the cultural landscapes category in 1992. Tongariro National Park was one of the key case-studies considered during this review process and was taken as a model for defining the subcategory of 'associative cultural landscapes',[21] the inscription of which on the World Heritage List is "justifiable by virtue of the powerful religious, artistic or cultural associations of the natural element rather than material cultural evidence, which may be insignificant or even absent".[22] At the same time as it adopted the revised cultural criteria, in 1992, the World Heritage Committee requested the New Zealand government to re-nominate Tongariro National Park as a cultural World Heritage site.[23]

After this request, the New Zealand Department of Conservation (DOC) appointed an independent consultant to prepare the supporting documentation on the cultural heritage of the Park for the World Heritage Committee. The nomination document was written in only a few months, between April and July 1993, and presented the associative cultural values of the *iwi* as inseparable from the natural qualities of the Park. However, an obvious oversight was that the DOC omitted to obtain, directly, the views of those tribal groups who have ancestral connections with the Park, including Ngāti Tūwharetoa and Ngāti Rangi. The consultant who was hired to write the nomination acknowledged that there was a "bare minimum of consultation" with Ngāti Tūwharetoa, and that "the time constraints... did shape the content of the report".[24]

The first meaningful input on indigenous cultural values from Ngāti Tūwharetoa occurred when case study reports were prepared for the World Heritage experts meeting on "Cultural

---

20   Te Heuheu, Sir Hepi 1995.
21   ICOMOS 1993, p. 138. The criteria for the inclusion of cultural landscapes on the World Heritage List were prepared by an expert group that met at La Petite Pierre, France, in October 1992.
22   UNESCO 2012, p. 88 (Annex 3, para. 10).
23   UNESCO 1992, p. 45; New Zealand Government 1993, p. 1.
24   Forbes 1993, p. 1.

Landscapes of Outstanding Universal Value" convened in October 1993 in Templin, Germany. The purpose of this meeting was to provide guidance to the World Heritage Committee on the inclusion of cultural landscapes on the World Heritage List, as well as illustrations and examples of cultural landscapes.[25] The Templin presentation on Tongariro National Park was important in that it was elaborated with the engagement of the Kaupapa Atawhai Tumuake (Head of Māori Section of the Department of Conservation), Ngāti Tūwharetoa elders and the eldest son of the Paramount Chief of Ngāti Tūwharetoa, Tumu Te Heuheu, who made the presentation at the Templin workshop.

In December 1993, at the World Heritage Committee's 17th ordinary session in Cartagena, Colombia, Tongariro National Park became the very first site to be listed as a cultural landscape. It was inscribed under cultural criterion (vi), which refers to sites that are "directly or tangibly associated with events or living traditions, with ideas, or with beliefs, with artistic and literary works of outstanding universal significance."[26] Tongariro National Park thus set an important precedent for the recognition and safeguarding of intangible cultural heritage under the World Heritage Convention. The justification for inscription provided in the technical evaluation of the nomination by ICOMOS states that: "The mountains that lie at the heart of the Tongariro National Park are of great cultural and religious significance to the Māori people and are potent symbols of the fundamental spiritual connections between this human community and its natural environment."[27]

Ngāti Tūwharetoa participation in decision-making associated with the Kāhui Maunga[28]

Horonuku's expectations with respect to the 'gift' were that he achieve a position of joint ownership over the Kāhui Maunga and be given a lifetime membership in a partnership arrangement with the Queen in order for him to assert proper decision-making over these *taonga* (tangible and intangible customary assets). This was an arrangement consistent with the concept of '*rangatiratanga*', a necessary precondition to exercise proper control over and protect the Kāhui Maunga and their associated values.

The 1894 National Park legislation failed to recognize the expectations of Horonuku and Ngāti Tūwharetoa despite the 1887 undertakings given by the Crown's Native Minister, John Ballance.[29] The Waitangi Tribunal has confirmed that this failure constituted a breach of the Crown's duty of active protection and the guarantee of *tino rangatiratanga* (full authority) under Article 2 of the *Treaty of Waitangi*.[30]

---

25 UNESCO 1993.
26 UNESCO 2013, para. 77.
27 ICOMOS 1993.
28 The term 'Kāhui Maunga' conveys the meaningful kinship associations between the mountains located within and adjacent to Tongariro National Park and the *iwi* who maintain ancestral connections to these mountains.
29 See Waitangi Tribunal 2013, chap. 7.
30 Waitangi Tribunal 2013, p. 524.

The existing legislative framework for governance and management of New Zealand's 14 national parks, including the Tongariro National Park, is provided by the *National Parks Act 1980* and the *Conservation Act 1987*. The Minister of Conservation and the Director-General of Conservation have ultimate oversight of New Zealand's conservation estates administered by the Department of Conservation (DOC). DOC is responsible for each park's planning and management. Each National Park is administered by a Conservation Board whose primary role is to ensure the development of Conservation Management Strategies (CMS) and Conservation Management Plans (CMP) for each Park. The Tongariro National Park is administered by the Tongariro/Taupō Conservation Board. At the national level, the New Zealand Conservation Authority (NZCA) is the statutory advisor on conservation matters to the Minister of Conservation and the Director-General of DOC.

Statutory provision exists for *iwi* representation on the NZCA and on each of the National Park boards. The Tongariro/Taupō Conservation Board membership may comprise up to 12 members, who are approved by the Minister of Conservation. The Paramount Chief of Ngāti Tūwharetoa is a permanent statutory member by virtue of the provisions of the 1894 legislation. This arrangement has been perpetuated for most of the life of the National Park boards and the descendants of Te Heuheu have been assigned an automatic right of representation. The effectiveness of this representation, however, has been judged by the Waitangi Tribunal as being "constrained and sporadic":

> "Our analysis, though, demonstrated that, until 1952 at least, the input of Tūreiti, Hoani and Sir Hepi in board governance was constrained and sporadic. The key reasons for this were (1) the inoperative state of the board between 1907 and 1914; (2) the abolition of the board between 1914 and 1921; (3) the ascendancy of the executive board from 1931, when recreational development boomed; and (4) the delegation of certain board functions to recreational groups in 1949. This limited the ability of Ngāti Tūwharetoa to prevent physical and cultural harm to their taonga." [31]

The *Conservation Act 1987* raised Ngāti Tūwharetoa's hopes that their sacred heritage would be given proper recognition and protection through Tongariro National Park's decision-making, planning and management regimes. This optimism arose because Section 4 of the Act states that this Act "shall so be interpreted and administered as to give effect to the principles of the Treaty of Waitangi."

The *Treaty of Waitangi*, signed in 1840, is regarded as New Zealand's founding document. The Treaty comprises a broad statement of principles on which the British and Māori made a political compact to found a nation state and build a government in New Zealand. The document has three articles. In the English version, Māori cede the sovereignty of New Zealand to Britain; give the Crown an exclusive right to buy lands they wish to sell and, in return, are guaranteed full rights of ownership of their lands, forests, fisheries and other possessions; and are given the rights and privileges of British subjects.

---

31 Waitangi Tribunal 2013, p. 873.

Matua Tu Tāua Group performing a haka with Sir Tumu Te Heuheu, Paramount Chief of Ngāti Tūwharetoa.
Photo: Tyrone Smith

The Treaty in the Māori language differs somewhat from the English version despite the apparent intention that it should convey the meaning of the English version. In the Māori version, the word 'sovereignty' was translated as '*kawanatanga*' (governance). Some Māori believed they were giving up government over their lands but retaining the right to manage their own affairs. The English version guaranteed 'undisturbed possession' of all their 'properties' but the Māori version guaranteed '*tino rangatiratanga*' (full authority) over '*taonga*' (treasures, which may be both tangible and intangible). Māori understanding was at odds with the understanding of those negotiating the Treaty for the Crown and, as Māori society valued the spoken word, explanations given at the time were as important as the wording of the document.

In 1994, Ngāti Tūwharetoa deemed that DOC had failed to adequately accommodate the principles of the Treaty within its policies and through its consultation processes and filed a claim under urgency with the Waitangi Tribunal.[32] Following a Waitangi Tribunal judicial conference, a joint working group was formed to resolve the matter. The outcome of this process was the adoption by DOC of nine Treaty-based principles within the Park's Conservation Management Strategy. The Treaty principles are to be implemented through the *He Kaupapa Rangatira* guidelines, which

---

32 Waitangi Tribunal 1994, Wai 480.

provide the basis for a cooperative partnership between DOC and *iwi* associated with the Park.[33] The following Treaty principles were adopted:

1. *Kāwanatanga*: the Crown's authority to make laws for the good order and security of the country (note: this cession of authority to the Crown was in exchange for the protection of *rangatiratanga* – see below);
2. *Tino rangatiratanga*: the right of *iwi* to exercise authority and control over their land, resources and *taonga* (tangible and intangible customary assets);
3. Exclusive and undisturbed possession: the right of *iwi* to exclusive and undisturbed possession of their land, forests, estates and fisheries, unless they gave their free consent to the contrary;
4. *Ōritetanga*: the right of Māori and non-Māori alike to equality, fair treatment and the privileges of state citizenship;
5. *Kaitiakitanga*: the right of *iwi* to undertake their duty of stewardship and guardianship over their land, resources and *taonga*;
6. *Whakawhānaungatanga*: the principle of good faith partnership between *iwi* and the Crown;
7. *Tautiaki ngangahau*: the duty of the Crown to ensure the active protection of *iwi* rights and interests;
8. *He here kia mōhio*: the duty of the Crown to make informed decisions and to engage in regular, active and meaningful consultation with *iwi*; and
9. *Whakatika i te mea he*: the duty of the Crown to provide appropriate redress for historical Treaty breaches and to prevent further breaches.[34]

The adoption of these Treaty-based principles within the Park's Conservation Management Strategy represents a significant conceptual step toward recognizing and embodying *iwi* values in Tongariro National Park. However, in practical reality, the Treaty principles are not implemented and the ethic of protecting the natural environment has continued to override efforts to recognize and protect the cultural heritage of *iwi* within the Park.

Protecting the *taonga* of the Kāhui Maunga

Horonuku's prime intention to protect the *taonga* (sacred heritage) of the Kāhui Maunga in perpetuity has been excluded from consideration in the policies, governance and management of the Park since 1894. It was never Horonuku's intention to establish the mountains as a national park. The Western concept of a national park as a pristine natural environment devoid of people is at odds with the Māori worldview that people are inextricably bound to the land, which they are obligated to protect as *kaitiaki* (guardians).

---

33 See Department of Conservation 2002, Section 3.7.3.
34 Department of Conservation 2002, Section 3.7; Department of Conservation 2006, p. 48 ff.

"At the outset, government representatives on the board did not determine a policy in partnership with iwi for how to manage the taonga it had acquired. The lack of policy created a vacuum that was filled by recreational groups willing to take an interest and invest in the park's development... In the process, the spiritual values and cultural beliefs of the [*iwi* of the Kāhui Maunga] were disregarded." [35]

The importance of maintaining a role as *kaitiaki* of the Kāhui Maunga is regarded by Ngāti Tūwharetoa as an essential extension of *rangatiratanga*. The need to protect and nurture their sacred heritage can only be achieved through active engagement in the control, governance and management of the Park. While the concept of *kaitiakitanga* is recognized within the Park's CMS, DOC has minimised the role of *kaitiaki*.[36] No delegation of authority has been given to *iwi* and input to decision-making is limited to non-substantive consultation.[37] The following observation of the Waitangi Tribunal is pertinent:

"The strengths and limitations of the general policy documents reflect the strengths and weaknesses of the Conservation Act 1987. There are positive statements about Treaty of Waitangi responsibilities... but far from complete policy guidance as to how these can be made operational across the wider spectrum of Crown conservation activities." [38]

As noted earlier, a major acceptance by DOC has been the inclusion within the CMS of the *He Kaupapa Rangatira* guidelines, a framework and protocol for giving practical expression to the principles of the *Treaty of Waitangi*. Unfortunately, these guidelines have become "largely detached from those portions of the [CMS] and the [Management Plan] that provide policy direction".[39] Policy parameters for the planning and management of the Tongariro National Park are contained in the Tongariro/Taupō CMS. The *Conservation Act 1987* states that the purpose of conservation management strategies is to:

"... implement general policies and establish objectives for the integrated management of natural and historic resources... and for recreation, tourism and other conservation purposes." [40]

The CMS contains six key management principles. Principle 3, "Development of an Effective Conservation Partnership with Tangata Whenua", pertains directly to *iwi* values. In implementing this management principle, the DOC is supposed to, among other things, "actively give effect to the principles of the Treaty of Waitangi" and "provide for an expression of iwi values in the management of conservation resources".[41]

---

35 Waitangi Tribunal 2013, p. 856.
36 Waitangi Tribunal 2013, p. 887.
37 Claimant Counsel submissions, 7 July 2007, Waitangi Tribunal 2007, p. 25.
38 Waitangi Tribunal 2013, p. 893.
39 Waitangi Tribunal 2013, p. 948.
40 *Conservation Act 1987*, Art. 17D(1).
41 Department of Conservation 2002, Section 2.1.2.

The imbalance in the application of the six principles is evidenced by the confirmation that Principle 1, "Protection and Enhancement of the Natural Environment within the Conservancy", is to be assigned the highest priority of the principles.[42] This is an anomaly that sits uncomfortably within the context of the Park's dual natural and cultural World Heritage status. The failure to protect the tangible and intangible cultural and spiritual values of *iwi* within the Park is well documented.

By ignoring the role of Ngāti Tūwharetoa and other *iwi* as *kaitiaki* over the natural resources of the Park, the Crown has also succumbed to practices that are inconsistent with its own role of maintaining protection of these natural resources. One of the most prolific 'pests' within the Park is heather, a low-lying scrub that is rapidly overtaking the native flora and transforming the original landscape of the Park. *Iwi* continue to experience frustration with Park officials because they are limited in or prevented from accessing traditional plants and resources for food, medicinal purposes or other traditional use.

The *iwi* associated with the Park are also concerned at the Park Board's well-documented favorable treatment of tourists and visitors[43] and, in particular, that huts for tourists have been allowed to be built on the *maunga*, at altitudes of 5,000 to 7,000 feet above sea level. The *iwi* regard the accommodation provided on the *maunga* as infrastructure that serves an exclusive few and believe that the huts should be removed.[44] In face of the concerns raised by *iwi*, the Park Board in 1996 granted the accommodation providers a 60-year extension of their licenses. The proliferation of accommodation and related service facilities has created problems with sewage disposal, an environmental matter that has been addressed at very high cost and one that *iwi* continue to regard as culturally objectionable. Other concerns raised by *iwi* include the increased generation of rubbish and erosion created by the increasing number of visitors to the Park. Despite these concerns, there is no decision to control visitor numbers or impacts.[45]

The greatest concern of *iwi* is the inability of the Crown, and in particular DOC, to protect the sacred areas of the Park. High on the list of concerns is the lack of protection for the tangible and intangible values associated with the *maunga*. The Park Board has allowed ski-field lifts to intrude into the original 'gift' area of 1887 demarcated by a 2,300m contour line on Mount Ruapehu. This area has always been regarded by Ngāti Tūwharetoa as a 'no go' area for any development. It appears that at least agreement may be able to be reached between *iwi* and DOC to prevent further encroachment of ski-field infrastructure into the 'gift' area.[46]

---

42 Ibid. p. 15: "Highest priority will be given to retaining and restoring natural biodiversity, and protecting threatened indigenous natural resources within the conservancy".
43 See Coombes 2007, chs. 3-6.
44 Te Hokowhitu Taiaroa, brief of evidence, 4 October 2006 (doc. G45), pp. 7-8. Referenced in Waitangi Tribunal 2013, sect. 12.5.3(3)(a).
45 Waitangi Tribunal 2013, p. 937.
46 Te Hokowhitu Taiaroa, brief of evidence, 4 October 2006 (doc. G45), p. 8. Referenced in Waitangi Tribunal 2013, sect. 12.5.3(3)(a).

The Waitangi Tribunal's National Park District Inquiry

Between 2005 and 2007, extensive Waitangi Tribunal hearings were held throughout the central area of the North Island to hear *iwi* submissions on claims against the Crown relating to breaches of the *Treaty of Waitangi*.[47] In 2006 and 2007, hearings focused on an especially constituted 'National Park inquiry district', mainly consisting of Tongariro National Park but also including additional lands surrounding the Park. The final report on the National Park District Inquiry, entitled *Te Kāhui Maunga*, was released by the Waitangi Tribunal in November 2013.

Many of the submissions made to the Waitangi Tribunal over the period 2005 to 2007 referenced the inadequacy of DOC's consultation processes and its failure to protect the cultural heritage of *iwi* in the centre of the North Island and, especially, within the National Park district. The Tribunal's in-depth enquiries and findings on DOC's application and exercise of its responsibilities to *iwi* within the National Park are particularly relevant. On claims relating to the CMS and the Tongariro National Park Management Plan (TNPMP) the Tribunal found that:

- No specific provisions exist to allow *iwi* of the Kāhui Maunga to exercise *rangatiratanga* (authority) over the Tongariro National Park;
- No specific provisions exist to allow *iwi* of the Kāhui Maunga to exercise *rangatiratanga* (authority) over the Tongariro National Park;
- Nothing exists in the Management Plan to ensure that *iwi* are able to exercise guardianship over the heritage resources of the Park;
- There is no provision for *iwi* to participate in economic development and share in the returns from development within the Park;
- There is a lack of guidelines to provide *iwi* with access to the Park's customary materials;
- Zoning methodologies do not provide adequate protection for the peaks of the mountains or sacred sites within the Park;
- The extension of accommodation and ski field licenses has been undertaken in breach of good faith, active protection and partnership;
- There are no provisions for *iwi* to establish partnership or co-management arrangements.[48]

The Tribunal's focus on consultations between DOC and *iwi* led to some interesting responses and conclusions. The Tribunal noted that, despite the Crown's Treaty obligations, DOC's changes in its consultation methodology "were not immediate and did not come evenly".[49] DOC staff cited the highlights of working closely with the late Sir Hepi Te Heuheu on the Centennial Celebrations in

---

47 Waitangi Tribunal 2008, 2013.
48 Waitangi Tribunal 2013, p. 914.
49 Waitangi Tribunal 2013, p. 915.

1987 and with both Sir Hepi and his son, Sir Tumu Te Heuheu, in obtaining recognition of the Park as a World Heritage site.[50]

DOC liaison with Ngāti Tūwharetoa has, until recently, been conducted mainly through the Tūwharetoa Māori Trust Board, an entity that has historically been considered to act as the tribal council for Ngāti Tūwharetoa. While this arrangement has been a helpful 'one stop shop', some *hapū* of Ngāti Tūwharetoa have preferred direct engagement and representation to ensure that their interests and values are better understood and recognized. The *hapū* of Ngāti Hikairo ki Tongariro have constantly advocated for direct engagement with DOC in recognition of the intimate ancestral relationship they maintain with Mount Tongariro and its surrounding landscapes.[51] Such a call is appropriate because the *hapū* (sub-tribe) of Ngāti Hikairo ki Tongariro reside at the northern base of Mount Tongariro. Their responsibility is similar and overlaps with other Ngāti Tūwharetoa *hapū* whose domains cover the northern, eastern and southern regions of the Park. These *hapū* assume their rightful role as *kaitiaki* of these areas on behalf of Ngāti Tūwharetoa. Other tribal groupings assume *kaitiaki* responsibilities in the western and southern regions of the Park and have connecting and overlapping interests with Ngāti Tūwharetoa; their connection with the Kāhui Maunga is also fully acknowledged by Ngāti Tūwharetoa.

Since 1987, *iwi* liaison has been the primary responsibility of DOC's Kaupapa Atawhai managers (Māori liaison officers, also called *Pou Tairangahou*). *Iwi* liaison managers face a major challenge in meeting their responsibilities to the diverse *iwi* and *hapū* groups associated with the Park as well as the other estates administered by DOC. The Waitangi Tribunal has noted that "consultation involves time costs and money costs and is not well resourced".[52] This appears to be a major factor in determining the effectiveness of consultation and the development of outcomes that may meet the expectations of *iwi* associated with the Park. The Tribunal further noted that:

> "There is, at present, a massive imbalance in the resources available to build relationships in a situation where both parties have very limited budgets. DOC allocates resources to fund the Crown side of the relationship but, despite the Treaty requirements of section 4 of the Conservation Act, allocates no budget to fund consultation or build up the capacity of the Treaty partner." [53]

This anomaly negates the development of a meaningful relationship in which *iwi* are able to assume their rightful position as guardians of their heritage within the Park. The Tribunal observed that "it is evident, in this context, that consultation does not equate to joint decision-making or co-management".[54]

The Tribunal's National Park hearings also highlighted a failure of the Crown to ensure that *iwi* and *hapū* are able to equitably share in the benefits of economic activities centred on Tongariro

---

50 Paul Green, amended brief of evidence on behalf of the DOC, 22 February 2007 (doc. H3(k)), pp. 11-12. Referenced in Waitangi Tribunal 2013, sect. 12.5.3(1).
51 Brief of Evidence of Te Ngaehe Wanikau, 2005. Waitangi Tribunal 2005b.
52 Waitangi Tribunal 2013, p. 915.
53 Waitangi Tribunal 2013, p. 918.
54 Waitangi Tribunal 2013, p. 918.

National Park. The Park provides significant commercial opportunities within the centre of the North Island. Visitors to the Ruapehu District in 2003 spent NZD $140 million on accommodation and tourist activities.[55] Several Ngāti Tūwharetoa *hapū* raised concerns about their incapacity to participate in the benefits of economic enterprises within the Park. For instance, the Ngāti Hikairo Ki Tongariro *hapū*, who have long established ancestral relationships with the Park and its mountains, noted:

> "Where tupuna [ancestors] ... once played host to those visiting the maunga, Ngāti Hikairo Ki Tongariro is now being denied the right to develop its own property and resources to take advantage of the recreational use of its traditional whenua [land]. The concessions process used by the Department of Conservation means that Ngāti Hikairo Ki Tongariro continues to be excluded." [56]

Ngāti Waewae representatives raised similar concerns, noting that DOC was

> "doing little or nothing to promote *hapū* business or commercial activity within the park".[57]

In summary the Tribunal found that:

> "[The *iwi* of the Kāhui Maunga] have not been given a share in the revenue from leases, licences, and concessions in Tongariro National Park. Nor have they been given a reasonable degree of preference in the tendering process for these commercial enterprises. The Crown has not recognised the principle of mutual benefit. National park iwi have been marginalised from past economic opportunities and are not provided for in present policies but must not be marginalised from future opportunities... It is entirely reasonable for [the *iwi* of the Kāhui Maunga] to expect to gain livelihoods and operate commercial ventures that serve the needs of those who use and enjoy the park... There are few provisions in the policy documents, the conservation strategies, the TNPMP, or the day to day management practices which enables [the *iwi* and *hapū* of the Kāhui Maunga] to exercise rangatiratanga over their lands, their resources, and their taonga." [58]

The Tribunal has emphasized that the lack of effective recognition of the *rangatiratanga* of the *iwi* is a failure of the Crown and a breach of the Treaty of Waitangi, which has significant consequences for the ability of the *iwi* to protect and nurture the tangible and intangible cultural and spiritual values of the Kāhui Maunga:

---

55 Wouters 2011, p. 31.
56 Ngaiterangi Smallman, brief of evidence, 28 September 2006, pp. 14-15. Cited in Waitangi Tribunal 2013, sect. 12.5.3(2).
57 Graeme Everton, brief of evidence, 29 September 2006, p. 11. Cited in Waitangi Tribunal 2013, sect. 12.5.3(2).
58 Waitangi Tribunal 2013, sect. 12.5.3(4).

"The core Treaty breach is the failure of the Crown to recognise the rangatiratanga of [the *iwi* of the Park]. Powers to care for wāhi tapu [sacred sites] have not been delegated, and management or governance partnerships have not been created. The consequence of this is a lack of opportunity for tangata whenua to exercise kaitiakitanga… within Tongariro National Park. Both of these, the breach and the consequence, reflect the organisational culture as well as the legislative and policy frameworks. DOC, at this point in time and under current frameworks, lacks the organisational confidence to participate in equitable and robust partnerships with [the *iwi* of the Park]." [59]

Developing an effective, operational framework would be a major step for both the Crown and *iwi* and would undoubtedly reinforce and help protect the authenticity and integrity of the cultural values recognized by the World Heritage Committee as having outstanding universal value. Clearly a better way forward must be found. The Waitangi Tribunal has outlined a number of prerequisites for a better way forward, which include:

- Recognition of the intentions of Horonuku to protect the Kāhui Maunga by the Crown and *iwi* working in concert;
- Recognition of the importance of the Park for everyone, including the *iwi* of the Kāhui Maunga, all New Zealanders and the global community;
- Working together in a co-management relationship based on the principles of the *Treaty of Waitangi*;
- Opening the way to a new and evolving relationship between the Crown and *iwi* of the Kāhui Maunga.[60]

Based on its findings, the Tribunal has made the following recommendations for a 'new' way forward:

"That the Tongariro National Park be held jointly by the Crown and [the *iwi* of the Park] and can never be alienated. This will require a new Tongariro National Park Act and a new form of title…

The creation by this Act of a statutory authority, comprising the Crown and [the *iwi* of the Park], for the governance and management of the Tongariro National Park…

The specifics of this arrangement will be worked out as part of the Treaty settlement process.

The world heritage status of the Tongariro National Park will be confirmed within the terms of reference of the statutory authority." [61]

---

59 Waitangi Tribunal 2013, p. 949.
60 Waitangi Tribunal 2013, p. 961.

The *iwi* of the Kāhui Maunga are currently considering these recommendations. Ngāti Tūwharetoa are now formally engaged in negotiations with the Crown to reach settlement of their historical claims and the Kāhui Maunga and the National Park are among the priority matters confirmed for resolution. While the recommendations of the Tribunal have received a mixed response from the Crown, they are, for the most part, viewed by Ngāti Tūwharetoa as having considerable merit. Ngāti Tūwharetoa are about to commence discussions with other *iwi* groups associated with the Kāhui Maunga in an attempt to develop a collaborative *iwi* approach and agreement on the way forward.

Conclusion

This chapter highlights systemic inconsistencies in the governance and management of the Tongariro National Park with respect to the realisation of its cultural heritage objectives. The failure to explicitly identify, protect and manage important cultural and spiritual values has been highlighted as a major concern. Important Treaty principles, which DOC is required by statute to adhere to, have been integrated into policy following external pressure from the *iwi* associated with the Park but the transformation of relevant policy into active programmes has not materialised to the satisfaction of the *iwi*. These issues have never been the subject of any formal report to UNESCO or the World Heritage Committee.

The concept of outstanding universal value (OUV) underpins the World Heritage Convention. Tongariro National Park's outstanding universal value lies both in its superlative natural features and the associated intangible heritage of the *iwi*, which is inseparable from the Park's natural features. The management and protection of the attributes that characterise this OUV are monitored through periodic State of Conservation reports which are used by the World Heritage Committee, as well as DOC, to quantify and evaluate the conservation status of Tongariro National Park within a regional and global context.

So far, two periodic reviews of the Park have been undertaken. The earliest, in 2002, affirmed DOC's viewpoint that the management and protection regimes of the Park were being progressed in a satisfactory manner. The 2002 Report stated, among other things:

> "Since [cultural inscription of Tongariro in 1993] there has been increased Maori participation in the management of the World Heritage Area. The Conservation Management Strategy for Tongariro Taupo Conservancy identified how the principles of the Treaty of Waitangi will be implemented in the management of Tongariro National Park and other conservation areas. Maori are now consulted on all significant management actions in Tongariro National Park, especially where cultural values are involved." [62]

In fact, Treaty principles have not received any substantial implementation in Park management during the 20 years in which they have been included in the Park's policy, as also highlighted by the

---

61 Waitangi Tribunal 2013, p. 961.
62 New Zealand Government 2002, p. 10.

Waitangi Tribunal in its 2013 final report on the National Park District Inquiry. This is a major concern for the *iwi* especially considering that their cultural values are an inextricable and extraordinary part of the outstanding natural attributes of the World Heritage property. The mountains and other natural entities are imbued with cultural and spiritual attributes and require appropriate and unique participatory management and protection mechanisms and a management approach that reflects the holistic nature of the Park's natural and cultural values. Unfortunately, the concerns of the *iwi* regarding the management of the World Heritage site have not been mentioned in New Zealand's periodic reporting to the World Heritage Committee. From the author's viewpoint, it would therefore be useful for the World Heritage Committee to revise the periodic reporting format and provide a section that incorporates indigenous peoples' and local communities' responses. This would ensure that indigenous peoples and local communities are able to directly respond to the key management issues relating to the OUV of cultural properties. It would also contribute to making the '5th C' of Community meaningful in practice.[63]

The author believes that the current situation relating to the *iwi* of the Park, while unacceptable, could be rectified. The findings of the Waitangi Tribunal and the recommendations presented in its 2013 Report on the National Park District Inquiry provide a basis for the establishment of a new framework for management in the future. As noted, the *iwi* of the Kāhui Maunga are now considering those recommendations, including a new Tongariro National Park Act, a new form of title and the establishment of a new Statutory Authority for the management of the Park which would comprise the Crown and the *iwi*.

In any event, real change in the National Park will require DOC to urgently commit to the implementation of its Treaty objectives, establish a meaningful engagement with all *iwi* and *hapū* and ensure their effective participation in decision-making. This will enable DOC to better understand the rich and expansive cultural heritage of the Park and lead to better informed governance and management. The indisputable fact in all this is that the Park's *iwi* and *hapū* are unique in being the only entities capable of "truthfully and credibly"[64] representing their culture and assessing the authenticity and integrity of the Park's OUV.

To some extent, DOC has begun to consider moving in this direction. In 2011, DOC and the National Conservation Authority worked through the completion of the latest Periodic Report on the state of conservation of the World Heritage site. To DOC's credit, it has successfully requested a delay in the finalisation of the Periodic Report while it liaises with *iwi* and *hapū* to obtain a clearer understanding of *iwi* perspectives and aspirations for Tongariro National Park's future management. ○

---

63 The "5th C" refers to the World Heritage Committee's fifth Strategic Objective: "Enhance the role of **Communities** in the implementation of the *World Heritage Convention*". The fifth Strategic Objective was adopted by the World Heritage Committee at its 31st Session in 2007, during the Chairmanship of Sir Tumu Te Heuheu, the present Paramount Chief of Ngāti Tūwharetoa.
64 Compare *Operational Guidelines for the Implementation of the World Heritage Convention* (paras. 80-82), according to which knowledge and understanding of credible and truthful information sources is a prerequisite for understanding and assessing the authenticity of a World Heritage site's cultural values.

References

Coombes, B. 2007. *Tourism Development and its Influence on the Establishment and Management of Tongariro National Park* (commissioned research report). Wellington, Crown Forestry Rental Trust. (doc I1)
Department of Conservation. 2002. *Tongariro/Taupo Conservation Management Strategy 2002-2012.* Tūrangi, Department of Conservation.
Department of Conservation. 2006. *Tongariro National Park Management Plan 2006-2016.* Tūrangi, Dep't of Conservation.
Forbes, S. 1993. *Consultant's Report – Nomination of Tongariro National Park for Inclusion in the World Heritage Cultural List.* August 1993. Wellington, Kotuku Consultancy Limited.
Grace, J. Te H. 1959. *Tūwharetoa.* Auckland, Reed Books.
ICOMOS. 1993. *World Heritage List – Tongariro – No. 421rev (Evaluation of World Heritage Cultural Nomination).*
Māori Members Hui. 1996. *Resolutions of the Conservation Boards, Maori Members Hui,* 1996. Wellington (unpublished document, on file with author).
Moller, H. et al. 2000. Co-Management by Māori and Pākehā for Improved Conservation in the Twenty-First Century. P. Menon and H. Perkins (eds.), *Environmental Planning and Management in New Zealand.* Palmerston, Dunmore.
New Zealand Government. 1993. *Nomination of Tongariro National Park for Inclusion in the World Heritage Cultural List.* Wellington, Department of Conservation.
New Zealand Government. 2002. *New Zealand Periodic report to the World Heritage Committee, October 2002 – Section 2 – Tongariro.*
New Zealand Government. 2007. *Proposal for a 'Fifth C' to be added to the Strategic Objectives.* UNESCO Doc. WHC-07/31.COM/13B.
Statistics New Zealand. 2004. *New Zealand: An Urban/Rural Profile – Report.* Available at: http://www.stats.govt.nz/browse_for_stats/people_and_communities/geographic-areas/urban-rural-profile.aspx.
Te Heuheu, Sir Hepi. 1995. Preface. In: C. Potton, *Tongariro – A Sacred Gift.* Auckland, Lansdown Press.
Te Heuheu, Sir Tumu. 2010. *Indigenous partnerships in protected area management: an NZ perspective.* Presentation to the 4th International Biennial Parks Leadership Conference, 24-26 August 2010, Sydney, Australia.
Te Puni Kōkiri. 2012. *Ngāti Tūwharetoa.* www.tkm.govt.nz/iwi/ngati-tuwharetoa (Accessed 14 February 2012).
UNESCO. 1992. *World Heritage Committee, Sixteenth session (Santa Fe, United States of America, 7-14 December 1994): Report.* Doc. WHC-92/CONF.002/12.
UNESCO. 1993. *Report of the International Expert Meeting on "Cultural Landscapes of Outstanding Universal Value", Templin, Germany, 12 to 17 October 1993.* Doc. WHC-93/INF.4.
UNESCO. 1994. *World Heritage Committee, Seventeenth session (Cartagena, Colombia, 6-11 December 1993): Report.* Doc. WHC-93/CONF.002/14.
UNESCO. 2007. *Decisions adopted at the 31st Session of the World Heritage Committee (Christchurch, 2007).* Doc. WHC-07/31.COM/24.
UNESCO. 2013. *Operational Guidelines for the Implementation of the World Heritage Convention.* Doc. WHC. 13/01.
Wai 575 Claims Cluster Steering Committee. 2006. *Te Taumarumarutanga o Ngāti Tūwharetoa: In the Shadow of Ngāti Tūwharetoa* (confidential commissioned research report). Wellington, Crown Forestry Rental Trust.
Waitangi Tribunal. 1994. Wai 480 (Claim by the Ngāti Tūwharetoa Trust Board regarding the Draft Tongariro/Taupo Conservancy Conservation Management Strategy).
Waitangi Tribunal. 2005a. Brief of evidence of Chris T. Winitana, 20 April 2005, National Park District Inquiry (doc. G1).
Waitangi Tribunal. 2005b. Brief of evidence of Te Ngaehe Wanikau to the Waitangi Tribunal, Central North Island Inquiry, 2005 (doc. E20).
Waitangi Tribunal. 2007. Claimant counsel, submissions by way of reply, 7 July 2007, National Park District Inquiry (paper 3.3.58).
Waitangi Tribunal. 2008. *He maunga rongo: report on Central North Island claims* (Wai 1200). Wellington, Legislation Direct.
Waitangi Tribunal. 2012. Letter of transmittal, 20 December 2012: *Te Kāhui Maunga: The National Park District Inquiry Report* (Pre-publication version). Signed by Chief Judge Wilson Isaac, Presiding Officer.
Waitangi Tribunal. 2013. *Wai 1130 Te Kāhui Maunga: The National Park District Inquiry Report.* Legislation Direct.
World Heritage Workshop for Pacific Island States. 2007. *Concluding comments to the Pacific Workshop at Waitetoko, February 2007.* 13 May 2007, Waitetoko Marae, New Zealand.
Wouters, M. 2011. *Socio-economic effects of concession-based tourism in New Zealand's national parks.* Wellington, Department of Conservation.

Rapa Nui National Park, Cultural World Heritage: The Struggle of the Rapa Nui People for their Ancestral Territory and Heritage, for Environmental Protection, and for Cultural Integrity[1]

Erity Teave and Leslie Cloud

The solemn desire of the Rapa Nui nation for justice and freedom authorises this trip through the history of Te Pito O Te Henua, the Rapa Nui Kingdom.[2] May this form a tribute to my parents, my family and those who forge justice, as well as to my ancestors for their great capacity to develop a Cultural Monument in which faith, the sciences, the arts, knowledge and great human talent come together and are projected wisely onto a mystical and spiritual world in which honour and respect form the foundations of man's existence.

Erity Teave

---

1   Parts of this chapter have been included in a document released by the Rapa Nui Parliament prior to the publication of this book (Parlamento Rapanui 2013).
2   In the article, the names 'Te Pito O Te Henua' ('Navel of the World') and 'Rapa Nui' ('Great Island') are used interchangeably and refer to the same territory.

Left: Moai on Rapa Nui, with Ahu Tongariki in the background. Photo: Christian Bobadilla

Introduction

Rapa Nui, also known as Easter Island, is a 16,600 ha triangular island in the eastern corner of Polynesia (27°9'S, 109°26'W), and an underwater platform extending as far as the Motu Motiro Hiva archipelago. To the north-west lie the Pitcairn Islands, 2,100 km distant, and to the north-east the Galapagos, 3,474 km away. To the east lies Chile, some 3,700 kilometres distant.

The inhabitants of Rapa Nui today number some 6,000, half of whom are native inhabitants of the island, and members of the Rapa Nui nation. The other half are immigrants, mostly from Chile although around 10% have family ties in France, Germany, Spain, the US and Italy.

The Rapa Nui nation lives on its ancestral territory under the colonial administration of the Chilean state, which still owns more than 70% of the island's territory in the form of public lands. This includes the Rapa Nui National Park, a UNESCO World Heritage site since 1995, within which the Rapa Nui no longer enjoy their rights to territory or natural resources.

In this article, we will illustrate the impacts that the declaration of the Rapa Nui National Park as a cultural World Heritage site has had on the rights of the Rapa Nui people, particularly on their collective rights to self-determination and to cultural heritage, and on their right to life. After a short historical overview of the Rapa Nui territory, its native population and its colonisation by the Chilean state, we will focus on the characteristics of Rapa Nui cultural heritage and the ways in which this has been appropriated by the Chilean state before moving onto the declaration of the Rapa Nui National Park as cultural World Heritage and the challenges that this designation presents with regard to the rights of the native inhabitants of Rapa Nui.

Colonisation, loss of territory and cultural damage in Rapa Nui: an historical overview

The native inhabitants of Rapa Nui

Oral tradition has it that Rapa Nui was discovered by the High Priest Haumaka through a dream. In his dream the spirit of Haumaka set off in the direction of the rising sun. First, he came across seven islands covered in mist. On reaching them, he explored them and discovered that they were not inhabitable. Continuing on his way, he spotted the reflection of the shadow of a land. Drawing closer, the spirit of Haumaka arrived at the islets of Motu Nui, Motu Iti and Motu Kaokao. Surprised, he said: "Here in the ocean rise the three kind sons of the former King (*Ariki Motongi*) Ta'anga VIII of the Oto Uta I Dynasty!" On awaking from his sleep, Haumaka immediately told the good news to his brother Hua Tava, and then also to King Matu'a IX of the Oto Uta I Dynasty.

On the first of June, the King's messengers, Ira and Raparenga, together with five other explorers, arrived at Rapa Nui, physically discovering the new territory for King Hotu Matu'a X, the son of Matu'a IX. After Matu'a IX had blessed his first-born Hotu Matu'a and the *Pakahera Mana* (skull of the first King, Oto Uta I), Hotu Matu'a embarked on a journey together with his sister Ava

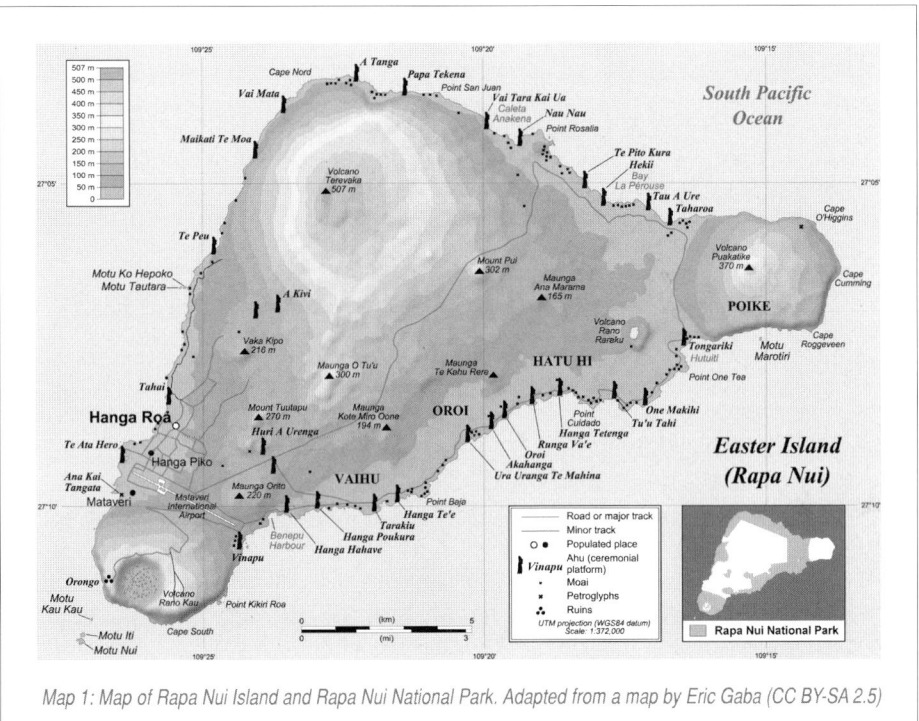

Map 1: Map of Rapa Nui Island and Rapa Nui National Park. Adapted from a map by Eric Gaba (CC BY-SA 2.5)

Rei Pua, leaving his native land behind him. Returning to the island, he named it Te Pito O Te Henua and divided it into two *Matas* (territories). Each *Mata* was subdivided between several tribes (*Ure*), with collective rights and practices. According to ancestral knowledge, the foundations of the Rapa Nui Kingdom and society were established by virtue of age-old ancestry, perpetuating the system of ancestral ownership by descent for the collective use and enjoyment of the descendants under the customary legal order.

From that moment on, a monarchy governed Te Pito O Te Henua, led by the *Ariki Mau* (King),[3] the highest authority on the island, invested with *Mana* (spiritual power) and advised by wise men, noted for their reliability, in addition to a Council of Chiefs designated by each tribe.

From the 19th century to 1966: times of slavery on Te Pito O Te Henua

The abduction of islanders into slavery

After first being reached by the Dutch Admiral Jacob Roggeven in 1722, the territory of Te Pito O Te Henua was visited by various explorers during the 18th century, with little lasting impact.

---

3 *Ariki* is usually translated as 'king'. For a history of the last *Ariki* and their designation see Moreno Pakarati 2010, p. 54.

However, in the 19th century, adventurers, pirates and vandals inflicted great harm on the native population of Rapa Nui. In 1862, the human population on Rapa Nui totalled approximately 6, 000.[4] In that year, a number of pirate ships arrived at the island and abducted men and women to be sold into slavery in Peru. The most destructive raid occurred on 23 December 1862 when six ships, some of them Chilean, flying Peruvian flags, arrived in Rapa Nui to obtain slaves. Eighty sailors fired a volley of shots; many Rapa Nui people were killed, others threw themselves into the sea and some fled to the mountains, while around a thousand remained to try and defend themselves but were finally captured. Many keepers of oral traditions were among the people captured as slaves, including those who knew how to read the *rongo-rongo* tablets,[5] *Ariki* (chiefs) and priests. A few months after the end of the Peruvians raids, the French Catholic mission demonstrated an interest in establishing itself in Rapa Nui. Tepano Jaussen, a bishop in Tahiti (a Polynesian territory colonised by France), intervened with the Lima government to repatriate the victims of slavery to the island. Some of the islanders relocated instead to Mangareva and to Pamata'i in Tahiti and some returned to Rapa Nui but, on the return voyage in August 1863, most of the 100 Rapa Nui on the boat died from smallpox and tuberculosis. Only a dozen or so actually returned to the island, many of them sick with smallpox, tuberculosis and other illnesses, and subsequently infected the disease-free population. As a result of the epidemic, by the year 1877 only 111 people remained on the island.[6]

The last quarter of the 19th century gave rise to two more milestones in Rapa Nui history: the elimination of the native Rapa Nui religion by the Catholic missions established in Hanga Roa in 1866 and Tarakiu in 1867[7] and the colonisation of the island by the State of Chile. For the Rapa Nui people, the 19th century was thus synonymous with slavery, violence and colonisation.

The colonisation of Rapa Nui by Chile

In 1888, a bilateral agreement was signed between the Kingdom of Te Pito O Te Henua, represented by King Atamu Tekena, and Chile, represented by Lieutenant Commander Policarpo Toro. According to the version written in Rapa Nui and ancient Tahitian, in this act the King retained the prerogatives of his Royal investiture, his territory and his institutions, making an act of faith and placing his trust in Chile, as a friend of the place; in return, through this act, Chile offered protection and development, as a friend of the place.

According to Rapa Nui oral tradition, in order to demonstrate Rapa Nui sovereignty over the territory, the King took a handful of soil and solemnly placed it in his bag; at the same time he took a

---

4 Cristino 2010, p. 25.
5 *Rongo-Rongo tablets*: the 'talking tablets' which bear carved figures on their surfaces symbolising a writing not yet deciphered.
6 Because of the tuberculosis, the population of Rapa Nui was reduced to 900 people by November 1866 and 600 by May 1869 (see Consejo de Jefes de Rapa Nui 1988, p. 286).
7 In 1868, a forced evangelisation of the resisting Rapa Nui took place, resulting in their transfer – along with the baptised Rapa Nui – closer to the missions. See Consejo de Jefes de Rapa Nui 1988, p. 285.

handful of grass and gave it to Chile's representative, thus making the foundations of the Treaty clear.

His Majesty the King added: "As from today, you can fly your flag from the same mast, mine at the top and yours under mine." He continued: "By flying your flag, Chile, you do not become the owners of this island because I have sold you nothing and I have gifted you nothing." This agreement culminated in the raising of both flags, that of Rapa Nui at the top and that of Chile beneath it. Fifteen years later in 1913, the Commander of the Chilean Navy ordered the Rapa Nui flag to be removed and sent to Chile, leaving orders that they would no longer allow any flag to be raised on Rapa Nui other than the Chilean.[8]

Not long after the 1888 Treaty was concluded, King Atamu Tekena handed over power to King Simeón Riroroko. Just seven years after the Treaty was signed, Chile began to systematically violate its provisions. On 6 September 1895, Chile signed a contract leasing out the island to the businessman Enrique Merlet who worked with the sheep farming company Williamson-Balfour Company. Under this lease signed by Enrique Merlet, and with the complicity of successive company administrators (Alberto Sánchez Manterola, Horacio Cooper and, later, Henry Percy Edmunds), the heritage and territory of the Rapa Nui Kingdom was divided up and stolen and sacred sites were destroyed. The Rapa Nui population were attacked, slaughtered, humiliated and forced into slavery following their violent eviction from their clans' ancestral territories, finally being incarcerated on a reserve measuring one square kilometre in size.[9] Any complaints made by the Rapa Nui population against the companies and administrators were violently suppressed. King Simeón Riroroko died in Valparaíso years later during a visit to demand respect for the Treaty signed by Chile.[10]

When the leasing agreement for the island expired in 1953 (having been extended once in 1917), Chile entrusted administration of the island to the Chilean Armed Forces. Ill-treatment of the Rapa Nui nation continued unabated. Forced labour was maintained, as were the previously established *"lunes fiscales"* by which all men were forced to work for the Chilean Army for free.

---

8   In 1990, Juan Teave Haoa, President of the Council of Chiefs, issued a Decree Law to raise the Reimiro Rapa Nui flag, communicating this decision to Governor Jacobo Hey Paoa and Mayor Pedro Edmunds Paoa; the Rapa Nui flag thus flew once more form the church mast, as part of a peaceful protest claiming their territory.
9   In 1896, the Chilean Maritime Governor and then administrator Alberto Sánchez Manterola, in complicity with Enrique Merlet, armed with guns and other weapons, evicted the sovereign Rapa Nui owners from their ancestral lands, seizing them and destroying the territorial integrity of the Rapa Nui Nation; they killed those that resisted, intimidating and raping women and children, burning crops and houses, and stealing all the animals. This inferno lasted three days. Fires were lit deliberately at points adjacent to the crops; the wind immediately spread the fire, forcing the people from their lands without food and turning them into slaves. They were violently evicted, amidst grief and tears, to be incarcerated in Hanga Roa, a reserve of approximately one square kilometre, deprived of their freedom to move outside of this area, slaves on their own land, prohibited from fishing or seeking other forms of sustenance. Many Rapa Nui died of hunger, over-exploitation and grief. The ban on their free movement around the island without the express authorisation of the Company lasted until the mid-1960s.
10 "Some time after his arrival at Valparaíso, H.M. King Riro Roko died and his prime minister Juan Araki, to whom the right to the Crown of Easter Island fell, was unable to return to his lands as he became seriously ill with consumption in the Andean town," newspaper *El Mercurio*, 8 April 1900 (unofficial translation).

Those who refused to follow orders or complained of ill-treatment had their heads shaved, were tied to fig trees on the public highway with nothing to eat or were taken off to prison.[11]

Until the enactment of Easter Island Law No. 16.441 of 1966,[12] the islanders had no civil or political rights on their island and until 1956 were unable even to leave their territory, despite having travelled throughout the whole of Polynesia – being a Polynesian nation – prior to colonisation by Chile.[13]

Appropriation of the island's lands by Chile

From 1928 to 1965, the Chilean Armed Forces granted some 500 provisional land titles.[14] However, these were not titles recognising ownership but simply allowing the occupation of the land, with rights of use and enjoyment. The titles were evenly split between urban and rural plots. The rest of the island's territory was occupied first by the Williamson-Balfour Company, which remained after its lease expired and continued to use land on the island until 1954, and then by the Chilean Navy.

In 1933, by means of a unilateral decision in violation of the 1888 Treaty, the Chilean government formally signed over the whole of the island's territory (16,600 ha) to the Chilean state, failing to recognise any indigenous Rapa Nui ownership rights.[15]

For the Rapa Nui nation, this formal annexation of the island by Chile meant not only the loss of their sovereignty and of title to their lands but also the loss of their tangible and intangible cultural heritage. This led the Rapa Nui nation to mobilise in an attempt to preserve and protect their cultural legacy.

Rapa Nui as heritage of Chile: seizure and denial of the Rapa Nui culture

The cultural heritage of the Rapa Nui nation

Cultural heritage provides a living record of everything that makes up the life and experiences of man, and it is the source of inalienable and fundamental rights that must be protected. The

---

11 When the author Erity Teave was 9 years old, they shaved the head of her aunt, María Atan, for complaining about unfair school punishments given to children and because the Governor claimed she had stolen a rabbit that his wife had in fact moved. H.M. King Valentino Riroroko also recalls in this regard: "Between 1944 and 1958 the ill-treatment continued, we were treated worse than animals, and so the alternative was to seek freedom in order to be able to denounce Rapa Nui's disaster; many managed to flee secretly in small boats with the hope of finding help or a better life." Don Valentino adds, "I am a survivor of this odyssey, many never arrived at their destination" (Personal interview, August 2011).
12 The 1966 Easter Island Law ('Ley Pascua') recognised the status of the island's inhabitants as Chilean citizens and established their duties and rights (including that of being able to leave the island). It created the Easter Island Department and the Island Municipality, and established different Chilean state public services on the island.
13 Polynesian triangle formed by Hawai'i, A'otearoa (New Zealand) and Rapa Nui.
14 Ramírez 2008, p. 10.
15 "The state owns Easter Island, known also as Rapa Nui... acquiring this island through occupation by virtue of Article 590 of the Civil Code..." (Registro de propiedades del Conservador de Bienes raíces y de Comercio de Valparaíso, Sheet 2400, N°2424, 1933; unofficial translation).

island culture, characterised by the mysteries of the island, its intangible cultural heritage and the archaeological remains, continues to be alive through cultural rituals, traditions and ancestor worship. The *Moai*, the island's iconic megalithic statues, represent the living faces of Rapa Nui ancestors. Alone or in groups, they are majestically placed on stone platforms called '*Ahu*', sacred sites where the remains of the leaders were deposited (ancient cemeteries), giving the place a solemnity that is difficult to describe.

The Rapa Nui language, music, culture and worldview are of Polynesian origin. The ancestral writings – still not deciphered – remain held in the *rongo-rongo* tablets. The last people able to read this writing died during the serious outrages committed against the Rapa Nui people and their culture from the 19th century onwards.

Rapa Nui has been considered an open-air museum because of its concentration of elements of Rapa Nui cultural heritage, which contribute significantly to the wealth and variety of cultural heritage of Polynesia and the South Pacific in general. Almost 900 *Moai* have been catalogued, more than 270 *Ahu* of varying sizes, thousands of cave figures (petroglyphs and paintings), and archaeological features of various kinds, including agricultural structures, residential sites, quarries, workshops and more. Most of these are located within the boundaries of the Rapa Nui National Park, formally established by Chile in 1935.

Aware of the immeasurable value of its culture, the Rapa Nui nation has continued to organise in an effort to preserve the legacy of its ancestors, its history, arts, language and worldview, and to oppose and minimise the impact of the policies implemented by the Chilean state in order to culturally assimilate the Rapa Nui people. In 1974 the Tu'u Hotu Iti group was formed to help preserve this legacy. Through dance, shows, songs, traditional dress and sets, this Rapa Nui group represented the legends and customs of its people and served as a reference for various generations of Rapa Nui who, in turn, have created new artistic and cultural Rapa Nui groups.[16]

When the military government of General Pinochet banned the Rapa Nui language in 1979, Juan Chávez (Teave) Haoa stood up at a general meeting of the parents' association for the only high school on the island, of which he was president, and said, "Never again shall a person be born who bans my mother tongue. I withdraw from this meeting. Let those who agree with this man remain." Everyone then got up and walked out. An audience was immediately obtained with Gen. Pinochet to demand a change of Military Governor and to demand a Governor native to the island, along with the lifting of the language ban.

The Rapa Nui language, its people, their culture, their worldview, their arts and sacred monuments, along with the island's territory (*Kainga* in the Rapa Nui language and worldview), a sacred site in itself, form the Rapa Nui cultural heritage, a tangible and intangible, indivisible heritage belonging to the Rapa Nui nation.

---

16 The Tu'u Hotu Iti group's first members and directors were Carlos Huke, as creator and legal representative, and Joel Huke as director. The rest of its members numbered between 17 and 20 islanders primarily from the Tuki and Huke families. Since it began, more than 300 young people from the Tuki, Huke, Teao, Hereveri, Pa, Pakomio, Pakarati, Ika, Haoa, Teave, Hotu, Pont, Tepihui and Tepano families have directly or indirectly participated (Hucke 1995, pp. 43-44).

The overwhelming link that binds the Rapa Nui to their Kainga

Rapa Nui ancestors named the territory, the land, '*Kainga*' (meaning 'Womb' or 'Uterus') "where human beings gestate". Mother Earth is viewed by the Rapa Nui as a sacred sanctuary in which humans are born with a physical and spiritual bond that makes them inseparable. Perhaps the closest analogy is the relation between mother and child before birth, bound eternally by an intrinsic, natural and inherent spirit. This worldview prevents the Rapa Nui from separating the land, environment, life or nature simply because everything is integrated, and was conceived under these principles. For the Rapa Nui the world is like the human body, internally interconnected, each organ having a different vital function of equal importance; down to the last cell, all is necessary, nothing is superfluous, and all contributes to the optimum conditions that permit life. Holistically, the world of the human being functions in precisely the same way: everything that makes up this world – environment, land, sea, way of life, development – is interdependent and obeys a natural order, and humans are a part of this interconnection.

The cultural practices of the Rapa Nui neither affect nor change the natural environment; on the contrary, tradition has established norms and codes of conduct for the use, enjoyment and care of the environment. Greed, the revolution of economic interests and a lack of respect on the part of the coloniser have, however, altered the island considerably. Since their arrival on the island, the Chilean state and its administrators have failed to respect the value of *Rapa Nui Kainga*; on the contrary, they have illegally robbed it, using excessive violence and arrogance, failing to respect its biodiversity and the transcendental relationship that binds it to its Rapa Nui children. Not only has Chile denied the Rapa Nui ownership of the majority of the island, it has also stolen their cultural heritage to form the Rapa Nui National Park, on an area of land that includes most of the Rapa Nui sacred sites. This park was declared Chilean natural heritage in 1935, without consideration for the rights, ownership and care provided by its sovereign owners: the Rapa Nui nation.

Chile's theft of Rapa Nui cultural heritage

Following the illegal transfer of all of Rapa Nui's lands into the name of the Chilean state in 1933, successively and without consulting the Rapa Nui nation, the Chilean state passed a series of laws aimed at turning a large part of the island's territory and Rapa Nui heritage into the historic heritage of Chile. In 1935, Chile declared the whole island to be a national monument and created the "Easter Island National Park", renamed the "Tourism National Park" in 1966, and then the "Rapa Nui National Park" in 1976. Also in 1976, and again without consulting the Rapa Nui nation, the three sacred islets of Motu Nui, Motu Iti and Motu Kao Kao were declared a "Nature Sanctuary". The National Park, along with the sacred islets (with which the island and the Rapa Nui maintain a sacred relationship), hold the largest number of *Moai, Ahu*, caves and sacred sites, including *Orongo*, a sacred religious site where the god *Make Make* used to be worshipped and where ceremonies are still conducted.

The park's boundaries were gradually extended by the Chilean administration until they reached today's area of 6,913.06 ha, equivalent to 41.64% of the whole island, while the sovereign Rapa Nui owners hold the title to only 14% of the island's land.

In this context, and with the aim of seeking help in protecting various archaeological sites that were in a state of decay (*Orongo, Ahu Tongariki*), the Chilean state submitted a nomination to UNESCO in 1994 for Rapa Nui National Park to be listed as a World Heritage site in the category of cultural landscape.

UNESCO's Declaration of the Rapa Nui National Park as a World Cultural Heritage site and the new challenges of protecting Rapa Nui's cultural heritage

In 1995, UNESCO inscribed Rapa Nui National Park on the World Heritage List as a cultural landscape, without any consultation with the Rapa Nui themselves and relying solely on the advice of international institutions. Despite the disregard shown to them, some Rapa Nui nevertheless thought that this declaration could perhaps help to protect both Rapa Nui's cultural heritage and respect for their rights as an indigenous people. However, almost 20 years have passed since the park was declared a World Heritage site and it has been predominantly the Chilean state and tourists who have profited from this declaration. The Rapa Nui nation and its people have not benefited, nor has their heritage been protected effectively enough. A letter sent on 24 June 2008 to the Chilean President Michelle Bachelet by the CONADI[17] National Advisor representing the Rapa Nui people, Rafael Tuki Tepano, complained that: "Our monuments are deteriorating day by day for lack of the necessary care, while the number of uncivilised people who are destroying them is increasing, without the necessary staff to look after them".[18] Furthermore, since 1995, despite visitors arriving from all over the world to visit the World Heritage site and the island, the rest of the Rapa Nui territory and the Rapa Nui nation have continued to face a series of major problems stemming from the failure to respect the fundamental right of the Rapa Nui nation to self-determination and to maintain, control, protect and develop their own heritage.[19]

Demographic collapse on the island: increasing migration and tourism and a controversial draft migration law

Since the designation of almost half of the island as a World Heritage site, Rapa Nui has experienced a significant increase in population, including an increase in the floating population

---

17 The National Indigenous Development Corporation (*Corporación Nacional de Desarrollo Indígena*), a national institution created by Indigenous Law No. 19.253 and responsible for implementing public policies on indigenous issues as determined by Chilean law.
18 Letter on file with author (unofficial translation).
19 See, e.g., *UN Declaration on the Rights of Indigenous Peoples*, Arts. 3, 11, 12, and 31.

due to uncontrolled Chilean and foreign tourism. In 1992, the island's population (both Rapa Nui and non-Rapa Nui) was estimated at 2,764 inhabitants; this increased to 3,791 in 2002, 4,231 in 2005 and in 2009 the population was estimated to total almost 6,000 people, of which only half are Rapa Nui and the rest are Chilean and foreign migrants.[20]

To this fixed population must be added the tourists, who double the population in the summer months and make tourism the dominant economic activity on the island around which most other activities revolve, including handicrafts, fishing, agriculture and other services.[21]

Between 2010 and 2011, visitors to the island fluctuated between 50,000 and 70,000 people per year, yet the National Forestry Corporation (CONAF) responsible for the park has not developed a tourism management plan aimed at preserving the island's biodiversity and the tangible and intangible Rapa Nui cultural heritage. The increase in both the fixed and floating populations has serious repercussions, not only in terms of the island's environment and preservation of its archaeological sites but also in terms of the preservation of the park and of Rapa Nui cultural heritage more generally. CONAF charges an entrance fee but has not implemented the necessary measures to provide protection for the park. By way of example, in 1995 the park recorded 7,760 visitors and had a body of nine park guards but, in 2005, with 20,000 visitors more, this had only increased to 12 guards.[22] This is woefully insufficient to cover the 6,000 ha of the park and ensure that tourists respect all areas of this open-air museum. As Bahamondez and González point out: "The resources intended for this purpose are absolutely insufficient and the fact is that tourists can move, freely and with virtually no controls, around all of the archaeological sites, with all the dangers and lack of care this implies."[23] Indeed, when around 4,000 people came to watch the solar eclipse in 2010, the intervention and improvisation of the Rapa Nui Parliament was necessary in order to safeguard the sacred sites. The Rapa Nui Parliament, discussed in greater detail below, is a representative authority of the Rapa Nui nation although it is largely unrecognised by the Chilean state.

Since 2003, the lack of action on the part of the Chilean state in the face of the island's over-population has led the Rapa Nui to call for controls on migration into the island and on tourist numbers. This is due to the irreversible consequences that over-population is having on Rapa Nui, threatening an imminent social and environmental collapse.[24] Migration and tourism have also led to the gradual deterioration of Rapa Nui living conditions and cultural integrity and the growing personal and family insecurity caused by increased crime coming from Chile.[25] The Rapa Nui

---

20 Statistics produced at the extraordinary session of the Chilean Senate, No. 78 of 22 December 2009.
21 In 2005, the tourist population comprised 30% Chilean tourists and 70% foreign tourists.
22 Data produced at a session of the Commission for the Development of Easter Island (CODEIPA), on the theme of Immigration and Transport, 8 April 2005.
23 Bahamondez and González 2007, p. 61.
24 Social and environmental problems on the island include: over-population in the Hanga Roa sector, a lack of drainage, which is threatening to contaminate the underground aquifers in the near future, the collapse of basic services such as electricity, leading to repeated black-outs, along with serious problems of waste management and in health services.
25 In 2003, the Chilean government was presented with a proposal to adopt a migration law. In 2009, with the aim of drawing the government's and international press attention to the need to control entry to the island, the Rapa Nui Parliament seized the airport in an attempt to force Chile to tackle the urgent issue of uncontrolled migration into Rapa Nui from Santiago de Chile. This is a critical problem for the island, and one that tremendously affects the environment, security, access to basic services such as health and the labour market, given that all contracts for work are put out to tender in Chile.

Tourists at Ahu Tongariki in Rapa Nui National Park. The Rapa Nui Parliament has called for Rapa Nui self-administration of the national park and for controls on tourist numbers to mitigate the significant adverse impacts of tourism on the island's environment and Rapa Nui tangible and intangible cultural heritage.
Photo: Mary Madigan (CC BY 2.0)

now want to ensure that anyone entering or remaining on Rapa Nui has to appear before a Rapa Nui legal commission to legalise their migratory status (distinguishing between permanent and temporary residents, and tourists) and pay a fine for any infractions committed against Rapa Nui tangible and intangible cultural heritage.

Despite the urgency with which such measures need to be implemented, the desire of the overwhelming majority of Rapa Nui to establish such controls[26] and the fact that establishing such controls is a right of the Rapa Nui nation protected by international law,[27] neither Chile's government nor Congress has agreed to adopt such a migration law. Instead, they prioritise economic income from tourism over respect for the most fundamental rights of the Rapa Nui nation. Illustrating this in 2009, the Vice-Minister of the Interior stated: "We are not seeking to restrict tourism or the inflow of

---

26 The results of a survey of 1,100 people (90% Rapa Nui and 10% married to Rapa Nui) conducted by the organisation Makenu Re o Rapa Nui showed that 99.9% of those surveyed were in favour of establishing immigration controls for the island. Makenu Re o Rapa Nui 2009, p. 7.
27 International human rights law, in particular the UNDRIP, recognises indigenous peoples' right to self-determination and to live in freedom, peace and security as distinct peoples (Arts. 1, 3 and 7 UNDRIP). It also recognises their right not to be subjected to forced assimilation or destruction of their culture, and gives the State responsibility for taking the necessary measures to prevent and compensate for any action which has the aim or effect of depriving them of their integrity as distinct peoples or of their cultural values or identities (Art. 8 UNDRIP).

visitors to the island but to stimulate tourism by improving the conditions under which tourists can discover the island's interior."[28]

Violations of the Rapa Nui nation's collective rights

Human rights and fundamental freedoms can only exist truly and fully when self-determination also exists, as established by Resolution 1514 of the 1960 UN General Assembly.[29] Therein lies the fundamental importance of self-determination as a human right, by virtue of which all peoples collectively determine their political, social and economic condition: it is a prerequisite for the enjoyment of all other human rights.

Violations of the Rapa Nui nation's right to self-determination

Indigenous Law No. 19.253 of 1993 recognises the Council of Elders as the only representative institution of the Rapa Nui nation, despite the continued existence of other Rapa Nui institutions. The Council of Elders is currently presided over by Alberto Hotus, someone whom the Rapa Nui nation does not feel represents them.[30] The Law also established CODEIPA, the Commission for the Development of Easter Island, with limited powers.[31] Alongside these institutions, the Rapa Nui nation's own representative institutions were re-established autonomously. In 1980, the Council of Chiefs was revived, from which emerged the *Koro o te Unahi Renga*, or Rapa Nui Parliament, composed of 12 Ministers and 36 Clan Chiefs.

The Rapa Nui Parliament represents the continuous resistance and historic struggle of the Rapa Nui nation to ensure the protection of their cultural heritage, the promotion of the interests of the Rapa Nui people and the recognition of the ancestral Rapa Nui ownership of their territory. This institution has assumed a social and political commitment to continue the peaceful struggle for the self-determination and territorial integrity of the Rapa Nui Kingdom, the eradication of colonialism, and the realisation of the UN Millennium Development Goals on Rapa Nui Island within the framework of the Third International Decade for the Eradication of Colonialism (2011-2020).

In line with Resolutions 1514 and 1541 of the 1960 UN General Assembly, which establish an obligation for colonising states to register nations such as Rapa Nui on the List of Non-Self-Governing Territories under Art. 73 of the UN Charter (especially if they are a territory

---

28 Minutes of a meeting between the Chilean government and Rapa Nui institutions on the draft of a migration law, 2009 (unpublished document on file with author, unofficial translation).
29 *Declaration on the Granting of Independence to Colonial Countries and Peoples.*
30 Alberto Hotus Chávez was removed from his post as President of the Council for failing to comply with his mandate not to occupy state posts or be a member of a political party (Consejo de Ancianos-Jefes de Rapa Nui 1994).
31 CODEIPA, which began operating in 1999, comprises five members of Rapa Nui origin, plus the President of the Council of Elders, the Mayor and the Governor, who is its chair. It also includes representatives from the National Indigenous Development Council, the Ministry of National Assets, Mideplán, CORFO, Ministry of Education, CONAF and the Chilean Army.

geographically separated by the ocean with a different origin, language and culture, as is the case with Rapa Nui), and with the 2007 *UN Declaration on the Rights of Indigenous Peoples* (UNDRIP, Arts. 1, 3, 4 and 5), the Rapa Nui Parliament demands respect for the Rapa Nui nation's right to self-determination. In exercise of this right, in 2011 the Rapa Nui Parliament proclaimed H.M. Valentino Riroroko King of Te Pito O Te Henua and drew up a Political Constitution for the Rapa Nui Kingdom.[32] However, neither the Rapa Nui's own institutions nor the demands made by its Parliament have been acknowledged in the draft special status drawn up by Chile for the special territory.[33] This draft, which proposes turning the Island of Rapa Nui into another sub-region of Chile, directly dependent upon the central authority, was not put out to consultation with the Rapa Nui representative institutions, in violation of the *Indigenous and Tribal Peoples Convention, 1989* (ILO Convention 169, Art. 6) and the UNDRIP (Arts. 18 and 19). It has been rejected on numerous occasions, not only by the Rapa Nui Parliament but also by the elected Rapa Nui members of CODEIPA, the Rapa Nui members of the Committee on the Special Status for Rapa Nui (Mesa de Estatuto Especial), the organisation Makenu Re'o Rapa Nui and the Rapa Nui representative within CONADI, Rafael Tucki, for violating inalienable rights such as the right to self-determination and for ignoring the rights of the native people.[34] This 'Proposed Special Statute of Administration for Easter Island' remains for now in draft form and has not become law.[35]

The Rapa Nui nation's struggle for recovery of their ancestral lands

"In the ancestral tradition that is respected to this day, land ownership had a corporate function deriving from a tribal conception in which each individual, to a greater or lesser extent, would receive the benefits of it [the land]; with this legislation [Chilean law] family ties are cut, ties that are a fundamental pillar of Polynesian societies and an innate part of their law (…)"

Paloma Hucke[36]

---

32 On 5 August 2011, the Rapa Nui Parliament proclaimed His Majesty Valentino Riroroko, grandson of the last king poisoned in Chile, as King. The next day, the King presented a legal complaint to the Valparaíso Appeals Court against the State of Chile for breach of the 1888 Treaty.

33 Since the 2007 constitutional reform, the territory of Rapa Nui has constituted a "special territory". By virtue of this, its government and administration are to be governed by a special status, envisaged in an organic constitutional law that has yet to be passed. In August 2005, President Lagos was presented with a Proposed Special Statute of Administration for Easter Island, which was submitted to Congress as a draft bill of law during 2008 and is still under consideration.

34 On 17 November 2003, the Special Rapporteur on the situation of human rights and fundamental freedoms of indigenous people, Mr. Rodolfo Stavenhagen, made the following recommendation: "The planned statute of autonomy for Easter Island (Rapa Nui) should contain guarantees for the protection of the rights of the native Rapa Nui people over their land and resources and their right to respect for their social organization and cultural life." (UN Commission on Human Rights 2004, para. 61).

35 In August 2005, President Lagos was presented with a Proposed Special Statute of Administration for Easter Island, which was submitted to Congress as a draft bill of law during 2008 and is still under consideration.

36 Hucke 1995, p. 56 (unofficial translation).

"Land ownership still has a corporate function, similar to the rest of Polynesia, in which rights over the land fall to groups in which there exist individual, extended family, lineage and clan rights, etc., and each piece of land is subject to a hierarchy of rights at different levels (...)"

Council of Rapa Nui Chiefs[37]

As previously noted, in 1933 the Chilean state declared that all the island's lands were to form part of the public domain, in violation of the provisions of the 1888 Treaty. As this was land traditionally occupied by the Rapa Nui people, the territorial area declared world and national heritage should belong to the Rapa Nui nation, in accordance with the UNDRIP (Arts. 25, 26, 27 and 28), ILO Convention 169 (Arts. 13, 14 and 15) and the jurisprudence of the Inter-American Court of Human Rights (IACHR).[38] However, currently only 13.65% of the land belongs to Rapa Nui people,[39] while 13.6% is in a state of irregular land tenure and the remaining 72.75% of the island (11,866 ha),[40] which includes most of the Rapa Nui sacred sites, falls under the domain of the Chilean state. This is considerably restricting the possibilities of livestock/agricultural production and fishing on the part of the Rapa Nui. Indigenous Law No. 19.253 did institute a mechanism by which rural lands began to be provided to the Rapa Nui population; however, only 1,500 ha (divided into five-hectare plots) have been set aside within the Vaitea Estate,[41] failing to take into consideration both traditional Rapa Nui territorial clan rights and international law relating to indigenous peoples. There are currently plans to begin negotiating a second phase of land distribution within the Vaitea Estate but this in no way envisages the return of lands located within the Rapa Nui National Park. Moreover, conditions are being placed upon lands of archaeological value within the Vaitea Estate, riding roughshod over the Rapa Nui nation's right to self-determination and territory.

Members of the Rapa Nui nation have demonstrated for the return of their ancestral lands,[42] for control over their natural resources and management of their cultural heritage but their protests

---

37 Consejo de Jefes de Rapa Nui 1988, p. 284 (unofficial translation).
38 See the judgments of the IACHR in the following cases: *Xákmok Kásek Indigenous Community v. Paraguay*, Judgment of 24 August 2010; *Saramaka People v. Suriname*, Judgment of 28 November 2007; *Sawhoyamaxa Indigenous Community v. Paraguay*, Judgment of 29 March 2006; *Yatama v. Nicaragua*, Judgment of 23 June 2005; *Moiwana Community v. Suriname*, Judgment of 15 June 2005; *Yakye Axa Indigenous Community v. Paraguay*, Judgment of 17 June 2005; *Mayagna (Sumo) Awas Tingni Community v. Nicaragua*, Judgment of 31 August 2001; *Aloeboetoe et al. v. Suriname*, Judgment of 10 September 1993.
39 This percentage corresponds to 973 individual titles. Of these, 9% were issued in the period 1990-2005, which included the so-called first stage of land restoration to the Rapa Nui, with 252 land titles granted in the 1998-2000 process. 530 are urban plots corresponding to 0.98% of the total area of the island and 35.01% of its urban area, and 443 are rural plots corresponding to 12.67% of the island's total area and only 13.04% of the total rural area (Ministry of National Assets 2008, pp. 1-5).
40 Rapa Nui National Park: 42% of the island, 6,900 ha; Vaitea Estate: 28% of the island, 4,600 ha.
41 The Vaitea country estate (Fundo Vaitea) in the centre of the island was formerly a sheep ranch managed by the Williamson-Balfour Company and is today in concession to state-owned livestock group SASIPA. It has an extension of 4.600 ha, which represents 28% of the total area of the island.
42 Many Rapa Nui reject the individuals titles promoted by the Chilean administration that endanger the cultural integrity of the Rapa Nui people.

Demonstration in January 2011 as part of a collective effort of the Rapa Nui people to recover their ancestral lands, protect sacred sites and regain self-government over clan issues. Photo: El Ciudadano

have been systematically and violently suppressed by the Chilean government. This repression came to a head in December 2010 when shots were fired at Rapa Nui individuals on 3 December and again on 29 December when a contingent of 200 or more special armed forces (G.O.P.E.) were sent to the island with police dogs and other equipment to brutally suppress and forcibly evict women, children and men, including members of the Rapa Nui Parliament, who were protesting in Riro Kainga Square. The peaceful demands of the Rapa Nui Parliament regarding their territory and decolonisation, their protests against the proposed special status and their calls for urgent controls to be placed on entry to the island from Chile and the right to remain on Rapa Nui were thus violently put down. As a consequence of the police violence, on 7 February 2011 the Inter-American Commission on Human Rights granted precautionary measures for the Rapa Nui people stating that "the Rapa Nui people's life and integrity are at risk due to acts of violence and intimidation reportedly carried out by police in the context of demonstrations and evictions".[43]

---

43 PM 321/10 - Rapa Nui Indigenous People, Chile.

In December 2010, Chilean armed police brutally suppressed peaceful protests of members of the Rapa Nui nation calling for respect for Rapa Nui rights over their ancestral lands and heritage. The police caused significant injuries to over 20 people, beating them and shooting them with rubber bullets. Photo: Save Rapanui (CC BY-NC-ND 3.0)

Violations of the Rapa Nui nation's right to control, protect and develop their cultural heritage

The Rapa Nui National Park is currently managed by CONAF and, until recently, all of its revenue was remitted to Chile. When in 1997 Rapa Nui groups wanted to get involved in the park administration and charge entry fees to tourists wishing to visit their sacred sites, the Chilean state invoked the Law on State Security against them. Today, thanks to the struggle of the Rapa Nui people, income from entrance fees remains on the island although it continues to be administered by the Rapa Nui municipality, an institution representing the Chilean state. Also when Rapa Nui people try to access, use or take over any well, plant or rock within their ancestral territory located in the park, they continue to be arrested by the police or sentenced to pay a fine for having broken Chilean cultural heritage rules.

Since the park was declared a World Heritage site, a UNESCO-Japan-Rapa Nui project has made it possible to undertake work to restore some of the cultural sites.[44] For its part, the Rapa Nui Parliament

---

44   UNESCO started promoting and supporting the conservation and restoration of Rapa Nui cultural heritage in 1966 (Charola 1994, pp. 53-57). For information on the restorations realised with the help of UNESCO since 1995, including the second stage of restoration of the *Ahu Tongariki* carried out by the UNESCO-Japan-Rapa Nui project, see Avilés 2006 and Bahamondez et al. 2007.

has revived its traditional laws in order to maintain, control, protect and develop the island's cultural heritage and intellectual property.[45] These laws, however, are being infringed on a daily basis by current Chilean law, in breach of international law and particularly Article 31 of the UNDRIP. In violation of this article, Indigenous Law No. 19.253 refers to indigenous cultures as part of Chile's national heritage[46] and legitimises the failure to protect indigenous peoples' rights to their own heritage.[47] Chilean Law No. 17.288 on national monuments continues to be applied, despite being incompatible with indigenous peoples' rights as recognised in international law. Although it does not specifically address indigenous cultural heritage, ILO Convention 169 (ratified by Chile in 2009) could be used to put an end to the violations of Rapa Nui cultural heritage, because of the obligation it places on the State to consult indigenous peoples in order to obtain their agreement or consent before approving measures that may affect them (Art. 6). In 2008-2009, when the Chilean government planned to take a *Moai* off the island to exhibit it in Europe, the Rapa Nui Parliament mobilised and requested that it be consulted, as a result of which it managed to prevent the removal of the *Moai* from the island. This consultation set a highly significant precedent as it was the first time that a *Moai* was implicitly recognised as forming the exclusive cultural heritage of the Rapa Nui. Prior to the ratification of ILO Convention 169 by Chile, various incidents of *Moai* being damaged both inside and outside the National Park were noted, without the Rapa Nui people having been consulted.[48] The Rapa Nui people's representative within CONADI in 2008 proposed establishing a Rapa Nui archaeological park, administered by a corporation run by Rapa Nui representative institutions, but this was rejected by the Chilean government.[49]

In conclusion, notwithstanding international human rights law relating to indigenous peoples, as contained in the UNDRIP, ILO Convention 169 and the evolving jurisprudence of UN and Inter-American human rights bodies, the Rapa Nui nation's rights to self-determination, territory, natural resources, participation, cultural heritage and intellectual property continue to be violated on a daily basis within a territory that has been declared a World Cultural Heritage site.

Recommendations to UNESCO

The Rapa Nui Parliament maintains that Rapa Nui cultural heritage can only be protected and promoted by safeguarding the native people's individual and collective human rights, which have

---

45 The *Moai* possess an importance and a sacred significance that Chile does not respect, committing sacrileges by using the *Moai* as a symbol in their tourist publicity, on their passports and in other uses.

46 "The State has a duty to promote the indigenous cultures that form part of the Chilean nation's heritage" (Art. 7 of Law No. 19.253). This provision violates the rights of the Rapa Nui nation, by which the Rapa Nui territory and its tangible and intangible heritage belong fully and exclusively to the native inhabitants of the Kingdom of Te Pito O Te Henua Rapa Nui, for the full use and enjoyment of their descendants.

47 Article 29(b) of Law No. 19.253 indicates that items of historical value may not be removed from the national territory with the aim of exhibiting them abroad; given that Rapa Nui is still considered a part of the Chilean territory, this provision enables the transfer of items of Rapa Nui heritage to continental Chile, located almost 4,000 km away from the island.

48 A few years back, the Chilean administration authorised archaeological studies of a *Moai*, located within the Rapa Nui National Park, permitting the buried part of the *Moai* to be excavated without consulting the Rapa Nui nation. Seismic activity was also conducted on state lands with the aim of removing construction materials, and this caused the demolition and destruction of various *Moai* for which no compensation was paid (the *Moai* are currently covered with nylon and wooden boards).

49 Letter sent by R. Tuki Tepano, CONADI National Advisor to President Bachelet on 24 June 2008.

been historically denied to them. Today the Rapa Nui people demand and desire that they be respected by others, commencing with UNESCO.

UNESCO should consider respect for human rights a fundamental factor in protecting Rapa Nui cultural heritage; this needs to be made concrete through respect and consideration for the native people, recognising, valuing and respecting their decision-making capacity over their heritage. The Rapa Nui people need to be the ones who define the guidelines on how to optimise the management, protection and promotion of their heritage. They are clearly the only people who know Rapa Nui culture deeply, and how best to rescue, protect and maintain their identity, which is today in danger.

Given the international legal framework for indigenous rights that is now in force and the fact that this is constantly being violated by the Chilean administration in Te Pito O Te Henua, despite part of the island having been declared World Cultural Heritage by UNESCO, and given that this organisation forms part of the UN system which is committed to protecting indigenous rights, it is recommended that UNESCO:

- Respect the intellectual property of the native people of Rapa Nui;
- Promote and recognise the political, administrative and decision-making capacity of the native people to manage and protect their own cultural heritage;
- Adapt the operational procedures for World Heritage to bring them into line with current international law on indigenous rights, particularly with regard to respecting indigenous peoples' right to consultation and to free, prior and informed consent when a World Heritage declaration affects part or all of their traditional territory;
- Make granting of World Heritage status conditional upon the participation of the indigenous peoples that traditionally own or occupy the area, and on the existence of internal regulations governing the administration and use of, and access to, the World Heritage site that are in accordance with the UNDRIP;
- Make retention of World Heritage status conditional upon respect for the UNDRIP, to be verified through a control mechanism implemented jointly with the UN Special Rapporteur on the Rights of Indigenous Peoples or another UN human rights institution.

To this day, Rapa Nui is suffering from the impacts of the injustices, atrocities and slavery that resulted from its colonisation by Chile, along with the alienation and seizure of its lands, territories and resources. This has prevented the Rapa Nui people from exercising their legitimate right to develop in accordance with their own needs and interests.

The survival of the Rapa Nui culture is dependent upon Chile and the United Nations respecting the Rapa Nui nation's right to self-determination, and so they must make a real commitment to cooperate with the Rapa Nui in order to achieve this, as the result of the historic struggle of this noble nation for justice.

"The Kingdom of Te Pito O Te Henua, Rapa Nui, its lands, its tangible and intangible heritage and its culture will be perpetuated for its descendants, via lineage and ancestry, in perpetual memory and via effective ownership of property, under the legal order of customary law, authorising full control over ancestral property."

Rapa Nui Parliament [50]

References

Avilés, M. 2006. *Concluye proyecto de restauración en Rapa Nui*. http://portal.unesco.org/es/ev.php-URL_ID=33345&URL_DO=DO_TOPIC&URL_SECTION=201.html (accessed 28 September 2014).

Bahamondez, M. and González, L. 2007. Principios de restauración y prospección arqueológica de Rapa Nui. P. Marambio (ed.), *Rapa Nui, Pasado, Presente y Futuro*. Santiago de Chile, UNESCO, pp. 55-62.

Bahamondez M. et al. 2007. Ahu Tongariki: trabajos de conservación de sus 15 moai. *Conserva*, No. 11, pp. 55-64.

Banderas, M. 1947. *La esclavitud en la Isla de Pascua*. Santiago, Imprenta Asís.

Charola, E. 1994. *Easter Island: The Heritage and its Conservation*. New York City, World Monuments Fund.

Comisión Verdad Histórica y Nuevo Trato. 2002. *La verdad Histórica de Rapa Nui y Planteamiento Final de la Comisión Provincial de Verdad Histórica y Nuevo Trato de Isla de Pascua* (Documento de Trabajo). Doc. CVHNT/GTRN/2002/056, Hanga Roa.

Comisión Verdad Histórica y Nuevo Trato. 2003. *Informe final*. Santiago de Chile.

Consejo de Ancianos-Jefes de Rapa Nui. 1994. Public statement. Rapa Nui, 4 February 1994.

Consejo de Jefes de Rapa Nui. 1988. *Te Mau Hatu 'O Rapa Nui – "Los Soberanos de Rapa Nui": Pasado, presente y futuro*. Santiago, Editorial Emisión.

Cristino, C. 2010. Colonialismo y neocolonialismo en Rapa Nui: una reseña histórica. C. Cristino and M. Fuentes (eds.), *La Compañia Explotadora de Isla de Pascua. Patrimonio, Memoria e Identidad en Rapa Nui*. Concepción, Escaparate Ediciones, pp. 19-52.

Fisher, S. 2005. *Island at the End of the World: The Turbulent History of Easter Island*. London, Reaktion Books.

Hucke, P. 1995. *Mata Tu'u Hotu Iti*. Santiago, Editorial Tiempo Nuevo.

Inter-American Commission on Human Rights. 2010. *Indigenous and Tribal Peoples' Rights over their Ancestral Lands and Natural Resources. Norms and Jurisprudence of the Inter American Human Rights System*. OEA/Ser.L/V/II. Doc.56/09, 30 December 2009.

Makenu Re o Rapa Nui. 2009. *Informe Técnico: Aplicación instrumento de consulta al Pueblo Rapanui. 'Apapa 'i te mana'u*. Hanga Roa.

McCall, G. 1994. *Rapanui: Tradition and Survival on Easter Island*. Honolulu, University of Hawai'i Press, 2nd ed.

Mendoza Uriarte, O. 2004. *Chile, un País Colonialista: El Caso del Pueblo Rapa Nui y el Territorio de Te Pito O Te Henua (Isla de Pascua)*. Undergraduate dissertation in legal sciences, Universidad Bolivariana, Santiago de Chile.

Métraux, A. 1995. *La Isla de Pascua*. Barcelona, Laertes, 3rd ed.

Ministry of National Assets. 2008. *Minuta: Situación de la Tierra y el Trabajo del Ministerio de Bienes Nacionales en Isla de Pascua*. Ministerio de Bienes Nacionales (Chile), Oficina Provincial Isla De Pascua.

Moreno Pakarati, C. 2010. El poder político nativo en Rapa Nui tras la muerte de los últimos 'Ariki Mau. C. Cristino and M. Fuentes (eds.), *La Compañia Explotadora de Isla de Pascua. Patrimonio, Memoria e Identidad en Rapa Nui*. Concepción, Escaparate Ediciones, pp. 53-73.

Parlamento Rapanui. 2013. Documento del Parlamento Rapanui. M. Fuentes (ed.), *Rapa Nui y la Compañía Explotadora*. Santiago, Rapanui Press, pp. 254-265. Also published at: http://www.lemondediplomatique.cl/Documento-del-Parlamento-Rapanui.html.

UN Commission on Human Rights. 2004. *Report of the Special Rapporteur on the situation of human rights and fundamental freedoms of indigenous people, Mr. Rodolfo Stavenhagen, on his mission to Chile*. Doc. E/CN.4/2004/80/Add.3, 17 November 2003.

---

50 Parlamento Rapanui 2013, p. 265 (unofficial translation).

Protecting Indigenous Rights in Denendeh: The Dehcho First Nations and Nahanni National Park Reserve

Laura Pitkanen and Jonas Antoine[1]

Introduction

This chapter chronicles the Dehcho First Nations' long-standing efforts to protect the South Nahanni River Watershed through the expansion of Nahanni National Park Reserve, a UNESCO World Heritage Site and homeland of tremendous cultural value for the Dehcho First Nations. The authors of this chapter have participated on behalf of the Dehcho First Nations in extensive negotiations for a co-management agreement and in a collaborative process for the expansion of Nahanni National Park Reserve. As such, we have an in-depth knowledge of the goals and objectives of the Dehcho First Nations regarding the park reserve and the challenges and successes along the way. Although the establishment of protected areas in Indigenous homelands in Canada and worldwide has often

---

1   Acknowledgements: The authors would like to thank Steve Catto, Georges Erasmus, David Murray, Lisa Myers and Chris Reid for helpful comments on a draft chapter. Any errors or omissions in the chapter are our own. The authors also acknowledge that the spelling of Naha Dehe in this chapter does not contain the Dene Zhatie symbols due to font incompatibility, and the correct font may be found in the original documents cited herein.

Left: Mt. Harrison-Smith and Glacier Lake in the expanded Nahanni National Park Reserve. Photo: Steve Kallick

constituted a neocolonial form of dispossession,² in this case we argue that the Dehcho First Nations objectives and actions towards the park reserve constitute a deliberate, comprehensive strategy of land management and stewardship for the Dehcho territory that seeks to meet the First Nations' goals regarding lands, resources and self-determination, while preserving their Aboriginal and Treaty rights. Yet more needs to be done. To this end, we conclude by making recommendations concerning the importance of including the Dehcho First Nations not only as a decision-making partner in the park reserve but also in any processes involving its international designation as a UNESCO World Heritage site.

Nahanni National Park Reserve

The Dehcho region is located in the south-west area of Denendeh, the homeland of the Dene peoples, in the Northwest Territories, Canada, and is the traditional territory of the Dehcho Dene and Metis peoples (Dehcho First Nations). Nahanni National Park Reserve is located within the traditional territory of the Dehcho First Nations, and primarily within the traditional territory of the Naha Dehe Dene Band, who have occupied the land since time immemorial.³ The Dehcho First Nations *Declaration of Rights* sets out their relationship with the land:

> "We the Dene of the Dehcho have lived on our homeland according to our own laws and system of government since time immemorial.
>
> Our homeland is comprised of the ancestral territories and waters of the Dehcho Dene. We were put here by the Creator as keepers of our waters and lands.
>
> The Peace Treaties of 1899 and 1921 with the non-Dene recognize the inherent political rights and powers of the Dehcho First Nation. Only sovereign peoples can make treaties with each other. Therefore our aboriginal rights and titles and oral treaties cannot be extinguished by any Euro-Canadian government.
>
> Our laws from the Creator do not allow us to cede, release, surrender or extinguish our inherent rights. The leadership of the Dehcho upholds the teachings of the Elders as the guiding principles of Dene government now and in the future.
>
> Today we reaffirm, assert and exercise our inherent rights and powers to govern ourselves as a nation.
>
> We the Dene of the Dehcho stand firm behind our First Nation government." ⁴

---

2   See, for example, Binnema and Niemi 2006, Sandlos 2001, and Dearden and Berg 1993.
3   Dehcho First Nations 2002.
4   Dehcho First Nations 1993. The website of the Dehcho First Nations contains information that is accessible to the public, including documents pertaining to the expansion of Nahanni National Park Reserve and Dehcho Process negotiations.

The *Declaration of Rights*, endorsed in 1993, is a guiding principle for the Dehcho First Nations in the Dehcho Process, a series of negotiations with the Government of Canada and the Government of Northwest Territories that began in 1999. The objective of the Dehcho Process is to conclude a *Dehcho Agreement* that will contain provisions for lands, resources and self-governance, and clarify and build upon the existing treaties (Treaties 8 and 11).

In 1971 and 1972, lands that would later become Nahanni National Park Reserve were set aside by the Government of Canada to protect the South Nahanni River and Virginia Falls from the threat of hydroelectric development.[5] Nahanni National Park Reserve was subsequently established in 1976. The original park reserve protected 4,766 square kilometers of the Mackenzie Mountains region in the south-west portion of the Dehcho region, Northwest Territories, Canada. While the park reserve was established within their traditional territory, the Dehcho First Nations assert that they "never ceded, released, or surrendered their aboriginal title and rights in the South Nahanni Watershed"[6] and the outstanding question of land title or ownership in the Dehcho territory is still a subject for negotiation in the Dehcho Process. The 1977 *Interim Management Guidelines* for the park reserve contain limited acknowledgement of the existence of Aboriginal claims to the area, noting that: "with the announcement of the establishment of Nahanni National Park in 1972, the Minister assured the native people of the area that traditional hunting, trapping and fishing would not be affected".[7] The 'Reserve' status of the park also reflects the outstanding claims of the Dehcho First Nations, for Nahanni National Park Reserve cannot be designated as a full national park until outstanding Aboriginal claims are settled.

Despite the unilateral declaration of park status by the Government of Canada and the limited recognition of Aboriginal claims, the Dehcho First Nations have, as noted by Grand Chief Samuel Gargan, viewed the potential of the park reserve and other protected areas initiatives "as tools that will help us manage our lands"[8] while protecting ecologically and culturally sensitive lands from oil and gas, mining and other developments that could negatively affect their rights and interests. As the park reserve is located in an extremely ecologically and culturally sensitive ecosystem that holds enormous traditional value for the Dehcho First Nations, this latter concern has formed the substantive basis for Dehcho support for the park reserve and reflects their self-determination. Further, the *Canada National Parks Act* recognizes the rights of the Dehcho First Nations to continue to use the area in the park reserve for traditional use.[9] The Dehcho strategy of land protection and land management through the park reserve also parallels the strategies of other First Nations in Canada, including the efforts of the Asatisiwipi First Nation to establish a UNESCO World Heritage site near Poplar River, northern Manitoba. These strategies are in effect "a preventative strike against the non-renewable development sector." [10]

---

5   For a detailed summary of the history of Nahanni National Park Reserve, see Tate 2004. For a critical analysis of national parks in Canada, see Dearden and Berg 1993.
6   Dehcho First Nations 2002.
7   Parks Canada 1977, p. 23.
8   Dehcho First Nations 2009a, p. 5.
9   *Canada National Parks Act* (S.C. 2000, c. 32), Section 40: "The application of this Act to a park reserve is subject to the carrying on of traditional renewable resource harvesting activities by aboriginal persons."
10 Pawlowska 2009, p. 116.

The lack of consultation and involvement of the Dehcho First Nations in the initial establishment and operation of the park reserve led them to take a proactive role in negotiating a strong partnership in park planning and management while advocating for the park reserve to confer benefits to the Dehcho people, including economic opportunities associated with employment and tourism. These negotiations are ongoing through the Dehcho Process. However, interim agreements have established a co-management body, the Naha Dehe Consensus Team, which is modeled on the agreement between the Government of Canada and the Council of the Haida Nation that established the cooperative Archipelago Management Board for Gwaii Haanas National Park Reserve and Haida Heritage Site.

In 2002, the Dehcho First Nations passed a Leadership resolution that specifically called for the protection of the entire South Nahanni Watershed through a formal park expansion process.[11] The Dehcho First Nations' campaign for the protection of the entire South Nahanni Watershed has been advanced through various channels. In addition to working directly with Parks Canada and through the Dehcho Process, the Dehcho First Nations have also utilized the support of the Canadian Parks and Wilderness Society, which launched its own national campaign for the protection of the South Nahanni Watershed and has been a staunch ally of the Dehcho First Nations.

UNESCO World Heritage site designation

In 1978, Nahanni National Park Reserve became one of the first sites to be designated a World Heritage site under the 1972 UNESCO World Heritage Convention due to the significant 'natural' features of the region.[12] The IUCN Advisory Body Evaluation that provided the basis for the designation by the World Heritage Committee described the area as an "unexploited natural area", concluding that the "ongoing geological processes and the superlative natural phenomena" were of outstanding universal value and therefore justified inclusion in the World Heritage List.[13] In 2006, the World Heritage Committee adopted a statement of significance for the property, which describes Nahanni National Park Reserve as an "undisturbed natural area" containing "one of the most spectacular wild rivers in North America, with deep canyons, huge

---

11 Dehcho Leadership meeting, Fort Providence, 29-31 October 2002, *Resolution #6: South Nahanni Watershed*. Subsequent Leadership resolutions that reference the protection of the watershed include: *Resolution #4: Nahanni National Park Reserve Interim Agreements* (Wrigley, 17-21 February 2003); *Resolution #3: Prairie Creek Road* (Hay River Reserve, 4-6 May 2004); *Resolution #32: Cyanide Removal Canadian Zinc (formerly Cadillac Mine)* (Kakisa Lake, 29 June - 2 July 2004); *Resolution #14: Protection of the South Nahanni Watershed* (K'atlodeeche First Nation, 22-24 February 2005); *Resolution #01: Nahanni Watershed Protection* (Kakisa Lake, 24-27 June 2008); *Resolution #01: Nahanni Watershed Protection* (Hay River Reserve, 28-30 April 2009).
12 UNESCO 1978, p. 7. Note: UNESCO refers to Nahanni National Park, not Nahanni National Park Reserve. The Park Reserve status is due to a pending agreement on Aboriginal and Treaty rights and interests that the Dehcho First Nations and Canada are negotiating through the Dehcho Process.
13 IUCN 1978. For the "Criteria for the inclusion of natural properties in the World Heritage List" that were applicable at the time see World Heritage Committee 1978, p. 4.

waterfalls, and spectacular karst terrain, cave systems and hot springs" and an "exceptional representation of on-going geological processes".[14]

There is no mention of any Indigenous values and cultural heritage associated with the World Heritage Site designation in any of these documents. Moreover, while UNESCO's technical documents for Nahanni National Park Reserve[15] provide significant detail about the geological and biophysical features of the area, the "Cultural Heritage" and "Local Human Population" are described as: "no information". Indigenous resource use and land rights are only mentioned under the category of "Management Problems", where it is stated that: "Native land claims exist and traditional hunting and fishing is undertaken by indigenous native peoples."[16] Despite there having been criteria for both 'natural' and 'cultural' heritage in the 1978 *Operational Guidelines for the Implementation of the World Heritage Convention*,[17] recognition and inclusion of Nahanni National Park Reserve for its cultural values as a living homeland of Indigenous peoples was clearly not advanced by Parks Canada, nor by IUCN or the World Heritage Committee during the nomination process for the establishment of the UNESCO designation. Further, the Dehcho First Nations' outstanding land claims were then considered a 'problem' for park management.

The nomination forms submitted by Parks Canada to UNESCO in 1978 reference the presence of Indigenous people in the following terms: "The conservation unit is basically unmodified by man. Hunters, trappers, and prospectors, both native and non-native, have used the region for many years, but their impacts on the parks lands have been negligible."[18] Importantly, however, Parks Canada did acknowledge to UNESCO that there were outstanding claims to the lands in the park, and described the park "as a Reserve for a National Park subject to native claims. Thus portions of the park could be claimed by natives as part of the overall settlement of native land claims in the Northwest Territories."[19] The rights of the Dehcho Dene, although not named, to continue to use the park are also referenced by Parks Canada in the *Interim Management Guidelines: Nahanni National Park* that were submitted to UNESCO along with the World Heritage Committee nomination forms.[20]

Co-management

Since the establishment of Nahanni National Park Reserve in 1976, and nomination for World Heritage status in 1978, Parks Canada has changed its policies to recognize Aboriginal rights

---

14 See World Heritage Committee Decision 30COM 11B (1996) and UNESCO 2006b.
15 See http://whc.unesco.org/en/list/24/documents (Accessed 24 January 2012).
16 WCMC Information Sheet, *Canada - Nahanni National Park* (Date 1982, updated November 1989), attached to the IUCN Advisory Body Evaluation posted at http://whc.unesco.org/en/list/24/documents.
17 World Heritage Committee 1978.
18 Government of Canada 1978, p. 9.
19 Ibid. p. 11.
20 Parks Canada 1977, p. 23.

and incorporate Aboriginal communities in the planning and management of national parks and reserves.[21] As noted by David Murray, Senior Planner for Parks Canada:

"[T]he North has changed Parks Canada, as policies, practices, and even legislation have been modified to adapt to northern realities. Parks Canada employees from southern parks have been posted to northern parks, worked alongside Aboriginal park staff and local people in cooperative management regimes, listened to the indigenous traditional knowledge, and then transferred their experiences to other parks when they move on. Policies have changed right across the system, partly because of changes that were happening in Canadian society but certainly because the experience of operating northern parks has demonstrated some new ways to manage national parks." [22]

These changes in federal policy and practice have informed the Dehcho Process. In 2001, as part of the Dehcho Process, Canada and the Dehcho First Nations entered into an *Interim Measures Agreement*. Section 59 of the Agreement provided that: "Canada and the Dehcho First Nations will negotiate for the purpose of reaching an interim management agreement that takes into consideration models found in existing arrangements between Canada and Aboriginal peoples respecting the management of national parks."[23] After two years of negotiations, Parks Canada and the Dehcho First Nations signed a subsequent agreement, termed the *Interim Parks Management Arrangement* for Nahanni National Park Reserve, which sets out the cooperative management framework for the park reserve until such time as a *Dehcho Agreement* is concluded. Importantly, the successful conclusion of a *Dehcho Agreement* is necessary before Nahanni National Park Reserve can be moved from park reserve status to full National Park status.

The co-management framework pursuant to the *Interim Park Management Arrangement* established the Naha Dehe Consensus Team (NDCT) as a management body to guide the planning and management of the park reserve. The Consensus Team comprises four representatives of the Dehcho First Nations, two of whom are from the community of Nahanni Butte and appointed by the Nahanni Butte Dene Band, and three representatives of Parks Canada. Of critical importance is the fact that the Consensus Team fulfills its roles and responsibilities through a consensus decision-making model. Any matter that affects the management of the park reserve is referred to the Consensus Team for deliberation, and their decisions are recommended to both the Minister responsible for Parks Canada and the Grand Chief of the Dehcho First Nations. The Superintendent of the park reserve is mandated "to endeavour to the best of his/her ability to carry out recommendations of the NDCT."[24] The Consensus Team also oversaw the drafting of the collaborative *Ecological Vision* for the park reserve, which states in part:

---

21 For an overview, see Dearden and Berg 1993.
22 Murray 2010, p. 211.
23 Dehcho First Nations, Government of Canada, and Government of Northwest Territories 2001, p. 12.
24 Parks Canada and Dehcho First Nations 2003a, *Interim Parks Management Arrangement*, p. 5 (Sections 19-25).

"Travelling through the land of the Naha Dene, who have lived on this land since time immemorial, local legends excite the imagination. Dene culture, so intimately linked to the ecology of Naha Dehe, is respected in this place of mystery, spirituality and healing. The life sustaining waters of Naha Dehe flow freely, protected through the wisdom and guidance of the Dehcho elders. Traditional subsistence harvesting continues as an integral and sustainable part of the ecosystem, occurring in accordance with Dene laws, values and principles. Dene are inseparable from the land.

Naha Dehe protects a wilderness watershed in the Mackenzie Mountains, where fires and floods shape the land, and naturally-occurring plant and animal species thrive. The park is a model of cooperative management, where excellence in the conduct of science is promoted and cultural resources are treated with care. Communities, volunteers and stakeholders are involved in the stewardship of Naha Dehe, ensuring respect for the land continues into future generations." [25]

The *Interim Parks Management Arrangement* clarifies that "the Parties agree to encourage greater understanding of and respect for the cultural heritage of the Dehcho First Nations and the natural environment in which it evolved" and that "the Parties agree to provide for the continuation of cultural activities and traditional renewable resource harvesting in Nahanni National Park Reserve", including the continuation of commercial "trapping of fur-bearing animals" and the "cutting of selected trees for ceremonial and artistic purposes".[26] The agreement further sets out that the Consensus Team has been mandated with the responsibility of making recommendations to the Dehcho First Nations in respect of Aboriginal and Treaty rights, and cultural and traditional activities, following consultation with the Dehcho First Nations communities.

The co-management model and the continuation of harvesting within the park reserve not only speak to the self-determination of the Dehcho First Nations as stewards of their lands but also disrupt the pervasive framing of national parks in the north as uninhabited 'wilderness' or as merely recreational or wildlife conservation areas for people from mostly southern urban locales. Indeed, as argued by scholar John Sandlos, "Northern peoples were colonized and at times physically excluded from the northern landscape by wildlife policies that imposed the southern aesthetic of the empty wilderness on the subsistence-oriented Inuit and Dene people."[27] The entrenchment of Aboriginal and Treaty rights into formal agreements with Parks Canada has been a key achievement for the Dehcho First Nations, especially given the historical dispossession of Aboriginal peoples in

---

25 Parks Canada 2010, *Nahanni National Park Reserve: Naha Dehe Management Plan*, p. 17. For an earlier version of the vision statement, see Parks Canada 2004, p. 12. As noted in the Management Plan, the vision statement is based on the Ecological Integrity Statement Workshop that was held in the Dehcho community of Fort Simpson, NT, from 29-30 January 2000 and on subsequent comments from participants on a draft statement.
26 Parks Canada and Dehcho First Nations 2003a, p. 2 (Sections 5-7).
27 Sandlos 2001, p. 23.

earlier national parks in Canada,[28] which constituted egregious violations of Indigenous rights and interests that unfortunately continue today in many protected areas worldwide.

The cooperative management model is reflected in many aspects of the planning and operation of the park reserve, including an oral history project, the documentation and incorporation of Dene language place names in the park reserve, and the development of cultural heritage interpretation programs. The full scope of the planning and management is beyond the scope of this chapter and, for full details, please refer to the 2004 and 2010 Management Plans.

Challenges: Third-party interests

While the Dehcho First Nations have been advocating for the protection of the entire South Nahanni Watershed for decades, one of the challenges in achieving full watershed protection has been the existence of third-party interests, notably lead, zinc, silver and tungsten mine operations and mineral dispositions, which the Dehcho First Nations have argued are incompatible with watershed protection. To this end, the Dehcho First Nations have been active partners in the protection of the entire South Nahanni Watershed both within and outside the park reserve expansion process, including acting as interveners and participants in environmental assessments, public hearings and regulatory processes for the Canadian Zinc Corporation and the North American Tungsten mining properties. The Dehcho First Nations also filed two judicial reviews that challenged decisions of regulatory bodies in relation to the Prairie Creek Mine development.[29]

The World Heritage Committee has also recognized the possible implications of mining operations for the ecological integrity of the watershed, and has brought the World Heritage site designation into question. In 2002, the World Heritage Committee expressed "strong concern with regard to the zinc mine, as well as the findings of the Mackenzie Valley Environmental Impact Review Board (MVEIRB) report, including the comments on the inadequacy of the Mackenzie Valley Resource Management Act (MVRMA) to resolve the issues of land use and policy conflicts involving the site and its surroundings."[30] Further, in 2003, the World Heritage Committee "Request[ed] the State Party to keep the World Heritage Centre informed on the development of the new management plan and environmental impact assessment of the proposed mine at Prairie Creek."[31] Subsequently, in 2006, the World Heritage Centre reported that the "IUCN remains very concerned that, through downstream effects, the various mining, mineral, oil and gas exploration activities around the property, including the CZN mine and road, could have major adverse cumulative impacts especially on the water quality and, thus, integrity of the World Heritage property" and the Committee

---

28 For example, see Binnema and Niemi 2006, Sandlos 2001, or Dearden and Berg 1993.
29 In 2008, both the Naha Dehe Dene Band and Liidlii Kue First Nations entered into Memoranda of Understanding with Canadian Zinc Corporation regarding the Prairie Creek development with the goal of negotiating Impact Benefit Agreements.
30 Decision 26COM 21B.3 (2002). For the full text of the World Heritage Committee concerns pertaining to mining developments in the area of Nahanni National Park Reserve, see the corresponding document "State of Conservation of Properties Inscribed on the World Heritage List", UNESCO 2002, p. 12.
31 Decision 27COM 7B.16 (2003).

encouraged "the State Party of Canada to proceed with the expansion of Nahanni National Park to protect the entire South Nahanni Watershed and the karstlands of the Ram Plateau." [32]

Of significance to the recognition and exercise of Indigenous rights and interests, the World Heritage Committee has not explicitly incorporated the Dehcho First Nations into its deliberations. While the Dehcho First Nations are acknowledged as supporting the expansion of the park reserve,[33] the World Heritage Committee makes no reference to the importance of these lands as a homeland of the Dehcho First Nations, nor mention of their Aboriginal and Treaty rights, nor of their long-standing efforts to protect the watershed, both within and outside of the Parks Canada national park reserve expansion process. This is a serious omission that has significant implications for if and how Indigenous rights are incorporated into the World Heritage Convention processes, not only for the Dehcho First Nations but also for all Indigenous peoples who have inherent rights and interests in proposed or established protected areas.

Despite the overall success and collaborative spirit and practice of planning and managing the park reserve, there have been significant challenges along the way that have tested the relationship between the Dehcho First Nations and Parks Canada, notably in relation to third-party interests. A significant example was the signing of a Memorandum of Understanding (MOU) between Parks Canada and the Canadian Zinc Corporation in July 2008 while the process to expand the park reserve was underway. The Dehcho First Nations recognize that Parks Canada may enter into agreements with other parties but they articulated that, pursuant to the spirit and letter of the *Interim Parks Management Arrangement*, Parks Canada had a prior obligation to consult with the First Nations and to bring the matter for discussion to the Consensus Team. As noted by the Dehcho Grand Chief:

> "It appears the MOU was signed in order for Parks Canada to be assured the Prairie Creek people would not oppose the Park Reserve expansion and at the same time for the mining company to reassure its stockholders that the expansion will not infringe on the company's property... [T]he DFN should have been involved in the development of the MOU and consulted by Parks Canada before it was signed off... The Dehcho First Nations have since the signing of the Treaties attempted to build trust and work [with] Canada, but Canada continues to make agreements with us then fails to honour them... We have never relinquished our rights to the area of the Park reserve and our people continue to occupy and use these lands as our Traditional lands... Signing and releasing this information sets a bad precedent for true co-management and sends the wrong signals when the DFN has been open and transparent in all its dealing regarding the park expansion." [34]

The signing of this MOU rattled the relationship between Parks Canada and the Dehcho First Nations at a critical moment in the park reserve expansion process, and it took an extensive effort

---

32 See UNESCO 2006a, p. 49-51 and World Heritage Committee Decision 30COM 7B.22 (2006).
33 World Heritage Committee 2006, p. 50.
34 Dehcho First Nations 2008.

by both parties to ameliorate the situation. This example not only demonstrates that the relationship between Indigenous rights-holders and colonial states is complex and can be fragile, but also highlights how the existence of third-party interests and the state's often conflicting mandates infringe upon Indigenous rights and interests. An area of significant tension can emerge when Indigenous peoples are treated as merely one more 'stakeholder' in a social or political negotiation. However, as pointed out by Stefan Disko, this only serves to alienate Indigenous peoples from the process as: "the stakeholder approach negates indigenous peoples' status and rights under international law, including their right to self-determination and their collective rights to their lands, territories and resources."[35] As will be discussed later, third-party interests were also a key area of contention in negotiating the expanded park reserve boundary.

Expansion of Nahanni National Park Reserve

While Parks Canada and the World Heritage Committee recognized early on that the original area of Nahanni National Park Reserve was insufficient to protect the ecological features of the Greater Nahanni Ecosystem, the Dehcho First Nations had their own long-standing interest in protecting the entire ecosystem due to its tremendous cultural values. To this end, in 2003, Parks Canada and the Dehcho First Nations entered into a Memorandum of Understanding to work collaboratively towards an expansion of Nahanni National Park Reserve that would "achieve sustainable boundaries for the ecological integrity" as well as "achieve compatible land use within the Greater Nahanni Ecosystem within the Dehcho territory".[36] The Memorandum of Understanding also stipulated that the study area proposed for park reserve expansion would be withdrawn from disposition[37] until the expansion process was completed. In 2003, the Dehcho First Nations and Minister of Indian and Northern Affairs Canada signed an agreement for a five-year interim land withdrawal of a study area for the expansion of the park reserve that included most of the Dehcho portion of the South Nahanni Watershed. In August 2007, a further land withdrawal was made that covered the entire Dehcho portion of the Greater Nahanni Ecosystem.

Pursuant to the Memorandum of Understanding, a Nahanni Expansion Working Group (NEWG) was formed to oversee research and feasibility studies and to recommend a park reserve expansion boundary to the Dehcho First Nations and the Government of Canada. The NEWG consisted of two representatives of the Dehcho First Nations and two representatives of Parks Canada, and reported to both the Grand Chief of the Dehcho First Nations and the Chief Executive Officer of Parks Canada.[38]

---

35   Disko 2010, p. 174.
36   Parks Canada Agency and Dehcho First Nations 2003b.
37   Disposition refers to the Government of Canada granting interests in land, including sales, leases, mineral claims, prospecting permits, and oil and gas rights.
38   The Dehcho First Nations representatives on the NEWG were Jonas Antoine and Petr Cizek. Laura Pitkanen joined the NEWG in 2006 as a representative of the Dehcho First Nations, replacing Petr Cizek. The representatives for Parks Canada were Steve Catto and David Murray.

As part of the expansion process, the NEWG oversaw research studies on the Greater Nahanni Ecosystem, including conservation values and wildlife studies (Woodland caribou, Dall's sheep, Grizzly bear, Bull trout, forest fire history, glacier mapping, karst landforms and existing third-party interests).[39] As noted by Doug Tate, Conservation Biologist for Nahanni National Park Reserve: "Although final decisions are more often than not based on political will rather than objective scientific information, without the ecological or cultural information to bring the importance of an area to light, it is unlikely to be considered for conservation at all."[40] As one example, Tate highlights the importance of combining scientific wildlife research and local traditional knowledge, including oral histories, of local First Nations in understanding the importance of watershed protection for caribou populations. In addition, Natural Resources Canada also undertook a detailed Mineral and Energy Resource Assessment study (MERA) to determine the potential oil and gas and mineral resources of the area.

In 2006 and 2007, the NEWG conducted extensive consultations, including open house meetings in Dehcho communities, and in Yellowknife and Ottawa. Throughout the entire park reserve expansion process, members of the Dehcho First Nations continued to press Parks Canada regarding the guaranteed continuance of Aboriginal and Treaty rights within an expanded Park. Indeed, Parks Canada noted that "there is support for protection of the whole watershed only if traditional hunting rights are protected".[41] The Dehcho First Nations administrative office also undertook to communicate with Dehcho communities, informing members that "the present Nahanni National Park Reserve is too small and narrow to protect animal ranges, birthing grounds, spiritual sites, harvesting areas, traplines, and the watershed" and stressing that "Dehcho members will keep their traditional harvesting rights in the Park".[42]

Despite the Dehcho First Nations' position that the entire South Nahanni Watershed should be protected in the final park reserve expansion boundary, the NEWG was faced with having to balance the interests of both parties and accommodate the existence of several third-party interests, notably mineral leases and authorizations. In December 2007, the NEWG submitted a recommendation that approximately 97% of the watershed should be included in an expanded Nahanni National Park Reserve.[43] Subsequently, Canada undertook an additional round of consultation at the ministerial level, returning with a position aimed at leaving out additional areas of high resource development potential based on the Mineral and Energy Resource Assessment study. As noted by Canada in the post-expansion press release: "The MERA results, along with the conservation research studies, were used to create a boundary that balances key conservation targets and potential future economic benefit."[44] In total, "all of the hydrocarbon potential and about half of the most important mineral potential identified by the MERA, as well as 100 percent of

---

39 Parks Canada 2006.
40 Tate 2004, p. 4.
41 Parks Canada 2007.
42 Dehcho First Nations 2004.
43 Nahanni Expansion Working Group 2007.
44 Government of Canada 2009, p. 2.

existing mineral claims and mineral leases, such as the operating Cantung Mine and the Prairie Creek Mine, currently under development" were left out of the final park reserve boundary.[45]

In April 2009, the Dehcho First Nations accepted this modified recommendation for the final park reserve expansion boundary through a Dehcho Leadership resolution that also reaffirmed that the "Dene and Treaty rights of DFN members would be fully protected within the boundaries of the expanded Park" and included a key principle that the Naha Dehe Dene Band would "continue to take a leading role in the management and protection of the Park Reserve through the Naha Dehe Consensus Team".[46] This direction stemmed from the acknowledgement of the Dehcho First Nations that the park was primarily located within the traditional territory of the community and that "the community dependence on the Watershed of the South Nahanni is engrained in their traditional occupancy of the area".[47]

In June 2009, the park reserve was expanded from 4,766 square kilometers to over 30,000 square kilometers, making Nahanni National Park Reserve the third largest national park or park reserve in Canada. The expanded area constitutes approximately 91% of the Dehcho portion of the South Nahanni Watershed and is considered by both parties to be a landmark achievement. Jonas Antoine, a member of Liidlii Kue First Nation and Dehcho Dene representative on the Nahanni Expansion Working Group, commented on the expansion: "Even when we don't walk on the land, our spirit is walking the land. This work has taken many years, many people working with passion and dedication."[48] In a Dehcho news release, Jonas further commented that: "This work represents a remarkable achievement for the Dehcho First Nations who have a long-held position to protect the South Nahanni Watershed. As we celebrate the expansion of Nahanni National Park Reserve, we must always remember our Elders: 'Take care of the land and the land will take care of us.'"[49] Importantly, the pivotal role of the Dehcho First Nations is recognized in the legislation passed by the Government of Canada to expand the park reserve: "The Dehcho First Nations, having a treaty relationship with Canada, have worked collaboratively with the Parks Canada Agency to protect the greater Nahanni ecosystem, and support the expansion of the Park Reserve",[50] demonstrating the importance of the Dehcho First Nations in the expansion process.

Conclusion: Moving forward in collaboration

The Dehcho First Nations are continuing to build upon and finalize the management arrangement for Nahanni National Park Reserve with Parks Canada staff and operations, and through the

---

45 Ibid.
46 Dehcho First Nations 2009d, *Resolution #1: Nahanni Watershed Protection* (Hay River Reserve, 28-30 April 2009). See also, Dehcho First Nations 2009b, *Letter to Minister Jim Prentice: Expansion of Nahanni National Park Reserve*.
47 Dehcho First Nations 2005. *Resolution #14: Protection of the South Nahanni Watershed* (K'atlodeeche First Nation, 22-24 February 2005).
48 Government of Canada 2009.
49 Dehcho First Nations 2009c.
50 *An Act to Amend the Canada National Parks Act to Enlarge Nahanni National Park Reserve of Canada* (S.C. 2009, c. 17), Preamble.

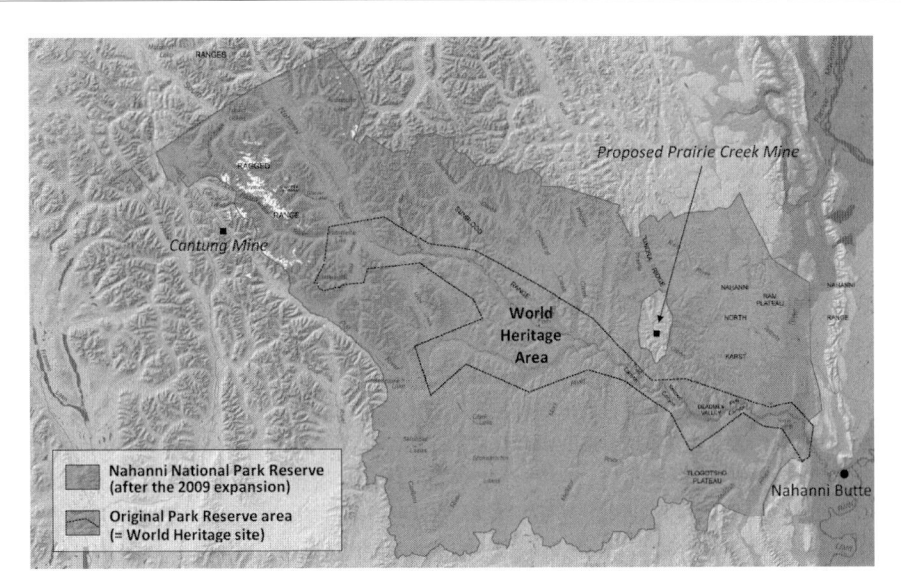

Map 1: Nahanni National Park Reserve before and after the 2009 expansion. Adapted from a map provided by Parks Canada

Dehcho Process. These negotiations will also culminate in an Impact Benefit Agreement that will mitigate impacts and confer benefits on the Dehcho First Nations in relation to the establishment and expansion of the park reserve. While these negotiations will at times present challenges, the parties have established a solid foundation for moving forward towards protecting an area of immense cultural and ecological value in a manner that recognizes and incorporates the rights and interests of the Dehcho First Nations.

In addition to changes in the policy, practice and legislation of Parks Canada in relation to Indigenous peoples and national parks, the World Heritage Committee has also, albeit more recently, started acknowledging the importance of including Indigenous peoples in the planning and management of areas recognized under the World Heritage Convention. In relation to Nahanni National Park Reserve, the Committee noted specifically the 'progress' made by Parks Canada in consultation with the Dehcho First Nations.[51] Yet more needs to be done in policy, planning and practice on the ground. This acknowledgement of the Dehcho First Nations by the World Heritage Committee is a key step towards recognizing the rights and interests of Indigenous peoples in World Heritage sites but UNESCO and the World Heritage Committee should take further concrete action to mandate and ensure that the Dehcho First Nations are

---

51 Decision 27COM 7B.16 (2003). For the background to the decision, see UNESCO 2003, p. 14.

Members of the Nahanni Butte Dene Band and Dehcho First Nations celebrate with Parks Canada over the expansion of Nahanni National Park Reserve in June 2009, Museum of Nature, Ottawa.
Photo: David Murray, Parks Canada

involved in any further process regarding Nahanni National Park Reserve and the World Heritage Convention, including any process to recognize the expanded park reserve area as a World Heritage site.

During the designation of Nahanni National Park Reserve as a World Heritage site in 1978, IUCN urged Canada to expand the Park boundaries, even going so far as to contemplate including the entire watershed in the World Heritage site even without its inclusion in the park reserve.[52] However, as previously discussed, the Dehcho First Nations were marginalized in the process. The World Heritage site designation has undoubtedly been beneficial in helping the Dehcho First Nations to protect the South Nahanni Watershed by bringing international recognition to the region and, in turn, to the objectives of the Dehcho First Nations in the Dehcho Process. However, in moving forward, it is vital that Parks Canada and UNESCO include the Dehcho First Nations in the World Heritage Convention processes.

Further, the statement of significance must be changed so that the outstanding universal value of the site reflects the Indigenous values and recognizes Dehcho cultural heritage as a vital, living part of the ecosystem of the park reserve. The dichotomy between 'natural' and

---

52 IUCN 1978.

'cultural' is a false distinction for the Dehcho First Nations, who hold a holistic view of the Dene people as inseparable from the land. Any new designation or expansion of the World Heritage site should therefore include the tremendous cultural values and ecological significance of the area for, and as determined by, the Dehcho First Nations rather than be based only on 'natural' features that focus on the physical environment and not its vibrant, dynamic and living cultural heritage. While this inclusion will not erase or hide the obvious omission of the Dehcho First Nations from the original designation of Nahanni National Park Reserve as a World Heritage site, it will recognize and demonstrate on an international scale that the cultural heritage of the Dehcho First Nations is an inextricable part of these lands. ○

References

Binnema, T. and Niemi, M. 2006. 'Let the line be drawn now': wilderness, conservation and the exclusion of Aboriginal people from Banff National Park in Canada. *Environmental History*, Vol. 11, No. 4, pp. 724-750.

Dearden, P. and Berg, L. 1993. Canada's National Parks: A model of administrative penetration. *The Canadian Geographer*, Vol. 37, No. 3, p. 194-211.

Dehcho First Nations. 1993. *Declaration of Rights*. Adopted at Kakisa, Denenat Kakisa, Denendeh, on 19 August 1993. Available at: www.dehcho.org/home.htm.

Dehcho First Nations. 2002. *Resolution #6: South Nahanni Watershed*. Dehcho Leadership meeting, Fort Providence, 29-31 October 2002.

Dehcho First Nations. 2004. *Naha Dehe (South Nahanni River Watershed) and the Dehcho Process*. An information pamphlet for Dehcho members, November 2004.

Dehcho First Nations. 2005. *Resolution #14: Protection of the South Nahanni Watershed*. Dehcho Leadership meeting, K'atlodeeche First Nation, 22-24 February 2005.

Dehcho First Nations. 2008. *DFN Leader Protests Prairie Creek Mine– MOU*. Press Release, 7 August 2008. Available at http://www.dehcho.org/press.htm.

Dehcho First Nations. 2009a. Grand Chief report. *2008-2009 Annual Report*.

Dehcho First Nations. 2009b. *Letter to Minister Jim Prentice: Expansion of Nahanni National Park Reserve*, 20 April 2009.

Dehcho First Nations. 2009c. Press Release, 18 June 2009 [Bill to Expand Nahanni National Park Passed in House of Commons]. Available at http://www.dehcho.org/press.htm.

Dehcho First Nations. 2009d. *Resolution #1: Nahanni Watershed Protection*. Dehcho Leadership meeting, Hay River Reserve, 28-30 April 2009.

Dehcho First Nations, Government of Canada, and Government of Northwest Territories. 2001. *The Dehcho First Nations Interim Measures Agreement*. 23 May 2001.

Disko, S. 2010. World Heritage Sites in Indigenous Peoples' Territories: Ways of Ensuring Respect for Indigenous Cultures, Values and Human Rights. D. Offenhäußer, W. Zimmerli and M.-T. Albert (eds.), *World Heritage and Cultural Diversity*. Bonn, German Commission for UNESCO, pp. 167-177.

Government of Canada. 1978. Nomination of Nahanni National Park to the World Heritage List (completed nomination form), 29 March 1978.

Government of Canada. 2009. *Government of Canada Announces the Expanded Boundary for Nahanni National Park Reserve of Canada*. Backgrounder and News Release, 9 June 2009.

IUCN. 1978. *IUCN Technical Review for 1978 – Nahanni, Canada* (Advisory Body Evaluation). Gland, Switzerland.

Murray, D. 2010. Canada's northern national parks: unfragmented landscapes, unforgettable landscapes, wilderness, and homeland. *The George Wright Forum*, Vol. 27, No. 2, pp. 202-212.

Nahanni Expansion Working Group. 2007. *Final Park Boundary Recommendation*, 11 December 2007.

Parks Canada. 1977. *Interim Management Guidelines: Nahanni National Park*, December 1977.

Parks Canada. 2004. *Nahanni National Park Reserve Management Plan*, April 2004.

Parks Canada. 2006. *Dehcho Community Update #1: Proposed Expansion of Nahanni National Park Reserve*, June 2006.

Parks Canada. 2007. *Dehcho Community Update #2: Proposed Expansion of Nahanni National Park Reserve*, January 2007.

Parks Canada. 2010. *Nahanni National Park Reserve: Naha Dehe Management Plan*, April 2010.
Parks Canada Agency and Dehcho First Nations. 2003a. *Nahanni National Park Reserve of Canada: Interim Park Management Arrangement*, 24 June 2003.
Parks Canada Agency and Dehcho First Nations. 2003b. *Nahanni National Park Reserve of Canada: Park Expansion Memo of Understanding*, 24 June 2003.
Pawlowska, A. 2009. *Using the Global to Support the Local: Community Development at Poplar River and the Establishment of a UNESCO World Heritage Site in Northern Manitoba*. Master of Arts Native Studies Dissertation, University of Manitoba.
Sandlos, J. 2001. From the outside looking in: aesthetics, politics and wildlife conservation in the Canadian North. *Environmental History*, Vol. 6, No. 1, pp. 6-31.
Tate, D. 2004. Expanding Nahanni National Park Reserve: the Contributions of Research, Consultation and Negotiation. Science and Management of Protected Areas Association (ed.), *Making Ecosystems Based Management Work: Proceedings of the Fifth International Conference on Science and Management of Protected Areas*, Chapter 9.
UNESCO.1978. Intergovernmental Committee for the Protection of the World Cultural and Natural Heritage, *Second Session, Washington, D.C. (USA) 5 to 8 September 1978: Final Report*. Doc. CC-78/CONF.010/10 Rev.
UNESCO. 2002. *State of Conservation of Properties Inscribed on the World Heritage List*. Doc. WHC-02/CONF.202/17.
UNESCO. 2003. *State of Conservation of Properties Inscribed on the World Heritage List*. Doc. WHC-03/27.COM/7B.
UNESCO. 2006a. *Examination of the State of Conservation of World Heritage Properties*. Doc. WHC-06/30.COM/7B.
UNESCO. 2006b. *Follow-up to the Periodic Report for North America, Annex*. Doc. WHC-06/30.COM/11B.Add.
WCMC. 1989. *Canada - Nahanni National Park* (WCMC World Heritage Information Sheet). Date 1982, updated November 1989.
World Heritage Committee. 1978. *Operational Guidelines for the Implementation of the World Heritage Convention (adopted by the Committee at its first session and amended at its second session)*. Paris, UNESCO.

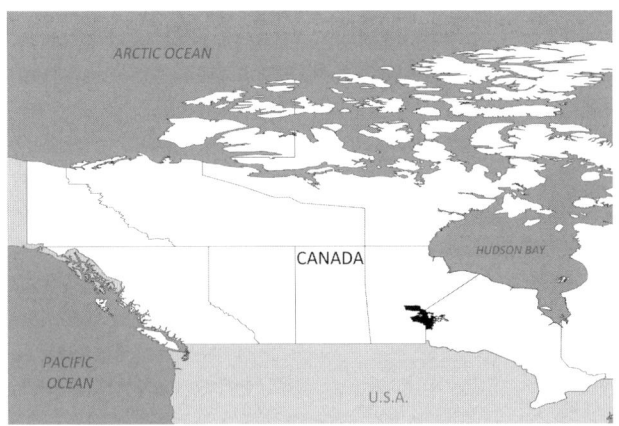

The Pimachiowin Aki World Heritage Project: A Collaborative Effort of Anishinaabe First Nations and Two Canadian Provinces to Nominate a World Heritage Site

Gord Jones[1]

Introduction

'Pimachiowin Aki' is a proposed mixed (cultural/natural) UNESCO World Heritage site covering over 33,400 square kilometres of land and water in central Canada. It is the ancestral home of the Anishinaabeg (Ojibwe) – a place where Indigenous people have co-evolved with the boreal forest landscape for more than 6,000 years. The name of the proposed World Heritage site, Pimachiowin Aki, means 'the Land that Gives Life' in the Ojibwe language and was chosen by Anishinaabe Elders. The term Pimachiowin speaks to life in the fullest sense: a good life in terms of enjoying longevity, good health, rewarding livelihood and freedom from misfortune. Aki ('land') includes all

---

1   This chapter has been drawn from the Pimachiowin Aki nomination document and is in parts an adapted version of that text. Sources other than the nomination document are cited. For more information about the Pimachiowin Aki World Heritage Project, visit www.pimachiowinaki.org.

Left: Anishinaabe healing ceremony. Photo: Hidehiro Otake

that is spiritual, living and non-living: the Creator's gifts that ensure the survival and well-being of the Anishinaabeg.

The site spans the border of two Canadian provinces, Manitoba and Ontario, and includes two provincial parks and a conservation reserve, as well as the traditional lands of five Anishinaabe First Nations (Bloodvein River First Nation, Little Grand Rapids First Nation, Pauingassi First Nation; Pikangikum First Nation and Poplar River First Nation). These five small isolated Anishinaabe settlements in Pimachiowin Aki have a total population of 6,200.

Situated at the heart of the North American continent, Pimachiowin Aki is located in what would have been the epicentre of Lake Agassiz, the largest post-glacial lake in the world. Lake Winnipeg, adjacent to the Pimachiowin Aki nominated area, is a remnant of Lake Agassiz. Today, Pimachiowin Aki's vast landscape mosaic of boreal forest communities, wetlands, myriad lakes and deranged watercourses is an outstanding representation of a healthy and whole boreal shield ecosystem forming a significant part of the global boreal biome.

The Aboriginal peoples of Pimachiowin Aki refer to themselves as Anishinaabeg ('the people') and their language as *Anishinaabemowin*. The Anishinaabeg are an Indigenous hunting-gathering-fishing people who continue to use and pervasively influence Pimachiowin Aki. Their land-use practices are grounded in and informed by their cosmology, spiritualism, traditional knowledge, customary governance and cultural values. There are many tangible signs of the long Anishinaabe presence on the land: ancient portages and travel routes still used to this day; ceremonial sites and rock pictographs; camps and cabin sites, both abandoned and actively-used. The Anishinaabeg have continuously adapted and employed different tools and technology in their traditional and modern resource-based livelihoods. The Anishinaabeg and their culture are an integral part of this vast boreal landscape.

The Pimachiowin Aki nomination is being led by the Anishinaabeg to gain international recognition of the significance of the boreal forest and Anishinaabe culture. In this way, they are seeking both to protect ancestral lands and resources and to create new livelihoods. The nomination is a collaborative effort between the five mentioned Anishinaabe First Nations and the Ontario and Manitoba provincial governments. The boundaries of the nominated area are an outcome of community-led land-use planning. Pimachiowin Aki is being nominated for both its outstanding cultural and natural value. What is especially significant is the symbiotic relationship between the Anishinaabeg and the boreal shield ecosystem, as the nomination and the proposed Statement of Outstanding Universal Value make clear. Pimachiowin Aki is a living and lived-in Anishinaabe cultural landscape and the nomination document, submitted by Canada to UNESCO in January 2012, emphasizes that "Canada wishes Pimachiowin Aki to be considered a cultural landscape".[2]

The free, prior and informed consent of the five Anishinaabe First Nations to the nomination is evidenced by a 'Message from the First Nation Partners of Pimachiowin Aki' at the very beginning of the nomination document, signed by the Chiefs of the respective First Nations. The Message states:

---

2   Government of Canada 2012, p. xiii.

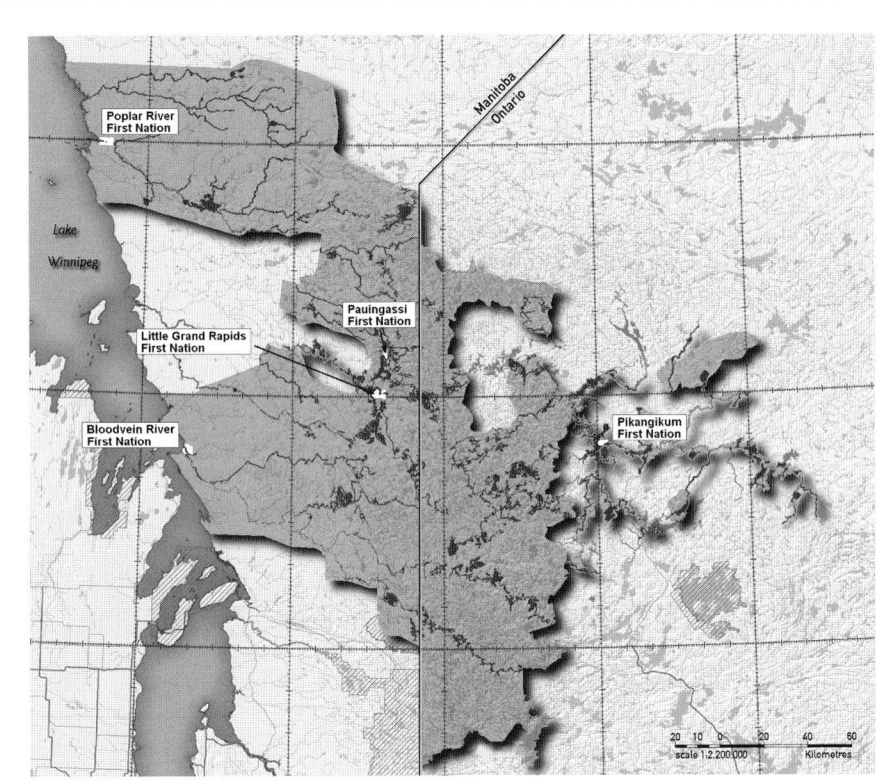

Map 1: Pimachiowin Aki nominated area. Source: Pimachiowin Aki Corporation

"On behalf of our First Nation communities, and along with the Government of Manitoba and the Government of Ontario, we are pleased to express our full support for the nomination of Pimachiowin Aki as a UNESCO World Heritage Site. We joined together in 2002 in a spirit of cooperation to protect our ancestral lands as a trust and duty to future generations, and to seek international recognition for the boreal forest and Anishinaabe culture. Preparing this nomination has been a wonderful experience, reaffirming the rich culture of our people... Pimachiowin Aki reminds us that we are inseparable from a land given to us by the Creator to take care of. Our home for thousands of years, this land is our very existence as a people, and it is important to protect for our children and children around the world. Situated in the heart of Canada, this boreal forest, the water, the air and the life it supports, is healthy and whole. The knowledge and teachings about living on and with the land, as told by our Ancestors and Elders, remain strong. What we have accomplished by taking care of the land is extraordinary, when we witness the destruction of our planet on a daily basis. Our Elders believe we should share our knowledge for the good of all people and that we must continue to protect this land for the good of the planet.

We believe that a UNESCO World Heritage site inscription would foster this protection and sharing."

History of the Pimachiowin Aki area

Throughout their long tenure, the Anishinaabeg of Pimachiowin Aki have remained comparatively autonomous from external domination and externally influenced cultural change, as Scott Hamilton has described.[3] The persistence of traditional land-use practices, economy, social organization and spirituality enabled the Anishinaabeg to confront change while maintaining their connection to the land. Following World War II, however, significant change was brought about by external forces such as government agencies and resource development. The more recent past reflects the beginnings of a resurgence in local decision-making autonomy aimed at taking a central and active role in planning the future. The Pimachiowin Aki World Heritage Project is an example of a new emerging Aboriginal reality within Canada.[4]

In the early19th century, the Anishinaabeg witnessed a brief period of frantic activity brought on by the fur trade. The unique geography of Pimachiowin Aki made travel into the area challenging and provided a layer of insulation from the negative impacts of the fur trade. The rugged interior, protected by dangerous rapids and precipitous waterfalls acted to shelter upriver communities. When the fur bearers declined and trading posts disappeared, the Anishinaabeg returned to traditional ways of life.[5]

Hamilton describes the complex interplay of events and pressures which began to appear in the mid-20th century. The iconic 'bush pilot' transportation industry transformed how Aboriginal and non-Aboriginal people accessed remote regions, and revolutionized how hunting, fishing and trapping were conducted. Provincial governments began to assert control over natural resources in the Pimachiowin Aki region in step with improved transportation networks as the resource frontier was expanded northward. By the 1970s, the inland commercial fisheries of Aboriginal families, made possible by improved transportation, gave way under pressure from provincial agencies to fly-in tourism resorts and outpost camps that catered predominantly for non-Native sports fishermen. In addition to the loss of the inland fisheries, fur trapping became increasingly non-viable as a cash income source, due to the combination of external market pressure and societal change.[6]

The loss of land-based livelihoods, along with centralized provision of healthcare, compulsory education and the provision of state subsidies, has influenced changes in land-use practices yet has not diminished the dependence of the Anishinaabeg on their ancestral lands for their material and cultural survival. As described in the above Message: "this land is our very existence as a people…"

---

3 Hamilton 2010.
4 Ibid., p. 17.
5 Lytwyn 2010, p. 7.
6 Hamilton 2010, pp. 15 f.

*Community Elders are helping to lead the Pimachiowin Aki World Heritage Project.
Photo: Pimachiowin Aki Corporation*

First Nations' aspirations to protect and manage their ancestral lands were significantly furthered with the 1982 *Constitution Act* which affirmed Aboriginal and treaty rights. An important driving force in this transformation has been a series of Court decisions that have upheld the Crown's treaty obligations towards Aboriginal nations and begun to fundamentally change the relationships between them and provincial and federal governments, particularly in the north where Aboriginal people form the majority, and where traditional land use remains important.[7]

The 2002 *Protected Areas and First Nation Resource Stewardship: A Cooperative Relationship Accord* (the Accord) between the five First Nations of Pimachiowin Aki sets out the essential vision for a World Heritage site and is the basis of the First Nations' leadership of the Pimachiowin Aki proposal. It opens with a pledge:

> "Our First Nations are joining together in the spirit of cooperation and mutual respect. We are joining together so that we may support each other and work together in our shared vision of protecting the ancestral lands and resources of our respective First Nations".[8]

---

7   Ibid., p. 16.
8   PRFN et al. 2002.

The Accord asserts that World Natural and Cultural Heritage designations provide a unique opportunity for the First Nations to cooperate with Canada and the international community. In turn, the Anishinaabeg are seeking to create new, ecologically-appropriate and sustainable livelihood opportunities for their future, thus maintaining positive relations with the forces which give them the divine gifts that sustain them in a good Ojibwe life, *bimaadiziwin*.

The Accord was influenced in part by the Elders' fear that the place of the Anishinaabeg on the land was under threat from outside forces moving inexorably onto their ancestral lands. Industrial forestry and mining, which in past decades opened up areas to the south and east of Pimachiowin Aki, were moving north with improved transportation networks. A proposed major hydro-line development in eastern Manitoba was a further concern. Moreover, in the 1980s, the provincial governments created the Atikaki Provincial Wilderness Park (Manitoba) and the Woodland Caribou Provincial Park (Ontario) within the traditional territories of several of the Pimachiowin Aki First Nations with little or no input from them, contributing to concerns about loss of access to ancestral lands and encroachment by tourist lodges and outcamps.[9]

Data on 'cumulative anthropogenic access', as illustrated in the map below, shows Pimachiowin Aki's vulnerability to land-use change and the urgency of a vision of a desired future as articulated in the Accord.[10] In 1999, Poplar River First Nation gained interim protection for its traditional territory under the Manitoba Provincial Parks Act based on a Memorandum of Understanding between First Nations and the Province of Manitoba. In Ontario, the Whitefeather Forest Initiative led by Pikangikum First Nation was a particularly important example of land-use planning that enabled local Aboriginal control over land-use and resource harvest planning. These significant individual initiatives preceded the outstanding collective action represented by the Accord, demonstrating both the First Nations' resilience and resolve to protect their traditional use of and relationship to the land. In the Proceedings of the IUCN Boreal Workshop held in 2003, the Accord was described as 'precedent setting'.[11]

In December 2002, the Accord First Nations joined with their provincial planning partners, the Ontario Ministry of Natural Resources and Manitoba Conservation, to submit a joint proposal to Canada for inclusion of their combined planning areas on Canada's Tentative List of sites to be considered for UNESCO World Heritage inscription. This partnership between First Nations and provincial governments was essentially an extension of the principles of the Accord to include the existing adjacent protected areas: Woodland Caribou Provincial Park and the Eagle-Snowshoe Conservation Reserve in Ontario and Atikaki Provincial Park in Manitoba. Canada included Pimachiowin Aki (then called the Atikaki/Woodland Caribou/Accord First Nations Site) on its Tentative List of World Heritage sites in 2004.

---

9   Hoole 2009, p. 11.

10 Lee and Hanneman 2010, p. 52 ff. 'Cumulative access' is the combined land surface anthropogenic disturbances caused mainly by industrial activities, which include, but are not limited to, roads, mines, clearcuts, wellsites, pipelines, transmission lines, and agricultural clearings.

11 IUCN 2004, p. 6.

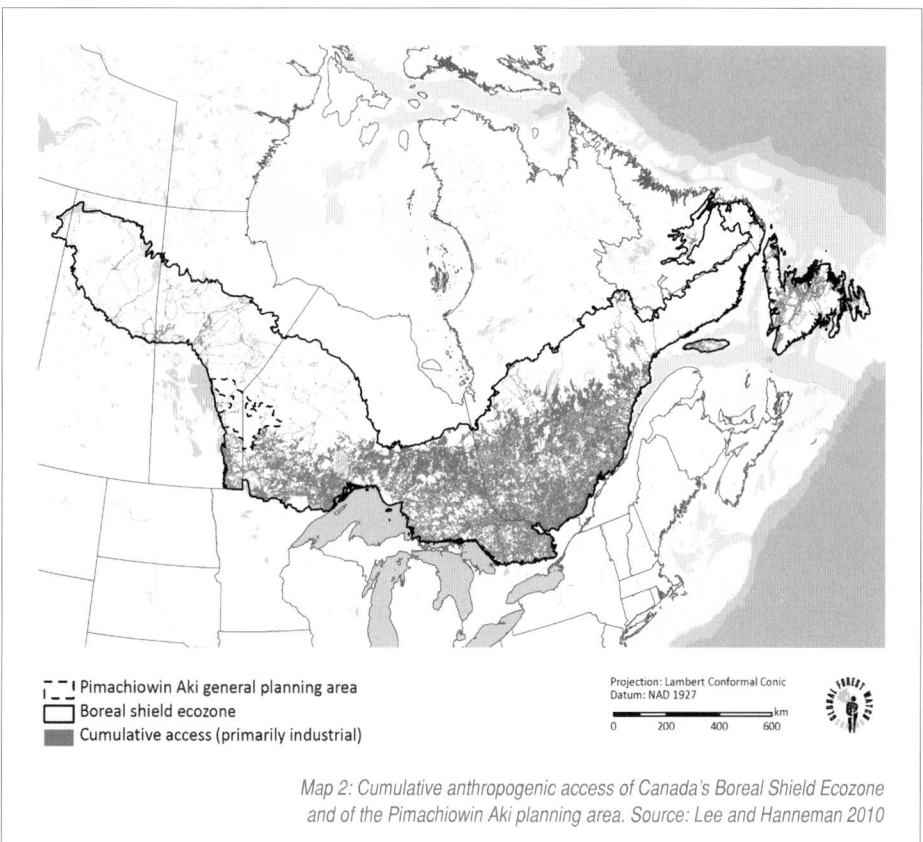

Map 2: Cumulative anthropogenic access of Canada's Boreal Shield Ecozone and of the Pimachiowin Aki planning area. Source: Lee and Hanneman 2010

Pimachiowin Aki organization and governance

The Pimachiowin Aki First Nations Accord initiative is significant in terms of the extent of cooperation between First Nations and provincial governments; decision-making is based on consensus building and cross-cultural understanding, which has enabled First Nations to move their vision of their ancestral lands as an Anishinaabe cultural landscape forward. Perhaps most importantly, the values of protection that were the impetus for the Accord are not focused merely on maintaining a healthy, functioning landscape for its own sake; rather, the Pimachiowin Aki initiative helps to address the ways in which effective First Nation-led stewardship of the land is important to the survival of the Anishinaabeg as a people.

In 2006, the partners created the Pimachiowin Aki Corporation as a non-profit, incorporated body, affirming the partnership of all seven parties, with a common goal of establishing the proposed World Heritage site. It is proposed that the Corporation's Board of Directors becomes the Pimachiowin Aki Management Board. This will meet regularly to set and support conservation policies, communications, collaboration and public awareness of managing the nominated area, and will be supported by a professionally staffed Secretariat.

Pimachiowin Aki Corporation has explicit by-laws and democratically represents all the participating partners. This not-for-profit corporation also has Canadian charitable status, permitting it to raise and receive donor funding. The Pimachiowin Aki Board of Directors is a collaborative partnership of First Nation communities and the two provincial governments.

The Board is co-chaired by a First Nation community representative and provincial government representative, both selected by the Board. Each First Nation community and each provincial government is represented by one Board member. Advisors, community elders and ex-officio parties are invited to participate in meetings of the Board as business may require. Dispute resolution is by consensus, focusing on the shared accountability for protecting the site's values. The Corporation's governance structure reflects the fact that each Board member is accountable to the respective community First Nation Chief and Council or provincial government that they represent. In addition, the governance structure reflects the partnership's collective accountability under the World Heritage Convention should Pimachiowin Aki be inscribed.

The governance and organizational structure with which the future needs of Pimachiowin Aki will be met is illustrated below.

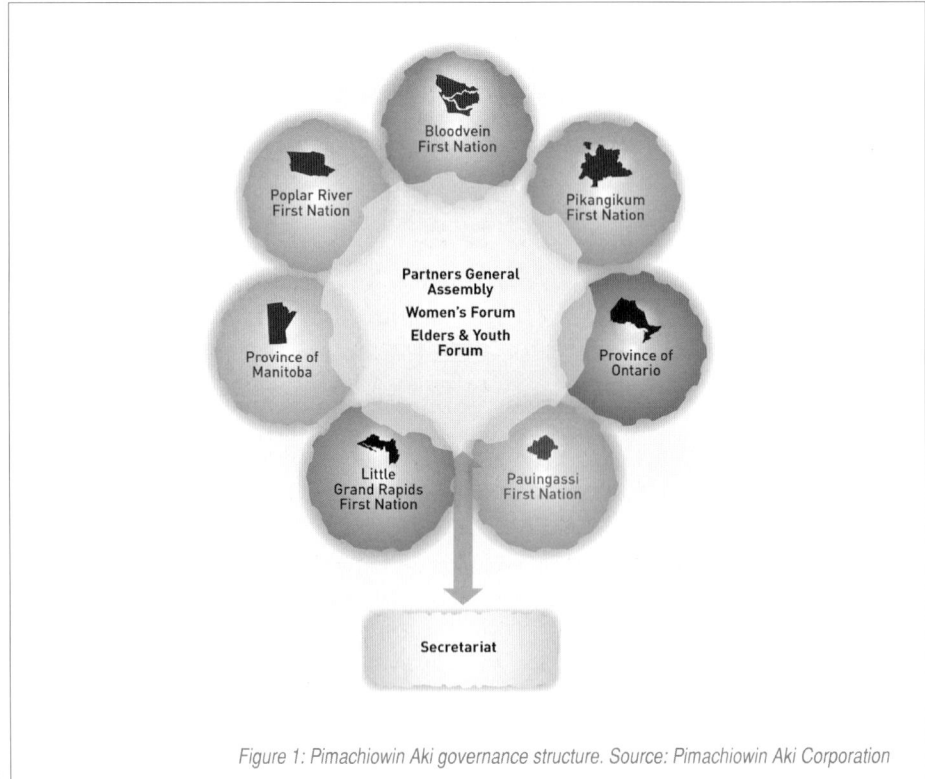

Figure 1: Pimachiowin Aki governance structure. Source: Pimachiowin Aki Corporation

The Board oversaw the development of the Pimachiowin Aki nomination between 2007 and 2012. In this same period, the Anishinaabe communities prepared community land-use plans with provincial support. Manitoba and Ontario each introduced new legislation to enable all First Nations in the Pimachiowin Aki region to create and implement community land-use plans for their traditional territories. Manitoba's *East Side Traditional Lands Planning and Special Protected Areas Act,* passed in 2009, enables First Nations on the east side of Lake Winnipeg to participate in land-use and resource management planning for areas of Crown land that they have traditionally used and to provide such areas with special protection from development. In Ontario, the *Far North Act,* passed in 2010, enables similar bilateral partnerships between Ontario First Nations. Pikangikum First Nation's land-use plan was completed and approved prior to the passing of the *Far North Act* but has since been deemed to be a Community-Based Land-Use Plan under the Act.

First Nation community land-use plans are approved and implemented by means of the above provincial legislation, giving them legal force. Through community land-use planning, 20,530 square kilometres of the nominated area have been allocated to protection. These First Nation Community Conserved Areas, together with the provincial parks and conservation reserve, create an interconnected network of legislated protected areas 32,730 square kilometres in size – larger than any existing protected area in the North American boreal shield. Potential community-led commercial forestry is permitted in a 690 square kilometre zone comprising 2% of the nominated area.

A management plan has been prepared as part of the nomination for the proposed Pimachiowin Aki World Heritage site and will constitute the official management plan if the nomination is successful. The Board of Directors of the Pimachiowin Aki Corporation oversaw, participated in and approved the management plan - their joint commitment to manage, protect and present the area's Outstanding Universal Value.

The plan draws its primary direction from the Accord, which envisaged an internationally recognized network of linked protected areas. It also reflects the proposed Statement of Outstanding Universal Value, the land-use plans that have been developed by the First Nation and provincial partners, and a series of ecological and cultural study reports prepared as part of the nomination process. As a unifying document, the management plan reflects the policies and land-use categories established in each of the local land-use plans, integrating and coordinating their provisions across the nominated area and focusing on safeguarding its Outstanding Universal Value.

Collaborative stewardship of Pimachiowin Aki by the Anishinaabeg and the provincial governments will support First Nation efforts to make decisions about how their land is managed; it will support continuity of Anishinaabe customary stewardship practices in ways that provide a range of livelihood benefits for First Nation members and provide a context for the re-affirmation and transmission of customary teachings. In their accession to the Accord, Bloodvein River First Nation stated the matter in direct terms: "It's always been a simple request from our community members: we just want to take control over our own destiny."[12]

---

12 Government of Canada 2012, p. 116

Potential outcomes of World Heritage inscription for the Anishinaabe people

Pimachiowin Aki was placed on Canada's Tentative List of possible future World Heritage sites based on its potential to meet four of the ten criteria described in the *Operational Guidelines for the Implementation of the World Heritage Convention*. The nomination submitted by Canada to the World Heritage Committee in January 2012 identified cultural criterion (v) and natural criterion (ix) as the proposed basis for inscription of Pimachiowin Aki as a cultural landscape. As underlined in the nomination document,[13] the Anishinaabe First Nations took a leading role in elaborating the proposed Statement of Outstanding Universal Value:

Criterion (v)
"Pimachiowin Aki is an outstanding example of Indigenous traditional land-use continuously adapted and evolved for more than 6,000 years to meet the social, cultural and livelihood needs of the Anishinaabeg in their harsh subarctic boreal shield environment. Anishinaabe oral traditions, traditional knowledge, customary governance and cosmology are integral to sustaining traditional land-use practices. Customary harvesting areas, travel routes, livelihood and ceremonial sites and ancient pictographs provide testimony to holistic connectedness with the environment. Pimachiowin Aki fully encompasses the tangible and intangible elements of a living Anishinaabe cultural landscape that is resilient but vulnerable to irreversible change."

Criterion (ix)
"Pimachiowin Aki is an outstanding example of a large, healthy multi-level and resilient boreal shield ecosystem encompassing a vast boreal forest biodiversity, free-flowing freshwater rivers, myriad lakes and wetlands. Pimachiowin Aki fully represents the significant ecological and biological processes in the evolution of the boreal shield ecosystem. Its size and ecosystem diversity fully support wildfire, an essential ecological process in the boreal forest. The rivers, lakes and tributaries provide ecological connectivity across the wide landscape of Pimachiowin Aki. Extensive wetlands and peat bogs store carbon and contribute significantly to biodiversity. Healthy predator-prey relationships are sustained among iconic boreal species such as wolf, moose and woodland caribou."

The proposed Statement of Outstanding Universal Value emphasizes that: "Through their land-use, customary governance and cultural values, Anishinaabeg engage in a form of reciprocity with the land (*Aki*) that sustains them" and that: "The Pimachiowin Aki partners commit to supporting the continuity of this unique relationship". Both the statement of authenticity and the statement of integrity further reinforce the importance of the continuity of the Anishinaabe relationship to the land. For instance, the statement of integrity states that: "Anishinaabeg cosmology, Ojibwe language retention, traditional knowledge, customary stewardship and governance impart integrity

---

13 Government of Canada 2012, p. 147.

Ancient pictographs along the Bloodvein River. Photo: Hidehiro Otake

to Pimachiowin Aki". Anishinaabe traditional land-use practices (which are continuously evolving and adapting, as the nomination emphasizes) such as hunting, trapping, fishing, gathering or the cultivation of native plants are treated as central to both the authenticity and the integrity of Pimachiowin Aki. The statement of authenticity also notes that the Anishinaabeg "modify the landscape to sustain their lives and culture" and that they "create new livelihood opportunities that provide for continuity of their Indigenous relationship to the land".

The outcomes and benefits of potential World Heritage inscription are yet to be fully determined for the Pimachiowin Aki partners and for the Anishinaabe people in particular. Preparation of the nomination has been an instructive and positive experience supporting the belief that this endeavor is truly meaningful, worthwhile and ultimately in the interests of everyone involved. The process has enabled and supported the growth and development of relationships and processes resulting in the completion of a complex and comprehensive nomination and fostering an approach to governance for Pimachiowin Aki that ensures that decision-making for the proposed World Heritage site is consensual and accountable, and reflects both the distinctive First Nations approach to leadership and the pluralism of the partnership.

This is also reflected in the proposed Statement of Outstanding Universal Value for the site:

"Protection and management of Pimachiowin Aki is based on Indigenous leadership in land management and governance, and on provincial laws and policies. Customary law and policy protection is achieved through Anishinaabe governance and traditional practices, community planning and conservation policies. Manitoba and Ontario provincial laws and policies contribute directly to protection and management through legal recognition of community-led planning and designation of protected areas, as well as the inclusion of two established provincial parks and a conservation reserve within Pimachiowin Aki. Community and provincial partners have established a not-for-profit corporation and developed a consensual, participatory governance structure, financial capacity and a management plan to protect, manage and commemorate the nominated area."

Community-based land-use planning marks a sea change in policy and perspective that reflects new and evolving relationships between First Nations and other levels of government. The Pimachiowin Aki nomination is built upon and guided by these plans. Nomination preparation required extensive community consultations, a series of major workshops and the development of a variety of technical reports. It also entailed documentation and mapping of tangible cultural landscape features that provide material testimony to the traditional hunting-gathering-fishing way of life of the Anishinaabeg (such as traditional travel routes, resource harvesting areas, seasonal camp and cabin sites, pictographs and other sites of archaeological significance, or place names). These activities and products have served to create broader awareness of the area's cultural and natural values within and among the partnership. Throughout this process, the partners have strived to build capacity through learning experiences and to create valuable relationships while developing the nomination. They have also sought to share the benefit of their experiences with others. These reciprocal learning experiences have given the partners a better understanding of opportunities and challenges, and have provided the basis for ongoing communication within a network of similar organizations.

To ensure its financial sustainability, the Pimachiowin Aki Corporation has developed a significant partnership with the Winnipeg Foundation, one of Canada's oldest charitable organizations to establish and manage an endowment fund. Based on a remarkable $10 million commitment from the government of Manitoba, the Corporation launched the 'Campaign for the Land that Gives Life' in 2010 with a goal to raise a further $10 million.

The Anishinaabe vision

In the context of the Pimachiowin Aki World Heritage Project, the Anishinaabe people of this area are hopeful and optimistic about the future. Completion of the nomination is a significant step towards achieving the vision set out in the Accord. The parties have worked together in a cooperative manner with goodwill and enduring commitment to further their goals through the Pimachiowin Aki Board structure, as well as other bilateral and multilateral arrangements. In particular, each of the First Nations' ancestral areas will be managed through new cooperative arrangements between the First Nations and their provincial planning partners. The collaborative partnership of the First Nations and the two provincial governments is also highlighted in the agreed management principles for the prospective World Heritage site, according to which the partners commit to collaborate, support and respect one another in protecting, celebrating and learning from Pimachiowin Aki.

The Pimachiowin Aki partners have agreed on a 'Shared Vision' of the site as an ancient, continuous and living cultural landscape in which:

- the Anishinaabeg, the forest, waters, fish and wildlife, and other beings of the ancestral lands, are understood and safeguarded as one living entity;
- five First Nations and two provincial governments work together in a spirit of cooperation and mutual respect, recognizing the authority of each partner to protect and care for this internationally significant cultural landscape;
- the tangible and intangible values of the landscape are celebrated and shared for the benefit of the partner communities, visitors and all humanity;
- Anishinaabe communities remain intricately tied to the landscape, engaging in activities and livelihoods that are continuously evolving and adapting but which are rooted in traditional cultural values, relationships with the land and with the other beings on the land; and,
- Anishinaabe beliefs, teachings and practices are respected as central to sustaining the living cultural landscape and fulfilling the sacred duty to protect the lands for future generations.[14]

The Pimachiowin Aki management plan recognizes the importance of viable Anishinaabe communities for the living landscape of Pimachiowin Aki and, in this regard, the plan notes that the partners will support investigations into sustainable community development initiatives and the creation of new land-based livelihoods to support communities and maintain Anishinaabe connections to the land.

Tourism is recognized in the management plan as a strong opportunity to celebrate and share the value of Pimachiowin Aki with international audiences. Expanded tourism services also represent a potential source of economic development and community-based livelihoods for the Anishinaabe communities. The Pimachiowin Aki Corporation will support destination marketing of the World Heritage site as a whole, and will support both new community-scale tourism development and community partnerships with existing operations. Cross-cultural education and interpretation will be central to tourism activities. The partners will develop communication, interpretive and educational messages aimed at building understanding and appreciation of the Anishinaabe connection to the land, and promoting and continuing the Anishinaabe role as stewards of Pimachiowin Aki.

The continued role of Anishinaabeg knowledge, values, practices and people in leading the protection and management of Pimachiowin Aki is recognized in the site's management principles as important and will be supported. This support will also include research into documenting, communicating and applying traditional stewardship practices. While provincial governments will continue to have obligations for Crown lands, Anishinaabe communities' relationships to the land, customary stewardship practices and governance of their Community Conserved Areas will continue. In this respect, the Anishinaabe and provincial governments will act as equal partners in the management of and decision-making for Pimachiowin Aki, and as lead partners for their respective areas of jurisdiction.

The management principles also commit the partners to fostering and applying the Anishinaabe language, values and teachings to managing Pimachiowin Aki. The Anishinaabe language,

---

14   Pimachiowin Aki Corporation 2011, p. 21.

traditions, teachings and practices will be celebrated in communication materials, and visitor education and interpretive programs. The Anishinaabe language will be prominent in publications, programs and at meetings of the Pimachiowin Aki partners. Educational, interpretive and cultural programs will target Anishinaabe youth, as well as national and international audiences.

With regard to research in Pimachiowin Aki, the management principles state that the partners will maintain and expand existing research partnerships while pursuing new collaborative research arrangements to support management, interpretation and communication programs. Research initiatives will aim to enhance understanding and communication in the areas of archaeology, traditional values and stewardship, livelihood opportunities, climate change and ecological processes. The Board will develop research agreements with all research partners, addressing community consent, information sharing, intellectual property and dissemination of research results.

The partners will continue to support wildlife research and trans-boundary communication with regard to wildlife management. Natural fire cycles will be maintained in as much of the World Heritage site as is feasible. Monitoring and reporting on values reflected in the Statement of Outstanding Universal Value and the requirement to protect the area's integrity and authenticity will be coordinated by the Pimachiowin Aki Corporation. Monitoring is guided by a shared vision to protect and care for the land as a trust and as a duty to future generations.

The First Nations communities of Pimachiowin Aki are an integral part of the nomination, and their persistence is essential to maintaining the cultural landscape. While remaining vulnerable to change from outside social, economic and political forces, the Anishinaabe cultural landscape of Pimachiowin Aki manifests continuity and resilience. The Anishinaabeg of Pimachiowin Aki are showing creativity and resolve in the face of social change; they have demonstrated leadership in fostering new planning relationships that will help to strengthen and maintain their tangible and intangible associations with Pimachiowin Aki. Additionally, they are leading this initiative for World Heritage inscription as a way of gaining recognition for their culture and asserting their place on 'the Land that Gives Life'.

Assessment of the nomination by the World Heritage Committee

From 25 August to 1 September 2012, the Advisory Bodies to the World Heritage Committee, IUCN and ICOMOS, carried out a field mission to Pimachiowin Aki as part of their technical evaluation of the World Heritage nomination. As the Advisory Body for natural heritage, IUCN was responsible for evaluating the applicability of natural criterion (ix), whereas ICOMOS was responsible for evaluating the relevance of cultural criterion (v). In May 2013, the Advisory Bodies advised Canada that they had recommended to the World Heritage Committee that the nomination of Pimachiowin Aki be deferred on both the natural and cultural criteria. The Board of Directors of Pimachiowin Aki Corporation, in concert with Parks Canada and after careful review of the Advisory Bodies' evaluation reports, decided to let the nomination stand on the agenda of the 37th session of the World Heritage Committee held in Phnom Penh, Cambodia in June 2013.

A showing of artefacts during the 2012 Evaluation Mission. These artefacts from Pauingassi First Nation are held at the Manitoba Museum by agreement with the First Nation. Photo: Pimachiowin Aki Corporation

The evaluation by ICOMOS commended the collaborative and community-based approach of the nomination and acknowledged that the cultural and spiritual associations between people and the natural environment were strong in Pimachiowin Aki. The evaluators also found that the "nominated landscape might have the potential to demonstrate Outstanding Universal Value for its cultural values", but considered that further clarifications were needed as to how the strong associations between the Anishinaabeg and the land in the nominated area could be seen to be 'outstanding' or 'exceptional' in comparison with other places and other Indigenous peoples with similarly strong relationships to their lands.[15]

ICOMOS noted that this task presented some difficulties and that further discussions were needed, as it had been made clear to the evaluators by the State Party that, out of respect for other Indigenous peoples, "the First Nations do not wish to see their property as being 'exceptional' as they did not want to make judgements about the relationships of other First Nations with their lands".[16] ICOMOS also noted that the nomination "raised fundamental issues in terms of how the indissoluble bonds that exist in some places between culture and nature might be recognised on the World Heritage List for the cultural value of nature". In particular, it was pointed out that there

---

15   ICOMOS 2013, pp. 35-46.
16   Ibid, p. 39. During the preparation of the nomination, Anishinaabe Elders also pointed out that defining their land in such terms as 'outstanding' or 'exceptional' was difficult for them insofar, as according to Anishinaabe belief everything that was created by the Creator is sacred and therefore everything has its value and has a unique purpose in life.

was "no way for properties to demonstrate within the current wording of the criteria, either that cultural systems are necessary to sustain the outstanding value of nature in a property, or that nature is imbued with cultural value in a property to a degree that is exceptional".[17]

IUCN recognized in its evaluation that "an argument... could be made for criterion (ix) to be applied in combination with cultural criteria", but did not believe the case for inscription under criterion (ix) on its own was compelling, despite the scale and naturalness of the area. "[A]pplication of only natural criteria would be inappropriate given the community-led nature of this nomination, and the central premise that traditional use would be recognized as intrinsic to the values of the property, if inscribed," IUCN noted. Consideration of criterion (ix) should therefore be deferred until the possible basis for inscription under cultural criteria was clarified.[18]

The World Heritage Committee upheld the recommendation to defer the nomination and recommended that Canada invite a joint ICOMOS and IUCN Advisory Mission in order to address the above mentioned issues. Recognizing that the current wording of the criteria might, in some cases, create difficulties in acknowledging interrelationships between culture and nature on the World Heritage List, and that "maintaining entirely separate evaluation processes for mixed nominations does not facilitate a shared decision-making process between the Advisory Bodies", the Committee requested that the World Heritage Centre, in consultation with the Advisory Bodies, "examine options for changes to the criteria and/or to the Advisory Body evaluation process" and decided to include a debate on this issue on the agenda of its 38th session in 2014.[19]

Pimachiowin Aki representatives who attended the World Heritage Committee meeting in Phnom Penh were encouraged by expressions of support from various State Parties and organizations, including ICOMOS and IUCN. Discussions with the Advisory Bodies in Cambodia led to the preparation of a draft terms of reference for an Advisory Mission that took place in October 2013. Subsequently, consistent with advice received during the mission, the Pimachiowin Aki partners decided to re-write the nomination, for re-submission at the earliest possible date.

The main lesson that can be learned by other Aboriginal peoples from the Pimachiowin Aki experience is the importance of early and active engagement with the Advisory Bodies during the preparation of World Heritage nominations regarding cultural landscapes and mixed sites. There is helpful literature on the preparation of nominations and much can be learned from a study of past decisions of the World Heritage Committee but, given the size of the World Heritage List, as well as the recognized need for changes to the current system, direct engagement with the Advisory Bodies is well advised.[20]

---

17 ICOMOS 2013, p. 45.
18 IUCN 2013, pp. 141-142. Both IUCN and ICOMOS indicated in their evaluations that the current practice, whereby nominations under both cultural and natural criteria are essentially treated as two distinct nominations that are evaluated separately by the Advisory Bodies and can be accepted without reference to the other, was problematic in cases where the interaction between people and nature is central. IUCN suggested that Pimachiowin Aki be taken as "a case study to evaluate the need for a revision to the IUCN and ICOMOS evaluation processes" (p. 142).
19 World Heritage Committee Decision 37 COM 8B.19.
20 Also see World Heritage Committee Decision 34 COM 12, Part III (2010), "Improvements to the processes and practices prior to consideration by the World Heritage Committee of a nomination (the 'upstream processes')". The decision encouraged the implementation of pilot projects to explore creative approaches and new forms of guidance that might be provided to State Parties in considering nominations before their preparation, as well as in relation to the nomination process.

In its 2013 deferral decision, the Committee commended the State Party and First Nations of Pimachiowin Aki and praised "their exemplary efforts to develop a nomination that will protect, maintain and restore the significant cultural and natural assets and values" associated with the site. The Pimachiowin Aki partners remain optimistic about achieving their goal of World Heritage recognition and are pleased to contribute in any way to the development of changes to the criteria and/or an improved evaluation process that could assist other Aboriginal peoples in the future.

One option for the World Heritage Committee to consider in discussing possible improvements to the criteria and the evaluation process is the re-insertion of references to cultural elements and human interaction with the environment into the natural heritage criteria.[21] The 1992 decision of the Committee to remove the references to 'man's interaction with his natural environment' and 'exceptional combinations of natural and cultural elements' from the natural heritage criteria makes it difficult if not impossible to appropriately acknowledge Indigenous peoples' relationship to the land when defining the Outstanding Universal Value of natural World Heritage sites.

References

Government of Canada. 2012. *Pimachiowin Aki World Heritage Project: Nomination for Inscription on the World Heritage List*. Winnipeg: Pimachiowin Aki Corporation. Available at: http://www.pimachiowinaki.org/sites/default/files/docs/Pim_Aki_Dossier_web_new.pdf.

Hamilton, S. 2010. *Recent aboriginal history in Pimachiowin Aki*. Report prepared for the Pimachiowin Aki Corporation. [Included in the nomination dossier as Appendix G.1.4].

Hoole, A. 2009. *Pimachiowin Aki governance study*. Report prepared for the Pimachiowin Aki Corporation. [Included in the nomination dossier as Appendix I.2]

ICOMOS. 2013. *ICOMOS 2013 Evaluations of Nominations of Cultural and Mixed Properties*. UNESCO Doc. WHC-13/37.COM/INF.8B1.

IUCN. 2004. *Proceedings of the World Heritage Boreal Zone Workshop held in St. Petersburg, Russia, 10-13 October 2003*. Available at: http://whc.unesco.org/uploads/activities/documents/activity-43-4.pdf.

IUCN. 2013. *IUCN World Heritage Evaluations 2013*. UNESCO Doc. WHC-13/37.COM/INF.8B2.

Layton, R. and Titchen, S. 1995. An Outstanding Australian Aboriginal Cultural Landscape. B. von Droste, H. Plachter and M. Rössler (eds.), *Cultural Landscapes of Universal Value – Components of a Global Strategy*. Jena, Gustav Fischer Verlag, pp. 174-181.

Lee, P. and M. Hanneman. 2010. *The Pimachiowin Aki World Heritage site planning area: Global and Canada boreal/taiga perspectives regarding key ecological criteria. Global Forest Watch Canada 10th anniversary report #7*. Report prepared for the Pimachiowin Aki Corporation. [Included in the nomination dossier as Appendix G.2.3]

Lytwyn, V.P. 2010. *The Anishinaabeg in the fur trade of the Petit Nord and Pimachiowin Aki*. Report prepared for Pimachiowin Aki Corporation. [Included in the nomination dossier as Appendix G.1.5]

Pimachiowin Aki Corporation. 2011. *Management Plan: Pimachiowin Aki World Heritage Project*. Prepared for the Pimachiowin Aki Corporation by Hilderman Thomas Frank Cram. December 2011.

PRFN et al. 2002. *Protected areas and First Nation resource stewardship: A cooperative relationship – Accord* (Accord between Poplar River First Nation, Pauingassi First Nation, Little Grand Rapids First Nation, Pikangikum First Nation and Bloodvein River First Nation).

---

21 For a similar view, see Layton and Titchen 1995.

A Refuge for People and Biodiversity: The Case of Manu National Park, South-East Peru

Daniel Rodriguez and Conrad Feather

Introduction

Manu National Park, a UNESCO World Heritage site in southeast Peru, is rightly famous for its unparalleled biodiversity. On a single tree in the Park, researchers have found 43 species of ant, as many as all the ant species found in the British Isles.[1] The Park and surrounding buffer zones extend over 1.8 million hectares, encompassing the entire watershed of the Manu River from its headwaters in the Andes Mountains (over 4,000 m above sea level) to the lowland tropical forests of the Manu floodplain. This combination of lofty Andean peaks, high montane cloud forest and dense steamy lowland jungle has made the area a haven not only for 43 species of ant but also at least 41,000 species of invertebrates[2] and threatened species such as the black caiman, giant otter and scarlet macaw.[3]

---

1 Wilson 2002.
2 Nature's Strongholds Foundation 2013.
3 Moreover, the Vilcabamba-Amboro corridor, of which Manu plays an integral part, includes a greater percentage of endemic plant and vertebrate species than any of the other 25 global hotspots for biodiversity identified as global conservation priorities (Myers et al. 2000).

Left: Mashco Piro men on the bank of the Upper Madre de Dios River, photographed in May 2011.
Photo: Karina Achahuanca

The Amazonian region of Manu National Park is also the ancestral territory of at least five different indigenous peoples for whom its rivers and forests are not only a haven for biodiversity but also their home. However, ever since the Park was established in 1968, initially as a reserve area, this protected area, superimposed on top of indigenous territories, has fuelled a fierce debate between two opposing viewpoints. The first is advocated by a strong conservationist lobby who view the continued occupation of the Park by indigenous peoples as incompatible with biodiversity conservation. This viewpoint is strongly opposed by indigenous peoples' organisations such as FENAMAD, who have consistently advocated for the legal recognition of indigenous territories within the borders of the Park.

Manu's indigenous inhabitants

Today, the Park's Amazonian region is occupied and used by at least five indigenous peoples, including the Arawakan-speaking Yine (also known as Piro), Matsiguenka and Mashco-Piro, the Harakmbut and the Panoan-speaking Nahua (also known as Yora).[4] Rock art, ceramics, stone axes and other archaeological evidence suggests an occupation of this area by lowland Amazonian groups for at least three thousand years.[5] Many of these groups engaged in direct trade with Andean societies: "copper tools, precious metals, jewellery, and other goods of Andean manufacture being exchanged for lowland products such as tobacco, resins, smoked meat, animal skins, and bird feathers".[6]

The Park's toponymy, particularly the names of rivers, reflects this long history of indigenous occupation. For example, the Nahua name for the Manu River is *Yoraya*, literally 'with people', referring to the dense historical occupation of the Manu basin, which today is sparsely populated.[7] In addition, most major tributaries of the middle and upper Manu River located inside the National Park (e.g., Sotileja, Cumerjali, Cashpajali and Serjali, amongst others) have a Yine derivation.[8]

Until the end of the 19th century, the Manu river basin and adjacent lowland areas had escaped the processes of colonization that affected other areas of the Peruvian Amazon. The expansion of the rubber frontier at this time, particularly from the Ucayali river basin, put an abrupt end to this isolation and brought profound political and socio-economic transformations to the region, including the demographic collapse of its indigenous peoples due to epidemics, slave raiding and exploitation.[9]

Today, the current distribution of Manu's inhabitants (Map 2) reflects both the ancestral occupation of these territories and more recent historical phenomena. These include the impact of

---

4   Manu is also home to Andean communities such as the Callanga, who occupy its southern tip (see Shepard et al. 2010).
5   Huertas and García 2003.
6   Camino, A. 1977. Trueque, correrías e intercambio entre los Quechas Andinos y los Piros y Machiguenga de la montaña peruana. *Amazonia Peruana*, Vol. 1(2), pp. 123–140, cited in Shepard et al. 2010, p. 255.
7   Feather 2010.
8   Naturally many of these are overlain with names in other indigenous languages such as Nahua (Feather 2009).
9   Von Hassel (cited in Shepard et al. 2010, p. 257) estimates that 60% of the native workers in the Manu River rubber camps died of disease or malnutrition.

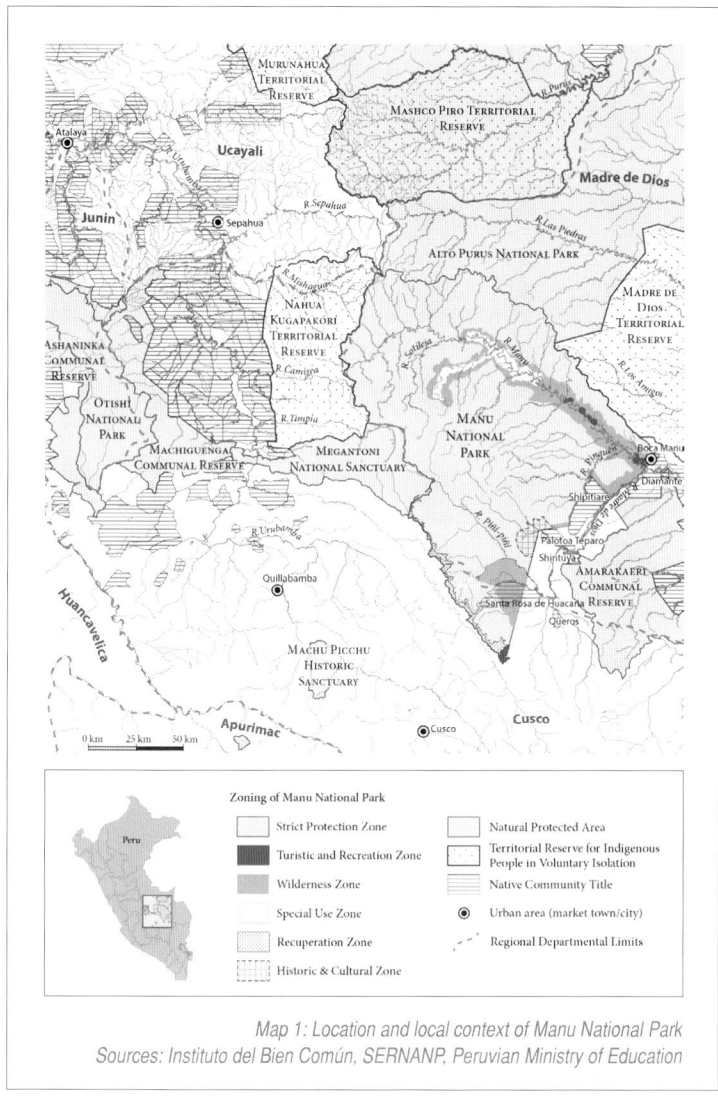

Map 1: Location and local context of Manu National Park
Sources: Instituto del Bien Común, SERNANP, Peruvian Ministry of Education

the rubber boom as well as more recent events such as the creation of the National Park and increasing pressure from the logging, oil and gas industries on areas surrounding the Park.

Harakmbut

The Harakmbut include several ethno-linguistic subgroups (Arakmbut, Toyeri, Huachipaeri, Arasaire Kisambaeri, Sapiteri) for whom the longstanding efforts of missionaries to contact them were concluded in the 1950s.[10] The last of the groups remaining in voluntary isolation, the Arakmbut ('Amarakaeri'), along with the Huachipaeri, were contacted in the 1940s and are the two most numerous subgroups at the present.[11] Their territory occupies the right bank of the Madre de Dios River, stretching from its headwaters to the Inambari River. Since 2002, part of this territory has been included in the Amarakaeri Communal Reserve (402,335 ha), which lies adjacent to Manu National Park (to the southeast). Today, some of the Harakmbut live in four native communities located in the buffer area ('multiple use zone') of Manu National Park: Shintuya, Queros, Boca Ishiriwe and Santa Rosa de Huacaria; in the latter case a significant part of the titled land is actually included within the Park.[12]

Yine

The Yine, an Arawakan-speaking indigenous people, continued to occupy several areas of the Manu river basin after the collapse of the rubber boom and remained there until the mid-1960s when they began to move downriver where they established the community of Diamante. Even after moving, they continued to use the lower Manu River for hunting and fishing and maintained small campsites there. However, after the Park was established in 1968, they stopped using the Manu River in response to the restrictions on their use of natural resources.[13] Today, they and their descendants live in the communities of Diamante and Isla de los Valles, which have a combined population of approximately 450.[14]

Matsiguenka

According to their oral histories, the Matsiguenka (the most numerous indigenous people currently living within the limits of the Park) had come to occupy the upper Sotileja, Cumerjali, and other tributaries on the south bank of the Manu River by the middle of the 20th century. They migrated from the headwaters of the Madre de Dios and Urubamba rivers, fleeing the pressures of the rubber boom. Today, the Matsiguenka live both within the Park's boundaries in the communities of Yomibato, Tayakome, Maizal and Sarigueminiki (Cacaotal) and also in the Park´s buffer zone in the communities of Shipetiari, Palotoa-Teparo and Santa Rosa de Huacaria. Besides these settled communities, there are also several Matsiguenka groups who live in the remote headwaters of the Piñi Piñi, Cumerjali, Sotileja, Yomibato and Palotoa rivers, either in 'initial contact'[15] with national

---

10   Gray 1996.
11   Current population numbers are estimated to be around 2,000 people (Alex Alvarez, pers. comm.).
12   Rummenhoeller and Aguirre 2008.
13   G. Shepard (pers. comm.).
14   Some of the inhabitants of these communities have also arrived from Yine communities on the Upper Urubamba river to the west of Manu.
15   'Initial contact' is a category officially recognised by Peruvian legislation, Law N° 28736, which defines it as the: "situation of an indigenous people, or part of it, which occurs when it has initiated a process of interaction with members of national society" (authors' translation).

Settlement of Matsiguenka in initial contact, Piñi Piñi River, Manu National Park, 2012.
Photo: Daniel Rodriguez, FENAMAD

society or in voluntary isolation.[16] The estimated total population of Matsiguenka communities inside the Park, including those living in initial contact or isolation, is between 1,000-1,500 people.[17]

Nahua

Oral histories of the Nahua indicate that they settled in the headwaters of the Manu, on the Cashpajali and Condeja rivers, at the end of the 19th century, having migrated from the Purús river basin where they were fleeing the ravages of the rubber industry.[18] In the mid-1980s, the Nahua experienced their first contact with loggers and migrated to the neighbouring Mishagua and Serjali river basins (in the buffer zone of the Park) seeking medical and humanitarian aid after the resulting epidemics wiped out almost half their population. Today, the Nahua have established one village outside the Park called Santa Rosa de Serjali but continue to access Manu for hunting and fishing.

---

16 These Matsiguenka groups avoiding contact are locally referred to as 'kugapakori'. *Kugapakori* is a derogatory term in Matsiguenka sometimes translated as 'assassin'.
17 Sources: FENAMAD; Alfaro and Nieto 2012
18 Feather 2010.

Their population has recovered to approximately 300. The Mishagua and Serjali river basins are now part of a 456,672 ha reserve for isolated indigenous peoples which is formally considered part of the buffer zone of the Park.[19]

Peoples living in voluntary isolation

In addition to the communities described, Manu National Park and adjacent river basins are also inhabited by indigenous peoples living in voluntary isolation who are actively rejecting direct contact with 'others'.[20] The available ethno-historical and anthropological sources indicate that these indigenous populations, commonly known as 'Mashco Piro', are part of the Arawak language family. Several authors have suggested that the present-day 'isolation' of the Mashco-Piro is a direct result of traumatic experiences of 'contact' in the past, specifically linked to the expansion of the rubber industry.[21] Although the existing demographic data is not precise,[22] it is believed that the Mashco Piro population includes several groups that inhabit a vast territory whose centre is the remote headwaters region at the intersection of the Ucayali, Purus and Madre de Dios river basins. Their characteristic highly mobile hunter-and-gathering lifestyles, involving long displacements whose patterns respond to the seasonal availability of specific resources, are also strongly affected by the existence of external pressures. The presence of the Mashco Piro has been extensively reported throughout the Manu National Park, particularly along the Manu River basin, both in its headwaters and in several of its lower tributaries (Pinquen, Condeja, Panagua), as well as on the left banks of the Upper Madre de Dios River. Local Yine populations living adjacent to the Park claim a common ancestry with the Mashco Piro and stress the mutual intelligibility of their languages.[23]

Fortress conservation: The impacts of Park policies on indigenous peoples

The establishment of protected areas in the Manu region began with the official declaration of a Reserve Zone[24] in 1968, and its subsequent categorization as a National Park on May 29, 1973 (total area 1,536,806 ha). With the creation of the Park, the loggers and hunters that operated in the area were expelled, as were Catholic and evangelical missionaries who had been working with indigenous communities. In March 1977, Manu National Park was incorporated as the core region

---

19 'Territorial Reserve in favor of the Kugapakori, Nahua, Nanti and other ethnic groups in voluntary isolation or initial contact in South East Peru'.
20 Alongside adjacent areas of Madre de Dios, Cusco and Ucayali and Acre in Brazil, Manu is part of a transnational 'corridor' for isolated indigenous peoples and one of the last existing refuges for isolated peoples in Amazonia.
21 For a full discussion of these indigenous peoples, see Shepard et al. 2010, pp. 260-261 and Gow 2006.
22 The Anthropological Plan of Manu National Park (2002) estimates that the total Mashco Piro population oscillates between 800 and 1,500 people, of which around 200 probably live inside the boundaries of the protected area.
23 Yine notions of relatedness regarding the Mashco Piro often stress the ancestral indigenous 'authenticity' of the latter, who are referred to as being Yine 'netos' or 'originales'.
24 A temporary legal status before definitive classification was finalized.

A REFUGE FOR PEOPLE AND BIODIVERSITY: THE CASE OF MANU NATIONAL PARK, SOUTH-EAST PERU

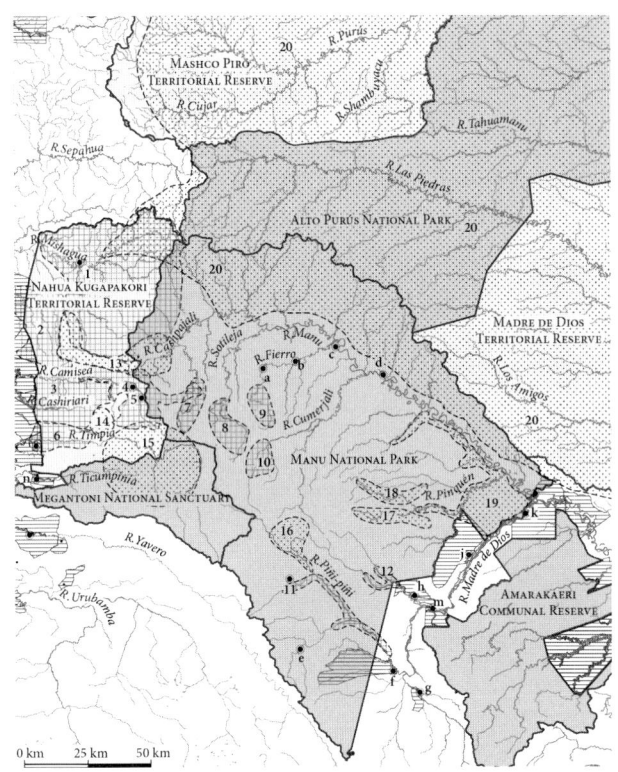

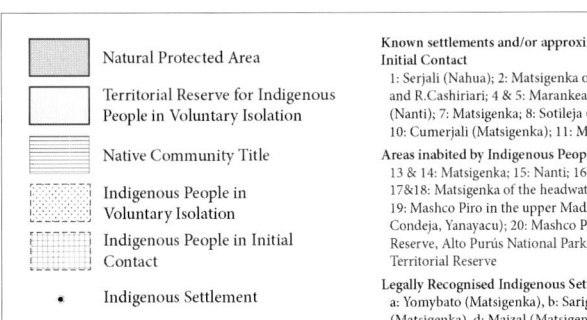

Known settlements and/or approximate areas of Indigenous Peoples in Initial Contact
1: Serjali (Nahua); 2: Matsigenka of R.Paquiria; 3: Matsigenka of R.Camisea and R.Cashiriari; 4 & 5: Marankeato and Montetoni (Nanti); 6: Kimaroari (Nanti); 7: Matsigenka; 8: Sotileja (Matsigenka); 9: Matsigenka; 10: Cumerjali (Matsigenka); 11: Mameria (Matsigenka); 12: Matsigenka

Areas inabited by Indigenous People in Voluntary Isolation
13 & 14: Matsigenka; 15: Nanti; 16: Matsigenka on R.Piñi-piñi; 17&18: Matsigenka of the headwaters of R.Pinquen/Pinquencillo; 19: Mashco Piro in the upper Madre de Dios and Manu (Pinqén, Panagua, Condeja, Yanayacu); 20: Mashco Piro in the Madre de Dios Territorial Reserve, Alto Purús National Park, Manu National Park, Mashco Piro Territorial Reserve

Legally Recognised Indigenous Settlements
a: Yomybato (Matsigenka), b: Sarigemini (Matsigenka), c: Tayakome (Matsigenka), d: Maizal (Matsigenka), e: Callanga (Quechua), f: Santa Rosa de Huacaria (Matsigenka, Huachipaeri), g: Queros (Huachipaeri, Matsigenka), h: Palotoa-Teparo (Matsigenka), j: Shipetiaari (Matsigenka), k: Diamante (Yine), m: Shintuya (Arakmbut-Huachipaire), n: Sababantiari (Matsigenka)

Map 2: Indigenous people in voluntary isolation and initial contact in and around Manu National Park. Sources: Cabeceras Aid Project, Daniel Rodriguez, Instituto del Bien Común, FENAMAD, Glenn Shepard, Shinai

of a larger conservation unit, the Manu Biosphere Reserve (RBM), through UNESCO's 'Man and the Biosphere' programme. Including its buffer zones, the RBM has a total area of 1,881,200 ha. The RBM includes areas where access is strictly prohibited as well as zones defined as 'multiple use' where people are permitted to carry out the sustainable use of natural resources.[25] In 1987, Manu National Park was inscribed on the list of UNESCO World Heritage sites.[26]

Park management and community participation

At the time of the Park's creation in 1968, the fundamental rights of indigenous peoples to lands and resources were not yet recognised in Peru. It was only in 1974 that the *Ley de Comunidades Nativas* (Law of 'Native Communities') was passed, which enabled indigenous peoples to secure collective land titles for the first time.[27] In this context it is not surprising, although it is disheartening, that there was no consultation of Manu's indigenous peoples when the Park was established.

Such a lack of consultation was particularly problematic given the immediate impacts that the declaration of the Park was to have on the indigenous peoples living within its boundaries. As a result of the designation as a 'National Park' (the highest category of protected area in Peru), limitations were immediately imposed on extractive activities, particularly those with a commercial objective, in favour of other 'non-intrusive' activities such as basic research or tourism. This resulted in restrictions for its indigenous inhabitants, including over the use of firearms for hunting, although "they were permitted to remain as long as they engaged in 'traditional' subsistence activities".[28]

This perception of indigenous societies, in which they were seen as acceptable only as long as they maintained their 'traditional subsistence activities', was reflected and acknowledged in the Park's first 'master plan' ('Plan Maestro') in 1985, which included among its objectives – besides the conservation of nature, scientific research and the promotion of tourism and educational activities – the "preservation of the cultural patrimony of the native populations of the area".[29] The master plan considered that there were only two acceptable options for its inhabitants: either to conserve their 'traditional lifestyles' and remain in the Park; or to opt for further integration into national society and leave. However, little action was taken in support of either option and it appears that relations with communities continued to be characterized by: "[t]he tacit hope of preservationist-minded conservationists... that the park would gradually become depopulated as native inhabitants were drawn toward trade centres and economic opportunities outside the park".[30]

---

25   The RBM includes, in addition to its 'core' (Manu National Park), an additional conservation unit: the Manu Reserved Zone ('*Zona Reservada del Manu*') and the "'Andean/Amazonian multiple use zone' (also known as 'Cultural' or 'Transition' Zone), which has no protected status but serves as a buffer zone of mostly titled lands where sustainable development can be promoted. This 'multiple use zone' comprises legally-titled native communities, Andean peasant communities and colonist settlements, semi-urban settlements, logging concessions and private landholdings, including private nature reserves associated with tourism (Shepard et al. 2010).
26   Decision 11COM VII.A, Doc. SC-87/CONF.005/9, p. 7.
27   Legal Decree N° 22175.
28   Shepard et al. 2010, p. 258.
29   Ríos and Ponce 1986.
30   H. Helberg, *Programa antropológico para del Parque Nacional del Manu* (1989). Cited in Shepard et al. 2010, p. 279.

The categorization of the National Park as a World Heritage site two years after the release of the Master Plan resulted in no change to this approach of paternalistic neglect towards the Park's indigenous peoples. Predictably, the nomination for World Heritage status was not put out to consultation with Manu's indigenous peoples or their organisations. The nomination document devoted little attention to the resident population, noting merely that there were "native populations in the Park area who have limited or no contact with modern civilization, such as the Machiguenga, Kogapakori, Amahuaca and Yaminahua".[31] IUCN added in its summary of the nomination that the native groups were nomadic and mostly subsisting on shifting cultivation, hunting, fishing, and gathering.[32] Despite the lack of consultation and inclusion in the process, the indigenous peoples of the Park and its surrounding areas were included as part of the government's proposed justification for designation as a World Heritage site under natural criteria (iii) and (iv):

(iii) "Exceptional combination of natural and cultural elements. Native populations living in the park are still largely unaffected by modern civilization and provide special opportunity for anthropological study."

(iv) "Habitat of Rare and Endangered Species. The biological diversity found in Manu National Park exceeds that of any other place on earth." [33]

At its eleventh session in December 1987, the World Heritage Committee approved the nomination and inscribed Manu National Park as a natural World Heritage site, although under natural criteria (ii) and (iv), rather than (iii) and (iv). While the reasons for this change are not clear from the record, it can be assumed that the rationale for applying natural criterion (ii) was the reference to 'man's interaction with his natural environment' which it contained at the time. The Committee and IUCN may have considered that this phrase better reflected the significance of the native peoples living in the park than the phrase 'exceptional combinations of natural and cultural elements' contained in natural criterion (iii).[34] In inscribing the Park, the Committee encouraged the Peruvian authorities to "continue to involve assistance agencies in providing support for this Park and to pursue the

---

31 Government of Peru 1986, p. 7 (authors' translation).
32 IUCN 1987a, p. 62.
33 Ibid., p. 63.
34 Neither the IUCN evaluation nor any other documents from the Committee's session provide an explanation as to why criterion (ii) was applied. This is unfortunate, as nothing in IUCN's evaluation (IUCN 1987b) is particularly relevant to this criterion, which at the time referred to "outstanding examples representing significant ongoing geological processes, biological evolution and man's interaction with his natural environment" (*Operational Guidelines*, 1984, 1987). It is therefore rather unclear as to which values of the Park are protected under this criterion. UNESCO and IUCN were contacted during the writing of this article but were not able to provide clarity on this question. Considering the justification for inscription proposed by the Government of Peru, and the fact that the Committee decision highlights the resident native population and the anthropological programme, it seems likely that the reason for applying natural criterion (ii) was the reference to 'man's interaction with his natural environment'. As this reference has since been removed from the text of the criterion, the authors consider that the Government of Peru and UNESCO should initiate a re-listing of the Park as a cultural landscape or mixed site in order to acknowledge the significance of the native peoples living inside the Park and ensure that Manu's outstanding universal values are adequately protected.

anthropological programme regarding the resident native population".³⁵ Thus, it appears that at the start the only role of the Park's indigenous inhabitants was as an object of study with no active role in the management of the Park.

By the late 1990s, the government's passive neglect of the Park's inhabitants had begun to change as growing pressure from communities and civil society organisations resulted in commitments from Park authorities to promote community participation in Park management, protect the rights and lives of isolated indigenous peoples, address the medical and educational needs of the communities and establish clear and transparent rules regarding subsistence resource use.

Changes instituted as a result of these pressures are reflected in the revised version of the Park's Master Plan of 2002, which aimed "to contribute to the acknowledgement and protection of cultural diversity, as well as the self-determination of the indigenous peoples of the area, in concordance with the rest of the objectives of the Park".³⁶ Although the new plan seemed to reflect a real shift in Park policy from 'preservation of cultures' to respecting indigenous peoples' rights to 'self-determination', it was careful to make indigenous self-determination conditional on its compatibility with the overall objectives of the Park.

Despite these improved statements of intention, the promised reforms have failed to result in significant changes to ensure the respect of indigenous peoples' rights and their meaningful participation in Park management. This point is clearly illustrated by the fact that the draft versions of two such essential instruments as the Anthropological Plan (2007) and the Contingency Plan in case of contact with voluntary isolated populations (2006) are still awaiting formal validation and implementation.³⁷ Moreover, several authors have pointed out an endemic lack of consistency in the application of anthropological policies in the Park, which have traditionally: "...responded to emergency decisions and possess little coherence".³⁸ Therefore, without a formal policy in place, relations between indigenous peoples and Park authorities have tended to vary depending on the particular political context or personal commitments of the different Park directors. In recent years, there have been increasing efforts to empower the 'Manu Management Committee' ('*Comité de Gestión del Manu*'), a key space that attempts to ensure the participation of local actors in the area.³⁹ Although this is a step in the right direction, there is a general consensus among the committee members that its capacity to address the issues facing the Park is extremely limited.⁴⁰ Despite the fact that community representatives regularly take part in the sessions of the committee, most of their long-standing demands remain unaddressed, thereby raising questions about the meaningful nature of indigenous participation. The failure to address indigenous peoples' issues is

---

35 Decision 11COM VII.A, Doc. SC-87/CONF.005/9, p. 7.
36 Instituto Nacional de Recursos Naturales (INRENA) 2003, p. 8 (authors' translation).
37 Rummenhoeller and Aguirre 2008; Rummenhoeller and Huertas 2006.
38 Rummenhoeller and Aguirre 2008, p. 9.
39 The *Comité de Gestión del Parque Nacional del Manu y la Reserva de la Biosfera Manu* was officially created in November 2005 in an assembly celebrated in Pilcopata with the participation of 95 public and private institutions (Rummenhoeller and Aguirre 2008).
40 In a series of workshops organised in the course of the process of revision ('*actualizacion*') of the Park's master plan, the members of the committee highlighted the need to strengthen this body as a priority issue for the management of the area.

further hindered by the fact that FENAMAD also does not participate regularly in this committee. In conclusion, while there are increasing efforts on the part of the Park to employ Matsiguenka as park staff, more meaningful participation in Park management remains elusive.

Since the Park's designation as a World Heritage site in 1987, the World Heritage Committee has reviewed the situation in the Park periodically, among other things expressing concern about the threats facing Manu Park from the oil and gas industry. The Committee has also repeatedly noted that it considers the deforestation and 'agricultural encroachment' occurring around the Park's indigenous communities as a threat to the integrity of the World Heritage site and has urged Peru to take measures to stop and reverse this threat.[41] The situation of the indigenous peoples of the Park and their lack of inclusion in Park management and decision-making, however, were not until very recently mentioned in the Committee's expressions of concern.

In 2010, a joint reactive monitoring mission of the World Heritage Centre and IUCN reviewed the state of conservation of the World Heritage property in response to growing concerns. The resulting report identified a range of threats to the property, including oil and gas exploration around the Park, expanding agricultural activity by the indigenous and other local communities, and hunting with firearms by sedentary indigenous communities. The report also raised the growing human population in the Park as a factor affecting the property, noting possible in-migration from areas affected by gas drilling in the nearby Camisea river basin, and that "[t]he sedentary indigenous communities within the property are likewise growing and there seems to be no clear policy in place for managing this growth".[42] The World Heritage Committee responded to the findings of the monitoring team by requesting that Peru focus on (among other things) "...protecting the indigenous peoples living in voluntary isolation and in initial contact from external pressures and engage with sedentary indigenous groups within the property in a more meaningful dialogue to define the future".[43] While there are increasing efforts on the part of the Peruvian government to engage in dialogue with the communities, 'meaningful participation' as yet remains elusive. The experience of the Manu Management Committee, while considered to be a model of participation for other protected areas, highlights the inherent difficulties for indigenous peoples in 'multi-stakeholder' spaces and raises the question as to whether such spaces can ever really work to ensure meaningful indigenous participation.

Impact of the Park on indigenous subsistence livelihoods

The creation of the Park resulted in dramatic changes for its indigenous inhabitants. Strict restrictions on resource use and a prohibition on any form of commercial activity resulted in limited choices for those peoples who chose to remain within its boundaries and were only permitted to carry out subsistence activities according to so-called 'traditional' practices. Shepard et al. describe how these restrictions included a prohibition on firearms for hunting, any form of commercial logging, the

---

41 See http://whc.unesco.org/en/list/402/documents/
42 Rhodes et al. 2010, p. 12.
43 Decision 35COM 7B.34 (2011).

sale of animal skins and hides and wild animals and the raising of cattle or swine. "Although freedom of movement for indigenous persons is guaranteed, searches and seizures of property can be carried out at any time. Further creating uncertainty, the enforcement of these regulations is unpredictable and dependent on the historical moment and the disposition of the park guard in question".[44]

Reactions to these increasing restrictions varied. It appears that after the creation of the protected area (initially as a Reserved Zone and subsequently as a National Park) the majority of the Yine (who had lived on the Manu River and worked in various extractive industries – rubber, logging, pelt hunting - but had begun to establish new communities outside the Park's borders) stopped using the Park for hunting and fishing, in large part due to the new restrictions.[45] Conversely, others such as the Matsiguenka, who today live in the community of Yomibato, relocated to even more remote areas within the Park.

For those who remained, the restrictions on resource use, access to external material goods, medical care and economic opportunities, which are dictated by national laws and policies regulating National Parks, continue to create severe tensions with Park authorities. For example, a recent research project associated with the Park, which involved measuring Matsiguenka farms, encountered problems due to community opposition. Community members suspected that the study was a precursor to limiting their farmland, alongside the general feeling that it represented a tacit form of control over their lives. Matsiguenka communities also continue to complain that they are not officially allowed to rear livestock, including chickens, a vital source of protein. If the concern is that they may be introducing pests, these communities are asking why the Park does not invest in a campaign of vaccination and quality control rather than simple confiscation. To date they have received no satisfactory response.

Income generation

Alongside the restrictions on their livelihoods, income-generating opportunities for communities living within Manu continue to be severely limited by Park regulations and national policies. Although Manu's abundant natural resources certainly meet their subsistence demands for food, construction materials and plant-based medicines, Matsiguenka communities also point out that, today, there are additional necessities that require money. "Now we know money, it's not like before" is a frequent statement one might hear from the Matsiguenka of Yomibato and Tayakome, for whom today's necessities include vital supplies for health posts and schools, tools such as machetes, axes and fish hooks and basic goods such as salt, sugar and soap. However, Park regulations prevent the Matsiguenka from engaging in any commercial activity such as small-scale timber harvesting or the sale of fish or game.

Shepard et al. summarise the impacts of these limited opportunities since the establishment of the Park:

---

44 Shepard et al. 2010, pp. 278-9.
45 G. Shepard, pers. comm.

"Though some Matsigenka worked as boat drivers or wage laborers in the tourist trade or for scientific researchers, overall such benefits were short-term and minimal, not truly building local capacities or social capital. During the particularly bleak years between PNM's establishment and the mid-1980s, some young men left the park for months at a time to work under appalling conditions as wage laborers in commercial logging or gold mining operations. Having almost no command of Spanish or notions of money, they often came back with little more than serious illnesses and a few pieces of used clothing. Throughout the first decade or more of the park's existence, virtually the only access to Western goods available to the Matsiguenka was charity or barter trade from Catholic missionaries, the poorly paid indigenous schoolteachers, visiting anthropologists, and scientists at Cocha Cashu station." [46]

To address their needs for money, the Matsiguenka frequently travel outside the Park - generally to the district capital, Boca Manu – to look for temporary employment in a variety of economic activities ranging from logging to boat construction. Pay and working conditions are typically poor. Additionally, these activities involve health risks as the Matsiguenka are still notoriously susceptible to external diseases. Within the boundaries of the Park, the opportunities to develop economic activities are very restricted and, as described below, the experiences to date have faced a variety of challenges.

Ecotourism

Most of the energy devoted to establishing a source of cash income has focused on the flagship 'Casa Machiguenga', a community-based ecotourism lodge within the Park that was inaugurated in 1997. The success of this enterprise has thus far been limited as the lodge has suffered from recurrent commercial, logistical and political problems. Lacking orientation and support, the communities persistently lament the challenges they meet in terms of running the lodge efficiently. A 2004 study suggests that the promotion of competition from external tourist operators inside the Park has contributed to the commercial weakness of the lodge.[47] Matsiguenka staff and managers have frequently complained that Park restrictions mean that they are unable to establish a small farm near the lodge to meet their own subsistence needs. This restricts their ability to remain in the lodge area, which is far from their farms and families, and makes their participation less economically viable.[48] In spite of the difficulties facing the lodge, Shepard et al. report that the Matsiguenka have continued to strive for its success but argue that its continuing existence appears

---

46 Shepard et al. 2010, p. 283.
47 Ohl, J. 2004. *El ecoturismo como oportunidad para un desarrollo sostenible? Laeconomía de los Matsiguenkas en el Parque Nacional del Manu, Peru.* Eschborn: GTZ. Cited in Shepard et al. 2010.
48 The challenges facing the 'casa Machiguenga' are by no means unique. Several other ecotourism initiatives involving indigenous communities in the Madre de Dios region have also failed to deliver the expected results. Communal lodges constructed as part of community conservation projects have simply fallen down in some communities such as Sonene, Shipetiari or Puerto Azul, while multi-communal initiatives such as *Wanamei,* in the Amarakaeri Communal Reserve, have also been unsuccessful.

to owe more to their own determination than to external support.[49] In the face of these tensions, the current Park management has now permitted the Matsiguenka to maintain a small farm close to the lodge and are supporting the Matsiguenka to resolve the many challenges that remain.

Timber harvesting

The Matsiguenka of Tayakome continue to claim the right to harvest the valuable hardwoods which fall naturally and float downriver during the rainy season. Peruvian legislation, however, prohibits the commercial extraction of natural resources within National Parks and, for this reason, the Matsiguenka are not allowed to harvest this timber within the limits of the protected area, which instead is harvested by a timber cooperative based outside the Park in the town of Boca Manu. The indigenous inhabitants of the Park view this situation as utterly unjust and have repeatedly asked FENAMAD and others: "Why should we not be allowed to take advantage of this timber when those living outside the park and not subject to its restrictions are able to benefit?" Although, with the intermediation of the Park and the local authorities, the Matsiguenka students resident in Boca Manu have recently gained access to a timber harvesting quota to support their expenses, the communities see this as insufficient and continue to claim a more direct access to these resources.

Park employment

Although the Park has restricted the Matsiguenka's economic activities, it has also become a major employer for the communities. Today, the majority of park guards and rangers in the lowland section of the protected area come from local Matsiguenka communities. In addition to providing a sustained wage income for some families, the increasing number of indigenous staff has contributed to improved communication and mutual understanding between Park authorities and local populations. The presence of indigenous park guards has also facilitated the joint efforts to protect peoples in isolation and initial contact that are being undertaken by the Park and the regional federation FENAMAD, whose leaders value, and feel more at ease amidst, the presence of other indigenous counterparts.

Health services

The Park has also had a major impact on community access to health services as its creation resulted in the suspension of the medical assistance that missionaries had previously been

---

49 Shepard et al. 2010.

Initial contact Matsiguenka seek medical attention in the health post of the community of Yomibato.
Photo: Daniel Rodriguez, FENAMAD

providing.[50] This gap in services has not been adequately filled by regional health authorities, who claim that they lack the necessary finance as well as the personnel willing to operate in such remote areas. As a result, outbreaks of epidemics are frequent even for the well-established community of Tayakome, which has more frequent and sustained contact with outsiders, greater immunological resistance and a functioning health post. The poor quality of health service provision in the community is made worse by the increasing exposure of community members to introduced diseases, as an increasing number of Matsiguenka now move back and forth outside the Park in order to travel, study or work.[51]

Although some of the health posts within the Park have recently been improved, there is an urgent need for an integrated health policy that addresses the specific and diverse needs of the Park's indigenous inhabitants.[52] The presence of indigenous populations in situations of 'initial

---

50 Analysis of demographic data from the village of Tayakome shows a 50% decline in the rate of population growth during the decade of 1975–1984, after the missionary exodus, when compared with the previous decade. Between 1974 and 1980, 15 of the 25 children born in Tayakome died during that period, a grim 60% rate of infant and child mortality (Shepard et al. 2010, p. 280).
51 Rodriguez 2008a; 2008b.
52 Several reports produced by FENAMAD describe in detail the context of indigenous health issues in Manu National Park and have been used to propose specific preventive and emergency policies in the area (see Rodriguez 2008b; 2010).

contact' or 'voluntary isolation' makes this issue even more complex given their susceptibility to introduced diseases. Currently, the Park lacks the mechanisms and resources required to address a 'contact' situation with some of the 'Mashco Piro' whose presence is regularly detected in the vicinity of the community of Tayakome (right bank of the Manu River) or in neighbouring areas of the communities of Diamante and Shipetiari (left bank of the Upper Madre de Dios River).[53] Equally, the Matsiguenka groups in initial contact who are living in areas upriver of the community of Yomibato and Piñi Piñi river basin are also known to have extreme levels of vulnerability and suffer from frequent outbreaks of epidemics. This vulnerability can be further aggravated by the presence of outsiders carrying new forms of contagious diseases. The lethal epidemics that took place along the Piñi Piñi River in 2002[54] and the headwater region of Yomibato in 2007,[55] which led to the reported deaths of up to 28 people, both coincided with encounters with unauthorized visitors in restricted areas of the Park.[56]

Despite these incidents, and the constant calls from indigenous organisations for improvements in health services, there is still no effective contingency or emergency plan in place that could be implemented effectively in case of epidemics resulting from contact with groups in voluntary isolation and initial contact. At the same time, the provision of appropriate medical assistance to those groups who have established 'initial contact' faces a host of additional challenges, including the lack of specially trained personnel, a lack of awareness on the part of the health authorities regarding the specific needs of these groups and a lack of sufficient resources to enable operation in remote areas of the Park.

Rights or relocation? Conflicting views on Manu and its indigenous peoples

The exclusion of indigenous peoples from processes of management and decision-making and the restrictions on their use of natural resources lie at the heart of the continued tensions between Park authorities and indigenous peoples. Although Park policy towards indigenous peoples has improved and Matsiguenka are now employed as park guards, the meaningful involvement of indigenous peoples is still a pending issue given the limitations of the Management Committee.

---

53 Although a contingency plan does exist, it lacks essential practical details and an awareness raising component amongst neighbouring communities if it is to be effective. Shepard et al. conclude that "throughout the park's history, no effective action has been taken to prepare for the immediate health emergencies or long-term consequences of such contact situations with isolated groups" (2010, p. 260).

54 According to the testimony of several representatives of the community of Santa Rosa de Huacaria, at least 24 Matsiguenka were reported to have died as a consequence of contagious respiratory diseases in the Piñi Piñi River area after their encounter with a large archaeological expedition team (Rodriguez 2008b).

55 In December 2007, Dr. Wilfredo Huamani Oblitas, Head Manager of the Manu provincial health services ('Micro Red Salvation Manu'), officially reported on an epidemic outbreak among the Matsiguenka living in a situation of 'initial contact' in the headwater areas surrounding the community of Yomybato. Dr. Huamani's team reported that about 80 Matsiguenka, all suffering from respiratory problems of different magnitudes, had arrived in the community seeking medical help. According to testimonies collected by the investigative team, four people (three children and one adult) had already died in that area.

56 Huamani 2008; Rodriguez 2008b.

Partly as a result, relations between Park authorities and the Park's inhabitants have remained problematic.

Ever since the Park's creation, views on its indigenous peoples have tended to fit into one of two conflicting positions. On the one hand, vocal proponents of a strict conservation approach have explicitly argued that the conservation of biodiversity is incompatible with the presence of indigenous communities. Notably, at the extreme of this ideological approach, conservation biologist John Terborgh has argued that the demographic growth of the Matsiguenka communities in Manu Park, with increasing access to modern health facilities and technologies, will ultimately degrade the Park's wildlife and ecosystem integrity. As a result, he has proposed "a carefully constructed and voluntary relocation programme built on the manifest desire of contacted indigenous groups to acquire goods and an education for their children and participate in the money economy".[57]

On the other hand, indigenous peoples' organisations, including the regional indigenous federation of Madre de Dios, FENAMAD, have defended the ancestral territorial rights of indigenous peoples to the lands and resources within the National Park and have advocated issuing land titles *within* the Park. FENAMAD has consistently pointed out that this is not only a fair solution to a long-standing problem but also the only solution that recognises indigenous peoples' rights to land and resources under both national and international law. From an indigenous peoples' rights perspective, the position of the conservationist lobby is untenable; both Peruvian and international law prohibit the forced or coerced resettlement of indigenous peoples from their ancestral lands, including where related to the creation of protected areas.[58] Nevertheless, the question of how certain sections of the Park might be titled to indigenous communities also presents its own legal and practical challenges.

From biodiversity conservation to indigenous refuge: Manu's invisible inhabitants

While relations with the Matsiguenka have been the main focus of the Park's anthropological policies to date, the Park authorities are increasingly being forced to address issues related to its less visible residents, the isolated indigenous peoples who sustain little or no communication with outsiders.

On 3 May 1984, four indigenous men armed with bows and arrows were captured from the upper Mishagua River (on the western edge of Manu National Park) by loggers from the nearby

---

57 Terborgh 1999, p. 56.
58 See, e.g., *UN Declaration on the Rights of Indigenous Peoples*, Art. 10 and *Indigenous and Tribal Peoples Convention, 1989* (ILO Convention 169), Art. 16. In Peru the Protected Areas Law (No. 26834) recognizes preexisting property rights (Art. 5) and therefore could not be used to justify displacement of either individuals or communities, indigenous or otherwise. More generally in Peru the Law Concerning Internal Displacements (No. 28223) recognizes that all human beings have the right to protection against arbitrary displacements that remove them from their home or place of permanent residence (Art. 7.1). The law also specifies that the State is obliged to take measures to prevent the displacement of indigenous peoples and other groups who have a special dependency on their land or special attachment to it (Art. 9).

town of Sepahua. The men were members of the Nahua, a Panoan-speaking indigenous people occupying the headwaters of the Manu and Mishagua rivers and who, until this point, had been actively rejecting all contact with outsiders. The contact between the loggers and the four men triggered an explosion of respiratory diseases, including pneumonia and influenza, which almost halved the Nahua population within a few months.[59] As a result of the epidemics and their need for constant medical and other humanitarian assistance, many Nahua began to leave the Park and they established a new village on the Mishagua River (Santa Rosa de Serjali), which provided them with better access to medical and other assistance. This process of relocation was complete by 1995 by which time all the surviving Nahua had left the Park.

The tragic story of the Nahua is relevant because it demonstrates very powerfully the extreme level of vulnerability of those indigenous peoples living in voluntary isolation in the Amazon as they lack resistance to disease variants that are common in large-scale societies but absent in their own. It also highlights the urgent need for effective contingency measures to prevent a repetition of this tragedy in Manu National Park, where the risk of a similar occurrence remains extremely high.

This is more important than ever for the authorities of Manu National Park and local and national health authorities because of the presence of Matsiguenka groups in 'initial contact' who live in the inaccessible headwaters of the Piñi Piñi, Cumerjali, Fierro and Sotileja rivers. These groups remain highly vulnerable to introduced diseases disseminated by a constant stream of adventure tourists, explorers seeking the secret city of Paititi, film-makers, colonists and missionaries.[60]

Since 1996, clear evidence of hitherto unrecorded isolated indigenous groups also identified as 'Mashco Piro' began to appear on the left (north) bank of the upper reaches of the Manu River. It appears that their arrival coincided with large-scale seismic exploration work being conducted by Mobil Oil in the Piedras River to the north-east of the Park.[61] In subsequent years, their presence became even more frequent as it appears they were fleeing from an intensive wave of illegal mahogany logging in the Las Piedras and Purús rivers, which pushed them into the headwaters of the Manu and Mishagua rivers.[62] A 2006 report from the Peruvian Human Rights Ombudsman records the appearance of isolated peoples on the left bank of the Manu River between the years 2002 and 2004 and notes that this coincided with the peak of the illegal logging activities in neighbouring territories.[63]

---

59   Feather 2010.
60   Rodriguez 2008a; 2008b.
61   According to Shepard, there is no record of isolated peoples on the left bank of the Manu River before 1994 (cited in Pro-Manu 2002).
62   This was corroborated by a UNESCO monitoring mission in 2010, which noted "reports of indigenous people moving into the property from the Camisea River in the Northwest of the property, possibly as a result of the decimation of wildlife in the Camisea River Basin. This would suggest that MNP may serve as a haven for indigenous peoples affected by developments outside of the property" (Rhodes et al. 2010, p. 11). Pressure on the Piedras River had increased due to Brazil's ban on mahogany exports, promoting mass invasions of armed loggers and frequent violent encounters with isolated peoples presumed to be Mashco Piro (Huertas 2002).
63   *Defensoría del Pueblo* 2006. The report also documents the presence of approximately 300 illegal loggers on the Amigos River in 2002. Schulte-Herbrüggen and Rossiter (2003) report 224 logging campsites along the length of the Piedras River within the Madre de Dios Territorial Reserve for Isolated Peoples.

In addition to the Mashco Piro on the upper reaches of the Manu, another group (also presumed to be Mashco Piro) have migrated along the southern bank of the lower Manu in close proximity to tour operations and native communities along the Upper Madre de Dios River.

There is thus now strong evidence that pressure on neighbouring areas from extractive industries is displacing isolated peoples into Manu National Park. The sightings of Mashco Piro continued despite the establishment of a Territorial Reserve for Isolated Peoples in Madre de Dios in 2002 to protect and safeguard their rights and territories. The reserve lacks the ability to enforce its borders and prevent invasions of loggers, despite the efforts of indigenous organisations and NGOs. Meanwhile, pressure is mounting from elsewhere as other territorial reserves for isolated peoples, including the Mashco Piro Reserve, the Murunahua Reserve and the Kugapakori/Nahua/Nanti Reserve, are also under siege from the logging and oil and gas industries (Map 3).[64]

The displacement of Mashco Piro into the Park triggered conflicts with the Matsiguenka as Shepard et al. report:

> "Since 2002, these isolated groups have encroached with increasing frequency and boldness on the territory of settled Matsiguenka communities on the upper Manu. They have taken metal implements and food from Matsiguenka houses, burned one Matsiguenka house located far up a north-bank tributary stream (perhaps as a warning not to return to that region) and fired arrows as warning shots at groups of Matsiguenka who inadvertently approached. Clearly, this group or groups are fleeing from turmoil in the Piedras area and seeking new territories within Manu Park."[65]

Tensions mounted as the presence of the Mashco Piro in the immediate vicinity of the Matsiguenka communities became a common feature, particularly during the dry season. In 2003, as a result of their continued presence on the left bank of the Manu River, the Matsiguenka community of Maizal decided to relocate to the right-hand side of the river, where they continue to live. In 2005, FENAMAD collected the testimony of one Matsiguenka man from the community of Tayakome, in which he recounts one such encounter with Mashco Piro on the opposite bank of the river:

> "From there a group of men and women appeared, totally naked with their penises tied with a string. The women had a little skirt…. and wore monkey teeth necklaces…. We began to speak with them using different sounds, they made the sounds of the monkey, the jaguar, the tapir. We did the same, they clapped and laughed. We were exchanging calls with 37 people! Their leader….he signaled to us by firing an arrow upriver, then downriver and then to the side. For sure he was saying that they are going upriver…"[66]

Despite the intensification of sightings and encounters, the presence of isolated peoples within the Park was not a new phenomenon. Nevertheless, the Park still lacks a comprehensive

---
64 Shinai 2004.
65 Shepard et al. 2010, p. 260.
66 Ponce 2005.

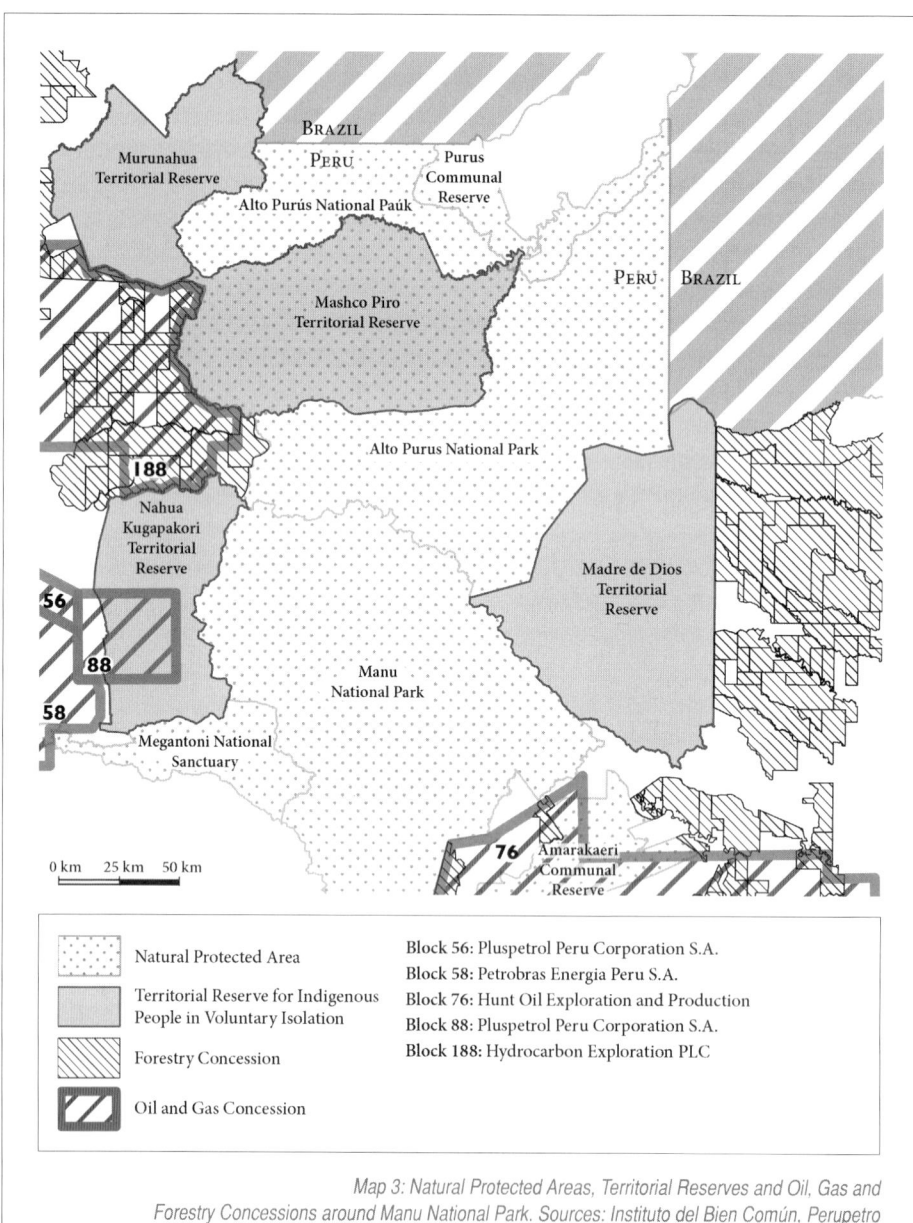

Map 3: Natural Protected Areas, Territorial Reserves and Oil, Gas and Forestry Concessions around Manu National Park. Sources: Instituto del Bien Común, Perupetro

medical contingency plan in case of a contact situation and has failed to work with neighbouring communities to raise their awareness of the risks of such contact. This was corroborated by the UNESCO monitoring mission in 2010, which reported that they were "not made aware of any concerted effort on the part of the authorities to better understand the dynamics of these groups, so as to plan for future situations. As it currently stands, the situation appears to develop in the absence of a particular policy".[67]

Despite the lack of a clear and overarching policy towards indigenous inhabitants (isolated or otherwise), recent events have marked a shift in the role of the Park as it becomes increasingly important as a refuge for isolated peoples, given the mounting pressures on neighbouring areas. This issue became even more relevant in May 2011 when a large group of Mashco Piro were spotted on the left bank of the Upper Madre de Dios River in a section of the river frequented by commercial and tourist traffic, known locally as 'Yanayaco'.[68]

Although their existence was already well-documented, the high visibility of the group on the river banks and their confident attitude towards passing boats was unprecedented. It was a distinct contrast with previous encounters with the Mashco Piro in the area, which had traditionally involved timid (or even hostile) reactions towards the presence of others. Many local people have interpreted the gestures and verbal signs of the Mashco Piro towards passing boats as clear evidence of their interest in establishing sustained contact.[69] This resulted in a proliferation of efforts to approach the Mashco Piro with metal tools, soft drinks or clothes. This was also fuelled by the increasing number of photographs that appeared in the press. Tourist boats on their way to Manu National Park even began to patrol the area looking for photo opportunities.

The situation prompted the start of hitherto unprecedented coordination between the Park authorities and FENAMAD in order to avoid forced or induced 'contact' and protect the lives of both isolated peoples and others from potentially violent encounters. Together, they joined forces to raise awareness of the extreme vulnerability of these peoples among local communities and state institutions and to reinforce the message that contact should not be initiated and any attempts to exchange objects should be avoided because of the obvious risks involved for both sides.[70]

FENAMAD and the Park worked together to persuade regional and local authorities to take action. This resulted in a series of measures, including a regional law in October 2011 that restricted river transit in order to prevent the recurrent attempts to approach the Mashco Piro.[71] Despite achieving a political and legal framework, the planned protection measures did not receive the support of the regional government or the Vice-Ministry of Culture, the national agency responsible for indigenous issues. As a consequence, in the absence of control mechanisms, efforts to

---

67 Rhodes et al. 2010, p. 11. The report issued the following recommendation to park authorities: "To protect indigenous residents living in voluntary isolation and in initial contact from external pressures and undesired attempts to contact them and engage in a more meaningful dialogue with sedentary indigenous groups within the property to define a clear policy for their future in the special use zones of the park taking into account natural resource management but also education and health" (ibid., p. 12).
68 El Comercio 2011.
69 Local people in the Upper Madre de Dios frequently say that the Mashco Piro 'want to be civilized' ('se quieren civilizar').
70 FENAMAD countered the discourse that the Mashco Piro should be approached and 'contacted' by pointing out that the real interests of the Mashco Piro people remained unclear and that it was vital to differentiate between their manifest desire for some manufactured goods and speculation that they desired to establish permanent relations with the national society.
71 Servindi 2011a.

approach the Mashco Piro and the resulting risks continued to increase. In October 2011, an indigenous park guard was shot with an arrow and severely wounded while he was carrying out patrolling duties in the Yanayaco sector.[72] Although this event reinforced the message of FENAMAD and the Park, given the lack of effective control mechanisms, some local inhabitants of the region actively continued to approach the Mashco Piro.

One of these people was a local indigenous man known as 'Shaco', a respected elder with a long-standing involvement and interest in efforts to contact the Mashco Piro and who was locally acknowledged as the key 'mediator' with the isolated group. From the beginning of the sightings, Shaco had repeatedly established verbal communication and exchanges of metal tools and farm produce with the Mashco Piro.[73] Tragically, in November 2011, for reasons that remain unclear, Shaco himself was killed in one such encounter.[74] Months later, the Mashco Piro are still active in the area while FENAMAD is in the final stages of completing the construction of a control post, in close coordination with the neighbouring communities, the Park authorities and the local and regional governments.[75]

Manu National Park: Rethinking its relationship with indigenous peoples

Despite its success in protecting biodiversity, the very existence of Manu National Park sits uneasily with the indigenous homelands with which it overlaps. Its classification as a World Heritage site has increased the international exposure of Manu National Park and served to further highlight the issues faced by its indigenous inhabitants, but has failed to lead to an improvement in the Park's relationship with indigenous peoples or greater indigenous participation in management and decision-making. The recent recommendation of the World Heritage Committee that Peru protect the indigenous peoples living in voluntary isolation and in initial contact from external pressures and engage with communities settled within the Park in a more meaningful dialogue to define the future has not yet been followed up and progress in recognising and respecting the rights of the Park's indigenous inhabitants has been limited.

One factor that may explain this is that UNESCO has consistently failed to ensure the participation of indigenous organisations such as FENAMAD or communities in its own efforts to monitor and assess Park policies and practices. For example, the joint World Heritage Centre / IUCN mission team that visited the Park in 2010 did not meet with a single indigenous organisation or any community representatives.[76] From March 2012 on, there were concerted efforts on the part of civil society groups to communicate to the World Heritage Centre the imminent threats facing

---

72   Servindi 2011b.
73   Over the years, Shaco and other Piro have been tireless in their efforts to contact the remaining, isolated Mashco Piro and have even temporarily captured Mashco Piro individuals (Gow 2006).
74   For more details, see Shepard 2012.
75   CNR 2012.
76   No indigenous organisation or community delegates were included in the various formal interviews and/or meetings conducted by the Mission team (Rhodes et al., p. 25 ff.).

Manu National Park from the likely expansion of the Camisea gas project. However, these were not addressed in either a timely or satisfactory fashion and, by November 2012, the World Heritage Centre had still taken no effective measures to address this threat with the appropriate authorities in the Peruvian government.[77]

Shepard et al. argue that, for much of the Park's history, its policy towards its indigenous inhabitants has effectively been one of social exclusion, one that would eventually encourage 'voluntary relocation' of its communities and satisfy the Park's vocal biodiversity conservation community. What is certain is that for much of its existence the Park has represented a restrictive force rather than a positive element in the lives of the communities concerned:

> "By the mid-1980s, most Matsiguenka inhabitants were of the opinion that the park was, at best, a nuisance, and at worst, an oppressor and a menace, providing no visible assistance, imposing arbitrary restrictions and prohibitions, hindering or expelling anyone who tried to help them, and denying them access to goods, services, and the market economy without providing any obvious benefits in return." [78]

Despite this history, today the Park seems to be moving towards a more progressive policy in which it is prioritising the rights of isolated indigenous peoples and beginning to work alongside other institutions to address the economic, social and medical concerns of its settled Matsiguenka communities.

From land titles to territories

Peru is bound by international human rights norms and jurisprudence to recognise and demarcate indigenous peoples' "lands, territories and resources which they have traditionally owned, occupied or otherwise used or acquired".[79] Nevertheless, throughout Peru, many indigenous communities are still awaiting land titles whilst countless others have received title to lands that are barely sufficient to meet their immediate subsistence needs let alone the needs of future generations, and are far more constricted than the boundaries of their traditional lands.[80] Given the severe restrictions and limitations imposed by the Park, for many years Matsiguenka political leaders, in association with FENAMAD, have called (unsuccessfully) for the exclusion of their lands from the Park and recognition of their collective land titles in line with Peruvian commitments on human rights.

More recently however, the perspective of Matsiguenka community members has appeared to shift. Today, they are placing less emphasis on their demand for land titles *per se* and focusing more on legal mechanisms to ensure that their *territorial rights* are respected, in addition to the

---

77 Forest Peoples Programme 2012b.
78 Shepard et al. 2010, p. 283.
79 *UN Declaration on the Rights of Indigenous Peoples*, Art. 26.
80 Espinosa and Feather 2011.

measures needed to address their economic, health and education concerns. During a meeting held in Tayakome in May 2011, community members explained to FENAMAD and representatives of the regional government that they were opposed to land titling because they believed that it would involve limitations to, rather than recognition of, their territorial rights. This is because many Matsiguenka associate community land titles in their region with small plots of land that barely include their homes and gardens let alone their hunting and fishing grounds or ancestral territory. As one resident of Yomibato said: "If they were going to title they would need to title the whole park." Other residents associate a land title with new elements of control: "I don't want a land title because this will mean that if a spider monkey crosses the boundary, I won't be able to hunt it," explained one resident of Tayakome.

Some advocates of the idea that land titles are the only way to improve the living conditions of the communities believe that the Matsiguenka have been misled by NGOs and the Park on the negative consequences of land titling. On the other hand, it is also true that the reality of neighbouring communities located outside the Park provides the Matsiguenka with persuasive examples illustrating that community land titles in other areas of Madre de Dios often fail to provide secure legal recognition over the entirety of a territory. Peru's titling policy has also frequently failed to provide its inhabitants with adequate security from extractive industries such as logging, mining, oil and gas. Knowledge of the experiences of those communities outside the Park has lent weight to the idea that, while the National Park presents its own set of complex problems, it also offers a haven of security in a sea of uncertainty.

In this light, the views of Matsiguenka today demonstrate the failure of community land titling policies within Peru to truly reflect indigenous conceptions of land and territory. The demands of the Matsiguenka now serve as a challenge to the Peruvian government and Manu National Park authorities to develop new models of indigenous land tenure in line with their rights.[81]

The end of fortress conservation: A rights-based approach

Protecting the territorial rights of indigenous peoples within the framework of a national park will require some significant changes to the Park management and will require a new consensus about the place of indigenous peoples in conservation areas. Shepard et al. try to pick out just such a middle ground between calls for territorial rights and the exclusionary model advocated by the conservation lobby by recommending a model of 'tenure for defense'.[82] Under this model, indigenous occupation of the Manu should be supported (but not recognised legally in the form of

---

81 This commitment (at least on paper) has been made by the Peruvian government in the context of its national REDD strategy. The Peruvian government's Readiness Preparation Package (RPP), which was approved by the World Bank's Forest Carbon Partnership Facility (FCPF) in March 2011, includes a commitment to: "analyze and propose actions to update national legislation with respect to the collective rights of indigenous peoples and communities over their lands and harmonization with applicable international obligations" (Peruvian Government Presentation to the FCPF Participants Committee 8, Vietnam, March 2012).
82 Shepard et al. 2010.

land titles), given their contribution to protecting the Park from external pressures, the likely social conflict that would ensue from their removal and the evidence that the impact of their current hunting activities on large mammal populations is negligible. They also show how biodiversity conservation is in the interest of the Matsiguenka, who rely on the abundant game for protein and who have noted the increasing scarcity for communities beyond the confines of the Park. The authors argue that, in this light, the Park should strongly support income-generating opportunities for the Matsiguenka that are consistent with sustainable resource use and the objectives of the Park.

The 'tenure for defense' model argues for the continued occupation of Manu's forests by its indigenous inhabitants on the basis that their interests are broadly aligned with the conservation objectives of the Park. Nevertheless, it does not fully capture either the perspectives of the Matsiguenka or their right to lands and resources as indigenous peoples. The *United Nations Declaration on the Rights of Indigenous Peoples* (UNDRIP) requires States to "consult and cooperate in good faith with the indigenous peoples concerned through their own representative institutions in order to obtain their free and informed consent prior to the approval of any project affecting their lands or territories and other resources".[83] Manu's indigenous inhabitants are bearers of rights and not simply another stakeholder whose interests can be traded off against other priorities; Manu National Park is primarily their home, rather than a tourist attraction or a biodiversity hotspot.

For Manu's indigenous inhabitants, the early history of Manu National Park was one of restriction and tension, one in which they consistently called for the exclusion of their lands from the Park. To date, the Park authorities have been slow to increase and promote community participation in Park management, provide support for the educational and health needs of communities or strongly back the Matsiguenka eco-tourism initiative. However, in spite of the Park's policies, in the present context, the often negative associations with the 'restrictive' nature of the protected area are increasingly contrasted with those that stress its quality as a 'refuge' for people. This has become particularly evident in the case of the highly vulnerable groups in 'initial contact' or isolation such as the Mashco Piro, as the Park has played a critical role working alongside FENAMAD to defend the rights of isolated peoples since 2011, and its authorities seem to be becoming aware that indigenous peoples are a critical ally in their efforts to protect Manu rather than a hindrance.

In the case of the Matsiguenka communities within the Park, some still maintain their demands for land titling. Others, while equally critical of the lack of basic services (including health, education

---

83 Article 32(2) UNDRIP. Corresponding obligations exist under several of the core international human rights treaties. See, e.g., Human Rights Committee, Communication No. 1457/2006, *Poma Poma v. Peru*, Views adopted on 27 March 2009, Doc. CCPR/C/95/D/1457/2006, para. 7.6: "In the Committee's view, the admissibility of measures which substantially compromise or interfere with the culturally significant economic activities of a minority or indigenous community depends on whether the members of the community in question have had the opportunity to participate in the decision-making process in relation to these measures and whether they will continue to benefit from their traditional economy. The Committee considers that participation in the decision-making process must be effective, which requires not mere consultation but the free, prior and informed consent of the members of the community." Similar observations have been made by the Committee on Economic, Social and Cultural Rights (e.g., *Concluding observations: Peru, 18 May 2012*, Doc. E/C.12/PER/CO/2-4, para. 23) and the Committee on the Elimination of Racial Discrimination (e.g., *Concluding Observations: Peru, 24 August 2009,* Doc. CERD/C/PER/CO/14-17, para. 14).

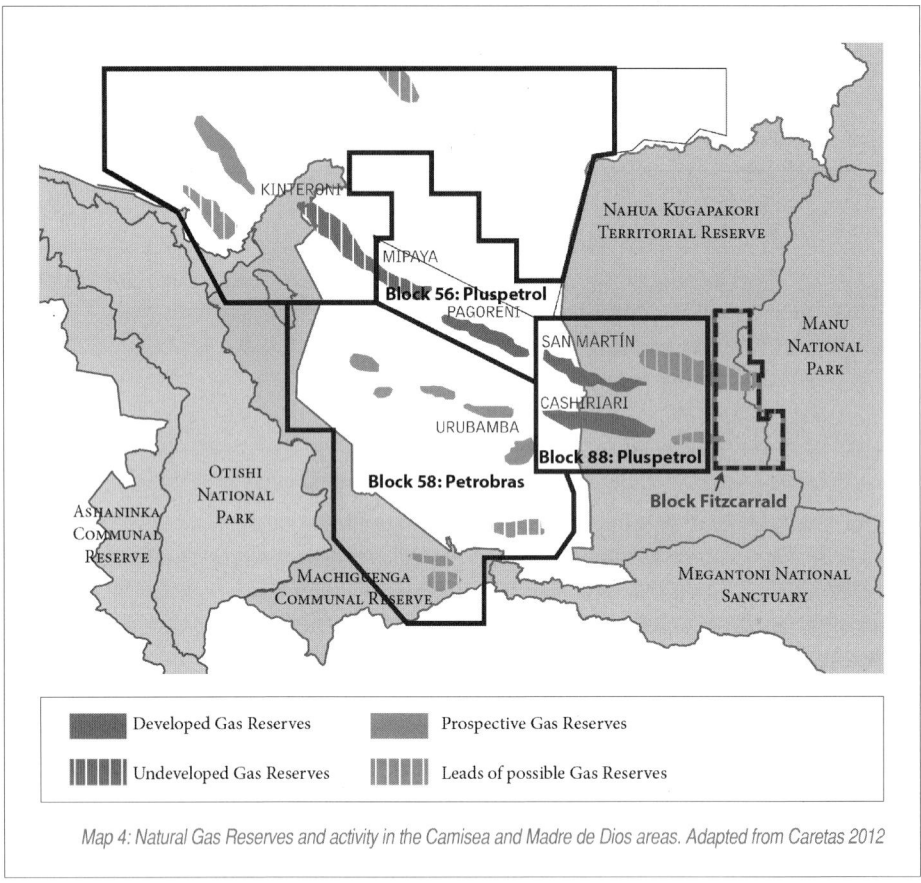

Map 4: Natural Gas Reserves and activity in the Camisea and Madre de Dios areas. Adapted from Caretas 2012

and income-generating opportunities) and their insufficient participation in Park management, also acknowledge the role of the Park in protecting their territories and the provision of some vital services. In this complex context, the challenge remains to find a new model for indigenous land tenure that respects indigenous peoples' right to land and resources and provides them with the autonomy to determine how they wish to live within the framework of a national park. To meet this challenge, it is necessary to strengthen the processes of dialogue between communities and the Park, in order to reach areas of consensus and develop concrete proposals, as well as to secure support from relevant authorities at regional and national levels to put these proposals into practice. These challenges also represent an opportunity for UNESCO and the Park to start a process in which Manu's future can be redrawn, not just on the strength of its biodiversity but based on the rights and concerns of its indigenous inhabitants. One important aspect that should be discussed in this context, together with indigenous communities and their representative organisations, is the possibility of re-listing the Park as a cultural landscape or mixed site, in order to give better recognition and protection to the exceptional indigenous cultural heritage contained within it, as initially contemplated at the time of World Heritage listing (see the discussion above).

In recent months, Peruvian government plans have emerged to open up an area for oil and gas exploration on the western border of the Park as part of the expansion of the Camisea gas project. Maps of the proposed concession even indicate that a section of the Park itself will be included within the new concession (Map 4). The exact location of the so-called 'Fitzcarrald concession' has yet to be formally confirmed but the Peruvian government is clearly intent on expanding the oil and gas industry in the region and even the Manu will not escape this.[84] Its role as a refuge for indigenous peoples is perhaps more important than ever before. ○

References

Alfaro, L. and Nieto, J. C. 2012. El Parque Nacional Del Manu Bajo La Lupa. *Rumbos de Sol & Piedra*, 24 October 2012.
Caretas. 2012. Por un Tubo: Salto al Futuro. *Caretas*, Vol. 2226, 4 April 2012, p. 22 ff.
CNR. 2012. Madre de Dios: Comunidad nativa de Diamante acepta construcción de puesto de vigilancia en su territorio'. *Coordinadora Nacional de Radio*, 16 February 2012. http://www.cnr.org.pe/nueva_web/nota.shtml?x=6088 (Accessed 18 March 2013).
Defensoría del Pueblo. 2006. *Informe Defensorial 101: Pueblos Indígenas en Situación de Aislamiento y Contacto Inicial*. Lima, January 2006.
El Comercio. 2011. Presuntos Indígenas En Aislamiento Voluntario Fueron Vistos En El Manu. *El Comercio.pe*, 25 May 2011. http://elcomercio.pe/actualidad/763053/noticia-presuntos-indigenas-aislamiento-voluntario-fueron-vistos-manu (Accessed 18 March 2013).
Espinosa, R. and Feather, C. 2011. *The reality of REDD in Peru: Between theory and Practice*. Moreton in Marsh, Forest Peoples Programme.
Feather, C. 2010. *Elastic selves and fluid cosmologies: Nahua resilience in a changing world*. PhD Thesis, University of St Andrews.
Forest Peoples Programme. 2012a. Peruvian government on brink of expanding oil and gas development in reserve for isolated peoples and UNESCO world heritage site. *FPP E-Newsletter July 2012*.
Forest Peoples Programme. 2012b. *UNESCO will urge Peruvian government to reconsider Camisea gas expansion plans that threaten the rights of isolated indigenous peoples and the integrity of Manu National Park*. 18 September 2012. http://www.forestpeoples.org/topics/extractive-industries/news/2012/09/unesco-will-urge-peruvian-government-reconsider-camisea-ga (Accessed 18 March 2013).
Government of Peru. 1986. World Heritage Nomination: Manu National Park. Lima, Corporación Departamental de Desarrollo de Madre de Dios (CORDEMAD) and Dirección General Forestal y de Fauna (DGFF).
Gow, P. 2006. "Stop annoying me": A preliminary report on Mashco voluntary isolation. Paper presented at Núcleo de Transformaçoes Indígenas/Abaeté, Museu Nacional, Rio de Janeiro, Brazil.
Gray, A. 1996. *The Arakmbut: mythology, spirituality, and history in an Amazonian community*. Providence, Berghahn Books.
Huamani, W. 2008. Informe de Ocurrencias en la Comunidad de Yomybato. OFICIO No 210 –2007-CSS-MRM- DRSMDD. Villa Salvación, Manu (07/01/08). Unpublished Report.
Huertas, B. 2002. *Los pueblos indígenas aislados de Madre de Dios*. Copenhagen, IWGIA.
Huertas, B. and García, A. (eds.). 2003. *Los pueblos indígenas de Madre de Dios: Historia, etnografía y coyuntura* (IWGIA Document No. 39). Puerto Maldonado, FENAMAD and IWGIA.
Instituto Nacional de Recursos Naturales (INRENA). 2003. *Plan Maestro del Parque Nacional del Manu*. Cusco, INRENA.
IUCN. 1987a. *World Heritage Nomination – IUCN Summary. 402: Manu National Park (Peru)*. Available at: http://whc.unesco.org/archive/advisory_body_evaluation/402bis.pdf.

---

84 Forest Peoples Programme 2012a.

IUCN. 1987b. *World Heritage Nomination – IUCN Technical Evaluation. 402: Manu National Park (Peru).* Available at: http://whc.unesco.org/archive/advisory_body_evaluation/402bis.pdf.

Myers, N. et al. 2000. Biodiversity hotspots for conservation priorities. *Nature*, Vol. 403, pp. 853-858.

Nature's Strongholds Foundation. 2013. *Manu National Park.* http://www.naturesstrongholds.com/south-america/manu-national-park.htm (Accessed 18 March 2013).

Ponce, M. 2005. Informe de los últimos avistamientos de los indígenas en aislamiento en la Comunidad Nativa de Tayakome, Parque Nacional Manu. FENAMAD, IUCN, TReeS-Perú.

Pro-Manu. 2002. Plan Antropológico del Parque Nacional del Manu. Documento de Trabajo. (Online Version)

Rhodes, A., Jaeger, T. and Patry, M. 2010. *Report on the Reactive Monitoring Mission to Manu National Park (Peru), 5-14 December 2010.* Paris, World Heritage Centre/IUCN.

Ríos, M. and Ponce, C.. 1986. *Plan Maestro. Parque Nacional del Manu.* Lima, Universidad Nacional Agraria La Molina.

Rodriguez, D. 2008a. An epidemic outbreak among the Matsiguenka in initial contact, Manu National Park, Peru. Report to the ASA (Association of Social Anthropologists of UK and Commonwealth).

Rodriguez, D. 2008b. *Diagnóstico básico para facilitar la protección de los Pueblos Aislados y en Contacto Inicial en el ámbito del Parque Nacional Manu.* Puerto Maldonado, FENAMAD/IWGIA.

Rodriguez, D. 2010. *Problemática de la atención en salud que afecta a las poblaciones indígenas ubicadas al interior del Parque Nacional del Manu.* Puerto Maldonado, FENAMAD.

Rummenhoeller, K. and Aguirre, Y. 2008. Plan Antropológico para el Parque Nacional del Manu elaborado con alcance para la Reserva de la Biosfera del Manu (2008-2012). Revisión del documento anterior elaborado por el Proyecto Pro-Manu (2002). INRENA/PNM.

Rummenhoeller, K. and Huertas, B. 2006. Plan de Contingencia en caso de contacto con Pueblos Indígenas en Aislamiento Voluntario en el ámbito del Parque Nacional del Manu. INRENA/ACCA.

Schulte-Herbruggen, B. and Rossiter, H. 2003. *A socio-ecological investigation into the impact of illegal logging activity in Las Piedras, Madre de Dios, Peru.* Project Las Piedras, The University of Edinburgh.

Servindi 2011a. Dan a Conocer Plan Conjunto Para La Protección De Los Aislados Del Alto Madre De Dios, *Servindi*, 27 October 2011. http://servindi.org/actualidad/53741#more-53741 (Accessed 18 March 2013).

Servindi 2011b. Indígenas En Aislamiento Voluntario Hieren a Guardaparques, *Servindi*, 17 October 2011. http://servindi.org/actualidad/53226 (Accessed 18 March 2013).

Shepard, G. 2012. Close Encounters of the Mashco Kind. *Anthropology News*, January 2012.

Shepard, G. and Izquierdo, C. 2009. Los Matsiguenka de Madre de Dios y del Parque Nacional del Manu. B. Huertas and A. García (eds.), *Los pueblos indígenas de Madre de Dios: Historia, etnografía y coyuntura* (IWGIA Document No. 39). Puerto Maldonado, FENAMAD and IWGIA, pp. 111–126.

Shepard, G. et al. 2010. Trouble in Paradise: Indigenous Populations, Anthropological Policies, and Biodiversity Conservation in Manu National Park, Peru. *Journal of Sustainable Forestry*, Vol. 29: 2, pp. 252-301.

Shinai. 2004. *Aquí vivimos bien. Kamyeti notimaigzi aka. Territorio y uso de recursos de los pueblos indígenas de la reserva Kugapakori Nahua.* Lima, Garfield Foundation.

Terborgh, J. 1999. *Requiem for nature.* Washington, DC, Island Press.

Wilson, E. O. 2002. *The Future of Life.* New York, Knopf.

Canaima National Park and World Heritage Site: Spirit of Evil?

Iokiñe Rodríguez[1]

Introduction

Canaima National Park and World Heritage site, internationally recognised as one of the world's natural wonders, is the homeland of the Pemon indigenous people. Despite their intimate connection with the environment and their strong historical and cultural ties with this area, their relationship with the National Park (henceforth CNP) has not been a happy one. The very name symbolises a long history of antagonism between the Pemon and environmental management agencies. To the detriment of park management, 'Canaima' means 'spirit of evil' in the Pemon language[2] and "refers to [a person who carries out] secret killing using specific methods which we would denote as sorcery".[3]

---

1   Acknowledgements: I wish to express my gratitude to the Pemon, with whom, over the last 15 years, I have learned all that I know about Canaima National Park. I also thank the School of International Development of the University of East Anglia (UEA), United Kingdom, for having been my host during the writing of this manuscript and to Audrey Colson and Chris Sharpe for their revision and constructive criticisms to an earlier version of this text.
2   Thomas 1982.
3   Butt-Colson 2009. The word 'Canaima' was popularised by the eponymous novel of the Venezuelan author Rómulo Gallegos, published in 1935.

Left: Kukenan Tepui at sunset. Photo: Paolo Costa Baldi (CC-BY-SA 3.0)

Thus, the name marked an inauspicious start to relations between Park and traditional inhabitants. A much more appropriate name would have been *Makunaimö* National Park, or '*Makunaimö Kowamüpö Dapon*', which means the 'Homeland of *Makunaimö*' (the Pemon supreme cultural hero).[4]

A lack of sensitivity to the significance of the park's name is one of the many ways in which the Pemon have been made to feel foreigners in their own land since the protected area was created. Although the designation of protected area status has helped to conserve this portion of the Pemon's territory, they have largely experienced the National Park as a threat to their existence, something expressed by a Pemon elder 40 years after the CNP was established:

> "They have decreed our lands as a national park so that they can be exploited one day, but not by ourselves, but by others, not by the poor, but by the rich…it is possible that one day we will be expelled from these lands. It looks like one day they will exterminate us, they will bury us or they will eat us. We have been told that in the past there used to be people that ate our ancestors. Others used fire-guns to kill us. Before they finished us physically, but today they are finishing us with their intelligence." [5]

This article examines why the National Park carries bad associations for the Pemon and suggests ways in which UNESCO and the World Heritage Committee could help to ensure that indigenous peoples' and traditional inhabitants' world views and rights receive greater consideration in the future implementation of the World Heritage Convention.

Setting the scene

The CNP is located in Bolívar State, south-east Venezuela, close to the borders with Brazil and Guyana, protecting the north-western section of the Guiana Shield, an ancient geological formation shared with Brazil, the Guianas and Colombia. The CNP was established in 1962 with an area of 10 000km², but its size was increased to 30 000km² in 1975 in order to safeguard the watershed functions of its river basins. The Guri Dam, which generates 77% of Venezuela's electricity, is located 200km downstream of the north-western border of the park. In recognition of its extraordinary scenery and geological and biological values, the CNP was inscribed on the World Heritage List as a 'natural site' in 1994.

The CNP is home to the Pemon indigenous people. The word 'Pemon' means 'people' and is used to differentiate this indigenous group from their neighbours, such as the Kapon (Akawaio and Patamona), found primarily in Guyana, and the Yekuana, found west of Pemon territories.[6] All these peoples are part of the Carib linguistic group.

---

4   This was the name given by the Pemon from the Gran Sabana to a self-demarcated map of their territory produced between 2000 and 2004 (Proyecto Cartográfico *Inna Kawantok* 2004).
5   Cited in *Roraimökok Damük* 2010, p.11. The name is not included in the quotation in order to protect identity.
6   Thomas 1980.

Within the Venezuelan border, the Pemon are roughly divisible into three subgroups on the basis of phonetic differences: the Arekuna, Kamaracoto and Taurepan.[7] There is also territorial differentiation between the three subgroups: the Arekuna are settled in the north of the Pemon territory, the Kamaracoto in the middle reaches of the Caroni River, and the Taurepan in the south. All three subgroups are found in the CNP.

The entire population of Venezuelan Pemon approaches 28 000,[8] the largest in population of all the Central Guiana Highlands people,[9] with about 18 000 living in the CNP.[10] Very few non-indigenous inhabitants live in the CNP. Most of the Pemon live in villages of between 100 to 1 000 inhabitants. However, some Pemon still follow the traditional settlement pattern of dispersed nuclear families.

The Pemon lifestyle is still based on traditional indigenous systems: subsistence activities include shifting cultivation, gathering, hunting and fishing, although today there is increasingly more work to be found in small-scale mining and tourism.

The date of settlement of the Pemon in their present-day territory is unknown, although they already occupied the south of what is now Bolívar State when the first European explorers and settlers arrived at the end of the 18th century.[11] Two pre-Hispanic archaeological sites are known, the estimated age of which is around 9 000 years, but no direct connection has yet been established with the Pemon.[12]

The Pemon have an intimate relationship with their landscape and environment. The *tepuis*, waterfalls, rapids, lakes and streams all have origins described in myth. Some of these names date from the time of the culture heroes, some from other mythological sequences.[13] In particular, the Pemon relationship with the *tepuis*, the characteristic flat-topped mountains for which the CNP is famous, is complex and profound: the *tepuis* are considered sacred mountains.[14] They are the 'guardians of the savannah', inhabited by the '*imawari*' – "the living forces of nature or nature spirits"[15] – and are consequently not to be disturbed, according to Pemon norms and traditions. Only in the last three decades, with the increase in visits from tourists, have some Pemon begun to disregard these traditional beliefs by taking groups of hikers to some of the more accessible *tepuis*, such as Roraima, Kukenan and Auyantepuy.

The vegetation of the CNP is strikingly divided between a savannah-forest mosaic in the eastern sector, known as the *Gran Sabana*, and evergreen forest in the west. The origin of this mixed forest-savannah landscape, and particularly of the savannahs, has bewildered many naturalists and ecologists over the centuries and is still the subject of controversy.[16] Explorers, scientists and managers assumed for years that the use of fire by the Pemon had turned much of the original 'primeval forest' into savannah, leaving a mixed forest-savannah landscape.[17]

---

7   Within the Brazilian border, the Pemon self-denominate themselves as Makuxi.
8   INE 2001.
9   Thomas 1982.
10 World Bank 2006.
11 Thomas 1980.
12 Schubert and Huber 1985.
13 Thomas 1982.
14 These mountains are known as '*tepuis*' from the local indigenous name *tüpü*. The *tepuis* were formed by a process of differential erosion of the surrounding lands over millions of years.
15 Butt-Colson 2009.
16 Rodríguez et al. 2009; Rull 2009.
17 Tate 1930; Christoffel 1939.

Fire does indeed help maintain the contemporary savannah landscape as it is widely used by the Pemon for a variety of purposes, including prevention of wildfires (see Table 1 for Pemon uses of fire and Section 3 for more details).[18] Furthermore, charcoal deposits found in paleoecological studies show that fire has been a permanent feature of this landscape for at least the last 7 000 years,[19] suggesting a long-term continuous human presence. However, paleoecological studies of the Guyanese and Venezuelan borders of the Guiana Shield reveal that these savannahs were not caused primarily by fire but by a combination of factors, of which climatic fluctuations during the last 12 000 years and low soil fertility are amongst the most important.[20]

| **Domestic use**
Cooking
Keeping warm
Lighting
Firewood (by-product of burning practices)
Cleaning around homes
Burning rubbish

Healing and spiritual use
Smoking out evil spirits when a person is ill
Chasing away dangerous spirits or, in some cases, summoning them (e.g. the rain spirits)

**Environmental protection
(wildfire prevention)**
Preventing large fires entering forests (savannah patch-burning and fire breaks)
Fighting big hazardous fires
(fighting fire with fire)

Communication
Signalling in hunting, fishing, gathering, emergencies

Aesthetic
Making the savannahs look pretty and green | **Safety**
Cleaning paths when going fishing, hunting, to agricultural plots, on visits, etc.
Clearing around houses
Chasing away dangerous animals (jaguars, snakes) and mosquitoes.

Grazing
Producing fresh green grass for cattle and deer

Fishing
Making the fish come out while fishing (the smoke resembles the dusk)

Gathering
Smoking out grasshoppers

Agriculture
Burning farmland
Fertilizing farmland

Hunting
Flushing out animals
Circle burning (rampüm)

Resistance to fire control policies
To irritate EDELCA and make the fire-fighters "work and get wet" |

Table 1: Uses given to fire by the Pemon. Adapted from Rodríguez 2007

---

18 Rodríguez 2007.
19 Leal 2010.
20 Eden 1964; Leal 2010.

The Pemon have their own explanation of the origin of the *Gran Sabana* landscape, found in the *Makuanima* legend, their creation myth, which tells that the *Gran Sabana* was formed by the *Makunaima* brothers, their supreme cultural heroes, sons of the sun and a woman made of jasper. The following is a condensed version of the myth, summarized from Armellada and Koch-Grünberg:

> Long before the *Makunaima* farmed their agricultural plots, they used to chase after animals to find out what they were eating. The younger of the two brothers had the bad habit of cutting down the trees where animals fed in order to eat as much fruit as he could. One day he persuaded his older brother to cut down a very big tree called *Wadakayek*, and the latter reluctantly accepted. It was a difficult tree to cut, as the wood was very hard and the tree was completely covered with vines and bees. Some of the vines turned into snakes when cut. Because of this, it fell towards what is now Guyana, or 'the other side'. Only very few of the branches fell towards 'this side'. The places where those branches fell, called *Tuai Waden* and *Muik*, are the forest patches where edible wild plants are now found. These are also the places preferred by the Pemon for cultivation and are now known to be areas of relatively fertile, less acidic soils. After the tree was felled, a vast quantity of water burst from inside the tree and together with it all sorts of large fish. Before the *Makunaima* could do anything to halt the flood, all the fruit (pineapples, sugar cane, papayas, etc.) and the big fish that the tree bore were carried away downstream.[21]

This is how the Pemon explain that all the forested and fertile areas (*Ingareta*) are found towards the west, east and north of their territory and that only small portions of fertile land and a few patches of forest and small fish can be found on their land. According to the Pemon, the stump of *Wadakayek* can be seen today in the shape of one of the table mountains: *Wadakapiapü*. Another mountain, Roraima (*Roroimö*), corresponds to the fallen trunk of the tree.

The history of the CNP from a Pemon perspective

Despite the historical and cultural ties that the Pemon have with their homelands, the CNP was created without local consultation. This, together with the fact that they have been excluded from practically all aspects of park management and that many of their traditional natural resource use practices clash with conservation objectives, caused great antagonism towards the park from the beginning:

> "Without any information, without any consultation with our communities, they turned the lands in which we live into a national park - into a park! Later they came to tell us that the indigenous communities had to be calm, that the national park designation would protect

---
21 Armellada 1989; Koch-Grünberg 1917, 1981.

us, that the national park would be a support to us so that we could live in peace, and that it would also protect our lands. But what we have seen is that INPARQUES [the National Parks Institute, the government agency with legal responsibility for national park management] came to impose rules for our ways of life, for hunting, fishing, shifting agriculture, burning. Those government officials from those institutions believe themselves to be authorities over us and our lands, so they impose other ways of life."

Pemon woman elder, meeting with the Minister of the Environment (1999)[22]

The rationale for the creation of the CNP followed environmental and economic criteria, although some importance was also given to its value in protecting the Pemon and their culture as long as they remained 'traditional'. This is noted in the CNP objectives, which read as follows:

- To preserve the structure of the ecosystems of the area, avoiding irreversible changes in the dominant vegetation of the different landscape units: savannahs, forests, shrubs, *morichales* and *tepuis*.
- To conserve the genetic resources representative of the wild fauna and flora, safeguarding the survival of autochthonous, endemic, threatened and endangered species.
- To maintain the natural levels of plant and animal communities and biodiversity.
- To preserve the quality of the landscape in the *Gran Sabana* and of the exceptional scenic values such as: *tepuis*, waterfalls, rapids, savannahs and vegetation.
- To safeguard the cultural values of the Pemon, their settlement areas and environmentally conceived traditions.
- To maintain the stability of river basins, protecting watercourses (Decree 1640, Art. 4).

The CNP has been divided into two sectors for management purposes: eastern and western, each approximately 1.5 million hectares in size. Since 1989 the eastern sector has become easily accessible due to the paving of an international highway to Brazil (Troncal 10). The western sector is accessible only by air or river and contains the CNP's main tourist attraction: the Angel Falls, the world's highest waterfall.

The two main legal instruments governing the management of the CNP are the 1989 Partial Regulation of the Constitutional Law for Territorial Planning pertaining to Administration and Management of National Parks and Nature Monuments (Decree 276) and the 1991 Zoning Plan of the Eastern Sector of CNP (Decree 1640).

Decree 276 was the first Venezuelan legal instrument to define in detail the administrative structure of INPARQUES as well as the general regulations governing national parks, prohibited activities in park areas and measures for ensuring compliance with the law. In line with the Western Hemisphere Convention,[23] this decree severely constrains local uses in national parks, although

---

22 Cited in Rodríguez 2003.
23 *Convention on Nature Protection and Wildlife Preservation in the Western Hemisphere*, ratified by Venezuela in 1941.

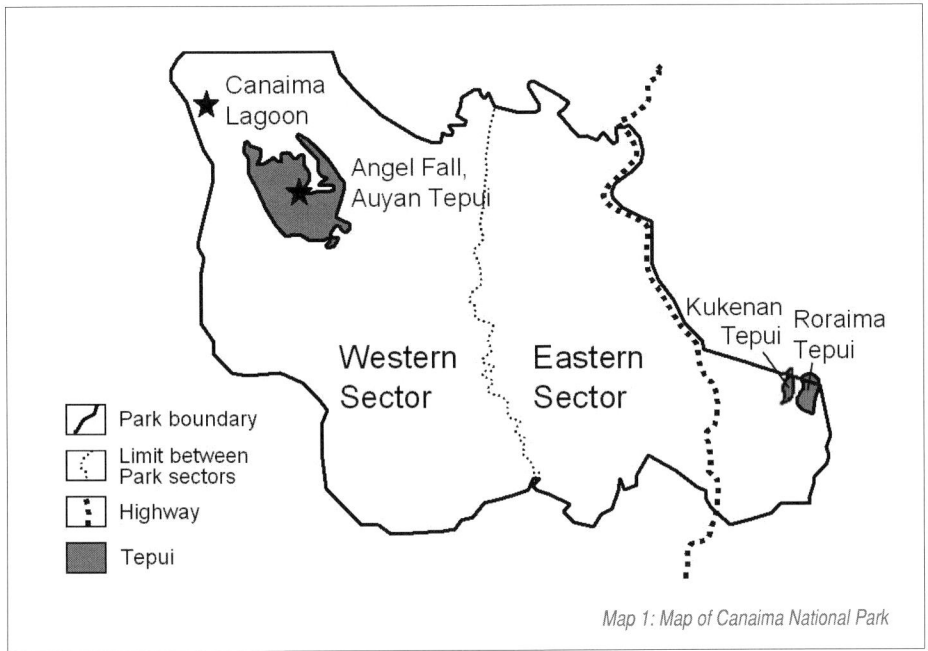

Map 1: Map of Canaima National Park

indigenous people have a 'regime of exception' which allows them to continue traditional activities. It stipulates, however, that specific uses are to be regulated in zoning plans.

National parks without zoning plans are managed according to more general guidelines provided in Decree 276, as in the case of the western sector of the CNP where there is no zoning plan.

The Zoning Plan for the Eastern Sector of the CNP provides "guidelines for planning and the gradual and balanced development of the park".[24] This plan defines the types of use that are permitted within different zones of the park, according to the fragility of the respective ecosystems. The eastern sector was divided into different zones according to the following categories of use and management: strict protection, special use, natural managed environment, recreation and natural recovery. Pemon practices are confined to the special use zone, corresponding to their settlement areas. Crucially, the areas used in subsistence activities, such as hunting, gathering, agriculture and fishing, which require an extensive use of the land, were omitted from the plan.

Attempts to regulate livelihood practices according to the management zones have met with serious Pemon opposition.[25] As a result, the zoning plan has been weakly enforced and the Pemon have continued to carry out traditional livelihood practices.

Although it is common practice in Venezuela to run consultation workshops prior to the approval of zoning plans, there was no consultation with the Pemon over the plan for the CNP. This was

---

24   Decree 1640, Art. 5 (translation by author).
25   Rodríguez 2003.

another lost opportunity for reaching a common understanding about land and natural resource use practices in the park and broader agreements for the management of the area. A revision of this plan should have been carried out (with consultation) in 1996 but was postponed indefinitely due to the intensity of conflicts in the park at that time.

Conflicts between the CNP authorities and the Pemon have gone through different phases. Between the 1970s and the early 1990s, before INPARQUES had a permanent presence in the area, the National Guard and the Venezuelan Corporation of Guyana (CVG) (an autonomous regional development corporation created in the 1960s in order to oversee the industrial development of the Guayana region and in charge of building the Guri Dam) had the institutional mandate to control traditional natural resource use practices, particularly shifting agriculture and savannah burning, which were considered particularly detrimental to the watershed functions of the CNP. During this time, repression and imprisonment were occasionally used to control these two activities.[26] Attempts were also made to change livelihood practices through the introduction of new farming techniques, fire suppression and environmental education activities aimed at teaching the Pemon 'appropriate environmental values'.

One of these attempts has been a fire control program, established in 1981 by the Electricity Company of Caroni (formerly known as EDELCA, now CORPOELEC), which has sought to:

- reduce the degree of fire damage to vegetation in priority sectors, by rapid intervention of a fire brigade
- reduce or minimize the start of fires through an intensive program of fire prevention (environmental education)
- ensure adequate fire management by the Pemon.[27]

Fire control policies have been based on the assumption that the use of fire gradually reduces forest cover,[28] even though there is no scientific proof for this.[29]

Many Pemon, especially from the older generations and more isolated communities, have resisted the fire control program and shifting agriculture and savannah-burning are still widely practiced. However, because of exposure to new values through the national education system and contact with extension and environmental education activities, the younger generation of Pemon have started experiencing a change in their identity and lifestyle and have gradually become more critical and disapproving of some traditional livelihood practices, such as savannah burning. As a result, intergenerational tensions over the use of fire are fairly common.[30]

Between 1991 and 1996, conflicts over tourism management in the *Gran Sabana* escalated sharply due to increasing pressure from economic sectors to open access up to non-Pemon

---

26 Ibid.
27 Gómez 1995.
28 Galán 1984; Gómez and Picón 1994.
29 Rodríguez 2004.
30 Rodríguez 2007.

tourism enterprises.[31] The most widely known tourism conflict was TURISUR, an ecotourism camp illegally authorized by INPARQUES in April 1996 without the consent of the Pemon, which was to be built on the Sierra de Lema in the *Gran Sabana*, and was to comprise 51 cabins with 157 rooms, and a capacity of 200 guests. Despite the offer of a community school, a local health centre, a tourism-training centre and approximately 200 jobs in the hotel, the Pemon unanimously resolved not to accept the project. They reasoned that the hotel would erode their right to provide tourism services in the CNP and that it would set a precedent for other entrepreneurs seeking to develop tourist operations. After six months of intense campaigning against the project in the regional and national press and protests to government agencies, the Pemon succeeded in halting the project. INPARQUES' construction permits were deemed invalid by the Ministry of the Environment because they violated the zoning plan.[32] Thus, TURISUR became a milestone for the Pemon in their struggles to retain their right to manage tourism in the CNP.

The Pemon continue to successfully assert their right to manage tourism in the CNP, particularly in the eastern sector (*Gran Sabana*). However, conflicts over tourism management have continued, albeit at a lower intensity, fuelled by unresolved struggles over authority and land ownership with INPARQUES. With regard to tourism management, INPARQUES has treated the Pemon as mere service providers rather than as right-holders, by imposing rules and regulations for tourism services rather than facilitating local development. One issue of recurrent contention has been the attempt to charge the Pemon tourism concession fees for providing services in the CNP, systematically rejected by the Pemon on account of their status as original settlers of the area:

> "I don't agree with INPARQUES' concession fee policy. The sum they want me to pay is too high... Plus, INPARQUES is acting as if the park was their property and as if my business was also theirs and they were renting it to somebody from the outside. But that hotel was built by my own sweat. I will not accept INPARQUES now trying to charge me for having established my own business and for doing my work."
>
> Pemon owner of a tourism camp (1999)[33]

The Pemon struggle over land rights found its strongest public expression in 1997 through the most controversial and widely known conflict in the CNP: the building of a high-voltage electricity power line through the CNP to export electricity to Brazil. CVG and EDELCA were in charge of building the project.

Once again, INPARQUES authorized the initiation of the project without Pemon consent. For five consecutive years, the Pemon from the CNP fought determinedly against the project because they saw it as a threat to their cultural and environmental integrity. Given that National Park status was now seen to be no guarantee of the protection of their lands from large-scale development, the Pemon systematically demanded territorial land rights in their struggle against the project. They were successful in temporarily suspending construction on various occasions and in forcing a change in the 1999 National Constitution

---

31 Rodríguez 2003.
32 Carrero 1996.
33 Pers. comm., cited in Rodríguez 2003.

Pemon demonstration against the power line project in Canaima National Park, Caracas, 1999.
Photo: Kumarakapay Community Archives

to include a chapter on indigenous rights, which now contemplates - for the first time in Venezuelan history - ownership rights for indigenous peoples over their habitats and traditionally occupied ancestral lands.[34] The constitutional reform was a vital condition in reaching an agreement in which the Pemon agreed to allow the completion of the project:

- Within a week of signing the agreement, the process of demarcation and titling of indigenous peoples' 'habitats' would be initiated.
- The government would ratify ILO Convention 169 on Indigenous and Tribal Peoples.
- The executive would ensure that the indigenous peoples were involved in monitoring the cultural and environmental impacts caused during the construction work for the power line.
- The management of protected areas would be carried out in a collaborative way between indigenous peoples and the State.
- The government would contribute to the formation of a Sustainable Development Fund for indigenous people. FIEB (the Indigenous Federation of Bolivar) would be in charge of managing the fund.[35]

Of these five points of agreement, the Government of Venezuela has subsequently complied only with the second, when it ratified ILO Convention 169 in 2002.

---

34 *Constitución de la República Bolivariana de Venezuela, 1999*, Art. 119.
35 República Bolivariana de Venezuela 2000.

Despite the government's lack of political will to initiate 'habitat' (land) demarcation, the Pemon took the lead by initiating their own processes in 2000 with the support of external facilitators, and two complementary self-demarcated territorial maps of the Pemon territory now exist.[36] None of these maps has been legally validated by the Venezuelan government. Lack of fulfilment of the power-line agreement conditions by the Venezuelan government has resulted in the Pemon being again in active conflict with the government over territorial rights.

Current involvement of the Pemon in protected area management/ decision-making

Although historically the Pemon have had little influence over official park policies, in practice they largely determine how the land and its natural resources are managed through their own livelihood practices, often resisting, confronting or simply ignoring park regulations and policies. There are, therefore, in a manner of speaking, two parallel park management systems: official and Pemon.

Official involvement of the Pemon has been limited to working as park guards for INPARQUES. Very little has been done to develop official collaborative processes in natural resource management, mainly because INPARQUES' top-down, autocratic style of decision-making has historically excluded this possibility, as an ex-Regional Director of INPARQUES has acknowledged:

> "INPARQUES' history in the area has given rise to a lot of distrust. At present at INPARQUES there is talk about the need to improve our relations with the community, but simultaneously decisions are made in the central office that create conflicts, no matter what efforts we might be making at the local level to improve things. We live in constant fear of what might come from above – the National Presidency, the Minister of the Environment, etc. – and spoil it all. The efforts that we make at the community level are lost. Instead of building trust we end up feeding the existing distrust." [37]

The possibilities of collaboration have also been hampered by a lack of acknowledgement of the rights of the Pemon as original settlers of the area in decision-making. As a Pemon woman elder once stated in a meeting with the Minister of the Environment:

> "I always say at every opportunity that I have that I am a native, I am an original settler of these lands. My grandparents died in these lands, their bones are here, and I ask the people from INPARQUES, where are the bones of your people, of INPARQUES, for you to

---

36 Perera et al. 2009; Sletto 2009.
37 Pers. comm., 1999. Cited in Rodríguez 2003.

say that you are the authorities of these lands? Where is your grandfather for you to say that you are the innate authorities of our lands, of our *Gran Sabana*?" [38]

The different meanings of 'the land' and of ownership over it has also been a constraining factor for collaboration:

> "The problem is that INPARQUES does not realize that we don't consider the *Gran Sabana* a national park but as our lands. For INPARQUES this is fundamentally an area for recreation... I agree with the principle of protection, but not of the park, of our territory."
>
> Pemon leader (1999)[39]

Besides impeding collaboration, this tension between different notions of authority and ownership over the CNP's territory also precludes the achievement of management objectives. For instance, in 1995 INPARQUES obtained a credit from the World Bank to improve on-the-ground park management.[40] This included building ten new park guard posts, six of which were to be located in the *Gran Sabana*. However, most of these park guard posts were not built due to Pemon opposition. Lack of participation in the decision-making process and of information about the project led to suspicion and distrust as to the intended aims of the park guard posts. Consequently, one of the strongest arguments against them became that, through the building of new park infrastructure, INPARQUES was seeking to exert more control over the lives of the Pemon, which would lead to their eventual displacement from their territories.[41]

Nevertheless, informal collaboration between the Pemon and INPARQUES does occasionally take place, particularly over tourism management, which is an area of common interest. During peak tourism seasons (Easter, Carnival and Christmas), the Pemon, local and regional INPARQUES personnel and tourism management agencies make improvised efforts to come together to control the influx of tourists. However, these collaborations have never become a structured or joint coordinated plan for tourism management.

Fire management is an area in which there is no collaborative work to achieve conservation objectives. Despite concerns over the use of fire, park managers have shown little interest in understanding local fire regimes and Pemon knowledge of fire management. While efforts have been made to involve young Pemon in some aspects of the fire control program as manual labourers (firemen) and as subjects in environmental education activities, Pemon elders have been systematically excluded. As a result, land managers have had little opportunity to understand traditional Pemon use of fire and the ecological knowledge that underlies it.

---

38 Cited in Rodríguez 2003.
39 Pers. comm., cited in Rodríguez 2003.
40 World Bank 1995.
41 Rodríguez 2003.

Pemon from Kumarakapay with photographs of their ancestors. Photo: Iokiñe Rodríguez

Social research carried out between 1999 and 2004 has shown that there are important cultural and environmental factors that explain the extensive use of fire, and which land managers must understand to be able to develop a fire management program that is well adapted to the area.[42]

Most significantly, for many Pemon - particularly elders and Pemon from isolated communities - fire is an integral part of their culture, deeply rooted in their practices through tradition. Any attempt to eliminate or restrict its use is perceived as a threat to cultural identity and to the Pemon sense of land ownership, and is likely to meet with Pemon resistance. Also, like other indigenous peoples living in similar environments,[43] the Pemon have developed a prescribed burning system that involves the selective and cooperative setting of savannah fires at various times of the year (savannah patch-burning and forest-edge fire breaks), in order to avoid large destructive forest fires.

Recent research on fire ecology shows that the heterogeneity of the savannah naturally restricts the extension of individual burns.[44] Rather than annual burnings in the same site, as was

---

42 Rodríguez 2004, 2007; Sletto 2006; Rodríguez and Sletto 2009.
43 Lewis 1989; Fairhead and Leach 1996; Mbow et al. 2000; Laris 2002.
44 Bilbao et al. 2010.

assumed to occur, these results suggest a pattern of many small fires in distinct sites every year. This is in accord with the system of fires described by the Pemon[45] and, moreover, explains why fire is a permanent component of the landscape of the *Gran Sabana*. Further, it indicates that their system of controlled burning is an adequate method for conserving biodiversity and reducing the occurrence of dangerous fires since it encourages heterogeneity in the vegetation of the savannah in time and space.[46] This system is similar to prescribed burning regimes increasingly used as forest-savannah management techniques in different parts of the world, particularly Australia, where interesting interaction between the cognitive traditions of scientists and local indigenous peoples has been taking place.[47]

In order to address the pressing need for a collaborative strategy for the management of the CNP, in 2006 a US$ 6 million project of the World Bank, financed by the Global Environment Facility (GEF) and entitled 'Expanding partnership for the National Parks System', was drafted. The three main project partners were INPARQUES, CVG-EDELCA and the Pemon's indigenous organization (*Federación Indígena del Estado Bolívar*, FIEB). They formally agreed to cooperate on the common objective of preserving the CNP's biodiversity, guaranteeing its environmental services and improving Pemon quality of life. To the project coordinators, this agreement denoted "a growing level of trust on the part of the Pemon and a growing willingness on the part of CVG EDELCA and INPARQUES to integrate the Pemon into a more effective and participatory governance system".[48]

The Project was to build upon this "historical achievement" and develop a participatory co-management model for the CNP based on four fundamental objectives: (i) threat prevention and mitigation, (ii) sustainable development of local communities by supporting local benefits, (iii) implementation of sustainable and long-term financial mechanisms to support PA management, and (iv) involvement of all stakeholders, including indigenous peoples, in the CNP Management Plan's design and implementation.[49]

However, although the World Bank approved the project, the Venezuelan government withdrew at the last minute due to a new political line from the central government that halted any collaboration with the World Bank. No further attempts have been made to establish a co-management model for the CNP.

Effects of World Heritage designation on the Pemon

The Pemon have had very limited interaction with the World Heritage Committee since the CNP became a World Heritage site, largely because the cultural significance of the area was ignored in the nomination of the site. The CNP was listed as a natural site only, on account of meeting all four of the established natural heritage criteria as follows:

---

45 Rodríguez 2004; Sletto 2006.
46 Bilbao et al. 2010.
47 Verran 2002.
48 World Bank 2006.
49 Ibid.

I) *"Outstanding examples representing the major stages of the Earth's evolutionary history*: Three different erosion surfaces are to be found within the park. The oldest rocks are Precambrian and, around 1 700 million years old, are some of the oldest on the planet. Above these are younger formations which have been weathered into mountains by 500 million years of erosion. The geology provides evidence that South America and Africa once formed part of a single continent."

II) *"Outstanding examples representing significant ongoing geological processes and biological evolution.* The *tepui* landscape is still undergoing the same type of geological evolution which has been taking place over the last 600 million years. Ongoing biological evolution is demonstrated by the response of endemic taxa to the very poor soils of *tepui* summits and the processes by which savannas are expanding at the expense of forests. The park demonstrates the interaction of the indigenous Pemon with the environment both because of the great use the Pemon make of the park's natural resources and because of the way the park's landscape and vegetation has been shaped by the Pemón."

III) *"Contains unique, rare or superlative natural phenomena, formations or features of exceptional natural beauty.* The *tepuis* are a unique natural formation of outstanding natural beauty and the park includes the Angel Falls, the world's highest waterfall."

IV) *"The most important and significant habitats where threatened species of plants and animals still survive.* The park protects a number of internationally threatened species, particularly in the floral communities on the summit of the *tepuis.*" [50]

The historical and contemporary presence and role of the Pemon was only a minor factor in the Venezuelan State's justification of the CNP's universal values, although their historic and continuing relationship with their lands in the CNP was noted, as was their role in creating and managing the natural environment in the park.[51] At the same time, however, the nomination document presented the Pemon as one of the main threats to the outstanding universal value of the site, by asserting that "more and more land is being burned and cleared for shifting agriculture" and that "the Park's

---

50 IUCN 1994a. Summary prepared by IUCN based on the information contained in the nomination dossier submitted by the Government of Venezuela.
51 In particular, the nomination document states: "The local population of Pemón indians in the Park provides a significant example of man's interaction with his natural surroundings. The ethnic group lives either in small settlements around the missions or, to a greater extent, in scattered dwellings all over the Park. They have their own culture which developed through the need to adapt to the peculiarities and demands of their environment. The huts they live in, the tools and weapons they use, the food they eat, their myths and customs all stem from a close relationship with their environment and the ecology of Canaima. Several multidisciplinary studies are being carried out to ascertain to what extent the Pemón affect the shape of the Park's landscape, especially in La Gran Sabana, where forest land is being taken over by savanna" (Government of Venezuela 1993, p. 48).

integrity is threatened by indiscriminate burning, shifting agriculture... and other activities which are incompatible with its national park status".[52]

As a result, IUCN wrote in its 1994 Advisory Body Evaluation that the conservation of the park was in jeopardy due to "the inability of the management to control activities within the park" and that one of the "main problems" was "excessive burning of vegetation by indigenous people".[53] IUCN found that the human factor clashed with the natural World Heritage Convention objectives and suggested that about one million hectares of savannah grasslands that had "been transformed into a human-dominated landscape" by the Pemon should be excluded from the nomination and that only the *tepui*-dominated portion of the CNP should be included "where the truly outstanding universal values are found".[54] For more than five years, the boundaries of the site remained undefined, until a 1999 UNESCO-IUCN monitoring mission recommended that the entire three million hectares of the CNP be taken as the boundaries of the World Heritage site, because of the "strong ecological and cultural linkages between the Tepuyes clusters and the Gran Sabana".[55] The mission report noted that: "Fires are a key element in the dynamic of ecosystems of the Great Plain" and that "the indigenous Pemon communities have been managing fires for centuries in this area and have their own traditional procedures for control".[56]

As in the case of the national park designation, the Pemon were not consulted when Canaima was nominated as a World Heritage site. Even though the World Heritage Committee was aware of this, and the interaction between the Pemon and the National Park had been part of the justification of the CNP's universal values, the Committee proceeded to inscribe the site without prior Pemon consent. According to the report of its 1994 session:

> "The Committee noted that a population of about 10,000 was resident in the savannah (nearly 1 million ha of the 3 million ha area of the Park) and have not been consulted regarding the nomination of the area. Nevertheless, the Committee was satisfied that the area met all four natural World Heritage criteria and decided to inscribe the site on the World Heritage List." [57]

In doing so, the Committee disregarded the view expressed by IUCN in the Advisory Body Evaluation that, "as a principle,...the Committee should have information on the views of local people who are resident within a nominated site. This is particularly important for Canaima as part of the justification for universal value is based on the interaction of the local people with the park." [58]

The Pemon only became aware that the CNP had been nominated a World Heritage site in 1997, when the conflict over the building of the power line broke out and they were seeking

---

52 Ibid., pp. 40, 50.
53 See the IUCN/WCMC Data Sheet attached to the Advisory Body Evaluation (IUCN 1994).
54 IUCN 1994b, p. 117.
55 UNESCO 1999a, p. 8.
56 Ibid., p. 2.
57 UNESCO 1995, p. 48.
58 IUCN 1994b, p. 117.

national and international support to halt the project. This became the only instance in which the Pemon sought to use UNESCO and the World Heritage designation to their advantage, although the results disheartened them.

Along with numerous national and international NGOs, the Pemon requested UNESCO's intervention in the hope that it would help stop the project.[59] The fact that the project contravened the CNP's and World Heritage regulations and that it entailed potential impacts in opening access to undisturbed forests and altering a landscape of outstanding natural beauty meant that the site could be placed on the List of World Heritage in Danger.[60] In 1999, a mission from the World Heritage Committee visited Venezuela in order to assess the situation.

Even though they owed their visit largely to the Pemon request, the mission made no effort to meet the traditional inhabitants during their field trip to Canaima National Park. The mission field visit team was composed solely of representatives from INPARQUES, the Ministry of the Environment (MARNR), Ministry of External Affairs (MRE), CVG-EDELCA, and a team of journalists from the national TV Channel Globovisión.[61] Site visits were limited to a two-day aerial inspection, as acknowledged in the report: "Due to time constraints the inspection was undertaken by helicopter, thanks to the contribution of EDELCA to this mission". During this inspection, no meetings were held in the CNP with the Pemon to listen to their concerns.[62]

However, on learning that a World Heritage mission was in Venezuela, and after the UNESCO mission had returned to Caracas, a group of Pemon leaders travelled to Caracas (a two day trip by land) to make their views heard.[63] During a meeting with the UNESCO mission, the Pemon made clear their opposition to the power-line project, as noted in the mission report:

"In a meeting with 22 representatives of indigenous peoples' communities [which took place in Caracas] they all ratified their strong position against the power line construction. The construction penetrates into land and territories traditionally occupied by them, without a proper process of consultation and endorsement. In addition, they are greatly concerned about its potential impact on their culture if the project promotes uncontrolled economic development around Canaima National Park, mainly related to the mining and tourism sectors.

The indigenous Pemón communities recognised the importance of Canaima National Park to preserve and maintain the natural and cultural values of this territory. It is important to note that they give strong emphasis to the spiritual and cultural linkages between the Gran Sabana and the Tepuyes and the need to consider them as one entity. However, they strongly claim their rights to be fully involved in the planning and management of Canaima National Park, allowing them to be key actors in its protection. To date they have been key

---

59 UNESCO 1999a, p. 1.
60 UNESCO 1998, pp. 15f.
61 UNESCO-IUCN 1999a, 1999b.
62 Rodriguez 2003.
63 Ibid.

players to stop illegal mining and other activities within their lands and territories, and this should be fully recognised".[64]

Despite the Pemons' demands for respect for the cultural integrity of the Gran Sabana landscape, the mission failed to give sufficient importance to this claim, concluding among other things that:

> "The posts for the transmission line have been installed practically in the entire sector [of the line] that penetrates into Canaima National Park. The implementation of this project has been done with the maximum possible care (installation using helicopters with no deforestation and using small and more transparent structures), so its environmental and visual impact is minimum. They do not interfere substantially with the main aesthetic values of the Park that are associated with its Western Sector".[65]

By giving more priority to protecting the aesthetic values of the western sector of the park than those of the eastern sector (where the power line was built), the UNESCO mission reproduced the view prevalent in the original World Heritage nomination according to which the eastern sector has less conservation value due to the fact that the savanna grasslands have "been transformed into a human-dominated landscape". Furthermore, it failed to give sufficient importance to the emphasis put by the Pemon on "the spiritual and cultural linkages between the Gran Sabana and the Tepuyes and the need to consider them as one entity".

What is perhaps more important is that as a result of their visit, the monitoring mission did not consider it necessary to include the CNP in the list of endangered sites. Thus, the World Heritage Convention failed to be of any use to the Pemon in their struggle against the power line and for the survival of their cultural identity:

> "The mission considers that the construction of the transmission line is not compatible with the objectives of Canaima National Park and World Heritage site. However, this construction is causing a localised impact and its environmental and visual impact have been minimised and *do not interfere with the main values for which this site was inscribed in the World Heritage List*. No significant impacts within the Park have been detected in relation to mining, deforestation or tourism. Thus, the mission considers that there is no evidence that justifies the inclusion of this site in the List of World Heritage in Danger".[66]

The recommendations made by the mission and subsequently endorsed by the World Heritage Committee include the following:

- that the Government of Venezuela "provide all possible support to INPARQUES and MARNR and [...] explore ways to enhance the institutional capacity of these institutions."

---

64 UNESCO 1999a, p. 5.
65 Ibid., p. 7.
66 UNESCO 1999a, p. 7 (emphasis added).

- that the State Party "create, as soon as possible, mechanisms to promote the dialogue between all relevant stakeholders interested in the conservation and management of this area… As a matter of priority this dialogue should seek to find common ground and acceptable solutions to all parties to conflicts arising from the construction of the transmission line. The Committee should request that the Centre and IUCN support this process as far as possible, including the provision of technical information on co-management arrangements in other World Heritage sites."
- that the State Party "submit to the World Heritage Centre a request for technical assistance to organise and implement a national workshop on Canaima National Park. This workshop should aim to prepare a project proposal for the long-term participatory management strategy for this site, to be submitted to international donors. It should count with the participation of all relevant national and local stakeholders, including indigenous peoples' representatives… This workshop should be seen as a main step in creating mechanisms for involving all relevant stakeholders in the planning and management of this site." [67]

The report makes clear that these recommendations were, not least, meant to address the following issue highlighted by the Pemon during their meeting with the UNESCO mission: "It is important that INPARQUES promote and implement as soon as possible co-management arrangements with the indigenous peoples living in the Park. At the present there is little dialogue between INPARQUES and the Pemón, despite the fact that co-management arrangements are in place in other national parks of Venezuela." [68]

In 1999, an international assistance request was submitted to the World Heritage Centre by Venezuela and, subsequently, US$ 30 000 was granted for an on-site training and awareness-building workshop in 2000. However, this international assistance resulted in neither the solution of the conflicts related to the power line nor in the establishment of co-management arrangements or other long-term participatory management mechanisms. In 2001, the World Heritage Centre reported the continuing and increasing opposition of the Pemon communities to the power line "due to the long-term consequences that the project will have on both the territories they occupy and their cultural integrity. They have been responsible for toppling over thirteen towers. The National Guard now has a permanent presence in the park in order to guarantee the continuation of the project".[69] In 2003, IUCN notified the Committee "that many national parks had been placed on the World Heritage List where existing management plans were in conflict with the needs and requirements of indigenous peoples" and that "Canaima National Park in Venezuela was a good example of this".[70]

Other responses to the UNESCO mission's recommendations were equally unsuccessful in establishing more inclusive management arrangements. They included the already mentioned 2006 Canaima GEF-financed World Bank Project, which was cancelled after some initial successes, and

---

67 UNESCO 1999a, pp. 9, 12.
68 Ibid., pp. 3-4.
69 UNESCO 2001, p. 11.
70 UNESCO 2004, p. 49.

Venezuela's participation in the 'Enhancing our Heritage Project',[71] a five-year project created by UNESCO in 2001 in 10 World Heritage sites to improve management effectiveness through new monitoring and evaluation systems and generating reports on each site for the World Heritage Centre. Canaima was selected as one of these sites. Pemon involvement in this project was limited to participating as informers in interviews and two workshops aimed at evaluating threats to the conservation values of the site.

However, rather than by a scarcity of evaluation and monitoring tools, management effectiveness of CNP and WHS is most severely impaired by a dwindling of resources for park management, insufficient personnel, lack of inter-institutional coordination[72] and the overwhelming lack of national government will to support the protected area system. This has a direct effect on the way the Pemon perceive the benefits of World Heritage status to them:

> "With respect to how we and our lands benefit from the World Heritage status... I think in NO WAY. Because what benefit is there in it being a Heritage, if the State does not invest anything in the park?"
>
> Pemon leader, pers. comm. (2011)[73]

The only benefit that the Pemon perceive is that protected area status has been relatively helpful in protecting their lands from natural resource extraction by non-indigenous concerns,[74] despite INPARQUES' laxity and complacency with some projects (e.g. Turisur and power line):

> "One way in which the national park status has helped could be by impeding invasions. I say this even though the government has been the 'invader'. It does not comply with or respect the established norms and regulations."
>
> Pemon leader, pers. comm. (2011)

Conclusions and recommendations

The Pemon have no specific expectations or hopes for the World Heritage site. Because of the poor relationship that they have had with it since it was established, the existence of the World Heritage site has no practical relevance for them. This is worsened by the fact that their only attempt to use the World Heritage designation to their advantage was rejected.

The fact that the site was nominated only on account of its natural values limits the extent to which they can relate to and benefit from it. This is clear from the power-line conflict, which

---

71 Novo and Díaz 2007.
72 Ibid.
73 Original emphasis by the interviewee.
74 Rodríguez 1998.

showed that the little importance given to protecting the Pemon's values, rights and priorities in the site's objectives prevented UNESCO and IUCN from adopting stronger opposition to the project. Furthermore, it showed that, as in the case of the National Park designation, priority given to protecting 'natural universal values' over 'cultural' ones turns the Pemon into 'threats' to the site, not only distorting their role in managing their land but also closing opportunities for engagement with the World Heritage system.

Relisting Canaima as a mixed cultural/natural site could represent an improvement by allowing the World Heritage Convention to become more meaningful for the Pemon in the future. Venezuela's current legal institutional framework regarding indigenous rights would certainly favour such a change but it is doubtful whether the institutional culture of INPARQUES and the other resource management institutions would be open to it. Any such move to re-list the site would have to be conducted with the full and effective participation of the Pemon and concluded only if their free, prior and informed consent had been obtained. A process of engaged and good-faith negotiation leading to consent could contribute to building the trust relationships necessary for effective co-management to occur.

A change that would help to make the World Heritage Convention more meaningful for the Pemon and indigenous peoples would be a requirement for future UNESCO monitoring missions to consult with any affected indigenous peoples through their own representative institutions. Such a requirement would be in line with indigenous peoples' right to participate in decision-making in matters which may affect their rights, through representatives chosen by themselves in accordance with their own procedures.[75] Independence of action should be ensured when site visits are carried out and the agendas of monitoring missions are defined (e.g. who to talk to and who not). In the case of the power-line conflict, it is clear that the UNESCO monitoring mission was constrained in its understanding of the situation and the depth of its recommendations to the World Heritage Committee by the fact that it was given very little freedom of movement by EDELCA and INPARQUES during the site visit, biasing to a great extent the information it received and the content of the final recommendations. If the Pemon themselves had not decided to travel to Caracas to meet with the monitoring mission, it is possible that the Pemon views would have been completely unaccounted for in the report.

Another way to ensure that the rights of the Pemon are protected and their needs and priorities considered in the World Heritage Area would be by assigning funds to support their own land management requirements, and not only INPARQUES' or UNESCO's. The Pemon have their own way of conceptualizing and working towards the sustainable management of their territory, which they have termed the Pemon 'Life Plan'.[76]

While land/territorial ownership is conceived as the primordial material base for cultural survival, the Life Plan is conceived as the ideological, spiritual and philosophical base for it. It seeks to help them visualize and define a desired future grounded in Pemon historical reconstruction and cultural identity. Thus, land ownership and the Life Plan are two mutually

---

75 *UN Declaration on the Rights of Indigenous Peoples*, Art. 18.
76 Pizarro 2006.

reinforcing pillars in their struggle for cultural reaffirmation, environmental integrity and the defence of the territory.

The Pemon Life Plan is conceived as a process of self-critical analysis of their current situation, their changes but also their values, helping them reflect on who they are and what they want to be as a society. By providing a clear vision of their identity, needs and desires, it seeks to help them negotiate more strategically the relationship with the institutions that have a presence in the area:

> "...our own Life Plan will not only strengthen us as a people, but also facilitate the necessary interactions with the institutions with which the Pemon interact, helping such institutions structure their initiatives and activities with the communities." [77]

A first attempt to start constructing a Pemon Life Plan was made in the preparation phase of the Canaima World Bank/GEF Project. At that time, one of the conditions for the Pemon forming part of participatory management planning for the CNP was that this process be carried out in coordination with Pemon indigenous communities' Life Plans. Through a series of workshops, a preliminary version of a Pemon Life Plan was thus developed, emphasizing the following components: 1. territorial and indigenous habitat, 2. education and culture, 3. organizational strengthening, 4. health and culture, 5. social infrastructure, and 6. production and economic alternatives.[78]

However, as the Canaima World Bank/GEF Project was never implemented, this preliminary version of the Life Plan was not validated. In some communities, progress has been made in initiating a process of historical reconstruction and self-reflection on their socio-cultural and environmental change and desired future.[79] Much effort is still needed to continue constructing this process and putting it into practice. UNESCO and the World Heritage Committee could play a positive role in ensuring the Pemon desire for cultural reaffirmation and sustainable use of their lands by supporting their Life Plan process and making it extensive in the World Heritage area.   ○

References

Armellada, C. 1989. *Tauron Panton. Cuentos y leyendas de los Pemon (Venezuela)*. Quito, Abya-Yala.
Bilbao, B., Leal, A. and Mendez, C. 2010. Indigenous Use of Fire and Forest Loss in Canaima National Park, Venezuela. Assessment of and Tools for Alternative Strategies of Fire Management in Pemón Indigenous Lands. *Human Ecology*, Vol. 38, No. 5, pp. 663-673.
Butt-Colson, A. 2009. *Land. Its occupation, management, use and conceptualization. The case of the Akawaio and Arekuna of the Upper Mazaruni District, Guyana*. Somerset, Last Refuge Publishing.
Carrero, M. A. 1996. *Declaración de Nulidad Absoluta de la autorización de afectación de recursos otorgada por la Dirección de Parques Nacionales al proyecto Aventura Gran Sabana*. Caracas, INPARQUES, 14 October 1996.

---

77 World Bank 2006, Annex 20.
78 Pizarro 2006.
79 *Roraimökok Damük* 2010, Rodríguez et al. 2010.

Christoffel, H. M. 1939. Informe definitivo sobre los suelos y posibilidades agrícolas en la Gran Sabana. S. E. Aguerrevere et al. (eds.), *Exploración de la Gran Sabana (Revista de Fomento*, Vol. 3, No. 19), pp. 596-631.
Eden, M. 1964. *The Savanna Ecosystem: northern Rupununi, British Guiana.* Montreal, McGill University (Department of Geography, Savanna Research Series No.1).
Fairhead, J. and Leach, M. 1996. *Misreading the African Landscape. Society and Ecology in a Forest-Savanna Mosaic.* Cambridge, Cambridge University Press.
Galán, C. 1984. *La Protección de la Cuenca del Rio Caroní.* Caracas, CVG-EDELCA.
Gómez, E. and Picón, G. 1994. Programa control de incendios forestales. *EDELCA,* Vol. 2, pp. 13-15.
Government of Venezuela. 1993. *World Heritage List Nomination: Canaima National Park, Venezuela.* Produced by: National Parks Division, National Parks Institute (INPARQUES).
INE. 2001. *Censo Nacional de Población y Vivienda.* Caracas, Instituto Nacional de Estadística, República Bolivariana de Venezuela.
IUCN. 1994a. *World Heritage Nomination – IUCN Summary: Canaima National Park (Venezuela).* Summary prepared by IUCN/WCMC (March 1994) based on the original nomination submitted by the Government of Venezuela.
IUCN. 1994b. *World Heritage Nomination – IUCN Technical Evaluation: Canaima National Park.*
Koch-Grünberg, T. 1981 (1917). *Del Roraima al Orinoco,* Vol. 2. Caracas, Armitano Editores.
Laris, P. 2002. Burning the seasonal mosaic: preventative burning strategies in the wooded savanna of southern Mali. *Human Ecology,* Vol. 30(2), pp. 155-186.
Leal, A. 2010. *Historia Holocena de la vegetación y el fuego en bordes sabana/bosque y turberas de la Gran Sabana, Guayana Venezolana.* Caracas, Universidad Simón Bolivar (Doctoral Thesis in Biological Sciences).
Lewis, H. 1989. Ecological and technical knowledge of fire: aborigines versus park rangers in northern Australia. *American Anthropologist,* Vol. 91, pp. 940-961.
Mbow, C., Nielsen, T. and Rasmussen, K. 2000. Savanna fires in east-central Senegal: distribution patterns, resource management and perceptions. *Human Ecology,* Vol. 28(4), pp. 561-583.
Novo, I. and Díaz, D. 2007. *Informe Final de la Evaluación del Parque Nacional Canaima, Venezuela, como Sitio de Patrimonio Natural de la Humanidad.* Caracas, INPARQUES and Vitales (Proyecto Mejorando Nuestra Herencia).
Perera, M., Rivas, P. and Gómez, S. **2009.** Los paradigmas ambientales del pueblo Pemón y la demarcación de tierras para la titulación colectiva. Cambios y resistencias. *Antropologica,* No. 111-112, pp. 115-147.
Pizarro, I. 2006. El plan de vida del pueblo Pemon. In: Medina Jose and Aguilar Vladimir (Eds) *Conservación de la biodiversidad en los territorios indígenas Pemon de Venezuela: una construcción de futuro.* Caracas, The Nature Conservancy.
Proyecto Cartográfico Inna Kawantok. 2004. *Autodemarcación del Sector Kavanayen.* Final Report, March 2004.
Real, M. et al. 2002. *Informe Preliminar, Primer año de Ejecución del Proyecto Mejorando Nuestra Herencia.* Caracas, Vitales and INPARQUES.
República Bolivariana de Venezuela. 2000. *Propuesta de negociación entre el Ejecutivo Nacional y las Comunidades Indígenas del Estado Bolívar para la prosecución de la obra de Sistema de Transmisión de Energía Eléctrica al sureste de Venezuela. República Bolivariana de Venezuela.* Caracas, Comisión para la Atención de los Asuntos Indígenas, April 2000.
Rodríguez, I. 1998. Using PRA in conflict resolution: lessons from a Venezuelan experience in Canaima National Park. *PLA Notes,* No. 33, pp. 3-10.
Rodríguez, I. 2003. *The Transformative Role of Conflicts in National Parks: Beyond the Managerial Conflict Resolution Approach. A Case Study of Canaima National Park, Venezuela.* Brighton, University of Sussex (Doctoral Thesis, Institute of Development Studies).
Rodríguez, I. 2004. Conocimiento indígena vs científico: el conflicto por el uso del fuego en la Gran Sabana. *Interciencia,* Vol. 29(3), pp. 121-129.
Rodríguez, I. 2007. Pemon perspectives of fire management in Canaima National Park, Venezuela. *Human Ecology,* Vol. 35(3), pp. 331-343.
Rodríguez, I. and Sletto, B. 2009. Apök hace feliz a Patá. Desafíos y sugerencias para una gestión intercultural del fuego en la Gran Sabana. *Antropologica,* No. 111-112, pp. 149-191.
Rodríguez, I., Leal, A., Sánchez Rose, I., Vessuri, H. and Bilbao, B. 2009. Facing up to the challenge of interdisciplinary research in Canaima National Park. *Human Ecology,* Vol. 37, pp. 783-785.
Rodríguez, I., Sánchez-Rose, I. and Vessuri, H. 2010. *El Plan de Vida de los Pemon de Kavanayen como escenario de articulación de conocimientos para la gestión socio-ambiental del Parque Nacional Canaima, Venezuela.* Buenos Aires, VI Jornadas de Antropología Social, Facultad de Filosofía y Letras de la Universidad de Buenos Aires, 3-6 August 2010.

Roraimökok Damük. 2010. *La Historia de los Pemon de Kumarakapay.* Edited by I. Rodríguez, J. Gómez and Y. Fernández. Caracas, Ediciones IVIC.

Rull, V. 2009. On the Use of Paleoecological Evidence to Assess the Role of Humans in the Origin of the Gran Sabana (Venezuela). *Human Ecology,* Vol. 37, pp. 783-785.

Schubert, C. and Huber, O. 1985. *The Gran Sabana: Panorama of a Region.* Caracas, Lagoven.

Sletto, B. 2008. The Knowledge that Counts: Institutional Identities, Policy Science, and the Conflict over Fire Management in the Gran Sabana, Venezuela. *World Development,* Vol. 36, pp. 1938-1955.

Sletto, B. 2009. Autogestión en representaciones espaciales indígenas y el rol de la capacitación y concientización: el caso del Proyecto Etnocartográfico Inna Kowantok, Sector 5 Pemón (Kavanayén- Mapauri), La Gran Sabana. *Antropologica,* Vol. 113, pp. 43-75.

Tate, G. 1930. Notes on the Mount Roraima Region. *Geographical Review,* Vol. 21(1), pp. 53-68.

Thomas, D. 1980. Los Pemon. R. Lizarralde and H. Seijas (eds.), *Los aborigenes de Venezuela. Etnologia Contemporanea.* Caracas, Fundación La Salle de Ciencias Naturales.

Thomas, D. 1982. *Order Without Government. The Society of the Pemon Indians of Venezuela.* Chicago, University of Illinois Press.

UNESCO. 1995. *Report: Convention Concerning the Protection of the World Cultural and Natural Heritage, World Heritage Committee, Eighteenth session, Phuket, Thailand, 12-17 December 1994.* Doc. WHC-94/CONF.003/16, 31 January 1995.

UNESCO. 1998. *Report: Convention Concerning the Protection of the World Cultural and Natural Heritage, World Heritage Committee, Twenty-second session, Kyoto, Japan, 30 November – 5 December 1998.* Doc. WHC-98/CONF.203/18, 29 January 1999.

UNESCO. 1999a. *Information Document: Report of the Mission to Canaima National Park (Venezuela), 16-19 May 1999.* Prepared for the twenty-third session of the Bureau of the World Heritage Committee. Doc. WHC-99/CONF.204/INF.18, 25 June 1999.

UNESCO. 1999b. *Informe de la Misión UNESCO-UICN al Parque Nacional Canaima, Caracas, Venezuela, del 19 al 26 de Mayo de 1999.* Prepared by Pedro Rosabal (IUCN) and José Pedro de Oliveira Costa (UNESCO).

UNESCO. 1999c. *World Heritage Committee: Report of the Rapporteur on the twenty-third extraordinary session of the Bureau held in Marrakesh, Morocco (26-27 November 1999).* Doc. WHC-99/CONF.209/6Rev, 30 November 1999.

UNESCO. 2001. *Reports on the state of conservation of properties inscribed on the World Heritage List.* Prepared for the twenty-fifth ordinary session of the Bureau of the World Heritage Committee. Doc.WHC-2001/CONF.205/5, 5 June 2001.

UNESCO. 2004. *Draft Summary Record of the Twenty-seventh session of the World Heritage Committee (Paris, 30 June - 5 July 2003).* Doc. WHC-04/28.COM/INF.6, 25 June 2004.

Verran, H. 2002. A Postcolonial Moment in Science Studies. Alternative Firing Regimes of Environmental Scientists and Aboriginal Landowners. *Social Studies of Science,* Vol. 32, pp.729–762.

World Bank. 1995. *Staff Appraisal Report. Venezuela INPARQUES Project.* Washington DC, World Bank, 12 May 1995.

World Bank. 2006. *Project brief on a proposed grant from the Global Environment Facility Trust fund in the amount of USD 6 million to the government of Venezuela for a Venezuela-expanding partnerships for the National Parks System Project.* World Bank, May 20

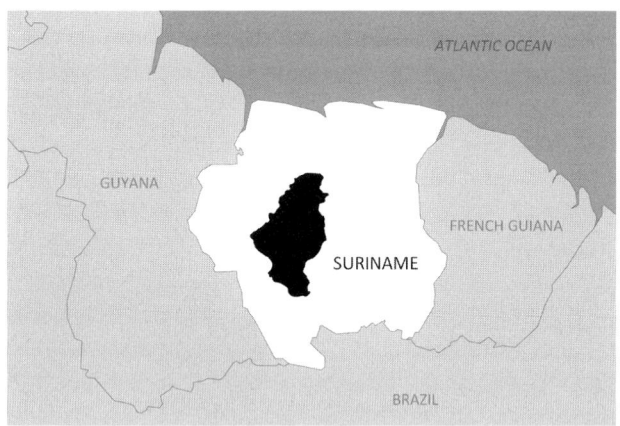

'We Heard the News from the Press':
The Central Suriname Nature Reserve and its Impacts on the Rights of Indigenous and Tribal Peoples

Fergus MacKay

Introduction

Nature conservation has a relatively long history in Suriname. Ten protected areas were created in 1954 specifically to compensate for resource exploitation (mostly bauxite mining and logging) in the coastal area. Currently, 16 protected areas have been established and six more have been proposed. Counting the Central Suriname Nature Reserve (CSNR), established in 1998 and the subject of this article, protected areas in Suriname now cover over 2 million hectares or approximately 12 percent of the national territory.

There are four indigenous peoples in Suriname and six tribal (Maroon) peoples.[1] Together they amount to approximately 20 percent of the national population of around 500,000 persons. Fifteen

---

1   Maroons are the descendants of African slaves that fought themselves free from slavery and established autonomous societies in the rainforest in the 17th and 18th centuries. Today, there are six Maroon peoples in Suriname with an estimated population of around 70,000. See, among others, CSQ 2001.

Left: Houses in Kwamalasamutu, a village of the Trio and related indigenous peoples who were brought together in this village by missionaries in the 1960s. Before that time the Trio inhabited and used much of the current-day Central Suriname Nature Reserve. Photo: Decio Yokota, Iepé Brazil

of the 22 existing and proposed protected areas are located within or in close proximity to indigenous and tribal peoples' traditional lands and territories.[2] Indigenous and tribal organisations have expressed great concern about nature conservation activities not least because Suriname has not legislated in any way to recognize and guarantee their ownership and other rights to traditional lands and territories.

The Kaliña and Lokono indigenous peoples of the Lower Marowijne River, for instance, have filed a case with the Inter-American Commission on Human Rights (IACHR) seeking, among other things, restitution of their traditional lands incorporated into three protected areas and challenging the management regimes in relation to human rights norms. Similar actions have also been discussed in relation to the CSNR. In addition to asserting that these protected areas violate their property rights, the Kaliña and Lokono also assert that there have been violations of a range of other rights, including cultural, spiritual and subsistence rights.[3] When declaring the case admissible in 2007, the IACHR explicitly identified the non-consensual establishment of nature reserves and the associated management regimes that fail to recognize and respect indigenous peoples' rights as "facts that, if proven, tend to establish violations of rights guaranteed under the American Convention [on Human Rights]."[4] It is expected that a decision will be made in this case shortly and that it will likely be transmitted to the Inter-American Court of Human Rights (IACtHR) for adjudication as a contentious case.

By virtue of the Constitution, the state is the owner of almost all land and resources in Suriname and, pursuant to land and resource legislation, indigenous and tribal peoples' 'de facto customary rights' to their villages and settlements can be (and routinely are) negated by activities classified as being in the 'national interest' or by conflicting grants of real title. Rights to due process, effective judicial remedies and basic consultation, let alone informed consent, are also not recognized and guaranteed and nor is the right to juridical personality. The latter, which may seem like a technical point for lawyers, essentially renders indigenous and tribal peoples invisible to the legal system and incapable of holding or seeking enforcement of their collective rights. That the preceding violates the rights of indigenous and tribal peoples has been confirmed by a variety of human rights bodies, including the IACtHR in its 2007 landmark judgment in the case of the Saramaka People v. Suriname.[5] The rights enunciated in this judgment are broadly consistent with and reflected in the UN Declaration on the Rights of Indigenous Peoples.[6]

Indigenous and tribal peoples' rights are not adequately guaranteed and protected in nature conservation laws and practice. In the 1954 Nature Protection Act, which directly governs 10 protected areas, there are no guarantees at all. The Nature Protection Act makes no reference to the existence of indigenous peoples nor does it recognize or protect their ownership or other rights

---

2   Kambel and MacKay 1999, p. 111.
3   This case is discussed in MacKay 2007.
4   IACHR 2007.
5   IACtHR 2007.
6   The Saramaka People judgment itself cites the UN Declaration, Article 32(2) as support for holding that indigenous and tribal peoples have the right to effective participation and to free, prior and informed consent in relation to activities that may affect the integrity of their territories.

View of the Coppename River in the Central Suriname Nature Reserve. Photo: Pierre-Michel Forget, MNHN

to their traditional territories. Article 1 of the Act provides that: "For the protection and conservation of the natural resources present in Suriname, after hearing the Council of State, the President may designate lands and waters belonging to the State Domain as a nature reserve." As indigenous and tribal peoples' territories are legally classified as state lands ('state domain'), this provision permits the state to unilaterally declare any indigenous or tribal territory or part thereof to be a nature reserve by decree and there is no mechanism available in law to challenge such declarations.

The Act also makes no provision for the exercise of indigenous and tribal peoples' rights within established nature reserves.[7] On the contrary, and to make matters worse, under the Act, nature reserves are the property of the state and hunting, fishing or any damage to the soil or the flora and fauna within the reserves are strictly prohibited and punishable as criminal offences.[8]

In 1986, the Nature Protection Resolution was adopted as subsidiary legislation pursuant to the Act. While it applies to only a small number of reserves, the resolution may be seen as an improvement to the extent that it at least acknowledges indigenous and tribal peoples' existence. It provides "that the forest inhabitants who live in or near the nature reserves will maintain their

---

7   Nature Protection Act (Natuurbeschermingswet), GB 1954, 26 (current text SB 1992, p. 80).
8   Id. Art. 5: "Within a nature reserve it is prohibited: a) to purposely or negligently damage the condition of the soil, the natural beauty, the fauna, the flora, or to perform acts which harm the value of the reserve itself;" and, Art. 8: "Violation of this law will be punishable with imprisonment not exceeding 3 months or with a fine of one thousand guilders maximum."

traditional rights and interests in the newly established protected areas (a) as long as the national goal of the nature reserves is not violated; (b) as long as the rationale for those traditional rights and interests remains valid; and (c) during the process of growing towards one Surinamese citizenship." [9]

In other words, indigenous and tribal peoples' rights are only to be respected during a certain period (when they are not yet assimilated into dominant Surinamese society) and only if they do not interfere with the conservation or other goals established (without indigenous and Maroon participation in all cases) by the state. It is also the state that decides – without any transparent criteria – whether the rationale for traditional rights continues to be valid (a question that also seems to be largely assimilationist in orientation). This is additionally complicated by the fact that there is no definition of or jurisprudence on the term 'traditional rights' in Suriname law, which leads to a great deal of uncertainty and confusion in practice. Moreover, it is questionable whether the Resolution could be upheld if challenged, as it directly contradicts the superior legal authority of the 1954 Act.

The Central Suriname Nature Reserve

Establishment and Legal Framework

Similar logic is present in the Nature Protection Resolution of 1998 that established the CSNR, an area of approximately 1.5 million hectares (9.7% of the total Surinamese land mass). Article 2 provides that the "villages and settlements of tribal bushland inhabitants will be respected, unless (a) the general interest or the national goal of the established nature reserve is harmed; or (b) it is provided otherwise." No explicit protection is provided for agricultural, hunting, fishing and gathering areas or for sites of religious and cultural significance and, pursuant to sub-section (b), protection of villages and settlements is entirely dependent on the good will of the state. Nor is it clear what is meant by 'respect for villages and settlements' nor whether this entails some form of recognition of rights. The CSNR was granted World Heritage status in 2000 as a 'natural site', on the basis of natural criteria (ii) and (iv).[10]

Initiated by Conservation International, the CSNR was officially announced in New York in June 1998, attracting substantial international media attention. The CSNR amalgamated and greatly expanded three previously existing reserves. "As far as is known," the 1998 Resolution's explanatory note reveals, "the area is uninhabited and there are no settlements." The description on the World Heritage Convention's web site, which is taken from the 2000 Advisory Body Evaluation by IUCN, additionally states that the CSNR is "one of the very few undisturbed forest areas in the Amazonian region with no inhabitants and no human use." [11]

These statements are surprising as the Maroon (Kwinti) communities of Witagron and Kaimanston, whose lands are located within and adjacent to the CSNR, had in 1997 been involved

---

9   Explanatory note to the 1986 Nature Protection Resolution, at p. 13 (original in Dutch).
10 See UNESCO 2001, p. 37.
11 UNESCO 2013; IUCN 2000, p. 78.

in discussions with the United Nations Development Programme (UNDP) about upgrading the Raleighvallen Reserve, the northernmost of the three nature reserves incorporated into the CSNR. It is also surprising given that the Trio indigenous peoples had made land use maps of their territory, which lies at the southern end of the reserve, showing that they have traditionally occupied and presently engage in subsistence and other activities within the CSNR. Moreover, a recent review of protected areas in Suriname states that conservation organisations had "advised the government to involve indigenous and tribal communities in the establishment of the CSNR, as the surrounding communities used the area for livelihood activities, but that the government set this advice aside."[12]

Discussing the Raleighvallen Reserve (created in 1961 and enlarged in 1986) at a 2001 conference on indigenous peoples and protected areas, Kwinti representative Orlando Emanuel observed that the "reserve was established without any notice and we did not participate in it. Management plans were made and implemented without any involvement of us. We do not share in the benefits (especially from tourism) which come out of it." [13]

Turning to the CSNR, he stated that "…the reserve comprises about one-third of lands[14] we consider to be our lands. It was established and proclaimed without any notice to us. We were not informed officially; we heard the news from the press."[15] In accord with this, Rudi Klemens, the representative of the Kwinti Granman (paramount chief), explains that the CSNR was established "without the people knowing about it".[16]

Emanuel further explains that:

"It took a year after the establishment before the government invited us to participate in so-called stakeholder activities. These activities were meant to write a management plan and to establish a trust fund for operation of the CSNR. Maybe it is funny, but we were stakeholders without knowing it. I need to stress that we were not invited because the government wanted us, but due to the fact that this was required by the funding organization. Lots of attention was given to this reserve, nationally as well as internationally; however, the negative effects of the reserve on our communities have never been discussed. The only opportunities we had to discuss these negative effects were at the subsequent stakeholder meetings. During these meetings we talked about issues such as: traditional use of the land, violation of our land rights, our right to hunt, to fish, to collect traditional medicinal plants, etc." [17]

He concluded by saying that: "Nowadays Non-Indigenous peoples … pretend to be the best conservationists. They deny our lifestyles, which have proven to be the best way to conserve the resources Mother Nature provides. They impose on us a way of conservation which is against our

---

12 FPP/VIDS 2009, p. 32
13 Emanuel 2001, p. 3.
14 There is an 1894 government resolution delimiting Kwinti territory (the only one of its kind in Surinamese history), at least in outline, that does include part of the CSNR. See Kambel and MacKay 1999.
15 Emanuel 2001, p. 3.
16 Rudi Klemens, quoted in Kambel 2006.
17 Emanuel 2001, at p. 4.

culture and lifestyles. In most cases their way of conservation implies serious violations of our basic human rights, our right to self-determination, our land rights, and our rights to control and manage our natural resources." [18]

The preceding shows that the Kwinti were not involved in decision-making about the establishment of the CSNR. Indeed, they learned that it had been established in the newspapers. This was the case despite the fact that some one-third of what they consider to be their traditional territory was expropriated when the CSNR was established and that the law that created it places potentially severe restrictions on the exercise of their rights therein. Some might argue that this expropriation took place when the Ralleighvallen Nature Reserve was established in 1961 and expanded in 1986, but the CSNR further confirmed these prior acts and further expanded the area that was expropriated. The Trio indigenous people to the south were also not involved in decision-making despite evidence of both traditional and contemporary occupation and use of lands in the CSNR.[19] Indeed, it has since become known that "members of the Trio community in Kwamalasamutu said that they did use areas within the CSNR (for hunting, fishing, and collecting) but that they 'were not allowed to indicate those activities in the reserve when mapping was done'." [20] The map in question was a land use map intended to support the recognition of Trio territorial rights.

The Upper Suriname River Saramaka Maroon people living to the east of the CSNR have also experienced problems. In 2002, they learned that Conservation International, reportedly at the request of one of their traditional leaders, intended to expand the CSNR to incorporate the Gaan and Pikin Rivers, together comprising around 35 percent of their territory. At that time, the entire area was subject to a precautionary measures order (roughly analogous to an interim injunction) issued by the IACHR, which requested that Suriname refrain from all resource development and other activities on lands occupied and used by the Saramaka.[21] In January 2003, the Saramaka requested that the precautionary measures order be reiterated and explicitly mentioned expansion of the CSNR. Their request was withdrawn after Conservation International agreed that it would not support protected area-related activities unless the Saramaka requested their assistance in the future.

Other than a sparsely attended meeting of a few hours held in July 2000 (almost one year after the World Heritage Nomination had been submitted to UNESCO), the Kwinti and the Trio were also not involved in decision-making about whether the CSNR should be inscribed as a World Heritage site. No meetings were held in the various communities and nor was any attempt made to adequately inform the Kwinti and Trio or to use culturally appropriate methods for participation. They are mentioned only three times in the July 1999 Nomination Dossier,[22] but not in IUCN's Advisory Body Evaluation or the World Heritage Committee's Decision. While the Nomination Dossier notes that both the Kwinti and the Trio are "potentially affected" and that the Trio should be "considered stakeholders as their land claims reach the southern border of the reserve",[23] the

---

18 Id.
19 FPP/VIDS 2009, p. 33.
20 Id.
21 IACHR 2002, Ch. III, para. 75.
22 Government of Suriname 2000, p. 11.
23 Id.

Meeting of Trio representatives from Suriname and Brazil, discussing issues such as land rights, strengthening traditional authority structures and the planned establishment of new protected areas in southern Suriname by international environmental NGOs. Photo: Decio Yokota, Iepé Brazil

Dossier asserts that the CSNR is "a region unchanged by man".[24] It repeats this statement a number of times in different ways, for example, stating that the CSNR "houses perhaps the largest tract of completely undisturbed, uninhabited and unhunted primary forest in the tropical world." [25]

These statements ignore the fact that the CSNR, or at least parts of it, have been occupied and used by both indigenous and tribal peoples for a variety of purposes and that there is additional archaeological evidence of traditional occupation, including cultural heritage sites such as petroglyphs.[26] They are also based on the erroneous assumption that the lack of current, permanent occupation means that the area is not subject to indigenous and tribal peoples' internationally guaranteed territorial and other rights. On the contrary, the existence of such rights is strongly supported by contemporary international law, including as explicated in a binding judgment of the IACtHR adopted in a case against Suriname in 2007. This judgment not only details indigenous and tribal peoples' property rights but also explains that such rights include the right to "effectively control and manage" their territories in accordance with their customary laws and institutions and to consent to any large-scale activities that may affect the integrity of those territories.[27]

---

24 Id. at p. 6.
25 Id. at p. 10.
26 UNEP/WCMC 2011, p. 4.
27 IACtHR 2007, at para. 194.

Management Planning

Paradoxically, while the World Heritage Nomination Dossier repeatedly asserts that the CSNR is uninhabited and devoid of human usage and impact, this document explains that the management planning process will involve 'stakeholder meetings', social impact assessment processes, sensitization for tourists about "local cultures" and developing "specific regulations to manage human activities, including customary uses by interior [indigenous and tribal] communities." [28] To what extent were these principles adhered to in the development of a management plan and to what extent did the affected indigenous and tribal peoples participate in developing this plan?

First, while there was a process established to develop a management plan that did involve some indigenous and tribal representatives as 'stakeholders' (as opposed to rights-holders in which rights provide parameters for management actions and benefit-sharing mechanisms), the outcome was more a negation of rights and participation than an affirmation of either. Indigenous and Maroon representatives have said that their input, which was to some extent incorporated in a preliminary version of the management plan, was later removed and is not reflected at all in the final plan. Kwinti leader, Rudi Clemens, describes the experience with the consultation and participation related to the CSNR management planning process as follows:

> "They called the people to participate like stakeholders and told them we will make a management plan for the reserve together. For two years the people have been going to Paramaribo, left their work, had to travel the bad road, and we sat down and made a plan which clearly said that the local population would also get control over the management. However, when the plan was finished, the reserve was declared a World Heritage Site, and when UNDP released the funding, the Minister of Natural Resources laid the document aside and produced a new document in which the local population has no, absolutely no, say. So it is back to where we started." [29]

Conservation International explained that the plan was changed because the government asserted that participatory forms of management would conflict with the 1954 Nature Protection Act.[30] This occurred despite the fact that some form of respect for indigenous and tribal interests is in principle guaranteed in the regulation establishing the CSNR. Moreover, the regulation itself subordinates the exercise of these interests to the terms of the management plan for the CSNR (the "goal of the nature reserve"). Thus, even the undefined respect for interests that is supposedly protected by the enabling law may have been negated in a management plan that was devised without formal participation and which, in its most critical terms, is directly contrary to the stated wishes of the affected peoples. The state took this decision consciously on the basis of out-dated and rights-

---

28   Government of Suriname 2000, at pp. 19-20.
29   Kambel 2006, pp. 9–10.
30   FPP/VIDS 2009, p. 39.

incompatible legislation. This unilateral action also directly contradicted the terms of financing from the Global Environment Facility (GEF), which states, as a project output, that "Management Plans will be drafted in close collaboration with relevant local and national stakeholders...." [31]

While formal participation in developing the plan was negated, the CSNR Management Plan 2004-2008 does propose the establishment of a "consultative and advisory body" for the CSNR, which will include two representatives of indigenous and tribal peoples. Its role will be to advise the responsible government agency and discuss and present suggestions for the management of the CSNR.[32] However, this body has yet to be formally established and as Suriname's national indigenous organisation has stressed:

> "[T]he proposed CSNR consultative and advisory body has the same shortcomings as the Galibi consultation commission, and [...] this should not be understood as providing meaningful participation. The communities still do not have effective decision-making authority. The management plan expressed the view that achieving consensus will be the aim in the consultative and advisory body, but if this fails the head of LBB [government agency] will take the final decision, after seeking advice from the Nature Conservation Commission." [33]

Not only has the advisory body not been established but the management plan has yet to be implemented. A Project Management Unit was, however, established in 2009 – without any representation from or consultation with indigenous and tribal peoples. According to recently published research, the "PIU held presentations for the different stakeholders about the implementation of the management plan. It was explained what was expected from different stakeholders and what role they were going to play." [34] This would appear to be a continuation of the top-down approach normally employed in state-indigenous relations in Suriname.

The extent to which the management plan exercise has in fact resulted in a curtailment of 'traditional rights' is not entirely clear. It certainly contains limits on hunting and other subsistence activities in the CSNR that, on their face, appear to limit the exercise of the associated rights. However, while community members have reported that they have become more cautious in terms of hunting, they do not attribute this to the management plan itself. In fact, they say little has changed because there has been no effort to implement and enforce the management plan and even the number of game wardens has decreased since the CSNR was established.[35] It is clear, however, that the establishment of the CSNR and its management plan have curtailed and denied the exercise of indigenous and tribal peoples' rights beyond the limited category of interests that are in principle recognized in the enabling law (see below).

The affected communities have also complained that they derive little in terms of benefits from the CSNR, are only eligible for the lowest rungs of employment, and are denied training opportunities

---

31 GEF/UNDP 1999, at p. 28.
32 CSNR Plan for Management, 2004–2008, Annex 1, p. 64.
33 Id. at p. 65.
34 Meddens 2011, at p. 52.
35 Id. p. 56.

because they do not hold sufficient educational qualifications.[36] They view this as grossly unfair and reneging on promises that were made during the drafting of the management plan. In the first place, they contend that the lack of qualifications is primarily due to the vastly substandard quality of education available in their areas and that this is a fault entirely attributable to years of neglect by the state education system.[37] Second, they highlight the biases that underlie such determinations of 'qualifications', stating that their traditional knowledge and expertise are thereby systematically denigrated and excluded. Neither of these issues is addressed in any of the management planning or other policy instruments related to the CSNR.

Conclusion

In 2004, the UN Committee on the Elimination of Racial Discrimination reviewed the situation of indigenous and tribal peoples in Suriname and, inter alia, recommended that laws and policies be changed to ensure "legal acknowledgement by the State party of the rights of indigenous and tribal peoples to possess, develop, control and use their communal lands and to participate in the exploitation, management and conservation of the associated natural resources...."[38] This recommendation was reiterated by the Committee in its 2009 review of Suriname.[39] In the 2007 Saramaka People judgment, the IACtHR specifically held that, pursuant to the rights to self-determination and property, indigenous and tribal peoples have the right to effectively control, manage and distribute their traditionally owned territories, and set forth seven preconditions that the state must comply with should it seek to engage in activities in those territories. These include the general requirements that any proposed restrictions to rights must be 'necessary' to meet a compelling public interest and 'proportional'. As noted above, in a pending case against Suriname, the IACHR has held that these norms also apply to the establishment and management of protected areas in indigenous territories. These norms of binding international law are all restated in the UN Declaration on the Rights of Indigenous Peoples, which calls on all UN bodies, including specialised agencies, to give full effect to its terms in their respective operations (Arts. 41 and 42).

The CSNR, both in its establishment and management, fails to comply with the rights of the affected indigenous and tribal peoples. In the first place, it is not 'necessary' to meet public interest nature conservation objectives by denying indigenous and tribal peoples' rights to own and control their territories. Such objectives could be met through much less intrusive means, such as the negotiation of consensual management plans for ecosystem and species management or by negotiating the creation of indigenous owned protected areas. The CSNR thus constitutes a non-consensual alienation and deprivation of indigenous and tribal peoples' ownership and related rights to their lands, territories and resources and they retain a right to restitution of the same irrespective of national law. Second, the affected peoples have suffered all the negative

---

36 Kambel 2006.
37 See IADB 2006, p. 19 et seq.
38 UN CERD 2004, at para. 11.
39 UN CERD 2009, para. 12.

consequences and derived few if any benefits, the majority of which have gone to tourism operators, researchers and the state. The CSNR thus places a disproportionate and negative impact and burden on the affected peoples. Third, in no way did the affected peoples meaningfully participate in or consent to either the establishment of the CSNR or its management regime, both of which constitute violations of their internationally protected rights. Fourth, their knowledge, cultural practices and heritage, their cosmovisions, and the interrelated and multi-faceted relationship between these and the exercise and enjoyment of their rights to their traditional territories have been wholesale disregarded and they are treated as little more than cheap labour and ignorant interlopers in need of education about conservation and sustainable use. The list could go on.

While obtaining World Heritage site status did not necessarily contribute to the preceding – other than yet again representing an instance where the affected peoples were rendered invisible due to the designs of others – it nonetheless appears to legitimise, and even celebrate, a series of serious human rights violations as well as reward the perpetrators. The designation of the CSNR solely in accordance with natural criteria, as opposed to recognising the cultural heritage dimensions inherent in the profound indigenous and tribal relations with the area, continues the process of making the affected peoples invisible and would appear to contradict a number of UNESCO Conventions and Declarations in addition to the above mentioned human rights norms.

These UNESCO Conventions are not, however, divorced from human rights norms. The 2005 Convention on the Protection and Promotion of the Diversity of Cultural Expressions, for instance, explains that "culture takes diverse forms across time and space" and this diversity is embodied "in the uniqueness and plurality of the identities and cultural expressions of the peoples and societies making up humanity."[40] Significantly, its adds that cultural diversity can only be protected and promoted through the safeguard of human rights, the same rights that have been disregarded by the CSNR.[41]

UNESCO thus recognizes that respect for rights is indispensable to the protection of cultural heritage and this should be translated into concrete and operational principles in relation to the designation of World Heritage site status. This, at a minimum, should include adequate assessment of these issues by the World Heritage Committee and its Advisory Bodies, even when a proposed site is presented as devoid of human use or otherwise solely on the basis of natural criteria. The need, again at a minimum, for such assessment should be amplified in connection with countries that have been held to deny indigenous and tribal peoples' basic rights and where the absence of effective domestic remedies essentially renders them defenceless in national law. While there is no ostensible reason that such assessments could not be undertaken within and by UNESCO, collaborative arrangements can be established or enhanced with the UN Permanent Forum on Indigenous Issues, the UN Expert Mechanisms on the Rights of Indigenous Peoples and the Special Rapporteur on the Rights of Indigenous Peoples. Additionally, it would be both prudent and highly advantageous to establish a mechanism comprised of indigenous peoples within the World Heritage Convention's secretariat and/or an independent advisory committee that could investigate and advise the World Heritage Committee on these issues. ○

---

40 Preamble, consideranda 1, 2 and 7 of the 2005 Convention.
41 Article 2(1) of the 2005 Convention.

References

CSQ. 2001. 25 Cultural Survival Quarterly, No. 4 ("Maroons in the Americas").

Emanuel, O. 2001. Presentation of the Kwinti at the Conference on Indigenous Peoples and Protected Areas in the Three Guyanas, April 2001, p. 3 (on file with author).

FPP/VIDS. 2009. Securing Indigenous Peoples' Rights in Conservation in Suriname: A review. Forest Peoples Programme / Vereniging van Inheemse Dorpshoofden in Suriname (Association of Indigenous Village Leaders in Suriname). Available at: www.forestpeoples.org/sites/fpp/files/publication/2010/04/wccsurinamepareviewoct09eng.pdf

GEF/UNDP. 1999. Conservation of Globally Significant Forest Ecosystems in Suriname's Guayana Shield Bio-Region. Project SUR/99/ G31/A/1G/31. Available at: www.thegef.org/gef/sites/thegef.org/files/repository/Suriname_Final_PAD.doc

Government of Suriname. 2000. Nomination Dossier Central Suriname Nature Reserve for the World Heritage List. Paramaribo, Ministry of Natural Resources, July 1999.

Government of Suriname. 2004. Central Suriname Nature Reserve Plan for Management 2004-2008. Paramaribo.

IACHR. 2002. Annual Report of the Inter-American Commission on Human Rights 2002.

IACHR. 2007. Report No. 76/07 (Petition 198-07, Admissibility, The Kaliña and Lokono Peoples, Suriname, October 15, 2007).

IACtHR. 2007. Case of the Saramaka People v. Suriname: Judgment of November 28, 2007. Series C No. 172. Available at www.corteidh.or.cr/docs/casos/articulos/seriec_172_ing.pdf.

IADB. 2006. Indigenous Peoples and Maroons in Suriname. Inter-American Development Bank, Economic and Sector Study Series, RE3-06-005, September.

IUCN. 2000. World Heritage Nomination – IUCN Technical Evaluation: Central Suriname Nature Reserve (Suriname). UNESCO Doc. WHC-00/CONF.204/INF.05, 6 October 2000, pp. 77-83.

Kambel, E-R. 2006. IADB consultation meeting with the traditional authorities of the indigenous peoples and Maroons of Suriname, 6–7 December 2005, North Resort, Paramaribo, Suriname. Report prepared for the Inter-American Development Bank, 16 January.

Kambel, E-R. and MacKay, F. 1999. The Rights of Indigenous Peoples and Maroons in Suriname. IWGIA Doc. No. 96. Copenhagen, IWGIA/Forest Peoples Programme.

MacKay, F. 2007. Indigenous Peoples and the Right to Restitution: Implications of Inter-American Human Rights Jurisprudence for Conservation Practice. IUCN Journal of Conservation Matters, Vol. 15, pp. 209-222.

Meddens, L. 2011. Local Government and Global NGO in a Struggle to Protect the Jungle: A case study of 'Conservation International' and the Central Suriname Nature Reserve. MSc Thesis, Wageningen University, 15 April 2011. Available at http://www.enp.wur.nl/UK.

UN CERD. 2004. Concluding Observations of the Committee on the Elimination of Racial Discrimination: Suriname. Doc. CERD/C/64/CO/9/Rev.2, 12 March 2004.

UN CERD. 2009. Concluding Observations of the Committee on the Elimination of Racial Discrimination: Suriname. Doc. CERD/C/SUR/CO/12, 3 March 2009.

UNEP/WCMC. 2011. Central Suriname Nature Reserve, Suriname. World Heritage Information Sheet, February 2000, updated May 2009 and May 2011. Available at http://www.unep-wcmc.org/world-heritage-information-sheets_271.html.

UNESCO. 2001. World Heritage Committee, Twenty-fourth session, Cairns, Australia, 27 November-2 December 2000: Report. Doc. WHC-2000/CONF.204/21, 16 February 2001.

UNESCO. 2013. Central Suriname Nature Reserve: Description. http://whc.unesco.org/en/list/1017/ (accessed 8 November 2013).

PART III

APPENDICES

Appendix 1

African Commission on Human and Peoples' Rights Resolution 197 (5 November 2011)

Resolution on the protection of indigenous peoples' rights in the context of the World Heritage Convention and the designation of Lake Bogoria as a World Heritage site

The African Commission on Human and Peoples' Rights (the African Commission), meeting at its 50th Ordinary Session held from 24th October to 5th November 2011 in Banjul, The Gambia:

Recalling its mandate to promote human and peoples' rights and ensure their protection in Africa under the African Charter on Human and Peoples' Rights (the African Charter);

Considering Article 22 of the African Charter which recognizes that all peoples have the right to their economic, social and cultural development and that States have the duty, individually or collectively, to ensure the exercise of the right to development;

Recalling its Decision on Communication 276 / 2003 - *Centre for Minority Rights Development (Kenya) and Minority Rights Group International on behalf of Endorois Welfare Council v Kenya* (Endorois Decision), adopted at the 46th Ordinary Session held from 11 – 25 November 2009 in Banjul, The Gambia;

Noting that this decision affirms the rights of ownership of the Endorois to their ancestral lands around Lake Bogoria and that these rights are protected by Art. 14 of the African Charter;

Noting Article 1 of the Constitution of the United Nations Educational, Scientific, and Cultural Organization (UNESCO) on the purposes and functions of the Organization, according to which UNESCO shall "further universal respect for justice, for the rule of law and for the human rights and fundamental freedoms which are affirmed for the peoples of the world, without distinction of race, sex, language or religion, by the Charter of the United Nations";

Recalling the United Nations Declaration on the Rights of Indigenous Peoples, a universal international human rights instrument that has attained consensus among UN Member States, and reaffirming the African Commission's commitment to fostering the values and implementing the principles enshrined in this Declaration;

Bearing in mind Advice No. 2 (2011) of the UN Expert Mechanism on the Rights of Indigenous Peoples, which calls on UNESCO and the World Heritage Committee to establish robust procedures and mechanisms to ensure that indigenous peoples are adequately consulted and involved in the management and protection of World Heritage sites and that their free, prior and informed consent is obtained when their territories are being nominated and inscribed as World Heritage sites;

Noting with concern that there are numerous World Heritage sites in Africa that have been inscribed without the free, prior and informed consent of the indigenous peoples in whose territories they are located and whose management frameworks are not consistent with the principles of the UN Declaration on the Rights of Indigenous Peoples;

Deeply concerned that the World Heritage Committee at its 35th session, on the recommendation of International Union for the Conservation of Nature (IUCN), inscribed Lake Bogoria National Reserve on the World Heritage List, without obtaining the free, prior and informed consent of the Endorois through their own representative institutions, and despite the fact that the Endorois Welfare Council had urged the Committee to defer the nomination because of the lack of meaningful involvement and consultation with the Endorois;

1. Emphasizes that the inscription of Lake Bogoria on the World Heritage List without involving the Endorois in the decision-making process and without obtaining their free, prior and informed consent contravenes the African Commission's Endorois Decision and constitutes a violation of the Endorois' right to development under Article 22 of the African Charter;

2. Urges the World Heritage Committee and UNESCO to review and revise current procedures and Operational Guidelines, in consultation and cooperation with the UN Permanent Forum on Indigenous Issues and indigenous peoples, in order to ensure that the implementation of the World Heritage Convention is consistent with the UN Declaration on the Rights of Indigenous Peoples and that indigenous peoples' rights, and human rights generally, are respected, protected and fulfilled in World Heritage areas;

3. Calls on the World Heritage Committee to consider establishing an appropriate mechanism through which indigenous peoples can provide advice to the World Heritage Committee and effectively participate in its decision-making processes;

4. Urges IUCN to review and revise its procedures for evaluating World Heritage nominations as well as the state of conservation of World Heritage sites, with a view to ensuring that indigenous peoples are fully involved in these processes, and that their rights are respected, protected and fulfilled in these processes and in the management of World Heritage areas;

5. Urges the Government of Kenya, the World Heritage Committee and UNESCO to ensure the full and effective participation of the Endorois in the decision-making regarding the "Kenya Lake System" World Heritage area, through their own representative institutions.

Done in Banjul, The Gambia, 5 November 2011

Appendix 2

IUCN World Conservation Congress Resolution 5.047 (15 September 2012)

Implementation of the United Nations *Declaration on the Rights of Indigenous Peoples* in the context of the UNESCO World Heritage Convention

RECALLING the adoption of the Declaration on the Rights of Indigenous Peoples by the United Nations General Assembly (UNGA) on 13 September 2007 and its endorsement by IUCN at the 4th World Conservation Congress through Resolution 4.052 *Implementing the United Nations Declaration on the Rights of Indigenous Peoples* (Barcelona, 2008);

ALSO RECALLING Resolution 4.048 *Indigenous peoples, protected areas and implementation of the Durban Accord*, which resolves "to apply the requirements of the UN Declaration on the Rights of Indigenous Peoples to the whole of IUCN's Programme and operations" and calls on governments "to work with indigenous peoples' organizations to… ensure that protected areas which affect or may affect indigenous peoples' lands, territories, natural and cultural resources are not established without indigenous peoples' free, prior and informed consent and to ensure due recognition of the rights of indigenous peoples in existing protected areas";

REAFFIRMING Resolution 4.056 *Rights-based approaches to conservation*, and Recommendation 4.127 *Indigenous peoples' rights in the management of protected areas fully or partially in the territories of indigenous peoples* and numerous other Resolutions which demonstrate IUCN's commitment to a rights-based approach to protected areas establishment and management;

NOTING that the World Heritage Convention is celebrating its 40th anniversary under the theme "World Heritage and Sustainable Development: the Role of Local Communities";

FURTHER NOTING that the World Heritage Convention can and has played a leadership role in setting standards for protected areas as a whole and that World Heritage sites with their high visibility and public scrutiny have the potential to act as "flagships" for good governance in protected areas;

RECOGNIZING the potentially positive role that the World Heritage Convention can and has played in ensuring and supporting the continued preservation of the traditional lands and territories of indigenous peoples, and WELCOMING Decision 35 COM 12E (2011) of the World Heritage Committee, which encourages States Parties to the World Heritage Convention to "Respect the rights of indigenous peoples when nominating, managing and reporting on World Heritage sites in indigenous peoples' territories";

ACKNOWLEDGING that injustices to indigenous peoples have been and continue to be caused in the name of nature conservation, and that indigenous peoples have suffered dispossession and alienation from their traditional lands and resources as a result of the establishment and management of protected areas, including many areas inscribed on the World Heritage List;

NOTING that the UN Permanent Forum on Indigenous Issues, the UN Expert Mechanism on the Rights of Indigenous Peoples and the African Commission on Human and Peoples' Rights (herein "African Commission") have all expressed concerns that current procedures and mechanisms are inadequate for ensuring that the rights of indigenous peoples are respected in the implementation of the World Heritage Convention, and have called on UNESCO and the World Heritage Committee to review and revise current procedures and operational guidelines;

IN PARTICULAR NOTING the African Commission's *Resolution on the protection of indigenous peoples' rights in the context of the World Heritage Convention and the designation of Lake Bogoria as a World Heritage site* (ACHPR/Res.197 (L) 2011) which reaffirms the Commission Decision on Communication 276 / 2003 - *Centre for Minority Rights Development (Kenya) and Minority Rights Group International on behalf of Endorois Welfare Council v Kenya* (Endorois Decision) and highlights the traditional ownership rights of the Endorois over Lake Bogoria;

SHARING the African Commission's concerns that Lake Bogoria National Reserve was inscribed on the World Heritage List in 2011 without the free, prior and informed consent of the indigenous Endorois people and "that there are numerous World Heritage sites in Africa that have been inscribed without the free, prior and informed consent of the indigenous peoples in whose territories they are located and whose management frameworks are not consistent with the principles of the UN Declaration on the Rights of Indigenous Peoples"; and

RESPONDING to the African Commission's recommendation urging IUCN to "review and revise its procedures for evaluating World Heritage nominations as well as the state of conservation of World Heritage sites, with a view to ensuring that indigenous peoples are fully involved in these processes, and that their rights are respected, protected and fulfilled in these processes and in the management of World Heritage areas";

The World Conservation Congress, at its session in Jeju, Republic of Korea, 6-15 September 2012:

1. REQUESTS the Council and Director General to:

    a. develop clear policy and practical guidelines to ensure that the principles of the United Nations *Declaration on the Rights of Indigenous Peoples* are respected in IUCN's work as an Advisory Body to the World Heritage Committee, and to fully inform and consult with indigenous peoples when sites are evaluated or missions are undertaken on their territories; and

b. actively promote and support the adoption and implementation of a rights-based approach to conservation by the World Heritage Committee and to promote the principles and goals of the *Declaration on the Rights of Indigenous Peoples*;

2. URGES the World Heritage Committee to:

   a. review and revise its procedures and Operational Guidelines, in consultation with indigenous peoples and the UN Permanent Forum on Indigenous Issues, to ensure that indigenous peoples' rights and all human rights are upheld and implemented in the management and protection of existing World Heritage sites, consistent with the principles and goals of the *Declaration on the Rights of Indigenous Peoples*, and that no World Heritage sites are established in indigenous peoples' territories without their free, prior and informed consent;
   b. work with State Parties to establish mechanisms to assess and redress the effects of historic and current injustices against indigenous peoples in existing World Heritage sites; and
   c. establish a mechanism through which indigenous peoples can provide direct advice to the Committee in its decision-making processes in a manner consistent with the right of free, prior and informed consent and the right to participate in decision making as affirmed in the *Declaration on the Rights of Indigenous Peoples*;

3. CALLS UPON State Parties to the World Heritage Convention to ensure respect for the rights of indigenous peoples in the management and protection of existing World Heritage sites, and to ensure that no World Heritage sites are established in indigenous peoples' territories without their free, prior and informed consent; and

4. URGES the Government of Kenya to ensure the full and effective participation of the Endorois in the management and decision making of the "Kenya Lake System" World Heritage area, through their own representative institutions, and to ensure the implementation of the African Commission's Endorois Decision.

Appendix 3

Call to Action of the International Expert Workshop on the World Heritage Convention and Indigenous Peoples, Copenhagen, Denmark (20-21 September 2012)

World Heritage and Indigenous Peoples – A Call to Action

Addressing the urgent need to make the implementation of UNESCO's World Heritage Convention consistent with the United Nations Declaration on the Rights of Indigenous Peoples

The International Expert Workshop on the World Heritage Convention and Indigenous Peoples was organized by the International Work Group for Indigenous Affairs (IWGIA) and financially supported by the Danish Agency for Culture, the Greenland Government, and the Christensen Fund. It took place in Copenhagen, Denmark from 20-21 September 2012 as part of the 40th Anniversary of the World Heritage Convention in 2012, celebrated by UNESCO under the theme "World Heritage and Sustainable Development: The Role of Local Communities".

The Expert Workshop was attended by, *inter alia*, Indigenous experts and representatives from all continents, including from several World Heritage areas, human rights experts, representatives of the UN Permanent Forum on Indigenous Issues, the UN Expert Mechanism on the Rights of Indigenous Peoples, UNESCO, the World Heritage Centre, IUCN, ICOMOS, the African World Heritage Fund and the Nordic World Heritage Foundation, as well as some government representatives.

This Plan of Action reflects the views of the Indigenous representatives and human rights experts who participated in the Expert Workshop but not necessarily those of the Danish Government's Agency for Culture and the Greenland Government.

Preamble

Recognizing the vibrant contribution that Indigenous peoples make to the maintenance of the common heritage of humankind through their world perspectives, knowledge, cultures, laws, customs, practices, lives, and institutions;

Recognizing the need to genuinely value, recognize and respect the cultural heritage of Indigenous peoples in the definition, management, and protection of World Heritage sites, and the positive outcomes that flow from valuing, recognizing and respecting Indigenous peoples' cultural heritage;

Emphasizing that Indigenous peoples' individual and collective human rights as affirmed in the

United Nations Declaration on the Rights of Indigenous Peoples must be recognized, respected, promoted, and realized by States, United Nations agencies, and intergovernmental organizations;

Recalling the purposes and principles of the Charter of the United Nations and the need for good faith in the fulfillment of the obligations assumed by States in accordance with the Charter;

Further recalling UNESCO's constitutional purpose, according to which the organization shall "further universal respect for justice, for the rule of law and for the human rights and fundamental freedoms which are affirmed for the peoples of the world, without distinction of race, sex, language or religion, by the Charter of the United Nations";

Stressing the need for the principles of justice, democracy, respect for human rights, non-discrimination, rule of law, good governance and good faith to guide the implementation of the World Heritage Convention at all levels;

Noting the theme of the 40th Anniversary of the World Heritage Convention, "World Heritage and Sustainable Development: the Role of Local Communities", and the fact that numerous World Heritage sites are situated within Indigenous peoples' lands and territories and therefore have significant ramifications for the human rights, conditions, integrity, and self-determined development of Indigenous peoples and communities;

Welcoming World Heritage Committee Decision 35 COM 12E, wherein the Committee encourages States to involve Indigenous peoples in decision-making, monitoring and evaluation of the state of conservation of World Heritage sites and to respect the rights of Indigenous peoples when nominating, managing and reporting on World Heritage sites within Indigenous peoples' territories;

Emphasizing the UN General Assembly's adoption of the Declaration on the Rights of Indigenous Peoples and the human rights framework that it provides for all States and the UN System, including UNESCO, the World Heritage Committee, and the Committee's Advisory Bodies, for ensuring the survival, dignity and well-being of the Indigenous peoples of the world;

Emphasizing in particular the rights of Indigenous peoples to self-determination, to free, prior and informed consent, to their lands, territories and resources, to cultural integrity, and their other economic, social, and cultural rights;

Convinced that respect for these rights will enable Indigenous peoples to maintain and strengthen their institutions, cultures and traditions, and to promote their development in accordance with their aspirations and needs;

Drawing attention to the fact that the UN General Assembly, the Permanent Forum on Indigenous Issues, the Expert Mechanism on the Rights of Indigenous Peoples, the Special Rapporteur on the

Rights of Indigenous Peoples, the African Commission on Human and Peoples' Rights, and the IUCN World Conservation Congress have all urged UNESCO and/or the World Heritage Committee to take measures to ensure that Indigenous peoples' rights are respected in all existing and future World Heritage sites and in the overall implementation of the World Heritage Convention (see Annex 1);[1]

Informed by detailed case studies from Indigenous peoples' representatives and experts from across the globe concerning the impacts of the nomination, designation, and management of World Heritage sites upon Indigenous peoples' rights, lives, communities, cultures, lands, and territories (see Annex 2);

Concerned about the legacy of past and ongoing injustices, and chronic, persistent human rights violations that have been and continue to be experienced by Indigenous peoples as a result of the establishment and management of protected areas, including many areas inscribed on the World Heritage List;

Recognizing the historical and persistent human rights violations and breaches of fundamental freedoms being perpetrated by States and others against Indigenous individuals and peoples as a direct result of the implementation of the World Heritage Convention and actions of the World Heritage Committee;

We therefore demand that States, the World Heritage Committee, UNESCO, the World Heritage Centre, and the Advisory Bodies give full attention to the following principles:

- The implementation of the World Heritage Convention must be consistent with the UN Declaration on the Rights of Indigenous Peoples and relevant international and regional human rights instruments and standards.

- Indigenous peoples must be recognized as rights-holders and not merely stakeholders in any decisions affecting them, in accordance with their distinct status and rights under international law and in particular, their right of self-determination.

- Effective, direct, and meaningful representation and participation of Indigenous peoples at all stages and levels of decision-making related to the World Heritage Convention must be recognized, respected, enabled and ensured.

- Indigenous peoples must be fully consulted and directly involved in the identification, decision-making and management of World Heritage sites within or affecting their lands, territories and resources, through representatives chosen by themselves in accordance with their own procedures and institutions.

---

1 The Annexes to the Call to Action are available at http://www.iwgia.org/news/search-news?news_id=678 and http://whc.unesco.org/en/events/906.

- States must respect the rights of Indigenous peoples when identifying, nominating, managing and reporting on World Heritage sites incorporating or affecting Indigenous peoples' lands, territories or resources.

- Indigenous peoples' free, prior and informed consent must be obtained when their territories are being identified, nominated or inscribed as World Heritage sites. This essential right must be fully respected and recognized.

- States, the World Heritage Committee, UNESCO, and the Advisory Bodies must effectively involve Indigenous peoples in all stages of monitoring and evaluation of the state of conservation of World Heritage sites in their territories.

To give effect to these principles, we call for the adoption of the following measures and actions:

1. That the World Heritage Committee urgently establish an open and transparent process to elaborate, with the direct, full and effective participation of Indigenous peoples, changes to the current procedures and operational guidelines and other appropriate measures to ensure that the implementation of the World Heritage Convention is consistent with the United Nations Declaration on the Rights of Indigenous Peoples and a human rights-based approach. Such changes must:

    a) Include, *inter alia*, new provisions that affirm and guarantee Indigenous peoples' right to free, prior and informed consent, consistent with the UN Declaration on the Rights of Indigenous Peoples, prior to any tentative listing or inscription of a World Heritage site incorporating or affecting their lands, territories or resources;
    b) Ensure that Indigenous peoples are recognized as rights-holders and not merely stakeholders;
    c) Ensure that historical and ongoing infringements of human rights, including those explicitly embraced by the UN Declaration on the Rights of Indigenous Peoples, are identified and addressed through periodic reporting, management and reactive monitoring, as well as by other means.

2. That the World Heritage Committee not inscribe any further sites incorporating or affecting Indigenous peoples' lands, territories or resources on the World Heritage List without proof or evidence that the free, prior and informed consent of the Indigenous peoples concerned has been obtained. In support of this:

    a) The World Heritage Centre must not accept any World Heritage nomination affecting Indigenous peoples as complete without proof or evidence of the free, prior and informed consent of the Indigenous peoples' concerned. The Operational Guidelines need to be revised to that effect;

b) The World Heritage Committee is urged to consider the immediate adoption of the amendments proposed in Annex 3.

3. That the World Heritage Committee and UNESCO urgently establish the necessary procedures to remedy the existing lack of transparency and accountability in the implementation of the World Heritage Convention, including in the identification, monitoring and management of World Heritage sites and in the processing of World Heritage nominations.

   a) Such procedures must ensure, *inter alia*, that World Heritage nominations, monitoring mission reports and State Party reports are made publicly available as soon as they are received by the UNESCO World Heritage Centre, so that affected Indigenous peoples, communities and other rights- and stakeholders have sufficient time to review these documents and provide input and comments in advance of any decision being taken by the World Heritage Committee;

   b) Further, to support increased transparency in the implementation of the Convention, the World Heritage Centre should establish and maintain a public list of those sites on the States Parties' Tentative Lists that may affect the lands, territories or resources of Indigenous peoples.

4. That the World Heritage Committee establish, with the full and effective participation of Indigenous peoples and through an open and transparent process, an advisory mechanism consisting of Indigenous experts, to assist in the implementation of these and other measures to ensure that all actions related to the World Heritage Convention uphold the rights of Indigenous peoples.

   a) While the exact role and functions of this mechanism must be determined in full consultation with Indigenous peoples, the advisory mechanism should play a consultative role to the World Heritage Committee in all processes affecting Indigenous peoples, to ensure that the Indigenous peoples concerned are adequately consulted and involved in these processes and that their rights, priorities, values, and needs are duly recognized, considered and reflected;

   b) A key mandate of the Indigenous advisory mechanism should be to identify and appoint appropriate Indigenous experts and representatives to take part in World Heritage processes impacting Indigenous peoples, including the evaluation of nominations, on-site evaluation missions, evaluation of the state of conservation of World Heritage sites and monitoring missions;

   c) The UN special mechanisms on Indigenous peoples' rights, including the Expert Mechanism on the Rights of Indigenous Peoples, the Permanent Forum on Indigenous Issues and the Special Rapporteur on the Rights of Indigenous Peoples, should be encouraged to collaborate with the advisory mechanism and assist in the execution of its functions as appropriate and consistent with their respective mandates.

5. That States, UNESCO and the World Heritage Committee provide sufficient financial and other resources to enable the World Heritage Centre to effectively support and advance the full realization of the provisions of the UN Declaration on the Rights of Indigenous Peoples in all matters concerning the World Heritage Convention, including by:

   a) Providing secretarial and other support, as required, to the above-mentioned advisory mechanism of Indigenous experts;
   b) Establishing a full time staff position to deal exclusively with the issues, concerns, and rights of Indigenous peoples;
   c) Joining the UN Inter-Agency Support Group on Indigenous Issues, which facilitates the dialogue between the Permanent Forum on Indigenous Issues and the various agencies and organs of the United Nations.

6. That the World Heritage Committee issue a standing invitation and provide support to the Permanent Forum on Indigenous Issues to participate in its sessions and provide sufficient speaking time to the Permanent Forum to effectively contribute to its sessions.

7. That States and the World Heritage Committee urgently respond to and redress conditions within existing World Heritage sites where human rights violations or conflicts continue to affect Indigenous peoples and communities.

8. That the World Heritage Committee request the Advisory Bodies to include experts on Indigenous peoples' rights on their World Heritage Panels and as desk reviewers of all nominations affecting Indigenous peoples.

9. That States ensure the equitable and effective participation of Indigenous peoples in the administration and management of World Heritage sites within Indigenous peoples' lands and territories and support Indigenous peoples' own initiatives to develop administration and management systems.

10. That States ensure that the benefits arising from the use of Indigenous peoples' lands, territories and resources as World Heritage sites are defined by and genuinely accrue to the Indigenous peoples concerned, in a fair and equitable manner.

11. That States, UNESCO and the World Heritage Committee provide sufficient financial resources to support the full realization of the rights of Indigenous peoples in the implementation of the World Heritage Convention and the measures outlined in this Call for Action.

Appendix 4

Report of UN Special Rapporteur on the rights of indigenous peoples, James Anaya, to the UN General Assembly (13 August 2012)[1]

32. In any event, the Special Rapporteur would like to take advantage of the unique opportunity that he has in reporting to the General Assembly, to bring the attention of Member States to some of the current programmes and processes within the United Nations system that are of particular interest to indigenous peoples. The following examples are by no means exhaustive, and the Special Rapporteur expects to provide further observations on these and other United Nations activities throughout the remainder of his mandate, especially in his assessment of specific country situations, where appropriate.

C. Specific programmes and processes within the United Nations system of particular interest to indigenous peoples

1. United Nations Educational, Scientific and Cultural Organization

World Heritage Convention

33. A recurring issue that has come to the attention of the Special Rapporteur relates to the impact on indigenous peoples of the United Nations Educational, Scientific and Cultural Organization (UNESCO) World Heritage sites. This issue has arisen in the context of the Special Rapporteur's communications with Governments regarding specific allegations of human rights violations, as well as in the context of his reports examining the situation of indigenous peoples in particular countries.[2] Indigenous peoples have expressed concerns over their lack of participation in the nomination, declaration and management of World Heritage sites, as well as concerns about the negative impact these sites have had on their substantive rights, especially their rights to lands and resources. The Permanent Forum and the Expert Mechanism have both raised concerns in this connection in the course of their work.[3]

34. The exact number of World Heritage sites that are within or near the traditional territories of indigenous peoples, or that otherwise affect them, is not certain and the World Heritage

---

1 UN Doc. A/67/301 (Excerpt).
2 See, for instance, A/HRC/21/47/Add.2, para. 50.
3 See, for instance, E/2010/43-E/C.19/2010/15, para. 131 and A/HRC/18/42, annex, para. 38.

Committee has apparently never undertaken a comprehensive review of this, but the indications are that there are dozens of such sites.

35. In the meantime, there is still no specific policy or procedure which ensures that indigenous peoples can participate in the nomination and management of these sites. The Operational Guidelines for Implementation of the World Heritage Convention, which set out the procedure for the inscription of properties on the World Heritage list and the protection and conservation of sites, are silent on the issue of participation by indigenous peoples. The guidelines provide only that States parties to the Convention are encouraged to ensure the participation of a wide variety of stakeholders in the identification, nomination and protection of World Heritage properties.

36. Furthermore, States are not specifically required to provide any information on the indigenous peoples and local communities living in or around a site they nominate for World Heritage designation, or review the kind of impact a site might have on the rights of these groups. In this connection, the templates provided in the operational guidelines for nominating sites do not contain fields requiring States to describe the potential impact a site might have on indigenous peoples or to provide information about whether affected peoples have been asked about and agree with the nomination, although States are asked to indicate the major categories of land ownership, including traditional or customary ownership.

37. At its thirty-fifth session, in July 2011, the World Heritage Committee took an important step in adopting decision 35 COM 12E, in which States parties are encouraged to involve indigenous peoples and local communities in decisionmaking, monitoring and evaluation of the state of conservation of World Heritage sites and to respect the rights of indigenous peoples when nominating, managing and reporting on World Heritage sites in the territories of indigenous peoples. However, until amendments are made to the operational guidelines, these proposals may not fully take root. It is worth noting also that in 2001, the World Heritage Committee rejected proposals put forward by indigenous peoples to establish a council of experts of indigenous peoples, which was to act as an advisory body to the Committee.

38. Other significant developments have taken place in cooperation with the advisory bodies to the World Heritage Committee, which play key roles in the declaration of sites. In 2011 the Permanent Forum on Indigenous Issues noted and welcomed the initiative of the Committee and its three advisory bodies, the International Union for Conservation of Nature (IUCN), the International Council on Monuments and Sites and the International Centre for the Study of the Preservation and Restoration of Cultural Property, to review current procedures and capacity to ensure free, prior and informed consent and the protection of the livelihoods and tangible and intangible heritage of indigenous peoples (E/2011/43 E/C.19/2011/14, para. 41). In addition, in its resolution 4.048, adopted at its fourth session in 2008, the IUCN World Conservation Congress resolved to apply the requirements of the Declaration on the Rights of Indigenous

Peoples to all of its programmes and operations and called on Governments to work with indigenous peoples' organizations to ensure that protected areas which affect or may affect the lands, territories and other resources of indigenous peoples are not established without their free, prior and informed consent and to ensure due recognition of their rights in existing protected areas.

39. In October 2011, the Special Rapporteur met with representatives of UNESCO programmes that are relevant to indigenous peoples. He observed during the meeting a willingness to improve the World Heritage nominations procedure related to indigenous communities and to explore methods for doing so. However, UNESCO representatives raised the issue of the limitations of their technical, human and financial resources for carrying out consultations with all affected indigenous peoples for all sites that have been nominated, as well as the political challenges they often face in this regard, including a lack of cooperation by Governments.

40. Nonetheless, it is worth noting that the Special Rapporteur has heard of positive examples of participation by indigenous peoples in the declaration and management of World Heritage sites, which demonstrate that these challenges can be overcome, at least in certain contexts. In one example, he learned about the designation of the Laponian area in northern Sweden as a World Heritage site, which the Sami people actively supported. He also notes as an example of good practice, the designation of Taos Pueblo in the United States as a World Heritage site, which was proposed by the Taos people themselves. In the view of the Special Rapporteur, proposals for the declaration of World Heritage sites that directly affect indigenous peoples should come from those peoples, something that the States parties to the World Heritage Convention and United Nations agencies should promote.

UNESCO policy on indigenous peoples

41. A potential tool for addressing concerns regarding the declaration and management of World Heritage sites lies in the anticipated, but not as yet developed, UNESCO policy on indigenous peoples. In October 2011, the Special Rapporteur and members of the Permanent Forum and the Expert Mechanism participated in a meeting at the headquarters of UNESCO in Paris, at which the organization launched its work to develop a policy on indigenous peoples. In a statement at the launch the Special Rapporteur emphasized that UNESCO programming, just as that of other United Nations agencies which touch upon the interests of indigenous peoples, must at a minimum be consistent with the relevant international standards, as well as with applicable national laws and policies.

42. Ideally, however, UNESCO programming would do more than avoid harm to indigenous peoples, but would actively support their rights, as it already has in numerous instances and through numerous programmes. The Special Rapporteur believes that a UNESCO policy could assist greatly in supporting the rights of indigenous peoples in three principal ways: first, by

assisting UNESCO to reflect on the effects of its existing programming on indigenous peoples, as part of an evaluative process; second, by assisting UNESCO in its strategic planning for programmes which affect indigenous peoples, incorporating the objective of protecting the rights of indigenous peoples into programmatic work; and third, by providing UNESCO with practical guidelines for consultation with indigenous peoples in relation to UNESCO programmes and activities. The Special Rapporteur will watch with interest the development of a UNESCO policy on indigenous peoples and expresses his willingness to provide input into this process if it would be considered useful. ○

Appendix 5

Letter of UN Special Rapporteur on the rights of indigenous peoples, James Anaya, to the Director of the World Heritage Centre (18 November 2013)[1]

Dear Director Rao,

I have the honour to address you in my capacity as United Nations Special Rapporteur on the rights of indigenous peoples pursuant to Human Rights Council resolution 24/9. As you are aware, I have been in contact with the World Heritage Centre and other UNESCO bodies on various occasions throughout my mandate as Special Rapporteur regarding aspects of the organization's work affecting indigenous peoples.

I am now writing in relation to recent developments regarding the nomination and declaration of World Heritage sites by the World Heritage Committee. In this connection, I am aware that the World Heritage Committee will include a discussion on potential reforms to site nomination criteria and the Advisory Bodies' evaluation process at its next annual session in Doha, Qatar from 15 to 25 June 2014.

I understand that reform efforts have arisen mainly due to the difficulties presented in the nomination process of the Pimachiowin Aki site in Canada, an indigenous-led nomination developed through a collaborative process between the Government of Canada and First Nations. The site was nominated as a "mixed property" for its both cultural and natural significance in accordance with criteria v and ix, respectively, of the Operational Guidelines for the Implementation of the World Heritage Convention.

I am aware, however, that the World Heritage Committee deferred the Pimachiowin Aki nomination in large part because the Advisory Bodies were unable to concurrently consider natural and cultural values under the present criteria and evaluation processes. Given that indigenous peoples around the world often have strong historical and cultural connections to the natural environments in which they live, I am aware that mixed proposals are common for potential World Heritage sites over lands occupied or used by indigenous peoples.

In anticipation of the upcoming discussion, I encourage the World Heritage Committee to consider options for modifying the current approach to mixed site proposals in a manner that reconciles the Advisory Bodies' separate evaluation processes and remedies gaps in existing criteria that delay or impede indigenous-centered nominations. Options for reform should facilitate shared decision-making between the Advisory Bodies of the World Heritage Committee in order to harmonize the evaluation processes for cultural and natural values in a single nomination.

---

1 Reference: OL Indigenous (2001-8), OTH 10/2013. Also contained in UN Doc. A/HRC/25/74, p. 127.

Within this context, I urge the World Heritage Centre and Advisory Bodies to also consider previous suggestions regarding the need to address inconsistencies in UNESCO's approach to natural and cultural world heritage of indigenous peoples as expressed by the United Nations Permanent Forum on Indigenous Issues (E/2011/43 E/C.19/2011/14, para. 41). In addition to recommendations by the Permanent Forum, I and numerous other United Nations bodies and mechanisms have also urged UNESCO to modify its approach as to ensure that indigenous peoples' rights and worldviews are fully valued and respected in all current and future World Heritage site designations as well as in the overall implementation of the World Heritage Convention.

I welcome the World Heritage Committee's efforts to improve existing nomination procedures and would like to emphasize the importance of consulting with indigenous peoples throughout the entirety of such a review process in order to address indigenous peoples' rights, interests and concerns. I would also like to encourage the Committee to consider other reforms to address concerns regarding the nomination and management of World Heritage sites that have been raised in years past in a variety of fora, including with respect to:

1) Ensuring meaningful representation and participation of indigenous peoples in the nomination of World Heritage sites;
2) Ensuring transparency throughout the World Heritage site nomination and implementation processes;
3) Safeguarding land and resource rights of indigenous peoples, both officially recognized and unrecognized, during the nomination process;
4) Ensuring that indigenous peoples derive benefits from World Heritage sites located where they live or that impact them;
5) Consulting indigenous peoples with a view towards obtaining their free, prior and informed consent regarding the establishment of World Heritage sites that may affect their land, natural resources and other rights;
6) Safeguarding against misuse and distortion of indigenous peoples' culture, practices and knowledge; and
7) Providing redress for past injustices and violations of indigenous peoples' rights to which the establishment of World Heritage sites have contributed.[2]

I look forward to keeping abreast of progress concerning the review of the nomination process and related criteria for World Heritage sites and will continue to monitor developments.

Should you or they require any additional information or clarifications concerning issues raised in this letter, please do not hesitate to contact me at indigenous@ohchr.org or Maia

---

2 *See generally*, Report of the United Nations Special Rapporteur on the rights of indigenous peoples to the General Assembly, A/67/301, paras. 33 – 35; United Nations Permanent Forum on Indigenous Issues, E/2011/43 E/C.19/2011/14, paras. 40 - 42; Expert Mechanism on the Rights of Indigenous Peoples, A/HRC/18/42, Annex, para. 38; and International Expert Workshop on the World Heritage Convention and Indigenous Peoples, Call to Action.

Campbell, who assists my mandate at the Office of the High Commissioner for Human Rights: mcampbell@ohchr.org.

I would be grateful if you could transmit this letter to relevant representatives at the World Heritage Committee and its Advisory Bodies.

Please accept, Excellency, the assurances of my highest consideration.

James Anaya
Special Rapporteur on the rights of indigenous peoples